Fodor Austria

Fodor's Travel Publications, Inc.
New York and London

Copyright © 1991
by Fodor's Travel Publications, Inc.

Fodor's Austria

Editors: Jillian Magalaner, Vernon Nahrgang
Contributors: Suzanne De Galan, George Hamilton, Alan Levy, Delia Meth-Cohn, Marcy Pritchard, Linda K. Schmidt, Earl Steinbicker, George Sullivan
Art Director: Fabrizio La Rocca
Cartographer: David Lindroth
Illustrator: Karl Tanner
Cover Photograph: E. Nagelle

Design: Vignelli Associates

Special Sales

Contents

Contents

Foreword

We would like to thank the directors of the Austrian National Tourist Offices in Vienna and in New York—especially Gabriele Wolf—and the individual tourist offices for each of the provinces for their generous and considerable assistance in preparing this new edition. Werner Fritz and the staff of the Austrian National Tourist Office in London have been of further help.

While every care has been taken to ensure accuracy of the information in this guide, tourism in Austria is a dynamic industry and changes will occur; consequently, the publisher can assume no liability for errors.

All prices and opening times quoted in this guide are based on information supplied to us at press time. Hours and admission fees may change; call ahead to avoid disappointment. Fodor's wants to hear about your travel experiences, both pleasant and unpleasant. When a hotel or restaurant fails to live up to its billing, let us know, and we will investigate the complaint and revise our entries where warranted.

Send your letters to the editors of Fodor's Travel Publications, 201 E. 50th St., New York, NY 10022.

Highlights'92 and Fodor's Choice

Highlights '92

Austria—and in particular, Vienna—has become the undisputed center of East–West activity following the collapse of communism in the East. Until 1918 those lands were part of the vast Habsburg empire, and despite language differences, ties are still fairly strong: Every Viennese is said to have an aunt in Prague (and every Czechoslovak an aunt in Vienna). The influence of East European cuisine is evident on every Viennese menu.

Politics and the Economy Long the "last oupost" of Western Europe, Austria today is struggling with the concept of integration with the European Community. The country wants to be a part of the bigger show, but it is not about to give up its claim to being the center of East–West trade. Many Western multinational companies use Vienna as a coordination center for their sales activities in the East, and the city is becoming the focal point for East–West financing. The airport is being expanded, new office complexes built, communications improved. Vienna is fighting to maintain its competitive edge as Eastern cities such as Budapest and Prague open up.

A formal application to join the EC was filed in 1990 and could be acted upon as early as 1994. A wave of liberalization has brought much legislation into line with European Community practice in anticipation of membership; old monopolies are disappearing and more competition is being encouraged, particularly in sectors (such as finance) once dominated by state-owned industry.

Austria this year expects an economic growth rate among the highest in Europe as a consequence of flourishing exports and tourism. The manufacturing side is led by production of parts and components for the German automotive industry. The nation's increased prosperity is reflected in the quality of goods (and their price ranges) in shop windows.

Travel Tourism has regained its position as the number one industry, and the emphasis is increasingly on quality. Planners, seeing limits to the number of tourists and tourist facilities, propose to preserve the country's virtues: sensational scenery, unpolluted air and water, and easy accessibility. Last year the railroads adopted a new schedule system that better coordinates trains between all parts of the country and speeds up many long-distance routes. More areas are now "off limits" to cars: the old centers of Innsbruck, Salzburg, and St. Wolfgang, for example. Tour bus traffic in Vienna is being restricted in order to make the environment more pleasant.

Noise-level limits are causing problems for charter flight operators to Salzburg. Because the airport is close to the city, the noisier (usually older) aircraft are restricted in the times they can land. Tourists headed for Salzburg from London or Scandinavia via charter may land instead in Munich (where controls are less stringent) and be bussed the last leg of the trip. For travelers headed to Austria from Canada or the northeastern United States, a new Singapore Airlines service flies Toronto–Vienna via Amsterdam twice weekly.

Air transportation within Austria is improving, with more competition on several routes. While this has resulted in greater frequency of services, domestic fares remain high.

Hotels have traditionally been independent enterprises in Austria, but an increasing number are joining reservation and referral groups such as Best Western or affinity organizations such as Romantik-Hotels, which groups hotels of unusual charm; Silencehotels, which are set in a particularly quiet environment; and Schlosshotels, which offer accommodation in castles and former palaces. The French Accor group is expanding under the names Mercure, Ibis, and Novotel; these variations offer fresh, modern accommodations but lack the personal touch of owner-management that many tourists find appealing in Austria. Hotels affiliated with the referral and affinity groups continue under private managment. The quality of accommodations has improved greatly in recent years, resulting in an upgrading of formerly lower-priced facilities; bargain accommodations are becoming harder to find in the major cities, while prices in the country remain low by any measure.

Few new top-class restaurants have appeared, and Innsbruck lost two last year. At the middle of the scale, local chains are setting up self-service restaurants that offer good value. Rosenberger, the operator of several excellent turnpike restaurants, opened an unusually attractive cafeteria in Vienna last year, and the Billa group is expanding its Wegenstein cafeterias. The Wienerwald chain has moved away from its chicken-only image to offer greater variety at reasonable prices. Many of the Anker bakery shops in the Vienna area now feature lighter but filling snacks along with coffee and other beverages.

Travelers who depend on credit cards for payment may lose some of this convenience in Austria. Many hotels and restaurants and virtually all travel agents canceled their contracts with credit card companies in 1991 in protest over high discount rates and often slow payment. At midyear the issue was in negotiation, with neither side showing an inclination to compromise.

The Arts Two themes will mark 1992: a comprehensive "In the tracks of the Habsburgs" series of exhibitions and events, and the 500th aniversary of Columbus's sailing. On the Habsburg theme, cities such as Innsbruck, Bad Ischl, Baden bei Wien, and Vienna will draw major attention, and many abbeys and castles throughout the country will feature special tours, exhibitions, and concerts. Linz and Graz will lay legitimate claim to the Habsburgs of an earlier era.

Austria's ties with North America will be emphasized in such exhibits as "Austria and the discovery of America" in the National Library in Vienna and "Emigration to America" in Güssing (Burgenland). The Habsburgs, with ties to the Spanish throne, helped finance Columbus's adventure, and this is the focus of the exhibition "Casa da Austria" and "The Catholic Kings" at Ambras Castle outside Innsbruck. On another theme, the exhibition in Schloss Rosenau (Lower Austria) covering "250 years of Freemasonry in Austria" includes a once-secret room in which the order met; because freemasonry came to Austria from England, many of the early documents are in English.

Music events of the year begin with the New Year's Concert and a performance of Beethoven's Ninth symphony, both in Vienna on New Year's Day. Then the spotlight moves to Salzburg for the Easter festival, to Vienna for the Festival Weeks (mid-May to mid-June) and onto Salzburg in August. For many people summer ends officially on September 1, when the opera in Vienna resumes its season after a two-month holiday.

This year should see a resumption of the "noble" balls, canceled last year in deference to the international crisis in the Gulf. The Philharmonic Ball will take place on January 23, in the Musikverein, and the noblest of all, the Opernball, on February 27 in the Opera. *Fasching*, the carnival season between New Year's and Lent, conludes with a great parade around the Ring in Vienna on February 29.

Special markets abound throughout the year. The Spring and Fall Markets, in late April and late September in Urfahr, the district of Linz just across the Danube, feature a huge range of handmade goods. There's a week-long Whitsun market at Braunau in Upper Australia. Of the many Christmas markets, one of the nicest is that on Freyung in Vienna in the weeks before the holiday, with many handmade goods.

Sports The year opens with international ski-jumping competitions at Bergisel in Innsbruck on January 4. In January and February, at nearby Igls, international skibob and tobagganing competitions are scheduled. An international indoor soccer tournament is planned for Vienna in January. In Filzmoos (Salzburg) the international hot air ballooning week will take place February 4–11. Perg (Upper Australia) will be site of the qualifying competitions for the world championship in parachuting scheduled for August 15–25 in Treiben (Styria). The sailing world championship will take place during the summer, starting at Gmunden on Traun Lake (Upper Austria).

As golf attracts more enthusiasts, the number of courses increases, popular courses become more crowded, and greens fees soar. Courses are under construction in Vienna (Am Wienerberg), Ulrichsberg (Upper Austria), Ellmau (Tirol), Kirchham (Upper Austria), ~~Linz~~ and Linz-Feldkirchen (Upper Austria), Luftenberg/St. Georgen (Upper Austria), Haag (Upper Austria), Timmersdorf (Carinthia), and Zöbern (Lower Austria). A number of hotels now offer package arrangements to ~~help~~ ease the costs.

Fodor's Choice

No two people will agree on what makes a perfect vacation, but it can be fun and helpful to know what others think. We hope you'll have a chance to experience some of Fodor's Choices yourself while visiting Austria. For detailed information on individual entries, see the relevant sections of this guidebook.

Times to Remember

Boating on Lake Neusiedl at sunset (Burgenland)

The Gauderfest in May in Zell am Ziller (Tirol)

Hearing a Benjamin Britten "church opera" in Ossiach (Carinthia)

High Mass on Sunday in the Augustinerkirche in Vienna

The trumpet and cannon salute from Salzburg's Fortress at noon on Christmas Day

Works of Art

Bosch's *Last Judgment* (Vienna)

Brueghel's *Hunters in the Snow* (Vienna)

Cellini's gold salt cellar (Vienna)

Klimt's *The Kiss* (Vienna)

Pacher's winged altar (St. Wolfgang)

Schiele's *The Family* (Vienna)

Vermeer's *Allegory of the Art of Painting: the Artist in his Studio* (Vienna)

Museums

Alpenzoo (Innsbruck)

Belvedere Palace (Vienna)

Historisches Museum der Stadt Wien (Museum of Viennese History, Vienna)

Kunsthistorisches Museum (Museum of Art History, Vienna)

Sights to Remember

Gesause Ravine (Styria)

The view up Maria Theresien-Strasse (Innsbruck)

Looking over Salzburg from Café Winkler's terrace

Memorable Drives

The Gerlos Pass on Route 165 from Zell am Ziller (Tirol)

Grossglockner Highway (East Tirol/Salzburg Province)

Over the Semmering Pass (Styria/Lower Austria)

On your own steam train in Mariazell (Styria)

Route 145 along the Traunsee (Upper Austria)

Taste Treats

Sampling wine at a romantic *Heuriger* in Rust (Burgenland)

Bosner Wurst (hot dog with Balkan spice) in the arcaded passageway off the Griesgasse (Salzburg)

Lake trout from the Ossiach lake (Carinthia)

Smoked trout at the Riedenburg (Salzburg)

A beer at Brauerei Hirt (Carinthia)

Architectural Gems

Ferstel Palace and Café Central (Vienna)

Gloriette (Schönbrunn Palace Gardens, Vienna)

Goldenes Dachl (Innsbruck)

Hundertwasserhaus (Vienna)

Looshaus (Vienna)

Reitschule theater (Salzburg)

Secession building (Vienna)

Hotels

Burg Bernstein (Burgenland)

Der Bär (Ellmau)

Goldener Adler (Innsbruck)

Goldener Hirsch (Salzburg)

König von Ungarn (Vienna)

Palais Schwarzenberg (Vienna)

Pension Zipser (Vienna)

Post (Villach)

Schlossberg (Graz)

Weisses Rössl (St. Wolfgang)

Restaurants

Bacher (Mautern)

Barth-Stuben (Neusiedl-am-See)

Deuring-Schlössle (Bregenz)

Glacisbeisl (Vienna)

Hofkeller (Graz)

Minichmayr (Steyr)

Römischer Kaiser (Vienna)

Stadtschänke zu den Grafen Lodron (Gmünd)

Weisses Kreuz (Mondsee)

Historic Towns/Picturesque Squares

Freistadt (Upper Austria)

Gmünd (Carinthia)

Hauptplatz, Linz (Upper Austria)

Mörbisch (Burgenland)

Steyr (Upper Austria)

Salzburg's interconnecting squares

Cafés

Central (Vienna)

Hawelka (Vienna)

Lewandofsky (Bad Aussee)

Schwarzenberg (Vienna)

Tomaselli (Salzburg)

Traxlmayr (Linz)

Zauner (Bad Ischl)

Churches and Abbeys

Dom (Salzburg)

Göttweig (Lower Austria)

Karlskirche (Vienna)

Kremsmunster (Upper Austria)

Melk (Lower Austria)

St. Florian (Upper Austria)

St. Peter's (Vienna)

St. Stephen's (Vienna)

The Franciscan church (Salzburg)

Parks and Gardens

Belvedere (Vienna)

Burggarten (Vienna)

Hellbrunn's Wasserspiele (Salzburg)

St. Sebastian's Cemetery (Salzburg)

Schlossberg (Graz)

Schönbrunn (Vienna)

Stadtpark (Vienna)

Austria

CZECHOSLOVAKIA

HUNGARY

GERMANY

YUGOSLAVIA

ITALY

SWITZERLAND

LIECHTENSTEIN

N

LOWER AUSTRIA (NIEDERÖSTERREICH)

UPPER AUSTRIA (OBERÖSTERREICH)

BURGENLAND

STYRIA (STEIERMARK)

CARINTHIA (KÄRNTEN)

SALZBURG

EAST TIROL

TIROL

VORARLBERG

Vienna

Poysdorf
Stockerau
Hainburg
Bruck
Neusiedler See
Eisenstadt
Mödling
Baden
Wiener Neustadt
Neunkirchen
Fürstenfeld
Feldbach
Bad Gleichenberg
Bad Radkersburg
Mura
Drava
Graz
Feldkirchen
St. Veit
Klagenfurt
Villach
Wolfsberg
Judenburg
Knittelfeld
Leoben
Kapfenberg
Bruck a. d. Mur
Mürzzuschlag
Mariazell
Horn
Waidhofen
Gmünd
Zwettl
Krems
St. Pölten
Melk
Scheibbs
Linz
Enns
Steyr
Wels
Ried
Efeading
Schärding
Braunau
Vöcklabruck
St. Wolfgang
Gmunden
Bad Ischl
Bad Aussee
Liezen
Radstadt
Bischofshofen
Salzach
Salzburg
St. Johann
Spittal
Feldkirchen
Badgastein
Heiligenblut
Bodensdorf
Matrei
Lienz
Zell am See
Saalfelden
Kitzbühel
Kufstein
Jenbach
Mayrhofen
Innsbruck
Landeck
Imst
St. Anton
Reutte
Lech
Zürs
Bregenz
Dornbirn
Feldkirch
Bludenz

Danube (Donau)
Inn
Enns
Salzach
Drau
Mur

A2
A1
A21
A10
A12
A13

Bodensee

50 miles
75 km
0
0

Ski Areas

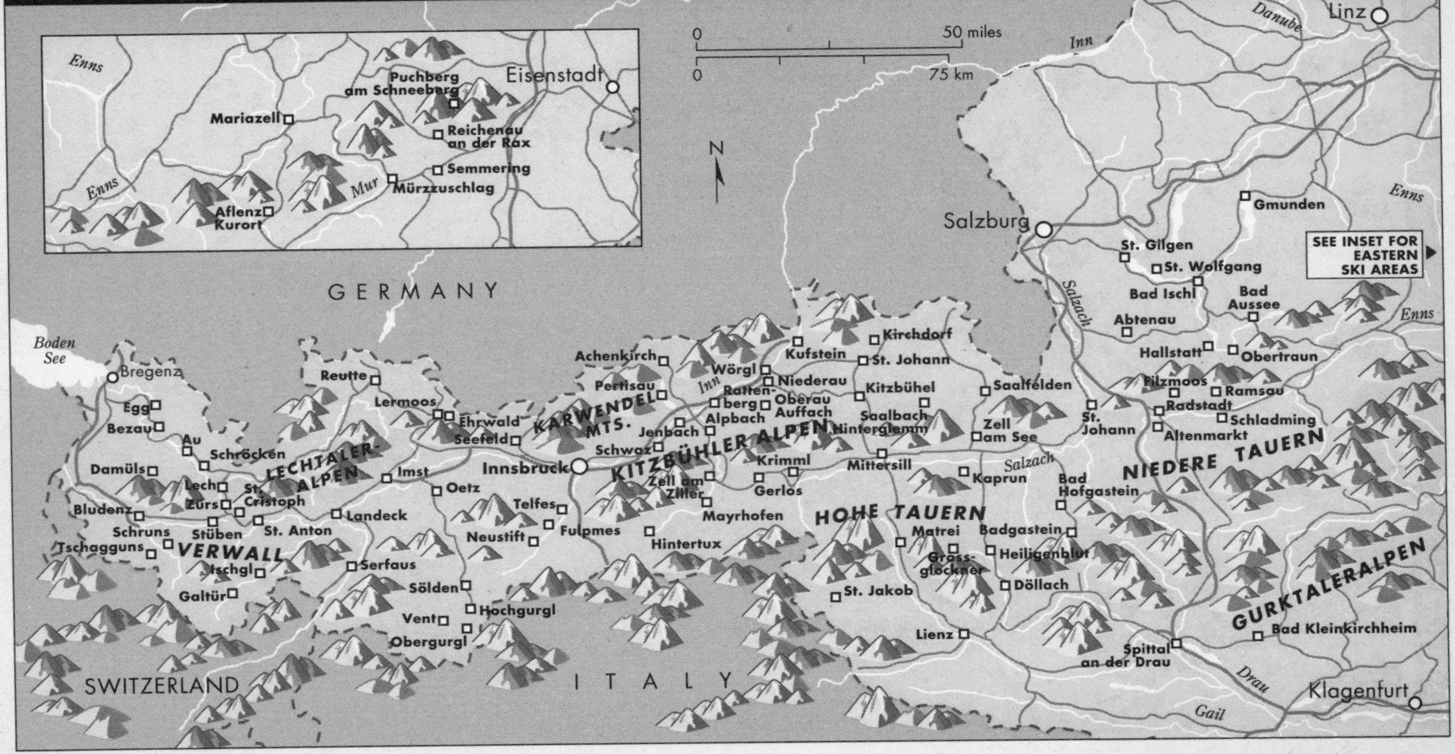

Enns
Enns
Puchberg am Schneeberg
Eisenstadt
Mariazell
Reichenau an der Rax
Semmering
Mur
Mürzzuschlag
Aflenz Kurort
0
50 miles
0
75 km
N
Danube
Linz
Inn
Enns
Gmunden
Salzburg
St. Gilgen
St. Wolfgang
SEE INSET FOR EASTERN SKI AREAS
GERMANY
Bad Ischl
Bad Aussee
Salzach
Abtenau
Enns
Boden See
Bregenz
Reutte
Achenkirch
Kufstein
Kirchdorf
St. Johann
Hallstatt
Obertraun
Wörgl
Niederau
Inn
Pertisau
Ratten-berg
Oberau
Auffach
Kitzbühel
Saalfelden
Filzmoos
Ramsau
Lermoos
Egg
Ehrwald
KARWENDEL MTS.
Alpbach
Saalbach Hinterglemm
St. Johann
Radstadt
Schladming
Bezau
Seefeld
Jenbach
Zell am See
Altenmarkt
Au
Schröcken
Schwaz
KITZBÜHLER ALPEN
LECHTALER-ALPEN
Krimml
Mittersill
Salzach
NIEDERE TAUERN
Damüls
Imst
Innsbruck
Zell am Ziller
Kaprun
Bad Hofgastein
Lech
St. Cristoph
Oetz
Gerlos
Zürs
Telfes
Bludenz
Landeck
Mayrhofen
HOHE TAUERN
Schruns
Stüben
St. Anton
Fulpmes
Neustift
Matrei
Badgastein
Tschagguns
VERWALL
Hintertux
Grossglockner
Heiligenblut
GURKTALERALPEN
Ischgl
Serfaus
Sölden
St. Jakob
Döllach
Galtür
Hochgurgl
Vent
Obergurgl
Lienz
Bad Kleinkirchheim
Spittal an der Drau
Drau
SWITZERLAND
ITALY
Klagenfurt
Gail

World Time Zones

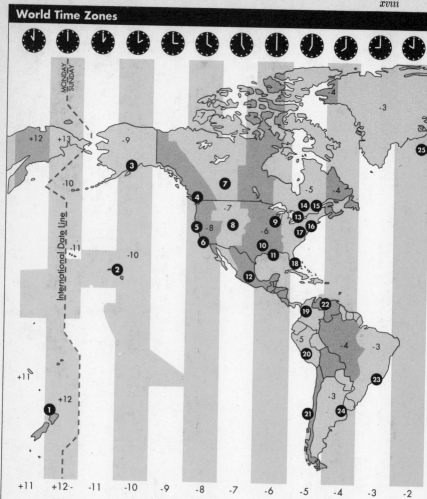

International Date Line

MONDAY
SUNDAY

+12 +13 -9 -7 -5 -4 -3

-10 -11 -10 -8 -7 -6 -5 -4

+11 +12

Numbers below vertical bands relate each zone to Greenwich Mean Time (0 hrs.).
Local times frequently differ from these general indications,
as indicated by light-face numbers on map.

+11 +12 -11 -10 -9 -8 -7 -6 -5 -4 -3 -2

Algiers, **29**   Berlin, **34**   Delhi, **48**   Istanbul, **40**
Anchorage, **3**   Bogotá, **19**   Denver, **8**   Jerusalem, **42**
Athens, **41**   Budapest, **37**   Djakarta, **53**   Johannesburg, **44**
Auckland, **1**   Buenos Aires, **24**   Dublin, **26**   Lima, **20**
Baghdad, **46**   Caracas, **22**   Edmonton, **7**   Lisbon, **28**
Bangkok, **50**   Chicago, **9**   Hong Kong, **56**   London (Greenwich), **27**
Beijing, **54**   Copenhagen, **33**   Honolulu, **2**   Los Angeles, **6**
   Dallas, **10**   Madrid, **38**
   Manila, **57**

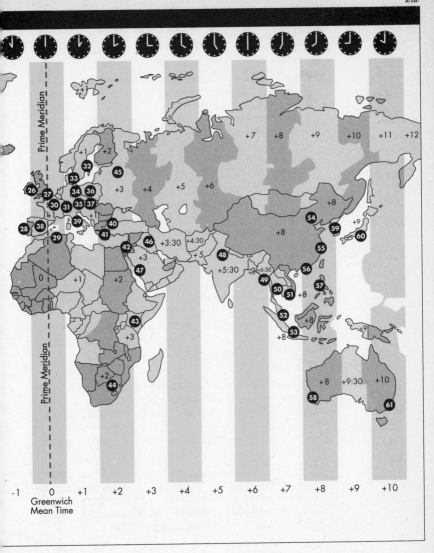

Mecca, **47**	Ottawa, **14**	San Francisco, **5**	Toronto, **13**
Mexico City, **12**	Paris, **30**	Santiago, **21**	Vancouver, **4**
Miami, **18**	Perth, **58**	Seoul, **59**	Vienna, **35**
Montreal, **15**	Reykjavík, **25**	Shanghai, **55**	Warsaw, **36**
Moscow, **45**	Rio de Janeiro, **23**	Singapore, **52**	Washington, DC, **17**
Nairobi, **43**	Rome, **39**	Stockholm, **32**	Yangon, **49**
New Orleans, **11**	Saigon, **51**	Sydney, **61**	Zürich, **31**
New York City, **16**		Tokyo, **60**	

Introduction

by Alan Levy

Alan Levy is an American author, librettist, and foreign correspondent who has lived in Vienna for 20 years.

Today's Austria—and, in particular, its capital, Vienna—reminds me of a formerly fat man who is now at least as gaunt as the rest of us, but still allows himself a lot of room and expects doors to open wide when he goes through them. After losing two world wars and surviving amputation, annexation, and occupation, a nation that once ruled Europe now endures as a tourist mecca and a permanently neutralized, somewhat Balkanized republic.

It takes any foreign resident in Austria, even a German or Swiss, the whole first year to find out what questions one should be asking. It takes the second year to start getting answers; beginning with the third year, one can sift the merits of the answers. This is why I tell our friends from embassies, agencies, banks, and businesses—people doing two or three-year stints in Austria—that they need a minimum of five years here to liquidate the investment of effort and utilize the contacts they've made. To tourists, I have just three words of advice: "Don't even try." Were you to succeed in thinking like the Viennese, for example, you would be a prime candidate for Doctor Freud's couch at Berggasse 19; but he and it aren't there anymore—it's now the Sigmund Freud Museum.

Sitting in a loge in the Vienna State Opera in the 1970s, my wife and I gasped with dismay when a young ballerina slipped and fell, but while we applauded the girl's quick recovery, the ancient dowager next to me merely murmured: "In the days of the monarchy, she'd have been taken outside and shot."

I hope it was hyperbole, but she had a point. In a world of tattered glitter and tacky taste, jet-lagged superstars and under-rehearsed choruses, opera and operetta aren't what they used to be (though Viennese ballet has climbed steadily uphill in the decades since that girl's fall).

Still, there are oases of perfection, such as those Sunday mornings from September to June, when—if you've reserved months in advance—you can hear (but not see) those "voices from heaven," the Vienna Choir Boys, sing Mass in the marble-and-velvet royal chapel of the Hofburg. Lads of eight to thirteen in sailor suits, they peal out angelic notes from the topmost gallery, and you might catch a glimpse of them after Mass as you cut across the Renaissance courtyard for the 10:45 performance of the Lippizaner Stallions in the Spanish Riding School around the corner. Beneath crystal chandeliers in a lofty white hall, expert riders in brown uniforms with gold buttons and black hats with gold braid put these aristocrats of the equine world through their classic paces.

Just past noon, when the Spanish Riding School lets out, cross the Michaelerplatz and stroll up the Kohlmarkt to No. 14: Demel's, the renowned and lavish pastry shop founded shortly after 1848 by the court confectioner. It was an instant success with those privileged to dine with the emperor, for not only was Franz Josef a notoriously stodgy and paltry eater, but, when he stopped eating, protocol dictated that all others stopped, too. Dessert at Demel's became a must for hungry higher-ups. Today's Demel's features a flawless midday buffet offering venison en croûte, chicken in pastry shells, beef Wellington, meat tarts, and frequent warnings to "leave room for the desserts."

Closer to the less-costly level of everyday existence, my family and I lay on a welcoming meal for visitors just off plane or train: a freshly baked slab of *Krusti Brot* to be spread with *Liptauer*, a piquant paprika cream cheese, and *Kräuter Gervais*, Austria's answer to cream cheese and chives, all washed down by a youngish white wine. Such simple pleasures as a jug of wine, a loaf of bread, and a spicy cheese or two are what we treasure as Austrian excellence in democratic days. Though our visitors manage to live well back home without *Grüner Veltliner* and *Rheinriesling* to drink and *Liptauer* and *Kräuter Gervais* to eat, they do find it hard to rejoin the outside world of white bread that wiggles. And if they really carry on about our wine, we can take them on the weekend to the farm it's from, for going to the source is one of the virtues of living in this small, unhomogenized land of 7½ million people that is modern Austria.

"Is it safe to drink the water?" is still the question I'm asked the most by visitors to Vienna. "It's not only safe," I reply, "it's recommended." Sometimes they call back to thank me for the tip. Piped cold and clean via Roman aqueducts from a couple of Alpine springs, the city's water has been rated the best in the world by such connoisseurs and authorities as the Austrian Academy of Sciences and an international association of solid waste–management engineers. Often on a summer evening, when our guests look as though a Cognac after dinner might be too heavy, I bring out a pitcher of iced tap water, and even our Viennese visitors smack their lips upon tasting this refreshing novelty. But don't bother to try for it in a tavern; except for a few radical thinkers and the converts I've made, virtually all Viennese drink bottled mineral water, and few waiters will condescend to serve you any other kind.

People say that after two decades in Vienna I must feel very Viennese, and maybe they're right, because here I am chatting about food and drink, which is the principal topic of Viennese conversation. So, before leaving the capital for the provinces, let me call your attention to three major culinary inventions that were all introduced to Western civilization in Vienna in the watershed year of 1683: coffee, the croissant, and the bagel.

That was the year the second Turkish siege of Vienna was at last repelled, when King Jan Sobieski of Poland and Duke Charles of Lorraine rode to the rescue, thereby saving the West for Christianity. The Sultan's armies left behind their silken tents and banners, some 25,000 dead, and hundreds of huge sacks filled with a mysterious brownish bean. The victorious Viennese didn't know what to make of it—whether to bake, boil, or fry it. But one of their spies, Franz George Kolschitzky, a wheeler-dealer merchant who had traveled in Turkey and spoke the language, had sampled in Constantinople the thick black brew of roasted coffee beans that the Turks called *"Kahve."* Though he could have had almost as many sacks of gold, he settled for beans—and opened history's first Viennese coffeehouse. Business was bad, however, until Kolschitzky tinkered with the recipe and experimented with milk, thus inventing the *mélange:* taste sensation of the 1680s and still the most popular local coffee drink of the 1990s.

While Kolschitzky was roasting his reward, Viennese bakers were celebrating with two new creations that enabled their customers truly to taste victory over the Moslems: a bun curved like a crescent, the emblem of Islam (what Charles of Lorraine might have called *croissant*, Austrians call *Kipferl*), and a roll shaped like Sobieski's stirrup, for which the German word was *Bügel*. The invention of the bagel, however, proved less significant, for it disappeared swiftly and totally, only to resurface in America centuries later, along with Sunday brunch.

Though Vienna's is more a wine culture than a beer culture, in its hundreds of *Heurige* (young-wine taverns identified by a bush over their door) the Viennese male indulges in a beer-garden ritual that I call "airing the paunch." With one or two buttons open, he exposes his belly to sun or moon or just passing admiration. One would be hard put to tell him that Wien (the German name for the capital) is not the navel of the universe, let alone of Austria, but the person who can tell it to him best would be a Vorarlberger. The 305,600 citizens of Austria's westernmost province live as close to Paris as they do to Vienna, which tries to govern them; their capital, Bregenz, is barely an hour's drive from Zurich, but eight or more from Vienna, and the natives sometimes seem more Swiss than Austrian.

The Kleinwalsertal, a remote valley of Vorarlberg that juts into Bavaria, cannot be reached directly from Austria by car, bus, or train. A couple of summers ago, I joined some intrepid Austrians on a strenuous and sometimes treacherous two-day up and downhill climb from Lech am Arlberg to the Kleinwalsertal. Along the way, we saw an eagle, vultures, and marmots—and I wouldn't have traded the trip for a sack of coffee beans; nor would I ever undertake such a venture again. When we tried to buy some coffee, the locals were reluctant to accept our schillings because the deutschemark is their official currency. While the rest of Austria strives for entry into the European Common Market after 1992, the Kleinwalsertal, through monetary union, has been quietly living in it from its outset.

The northern reaches of Tirol and the western parts of Upper Austria also border on Germany and have a heartier, beerier character than the eastern and southern provinces. (There are nine provinces in all; Vienna, the capital, counts as a state, too, and its mayor is also a governor.) Although the glittering city of Salzburg, capital of rugged Salzburg province, perches right on the German border 16 miles from Berchtesgaden, Austrian traditions, folk customs and costumes, and the music of native son Mozart flourish there as nowhere else in the country—revered and cherished, revived and embroidered. And defended! Once, sitting at sundown in the Café Winkler high up on the Mönchsberg, watching the lights of the city come on below, I heard a man from Munich exclaim in admiration of the same view: "Ah, Salzburg! Still the most beautiful of Bavarian cities." From three sides of the restaurant, three glasses smashed in Austrian hands. The man from Munich hastily paid up and left.

Austria borders not just on Germany and Switzerland, but on Liechtenstein, Italy, Yugoslavia, Czechoslovakia, and Hungary. In Austria's greenest province, Styria, one side of the road is sometimes in Yugoslavia, and you're never far from Hungary or Italy. Styria is so prickly about its independence, even from Austria, that it maintains its own embassies in Vienna and Washington. It is the source of Schilcher, Austria's best rosé wine, which you almost never see in Viennese restaurants. A few years ago, at a farmhouse near Graz, the Styrian capital, I was sipping some Schilcher that went with some wonderful lamb. "Where is this lamb from?" I asked my host.

"Right here," he replied. "Styrian lamb wins all kinds of prizes."

"Then why can't we find it in Vienna?" I wondered. "When we do get lamb, it comes all the way from New Zealand and costs a fortune."

"That's because we don't grow lambs or Schilcher for export," he replied, dead serious.

The influx and tastes of Yugoslav and Turkish workers have made lamb cheaper and plentiful all over Austria, and now, with the crumbling of the Iron Curtain, Austria will reluctantly become even more of a melting pot than it was in the days of the Habsburg empire. The most assimilable province will surely be Burgenland, which used to be part of Hungary. It retains much of its Magyar character in villages where you open a door and find, instead of a courtyard, a whole street full of steep-roofed houses, people, and life. With the dissolution of the Austro-Hungarian empire after World War I, Burgenland was ceded to Austria, pending a plebiscite in 1921. The population voted overwhelmingly to stay Austrian—except for the people of Ödenburg, which was then its capital and is now Sopron in Hungary. Later, but too late, it was discovered that Ödenburg's pro-Hungarians had registered the inhabitants of several cemeteries to achieve a majority. By enlisting their ancestors, they doomed their descendants to two generations behind the Iron Curtain and a difficult job of catching up. Their move also meant, until lately, that to go from one point in Burgenland to another 20 km (12.5 mi) away, Westerners sometimes had to detour up to 100 km (62 mi).

Burgenland also boasts a culturally active Croatian minority, while Carinthia, Austria's southernmost province, has a proud Slovenian minority that is still fighting for the legal right not to Germanize the names of its villages.

The ultimate identity problem, however, belonged until recently to the province of Lower Austria, which is neither low nor south but takes its name from the part of the Danube it dominates on the map. Before 1986, Lower Austria had no capital city; its state offices were scattered around Vienna, the metropolis it envelops with forest. Upon its selection as the provincial seat, the small city of St. Pölten, with a core of lovely churches and cloisters that swirl around you like a Barococo ballet, danced onto the map of tourist destinations. Already coming to life as a sightseeing attraction, St. Pölten is starting to thrive as a center of government, though Lower Austria's bureaucrats in Vienna are relocating slowly and grudgingly, if at all; many are contemplating early retirement.

Any day of the year, you can take an express train at Wien's Westbahnhof for an eight hour, 770-km (480-mi) east-west crossing of most of the country, stopping at five of Austria's nine provincial capitals: St. Pölten; Linz, the Upper Austrian seat; Salzburg; Innsbruck in Tirol, and Bregenz in Vorarlberg. But you would be well rewarded, as the pages that follow will demonstrate, by disembarking at each one and giving it a day or two or more of your life.

1 Essential Information

Before You Go

Government Tourist Offices

by George W. Hamilton

A longtime resident of Vienna, George Hamilton writes on travel and tourism in Eastern Europe.

In the United States the primary source of information for anyone planning a trip to Austria is the **Austrian National Tourist Office**, 500 5th Ave., 20th floor, New York, NY 10110, tel. 212/944–6880; 11601 Wilshire Blvd., Suite 2480, Los Angeles, CA 90025, tel. 213/477–3332; 1300 Post Oak Blvd., Suite 960, Houston, TX 77056, tel. 713/850–9999; 500 N. Michigan Ave., Suite 1950, Chicago, IL 60611, 708/644–5556. These offices have detailed material on all kinds of specific holiday offerings, so indicate what you most want to do or see. They can also tell you about snow and ski conditions at various resort centers.

In Canada the tourist offices are at 2 Bloor St., Toronto, Ontario M4W 1A8, tel. 416/967–3348; 1010 Sherbrooke St. W, Suite 1410, Montreal, Quebec H3A 2R7, tel. 514/849–3709; 200 Granville St., Suite 1380, Granville Square, Vancouver, BC V6C 1S4, tel. 604/683–5808 or 683–8695. For current snow conditions, tel. 416/967–6870.

In the United Kingdom, check with the tourist office at 30 George St., London W1R 0AL, tel. 071/629–0461. Ask for the *Holiday Hotline* for the latest resort and price information.

Tour Groups

If you want to see the best and most of Austria in a limited time, then consider an escorted tour. Imaginative itineraries abound, hitting out-of-the-way places you might not be able to get to on your own as well as the traditional tourist spots. Because Austria is a major travel destination, a number of operators offer packages covering every conceivable interest. These packages also tend to save you money on airfare and hotels. If group travel is not your thing, look into independent packages (described below). Here, too, variety abounds. You can design your own itinerary by stringing together mini hotel packages in various cities, taking a self-drive tour, castle-hopping, riding the rails, or whipping up a unique combination of all of the above.

Nearly all operators offer both general and special-interest tours year-round. For specifics, see below or check with one of the Austrian National Tourist Offices, major international airlines, and, of course, travel agents.

When evaluating any tour, be sure to find out exactly what expenses are included (particularly tips, taxes and service charges, side trips, additional meals, and entertainment); ratings of all hotels on the itinerary and the facilities they offer; the policy regarding complaints, tour-interruption insurance, and cancellation by either you or the tour operator; the number of travelers in your group; and, if you are traveling alone, the cost for a single supplement. Note whether the tour operator reserves the right to change hotels, routes, or even prices after you've booked.

Listed below is a sampling of operators and packages to give you an idea of what is available. Most tour operators request that bookings be made through a travel agent—there is no additional charge for doing so.

General-interest Tours **Adriatic Tours** (691 W. 10th St., San Pedro, CA 90731, tel. 213/548–1446 or 800/272–1718) offers a nine-day escorted tour that includes Vienna, Salzburg, and Innsbruck.

For shorter stays, **Hapag Lloyd Tours** (1640 Hempstead Tpke., East Meadow, NY 11554, tel. 516/794–1253 or 800/334–2724) offers eight-day tours. **Intropa International** (1066 Saratoga Ave., San Jose, CA 95129, tel. 408/247–5574 or 800/468–7672) specializes in music tours of Austria. At the upper end of the price spectrum, **Abercrombie & Kent** (1420 Kensington Rd., Oak Brook, IL 60521, tel. 708/954–2944 or 800/323–7308) has a seven-day luxury rail and road tour through Austria.

With **Maupintour** (Box 807, Lawrence, KS 66044, tel. 913/843–1211 or 800/255–4266), you can spend a week at a luxury resort in the Tirol and take daily motorcoach and rail excursions into the Bavarian, Austrian, and Italian Alps. The 14-day Bavarian Alpine Adventure takes in Vienna, Salzburg, Zell Am See, and Innsbruck.

Tour operators that combine Austria with other Alpine destinations include **American Express Vacations** (Box 5014, Atlanta, GA 30302, tel. 800/241–1700 or 800/282–0800 in GA), **Trafalgar Tours** (21 E. 26th St., New York, NY 10010, tel. 212/689–8977 or 800/854–0103), **Globus Gateway** (150 S. Los Robles Ave., Pasadena, CA 91101, tel. 818/449–0919 or 800/556–5454), **Olson-Travelworld** (100 N. Sepulveda Blvd., Suite 1010, El Segundo, CA 90245, tel. 213/615–0711; 800/421–2255; in CA 800/421–5785), and **TWA Getaway Vacations** (tel. 800/438–2929).

Special-interest Tours From the United States, you can book ski tours, rail tours, self-drive tours, ballooning tours, Vienna-only tours, Danube cruise tours, and budget tours, among others. Fly/drive tours combining Austria with the southern part of Germany, northern Italy, or Switzerland are a popular way of seeing more than one country. Pan Am offers several ski tours in the Austrian provinces during the winter. Buddy Bombard's popular Great Balloon Adventures (*see* below) features balloon rides, picnic lunches, and afternoon sightseeing in the Salzburg region, the Alpine foothills, and the Lake District.

Austrian Airlines (17–20 Whitestone Expressway, Whitestone, NY 11357, tel. 718/760–8630 or 800/843–0002) has Ski Escapade tours to Salzburg, Innsbruck, and Kitzbühel.

Value Holidays (10224 N. Port Washington Rd., Mequon, WI 53092-5755, tel. 414/241–6373 or 800/558–6850) sells a Royal Castle Vacation, which includes seven nights or more in romantic castles or historic hunting lodges in Austria and unlimited use of a rental car.

The Bombard Society (6727 Curran St., McLean, VA 22101, tel. 703/448–9407 or 800/862–8537) meets clients in Salzburg for the start of land packages that include lodging and meals, sights and ballooning.

For Britons Austria has long been a popular destination for British travelers, so a great many tour operators—about 75 in fact—have vacation packages for all seasons. These cover every interest from guided art tours to excellent budget ski trips. With so many firms offering good Austrian package tours, only a few can be listed here; for a full list, check with the Austrian National Tourist Office or your travel agent.

Austria Travel (46 Queen Anne's Gate, London SW1H 9AU, tel. 071/222–2430), run by the Anglo-Austrian Society, is one of the best sources of well-organized tours that are good value. As you might suspect, the society arranges economical packages to encourage more Britons to visit Austria. The tours take in the countryside as well as the major cities, and side trips to Budapest and Prague can be arranged.

DER Travel Service (18 Conduit St., London W1R 9TD, tel. 071/408–0111) offers two-center stays in Austrian cities, resort holidays in the Tirol, and 10-night Christmas and New Year packages.

GTF Tours (182–186 Kensington Church St., London W8 4DP, tel. 071/792–0311) offers city breaks in Vienna, Salzburg, and Innsbruck, fly/drive holidays, and Danube river cruises.

Page & Moy (136–140 London Rd., Leicester LE2 1EN, tel. 0533/552521) offers an eight-day Austria and Switzerland Alpine trip that takes in Innsbruck and St. Anton, art and music holidays in Vienna, and tours of Austrian cities and the Salzkammergut region.

Prospect Music & Art Ltd. (454–458 Chiswick High Rd., London W4 5TT, tel. 081/742–2323) has art tours and opera and music tours in Salzburg and Vienna.

Shearings Holidays (Miry La., Wigan, Lancashire WN3 4AG, tel. 0942/824824) and **Wallace Arnold Tours** (Gelderd Rd., Leeds LS12 6DH, tel. 0532/310739) have a selection of coach tours around Austria.

Swan Hellenic (77 New Oxford St., London WC1A 1PP, tel. 071/831–1616) provides guided art and culture tours with lectures by eminent scholars and Oxford and Cambridge dons.

Tyrolean Travel (10–18 Putney Hill, London SW15 6AX, tel. 081/789–6555) is an Austrian specialist with a wide range of tours and resort-based vacations. Its 15-day Grand Austrian Tour, for example, covers all major tourist regions and cities.

A large number of companies offer skiing holidays. Among them are **Active Learning and Leisure** (Northumberland House, 2 King St., Twickenham, Middx. TW1 3RZ, tel. 081/891–4400); **Austro Tours Ltd.** (5 St. Peter's St., St. Albans, Herts. AL1 3DH, tel. 0727/838191); **Nielson Ski** (Arndale House, Otley Rd. Heatingly, Leeds LS6 2UU, tel. 0532/744422); **Winter World** (Summerville House, 58A The Grove, Ilkley, West Yorks. LS29 9PA, tel. 0943/816317).

Package Deals for Independent Travelers

Independent travel usually costs more than going in a group, but you will have far more flexibility in terms of what you can see and how you spend your time; it may be a good idea in a country like Austria, with so much tempting variety. And you will get far better value for money when dining on your own. Many of the independent packages that include lodging will work out to be less expensive than the flight alone would be if you booked a regular economy fare. American Express or your travel agency can also assist with rail passes, Danube river boats, and other surface transportation; airline packages tend to get you to one city and leave you there, which is fine if you'll be on a ski holiday, less useful if you want to see more of Austria.

Austrian Airlines (*see* above), offers a series of air/hotel packages in Vienna and Salzburg ranging from five to nine days. **Pan Am Holidays** (tel. 800/843–8687) provides special rates at select hotels when you fly round-trip to Vienna on Pan Am; stay for just one night or as many as you choose. Pan Am also serves up fly/drive packages.

American Airlines Fly Away Vacations (tel. 817/355–1234 or 800/433–7300) lets you design your own fly/drive itinerary, choosing from among dozens of hotels in all price ranges, rental cars, and rail passes. Three-day packages to Innsbruck, Vienna, and Salzburg are available. **TWA Getaway Vacations** (tel. 800/438–2929) has three-night and six-night Vienna packages.

Travel Bound (599 Broadway, New York, NY 10012, tel. 212/334–1350 or 800/223–6243) offers both fly/drive and Eurail packages, which include six nights' hotel accommodations and either seven days' use of a rental car or a rail pass.

Jet Vacations (888 7th Ave., New York, NY 10106, tel. 212/247–0999 or 800/538–0999) has preferred nightly rates at hotels in Innsbruck, Salzburg, and Vienna. Sightseeing in a chauffeured Mercedes limo or sedan can be arranged.

When to Go

Austria has two main tourist seasons. The weather usually turns glorious about Easter to mark the start of the summer season and holds until about mid-October, often later. Because much of the country remains "undiscovered," you will usually find crowds only in the major cities and resorts. May and early June, September, and October are the pleasantest months for traveling around; there is less demand for restaurant tables, and hotel prices tend to be lower.

An Italian invasion takes place over the long Easter weekend, and hotel rooms in Vienna are at a premium, but otherwise July and August and when the main festivals take place are the most crowded times.

The winter-sports season starts in December, snow conditions permitting, and runs through April. You can ski as late as mid-June on the high glaciers, at altitudes of 2,500 meters (8,200 ft) or more. Reservations are essential in the major ski resorts in season, although even then, travelers on their own can frequently find rooms in private houses or small pensions if they're prepared to take a slight detour off the beaten path.

Climate Austria has four distinct seasons, all on the whole fairly mild. But because of altitudes and the Alpine divide, temperatures and dampness vary considerably from one part of the country to another; for example, northern Austria in winter is often overcast and dreary, while the southern half of the country basks in sunshine. In winter it's wise to check with the automobile clubs for weather conditions, since mountain roads often get blocked and ice and fog are hazards.

Average daily maximum and minimum temperatures in Austria:

Vienna	Jan.	34F	1C	May	66F	19C	Sept.	68F	20C
		25	−4		50	10		52	11
	Feb.	37F	3C	June	73F	23C	Oct.	57F	14C
		27	−3		57	14		45	7
	Mar.	46F	8C	July	77F	25C	Nov.	45F	7C
		34	1		59	15		37	3
	Apr.	59F	15C	Aug.	75F	24C	Dec.	37F	3C
		43	6		59	15		30	−1

Salzburg	Jan.	36F	2C	May	66F	19C	Sept.	68F	20C
		21	−6		46	8		50	10
	Feb.	39F	4C	June	72F	22C	Oct.	57F	14C
		23	−5		52	11		41	5
	Mar.	48F	9C	July	75F	24C	Nov.	46F	8C
		30	−1		55	13		32	0
	Apr.	57F	14C	Aug.	73F	23C	Dec.	37F	3C
		39	4		55	13		25	−4

Innsbruck	Jan.	34F	1C	May	68F	20C	Sept.	70F	21C
		19	−7		46	8		50	10
	Feb.	39F	4C	June	75F	24C	Oct.	59F	15C
		23	−5		52	11		41	5
	Mar.	52F	11C	July	77F	25C	Nov.	46F	8C
		32	0		55	13		32	0
	Apr.	61F	16C	Aug.	75F	24C	Dec.	36F	2C
		39	4		54	12		25	−4

Current weather information for more than 750 cities around the world may be obtained by calling **WeatherTrak** information service at 900/370–8728 (the cost is 95¢ per minute). A taped message will tell you to dial the three-digit access code for the destination you're interested in (either SAL or VIE in Austria). For a list of all access codes, send a stamped, self-addressed envelope to Cities, 9B Terrace Way, Greensboro, NC 27403. For further information, phone 800/247–3282.

Festivals and Seasonal Events

Jan. 1 The **New Year** opens in Vienna with the world-famous concert by the Vienna Philharmonic Orchestra (tickets from Vienna Philharmonic, Musikverein, Bösendorferstr. 12, A–1010 Vienna, tel. 0222/505–6525; they may be charged to your credit card, but you may need to write a year—or more—in advance). Those who can't get into the Philharmonic concert try for one of the performances of the Johann Strauss operetta *Die Fledermaus* in the State Opera and Volksoper (tickets from Bundestheaterverband, Goethegasse 1, A–1010 Vienna, by credit card; tel. 0222/513–1513) or for Beethoven's Ninth (Choral) Symphony by the Vienna Symphony Orchestra (tickets by credit card from Konzerthaus, Lothringerstr. 20, A–1030 Vienna, tel. 0222/712–1211). Those who want to dance their way into the new year can do so at the Kaiserball in the elegant rooms of the Hofburg (information and tickets: WKV, Hofburg, Heldenplatz, A–1014 Vienna, tel. 0222/587–3666–14).

Mid-Jan. **Mozart Week** in Salzburg features opera and orchestral works (tickets from Mozarteum, Schwarzstr. 26, A–5020 Salzburg, tel. 0622/73154).

Early Mar. **Viennale** in Vienna shows films ranging from the latest of the avant-garde to retrospectives (tickets, information: Wiener Festwochen Viennale, Uraniastr. 1, A–1010 Vienna, tel. 0222/753285).

Easter **Easter Festival,** Salzburg's "other" major music festival, now under the sure hand of Sir Georg Solti, offers opera and concerts of the highest quality, with ticket prices to match (tickets: Hofstallgasse 1, A–5020 Salzburg, tel. 0662/842541–361).

May 30 **Corpus Christi** is a religious holiday celebrated throughout Austria with colorful processions and parades. In the Lungau region of Land Salzburg, villagers dress up in local costumes that appear only on the most special occasions. Equally colorful are the water processions with gaily decorated boats and barges on the Traun and Hallstätter lakes.

Mid-May–mid-June **Wiener Festwochen** takes place in Vienna—a festival of theater, music, films, and exhibitions (tickets: Wiener Festwochen, Lehargasse 11, A–1060 Vienna, tel. 0222/586–1676).

Mid-June **A Schubert Festival** is held in Hohenems in Vorarlberg.

June 21 **Midsummer Night** is ablaze with bonfires throughout the country, with the liveliest celebrations taking place in the mountains of Tirol and in the Wachau region along the Danube in Lower Austria.

July–Aug. **Carinthian Summer** combines concerts, opera, and literature in the modern Congress House in Villach and in the exquisite monastary and baroque chapel in Ossiach (tickets: through May, Carinthischer Sommer, Gumpendorfer Str., A–1060 Vienna, tel. 0222/568198; May through Aug., Carinthischer Sommer, Stift Ossiach, A–9570 Ossiach, tel. 04243/2510 or 2502).

Musical Summer in Vienna gives you a choice every night of a recital in one of the city's many palaces or an orchestral concert in the courtyard of the city hall. (Tickets and information: Musikalischer Sommer, Friedrich Schmidt-Platz 5, A–1082 Vienna, tel. 0222/4000–8400).

The Salzburg Festival brings together the world's greatest musical artists for a celebration that involves the whole city. (For tickets, write several months in advance to Salzburger Festspiele, Postfach 140, A–5010 Salzburg, tel. 0662/842541).

Sept. 1 Marks the start of the **theater and music season** in Vienna, and life gets back to normal for the Viennese. (Information from the Wiener Fremdenverkehrsverband, Obere Augartenstr. 40, A–1020 Vienna, tel. 0222/211–1400).

Early Sept. The **Autumn Trade Fair** packs Vienna during the first weeks of the month; the international event promotes everything from Eastern Europe's heavy machinery to canned goods, wine, and office supplies from almost everywhere.

The **Haydn Festival** takes place in Eisenstadt in Burgenland. (Tickets and information from Burgenländische Haydn Festspiele, Schloss Esterhazy, A–7000 Eisenstadt, tel. 02682/61886).

The **International Bruckner Festival** makes Linz come alive: theater, concerts, fireworks, and art exhibits spread to the St. Florian monastery, where the composer Anton Bruckner

worked and is buried (tickets and information: Untere Donaulände 7, A–4010 Linz, tel. 0732/775230).

Nov. 11 **St. Martin's Day** is as good as a holiday; restaurants throughout
the country serve traditional roast goose and red cabbage in
honor of the patron saint of publicans and innkeepers. Called
Martinigansl, or *Ganslessen* ("Martin's goose," or "goose eating"), it's much more than just a feast of goose; people celebrate
with parties and processions, church services, and village parades. The most enthusiastic celebrations take place in Burgenland, of which Martin is the patron saint.

Nov. 15 On **St. Leopold's Day,** the name day of the ruler Leopold III
(1075–1136), a splendid folk and religious festival takes place at
Klosterneuburg, outside Vienna, where the saint is buried in
the great monastery.

Dec. 6 On **St. Nicholas's Day** the patron saint of children is honored at
Christkindl (Christchild) festivals, open-air markets throughout the country selling toys, favors, decorations, and food. The
town of Christkindl in Styria comes into its glory each year at
this time.

Dec. 24 The **Christmas Eve** service in the tiny memorial chapel at
Oberndorf, north of Salzburg, features the singing of *Silent
Night, Holy Night,* which Franz Gruber wrote when he was organist here in the early 19th century. **Christmas Eve midnight
mass** in St. Stephen's cathedral in Vienna is an impressive if
crowded event; get an entrance pass at the cathedral in advance.

What to Pack

Clothing The Austrians are conservative in dress; slacks on women are
as rare as loud sports shirts are on men. Jeans are ubiquitous in
Austria as everywhere, but are considered inappropriate—
even the designer versions—at concerts (other than pop) or
formal restaurants.

If concerts and opera are on the schedule, women may want a
skirt or dress, men a jacket, and both, dress shoes. Even in the
summer, gala performances at even the small festivals tend to
be dressy affairs. And since an evening outside at a *Heuriger*
(wine garden) may be on your schedule, be sure to take a sweater or light wrap. Unless you're staying in an expensive hotel or
will be in one place for more than a day or two, take hand-
washables; laundry service gets complicated. And pack sturdy,
comfortable shoes. Austria is a walking country, in the cities or
the mountains. The most interesting sections of many cities are
now pedestrian zones, and you'll need flat heels to cope with
the cobblestones.

Miscellaneous An extra pair of glasses, contact lenses, or prescription sun-
glasses is always a good idea. Mountainous areas are bright, so
you will need sunscreen lotion, even in winter. Bring skin and
lip lotion, too, against the drier air. Consider packing a small
folding umbrella, particularly if you'll be going to Salzburg; the
city is noted for its brief but sudden deluges.

Austria, like the rest of Europe, runs on 220V electric current,
so if you pack a hairdryer or other appliance, bring along a con-
verter and the appropriate adapter plugs.

Carry-on Luggage Airlines generally allow each passenger one piece of carry-on luggage on international flights from the United States. The bag cannot exceed 45 inches (length + width + height) and must fit under the seat or in the overhead luggage compartment. Experienced travelers often include essential personal-care items in the carry-on bag as insurance against their checked luggage getting lost.

Checked Luggage Passengers are generally allowed to check two pieces of luggage (or one piece in addition to skis), neither of which can exceed 62 inches (length + width + height) or weigh more than 70 pounds. Baggage allowances vary slightly among airlines, so be sure to check with the carrier or your travel agent before departure. If you're going to ski, ask the airline about appropriate packing for your skis, poles, and boots.

Taking Money Abroad

Traveler's checks and major U.S. credit cards are widely accepted, but in 1991 a dispute with the credit card organizations made many hotels, restaurants, and travel agencies in Austria unwilling to take credit cards. Yet some hotels whose stated policy is "No credit cards" may be announcing their reluctance, not a refusal, to accept the cards, and in some circumstances they may take them. Cards are more welcome in the major tourist centers of Vienna, Salzburg, and Innsbruck; in some wildly expensive winter resort communities, such as Lech and Zürs, credit cards simply aren't recognized. Whether or not this situation continues in 1992, the prudent consumer will confirm a facility's credit card policy before using its services.

You will need cash for some of the smaller restaurants and shops, for snacks and coffee, for taxis, and for museum admissions. Although you won't get as good an exchange rate at home as abroad, it's wise to change a small amount of money into Austrian schillings before you go; lines at airport currency-exchange booths can be long. Most U.S. banks will convert dollars into schillings. If your local bank can't provide this service, you can exchange money through **Thomas Cook Currency Services** (29 Broadway, New York, NY 10006, tel. 212/635–0515).

For safety and convenience, it's always best to take traveler's checks. The most recognized ones are American Express, Barclays, Thomas Cook, and those issued through major commercial banks, such as Citibank and Bank of America. Some banks will issue the checks free to established customers, but most charge a 1% fee. Buy part of the traveler's checks in small denominations for the end of your trip, to save you from having more foreign money left than you need; but note that in Austria, all banks and exchange offices have a base fee for cashing a check of any size, which could eat up 15% or more of a small check. (Hold on to your receipts after exchanging your traveler's checks in Austria; it's easier to convert leftover foreign currency back into dollars if you have the receipts. You can exchange any surplus schillings as you are leaving Austria and will probably get a better rate than you will through your bank at home.) You can also buy traveler's checks in West German deutschemarks, which have a fixed exchange rate of 1:7 to the Austrian schilling. Traveler's checks in deutschemarks are a good idea if the American dollar is falling and you want to lock in the current rate. Remember to take the addresses of offices where you can get refunds for lost or stolen traveler's checks and be sure to keep a list of the check numbers separate from the checks themselves.

In Austria, you will get the best exchange rate at one of the larger banks or, if you're carrying American Express checks, at American Express offices. Shops, hotels, and smaller banks and exchange offices often charge a higher fee and may not offer as favorable a rate.

Getting Money from Home

There are at least four ways to get money from home:

(1) Have it sent through a large commercial bank that has a branch where you are staying. The only drawback is that you must have an account with the bank; if not, you'll have to go through your own bank, and the process will be slower and more costly.

(2) Have it sent through American Express. If you are an American Express credit-card holder, you can cash a personal check or a counter check at American Express offices for up to $1,000; $200 will be in Austrian schillings and $800 in traveler's checks (which you can immediately cash if you need the funds). There is a 1% commission on the traveler's checks. You can also obtain up to $10,000 in cash through an American Express MoneyGram. It works this way: You call home and ask someone to go to an American Express office or an American Express MoneyGram agent located in a retail outlet, and fill out a MoneyGram form. It can be paid for in cash or with any major credit card. The person making the payment is given a reference number and telephones that number to you. The MoneyGram agent calls an 800 number and authorizes the transfer of funds to the American Express office or participating agency where you are staying. In most cases, the money is available immediately on a 24-hour basis. You pick it up by showing identification and giving the reference number. Fees vary with the amount of money sent. For $300, the fee is $30; for $5,000, the fee is $195. For the American Express MoneyGram location nearest your home and to find the Austrian locations, call 800/543–4080. You do not have to be a cardholder to use this service.

(3) Present your MasterCard or Visa card at one of the participating banks in Austria (in Vienna, at any branch of the Zentralsparkasse) and ask for schillings. You will receive the cash, sometimes minus a fee, and your card account will be billed in dollars just as though you had made a purchase. Be aware, though, that interest at your own bank's regular rate will begin immediately and accrue until you repay the advance.

(4) Have money sent through Western Union. If you have MasterCard or Visa, you can have a friend in the United States call 800/325–6000 and have money sent for any amount up to your credit limit. If not, have someone take cash or a certified check to a Western Union office. The money will be delivered to a bank where you are staying. Fees vary with the amount of money sent and the location of the recipient.

U.K. citizens holding a Eurocheque card and the Eurocheques themselves—obtainable from a bank—can write checks for up to AS2,500 a day and receive cash at virtually any bank. The checks may also be used for purchases, although no single check can be written for more than AS2,500.

All major British banks have correspondents in Austria and can arrange for a telex transfer of cash usually overnight.

Cash Machines American Express has cash machines in Vienna at the airport and at its office at Liebenberggasse/Parkring 10, A–1010 Vienna. More such machines are appearing. For U.K. citizens, the possibility exists that by 1992, Eurocheque cards can be used to obtain schillings from any of the Bankomat cash machines throughout the country.

Austrian Currency

The Austrian unit of currency is the schilling (AS), subdivided into 100 groschen. At this writing, the exchange rate was about AS11.7 to the dollar, AS20.7 to the pound sterling. These rates can and will vary. The schilling is pegged to the West German deutschemark at a 7-to-1 ratio that remains constant.

There are Austrian coins for 5, 10, and 50 groschen and for 1, 5, 10, and 20 schillings. The paper notes have AS20, AS50, AS100, AS500, AS1,000 and AS5,000 face value. There is little visible difference between the 100- and 500-schilling notes, so be careful, since confusion could be expensive!

Foreign currency and Austrian schillings may be taken in and out of the country in any amount. Legally, foreign exchange is limited to licensed offices (banks and exchange offices); in practice, the rule is universally ignored.

What It Will Cost

Austria remains one of Europe's best buys. Indeed, this is the reason behind the annual invasion of Italians, Germans, and Dutch, in particular; a holiday in Austria for them is relatively inexpensive. The Austrians, in turn, are shocked by prices in neighboring countries. Inflation in Austria is negligible, so prices go up slowly if at all. Generally, costs directly related to tourism (hotels, restaurants, ski lifts, and such) increased less, despite high taxes, than in other major tourist countries.

Vienna and Salzburg are the expensive cities in Austria, followed by Innsbruck, but many attractive places—Graz, Linz, Krems, Hallstatt, Feldkirch, Dürnstein, and Steyr, to name but a sampling—offer almost as much history and some notable architecture at a much lower cost. The high-priced resorts are Kitzbühel, Lech, St. Anton, Seefeld, Badgastein, Bad Hofgastein, Bad Kleinkirchheim, Velden, Saalbach, Zell am See, and Pörtschach.

Ample bargains can be found off the beaten path and in rural areas. You can also cut your vacation costs by staying in one place for at least a week and making it a base for daily excursions. Many hotels of all classes offer special weekly rates, although not all of them during the high season. In many resort areas, a longer stay will entitle you to a Visitor's Card, carrying substantial reductions at local swimming pools, saunas, ski lifts, bowling alleys, and such.

In many localities, including the expensive resort towns, you can cut costs by taking an apartment or a bungalow. And if your German is up to it, you can find room and board in the kind of alpine-style farmhouse that's the original model for every balconied inn and luxury country hotel in Austria (*see* Lodging, below).

Off-season travel is recommended if you are willing to pass up the big events that take place in—or create—the peak season. Air travel and hotel rates are lower out of season. The hotel reductions, especially for full-board, can amount to one-third or more.

Taxes Austrian prices include 20% VAT (value-added tax) on most items, 10% on some goods and services. If you buy goods totaling AS1,000 or more in one shop, ask for the appropriate papers *when you make the purchase,* and you can get a refund of the VAT either at the airport when you leave or by mail. You can have the refund credited to your credit card account and not have to worry about the exchange rates. In Austria tax upon tax is piled onto beverages, but don't worry about it—they are all included automatically in the prices. In some resorts, a small local hotel-room tax is added to the bill.

Sample Costs A cup of coffee in a café will cost about AS22; a half-liter of draft beer, AS27–30; a glass of wine, AS32; a Coca-Cola, AS22; an open-face sandwich, AS20; a mid-range theater ticket AS200; a concert ticket AS250; an opera ticket AS600; a 1-mile taxi ride, AS27. Outside the hotels, laundering a shirt costs about AS30; dry cleaning a suit costs around AS100; a dress, AS70. A shampoo and set for a woman will cost around AS400, a manicure about AS60; a man's haircut (without shampoo) will cost about AS120.

Passports and Visas

Americans All U.S. citizens need a passport to enter Austria. Application for your first passport must be made in person; renewals can be obtained in person or by mail. First-time applicants should apply at least five weeks in advance of their departure date to one of the 13 U.S. Passport Agency offices. In addition, local county courthouses, many state and probate courts, and some post offices accept passport applications. Necessary documents include (1) a completed passport application (Form DSP–11); (2) proof of citizenship (birth certificate with raised seal or naturalization papers); (3) proof of identity (unexpired driver's license, employee ID card or any other document with your photograph and signature); (4) two recent, identical, two-inch-square photographs (black-and-white or color) with a white or off-white background; (5) $42 application fee for a 10-year passport (those under 18 pay $27 for a five-year passport). When you pay in cash, you must have the exact amount; no change is given. Passports should be mailed to you in about 10 working days, but it can take longer in the early summer.

To renew your passport by mail, you'll need to complete Form DSP–82 and submit two recent, identical passport photographs, your current passport (less than 12 years old), and a check or money order for $35.

A visa is not required to enter Austria for a stay of up to three months. For longer stays, check with the Austrian Embassy

(2343 Massachusetts Ave. NW, Washington, DC 20008, tel. 202/232–2674) or the nearest Austrian Consulate General.

Canadians All Canadians need a passport to enter Austria. Send your completed application (available at any post office or passport office) to the Bureau of Passports (Suite 215, West Tower, Guy Favreau Complex, 200 Rene Levesque Blvd. W, Montréal, Québec H2Z 1X4). Include $25, two photographs, a guarantor, and proof of Canadian citizenship. Applications can be made in person at the regional passport offices in Edmonton, Halifax, Montreal, Calgary, St. John's (Newfoundland), Victoria, Toronto, Vancouver, or Winnipeg. Passports are valid for five years and are nonrenewable.

A visa is not needed by Canadians to enter Austria for stays of up to three months.

Britons British subjects do not need a visa to enter Austria, but they do need a valid passport or a British Visitor's Passport. Application forms are available from most travel agents and major post offices or from the Passport Office (Clive House, 70 Petty France, London SW1H 9HD, tel. 071/279–3434). The cost is £15 for a standard 32-page passport, £30 for a 94-page passport. British Visitor's Passports are valid for one year only, cost £7.50, and are nonrenewable. All applications must be accompanied by two photographs and be countersigned by your bank manager or by a solicitor, a barrister, a doctor, a clergyman, or a justice of the peace.

Customs and Duties

On Arrival Austria follows the general European regulations, with the honor system of green and red gates ("Nothing to Declare" or "Goods to Declare") at the airports. If you are entering by highway, officials may ask what you are bringing into the country. In general, though, there is no need to worry about the letter of the regulations. Customs officials are as a rule so overworked that they are not too concerned whether you have 400 or 420 cigarettes with you. Travelers over 17 *coming from European countries*—regardless of citizenship—may bring in duty-free 200 cigarettes *or* 50 cigars *or* 250 grams of tobacco, two liters of wine and one liter of spirits, one bottle of toilet water (approx. 300 ml), and 50 milliliters of perfume. *Travelers from all other countries* (such as those coming directly from the United States or Canada) may bring in *twice* these amounts.

If you take into Austria any foreign-made equipment from home, such as cameras, it's wise to carry the original receipt with you or register it with U.S. Customs before you leave (Form 4457). Otherwise you may end up paying duty on your return.

On Departure You may take any reasonable quantity of goods with you when you leave, but you may need an export permit for certain art objects and some antiques. The shop where you bought the goods will advise you and help with any formalities.

U.S. Customs U.S. citizens may bring home duty-free up to $400 worth of foreign goods, as long as they have been out of the country for at least 48 hours and haven't made an international trip in 30 days. Each member of a family is entitled to the same exemption, regardless of age, and exemptions may be pooled. For the next $1,000 worth of goods, a flat 10% is assessed; above $1,000 the duty varies with the merchandise. Travelers 21 years or older may include in the duty-free allowance one liter of alcohol, 100 cigars (non-Cuban), and 200 cigarettes. Only one bottle of perfume trademarked in the United States may be imported. Anything exceeding these limits will be taxed at the port of entry and may be taxed additionally in the traveler's home state. There is no duty on original works of art or on antiques over 100 years old. Gifts valued at under $50 may be mailed to friends or relatives at home duty-free, but you may not send more than one package per day to any one addressee, and packages may not include tobacco, liquor, or perfumes costing more than $5.

Canadian Customs   Exemptions for returning Canadians range from $20 to $300, depending on length of stay out of the country. For the $300 exemption, you must have been out of the country for one week. In any given year, you are allowed only one $300 exemption. You may bring in duty-free up to 50 cigars, 200 cigarettes, 2.2 pounds of tobacco, and 40 ounces of liquor, provided these are declared in writing to customs on arrival and accompany you in hand or checked-through baggage. Personal gifts should be mailed labeled "Unsolicited Gift—Value under $40." Obtain a copy of the Canadian Customs brochure *I Declare* for further details.

U.K. Customs   Returning to the United Kingdom, those who are 17 years or older may bring home duty-free: (1) 200 cigarettes or 100 cigarillos or 50 cigars or 250 grams of tobacco; (2) two liters of still table wine and, in addition, (a) one liter of alcohol over 22% by volume (most spirits) or (b) two liters of alcohol under 22% by volume (fortified or sparkling wines) or (c) two more liters of still table wine; (3) 60 milliliters of perfume and 250 milliliters of toilet water; (4) other goods to the value of £32, but not more than 50 liters of beer or 25 lighters.

In addition, *no animals or pets of any kind* may be brought into the United Kingdom. The penalties for doing so are severe and the regulation strictly enforced; there are *no* exceptions. Similarly, fresh meats, plants and vegetables, controlled drugs, and firearms and ammunition may not be brought into the United Kingdom.

For further information, contact **HM Customs and Excise** (Dorset House, Stamford St., London SE1 9PS, tel. 071/620–1313).

Traveling with Film

If your camera is new, shoot and develop a few rolls of film before leaving home. Pack some lens tissue and an extra battery for your built-in exposure meter. Invest about $10 in a skylight filter; it will protect the lens and reduce haze, particularly if you're taking pictures at high altitudes.

Film doesn't like hot weather, so if you're driving in summer, don't store it in the glove compartment or on the shelf under the rear window. Put it on the floor behind the front seat on the side opposite the exhaust pipe.

On a plane trip, never pack unprocessed film in check-in luggage; if your bags get X-rayed, say goodbye to your pictures. Always carry undeveloped film with you through security and ask to have it inspected by hand. (It helps to have your film in a plastic bag, ready for quick inspection.)

The old airport scanning machines, still in use in some countries, administer heavy doses of radiation that can turn a family portrait into an early morning fog. The newer models used in all U.S. airports are safe for many more scans, depending on the speed of your film. But the effects are cumulative; you can put the same roll of film through several scans without worry. After five scans, however, you're asking for trouble.

If your film gets fogged and you want an explanation, send it to the National Association of Photographic Manufacturers (550 Mamaroneck Ave., Harrison, NY 10528), which will try to determine what went wrong. The service is free.

Language

German is the official national language in Austria. In larger cities and in most resort areas, you will have no problem finding people who speak English; hotel and restaurant staffs in particular speak it reasonably well. Most young Austrians speak at least passable if not fluent English.

Staying Healthy

No health certificate or special shots are required before visiting Austria, but if you will be cycling or hiking through the eastern or southeastern parts of the country, get inoculated against encephalitis; it can be carried by ticks.

If you have a health problem that may require the purchase of prescription drugs, have your doctor write a prescription using the drug's generic name, as brand names vary from country to country.

Water throughout Austria is safe and drinkable unless marked *"Kein Trinkwasser"* (not drinking water).

The **International Association for Medical Assistance to Travelers (IAMAT)** is a worldwide organization that offers a list of approved physicians and clinics meeting British and American standards. For a list of Austrian physicians and clinics that are part of this network, contact IAMAT (417 Center St., Lewiston, NY 14092, tel. 716/754–4883; in Canada, 40 Regal Rd., Guelph, Ontario N1K 1B5; in Europe, 57 Voirets, 1212 Grand-Lancy, Geneva, Switzerland). Membership is free.

Insurance

We recommend strongly that you take out adequate insurance to cover you in three areas, where applicable: health and accident, lost or stolen luggage, and trip cancellation. First review your existing insurance policies; some health plans cover you while traveling, some major-medical plans cover emergency transportation, and some homeowner policies cover the theft or loss of luggage.

Travel-accident insurance and extra coverage against baggage loss or damage are often included in the price of a ticket when paid for with American Express, Visa, or another major credit card.

In the United Kingdom, for free general advice on all aspects of holiday insurance, contact the **Association of British Insurers** (Aldermary House, 10–15 Queen St., London EC4N 1TT, tel. 071/248–4477). A proved leader in the holiday-insurance field is **Europ Assistance** (252 High St., Croydon, Surrey CRO 1NF, tel. 081/680–1234).

Health and Accident
Several companies offer coverage designed to supplement existing health insurance for travelers:

Carefree Travel Insurance (Box 310, 120 Mineola Blvd., Mineola, NY 11501, tel. 516/294–0220 or 800/323–3149) provides coverage for emergency medical evacuation and accidental death and dismemberment. It also offers 24-hour medical advice by phone.

International SOS Assistance (Box 11568, Philadelphia, PA 19116, tel. 215/244–1500 or 800/523–8930), a medical assistance company, provides emergency evacuation services, worldwide medical referrals, and optional medical insurance.

Travel Assistance International (1133 15th St. NW, Suite 400, Washington, DC 20005, tel. 202/331–1609 or 800/821–2828) provides emergency evacuation services and 24-hour medical referrals.

Travel Guard International, underwritten by Transamerica Occidental Life Companies (1145 Clark St., Stevens Point, WI 54481, tel. 715/345–0505 or 800/782–5151), offers emergency evacuation services and reimbursement for medical ex-penses with no deductibles or daily limits.

Wallach and Company, Inc. (243 Church St., Suite 100D, Vienna, VA 22180, tel. 703/281–9500 or 800/237–6615) has comprehensive medical coverage, including emergency evacuation services worldwide.

WorldCare Travel Assistance Association (1150 S. Olive St., Suite T-233, Los Angeles, CA 90015, tel. 213/749–0909 or 800/666–4993) provides unlimited emergency evacuation, 24-hour medical referrals, and an emergency message center.

Lost Luggage
Before you go, itemize the contents of each bag in case you need to file an insurance claim. Be certain to put your business address and telephone number on and inside each piece of luggage, including carry-on bags. If your luggage is lost or stolen and later recovered, the airline will deliver it free of charge.

On international flights, airlines are responsible for lost or damaged property to a limit of $9.07 per pound (or $20 per kilo) for checked baggage and up to $400 per passenger for unchecked baggage. If you're carrying valuables, either take them with you on the plane or buy additional insurance for lost luggage. Some airlines sell extra luggage insurance on request when you check in, but many do not. You can buy insurance for lost, damaged, or stolen luggage through travel agents or directly from various insurance companies. Luggage loss is usually part of a comprehensive travel-insurance package that includes personal accident, trip cancellation, and sometimes default or bankruptcy.

Two companies that offer luggage insurance are **Tele-Trip** (Box 31685, 3201 Farnam St., Omaha, NE 68131, tel. 800/228–9792), a subsidiary of Mutual of Omaha, and **The Travelers Insurance Corporation** (Ticket and Travel Dept., 1 Tower Sq., Hartford,

CT 06183, tel. 203/277–0111 or 800/243–3174). Tele-Trip operates sales booths at airports and also sells insurance through travel agents. Tele-Trip will insure checked luggage for up to 180 days; rates vary according to the length of the trip. The Travelers will insure checked or hand luggage for $500 to $2,000 valuation, also for a maximum of 180 days. Rates for $500 coverage for one to five days are $10; for 180 days, $85. Some other companies whose comprehensive policies cover loss of luggage are **Access America Inc.**, a subsidiary of Blue Cross–Blue Shield (Box 11188, Richmond, VA 23230, tel. 800/334–7525 or 800/284–8300); **Near Services** (450 Prairie Ave., Suite 101, Calumet City, IL 60409, tel. 708/868–6700 or 800/654–6700); **Carefree Travel Insurance** and **Travel Guard International** (*see* Health and Accident Insurance, above).

Trip Cancellation This is usually included in combination travel-insurance packages available from most tour operators, travel agents, and insurance agents.

Renting and Leasing Cars

Car-rental firms, both local and international, will supply self-drive and chauffeured cars, which you can pick up at an airport, rail station, or hotel in large cities. You will need a valid license; for U.S. or Canadian residents, an international driver's license is preferred.

It is considerably cheaper to arrange car rental in the United States than to wait until you get to Austria; the variety of rates and packages—prepaid and deposit-only, daily and weekly, "Supersaver" and "Super-value"—offers you a multitude of choices. Two companies that give good value are Kemwel (800/678–0678) and Europcar, an affiliate of National (800/227–3876), both of which have one-week packages on a two-door manual-shift hatchback with unlimited mileage for well under $200 plus tax (price guaranteed in schillings). You can choose to take the rental company's insurance, which will add about $8–$10 per day to the cost, or you can charge the rental to a major credit card, which will become your primary insurer in case of an accident.

The approximate cost of a comparable car rented locally is $500 per week, plus 23¢ per km, insurance extra. In either case the tax is 20%, so it may be cheaper to hire the car in a neighboring country (Switzerland has no tax, for example), and drive it into Austria even if there's a one-way charge. Shop around, as rates and tax vary widely. Among the cheapest local rental firms is **Autoverleih Buchbinder** (Schlachthausgasse 38, A–1030 Vienna, tel. 0222/71750, 0222/717–5021, and offices throughout Austria).

Car leasing in Austria is practical only if you will be using a car for six months or longer; when you need a car for more than one or two weeks, make a deal with one of the regular rental firms.

Rail Passes

The **EurailPass**, valid for unlimited first-class train travel through 17 countries including Austria, is an excellent value if you plan on traveling around the Continent. The pass must be bought from an authorized agent before you leave for Europe. Apply through your travel agent or through **Rail Europe** (610

5th Ave., New York, NY 10020, tel. 800/345–1900). It does not cover Great Britain and is not available to people who live in Europe or North Africa.

In Austria, the pass is good on the extensive rail network, on Danube river boats of the DDSG (Erste Donau–Dampfschif-fahrts–Gesellschaft) Company between Passau and Vienna, on the steamers on Wolfgangsee, and on the Puchberg am Schneeberg/Hochschneeberg cog railway. The ticket can be bought for periods of 15 days ($390), 21 days ($498), one month ($616), two months ($840), and three months ($1,042). When two or more people travel together, a 15-day rail pass costs each of them $298. Between April 1 and September 30, you need a minimum of three in your group to get this discount. For discount travel within Austria, *see* Getting Around, By Train, below.

For those 25 or younger, the **Eurail Youthpass** is good for one or two months' unlimited second-class travel for $425 or $560. And travelers who like to spread out their train journeys may opt for the **Eurail Flexipass.** With the 15-day pass ($230), you get five days of unlimited travel within the 15 days; a 21-day pass gives you nine days of travel ($398), and a one-month pass gives you 14 days ($498).

Student and Youth Travel

The **International Student Identity Card** (ISIC) entitles full-time students of any age to rail passes, special fares on local transport, student charter flights, and discounts at museums, theaters, sports events, and many other attractions. If bought in the United States, the $14 cost of the ISIC card also includes $3,000 in emergency medical coverage, $100 a day for up to 60 days of hospital coverage, as well as a phone number to call collect in case of emergency. Apply to the Council on International Educational Exchange (CIEE, 205 E. 42nd St., New York, NY 10017, tel. 212/661–1414 and 35 W. 8th St., New York, NY 10011, tel. 212/254–2525). In Canada, the ISIC is available for $CN12 from **Travel Cuts** (187 College St., Toronto, Ontario M5T 1P7, tel. 416/979–2406).

Travelers under age 26 can apply for a **Youth International Ed-ucational Exchange Card** (YIEE) issued by the Federation of International Youth Travel Organizations (FIYTO, 81 Islands Brugge, DK–2300 Copenhagen S, Denmark). It provides ser-vices and benefits similar to those of the ISIC card. The YIEE card is available in the United States from CIEE (*see* above) and in Canada from the Canadian Hosteling Association (CHA, 1600 James Naismith Dr., Suite 608, Gloucester, Ont. K1B 5N4, tel. 613/748–5638).

An **International Youth Hostels Federation** (IYHF) member-ship card is the key to inexpensive dormitory-style accommoda-tions at more than 5,000 youth hostels in 75 countries around the world. Hostels aren't only for young travelers on a budget, though; many have family accommodations. Hostels provide separate sleeping quarters for men and women at rates ranging from $7 to $20 a night per person and are situated in a variety of facilities, including converted farmhouses, villas, restored cas-tles, even lighthouses, as well as specially constructed modern buildings. IYHF memberships, which are valid for 12 months from the time of purchase, are available in the United States through the CIEE (*see* above) or **American Youth Hostels** (AYH, Box 37613, Washington, DC 20013, tel. 202/783–6161). The cost of a first-year membership is $25 for adults 18 to 54; renewal is $15. For those under 18, the rate is $10; for seniors (55 and older), the rate is $15; and for families of two adults and two children, it's $35. Every national hostel association arranges such benefits as discounted rail fares and free bus travel, so be sure to ask for an international concessions list when you join.

In Austria, youth hostels are coordinated through the **Jugend-herbergverband** (Gonzagagasse 22, A–1010 Vienna, tel. 0222/533–5353), which can help you plan a hostel holiday of hiking, cycling, or camping.

Council Travel, a CIEE subsidiary, is the foremost U.S. student travel agency, specializing in low-cost charters and serving as the exclusive U.S. agent for many student airfare bargains and student tours. CIEE's 80-page *Student Travel* catalogue and *Council Charter* brochures are available free from any Council Travel office in the United States (enclose $1 postage if ordering by mail). In addition to the CIEE headquarters and branch office in New York City (*see* above), there are Council Travel offices in Berkeley, La Jolla, Long Beach, Los Angeles, San Diego, San Francisco, and Sherman Oaks, CA; Boulder, CO; New Haven, CT; Washington, DC; Atlanta, GA; Chicago and Evanston, IL; New Orleans, LA; Amherst, Boston, and Cambridge, MA; Minneapolis, MN; Durham, NC; Portland, OR; Providence, RI; Austin and Dallas, TX; Seattle, WA; and Milwaukee, WI.

The **Educational Travel Center** (438 N. Frances Street, Madison, WI 53703, tel. 608/256–5551) is another student travel specialist.

ÖKISTA-Reisen (Türkenstr. 4, A–1090 Vienna, tel. 0222/317526 or 318681, with a branch at Karlsgasse 3, A–1040, tel. 0222/505–0128) is a leader in organizing student travel and cheap charters in Austria. It arranges for standby and other inexpensive flights and weekend excursions to Budapest, Prague, and other eastern European cities.

Students who want to work abroad should contact CIEE's Work Abroad Department (205 E. 42nd St., New York, NY 10017, tel. 212/661–1414, ext. 1130) for information on paid and voluntary jobs overseas for up to six months. CIEE also sponsors study programs in Europe, Latin America, Asia, and Australia and publishes such books as *Work, Study, Travel Abroad: The Whole World Handbook* ($10.95 plus $1 book-rate postage or $2.50 first-class postage) and *Volunteer! The Comprehensive Guide to Voluntary Service in the U.S. and Abroad* ($6.95 plus $1 book-rate postage or $2.50 first-class postage).

The Information Center at the **Institute of International Education** (IIE, 809 UN Plaza, New York, NY 10017, tel. 212/984–5413) has reference books, foreign-university catalogues, study-abroad brochures, and other materials, free for consultation.

Traveling with Children

Publications *Family Travel Times* is a newsletter published 10 times a year by Travel With Your Children (TWYCH, 80 8th Ave., New

York, NY 10011, tel. 212/206–0688). A one-year subscription costs $35 and includes access to back issues and a phone number you can call for specific advice.

Hotels Most hotels in Austria happily welcome children and will arrange special beds and baby-sitters. There's even a hotel in Carinthia named **Austria's First Baby Hotel** (Trebesing Bad 1, A–9852 Trebesing, tel. 04732/2350) where parents accompany the babies instead of the other way around! Ask for the brochure on hotels with special facilities for children at any of the Austrian National Tourist Offices. Many of the smaller holiday hotels are family-run and have special programs for younger guests that leave parents free.

Getting There On international flights, children under 2 years of age not occupying a seat pay 10% of adult fare. Various discounts apply to children aged 2–12, so check with your airline when booking. Reserve a seat behind the bulkhead of the plane, since there's usually more leg room and enough space to fit a bassinet, which the airline will supply. At the same time, ask about special children's meals and snacks; most airlines offer them. See TWYCH's "Airline Guide," published in the February 1990 and 1992 issues of *Family Travel Times* (and scheduled again for February 1992) for a rundown on the services for children offered by 46 airlines. Ask in advance if you can bring aboard your child's car seat. For the booklet "Child/Infant Safety Seats Acceptable for Use in Aircraft," contact the Federal Aviation Administration (APA–200, 800 Independence Ave. SW, Washington, DC 20591, tel. 202/267–3479).

Home Exchange Exchanging homes is a surprisingly low-cost way to enjoy a vacation abroad, especially a long one. The largest home-exchange service, **International Home Exchange Service** (Box 190070, San Francisco, CA 94119, tel. 415/435–3497), publishes three directories a year. Membership, which costs $45, entitles you to one listing and all three directories. Photos of your property in the listing cost an additional $10, and including a second home costs $10.

A good choice for domestic home exchange, **Vacation Exchange Club, Inc.** (Box 820, Haleiwa, HI 96712, tel. 800/638–3841) publishes three directories a year as well as updated, late listings. Annual membership, which includes your listing in one book, a newsletter, and copies of all publications, is $50.

Loan-a-Home (2 Park La., 6E, Mount Vernon, NY 10552, tel. 914/664–7640) is popular with the academic community on sabbatical and businesspeople on temporary assignment. There's no annual membership fee or charge for listing your home; however, one directory and a supplement costs $35. Loan-a-Home publishes two directories (in December and June) and two supplements (in March and September) each year. All four books cost $45 per year.

Baby-sitting Services Children are generally welcome in Austrian hotels, and concierges can arrange reliable baby-sitting. But make your request a day in advance; don't expect baby-sitters at a moment's notice. In Vienna, you can call on the **Babysitter** of the Austrian Academic Guest Service (Mühlgasse 20, A–1040, tel. 0222/587–3525), or the **Babysitterzentrale** (Herbststr. 6–10, A–1160, tel. 0222/951135). Since both organizations draw mainly on students for their sitters, you can arrange for someone who speaks English.

Hints for Disabled Travelers

The Austrian National Tourist Office nearest you can provide a
guide to Austrian hotels that are accessible to disabled visitors, and the tourist office in New York City also has a guide to
Vienna for the disabled, a special map of the city that locates
accessible sights, and a booklet on Vienna's hotels with facilities for the disabled. The Hilton, InterContinental, and
Marriott chain hotels plus a number of smaller ones are accessible to handicapped travelers. The railroads are both under-
standing and helpful. If prior arrangements have been made,
taxis and private vehicles are allowed to drive right to the train
platform; railway personnel will help with boarding and leaving trains; and with three days' notice, a special wheelchair can
be provided for getting around train corridors.

Once in Austria, check with the Österreichischer Zivilin-
validenverband (Lange Gasse 60, A–1080 Vienna, tel. 0222/
408–5505) for more information. The **Sozialamt der Stadt Wien**
(Schottenring 24, A–1020, tel. 0222/531140) and the **Vienna
Tourist Office** (Obere Augartenstr. 40, A–1020, tel. 0222/
211140) also have the booklet on Vienna hotels and the city
guide for the disabled. The biggest problem in Vienna is the
subway system; a number of stations have only stairs or escalators, no elevators.

The **Information Center for Individuals with Disabilities** (Fort
Point Pl., 1st floor, 27–43 Wormwood St., Boston, MA 02210,
tel. 617/727–5540; TDD 617/727–5236) is good at problem solv-
ing and has lists of travel agents who specialize in tours for the
disabled.

Moss Rehabilitation Hospital Travel Information Service (1200
W. Tabor Rd., Philadelphia, PA 19141, tel. 215/456–9600; TDD
215/456–9602) provides information on tourist sights, transportation, and accommodations in destinations around the
world for a small fee.

For a $15 per person annual membership fee, the **Travel Indus-
try and Disabled Exchange** (TIDE, 5435 Donna Ave., Tarzana,
CA 91356, tel. 818/368–5648) provides a quarterly newsletter
and a directory of travel agencies and operators of tours to Europe, Canada, Great Britain, New Zealand, and Australia, who
specialize in travel for the disabled.

Mobility International USA (Box 3551, Eugene, OR 97403, tel.
503/343–1284) has 500 affiliated members. For a $20 annual fee,
it coordinates exchange programs for disabled people around
the world and offers information on accommodations and organized study programs.

In the United Kingdom, excellent guides, *Holidays and Travel
Abroad* and *Holidays in the British Isles*, published by the
Royal Association for Disability and Rehabilitation (25 Morti-
mer St., London W1N 8AB, tel. 071/637–5400), can be ordered
for £3 each from W. H. Smith bookseller or direct from RA-
DAR, with no charge for postage or packing.

Hints for Older Travelers

Austria itself has so many senior citizens that facilities almost
everywhere cater to the special needs of older travelers, with
concessions like smaller portions in restaurants and discounts

for rail travel and museum entry. Check with the nearest branch of the Austrian National Tourist Office to find what form of identification is needed for various advantages.

The **American Association of Retired Persons** (AARP, 1909 K St. NW, Washington, DC 20049, tel. 202/872–4700), open to anyone 50 or older for an annual membership fee of $5 per person or couple, has a Purchase Privilege Program that gives discounts on hotels, airfare, car rentals, RV rentals, and sightseeing to the member and member's spouse or another person who shares the member's household. The AARP Travel Service (800/227–7737) also arranges group tours, including apartment living in Europe, through **AARP Travel Experience from American Express** (Box 5850, Norcross, GA 30091, tel. 800/927–0111).

When using an AARP or other identification card, ask for the reduced hotel rate at the time you make your reservation, not when you check out. At restaurants, show your card to the maître d' before you're seated, since discounts may be limited to certain set menus, days, or hours. When renting a car, remember that economy cars, priced at promotional rates, may cost less than cars available with your discount ID card.

Elderhostel (75 Federal St., 3rd floor, Boston, MA 02110, tel. 617/426–7788) is an innovative educational program for people 60 years and older. Participants live in dorms on some 1,200 campuses around the world. Mornings are devoted to lectures and seminars, afternoons to sightseeing and field trips. Fees for two- to three-week trips, including room, board, tuition, and round-trip transportation, range from $1,800 to $4,500.

National Council of Senior Citizens (925 15th St. NW, Washington, DC 20005, tel. 202/347–8800) is a nonprofit advocacy group with some 5,000 local clubs across the country. Annual membership is $12 per person or per couple. Members receive a monthly newspaper with travel information and an ID card for reduced-rate hotels and car rentals.

Saga International Holidays (120 Boylston St., Boston MA 02116, tel. 800/343–0273) specializes in group travel for people 60 and over, with a selection of variously priced tours.

Further Reading

Edward Crankshaw, *The Habsburgs* (Weidenfeld & Nicolson, 1972): a good and brief history of the royal house that ruled Austria from 1278 to 1918.

Vienna: The Image of a Culture in Decline (Macmillan, 1938; out of print, check your library).

Sarah Gainham, *Night Falls on the City* (Collins, 1967; out of print): an extraordinary novel about the struggle of an actress to hide her Jewish husband from the Nazis in wartime Vienna.

Henriette Mandl, *Vienna Downtown Walking Tours* (Ueberreuter, 1987): an excellent and compact guide to seeing Vienna on foot.

Christian Nebehay, *Vienna 1900* (Brandstätter, 1984): a set of profusely illustrated guides to architecture and painting, music, and literature in turn-of-the-century Vienna.

Richard Rickett, *A Brief Survey of Austrian History* (Heinemann, 1983): a good overview, and *Music and Musicians in Vienna* (Heinemann, 1973): a compact guide to those musicians
who helped make Vienna the musical capital of the world.

Arriving and Departing

From North America by Plane

When booking a flight, air travelers will want to keep in mind
the distinction between *nonstop flights* (your destination is the
only scheduled stop), *direct flights* (one or more stops are
scheduled before you reach your destination), and *connecting
flights* (you'll stop and change planes before you reach your destination).

Airports and Airlines Scheduled international flights from North America all fly into
Vienna's Schwechat airport, about 12 miles southeast of the
city. Other Austrian cities with international service—but not
from North America—are Linz, Salzburg, Innsbruck, Graz,
and Klagenfurt. Airlines specifically serving Austria from major U.S. cities (usually New York) include the following:

Austrian Airlines (tel. 800/843–0002) offers nonstop service
Wednesday–Monday from New York/JFK.

Pan Am (tel. 212/687–2600) flies three times weekly from New
York/JFK, once nonstop, twice via Budapest.

Tarom/Romanian Airlines (tel. 212/687–6013) has, depending
on the season, one or two nonstop flights weekly from New
York/JFK.

Air Canada (tel. 416/925–2311 or 800/268–7240) flies from Toronto via Frankfurt or Zurich three times a week.

Singapore Airlines (tel. 416/323–1911) flies Toronto–Vienna via
Amsterdam three times weekly.

Flying Time From New York, a nonstop flight to Vienna takes just over
eight hours. From Toronto, a direct flight takes about 11 hours.

Enjoying the Flight If you're lucky enough to be able to sleep on a plane, it makes
sense to fly at night. Many experienced travelers, however,
prefer to take a morning flight to Europe and arrive in the evening, just in time for a good night's sleep. Because the air on a
plane is dry, it helps, while flying, to drink plenty of nonalcoholic beverages; alcohol contributes to jet lag, as does eating
heavy meals on board. Feet swell at high altitudes, so it's a good
idea to remove your shoes at the beginning of your flight. Sleepers usually prefer window seats to curl up against; those who
like to move about in the cabin ask for aisle seats. Bulkhead
seats (located in the front row of each cabin) have more
legroom, but seat trays are attached rather awkwardly to the
arms of the seat rather than to the back of the seat ahead. Bulkhead seats are generally reserved for the disabled, the elderly,
or parents traveling with babies.

Discount Flights As a rule, the farther in advance you buy an airline ticket, the
less expensive it is, but these tickets carry certain restrictions.
An APEX (advance-purchase) ticket must be bought in advance (usually 21 days); it limits your travel, usually with a
minimum stay of seven days and a maximum of 90; and it pena-

lizes you severely (up to 100%) for changes—voluntary or not—in your travel plans. But if you can work around these drawbacks (and most travelers can), they are among the best values. For example, you can fly round-trip New York–Vienna in peak periods for around $700, versus $1,800 on regular coach or $4,400 in first class.

Other discounted fares can be found through consolidators, companies that buy blocks of tickets on scheduled airlines and sell them at wholesale prices—up to 50% below APEX fares. Seats are limited on any one flight, so passengers must have flexible travel schedules. Here again, you can lose all or most of your money if you change plans, but you will be on a regularly scheduled flight, with less risk of cancellation than on a charter. As an added precaution, you might want to purchase trip-cancellation insurance. Once you've made your reservation, call the airline to confirm it. Among the best-known consolidators to Europe are **UniTravel** (Box 12485, St. Louis, MO 63132, tel. 314/569–2501 or 800/325–2222) and **Access International** (101 W. 31st St., Suite 1104, New York, NY 10001, tel. 212/465–0707 or 800/825–3633). Others advertise in Sunday newspaper travel sections.

Another option is to join a travel club that offers special discounts to its members. Several such organizations are **Discount Travel International** (114 Forrest Ave., Narberth, PA 19072, tel. 215/668–7184), **Moment's Notice** (425 Madison Ave., New York, NY 10017, tel. 212/486–0503), **Travelers Advantage** (CUC Travel Service, 49 Music Sq. W, Nashville, TN 37203, tel. 800/548–1116), and **Worldwide Discount Travel Club** (1674 Meridian Ave., Miami Beach, FL 33139, tel. 305/534–2082). These cut-rate tickets should be compared with APEX tickets on the major airlines.

Travelers willing to put up with some restrictions and inconvenience, in exchange for substantially reduced airfares, may be interested in flying as air couriers, to accompany shipments between designated points. For a telephone directory listing courier companies by the cities to which they fly, send $5 and a self-addressed, stamped business-size envelope to **Pacific Data Sales Publishing** (2554 Lincoln Blvd., Suite 275–F, Marina del Rey, CA 90291). For "A Simple Guide to Courier Travel," send $14.95 postpaid to the **Carriage Group** (Box 2394, Lake Oswego, OR 97035). For more information call 800/344–9375.

Smoking   On long-distance flights where smoking is still permitted, U.S. carriers are required to find seats in a nonsmoking section for travelers who request them on the day of the flight and meet check-in time restrictions. But the best move for nonsmokers may be to request a nonsmoking seat when you book your ticket.

From the United Kingdom by Plane, Car, Train, and Bus

By Plane   **British Airways** (tel. 071/897–4000), **Austrian Airlines** (tel. 071/439–0741), and **Lauda Air** (tel. 071/494–0702) have nonstop services from London to Vienna and Salzburg. There are at least four flights daily to Vienna from London Heathrow, a trip of a little more than two hours, and nonstop service three days a week to Salzburg on Austrian Airlines (about two hours). You can fly to Linz, Graz, and Innsbruck via Frankfurt or Zurich.

Austrian Air Transport, a subsidiary of Austrian Airlines, has daily "scheduled charter" service to Vienna, Innsbruck, Graz, Klagenfurt, and Salzburg from Gatwick; **DanAir** and **British Airways** have additional scheduled charter flights. You can book these flights through **GTF Tours** (tel. 071/792–0311); **Austria Travel** (tel. 071/222–2430), the travel arm of the Anglo-Austrian Society; or a travel agent or charter operator. Scheduled charter flights must be booked well in advance, and you can't change your plans without losing your money, but the round-trip fares start at about £100, instead of £180 for APEX or £460 for business class. Several bucket shops also offer flights to Austria; check the ads in *Time Out* and the Sunday papers.

By Car The best way to reach Austria by car from England is to take one of the North Sea/Cross Channel ferries to Oostende or Zeebrugge in Belgium or Dunkirk in northern France. Then take the toll-free Belgian motorway (E5) to Aachen, and head via Stuttgart to Innsbruck and the Tirol (A61, A67, A5, E11, A7) or east by way of Nürnberg and Munich, crossing into Austria at Walserberg and then on to Salzburg and Vienna. Total distance to Innsbruck is about 1,100 km (650 mi); to Vienna, about 1,600 km (1,000 mi). The most direct way to Vienna is virtually all on the autobahn via Nürnberg, Regensburg, and Passau, entering Austria at Schärding. In summer, border delays are much shorter at Schärding than at Salzburg.

The trip to Innsbruck via this route will take 2–3 days. The ferry crossing to Dunkirk from Ramsgate on the Sally Line (tel. 0800/636465) takes about 2½ hours. Sailings to Oostende (4 hours) and Zeebrugge (4½ hours from Dover, 6 hours from Felixstowe) are on **P&O European Ferries** (tel. 0800/456456). The best arrangement is to take a morning ferry, then stop overnight in Belgium or Germany.

If this seems like too much driving, in summer you can put the car on a train in s'Hertogenbosch in central southern Netherlands, on Thursday, or in Schaerbeek (Brussels) on Friday, for an overnight trip, arriving in Salzburg early the following morning and in Villach three hours later. **DER Travel Service** (18 Conduit St., London W1R 9TD, tel. 071/408–0111) has details of fares and schedules.

By Train There's a wide choice of rail routes to Austria. You can take a daily train via Calais to Innsbruck, leaving London's Victoria Station in the afternoon; running via Basel, Zurich, and Bludenz; and arriving late morning the next day. For the overnight run from Calais, second-class couchettes are available and light refreshments are provided from Basel onward. Alternatively, you could take the *Oostende Wien* direct link from London to Vienna, leaving London at 9:15 AM and arriving in Vienna at 9:40 AM the next day. If you don't mind changing trains, you can travel more comfortably via Paris, where you catch the *Arlberg Express* at 10:40 PM for Vienna via Innsbruck. First- and second-class sleepers and second-class couchettes are available as far as Innsbruck.

When you have the time, a strikingly scenic route to Austria is via Cologne and Munich; after an overnight stop in Cologne, you take the EuroCity Express *Johann Strauss* to Vienna.

Fares represent reasonable value for money. One-way London–Vienna costs around £150 first class, £105 second class.

Eurotrain (52 Grosvenor Gardens, London SW1W OAG, tel. 071/730–3402) and **Transalpino** (71–75 Buckingham Palace Rd., London SW1W ORE, tel. 071/834–9656) both offer excellent deals for those under 26. Otherwise, book through **British Rail Travel Centers** (tel. 071/834–2345). For additional information, call **DER Travel Service** (071/408–0111) or, in the United States, **GermanRail** (747 3rd Ave., New York, NY 10017, tel. 212/308–3100).

By Bus   There are no direct bus services from the United Kingdom to Austria; the closest you can get is Munich, and from there, the train is your best bet. **International Express** (Coach Travel Center, 13 Lower Regent St., London SW1Y 4LR, tel. 071/439–9368) operates daily in summer, leaving London's Victoria coach station in mid-evening and arriving in Munich about 23 hours later.

Staying in Austria

Getting Around

By Plane   Austria has domestic air service, but the fares are high. The train is much cheaper and, in most cases, about as convenient as flying. **Austrian Airlines** or its subsidiary **Austrian Air Services** has flights connecting Vienna with Linz, Salzburg, Graz, and Klagenfurt. **Tyrolean** flies between Vienna and Innsbruck, and it has a fly/drive combination with Avis that can save you money. Tyrolean also connects to points outside Austria, and Rheintalflug flies between Vienna and Altenhausen, in Switzerland, just over the border from the province of Vorarlberg. Winter schedules on all domestic lines may vary, depending on snow conditions. There is helicopter service between St. Anton and St. Christoph, which can be combined with ski tours in the high mountain regions of the Arlberg. For private charter flights contact **Alpenair** (tel. 0222/945228), **Jetair** (tel. 0222/533–6033), or **Polsterer Jets** (tel. 0222/71110–2077).

By Train   Austrian train service is excellent: it's fast and, for Western Europe, relatively inexpensive, particularly if you take advantage of the discount fares. The main intercity lines run at fixed intervals, so trains usually run hourly and leave at set times after or before each hour. Although speeds are improving, trains on the mountainous routes are slow. But driving is no faster. And what difference does it make that the 580-km (360-mi) run from Vienna to Innsbruck, for example, takes 5½ hours? The scenery is gorgeous! Many of the remote rail routes will give you a look at traditional Austria, complete with alpine cabins tacked onto mountainsides and a backdrop of snowcapped peaks even in summer.

Your hotel desk can often provide a train schedule, but in any case, planning a train trip is simple. In every station and in many hotels, you will find large posters labeled *Abfahrt* (departures) and *Ankunft* (arrivals). Look through the Abfahrt glisting for a train to your destination. You'll find the departure time in the main left-hand block of the listing and, under the train name, details of where it stops en route and the time of each arrival. There is also information about connecting trains and buses, with departure details.

Austrian Federal Railways trains are identifiable by the letters that precede the train number on the timetables and posters. The *Ex* and *D* trains are fastest, but a supplement of AS30 is automatically included in the price of the ticket. All tickets are valid without supplement on *Eilzug* (fast) and local trains. Seat reservations are required on some trains; on most others you can reserve for a small extra charge up until a few hours before departure. Be sure to do this on the major trains at peak holiday times.

The difference between first and second class on Austrian trains is mainly a matter of space. First- and second-class sleepers, and couchettes (six to a compartment) are available on international runs, as well as on long trips within Austria.

If you're driving and would rather watch the scenery than the traffic, you can put your car on a train in Vienna and take it to Salzburg, Innsbruck, Feldkirch, or Villach. You relax in a compartment or sleeper for the trip, and the car is unloaded when you arrive.

The railroad also has an arrangement whereby you can rent a bicycle for AS80 per day at any one of many stations and leave it at another. You don't have to be a rail passenger to take advantage of this scheme, but if you are, the rental is half the price. Virtually all the major stations—well over 100 of them—will take credit cards.

Discount Fares   Even if you'll be in Austria for only a short time, you can save money on one of the discount rail fares. For AS200 and a passport photo, senior citizens (women 60 years, men 65) can obtain a *Seniorenpass*, which carries discounts up to 50% on rail tickets. The pass is also accepted as identification for reduced-price entry into museums and has a host of other useful fringe benefits. Most rail stations can give you information.

Travelers under 26 should inquire about discount fares under the Billet International Jeune (BIJ). The special one-trip tickets are sold by **Eurotrain International** (no connection with Eurailpass) at its offices in London, Dublin, Paris, Madrid, Lisbon, Rome, Zurich, Athens, Brussels, Budapest, Hanover, Leiden, Vienna, and Tangier and at travel agents, main-line rail stations, and youth-travel specialists.

The **Rabbit Card** is good on any four days within a 10-day period for unlimited travel on any rail route, including the private lines, the cog railways, and the Wolfgangsee ships. It carries a 50% reduction on ships on Lake Constance run by the railroad and 30% off on any one of the 10 days on the DDSG Danube river boats. The Rabbit Card costs AS1,390 first class, AS950 second class. If you're 27 or under, prices are AS860 first class, AS590 second. (The rates are scheduled to be higher in 1992.) You'll need identification when you buy the ticket. But unless you'll be confining your rail travel to Austria, the *Eurailpass* (*see* Rail Passes, above) will probably be cheaper.

A *Bundesnetzkarte* (full-network pass) gives you unlimited travel for a month (AS4,650 for first class, AS3,100 second class) or a year (check on current prices) and will allow you a 50% reduction on Austrian intercity buses and private rail lines. The ticket is also good on the suburban rail system (*S-Bahn*) around Vienna and ships on the Wolfgangsee. Apply for a *Bundesnetzkarte* at any large rail station, and expect the cost to be higher in 1992. You will need a passport photo.

Zonenkarten, or regional tickets, both first class (AS500) and second class (AS400), are available for some 18 different areas and are good for any four days within a 10-day period. Again, you'll need a passport photo when you buy the ticket. Note that the *Zonenkarten* may be discontinued and that prices are likely to be higher in 1992.

You can buy regular rail tickets through travel agents and at any station, but for the special passes and tickets, you'll usually have to go yourself to a train station.

Railroad enthusiasts and those with plenty of time can treat themselves to a ride on narrow-gauge lines that amble through alpine meadows; some even make flower-picking stops in season. A few lines still run under steam power, and summertime steam excursions are becoming more frequent. Local stations have descriptive brochures with dates, points of origin, and fares.

By Bus Where Austrian trains don't go, buses do, and you will find the yellow railroad and post-office buses in some of the remotest outposts you might imagine, carrying passengers as well as the mail. You can get tickets on the bus itself, and in the off season there is no problem getting a seat, but on routes to favored ski areas and during holiday periods reservations are essential. Most towns with bus service have a ticket office, or tickets can be booked with a travel agent. In most communities, the bus routes begin and end at or near the railroad station, making transfers easy. Increasingly, coordination of the bus service with that of the railroads means that many of the discounts and special tickets available for trains apply to the buses as well. Bus services also tie together the outskirts of many Austrian cities, both with circumferential and crosstown routes.

By Car The Austrian highway network is excellent, well maintained, and well marked. Secondary roads may be somewhat narrow and winding, but these are so shown on maps. The main through routes (autobahn) are packed during both Austrian and West German school holidays, and weekends in summer can also be hectic. As a nod to the ecology, less salt is being used on highways in winter, but few drivers seem to take heed of the greater hazard. In bad weather you will need snow tires and often chains in winter, even on the well-traveled roads. Austrians are fairly poor drivers, inclined to take chances and aggressive; defensive driving is the best policy.

Tourists from European Community countries may bring their cars to Austria with no documentation other than the normal registration papers and their regular driver's license. A Green Card, the international certificate of insurance, is recommended for EC drivers and compulsory for others. All cars must carry a first-aid kit and a red warning triangle (obtainable at border crossings or from the Automobile Club—*see* below) to use in case of accident or breakdown.

A set of eight excellent detailed roadmaps is available at a nominal price from the **Austrian Automobile Club/ÖAMTC** (Schubertring 1–3, A–1010 Vienna, tel. 0222/711–9955), at most service stations, and at many bookstores. The maps supplied without charge by the Austrian National Tourist Office are adequate for most needs, but if you will be covering much territory, the better ÖAMTC maps are a worthwhile investment.

The minimum driving age in Austria is 18, and children under 12 years must ride in the back seat. Passengers in the front seats must use seat belts. Vehicles coming from the right have the right of way, except that at unregulated intersections, streetcars coming from either direction have the right of way. No turns are allowed on red.

Unless otherwise marked, the speed limit on autobahns is 130 kph (80 mph), although this is not strictly enforced, as you will discover. On other highways and roads, the limit is 100 kph (62 mph), 80 kph (49 mph) for RVs or cars pulling a trailer weighing more than 750 kilos (about 1,650 lbs). In built-up areas, a 50 kph (31 mph) limit applies and is likely to be taken seriously.

Gasoline is readily available, but remember that on Sunday, rural stations may be closed. Virtually all stations now carry unleaded (*bleifrei*) gas, both regular and premium (*Super*). Diesel fuel may not be easy to find off the beaten path. Gasoline prices are the same throughout the country, slightly lower at discount filling stations and self-service stations. Expect to pay about AS10 per liter for regular, AS11.50 for premium. If you're driving into Austria, consider tanking up on the other side of the border, particularly if you're entering from West Germany, where gasoline is consistently cheaper. Oil in Austria is expensive, retailing at AS50–AS80 per liter.

Austria has two automobile clubs, ÖAMTC and ARBÖ, both of which operate motorist service patrols. You'll find emergency phones along all the key highways. Otherwise, if you have problems, call ARBÖ (tel. 123) or ÖAMTC (tel. 120) anywhere in the country. No area or other code is needed for either number. Both clubs charge nonmembers for emergency road service.

Along the autobahns, the roadside food services run by the **Rosenberger** chain are excellent. They are well designed, and the food is good and varied, with a salad bar and children's menus.

By Boat For leisurely travel between Vienna and Linz or eastward across the border into Czechoslovakia or Hungary, consider taking a Danube boat. More than 300 km (187 mi) of Austria's most beautiful scenery awaits you, as you glide past romantic castles and ruins, medieval monasteries and abbeys, and lush vineyards. One of the high spots, particularly in spring, when the apricot and apple trees are in blossom, is the Wachau valley near Vienna.

The trip from Passau (West Germany) to Vienna takes two days, including an overnight stop in Linz (on board, if you like), and runs from late June to late September. The boat leaves Passau at 3 PM, arriving at Linz at 8 PM and departing the next morning at 10 for arrival in Vienna at 8:15 PM. Check for current fares with your travel agent or, in Austria, with the **DDSG/Danube Steamship Company** (Handelskai 265, A–1020 Vienna, tel. 0222/217100). Fares vary according to the type of accommodation and the ship itself; the new river cruiser *Mozart*—complete with swimming pool—is in the luxury category.

Day trips are also possible on the Danube, and in the Wachau, you can use the boats to move from one riverside community on or across to the next. The Eurailpass includes the DDSG network.

Daily hydrofoil services run from Vienna to Bratislava in Czechoslovakia and to Budapest in Hungary. You need no visa for these trips, but be sure to have your passport with you. Both routes offer on-board, duty-free shopping. If you want adventure, you can travel via the Danube to the Black Sea and back on river passenger ships flying the Soviet or Romanian flag.

Telephones

Austria's telephone service is in a state of change as the country converts to a digital system. We make every effort to keep numbers up to date, but do check—particularly in Innsbruck, Linz, and Vienna—if you have problems getting the connection you want. All numbers given here include the city or town area code; if you are calling within that city or town, dial the local number only.

Basic telephone numbers in Austria consist only of numerals, of three to seven digits; longer numbers are the basic number plus a direct-dial extension of two to four digits.

Coin-operated pay telephones are numerous and take a one-schilling piece for local calls. Drop in the coin, pick up the receiver and dial; when the party answers, push the indicated button and the connection will be made. If there is no response, your coin will be returned into the bin to the lower left.

If you plan to make many calls from pay phones, a *Wertkarte* is a convenience. At any post office you can buy an electronic credit card for AS95 or AS48 that allows AS100 or AS50 worth of calls from any *Wertkartentelephon*. You simply insert the card and dial; the cost of the call is automatically deducted from the card.

Calls within Austria are one-third cheaper between 6 PM and 8 AM on weekdays and from 1 PM on Saturday to 8 AM on Monday.

International Calls You can dial direct to almost any point on the globe from Austria. The international access code for the United States and Canada is 001, followed by the area code and number. For Great Britain, first dial 0044, then the city code *without the usual "0"* (71 or 81 for London), and the number. Other country and many city codes are given in the front of telephone books (in Vienna, in the *A–H* book). By 1992, reduced off-peak rates may be in effect for out-of-country calls, but at press time, these calls are all billed at the same rate no matter when you phone.

Don't make long-distance calls from your hotel room without first checking carefully on the cost of the call. Hotels in Austria, as in many countries, frequently add several hundred percent to such calls. AT&T's USA Direct plan enables you to charge the call to your card or call collect. The access number, 022–903011, is a local call all over Austria. You can also make a quick call asking the called party to phone you back at the number in Austria. All post offices in Austria have public telephone facilities, and you can get assistance in placing a long-distance call. In large cities, these centers are open around the clock.

Operators and Information For information on local calls, dial 16; for assistance with long-distance service, dial 09; and for information on direct dialing out of Austria, call 08.

Mail

Postal Rates Within Europe, all mail goes by air, so there's no supplement on letters or postcards. A letter of up to 20 grams (about ¾ ounce) takes AS7, a postcard AS6. To the United States or Canada, a letter of up to 20 grams takes AS9 minimum, plus AS1.50 per 5 grams for airmail. If in doubt, mail your letters from a post office and have the weight checked. The Austrian post office also adheres strictly to a size standard; if your letter or card is outside the norm, you'll have to pay a surcharge. Postcards via airmail to the United States or Canada need AS7.50. Post offices have air-letter (aerogram) forms for AS11 to any overseas destination.

Receiving Mail When you don't know where you'll be staying, **American Express** mail service is a great convenience, with no charge to anyone either holding an American Express credit card or carrying American Express traveler's checks. (American Express: Kärntner Str. 21–23, A–1015 **Vienna,** tel. 0222/515400; Mozartplatz 5, A–5020 **Salzburg,** tel. 0662/842501; Brixner Str. 3, A–6020 **Innsbruck,** tel. 0512/582491; Bürgerstr. 14, A–4021 **Linz,** tel. 0732/669013.) You can also have mail held at any Austrian post office, but the letters should be marked *Poste Restante* or *Postlagernd*. You will be asked for identification when you collect mail. In Vienna, this service is handled through the main post office (Fleischmarkt 19, A–1010 Vienna, tel. 0222/512–76810), now temporarily located at Postgasse/Barbaragasse 2 until renovations on the Fleischmarkt building are completed.

Tipping

Although virtually all hotels and restaurants include service charges in their rates, tipping is still customary, but at a level lower than in the United States. Tip the hotel doorman AS10 per bag, and the porter who brings your bags to the room another AS10 per bag. In very small country inns, where the staff doubles in a number of jobs, such tips are not expected but are appreciated. Tip the hotel concierge only for special services or in response to special requests. Room service gets AS10 for snacks or ice, AS20 for full meals. Maids normally get no tip unless your stay is a week or more or service has been special.

In restaurants, round up the bill by AS5 to AS50, depending on the size of the check and the class of the restaurant. Big tips are not usual in Austrian restaurants, since 10% has already been included in the prices. Hat-check girls get AS7–AS15, depending on the locale. Washroom attendants get about AS2–AS5. Wandering musicians and the piano player get AS20, AS50 if they've filled a number of requests.

Round up taxi fares to the next AS5 or AS10; a minimum AS5 tip is customary. If the driver offers (or you ask for) special assistance, such as carrying your bags beyond the curb, an added tip of AS5–AS10 is in order.

Opening and Closing Times

Banks in most cities are open weekdays from 8 to 3, on Thursday until 5:30 PM. Smaller bank offices close from 12:30 to 1:30. All are closed on Saturday, but you can change money at various locations (such as American Express offices on Saturday morning and major railroad stations around the clock) at other than bank hours.

Museum hours vary from city to city and museum to museum; if there's a closing day, it will usually be a Monday. Few Austrian museums are open at night.

In general, you'll find shops open weekdays from 8:30 or 9 AM until 6 PM, with a lunchtime closing from noon to 1 or 1:30. In smaller villages, the midday break may run until 3 PM. Many food stores, bakeries, and small grocery shops open at 7 or 7:30 AM and, aside from the noontime break, stay open until 6:30 PM. Shops in large city centers take no noon break. On Saturday, shops stay open until noon or 1 PM, except on the first Saturday of the month, when (except for food stores) they stay open until 5, a few until 6 PM. Barbers and hairdressers traditionally take Monday off, but there are exceptions.

All banks and shops are closed on national holidays: Jan. 1; Jan. 6, Epiphany; Apr. 19–20, Easter Sunday and Monday; May 1, May Day; May 28, Ascension Day; June 7–8, Pentecost Sunday and Monday; June 18, Corpus Christi; Aug. 15, Assumption; Oct. 26, National Holiday; Nov. 1, All Saints' Day; Dec. 8, Immaculate Conception; Dec. 25–26, Christmas. Museums are open on most holidays and closed on Good Friday and Dec. 24.

Shopping

You'll find specific shopping tips in the individual chapters, but in general, such locally produced goods as textiles, crystal, porcelain figurines, leather goods, wood carvings, and other handicrafts are good value. Prices are similar throughout the country, but higher, of course, in the major tourist centers. Shops will ship your purchases, but if you can, take them with you. If you do ship goods, be sure you know the terms in advance, how the items will be sent, when you can expect to receive them, *and get all these details in writing*.

All purchases made in Austria are subject to a 20% value-added tax (VAT). You can get this refunded on goods you personally take or have shipped out of the country, when the purchases amount to AS1,000 or more from one shop and the shop will handle the necessary paperwork. Ask for details on the spot. The refund can be arranged and later credited to your credit card by the shop, or you can present the papers at the Post Office window at the airport upon departure (look for "VAT Refund" signs) and get an immediate cash refund. (The banks at the airports usually slap on a healthy handling fee, which may cancel out a substantial chunk of your refund.) You may be asked to show the purchases at Customs as you depart, so don't pack them in the bottom of the suitcase you have just checked through!

Sports and Outdoor Activities

Austria is one of the most participant-sports-minded countries anywhere. At a snowflake's notice, half the population will take to their skis; in summer, water sports are just as popular. But new attractions are appearing; golf, for example, is becoming more common. The National Tourist Offices have information on many specific sports.

Ballooning   **Filzmoos** in the Tirol is one of several centers for those who want to glide peacefully over Alpine meadows. Get details of the sport for the whole country from the **Austrian Ballooning Club** (Endresstr. 65, A–1230 Vienna, tel. 0222/888222); **Austrian Aero-Club** (Prinz Eugen-Str. 12, A–1040 Vienna, tel. 0222/ 505–1028); or from the **Vienna Ballooning Club** (tel. 0222/ 692913, 692916, or 883–0353).

Bicycling   Cyclists couldn't expect much more than the new cycle track that runs the length of the Danube or the many cycling routes that crisscross the country, major cities included. You can rent a bicycle for AS80 per day (AS40, if you've a rail ticket in your hand) at any of about 100 railroad stations throughout the country and return it to another. Special brochures available from the national tourist offices have details, including maps and hints for trip planning and mealtime and overnight stops. Ask for the booklet *Radfahren in Österreich,* or contact **Austria Radreisen** (A–4780 Schärding, tel. 07712/2409), which organizes cycling tours.

Boating and   Small boats can be rented on all the lakes of the Salzkammergut
Sailing   region and on the large lakes in Carinthia. You can rent a rowboat on almost all of Austria's lakes and on the side arms of the Danube (Alte Donau and the Donauinsel) in Vienna. Information is available from the **Österreichischer Segel-Verband,** the Austrian Yachting Club (Grosse Neugasse 8, A–1040 Vienna, tel. 0222/587–8688).

You can go white-water kayaking on the Enns River between Schladming and Gesäuse—it's extremely difficult through the narrow Gesäuse—and on most of the Mur River, an easy run beyond Graz. Boats can be rented at Gröbming and Aich-Assach for the Enns run. Kayaking is possible on the Danube but a bit hazardous in some areas because of the commercial traffic.

Windsurfing (*Windsegeln*) is extremely popular, particularly on Neusiedler See in Burgenland, Attersee in Upper Austria, and on the side arms of the Danube in Vienna. There are schools at all these locations where you can learn the art and rent sailboards.

Camping   You'll find more than 400 campsites throughout the country, usually run by regional organizations, a few private. Most have full facilities, often including swimming pools and snack bars or grocery shops. Charges range from about AS30 to AS40 per person per day, depending on the range and quality of services offered, plus AS30–AS40 for car parking. For details, check with the **Österreichischer Camping Club** (Johannesgasse 20, A–1010 Vienna, tel. 0222/512–5952) about sites, prices, and availability and with the tourist offices of the individual Austrian provinces. Camping is not restricted to the summer season; some sites are open year-round, with nearly 80 specifically set up for winter camping.

Fishing   Among Austria's well-stocked lakes are the Traunsee, Attersee, Hallstätter See, and Mondsee in Upper Austria; the Danube, Steyr, Traun, Enns, Krems, and Alm rivers also provide good fishing. Tirol is another good region; try the Achensee, Traualpsee, Walchsee, Plansee, and nearby streams. Also try the Inn and Drau in East Tirol and the Ziller in the Zillertal. Styria provides some of the best trout fishing in Austria, as do the lakes in the Styrian Salzkammergut. Carinthian lakes and the streams in Lower Austria also abound in fish. Ask the Austrian National Tourist Office for the guidebook "Fishing in Austria"; it includes details of licensing. Unfortunately for anglers, the rights along many of the best streams have been given, meaning that no additional licenses will be issued, but ask at the local tourist office.

Gliding   If you're set for adventure, from May to September you can glide solo or learn to glide at one of Austria's schools, at Zell am See (Salzburg province); Niederöblarn and Graz-Thalerhof (Styria); in Wiener Neustadt and Spitzberg bei Hainberg (Lower Austria). In Zell am See and at Wien-Donauwiese (Vienna), there are two-seater gliders, for instructor and passenger; at the other airfields you're on your own. For details, contact the **Austrian Aero Club** (Prinz Eugen-Str. 12, A–1040 Vienna, tel. 0222/505–1028).

Golf   Austria is changing quickly from a golfing no-man's-land into a place where golfers can now find more than 50 courses. Most of them are private, but for a greens fee, you can arrange a temporary membership. Several of the courses are associated with hotels, so package arrangements can be made. The Austrian National Tourist Offices have special golfing brochures, or you can write **Golf Green Austria** (Panzaunweg 1g, A–5071 Wals, tel. 0662/851355).

Hiking and Climbing   With more than 50,000 km—that's about 35,000 miles—of well maintained mountain paths through Europe's largest reserve of unspoiled landscape, the country is paradise for hikers. Three long-distance routes traverse Austria: E-4, the Pyrenees–Jura–Neusiedler See route, ending in Burgenland on the Hungarian border; E-5 from Lake Constance in Vorarlberg to the Adriatic; and E-6 from the Baltic, cutting across mid-Austria via the Wachau valley region of the Danube and on to the Adriatic. Wherever you are in Austria, you will find shorter hiking trails requiring varying degrees of ability. Routes are well marked and maps are readily available. Hikers' maps on a scale of 1:20,000 or 1:25,000 will be the most useful.

If you are planning high-altitude hiking, remember that cable cars and other transportation facilities are often closed during off-season months. Always take protection against rain, and tell your hotel desk where you're headed. In winter, be careful not to stray from the marked paths; the sad side of winter hiking in Austria is the number of deaths owing to carelessness and inattention to avalanche warnings.

Tourist offices all have details on hiking holidays, and serious climbers can write directly to **Österreichischer Alpenverein/ ÖAV** (Austrian Alpine Club, Wilhelm-Greil-Str. 15, A–6020 Innsbruck, tel. 0512/595470) for more information. Membership in the club ($35) will give you a 50% reduction from the regular fees for overnights in the 275 mountain refuges it operates.

Of the more than 700 refuges, all told, in Austria, about a quarter are at altitudes of between 2,500 and 3,000 meters (8,200 and 9,843 ft). Mountain guides will charge up to AS950 a day for glacier tours and easy-to-moderate climbs, with the guides responsible for their own food. For more strenuous climbing and longer periods, you can arrange a fixed fee in advance. A tip is usual at the end of the climb.

If you're a newcomer to mountain climbing or want to improve your skill, schools in Tirol, Carinthia, Styria, and Salzburg province will take you on. Ask the ÖAV for addresses. All organize courses and guided tours for beginners and more advanced climbers.

British mountaineers can get details via a branch of the ÖAV (13 Longcroft House, Fretherne Rd., Welwyn Garden City, Herts.) and arrange membership in the parent organization.

Horseback Riding Whether you want to head off cross-country or just canter around a paddock, Austria offers many kinds of equestrian holiday, and some hotels have their own riding schools. Ask for the booklet "Equestrian Sports in Austria" from the tourist office. The provinces of Styria, Burgenland, and Upper and Lower Austria are particularly popular with riders.

Skiing Since skiing is the Austrian national sport, you'll have plenty of company wherever there's a slope and a snowflake. Here babies barely out of diapers literally learn to walk and ski at the same time. The season runs from late November to April, depending on snow conditions. But there are enough year-round skiing regions on glaciers at 3,300 meters (11,000 ft) or more to satisfy even the wildest skiing freak. The well-established winter–summer regions include Kitzsteinhorn (Kaprun) in Salzburg province, Rettenbachferner (Sölden), Stubaier Glacier (Renalt), Wurmkogel (Hochgurgl), Tuxer Ferner (Hintertux), St. Leonhard (Pitztal), Kaunertal Glacier in Tirol, and Dachstein (Ramsau) in Styria.

In many areas, cable cars, chair lifts, and T-bars have been so arranged that you can ski all day long on the same ski pass without using the same slope twice and end up in the afternoon exactly where you started in the morning. Nor is the beginner forgotten in all this. At all centers, you will find experienced instructors, many with substantial international credentials, and the schools take children at age 3. You can bring your own gear or rent skis, boots, and poles—even clothes in some areas—at the resorts.

Austrians lean toward downhill skiing, though in recent years a number of cross-country routes have been developed. Depending on the local terrain, most ski resorts now have some cross-country trails, but you'll have to look harder to find them.

Of course, you can head for the popular and known resorts, but if a skiing holiday without all the frills (and expense) is what you want, you'll find good facilities and excellent slopes with far lower prices in East Tirol, Styria, Lower Austria, Carinthia, and parts of Salzburg province and Upper Austria. Ski areas offer a weekly pass for use on all lifts, cable cars, and usually swimming pools, at 20%–30% reductions. Your hotel or the local tourist office will have details. Many resorts, including several of the more expensive and fashionable towns, offer all-inclusive weekly rates, sometimes including ski schools and lifts. Not surprisingly, the Austrian National Tourist Office will overwhelm you with detailed information on the various packages.

Student ski trips are organized in the December–April period by the **Büro für Studentenreisen,** the Office for Student Tours (Schreyvogelgasse 3, A–1010 Vienna, tel. 0222/533–3589) and by two other student-travel organizations: **ÖKISTA** (Türkenstr. 4, A–1090 Vienna, tel. 0222/347526) and its partner **OS-Reisen** (Reichstratstr. 13, A–1010 Vienna, tel. 0222/408–7821).

Water Sports and Swimming Waterskiing and sail skiing are popular on the Wörther See (where there's also spectacular night waterskiing with torches) and Millstätter See in Carinthia; on the Traunsee, Attersee, and Wolfgangsee in Salzkammergut; in Zell am See in Salzburg province; and on the Bodensee (Lake Constance) in Vorarlberg. Waterskiing is not permitted on many of the smaller Austrian lakes, however, so check first. There are hundreds of places to swim throughout Austria, and with very few exceptions, the water is unpolluted. All the lakes in the Salzkammergut, Carinthia, and Tirol have excellent swimming, but all are crowded in the peak season. In the Vienna area, the Alte Donau and Donauinsel arms of the Danube are accessible by public transportation and are suitable for families, so it's best to go early to avoid the crowds on hot summer weekends. The Alte Donau beaches have changing rooms and checkrooms. Swimming in the Neusiedler See in Burgenland is an experience; you can touch bottom at virtually any place in this vast brackish lake.

Spectator Sports Soccer is a national favorite. Every town has at least one team, and rivalries are fierce. Matches are held regularly in Vienna and Innsbruck. When Austrians aren't skiing, they like to watch the national sport. Downhill and slalom races are held regularly in Innsbruck, Kitzbühel, Seefeld, and St. Anton. There's horse racing with parimutuel betting at the track in the Prater in Vienna. Tennis matches are held in Vienna, Linz, and Innsbruck.

Dining

Restaurant food in Austria ranges from fine (and expensive) offerings at elegant gastronomic temples to the simple, inexpensive, and wholesome good meals in small country inns. Wherever you go, you will find traditional restau-rants, with all the atmosphere typical of such places—good value included. In this regard, Austria still has much to offer. If you crave a Big Mac you can find it, and you can even get a bad meal in Austria, but it will be the exception; the simplest *Gasthaus* takes pride in its cooking, no matter how standard it may be.

Austrian cuisine is heavily influenced by that of its neighbors, which were once parts of the Austro-Hungarian empire. This accounts for the cross-fertilization of tastes and flavors, with Hungarian, Czechoslovak, Polish, Yugoslav, and Italian cooking all in the mix. The delicious, thick Serbian bean soup came from an area of modern Yugoslavia; the bread dumpling (*Knödel*) that accompanies so many standard dishes has its parentage in Czechoslovakia; the exquisitely rich (more butter than sugar) *Dobostorte* comes straight from Hungary.

Alas, justice is all too often not done to the relatively few Austrian national dishes. You're likely to get a soggy Wiener schnitzel as often as a supreme example, lightly pan-fried in a dry, crisp breading. Now at least it will be honestly presented, as pork or the real thing, veal. Austrian cooking on the whole is more solid than delicate. Try, for example, *Tafelspitz*—boiled beef, if you will, but when well done, it's outstanding in flavor and texture. Reflecting the Italian influence, Austrian cooking also leans heavily on pastas and rice. *Schinkenfleckerl* is a good example: a casserole of confettilike flecks of ham baked with pasta. A standard roast of pork (*Schweinsbraten*) served hot or cold can be exquisite, as the Austrians do not cook it to shoeleather consistency. But since many Austrian dishes are basically simple, they depend on the quality of the ingredients.

Austria's best restaurants—and not just in Vienna—have bounded in recent years into a class and quality earlier unthinkable. A school of inventive chefs has spawned a generation willing to try ideas wholly new to Austria; many of the most successful of these experiments involve imaginative, lighter variations on traditional themes of game and freshwater fish, relying as well on the abundant local produce.

When dining out, you'll get best value for money at the simpler restaurants. Most post menus with prices outside. If you begin with the *Würstelstand* (sausage vendor) on the street, the next category would be the *Imbisstube,* for simple, quick snacks. You'll find many of them at city markets, serving soups and a daily special at noon. Many cafés also are open for lunch, but watch the prices; some can turn out to be more expensive than restaurants. *Gasthäuser* are simple restaurants or country inns with no pretensions. From that basic level of cuisine everything else is upward, ranging from intimate finds to the most elegant. Austrian hotels have some of the best restaurants in the country, and they have hired outstanding chefs to attract the paying customers.

Wine cellars and wine gardens, or *Heuriger* (for new wine), are a special category among Austrian eateries. Mainly in Vienna and Lower Austria, they also can be found throughout the country, serving everything from a limited selection of cold cuts and cheeses to full meals. And some urban wine cellars are known as much for their food as for the wines.

Austrian vintage wines range from good to outstanding. Don't hesitate to ask waiters for their advice, even in the simpler restaurants. The best whites come from the Wachau and Kamptal, Weinviertel (Lower Austria), Styria, and the area around Vienna. Grüner Veltliner, a light, dry to medium-dry that goes well with many foods, is the most popular. The Welschriesling is a slightly heavier, fruitier wine. The favored Austrian reds are those of Burgenland. No single variety dominates. Blauer Portugieser and Zweigelt tend to be lighter. For a slightly heavier red, select a Blaufränkisch, Blauer Burgunder, or St. Laurent. These are all good value, and there is little difference among the years. Most of these wines can be bought by the glass. Look for labels from vintners Beck in Gols; Brundlmayer in Langenlois; Hirtzberger in Spitz/Donau; Jamek in Joching; Sonnhof in Langenlois; Kierlinger in Vienna, and Winzergenossenschaft Wachau in Dürnstein.

For Grüner Veltliner, Blaufränkisch, and St. Laurent, the recommended vintages are '81, '83, '85, '86, and '88. For Rheinriesling and Welschriesling, they are the same years plus '87. In every case '86 was outstanding.

Lunch in Austria is usually served between noon and 2 PM, dinner between 6 and 9 PM, tending toward the later hour. Many restaurant kitchens close in the afternoon, but some post a notice saying *Durchgehend warme Küche*, meaning that hot food is available even between regular mealtimes.

Restaurants in our listings are divided by price into four categories: Very Expensive, Expensive, Moderate, and Inexpensive. *See* Dining in individual chapters for specific prices, which vary from region to region. Prices quoted are for a three-course meal with house wine, including all service and taxes.

Lodging

You can live like a king in a real castle in Austria or get by on a modest budget. Starting at the lower end, you can find a room in a private house or on a farm or dormitory space in a youth hostel. Next up the line come the simpler pensions, many of them identified as *Frühstückspension*, meaning bed-and-breakfast. Then come the *Gasthäuser*, the simpler country inns. The fancier pensions in the cities can often cost as much as hotels; the difference lies in the services they offer. Most pensions, for example, do not man the front desk around the clock. Among the hotels, you can find accommodations ranging from the most modest, with a shower and toilet down the hall, to the most elegant, with every possible amenity.

Among the familiar names you will find in Austria are Hilton, Holiday Inns, InterContinental, Marriott, Novotel, Penta, Ramada, and Sheraton. Most of these chain establishments are in the upper price category, even those you may associate with budget prices at home.

We divide hotels into four price categories: Very Expensive, Expensive, Moderate, and Inexpensive, giving rates for a standard double room with private bath in peak season (where applicable).

All hotel prices include service charges (usually 10% but occasionally higher) and federal and local taxes—and in a few places, a small local tourism tax is added later. Some country hotels may add a heating supplement in winter.

Breakfast is included at virtually all hotels *except* those in the Very Expensive category, where it is extra—and expensive. It may range from rolls, marmalade, and coffee to an expansive buffet with eggs and meat dishes. You can usually get juice or an egg, but, in some cases, you'll be asked to pay extra. Some of the top resort hotels insist on half or full board in season; at other times, you can set your own terms.

Austria has few Very Expensive hotels outside Vienna, Salzburg and the major resorts, but numerous Expensive ones (usually with swimming pools—sometimes indoor and outdoor—saunas, fitness rooms, and other amenities). The Moderate accommodations in country areas or smaller cities and towns are generally more than adequate: food, service, and cleanliness are of high standard. The newer Inexpensive hotels have private showers. *See* Lodging in individual chapters for prices, which vary widely among large cities, resorts, and small country towns, in peak season and in low.

Credit Cards

The following credit card abbreviations are used: AE, American Express; DC, Diner's Club; MC, MasterCard/Access/Barclays; V, Visa.

Great Itineraries

The Wine Country

Austria's vineyards, spread out over the northern and eastern countryside, offer a splendid excuse to see areas that are well off the usual tourist routes. Here you can sample local wines, many of which are very good indeed but—because their output is low—don't travel far beyond private wine cellars. The countryside is relaxed and rolling in the north, a bit more dramatic as you head south. You could break the trip at any stage, but as the scenery keeps changing, so does the attraction of continuing. Although public transport penetrates these areas, you will do much better by car.

Length of Trip 4 to 6 days

Getting Around The trip by car will run about 810 km (507 mi), and the total
By Car driving time will be 13–16 hours.

By Public Klosterneuburg and Krems can be reached from Vienna by
Transportation train. A local train goes up the Kamp valley to Horn, where a post office bus goes on to Retz and back to Vienna. Laa an der Thaya is served by bus from Vienna; so is Poysdorf. A train runs from Bruck an der Leitha via Neusiedl to Eisenstadt. While the southernmost section of this itinerary can be covered by post office bus, the service is infrequent. A train from Graz goes to Bad Gleichenberg. The vineyards south of Vienna in Mödling, Baden, Gumpoldskirchen, and Bad Vöslau are easily reached by rail or bus.

The Main Route **One night: Krems.** A wine-tasting in Kloster Und will give some idea of the wines of the area. The Göttweig abbey, across the river, also produces wines and sells them by the bottle in the abbey shop.

One night: Laa an der Thaya. For variety, you might visit the beer museum associated with the Hubertus brewery, in business since 1454. The "Weinschlössl" offers tastings of area wine specialties.

One night: Eisenstadt. The road down from Jois is part of the "Red Wine Highway" through Burgenland's best vineyards. At Donnerkirchen the Vinarium (Leisserhof) has tastings of local wines. A side trip to the "Weinakademie" in Rust allows the opportunity to sample the wines of the Rust and Neusiedler lake region. Nearby Siegendorf produces outstanding wines.

One night: Bad Gleichenberg. There's no wine involved, but don't overlook nearby Riegersburg castle. The north–south valleys lying to the west are covered with vineyards. Parallel to Route 66 to the east, from Höflach south to Halbenrain, lies the

Klöcher wine highway. West of Strass on Route 69, Gamlitz is the northern end of the South Styrian Wine Road. Off Route 74 west of Leibnitz, Kitzeck in Sausal, at the lower end of the Sausal Wine Road, boasts a wine museum.

One night: Baden. The region around Bad Vöslau is home to one of Austria's most widely known white wines, Gumpoldskirchen, named for a nearby town. Traiskirchen offers a wine festival in the city park near the beginning of July, and from spring to late fall hundreds of vintners offer their wares at tiny Heurige cellars throughout the area.

Information   *See* Excursions from Vienna in Chapters 3, 4, and 5.

Alpine Vistas and Medieval Squares

Views over the Austrian Alps can rival any in the world, and when juxtaposed with medieval walled cities, the experience is memorable. This trip provides encounters with two aspects of Austria seldom seen by most tourists: the Alps from the topside and two colorful and fascinating town squares. It includes sweeping alpine valleys, stately churches, mountaintop castles, and a folk that owes its existence to the land. Our route takes us from Salzburg over Zell am See and down into Carinthia via the 3,800-meter (12,500-ft) Grossglockner mountainpass highway, follows the Möll river valley to the walled town of Gmünd, continues up the south side of the Dachstein mountain and along the Enns river valley, and turns north over the Pyhrn pass to Steyr and on to Linz.

Length of Trip   3 to 4 days

Getting Around   The trip by car will run about 520 km (325 mi), the driving time
By Car   about 10 hours, with the drive up and over the Grossglockner taking 2–2½ hours. If you avoid the autobahns and use parallel roads, allow another hour in all.

By Public   Tourist buses make this trip, but few will (or can) cope with the
Transportation   Grossglockner hairpin turns. You can reach Gmünd via Spittal an der Drau. No trains traverse this rugged terrain, but bus service is available to Schladming and the stretch through the Enns valley. Steyr is accessible by train from St. Valentin on the main east–west line.

The Main Route   **One night: Gmünd.** You can climb to the castle ruin that overlooks the town and visit the Porsche auto museum (Porsche set up his design studio in Gmünd after the German quarters were bombed), but the main attraction is the 15th-century town square and the fasinating side streets and back alleys. The great hydroelectric dam and reservoir at the top of the Malta valley are also impressive.

One night: Steyr. This city of the 15th and 16th centuries, perched above the confluence of the Enns and Steyr rivers, was well positioned for defense purposes. Its attractions are the restored town square, the arched and stepped alleyways that lead to the castle above the old square, and an industrial museum.

One night: Linz. The main square in Linz is similar in style to those of Gmünd and Steyr but on a larger scale. Visitors wander the narrow side streets and take a tram excursion up the Pöstlingberg. For all its industry, Linz is a relaxed city, with wine gardens along the Danube on the Urfahr side of the river.

An outing on a river boat reveals more of the immediate countryside.

Information *See* Chapters 5, 8, and 9.

Castles against the Invaders

During the Middle Ages, hordes of invaders periodically swept down from the north into what is now Lower Austria. Lacking natural defenses such as mountains or a river, local rulers set up a chain of castles to protect their lands and to display their wealth and position. To visit these fortifications is to appreciate what life was like more than 300 years ago for the ruling elite. The chain includes the castles at Ottenstein, Weitra, Gmünd, Heidenreichstein, Raabs an der Thaya, Riegersburg, and Hardegg.

Length of Trip 2 to 3 days

Getting Around The distance by car is about 340 km (215 mi), and the total driv-
By Car ing time will be more than 6 hours.

By Public Trains run from Vienna to Gmünd, and bus service is available
Transportation from Gmünd to Weitra and Heidenreichstein. Raabs can be reached by bus from Horn. Post office buses connect Riegersburg and Hardegg with Retz, which has a bus link to Vienna.

The Main Route **One night: Heidenreichstein.** Neunagelberg, on the Czechoslovak border southwest of Heidenreichstein, is a center of handmade ornamental glass in the old tradition, and several glassworks are open to the public. In Heidenreichstein you can easily spend the better part of a morning or an afternoon in the moated castle and its grounds.

One night: Raabs an der Thaya. The idyllic setting alongside the Thaya river, with the castle perched on a promontory above, is a splendid place for relaxation. Nearby is the mysterious ruin of Kollmitz castle. At Hardegg, the castle tour (allow two hours) includes kitchens and other utility areas as well as the more elegant reception rooms.

Information *See* Excursions from Vienna in Chapter 3.

Austrian Highlights from West to East

When you want to see the major cities of Austria in a compact tour, Innsbruck, Salzburg, and Vienna can be combined on one itinerary that contrasts the resolutely patriotic Tiroleans, the quieter Salzburgers, and the more cosmopolitan yet stoutly conservative Viennese. If you're driving, try to allow an extra day or more for the attractions along the way. The boat from Melk to Krems, and even on to Vienna, is a relaxing way to see magnificent countryside swept with vineyards and dotted with castles.

Length of Trip 7 to 8 days

Getting Around You'll find the scenery far more attractive by avoiding the
By Car heavy traffic of the autobahn and instead following the parallel highways. The distance is 552 km (345 mi) when you take the longer variation; the "German corner" shortcut trims 83 km (52 mi) and more than an hour off the trip. Otherwise, allow about 9 hours driving time for the full trip. The Salzburg–Vienna

stretch on the autobahn is only slightly shorter than Route 1 but considerably faster, taking about 3 hours against 4–4½ on A1.

By Public Transportation Fast trains link the three cities on the route, and you have the choice of going via the "German corner" (Bad Reichenhall) between Innsbruck and Salzburg or staying in Austria and taking the longer and more scenic Zell am See–Bischofshofen route. Trains run nearly every hour from Salzburg to Vienna. You can combine rail and boat by getting off the train at Melk and taking the Danube river boat to Vienna.

The Main Route **Two nights: Innsbruck.** Allow at least one day for town sightseeing and museums, a half day or more for Schloss Ambras or the Stubai valley south of the city, and a half day for travel.

Two nights: Salzburg. Allow a half day for the fortress, another for the old city, and a half day each for the new city or Hellbrunn and the salt mines in Hallein. You can reach Vienna in a matter of hours, but Linz warrants a stop for a look around Austria's largest city on the Danube.

Three nights: Vienna. Organized sightseeing takes half a day at minimum; allow another half day for an excursion to the Vienna Woods, a day for exploring the city on your own, and another day for some of the world's great museums.

Information *See* Chapters 3, 5, 7, and 10.

In Pursuit of the Great Abbeys

Austria's abbeys were centers of learning and education, repositories of books and documents, scientific papers, music manuscripts, and art. The church's special position allowed the abbeys the freedom to engage in commercial activities in order to support less worldy pursuits. The bishopric in Salzburg ruled over a vast area, drawing on income from the salt mines to pay for elaborate libraries and galleries. A visit to these abbeys, still very much in operation, can give you a feeling for the sequestered life of 100–200 years ago and the magnificence these treasuries hold. Our tour highlights Klosterneuburg, Göttweig, and Melk in Lower Austria; St. Florian and Kremsmünster in Upper Austria; Admont and Seckau in Styria; and St. Paul in Lavantal in Carinthia. The St. Paul abbey was rescued from ruin in the 1930s when the abbotts sold a Gutenberg Bible to the U.S. Library of Congress for $250,000; the abbey library still holds priceless treasures.

Length of Trip 3 to 4 days

Getting Around *By Car* This is the only practical way to tackle this tour, as public transportation is scarce in the out-of-the-way locations which early bishops and church worthies chose for their abbeys. The itinerary by car covers 825 km (515 mi) and will take about 13–15 hours to drive.

By Public Transportation Klosterneuburg is easily reached by fast suburban train from Vienna. Göttweig lies some distance from public transport. Melk is reached by train from Vienna. Buses run to St. Florian and Kremsmünster from Linz. Post office buses go to Admont and St. Paul. Seckau is off the usual path.

The Main Route **One night: Krems.** Klosterneuburg and Melk can be seen in a day, Göttweig as well if you hurry. Yet Krems is a pleasant base for a more leisurely visit to Göttweig, and you'll want time to stroll Krems' old streets and squares.

One night: Bad Hall. This spa near Kremsmünster offers a refreshing stop after a busy day of sightseeing.

One night: Judenburg. Seckau is not far distant from Judenburg, and this is a good starting point for making the trip to St. Paul.

Information *See* Chapters 4 and 5.

The Danube from Passau to Vienna

The Danube's tranquility contrasts markedly with the busy character of the Rhine and Main rivers in Germany, but the relative quiet of today will disappear in the 1990s on completion of the Rhine-Main-Danube canal, and now may be a good time to enjoy the river before commercial shipping gets the upper hand. On the Austrian stretch down to Vienna the river is in places docile and a bit insignificant; in other places it is the kind of mighty stream you'd associate with one of the great rivers of the world. The course through the Wachau is as impressive as any part of the Rhine, and the Danube also boasts its Lorelei.

Length of Trip 2 to 3 days

Getting Around This tour is a little more than 300 km (190 mi) long and will take
By Car 13–15 hours to drive.

By Public From early May to late October you can travel the stream itself
Transportation on the comfortable river ships run by the tongue-twisting DDSG/Donaudampfschiffahrtsgesellschaft. You have the choice of deck or cabin passage, with ships docking overnight in Linz on the Passau run. From Melk to Krems, local services crisscross the river from town to town. The main rail line from Passau via Linz to Vienna parallels the river closely as far as Melk, but you miss the intimacy when you see the Danube fleetingly through a train window. The Tulln–Vienna rail line also hugs the river bank, sharing it with the highway.

The Main Route **One night: Eferding or Linz.** The choice depends on whether you prefer a quiet, smaller city or the attractions of a major center.

One night: Krems. Outings to Dürnstein, Weissenkirchen, Spitz, and Melk—by car, boat, or public transportation—are easy from this convenient base. If you're driving, don't overlook the Göttweig abbey across the river or the wine cellars around nearby Langenlois.

Information *See* Chapter 5.

2 Portraits of Austria

Austria at a Glance: A Chronology

c. 800 BC Celts move into Danube valley.

c. 100 BC Roman legions, and Roman civilization, advance to Danube. Carnuntum (near Petronell, east of Vienna) is established as a provincial capital.

AD 180 Emperor Marcus Aurelius dies at fort of Vindobona, site of the Innere Stadt of Vienna. Other Roman settlements include Juvavum (Salzburg), Valdidena (Innsbruck).

c. 400–700 Danube valley is the crossing ground for successive waves of barbarian invaders. Era of the events of the Nibelung saga, written down c. 1100.

c. 700 Christian bishop established at Salzburg; conversion of pagan tribes begins.

791–99 Charlemagne, king of the Franks, conquers territory now known as Austria.

800 Pope Leo III crowns Charlemagne Emperor of the West.

814 Death of Charlemagne; his empire divided into three parts.

c. 800–900 Invasion of Magyars; they eventually settle along the Danube.

962 Pope John XII crowns Otto the Great, of Germany, Emperor of the Holy Roman Empire, constituting the eastern portion of Charlemagne's realm. Neither Holy, nor Roman, nor an Empire, this confederation continued until 1806.

The House of Babenberg

976 Otto II confers the eastern province of the *Reich*—i.e., *Oesterreich*, or Austria—upon the Margrave Leopold of Babenberg.

1095–1136 Reign of Leopold III, later canonized and declared patron saint of Austria.

1156 Austria becomes a duchy. Duke Heinrich II makes Vienna his capital, building a palace in Am Hof.

1192 Leopold V imprisons King Richard I (the Lionheart) of England, who is on his way to a crusade. Parts of Vienna and several town walls are later built with the ransom money.

1246 Death of Friedrich II (the Quarrelsome), last of the Babenbergs; a long interregnum follows.

The House of Habsburg

1273 Rudolf of Habsburg in Switzerland is chosen duke by the Electors of the Rhine; his family rules for 640 years.

1282 Habsburgs absorb the land of Austria.

1365 University of Vienna founded.

1477 Duke Maximilian I marries Maria of Burgundy, whose dowry comprises Burgundy and the Netherlands.

1496 Maximilian's son, Philip, marries Juana of Castile and Aragon, daughter of Ferdinand and Isabella of Spain.

1519 Death of Maximilian; his grandson, Charles I of Spain, inherits Austria, Burgundy, and the Netherlands; he is elected Holy Roman Emperor as Charles V.

1521 Charles divides his realm with his brother, Ferdinand, who becomes archduke of Austria and the first Habsburg to live in the Hofburg in Vienna.

1526 When his brother-in-law, Louis II, king of Hungary and Bohemia, dies fighting the Turks, Ferdinand inherits these crowns and some of their territories; the Turks take the rest.

1529 Turks lay siege to Vienna.

1556 Charles V abdicates; Ferdinand becomes Holy Roman Emperor. A Catholic with many Protestant subjects, he negotiates the Peace of Augsburg, which preserves a truce between the Catholic and Protestant states of his realm until 1618.

1618–48 Thirty Years' War: begins as a religious dispute, but becomes a dynastic struggle between Habsburgs and Bourbons, fought on German soil by non-Germans. The Peace of Westphalia, 1648, gives Austria no new territory and reestablishes the religious deadlock of the Peace of Augsburg; the Holy Roman Empire remains a loose confederation.

1679 Plague strikes Vienna, leaving 100,000 dead.

1683 Turks besiege Vienna; are routed by combined forces of Emperor Leopold I, the duke of Lorraine, and King Jan Sobieski of Poland. By 1699, armies led by Prince Eugene of Savoy drive the Turks east and south, doubling the area of Habsburg lands. The Turkish legacy: a gold crescent and a sack of coffee beans; Vienna's coffeehouses open for business.

1713 As a result of the War of the Spanish Succession, Austria gains Spanish territories in Italy and Flanders.

1740 Last male Habsburg, Charles VI, dies; succession of his daughter Maria Theresa leads to attack on the Habsburg dominions; long-term rivalry between Austria and Prussia begins.

1740–80 Reign of Maria Theresa, a golden age, when young Mozart entertains at Schönbrunn Palace and Haydn and Gluck establish Vienna as a musical mecca. Fundamental reforms modernize the Austrian monarchy.

1780–90 Reign of Maria Theresa's son Joseph II, who carries her liberalizing tendencies too far by freeing the serfs and reforming the Church. Her daughter, Marie Antoinette, has other problems.

1806 Napoleon forces Emperor Franz II to abdicate, and the Holy Roman Empire is no more; Franz is retitled emperor of Austria and rules until 1835.

1814–15 The Congress of Vienna defines post-Napoleonic Europe; Austria's Prince Metternich (who had arranged the marriage between Napoleon and Franz II's daughter Marie Louise) gains territory and power.

1815–48 Rise of nationalism threatens Austrian Empire; as chief minister, Metternich represses liberal and national movements with censorship, secret police, force.

1848 Revolutions throughout Europe, including Budapest, Prague, Vienna; Emperor Ferdinand I abdicates in favor of his 18-year-old nephew, Franz Josef. Under his personal rule (lasting until 1916), national and liberal movements are thwarted.

1856–90 Modern Vienna is created and much of the medieval city torn down; the "waltz kings," Johann Strauss, father and son, dominate popular music. Sigmund Freud (1856–1939) begins his research on the human psyche with his patients in Vienna. By 1900, artistic movements include the Wiener Werkstatte and Expressionism.

1866 Bismarck's Prussia defeats Austria in a seven-weeks' war, fatally weakening Austria's position among the German states.

1867 In response to Hungarian clamor for national recognition, the *Ausgleich,* or compromise, creates the dual monarchy of Austria-Hungary with two parliaments and one monarch.

1870–71 Bismarck's victory in the Franco-Prussian war unifies German states under Prussian dominion.

1882 Austria-Hungary, Germany, Italy join in the Triple Alliance.

1889 Franz Josef's only son, Rudolf, dies mysteriously in an apparent suicide pact with his young mistress, Baroness Marie Vetsera.

1898 Empress Elisabeth is murdered by an anarchist.

1907 Universal manhood suffrage is gained in Austria, but not in Hungary.

1914 June 28: Archduke Franz Ferdinand, nephew and heir of Franz Josef, is assassinated by a Serbian terrorist at Sarajevo (now in Yugoslavia). August 4: Europe is at war: Germany and Austria-Hungary versus Russia, France, and Britain.

1916 Death of Franz Josef.

The Republic

1918 End of World War I; collapse of Austria-Hungary. Emperor Karl I resigns; Republic of Austria is carved out of Habsburg crown lands, while nation-states of the Empire declare autonomy. Kept afloat by loans from the League of Nations, Austria adjusts to its new role with difficulty. Culturally it continues to flourish: Arnold Schoenberg's 12-tone scale recasts musical expression, while the Vienna Circle redefines philosophy.

1927 General strike; antigovernment riots.

1933 Chancellor Dollfuss suspends Parliament.

1934 Dollfuss suppresses the socialists and creates a one-party state; later in the year he is assassinated by Nazis. His successor, Kurt von Schuschnigg, attempts to accommodate Hitler.

1938 *Anschluss:* Hitler occupies Austria without resistance.

1945 Austria, postwar, is divided into four zones of occupation by the Allies; free elections are held.

1955 Signing of the Austrian State Treaty officially ends the occupation.

1979 SALT II treaty signed in Vienna.

1989 Austria becomes the first destination for waves of Eastern European emigrants as the borders of Warsaw Pact nations are opened.

The Land of the Waltz

by Hans Fantel

A native of Austria and longtime resident of the United States, Hans Fantel is currently a syndicated columnist for the New York Times.

The Viennese traditionally live in two countries. One is on the map. The other is the imaginary region where wine flows, love triumphs, and everything is silk-lined. This is the land of the waltz.

A century ago, during the sunset years of Austria's 1,000-year-old empire, there was no clear demarcation between the real world and that mythical land of the waltz. The two realms merged along the hazy boundary that never quite separates fact from fancy in Vienna.

This region of the Viennese mind is not just a shallow, sybaritic fantasy. Like Viennese music itself, it embodies a substantial premise. If melody could be translated, a Viennese waltz would add up to 100 ways of saying that, all considered, and with due allowance for everything, simply being alive is a cause for celebration.

At its surprising best—in such creations as *The Blue Danube*, the *Emperor Waltz*, or *Tales from the Vienna Woods*—the waltz is perhaps the closest description of happiness ever attained in any art.

Paradoxically, the music is not merry. A haze of wistfulness lies over the sunniest tunes, and their sweetness sometimes touches on melancholy. Though the dance is a swirling embrace, the music countermands sensual abandonment. It insists on grace; it remains pensive in the midst of pleasure. And in this blending of the sensual with the reflective, the Viennese waltz expresses and creates a condition of durable bliss—a measured joy.

For almost 100 years, while the last Habsburg emperors ruled the real Austria, the land of the waltz had its own dynasty—the Waltz Kings. Both were named Johann Strauss.

Johann Strauss I ruled over this mythical realm of music during the first part of the 19th century. A generation later, his son, Johann Strauss II, extended the scope of the waltz to symphonic proportions, writing dance music in the form of orchestral tone poems that transformed the ballroom into a concert stage.

These two men welded their city and their music into a single identity, making Vienna and the waltz almost a single thought. Viennese historians are fond of florid metaphors suggesting that Johann Strauss—father and son—did not so much compose their waltzes as ineffably transmute their city into music. Such notions seem altogether plausible to the romantic Viennese, including the younger Strauss himself. "If it is true that I have talent," he wrote during the latter part of his life, "I owe it, above everything else, to my beloved city of Vienna . . . in whose soil is rooted my whole strength, in whose air float the melodies which my ear has caught, my heart has drunk in, and my hand has written down."

Sentimental, yes. Unrealistic, no. Strauss's own assessment of his creative act is probably accurate. *Zeitgeist* and *genius loci*—the spirits of time and place—have always whispered to the creative imagination, and Strauss, being a musician, surely had a fine ear for such promptings.

It is impossible to weigh such ephemeral influences, but one can hardly dispute the perceptive comment made by Marcel Brion on Vienna's matchless array of musicians: "They would not have been what they were, what they had to be, if chance had forced them to live anywhere but in Vienna."

Music, like wine, takes its flavor from the soil and the season in which it grows, and the roots of the waltz were nourished by a moment of history in which an aging civilization had reached the peak of mellowness. No other city has ever been so suffused by an art as Vienna was by music. Painting, perhaps, was of similarly intense concern to the Florentines of the Renaissance. But this enthusiasm was confined to a relatively small circle of aristocratic sponsors centering around the Medicis, and it seems unlikely that painting played a major part in the life of the ordinary Florentine.

By contrast, Vienna's involvement with music was shared by its shopkeepers and janitors. The barriers between serious and popular music had not yet become impassable. There was no "music business" in the modern sense, for commercial pressures had not yet debased and polarized public taste. In the crowds who thronged to hear performances of Beethoven symphonies, Haydn oratorios, or Mozart operas, burghers and artisans easily joined princes of the realm. Conversely, in the little rustic inns tucked among the hillsides of the Vienna Woods, members of the nobility mixed quite casually with lesser folk to dance to the sweet and giddy folk tunes of the region. Here lay the tree-shaded courtyards of the *Heurigen*, the vintners' houses where the Viennese sampled the new wine. And if the white wines that grow along the Danube lack the finesse of more famous vintages from the Rhine or the Moselle, they have a tart freshness and a light headiness that make them all the more inviting for casual tippling.

During the long spring and fall seasons, and during the mild summers, these spacious gardens and courtyards were filled daily from about four in the afternoon until the early hours, and their mood of easy conviviality shaped the pattern of Viennese leisure. Drunkenness was not tolerated; the typical Viennese was a thoughtful drinker who made a glass last a long time by puffing, between sips, on a pencil-thin, foot-long cigar that he smoked through a straw. Groups of strolling musicians would pass from one to another of these inns, entertaining the patrons with tunes of the Austrian countryside—the lilting *Ländler*, which was the rural precursor of the not yet invented waltz, and the *Schnadahüpfl*, a jaunty country hop. Here, too, the sound of music created an instant democracy of manners, and class barriers melted in the balmy atmosphere of relaxed hedonism.

This aspect of Vienna's life invariably amazed foreign visitors, particularly those from France, where such casual friendliness between people of widely different social standing was unthinkable either before or after the revolution. "Ancestors and rank seem to be forgotten," reports one traveler, "and aristocratic pride laid aside. Here we see artisans, artists, merchants, councillors, barons, counts and excellencies dancing together with waitresses, women of the middle class, and ladies."

At private concerts, too, there was congenial mingling of persons from different social strata. Tradespeople with sincere musical interests often found access to the musical soirées which were the chief entertainment in the Baroque town houses of the high bourgeoisie.

In an ancient monarchy whose minutely graded class structure might otherwise have calcified into social arthritis, music thus served a vital limbering function. In an order where status—being mostly fixed by birth—could rarely be achieved, music provided the safety valve that kept the pressure of social unrest from building up and enabled absolutism to maintain its sway over Austria long after the American and French revolutions had shaken other thrones.

For centuries, the Habsburg rulers maintained a tradition of fostering the arts. The theater, as long as it confined itself to entertainment and did not become a platform for ideas, received royal encouragement, as did the pictorial arts; sculpture; and, above all, music, architecture, and landscaping.

The implicit tenet was that beauty begets pleasure, and pleasure begets contentment. The great cities of imperial Austria—Vienna, Prague, Salzburg, and Budapest—owe their splendor to the endearing assumption that civic beauty is the key to civic tranquillity.

To accuse the Habsburgs of prostituting art for political aims would be unjust. Its furtherance was no cynically contrived policy. In fact, it was no policy at all, never having been consciously formulated. The state of the arts in Austria sprang quite naturally from a naïvely mystic faith—not uncommon in Catholic countries—that aesthetic grace was akin to divine grace and that to invest a country with outward beauty would somehow bestow civic virtues that would hold it together inwardly. This sort of intuition is legitimate to statecraft. What, after all, is a nation but an agreement on style and a cohesive sharing of myths?

Under these conditions, the whole country seemed pervaded by a certain musicality—an innate, casual feeling for form and harmony. It was evident in the visual charm of the Austrian Baroque that left its mark not alone on the great cities but also on many of the smaller towns and villages.

A feeling for the Baroque and its later, lighter variants, with their graceful, almost melodic lines, was by no means confined to the leading architects employed in the design of palaces and manors. It filtered down to the humblest mason molding garlanded cherubs above the gate of an ordinary house. It shaped the vision of the local builder who quite matter-of-factly bestowed an exquisite harmony of proportions. It guided the hand of the cabinetmaker who filled the house with the playful curves of Rococo and Biedermeier furniture. It influenced the gardener and blacksmith alike, one arranging flowerbeds like calligraphy, the other echoing the scrolls in wrought iron. The tailor and the pastry cook shared a concern for graceful shape, and even the gestures of ordinary citizens reflected a certain elegance as they went about their business.

Industrial manufacture had not yet cast its equalizing pall on the design of objects that fill the household and pass through hands in daily use. Far longer than the more industrialized countries to the west, Austria retained the practice and attitudes of individual craftsmanship. The decorative merit of a product ranked at least as high as its utility. Beauty had market value, and the combination of commercial worth and aesthetic joy bestowed on tradesmen and their customers alike a measure of dignity and satisfaction.

In such an ambience, the ear, too, became attuned to the refinements and delights of form. Music derived from the surroundings. It was inescapable. It lay before the eyes.

Vienna, and much of Austria, thus became a natural breeding ground for musicians. A contemporary chronicler, Eduard Bauernfeld, observes that "every hole is full of musicians who play for the people. Nobody wants to eat his *Bratl* at the inn if he can't have table music to go with it." No feast or celebration was complete without a special overture composed for the occasion. Virtually every bourgeois family could muster a passable string quartet among its members, creating a constant demand for new scores. More than 60 piano factories flourished in the city, which numbered a mere 250,000 inhabitants, and next to good looks and a dowry, musical talent was considered a girl's chief asset.

Every Sunday, the churches resounded with musical settings of the Mass—"operas for the angels," as Mozart called them. Performed by choirs and orchestras of remarkable proficiency, these compositions by Mozart, Haydn, and Schubert were splendidly melodic, and the occasion, despite its ecclesiastical setting, was often more of a public concert than a divine service. The clergy never objected to mixing devotion and enjoyment. In fact, the monasteries owned some of the best vineyards and maintained some of the coziest inns to dispense their wine. Austrian Catholicism had been spared the more Puritan notions of sin that had shaped the restrictive attitudes of northern Europe. It had also escaped much of the cruel virulence of the Counter Reformation. Austria's faith, touchingly expressed in countless sculptures of smiling, childlike Madonnas, never really clashed against that other trinity in Vienna's heaven—wine, women, and song.

Perhaps the most significant aspect of Vienna's musical life was the attitude of the typical listener. In Paris or London, for example, music was regarded as an entertainment. Not so in Vienna. Here it was a personal necessity, an indispensable part of everyday life. In its lighter forms, music was a needed refreshment; in its more demanding forms, an exercise of the spirit in search of illumination.

It is hardly surprising that such a society left considerable room for individuality. The forces of regimentation and efficiency were traditionally resisted, thus preparing the ground for Vienna's famed *gemütlichkeit*, the characteristic attitude of unhurried bonhomie.

No doubt the most benign economic influence on the social climate was the virtual absence of extreme poverty. To be sure, Vienna had its share of improvidents and people suffering ill fortune. But the causes of their plight were personal rather than built into an exploitive system. Hence their number was small and they did not constitute an embittered group endangering the balance of the community. Where in Paris a Jacobin majority marshaled the envy and fear of the deprived into an orgy of class hatred, the Viennese joined all classes in self-indulgent epicureanism.

Even lowly citizens ate well in Vienna. A surviving restaurant menu lists a complete meal for 13 *Kreuzer*—the equivalent of about 25¢. For this modest sum one could regale oneself on soup, smothered liver, roast beef, vegetables, bread, and a quarter-liter of wine. A remarkable document survives in the City Archives showing that during one typical year (1786) some 200,000 Viennese managed to do away with 42,197 oxen, 1,511 cows, 66,353 calves, 43,925 sheep, 164,700 lambs, 96,949 pigs, 12,967 suckling pigs, 454,063 buckets of local wine, 19,276 buckets of Hungarian and Tirolean wine, and 382,478 buckets of beer. No one seems to have made per-capita comparisons, but this document is generally taken as historic proof of an ample appetite.

Such statistics are not irrelevant to music, for they bespeak a love of life and a general greediness for good things, be they products of art or of the kitchen.

With comforts of mind and body abundant and readily available, economic incentive never was honed to an irritant edge. Material possessions alone could not change one's social standing in a fixed-status society, and since the public environment was generally delightful, there was less need for private luxury. Consequently, acquisitive drive, the dominant motivating force in open and industrial societies, rarely inspired the Viennese. Their motivation was not so much material success but satisfaction with the task at hand, or, quite often, simply the leisurely enjoyment of the day. To the Viennese, this was the utmost practicality and realism.

As long as external conditions supported this mode of existence, remarkably little cruelty or vulgarity crept to the surface of Austrian life. The feral substrate at the bottom of any society remained nicely covered. And those who, by dark intuition, knew it was there said nothing of it.

Of course, not even an unfailing surfeit of music and Wiener schnitzel could remove all challenges from life, but in an age of indulgent epicureanism, these challenges could usually be surmounted by not trying too hard. That, too, lies in the music. The cardinal rule for playing a waltz is the same as for mastering other phases of life in Vienna: Don't push it—and keep the tempo loose.

Its cushioned resilience made Vienna relatively crisis-proof—at least until the final, cataclysmic collapse of the empire. Nonchalant self-irony lent Vienna, and all Austria, the buoyancy to clear minor hurdles. For example, during a government scandal involving payoffs at the ministerial level, the noted Viennese journalist Karl Kraus soothed tempers by explaining that the accused civil servant "took such small bribes as to border on incorruptibility."

Scanning 1,000 years of Austrian history, John Gunther observed that the country "in its own inimitable, slippery way wriggled out of any difficulty. Something of the very softness of the Austrian character had been a factor of strength, because the horns of a crisis were apt to disappear through absorption—the crisis lost its point, melted in the prevailing solvent of easygoing compromise."

This is hardly a country to be admired by moralists. Philosophers may not find it much to their liking, either. But poets and musicians have always felt at home there, for the land pulses with the heartbeat of humanity.

Johann Strauss felt that pulse and shaped it into a special music that lifted Vienna from its moorings on the map, wafting the city across that misty line between reality and dream into the land of the waltz.

The Once and Future Lech

by John Skow

John Skow is a freelance writer who lives in New Hampshire. He writes on skiing, mountaineering, and environmental subjects.

Never mind that you can't go home again; you can't even go *skiing* in that snowbound little village in the Arlberg again. Not the way it was, not the way you were. When I first skied at Lech am Arlberg in 1969, my knees were strong and my technique was wobbly; the dollar was strong and the schilling was weak. I could pick up all three of my children at the same time, and sometimes did. We were all living in the province of Salzburg, in half of a 35-room lakeside villa listed on the maps as a *schlossl*, or small castle. At Lech, my wife and I each bought our first buckle boots, made to order, of plastic-leather laminate, fitted by Martin Strolz himself. And then went home to learn that I had lost my job with the *Saturday Evening Post* because that great old magazine had hit an iceberg and sunk. We joked, hollowly, about whether you could boil plastic-leather boots and eat them.

Some of this is personal and irrelevant, some not. I don't even want to go home again to the schlossl, which is now owned, I suppose, by a German rock star or a deposed Central American dictator.

And Lech?

It was the best ski town in Austria: at 1,450 meters, higher than Kitzbühel, which already had become a bit too glossified; cozier, more *gemütlich*, than Badgastein, Zell am See, or Innsbruck; part of a formidable on-and-off-*piste* ski network that, with a little bus hopping, took you to Zürs and as far as St. Anton and back. A few years later, visiting Lech again on assignment, I noted that the farmers who owned the lifts no longer stopped them for an hour at noon (so that the sons and nephews who ran them could hustle bratwurst at the mountainside restaurants the farmers also operated), though lunch was still taken very seriously. And I noted that concrete avalanche galleries had been built over the highway that wound from the Arlberg pass up over the Flexen pass to Zürs and on to Lech. This meant, alas, an end to a fine old falsehood (occasionally a truth) that involved calling up your boss and telling him that you had fully intended to assist in the decline of the West that week, except that a huge snowslide had blocked the road and—bad luck—you were marooned in Lech for a few more days.

Even if progress *had* munched one of the world's great excuses, Lech was still what it had been: the settlement where the highway plows stopped, a lost valley where the world seemed not to intrude or matter much. And, of course, it was still the center of a superb ski network of broad-shouldered mountains, rising up through spruce and fir forests to the moderate altitude of about 2,300 meters, on both sides of the little Lech river and what was still a small and unpretentious town.

Development pressure has been increasing throughout the '80s, however, and by 1989 Lech was straining hard to retain what was now, to some extent, an illusion: that it was still a small mountain village. True, it is the sort of small village where former Queen Juliana of the Netherlands vacations in winter. She stays, of course, at the small and elegant Gasthof Post, Lech's best address since the glaciers receded. "And you know, at 80, she still skis, and not so badly either," says Kristl Moosbrugger, who runs the Post with her husband Franz. Frau Moosbrugger skis with her royal guest, it should be noted; she is 83.

So far, Lech has resisted efforts to build giant, chain-run hotels and massive condo and apartment complexes. Lifts, restaurants, and hotels here are locally owned. New construction occurs mostly when a landowner has several children and wants to establish each in a business.

Cars of day skiers jam the town on weekends despite relatively high lift prices, and some of Lech's hotelmen and lift owners think that a big, underground parking garage should be built between Zürs and Lech. A more subtle sort of pressure arises from an escalating status war among hotel owners. "Everyone wants to have the fanciest," says Othmar Schneider, the 1952 Olympic slalom gold medalist who went on to ski schools at Stowe, Boyne Mountain, and Portillo. "I don't think skiers want three waiters in white gloves to serve dinner, but. . . ." Schneider's Kristiania Hotel is relaxed about its four stars, but it is now the exception in Lech. *Bürgermeister* Johann Schneider (no relation), who runs the glossy Arlberg Hotel, says defensively that "we aren't as stiff as St. Moritz." Not yet, a visitor decides, but it is harder to find country food in Lech and to avoid the expensive and characterless cuisine referred to as "continental."

We came to ski, though, didn't we? And no question about it: Even though snowfall throughout Europe was low, skiing at Lech was better than ever. Twenty years ago in early March—which was when we arrived this time—the lower slopes would have been burned out. Now, snowmaking fills in the bare spots. The early-morning liftline bottlenecks that plague many of Europe's great ski stations have never been a problem at Lech, and now getting up to the slopes is even easier. Two parallel cable cars rise from the center of town up the Rufikopf, which is the starting point for the long, easy swing down to Zürs (also, if you are going off-piste, for the long, arduous, deep-snow adventure down to Zürs). A couple of chair lifts and the Oberlech cable car start you up the Schegelkopf, across the river. Ah, yes, Oberlech: a settlement of several hotels at 1,700 meters above the town, reachable by a *seilbahn* that runs till midnight; great for dinner, superb for eating lunch (chewing the beer, sucking in the schnitzel) on the terrace, in the sun. But we came to ski. . . .

Above the tree line, not much higher than Oberlech, lifts ramify amiably in the direction of Zug and Zürs. There is almost no destination that can't be managed by anyone who can stretch a point and call himself an intermediate skier; and almost no broad, cruising trail from which an expert cannot peel off with a yodel into the white and hairy. All that is lacking is through-the-trees skiing, because woodland terrain here is protected by environmental laws. Almost everything works smoothly; lifts are quick and modern; lines at mountain restaurants are tolerable. The exception is the second lift of three on the way back from Zürs, a slow and vexatious chair lift up the Madloch. For obscure environmental reasons that made even less sense in English than in German, this clunker cannot be replaced, and everyone stands around on a frozen lake, telling jokes and muttering while it grinds.

Because the territory is so vast, and because so much skiing here is from one town to another, over one peak and another, guides are more than useful. You won't get lost without one if you follow the signs, but you will miss some of the best, hidden-away, alternative runs, and the better you ski, the more you will miss. What this leads up to is that although American males would sooner take hookworm medicine than ski lessons, a ski class is a good idea at Lech.

My grown daughter and I skied with a private instructor for a day that would have been hopeless without him. A foggy whiteout fuzzed everything beyond the ski tips. We followed his jacket, not believing that we were doing this, down deep-snow slopes that even the next day, in bright sun, were impressive. Then we joined a class, and kept at it for six days. What I got out of it was a lot of rowdy stamina. After years of skiing, I could manage all the instructor's drills easily, but at the outset, because of knee operations, too little conditioning, and too much beer and schnitzel, I had to stop every 500 meters. By the end of the week, we were stopping only to ease onto another chair lift.

And, yes, for lunch. One day, sitting outside at a restaurant on the Zugerberg, I happened to notice a black dot just below a broad, snowy peak perhaps a kilometer away through the clear air. Then another: two skiers. They cut two tracks down the highest face, then slowly disappeared behind a rock mass, reappeared, and did a lovely series of eights down an enormous, untracked wall of powder. *"Ja, ski schule,"* our instructor said with a sly smile. Practice hard, and one day. . . .

Maybe. Why not? An old friend, an Austrian well into his seventies, has been skiing at Lech since the 1930s. Horses trailing ropes used to pull skiers up the road from Lech to

Zürs. You would wrap the rope around one ski pole and use the other pole to whack the horse behind you in case he started to step on your skis. Once, he said, he and a friend climbed the Valluga, above St. Anton—with skis and skins, of course—then skied down and skied the Madloch above Zürs using the new lift. "All on one day," he said. "It seemed a marvel." Skiing at Lech, he said, is "the salt in the soup," the spice of life. He says he'll be back next spring.

The Law of the Heuriger

by Alan Levy

Maria Theresa's son, Emperor Joseph II (1741–90), who wanders in and out of the play and movie *Amadeus* muttering, "Well, there you are," uttered far more enduring words on August 17, 1784, when he proclaimed to the Austrian people that "we give every man the freedom to sell or dispense—year-round, in any form, at any time, and at whatever price he wants—food, wine, or fruit juice that he has produced himself."

Handed this entrepreneurial key by royalty, the farmers of the Vienna Woods unlatched the *Heuriger:* a unique wine tavern that proliferates in the capital and eastern Austria. Heuriger is a noun derived from an adjective meaning "this year's," which applies not only to young wines, but also to such crops as cabbage and potatoes. To the thirsty, however, the only real heuriger is the farmhouse facade adorned by a sprig of pine, a branch of fir, or a wreath of holly and a plaque on the door signifying that the new wine is in and has been pressed on the premises. Open that door in summer and you'll feast your eyes upon an inviting courtyard lined with picnic tables and crowded with Austrians making merry (which, often as not, means intense intellectual conversations about trivia), frequently hoisting glasses for toasting or refilling, and occasionally lifting voices, too, in song.

Inside the house you'll usually find a buffet from which you can buy hot or cold food and, in those that stay open year-round, a cozy hearth around which you can also eat, drink, and revel. In the larger heurige (plural) or posher ones that cater to tourists and businesspeople, you'll find live music—usually *schrammelmusik*, named after a 19th-century family who composed, played, sang, and ordained the wistful sound of music still heard in the heuriger.

Rendered by violins, guitar, and clarinet or accordion and sung in an impenetrable Austrian dialect, the songs counterpoint the conversation by treating such earthy themes as a lover's lane in the Vienna Woods that's too small for one person but big enough for two, or lamenting that "the old cog-wheel railway is scrap iron now," or wrestling with the dilemma of a would-be lover who's making headway but watching the clock in the knowledge that the last streetcar leaves soon and he doesn't have money for the taxi ride that would clinch his case. This song is called "The Little Blue Light," and, while the last No. 38 streetcar from the wine suburb of Grinzing no longer wears a blue lamp on its tail, its illuminated destination signs bear equally ominous blue squares of cardboard.

In Grinzing, in particular, one must be wary of places where the Vienna-by-night tour buses draw up every half hour and the schrammel musicians drop everything to play "Deep in the Heart of Texas" or "If I Were a Rich Man." Stick around there and you won't be rich for long. Far better to follow a Viennese drinking song with lyrics that list virtually every wine village within easy reach, starting with "a little Grinzing, a little Sievering, a little Neuwaldegg, Nussdorf, Ottakring and Petersdorf." Or play it safe at the elegantly rustic Grinzinger Hauermandl, where the music, chicken, and wine are consistently first-rate.

Today, within the city limits of Vienna, there are some 800 families growing wine on more than 1,800 acres to produce about 12 million quarter-liter glasses of wine per year. Heuriger wine is mostly white: clear, sparkling, dry, and, thanks to its high acidity, possessed of a fresh bite that can bite back the morning after. It is wise to switch, after a couple of glasses, from new wine to old *(alt)*. The price may be a dime more tonight, but tomorrow's pain will be less.

The Vienna Tourist Board publishes a free brochure in German, English, French, and Italian, "Heurige in Wien," listing 150 of them by neighborhood with helpful maps. There are at least five times that many, and one of the charms of a summer night is to discover your own. Even the farsighted Joseph II, "The People's Emperor" who encouraged Mozart and tried to democratize the Habsburg monarchy, might be astonished at how the cottage industry he envisioned has become a backbone of both Austrian tourism and Viennese life.

"During the warm season, from May to September, people go early, around six o'clock in the evening," says Traudl Lessing, a Viennese chronicler and connoisseur of heuriger living. "They take their children and dogs along, as both provide excellent starting points for conversation and friendly relations. As soon as the benches around the rough wooden tables have filled, people sit down with strangers and begin to confide in each other. They tell their unknown friends about the wife's illness, the cranky boss, and how they avoid the burdens of taxation."

Frau Lessing and her husband, Erich, gave their daughter Hannah's wedding party indoors last January at the spacious and lively Heuriger Schübel-Auer in the Heiligenstadt neighborhood. Beethoven once lived in this district and cursed the church bells he could see tolling but not hear. In fact, just around the corner, a 17th-century house where the peripatetic composer resided for part of 1817 is now one of Vienna's most famous heurige: Mayer am Pfarrplatz.

After Joseph II's 1784 proclamation, known in Vienna as "the law of the heuriger," farmers started selling pork, poultry, and sometimes beef from their own livestock in the front rooms where their customers used to sample their wines. Farmers' daughters found work at home as cooks and waitresses instead of migrating to the city or marrying for survival. Soon, whole families were making cheese and peddling their produce to a market that came to them.

Early in the 20th century, this laissez-faire law of the heuriger was modified for the only time in its 207-year history. Its provisions had spawned too many child alcoholics and adult workaholics—the former souring on not-always-unfermented grape juice; the latter missing church—so certain soft drinks were sanctioned (usually Almdudler Limonade, which tastes like ginger ale), and farmers were forbidden to sell their wines on more than 300 days a year. The amendment also permitted ham and cheese and fowl to be sold by wine farmers who didn't have their own pigs and cows and chickens. Even today, though, a wine tavern peddling beer, coffee, or Coca-Cola isn't an authentic heuriger and shouldn't be displaying the symbolic green bush outside.

During and after two devastating world wars, the heuriger assumed a new social role in Viennese lives. Rather than entertain in cramped, shabby, or bomb-damaged quarters, hosts invited their guests to meet them at "our heuriger," where they would buy drinks and sometimes dinner—though it is still good form in many heurige to bring your own picnic and buy just wine. If the coffeehouse, a tradition a century older than the heuriger, remains the living room of the Viennese—"neither at home nor in the fresh air," they like to say—the heuriger is their summer garden and year-round retreat.

How the heuriger has kept pace with modern times, trends, and thinking can be experienced most happily on a visit to Gumpoldskirchen, a wine village some seven miles outside the city. On the dividing line between the slopes of the *Wienerwald* (Vienna Woods, the northeastern foothills of the Alps) and the *Puszta* (the flat Hungarian plain that begins in Austria), Gumpoldskirchen is a more early-to-sing, early-to-bed place than Grinzing—and the prices are better. If you arrive around 3 or 4 PM, there is ample light to explore some of the 100 charming courtyards behind welcoming green laurels and tarry perhaps in the Renaissance sobriety of the Benedictine monks' heuriger or the cozy nook carved out of a wine barrel in Schabl's Pressehaus (both on the main street) before bearing left at the onion-domed church around which the town was built several centuries ago.

This will put you on a *weinwanderweg* through the vineyards: a 30- to 45-minute circle walk designed and decorated in 1975 by the vintners of Gumpoldskirchen. An ancient wine press looms up on a hillside like a gallows. A modern metal sculpture of an insect magnifies and gentrifies the *reblaus* (phylloxera), a plant pest that came over from California in the 1870s and destroyed most of Europe's wines; the vines were restored only when reblaus-resistant strains were also imported from California.

Along its way, the weinwanderweg relates the history of Austrian wines from the third century, when the Roman Emperor Probus first allowed grapes to be grown outside Italy, up through Joseph II to the present day, when Gumpoldskirchen leads all of Austria in the production of Zierfandler, another white wine deceptively called Rotgipfler, and Blau Portugiese, which is red and Austrian.

Somehow, one develops a thirst along the weinwanderweg, and in gathering darkness, dozens of pine bushes of Gumpoldskirchen are already illuminated and beckoning below. Safely down, you should head for one of the twin heurige of the Bruckberger family at Wienerstrasse 1 and Kirchenplatz 1, where the music has already started and the partying has been going on for hours.

The Bruckbergers have been in the wine business for more than three centuries. They slaughter their homefed livestock once a week. Apple-cheeked young Hans Bruckberger presides over the noisy, happy, 800-seat heuriger that bears the family name on the main street. A couple of blocks away, right where the weinwanderweg begins and ends, his sister Elisabeth runs a more intimate cellar heuriger for romantic dining by candlelight and softer music. The wine, music, and strudel in both places are just right—and so are the duck at Elisabeth's and the crisp bread and spicy Liptauer cheese, roast chicken, and steamy pigs' knuckles at Hans's.

Hans's and Elisabeth's sister, Hansi, runs a *heuriger-proviant*, a food-supply store adjacent to the larger heuriger. Here you can buy cold cuts and bread for snacking along the weinwanderweg or on a wienerwald hike or if you just don't feel like hacking the buffet in the heuriger. At the end of an evening, when a Bruckberger patron expresses the need for a cup of coffee before heading back to the real world, particularly by car, the dirndled wine waitress will respond demurely with: "That would be against the law of the heuriger. But we can send out. Give me the money and I'll go next door and buy you one."

Taking your schillings and accepting a small tip, she strides through Hans's kitchen into Hansi's store. As a shopkeeper, Hansi is allowed to brew and sell coffee. The law of the heuriger has been circumvented, but if it helps a drinker to arrive home safely, well, as Joseph II might say, there you are.

3 Vienna

Introduction

by George H. Sullivan

Vienna is a city that deeply loves its past. For many centuries it was one of the great capitals of Europe, home to the Habsburg rulers of the Austro-Hungarian Empire. Today the Empire is long gone, but many reminders of the city's Imperial heyday remain, carefully preserved by the tradition-loving Viennese. Most of Vienna's renowned 18th- and 19th-century buildings have been preserved as well, attesting to a brilliant architectural past that few cities can match.

From the late 18th century until World War I, Vienna's culture—particularly its musical culture—was famous throughout Europe. Haydn, Mozart, Beethoven, Schubert, Brahms, Strauss, Mahler, and Bruckner all lived in the city, producing music that is still played in concert halls all over the world. And at the tail end of the 19th century the city's artists and architects—Gustav Klimt, Egon Schiele, Oskar Kokoschka, Josef Hoffmann, Otto Wagner, and Adolf Loos among them—brought about an unprecedented artistic revolution, a revolution that swept away the past and set the stage for the radically experimental art of the 20th century.

At the close of World War I the Austro-Hungarian Empire was dismembered, and Vienna lost its cherished status as the seat of Imperial power. Its influence was much reduced, and (unlike most of Europe's other great cities) its population began to decline, from around 2 million to the current 1.5 million. Today, however, the city's future looks bright, for with the collapse of the Iron Curtain, Vienna may at long last regain its traditional status as the hub of central Europe.

For many first-time visitors, the city's one major disappointment is the Danube River. The inner city, it turns out, lies not on the river's main stream but on one of its narrow offshoots, known as the Danube Canal. As a result, the sweeping river views expected by most newcomers fail to materialize.

The Romans are to blame, for when Vienna was founded as a Roman military encampment around AD 100, the walled garrison was built not on the Danube's main stream but rather on the largest of the river's eastern branches, where it could be bordered by water on three sides. (To this day the outline of the Roman walls, a lopsided square, can be seen in the street plan of the inner city: Naglergasse and the Graben to the southwest, Kramergasse and Rotgasse to the southeast, Salzgasse to the northeast, and Tiefer Graben to the northwest.) The wide present-day Danube did not take shape until the late 19th century, when its various branches were rerouted and merged to prevent flooding.

The Romans maintained their camp for some 300 years (the emperor Marcus Aurelius is thought to have died there in AD 180) and finally abandoned it around AD 400. The settlement survived, however, and by the 13th century growth was sufficient to require new city walls to the south. According to legend, the walls were financed by the English: In 1192 the local duke kidnapped King Richard I, who was on his way home from the Third Crusade, and held him prisoner for two years until he was expensively ransomed.

Vienna's third set of walls dates from 1544, when the existing walls were improved and extended. The new fortifications were built by the Habsburg dynasty, who ruled the Austro-Hungarian Empire for an astonishing 640 years, beginning with Rudolf I in 1273 and ending with Karl I in 1918. The walls stood until 1857, when Emperor Franz Josef finally decreed that they be demolished and replaced by the famous Ringstrasse ("Ring Street").

During medieval times the city's growth was relatively slow, and its heyday as a European capital did not begin until 1683, after a huge force of invading Turks laid siege to the city for two months and were finally routed by an army of Habsburg allies. Among the supplies left behind by the fleeing Turks were sacks filled with coffee beans. It was these beans, so the story goes, that gave a local entrepreneur the idea of opening the first public coffeehouse. Cafés remain a Viennese institution to this day.

The passing of the Turkish threat produced a Viennese building boom, and the Baroque style was the architectural order of the day. The style had originated in Italy around 1600, when a group of brilliantly inventive Italian architects began to embroider and transform the classical motifs that the High Renaissance had copied from ancient Rome. Architects in other countries throughout Europe followed suit, and during the 17th century England, France, and Austria all developed Baroque styles that were very much their own. Austrin Baroque possessed a special grace, described in detail in the walking tours to follow, and it is this grace that gives Vienna the distinctive architectural character that sets the city so memorably apart from its great rivals London, Paris, and Rome.

Essential Information

Important Addresses and Numbers

by George W. Hamilton

We show the Vienna telephone area code (0222) with all numbers; if you are calling within the city or to or from the airport, dial only the other numbers in the series.

Tourist Information
The main point for information is the **Vienna City Tourist Office** *(Fremdenverkehrsstelle der Stadt Wien)*, around the corner from the Hotel Sacher, at Kärntner Strasse 38 (tel. 0222/513–8892). From 9 to 7 daily, the extremely helpful and knowledgeable staff will assist you with everything from museum and transportation information to room reservations. The **Österreichisches Verkehrsbüro** (in Opernpassage, underground in front of the Opera, tel. 0222/586–2352) offers similar services and can provide theater tickets, Monday–Saturday 9–6, Sunday 9–2. Good, detailed city maps and public transport maps are available at all these offices (look for the *i* sign).

If you need a room, go to **Information-Zimmernachweis** in the Westbahnhof (tel. 0222/835185, open daily 6:15 AM–11 PM) and in the Südbahnhof (tel. 0222/505–3132, open daily 6:15 AM–10 PM). At the airport, the information and room-reservation office (tel. 0222/71110–2617) is open daily 9 AM to 10:30 PM. The information office at the DDSG dock on the Danube (tel. 0222/218–0114 or 218–1954) is open when ships are docking and embarking. But none of these offices can arrange room bookings by telephone.

If you're driving into Vienna, get information or book rooms at **Information-Zimmernachweis** at the end of the Westautobahn at Wientalstrasse/Auhof (tel. 0222/971271) or at the end of the Südautobahn at Triesterstrasse 149 (tel. 0222/674151 or 0222/677100).

Embassies The **U.S. embassy** is at Boltzmanngasse 16, tel. 0222/315511; the **consulate** is at Gartenbaupromenade, Parkring 12a, in the Marriott building, tel. 0222/51451. The **Canadian embassy** is at Dr. Karl Lueger–Ring 10, tel. 0222/533–3691. The **U.K. embassy and consulate** are at Jauresgasse 10; embassy tel. 0222/713–1575, consulate tel. 0222/713–6117.

Emergencies The emergency numbers are 133 for the **police,** 144 for an **ambulance,** 122 for the **fire department.** If you need a doctor and speak no German, try calling the **American Medical Society of Vienna** (Lazarettgasse 13, tel. 0222/424568).

English-language **Big Ben Bookstore** (Porzellangasse 24, tel. 0222/316412), **Brit-**
Bookstores **ish Bookstore** (Weihburggasse 8, tel. 0222/512–1945), **English Bookshop Heidrich** (Plankengasse 7, tel. 0222/512–3701), **Pickwick's** (Marc-Aurel-Str. 10–12, tel. 0222/630182), **Shakespeare & Co.** (Sterngasse 2, tel. 0222/535–5053).

English-language "Blue Danube Radio" on FM at 103.8 MHz carries news, music,
Radio and information in English (and some in French) from 7 AM to 1 PM and again from 6 to 8 PM.

Late-night In each area of the city one pharmacy stays open 24 hours; if a
Pharmacies pharmacy is closed, a sign on the door will tell you the address of the nearest one that is open. Call 0222/1550 for names and addresses (in German) of the 24-hour pharmacies open that night.

Lost and Found Check with the police at the **Fundamt** (Wasagasse 22, tel. 0222/313440). If your loss occurred on a train, check the *Bundesbahn Fundamt* (railway lost property office, Westbahnhof, tel. 0222/5650–2996).

Travel Agencies **American Express** (Kärntner Str. 21–23, tel. 0222/51540, and at Parkring 10, actually around the corner in Liebenberggasse, tel. 0222/515–1180), **Thomas Cook/Wagon-Lits** (Kärntner Ring 2, tel. 0222/50160), **Cosmos** (Kärntner Ring 15, tel. 0222/515330), **Ruefa Reisen** (Fleischmarkt 1, tel. 0222/53404), **Österreichisches Verkehrsbüro** (Friedrichstr. 7, opposite Sezession, tel. 0222/588000).

Arriving and Departing by Plane

Vienna's airport is at Schwechat, about 19 km (12 mi) southeast of the city. For flight information, call 0222/71110–2231. **American Airlines, Pan American, Air Canada, Singapore Airlines,** and **Tarom/Romanian Airlines** fly into Schwechat from North America.

Between the A bus leaves the airport every 20 minutes for the city air termi-
Airport and nal beside the Hilton Hotel. The trip takes about 25 minutes
City Center and costs AS50; you buy your ticket on the bus, so be sure to
By Bus have Austrian money handy. A bus also runs every half hour to the Westbahnhof (West rail station) via the Südbahnhof (South station); this bus might land you closer to your hotel, and taxis are available at the station.

By Taxi Taxis will take about 30 minutes to most downtown locations, longer when traffic is heavy (7–8:30 AM and 4:30–6:30 PM on weekdays). Taxis from Vienna are not allowed to pick up passengers at the airport unless they've been ordered; only those from Lower Austria (where the airport is located, beyond the city limits) can take passengers into town. This means that taxis travel one way empty, so the meter fare is doubled; you'll end up with a bill of about AS350. You can cut the charge in half by phoning one of the Vienna cab companies from the airport (tel. 0222/31300, 0222/60160, 0222/40100, or 0222/91011) and asking for a taxi to take you into town. They'll give you the last couple of digits of the taxi license, and you wait until it arrives. Be sure to arrange where the taxi will meet you. The same scheme applies when you leave: not all Vienna cabs have permits for airport service, so call in advance to get one that can take you out for about AS220–AS270.

By Limousine *Mazur* limos provide door-to-door transportation cheaper than a taxi. Look for the *Mazur* stand at the airport, or call 0222/604–9191 or 0222/604–2233.

By Train Fast trains run from the airport to the **Wien Mitte** station across the street from the Hilton Hotel and to the **Wien Nord** station, Praterstern, but the rail service is less frequent than the bus (about one train an hour), and both land you in virtually the same spot. Fare: AS30, or a Vienna streetcar ticket plus AS15. Both the frequency and the fare may increase by 1992.

Arriving and Departing by Car, Train, Boat, and Bus

By Car On the road from the airport and on highways from points south or west, *Zentrum* signs clearly mark the route to the center of Vienna. From there, however, finding your way to your hotel can be no mean trick, for traffic planners have installed a devious scheme prohibiting cars in the city core (the First District) and scooting them out again via a network of exasperating one-way streets. In the city itself a car is a burden, though very useful for trips outside town.

By Train Trains from Germany, Switzerland, and western Austria arrive at the **Westbahnhof** (West Station), on Europaplatz, where the Mariahilfer Strasse crosses the Gürtel. If you're coming from Italy or Hungary, you'll generally arrive at the **Südbahnhof** (South station, Wiedner Gürtel 1). The current stations for trains to and from Prague and Warsaw are **Wien Nord** (North Station, Praterstern) and **Franz-Josef Bahnhof** (Julius-Tandler-Platz). Central train information will have details (tel. 0222/1717 or tel. 0222/1552 for taped schedule information).

By Boat If you arrive in Vienna via the Danube, the DDSG ship will leave you at **Praterlände** near Mexikoplatz (Handelskai 265, tel. 0222/217100), although some downstream ships also make a stop at **Nussdorf** (Heiligenstädter Str. 180, tel. 0222/371257). The Praterlände stop is a short taxi ride from the Vorgartenstrasse subway station, or you can take a taxi directly into town.

By Bus There is virtually no long-distance bus service into Vienna, but the postal and railroad buses arrive at the **Wien Mitte** central bus station (Landstrasser Haupstr. 1b, tel. 0222/711070 or 0222/71101), across from the Hilton Hotel.

Getting Around

Vienna is divided into 23 numbered districts. Taxi drivers may need to know which district you seek, as well as the street address. The district number is coded into the postal code with the second and third digits; thus A–1010 (the "01") is the First District, A-1030 is the Third, A–1110 is the 11th, and so on. Some sources and some maps still give the district numbers, either in roman or arabic numerals, as Vienna X or Vienna 10.

Vienna is a city to tackle on foot. With the exception of the Schönbrunn and Belvedere palaces and the Prater amusement park, most sights are concentrated in the center, the First District (A–1010), much of which is a pedestrian zone anyway.

Get public-transport maps at a tourist office or at the transport-information offices (*Wiener Verkehrsbetriebe*), underground at Karlsplatz, Stephansplatz, and Praterstern. Vienna's public transportation system is fast, clean, safe, and easy to use. You can transfer on the same ticket between subway, streetcar, bus, and long stretches of the fast suburban railway, *Schnellbahn (S–Bahn)*. You can buy single tickets valid for the subway, streetcars, and buses for AS20 from dispensers on the streetcar or bus or at one of the subway stations. You'll need exact change. At *Tabak-Trafik* (cigarette shops/newsstands) or the underground *Wiener Verkehrsbetriebe* offices you can get a block of five tickets for AS75, each ticket good for one uninterrupted trip in more or less the same general direction with unlimited transfers. Or you can get a three-day ticket for AS115, good on all lines for 72 hours from the time you validate the ticket; there's also a 24-hour ticket for AS45. If you're staying longer, get an eight-day (AS235) ticket, which can be used on eight separate days or by any number of persons (up to eight) at any one time.

You validate any ticket by inserting it into the small blue canceling maching (*Entwerter*) found on all buses and streetcars and at the entrance to subway stations. The multiple-ride tickets have to be folded back so the indicated strip can be stamped.

By Rental Car Avis (at airport, tel. 0222/71110–2700), *Opernring 1, tel. 0222/587–6241.*
Budget (at airport, tel. 0222/71110–2711), *Hilton Hotel, Am Stadtpark, tel. 0222/756–565.*
Hertz (at airport, tel. 0222/71110–2661), *Kärntner Ring 17, tel. 0222/512–8677; international reservations, tel. 0222/713–1596.*
National (Europcar/interRent at airport, tel. 0222/71110–3316), *Denzel Autovermietung, Kärntner Ring 14, tel. 0222/505–4166.*

By Subway Five subway lines (*U-bahn*), whose stations are prominently marked with blue *U* signs, crisscross the city. Karlsplatz and Stephansplatz are the main transfer points between lines. The last subway (U4) runs at about 12:20 AM.

By Streetcar and Bus The first streetcars run about 5:15 AM, for those Viennese who start work at 8. From then on, service (barring gridlock on the streets) is regular and reliable, and most lines operate until about midnight. Where streetcars don't run, buses do; route maps and schedules are posted at each bus or subway stop.

Vienna Subways

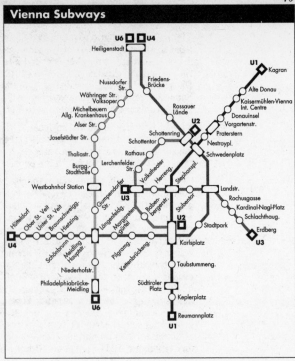

Should you miss the last streetcar or bus, special night buses with an *N* designation operate at half-hour intervals on weekends over several key routes; the starting (and transfer) point is Schwedenplatz. The night-owl buses take a special fare of AS25, tickets available on the bus; normal tickets are not valid.

Within the heart of the city, bus lines 1A, 2A and 3A are useful crosstown routes. These carry a reduced fare of AS7.50 per trip if you have bought the *Kurzstrecke* ticket (AS30), good for four trips or up to four people on one trip (with no transfer). The *Kurzstrecke* tickets are also valid for two stops on the subway or shorter distances on the streetcar lines.

By Taxi Taxis in Vienna are relatively inexpensive. The initial charge is AS22 for as many as four people. AS10 is added for each piece of luggage that must go into the trunk, and a charge is added for waiting beyond a reasonable limit. A night and weekend surcharge of AS10 is also added to the meter reading. It's customary to round up the fare to cover the tip. Taxis can be flagged on the street (when the roof light is on), taken from regular stands, or ordered by phone. To get a radio cab, call 0222/31300, 0222/40100, 0222/60160, or 0222/91011. Service is usually prompt, but at rush hour, when weather is bad, or if you need to keep to an exact schedule, call ahead and order a taxi for a specific time. If your destination is the airport, say so, and ask for a reduced-rate taxi.

By Limousine For a chauffeured limousine call **Avis-Adler** (tel. 0222/216–0990), **Göth** (tel. 0222/713–7196), **Mazur** (tel. 0222/604–2233),

Mietwagen Sidlo (tel. 0222/312514), or **Peter Urban** (tel. 0222/
713–5255 or 713–3781).

Guided Tours

Orientation When you're pressed for time, a good way to see the highlights
of Vienna is via a sightseeing-bus tour, which gives you a once-
over-lightly of the heart of the city and allows a closer look at
Schönbrunn and Belvedere palaces. **Vienna Sightseeing Tours**
(Stelzhammergasse 4/11, tel. 0222/712–4683; a booking office is
downstairs in the Opernpassage) runs a 1¼-hour "get acquainted" tour daily, leaving from in front of the Opera at 10:30
and 11:45 AM and 3 PM (Adults AS170, children AS60). You can
cover almost the same territory on your own by taking either
the No. 1 or No. 2 streetcar around the Ring, and then walking
through the heart of the city. Vienna Sightseeing and **City-
rama/Gray Line** (Börsegasse 1, tel. 0222/534–130) both have
tours of about three hours (Adults AS340, children AS120), including visits to Schönbrunn and Belvedere palaces (check to
be certain you will go *inside* both; some tours just drive past).
Both depart at 9:30 AM and 2:30 PM; Vienna Sightseeing also has
one at 10:30 AM. Both firms offer a number of other tours as well
(your hotel will have detailed programs), and both provide hotel pickup for most tours. For other than the "get acquainted"
tours, the Vienna Sightseeing buses leave the central loading
point in front of the Opera 10 minutes before scheduled tour departures to make the hotel pickups. Cityrama tours start from
Johannesgasse at the Stadtpark station on the U4 subway line,
across from the InterContinental hotel.

Streetcar Tours From early May through mid-October, a 1929 vintage streetcar
leaves each Saturday at 2:30 PM and Sundays and holidays at 10
AM from the Otto Wagner Pavilion at Karlsplatz for a guided tour.
For AS150 (children AS50), you'll go around the Ring, out past
the big Ferris wheel in the Prater and past Schönbrunn and Belvedere palaces in the course of the two-hour trip. Get tickets in
advance at the transport-information office underground at
Karlsplatz, weekdays 7–6, weekends and holidays 8:30–4 (tel.
0222/587–3186).

Boat Tours The **Donau-Dampfschiffahrts-Gesellschaft** (DDSG; tel. 0222/
217100) runs a three-hour boat tour up the Danube Canal and
down the Danube, from Schwedenbrücke, by Schwedenplatz,
May through September, daily at 1 and 4:30 PM. There are occasional moonlight cruises and weekly on-board evening
Heuriger (new wine) parties, "golden oldies" dancing cruises,
and Saturday night disco trips as well, with departures at 8:30
PM.

Personal Guides Guided tours (in English) on foot are a great way to see the city
highlights. Tour topics range from "Unknown Underground
Vienna" through "1,000 Years of Jewish Tradition" to "Vienna
Around Sigmund Freud." Tours take about 1½ hours, are held
in any weather provided at least three persons turn up, and cost
AS100 (ages 15–18, AS50; plus any entry fees. No reservations
are needed. Get a list of the guided-tour possibilities at the city
information office at Kärntner Strasse 38 (tel. 0222/513–8892),
or phone 0222/512–9735, 0222/468–5322, 0222/216–0466, 0222/
220–6620, 0222/365–7033, or 0222/513–1261 for details. You can
also arrange to have your own privately guided tour for AS900.

Self-guided   Get a copy of *Vienna: Downtown Walking Tours* by Henriette
Mandl (Ueberreuter, 1987), from any bookshop. The six tours
take you through the highlights of central Vienna with excellent commentary and some entertaining anecdotes, which most
of your Viennese acquaintances won't know. The booklet "Vienna from A to Z" (in English; available at bookshops) explains
the numbered plaques attached to all major buildings.

Horse Cab   A *Fiaker*, or horse cab, will trot you around to whatever destination you specify, but today this is an expensive way to have a
look at the city. A short basic tour (just under ½ hour) costs
AS400, and a longer one (about an hour) costs AS800, for the
whole Fiaker. The carriages accommodate four (five if someone
sits next to the coachman). Starting points are Heldenplatz in
front of the Hofburg, Stephansplatz beside the cathedral, and
across from the Albertina, all in the First District. For longer
trips, or any variation of the regular route, agree on the price
first.

Exploring Vienna

Orientation

*by George H.
Sullivan*

To the Viennese, the most prestigious address of Vienna's 23
Berzirke, or districts, is the First District (the inner city,
bounded by the Ringstrasse and the Danube Canal). The Second through the Ninth Districts surround the inner city (starting with the Second District across the Danube Canal and
running clockwise); the 10th through the 23rd Districts form a
second concentric ring of suburbs. The vast majority of sightseeing attractions are to be found in the First District. For
hard-core sightseers who wish to supplement the walking
tours that follow, the Tourist Office (*see* Important Addresses
and Numbers in Essential Information, above) has a booklet
"Vienna A to Z" (AS30) that gives short descriptions of some
250 sights around the city, all numbered and keyed to a fold-out
map at the back, as well as to wall plaques on the buildings
themselves. The more important churches possess coin-operated (AS10) tape machines that give an excellent commentary
in English on the history and architecture of the church.

The description of the city on the following pages is divided into
seven tours: six walks that explore the architectural riches of
central Vienna, and a seventh tour that describes Schönbrunn
Palace and its gardens. If you arrive in the city in the early afternoon and do not want to plunge into inner-city sightseeing, a
visit to Schönbrunn is highly recommended.

Before beginning the walking tours, a word about Viennese
palaces is perhaps in order. In most cases, the term "palace" is
a misnomer, for by English-language standards only the
Hofburg, Schönbrunn, and Belvedere palaces are large enough
to be described as palatial. The remainder of the Viennese palaces are in fact very large town houses that originally served as
the inner-city residences of the aristocracy. Many of them have
been restored in recent years, and the facades have been re-
painted in beautiful old pastel colors that somehow manage to
look refreshingly cool in summer and comfortably warm in
winter. Many more facades remain unpainted, however; try to
envision them as they were meant to be, dressed up in softly

contrasting colors like their more fortunate peers. It will be well worth the effort.

Highlights for First-time Visitors

St. Stephen's Cathedral (*see* Tour 1: The City's Ancient Core)

The Hofburg (*see* Tour 4: The Hofburg and the Ringstrasse)

Schönbrunn Palace (*see* Tour 7: Schönbrunn Palace)

Belvedere Palace (*see* Tour 6: South of the Ring to the Belvedere)

Museum of Art History (*see* Tour 4: The Hofburg and the Ringstrasse)

Museum of Viennese History (*see* Tour 6: South of the Ring to the Belvedere)

Tour 1: The City's Ancient Core

Numbers in the margin correspond with points of interest on the Vienna map.

The citizens of Vienna, it has often been said, waltz only from the waist down, whirling around the crowded dance floor while holding their upper bodies motionless and ramrod straight. The sight can be breathtaking in its sweep and splendor, and its elegant coupling of freewheeling exuberance and rigid formality—of license and constraint—is quintessentially Viennese.

Architecture is frozen music, said the German poet Goethe, and the closest that European architecture ever came to embodying the Viennese waltz, appropriately enough, is the Viennese town palace. Built mostly during the 18th century, these Baroque mansions can be found all over the inner city, and they present in stone and stucco the same artful synthesis of license and constraint as the dance that was so often performed inside them. They make Vienna a Baroque city that is, at its best, an architectural waltz.

The inner city is by no means exclusively Baroque, however. Occasional survivors from medieval times as well as many additions from the 19th and 20th centuries dot the cityscape, and sometimes they present startling alternatives to the city's prevailing architectural style. These anomalies are of inestimable value to the city, however, for they supply surprise, variety, and the spice of argument, keeping the urban architectural dialogue alive and vital. Without them Vienna would be a much duller place.

❶ Tour 1 begins with the most prominent of these anomalies: **St. Stephen's Cathedral**, at the heart of the inner city. Consecrated in 1147, St. Stephen's is the hub of the city's wheel; for more than eight centuries its enormous bulk has served as the nucleus around which the city has grown. The top of its tall south tower is the city's preeminent lookout point, offering fine views in all directions. Be warned, however, that the 345-step ascent is long and arduous; you may want to postpone it until the last day of your visit, when the city's landmarks will be familiar and the views will serve to fix them in your memory. *Admission: AS20. Tower ascent open daily 9–4:30; closed Jan. 8–31.*

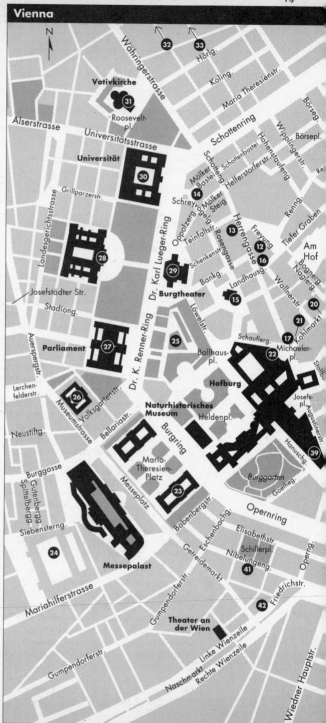

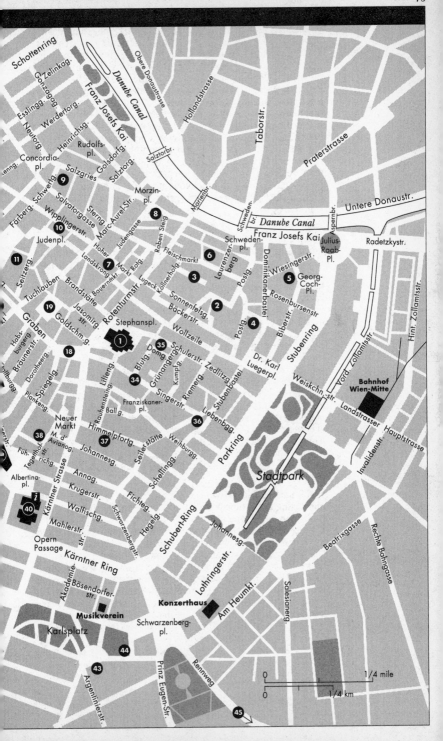

As architecture, St. Stephen's possesses a fierce presence that is blatantly un-Viennese. Hunkering down rather than soaring up, its hulking frame bristles with prickly Gothic outgrowths, and the overall effect is far from refined. This is an architecture of encrustation, of bits and pieces—towers and pinnacles and gables—added here and there over hundreds of years. The result is a stylistic jumble, ranging from 13th-century Romanesque (the primitive and sometimes ill-matched arrangement of windows and decoration on the front facade) to 15th-century Gothic (the sophisticated stone tracery of the gables along the base of the roof on the sides). Such a hodgepodge ought to be indigestible, but the cathedral's magnificent steeply pitched roof comes to the rescue; with its forceful zigzag tiles (the design derives from Oriental carpeting) it locks the bits and pieces together with tremendous authority and gives the main body of the church the power to stand up to the massive southside Gothic tower.

Like the exterior, St. Stephen's barnlike interior lacks the soaring unity of Europe's greatest Gothic cathedrals, with much of its decoration dating from the later Baroque era. The change in style from Gothic to Renaissance to Baroque is best illustrated at the southwest corner of the crossing (where the nave and transept meet). The small 15th-century choir gallery, with its fancifully carved balcony above and spindly columns below, is typically Gothic, but the 17th-century doorway immediately to the right is framed in an entirely different style. Classical elements (plain columns with Corinthian capitals supporting a triangular pediment) have taken over—a sure sign of the Renaissance, with its passionate rediscovery of the architecture of ancient Rome. Baroque architects, in their turn, continued to use this classical vocabulary, but they molded and twisted and broke the ancient motifs into forms that had never been seen before. The ornate altars that dot the nave and side aisles (at the bases of the freestanding piers and against the side-aisle walls) beautifully illustrate this later change in taste. The altars were added in the early 18th century, and although most of them still use plain columns to frame their altarpiece paintings, the pediments on top have erupted into full-blown Baroque.

The wealth of decorative sculpture in St. Stephen's can be demoralizing to the nonspecialist, so if you wish to explore the cathedral in detail, you may want to buy the admirably complete English-language description sold in the small room marked *Schriften und Opferkerzen* (Pamphlets and Votive Candles). One particularly masterly work, however, should be seen by everyone: the stone pulpit attached to the second freestanding pier on the left of the central nave, carved by Anton Pilgram around 1510. The spun-sugar delicacy of its decoration would in itself set the pulpit apart, but even more intriguing are its five sculpted figures. Carved around the outside of the pulpit proper are the four Latin Fathers of the Church (from left to right: Saint Augustine, Saint Gregory, Saint Jerome, and Saint Ambrose), and each is given an individual personality so sharply carved as to suggest satire, perhaps of living models. (The four figures may also have been meant to represent the Four Temperaments of ancient lore: melancholic, phlegmatic, choleric, and sanguine.) There is no satire suggested by the fifth figure, however; below the pulpit's stairs Pilgram sculpted a fine self-portrait, showing himself peering out a half-open window.

St. Stephen's was devastated by bombing during World War II, and the extent of the damage may be seen by leaving the cathedral through the south porch, where a set of prereconstruction photographs commemorates the disaster. Restoration was protracted and difficult, but today the cathedral once again dominates the center of the city. The final effect is of crude power rather than polished sophistication, but in a city that sometimes suffers from a surfeit of refined architectural manners, St. Stephen's serves as a bracing and enlivening centerpiece.

Works of art associated with the long history of the cathedral can be found in the **Dom und Diözesanmuseum** (the Cathedral and Diocese Museum), located in a passageway at the northeast corner of the cathedral square. Despite the wide range of styles represented (Gothic carving to Baroque printing) the collection is not overly large; its exclusively religious focus, however, does make it somewhat specialized in its appeal. *Stephansplatz 6, tel. 0222/51552-429. Admission: AS30. Open Tues.-Wed., Fri.-Sat. 10-4, Thurs. 10-6, Sun. 10-1.*

On the north side of Dr.-Ignaz-Seipel-Platz (named for the theology professor who was chancellor of Austria during the 1920s) is the **Jesuitenkirche**, built around 1630. Its flamboyant Baroque interior contains a fine trompe l'oeil ceiling fresco by that master of visual trickery, Andrea Pozzo, who was imported from Rome in 1702 for the job. Pozzo's painted dome is worth examining twice, first from the entrance end of the nave and then from the altar.

The exterior of the church provides an illuminating contrast to the **Academy of Science** on the west side of the square. While the church's facade exhibits a rudimentary classicism—the decorative pediments above the windows and the double-story pilasters are plain and rather awkwardly arranged—there is nothing awkward about the Academy of Science, built more than a century later, in 1753. Here the Baroque style is in full flower. The classical elements no longer look pasted on; instead, the columns and pediments act both to frame the building's windows and to organize the facade into a carefully balanced composition of considerable complexity.

The architect, J. N. Jadot de Ville-Issey, was French, and the influence of French architecture is strong; indeed, the plain ground floor, the recessed windows separated by paired columns on the floor above, and the pilastered end pavilions are all facade features of that most famous of French buildings, the Louvre. Here, however, Jadot de Ville-Issey added extra touches, which, though far from lavish—mostly limited to decorative carving above the windows—nevertheless transform the facade, adding insouciant grace notes to what might otherwise be sober plainsong. The result is impeccably elegant: a proud classical facade decked out in high-style special-occasion Baroque finery. Like so many of Vienna's great Baroque buildings, the Academy of Science looks as if it is about to set out for the Opera Ball.

In contrast to the academy, more modest buildings of the period tended to be less concerned with classical dignity. The house at No. 3 Sonnenfelsgasse (the street on the north side of the academy) is a case in point. Known as **Hildebrandthaus** (it was designed in 1721 by an unknown follower of the architect Johann Lukas von Hildebrandt), the facade is a purist's nightmare. Not only are the pilasters between the lower windows elaborately carved, they are then merged with (and visually made to support) far weightier uncarved pilasters above, thus breaking one of the cardinal rules of traditional classical facade design: weightier elements on the bottom, lighter elements on top. Renaissance propriety has here given way to Baroque license, and anything goes. But with carving like this, who could complain? The Academy of Science may present a more balanced architectural meal, but this is pure Viennese pastry.

In their own small way, the Academy of Science and Hildebrandthaus mark the extremes of Viennese Baroque architecture—the one urbane and patrician, the other frivolous and frothy. Most of the famous Viennese Baroque facades fall somewhere in between these extremes, but the fundamental architectural dialogue—the interplay between classical dignity and decorative vivacity—remains a constant, and it can be found all over the inner city.

Turn north from Sonnenfelsgasse on Köllnerhofgasse, then immediately right onto the short Grashofgasse. The door at the far end leads into **Heiligenkreuzerhof** (Holy Cross Court), one of the city's most peaceful backwaters. This complex of buildings, owned by the Holy Cross Abbey, 32 km (20 mi) south of the city, dates from the 17th century (but with an 18th century face-lift). Appropriately, the restraint of the architecture—with only here and there a small outburst of Baroque spirit—gives the courtyard a distinct feeling of retreat. The reigning tranquillity is a welcome respite from the bustle of the narrow streets outside.

Through the far gate of Heiligenkreuzerhof is Schönlaterngasse (Beautiful Lantern Street), named for the wall lantern at No. 6. No. 7, the house known as the **Basiliskenhaus,** was according to legend first built for a baker; on June 26, 1212, a foul-smelling basilisk (half rooster, half toad, with a glance that could kill) took up residence in the courtyard well, poisoning the water. An enterprising apprentice dealt with the problem by climbing down the well armed with a mirror; when the basilisk saw its own reflection it turned to stone. The petrified creature can still be seen in a niche on the building's facade. Today, modern science accounts for the contamination with a more prosaic explanation: natural-gas seepage.

To the east of Schönlaterngasse, on Postgasse, is an unexpected visitor from Rome: the **Dominikanerkirche.** Built in the 1630s, some 50 years before the Viennese Baroque building boom, its facade is modeled after any number of Roman churches of the 16th century. The interior, too, is Italian in design and detail; only the extensive use of plain white paint fails to suggest Rome (the Italians would have gilded the carved stucco and painted any flat surfaces to look like colored marble). The interior illustrates why the Baroque style came to be considered the height of bad taste during the 19th century and still has many detractors today. "Sculpt 'til you drop" seems to have been the motto here, and the viewer's eye is given no respite. Happily, this sort of Roman architectural orgy never really gained a foothold in Vienna, and when the great Viennese architects did pull out all the decorative stops—Hildebrandt's interior at the Belvedere Palace, for instance (*see* Tour 6, be-

low)—they did it in a very different style and with far greater
success.

Two blocks northeast of the Dominikanerkirche is the **Georg-
Coch-Platz,** a small square bounded on the east by the **former
⑤ War Ministry** and on the west by the **Post Office Savings Bank.**
The War Ministry was constructed in 1909 at the tail end of the
19th-century Viennese building boom. Its Baroque Revival facade derives from the Academy of Science, but here the small
scale of the academy is blown up to ponderous proportions, and
the earlier building's delicate decoration has been transformed
into bellicose piles of carved weaponry meant to symbolize Imperial might.

The Post Office Savings Bank is one of Modern architecture's
greatest curiosities. It was designed in 1904 by Otto Wagner,
whom many consider the father of 20th-century architecture.
In his famous manifesto, *Modern Architecture,* Wagner con-
demned 19th-century revivalist architecture and pleaded for a
modern style that honestly expressed modern building methods. Accordingly, the exterior walls of the Post Office Savings
Bank are mostly flat and undecorated; visual interest is supplied merely by varying the pattern of the bolts that were used
to hold the marble slabs in place on the wall surface during construction. Later architects were to embrace Wagner's beliefs
wholeheartedly, although they used different, truly modern
building materials: glass and concrete rather than marble. As a
result the oddly metallic look Wagner created here has today
the air of a failed futuristic fantasy, akin to the clunky space-
ships in an old Buck Rogers movie serial. The Post Office Savings Bank was indeed a bold leap into the future, but
unfortunately the future took a different path.

Next go to Fleischmarkt, where between Nos. 9 and 11 the picturesque Griechengasse forks off to the right, just beyond the
glittering 19th-century Greek Orthodox church. This corner of
the inner city has a medieval feel that is quite genuine; there
⑥ has been a tavern at **No. 11 Fleischmarkt** for some 500 years.
The wooden carving on the facade of the current Griechenbeisl
restaurant commemorates Max Augustin—known best today
from the song "Ach du lieber Augustin"—an itinerant musician
who sang here during the plague of 1679. Augustin survived
being thrown alive into a pit filled with dead plague victims; he
had been thought dead by the body collectors, when in fact he
had only been dead drunk.

Time Out Take a break for coffee at the corner of Fleischmarkt and
Wolfengasse, at the **Café Vienne,** famous for baking the biggest
cakes in the city. Or for a snack on the run, pick out one of the
mouth-watering pastries at **Elias Bäckerei,** a few doors along
Fleischmarkt (opposite No. 9).

No. 14 Fleischmarkt is an oddity for Vienna but an instructive
one: a bad example of Jugendstil, the crisper, more geometric,
Austrian version of French Art Nouveau that enjoyed its heyday around the turn of the century. Jugendstil motifs, when
successfully applied to building facades, sometimes look
poured, sometimes look hung, and sometimes look draped; they
sometimes look as if they are climbing up the wall, and sometimes look as if they're creeping down. But they never, as here,

look merely stuck on; they are never mere space fillers; and they are never randomly and aimlessly gilded.

From Fleischmarkt, a turn south onto Rotenturmstrasse and a right turn onto Lichtensteg leads into **Hoher Markt.** The square was badly damaged during World War II, but the famous Anker Clock at the east end survived the bombing. The huge mechanical timepiece took six years to build (1911–17) and still attracts crowds at noon when the full panoply of mechanical figures representing Austrian historical personages parades by. The graceless buildings erected around the square since 1945 are not aging well and do little to show off the square's lovely Baroque centerpiece, the St. Joseph Fountain, designed in 1729 by Joseph Emanuel Fischer von Erlach, son of the great Johann Bernhard Fischer von Erlach. The Hoher Markt does harbor one wholly unexpected attraction, however: ❼ **underground Roman ruins.** This is what was once the main east–west axis of the Roman encampment of Vindobona, and the foundations of several officers' houses built in the 2nd century have been uncovered. The excavations are entered through the snack bar in the passageway at No. 3; a short descriptive pamphlet in English is available at the ticket-table. *Hoher Markt 3, tel. 0222/535–5606. Admission: AS 15. Open Tues.–Sun. 9–12:15 and 1–4:30.*

Beginning beneath the Anker Clock, follow Bauernmarkt back to Fleischmarkt. To the left, next to the steps leading up to Ruprechtsplatz, is one of the city's most eccentric buildings: the **Kornhäusel Tower,** built around 1825. Joseph Kornhäusel was the most puritanical of Vienna's great architects; his restrained classicism rejected all but the plainest decoration and ran distinctly counter to the Viennese love of architectural finery. Apparently he had a misanthropic personality to match, for the starkly unornamented tower here, which was attached to his home, was reportedly built so he could get away from his wife (the studio at the top could be reached only by climbing up a ladder and through a trap door). Whatever the truth may be, the Kornhäusel Tower remains a profoundly antisocial building.

Several of Kornhäusel's more conventional buildings can be seen up the steps and around the corner to the right, at Seitenstettengasse at **Nos. 2–4** and at **No. 5.** The building at Nos. 2-4 houses the only synagogue in Vienna to survive the Nazi holocaust; its lack of an appropriate facade results from the 19th-century Viennese law that required all synagogues to be hidden from street view.

To the north of the Kornhäusel Tower lies Ruprechtsplatz, another of Vienna's time-warp backwaters. The church in the ❽ middle, **Ruprechtskirche** (St. Rupert's), is the city's oldest. According to legend it was founded in 740; the oldest part of the present structure (the lower half of the tower) dates from the 11th century. Set on the ancient ramparts overlooking the Danube Canal, it is serene and unpretentious, and its modest church-on-the-village-green feel lends to the tiny square a welcome breath of rural fresh air.

To the west of the Ruprechtsplatz entrance, steps on Sterngasse lead down to Marc-Aurel-Strasse. The lump of stone set into a wall niche at Sterngasse 3, at the top of the stairs, is a cannonball fired into the city during the unsuccessful Turkish siege of 1683; the larger lump of stone near the bottom of the stairs is a section of wall from the ancient Roman baths.

Continue west; at the end of Sterngasse a left turn and a short flight of steps lead to Salvatorgasse, with a timeworn Renaissance doorway at No. 5 (circa 1525). As you walk west, Salvatorgasse curves slightly, skirting the edge of the Gothic church of **Maria am Gestade** (St. Mary on the Banks). Built around 1400 (but much restored in the 17th and 19th centuries), the church incorporated part of the Roman city walls into its foundation; the north wall, as a result, takes a slight but noticeable dogleg to the right halfway down the nave. Like St. Stephen's, Maria am Gestade is rough-hewn Gothic, with a simple but forceful facade. The church is especially beloved, however, because of its unusual details—the pinnacled and saint-bedecked gable that tops the front facade, the stone canopy that hovers protectively over the front door, and (most appealing of all) the intricate openwork lantern atop the south-side bell tower. Appropriately enough in a city famous for its pastry, the lantern lends to its tower an engaging suggestion of sugar caster.

The small square in front of Maria am Gestade overlooks Tiefer Graben, which until the 15th century was a tributary of the Danube that served as a moat just outside the city walls. The view is worth noting, for on clear days the famed Vienna Woods can be seen to the west, down the line of Börsegasse.

Tour 2: Baroque Gems

From Maria am Gestade, walk south on Schwertgasse and turn left onto Wipplingerstrasse. At No. 7 is the former **Bohemian Court Chancery**, built between 1708 and 1714 by Johann Bernhard Fischer von Erlach. Fischer von Erlach and his contemporary Johann Lukas von Hildebrandt were the reigning architectural geniuses of Baroque Vienna; they designed their churches and palaces during the building boom that followed the defeat of the Turks in 1683. Both had studied architecture in Rome, and both were deeply impressed by the work of the great Italian architect Francesco Borromini, who had brought to his designs a wealth and freedom of invention that was looked upon with horror by most contemporary Romans. But for Fischer von Erlach and Hildebrandt, Borromini's ideas were a source of triumphant architectural inspiration, and when they returned to Vienna they between them produced many of the city's most beautiful buildings.

Like Jadot de Ville-Issey's Academy of Science (*see* Tour 1), the Chancery facade displays a beautifully calculated balance between plain and fancy. The central and end sections of the building are quite staid, but their simplicity serves an obvious purpose: It frames and contrasts with the entryway portals, where Fischer von Erlach gives his Baroque ingenuity free reign. The use of atalantes—muscular figures growing out of the tapered pilasters on the ground floor—is typically Baroque in its denial of the earlier Renaissance convention by which facade compositions were supposed to be carefully graduated, from heavier bottoms to lighter tops. Fischer von Erlach flouts this dogma with breathtaking assurance: His pilasters taper away to nothing at the bottom and grow heavier as they move upward, leaving the atalantes to struggle mightily with the weight of the massive protruding cornice. Likewise, the ornate window treatments on the upper floor would have shocked the Renaissance—such swoops and swirls and sinuous curves would have been viewed as an insult to the dignity and straight-forward nobility of ancient Greek and Roman architecture. But like all the great Baroque architects, Fischer von Erlach wanted to eat his cake and have it, too: He wanted dignity *and* panache, nobility *and* grace. And so he softened and melted and molded the plain geometric window pediments of old, and he embellished them with sumptuous carved decoration. The facade that resulted is Baroque Vienna at its best.

Across the street from the Bohemian Chancery is the **Altes Rathaus** (Old City Hall), dating from the 14th century but sporting 18th-century Baroque motifs on its facade. The interior passageways and courtyards, which are open during the day, house a Gothic chapel (open at odd hours), a much-loved Baroque wall fountain (Georg Raphael Donner's **Andromeda Fountain** of 1741), and display cases exhibiting maps and photos illustrating the city's history.

From Wipplingerstrasse, follow the short Fütterergasse south to **Judenplatz,** from the 13th century onward the center of Vienna's ghetto. An old carved plaque at No. 2 recounts the events of 1421, when more than 200 Jews—the plaque calls them "Hebrew dogs"—were burned alive and the rest of the Jewish community was banished en masse to Hungary. Today the square's centerpiece is a statue of the 18th-century Jewish playwright Gotthold Ephraim Lessing, erected after World War II; disconcertingly, the statue suggests the work of the American artist R. Crumb, famous during the 1960s for his underground comics.

Kurrentgasse leads south from the square's east end; the beautifully restored 18th-century houses on its east side make this one of the most unpretentiously appealing streets in the city. And at the far end of the street is one of Vienna's most unpretentiously appealing museums: the **Uhrenmuseum,** or Clock Museum (entrance around the corner to the right on the Schulhof side of the building). The museum's three floors display a splendid array of clocks and watches—more than 3,000 timepieces—dating from the 15th century to the present. *Schulhof 2, tel. 0222/533–2265. Admission: AS 30. Open Tues.–Sun. 9–4:30.*

Time Out A number of restaurants in the Kurrentgasse area serve good traditional Viennese food at moderate prices, among them **Ofenloch** (Kurrentgasse 8), **Gösser Bierklinik** (Sterndlgasse 4), and **Stadtbeisl** (Naglergasse 21). All three will supply English menus on request.

From the Clock Museum, Schulhof leads into Am Hof, one of the city's oldest squares. In the Middle Ages, the ruling Babenberg family built their castle on the site of No. 2; hence the name of the square, which means simply "at court." The Baroque **Column of Our Lady** in the center dates from 1667; the **Civic Armory** at the northwest corner has been used as a fire station since 1685 (the high-spirited facade, with its Habsburg eagle, dates from 1731) and today houses the headquarters of Vienna's fire department.

⓫ The **Kirche Am Hof,** on the east side of the square, can lay fair claim to being the least successful piece of important architecture in the city. The flaccid, sprawling Baroque facade (1662) is thoroughly mediocre; there is no special Viennese grace here, only a hapless overall plastering-on of conventional Baroque motifs. Inside, though the ceiling remains Gothic, the rest is later decoration at war with itself. The nave piers have been given clumsy classical capitals, the side chapels are entered through fussy Baroque triumphal arches, and the choir carries a heavy mock-Roman coffered ceiling that is visually (and insufficiently) supported by spindly, hideously painted pilasters. Only the tall altars on either side of the choir entrance manage to muster up a bit of real Baroque conviction, but the surrounding muddle destroys their impact almost completely.

Bognergasse leaves the square to the right of the church. At No. 9 is the **Engel Pharmacy,** with a Jugendstil mosaic depicting winged women collecting the elixir of life in outstretched chalices. At the turn of the century the inner city was dotted with storefronts decorated in a similar manner; today this is the sole survivor.

From Bognergasse, the tiny Irisgasse—only a few yards long—leads to Naglergasse, another of Vienna's beautifully restored Baroque streets. The curve at the street's west end is due to the much earlier curve of the Roman city wall, which turned north here to run along Tiefer Graben to the Danube.

Naglergasse leads, at its curved end, into Heidenschuss, which in turn leads down a slight incline to Freyung, meaning "freeing." The square was so named because for many centuries the monks at the adjacent Schottenkirche (Scottish Church, though in fact the original monks were probably Irish) possessed the privilege of offering sanctuary. In the center of the square stands the allegorical **Austria Fountain** (1845), notable because its Bavarian designer, one Ludwig Schwanthaler, had the statues cast in Munich and then supposedly filled them with cigars to be smuggled into Vienna for black-market sale.

12 At Freyung 2 stands the recently restored **Palais Ferstel,** which is not a palace at all but a commercial shop-and-office complex designed in 1856 and named for its architect, Heinrich Ferstel. The facade is Italianate in style, harking back, in its 19th-century way, to the Florentine palazzi of the early Renaissance. The interior is unashamedly eclectic: vaguely Romanesque in feel and Gothic in decoration, with here and there a bit of Renaissance or Baroque sculpted detail thrown in for good measure. Such eclecticism is sometimes dismissed as mindlessly derivative, but here the architectural details (recently restored) are so respectfully and inventively combined that the interior becomes a pleasure to explore. Pastiche the building may be, but it is pastiche brought alive by a manifestly genuine love of architectural history.

Returning to Freyung, proceed to its west end, dominated by the hulking and haphazardly decorated Schottenkirche. The square's best-known palace, one of the most sophisticated pieces of Baroque architecture in the city, is across the street at **13** No. 4: the **Kinsky Palace,** built between 1713 and 1716 by Hildebrandt. As at Fischer von Erlach's Bohemian Chancery, the facade is a happy marriage of plain and fancy: The two pairs of outer double-story pilasters are left undecorated, while the four central pilasters are fancifully carved; the middle row of windows is given simple window-surrounds, while the upper row is decorated in full-blown Baroque style (these are the beloved Viennese "eyebrows" that are a recurring motif all over the city). The entire composition thus becomes an essay in carefully controlled vertical and horizontal contrasts, with the contrasts arranged so that the simple and the complex are inextricably interlocked.

Compared to the Kinsky Palace, the buildings on either side fall distinctly short: The 16th-century facade on the left looks like a plain-jane wallflower, while the 19th-century facade on the right looks like an overdressed fussbudget. The Kinsky Palace's only real competition comes a few yards farther on: the Greek temple facade of **Schottenhof,** attached at right angles to the church. Designed by Joseph Kornhäusel in a very different style from his antisocial tower seen earlier, the Schottenhof facade typifies the change that came over Viennese architecture during the Biedermeier Era (1815–48). The Viennese, according to the traditional view, were at the time so relieved to be rid of the upheavals of the Napoleonic Wars that they accepted without protest the iron-handed repression of Prince Metternich, chancellor of Austria, and retreated into a cozy and complacent domesticity. The era's passion for conventional rectitude was later satirized in a famous series of poems, published in 1855–57 and ostensibly written by Gottfried Biedermeier, an upright (but fictitious) German schoolteacher whose name soon became synonymous with mindless bourgeois respectability.

During the Biedermeier Era restraint also ruled in architecture, with Baroque license rejected in favor of a new and historically "correct" style that was far more controlled and reserved. Kornhäusel led the way in Vienna; his Schottenhof facade is all sober organization and frank repetition. But in its marriage of strong and delicate forces it still pulls off the great Viennese-waltz trick of successfully merging seemingly antithetical characteristics.

Follow Teinfaltstrasse (just opposite the Schottenkirche facade) one block west to Schreyvogelgasse on the right. The doorway at No. 8 (up the incline) was made famous in 1949 by the film *The Third Man;* it was here that Orson Welles, as the malevolently knowing Harry Lime, stood hiding in the dark, only to have his smiling face illuminated by a sudden light from the upper-story windows of the house across the alley.

⑭ Around the corner at No. 8 Mölker Bastei is the **Pasqualatihaus,** where Beethoven lived while he was composing his only opera, *Fidelio,* as well as his Seventh Symphony and Fourth Piano Concerto. Today his apartment houses a small commemorative museum. *Tel. 0222/637-0665. Admission: AS15. Open Tues.–Sun. 9–12:15 and 1–4:30.*

⑮ Four blocks south of Schreyvogelgasse is the Minoritenplatz, named after its centerpiece, the **Minoritenkirche** (Church of the Minorite Order), a Gothic stump of a church built mostly in the 14th century. The front is brutally ugly, but the back is a wonderful (if predominantly 19th-century) surprise. The interior contains the city's most imposing piece of kitsch: a large mosaic reproduction of Leonardo da Vinci's *Last Supper,* commissioned by Napoleon in 1806 and later purchased by the Emperor Franz I.

From the east end of Minoritenplatz, follow Landhausgasse one block east to Herrengasse. Across the street to the left is the entrance to the **Café Central,** part of the Ferstel Palace complex and one of Vienna's most famous cafés, recently restored. No matter how crowded the café may become, you can linger as long as you like over a single cup of coffee and a newspaper from the huge international selection the café keeps on hand.

In its prime (before World War I), the Café Central was home to some of the most famous literary figures of the day—home in the literal as well as the figurative sense. In those days, housing was one of the city's most intractable problems. The large apartment houses that had gone up to accommodate the surge in Vienna's population were often (despite their imposing facades) no better than tenements, and overcrowding was so extreme that many apartment dwellers sublet space by the square foot—just enough room for a spare bed. As a result, many of Vienna's artists and writers spent as little time as possible in their "homes" and instead ensconced themselves at a favorite café, where they ate, socialized, worked, and even received mail. The denizens of the Central favored political argument; indeed, their heated and sometimes violent discussions became so well known that in October 1917, when Austria's foreign secretary was informed of the outbreak of the Russian Revolution, he dismissed the report with a facetious reference to a well-known local Marxist, the chess-loving (and presumably harmless) "Herr Bronstein from the Café Central." The remark was to become famous all over Austria, for Herr Bronstein had disappeared and was about to resurface in Russia bearing a new name: Leon Trotsky.

Herrengasse is lined with Baroque town houses and is also home to the inner city's first "skyscraper," on the corner of Herrengasse and Fahnengasse. This 20th-century addition to the cityscape (called *Hochhaus,* or high house) is much decried by the Viennese, although it will seem innocuous enough to visitors from New York or London. At No. 13 is the Palace of the Lower Austrian Diet, more familiarly known as the **Landhaus.** In front of this building on March 13, 1848, Imperial troops fired into a crowd of demonstrators, killing four men and one woman and signaling the beginning of the abortive Revolution of 1848.

Tour 3: From Michaelerplatz to the Graben

At the south end of Herrengasse, in **Michaelerplatz,** one of Vienna's most evocative squares, the feel of the medieval city remains very strong; the buildings seem to crowd in toward the center of the small plaza as if the city were bursting at its seams, desperate to break out of its protective walls. The buildings around the perimeter present a synopsis of the city's entire architectural history: medieval church spire, Renaissance church facade, Baroque palace facade, 19th-century apartment house, and 20th-century bank (originally a clothing store). In the center, recent excavations have turned up extensive traces of the old Roman city and relics of the 18th and 19th centuries. **Michaelerkirche** (the Church of St. Michael's), with its unpretentious spire, dates from the 13th and 14th centuries, although the ground-floor entrance porch and upper-story decoration were not added until several hundred years later. The result is awkward, to say the least.

The curved, domed **entrance to the Imperial Palace** (part of the Hofburg, which we'll explore at length in Tour 4) is far from awkward, but unfortunately it is also far from inspired. It was designed by Joseph Emanuel Fischer von Erlach in the first half of the 18th century, although the design was not executed until the 1890s, and then in a somewhat modified form. It is a competent, conventional, French-influenced work that possesses very little decorative exuberance and therefore ends up looking more Parisian than Viennese.

The **Palais Herberstein,** across Herrengasse, echoes some of the motifs of the palace entrance, but it is not afraid of showing off. It was built in 1903, and its recognizably Viennese decoration is typical of the neo-Baroque style of the day. Eight years later Adolf Loos, one of the founding fathers of 20th-century Modern architecture, built the **Looshaus** next door, facing the palace entrance. It was anything but typical—it was more like an architectural declaration of war. After two hundred years of Baroque and neo-Baroque exuberance, the first generation of 20th-century architects had had enough. Loos led the revolt against architectural tradition; *Ornament and Crime* was the title of his famous manifesto in which he inveighed against the conventional architectural wisdom of the 19th century—against the style of the Palais Herberstein—and denounced Vienna's decorative vivacity. Instead, he advocated buildings that were plain, honest, and functional. When he built the Looshaus for Goldman and Salatsch (men's clothiers) in 1911 the city was scandalized. "The house without eyebrows," hooted his critics. Archduke Franz Ferdinand, heir to the throne, was so offended that he vowed never again to use the Michaelerplatz entrance to the Imperial Palace. Everyone in the city took sides, and the debate over the merits of Modern architecture began. Nowadays the Looshaus has lost its power to shock, and the facade seems quite innocuous. The recently restored interior, however, remains a breathtaking suprise. Loos's plain surfaces allow his carefully selected materials, particularly the richly grained wood he so loved, to shine with a luster that positively dazzles. This is plainness, to be sure, but it is a plainness that is downright voluptuous. Here, for once, less really *is* more.

The passageway just to the right of St. Michael's, with its large 15th-century relief depicting Christ on the Mount of Olives, leads into the Stallburggasse, named after the Imperial Stables on the right. The area is dotted with antiques stores, attracted by the presence of the **Dorotheum,** the famous Viennese auction house that began as a state-controlled pawnshop in 1707 (known as "Aunt Dorothy" to its patrons). Merchandise coming up for auction is on display at Dorotheergasse 11, at the far end of Stallburggasse to the left.

At No. 6 Dorotheergasse, hidden behind an unprepossessing doorway, the **Café Hawelka** is one of the few famous inner-city cafés that has survived without major restoration. The Hawelka's air of romantic shabbiness—the product of Viennese *fortwursteln,* or "muddling through"—is especially evocative; long may it muddle along, exactly as it is.

The Dorotheergasse leads out into the Graben, a pedestrian mall lined with luxury shops and open-air cafés. Turn right into Stock-im-Eisenplatz, where opposite the southwest corner of St. Stephen's, set into the corner of the building on the west side of Kärntner Strasse, is one of the city's most revered relics: the **Stock-im-Eisen,** or iron tree stump. Chronicles first mention the Stock-im-Eisen in 1533, but it is probably far older, and for hundreds of years any apprentice metalsmith who came to Vienna to learn his trade hammered a nail into the tree trunk for good luck. During World War II, when there was talk of moving the relic to a museum in Munich, it mysteriously disappeared; it reappeared, perfectly preserved, after the threat of removal had passed.

Across the street from Stock-im-Eisen is Vienna's newest and (for the moment, at least) most controversial piece of architecture: **Neues Haas Haus.** It was designed by Hans Hollein, Austria's best-known living architect; *The Architectural Review* described it as "a collagist collision of heavy concrete and masonry with suave metal and glass cladding." Detractors consider its aggressively contemporary style out of place opposite St. Stephen's, while advocates consider the contrast enlivening; whatever the verdict, it should be noted that the banal postwar building it replaced was no great loss.

The **Graben,** leading west from Stock-im-Eisenplatz, is a street whose unusual width gives it the presence and weight of a city square. Its shape is due to the Romans, who dug the city's southwestern moat here, adjacent to the original city walls. The Graben's centerpiece is the **Pestsäule,** or Plague Column, erected by Emperor Leopold I between 1687 and 1693, in thanks to God for delivering the city from a particularly virulent plague. The style (High Baroque) is immediately clear from the frenzied feel of the piece, but the subject matter (the Trinity supported by an angel-covered cloud) may not be so apparent. Still, the monument proved extremely popular, and imitations of it can be found all over Austria.

The real glory of the Graben, however, is not the Plague Column but the architecture that surrounds it, creating the city's finest ensemble of buildings. Most of the buildings date from the late 19th century, but a few of them are earlier or later, and the contrast is illuminating.

The oldest building is **No. 11,** near the square's southeast corner. It was probably designed around 1720 by the great Johann Lukas von Hildebrandt, architect of the Kinsky Palace (*see* Tour 2) and the Belvedere Palace (*see* Tour 6); the top story is a later addition. This was a modest building, and Hildebrandt's facade is quite simple. But his love of decoration still comes through above the windows, where the traditional classical pediments, usually plain triangles, are reshaped and embroidered to become the famous Viennese "eyebrows" (in this case, raised eyebrows).

By the first half of the 19th century a reaction against Baroque decoration had set in, as can be seen at **No. 21,** at the northwest corner. Designed by Alois Pichl in 1835, the building's middle-story window pediments are impeccably traditional, and in its sober organization Pichl's facade clearly shows the influence of the leading architect of the day, Joseph Kornhäusel. Still, the overall effect is surprisingly fragile. Viennese exuberance has (for the moment) been banished, but Viennese delicacy remains.

There is nothing delicate about the **Graben-Hof,** built in 1873 (Nos. 14–15, on the south side). The overall organization of the facade is similar to the Academy of Science (*see* Tour 1), but the general effect is quite different, for the classical elements are used to give the building a weighty and imposing presence—to make it stand proud. The result here is more than a little ponderous, and if Otto Wagner, the building's codesigner, had continued to build in this style, he would today be as forgotten as his collaborator, Otto Thienemann. But Wagner was an experimenter, and he later came to reject the classical vocabulary entirely, as can be seen in his 1895 design at **No. 10** (southeast corner), which employs an entirely new free-form style of decoration. The building was structurally unconventional as well, using iron and glass in new ways on the ground floor and roof. Wagner was to continue his experiments (*see* the Post Office Savings Bank, Tour 1) to become a pioneer of 20th-century architecture.

Wagner's influence can be seen clearly at **No. 16,** one of the Graben's youngest buildings (1911). Again, iron and glass are used in a novel way at the top and bottom. But a special feel to the decoration, and a suggestion of sleekness to the building's curved corner, proclaims the arrival of Jugendstil, the Austrian version of Art Nouveau (and a forerunner of Art Deco). The upper-story stucco-work motifs in particular stand out; hanging from the corner windows like jewelry, they give the facade an air of glamour that, in its day, must have seemed as modern as the automobile and the flapper.

⑲ Just north of the Graben is Petersplatz, site of **Peterskirche** (St. Peter's Church), constructed between 1702 and 1708 by Hildebrandt, using an earlier plan by the Italian Gabriele Montani. The facade possesses angled towers, graceful towertops (said to have been inspired by the tents of the Turks during the siege of 1683), and an unusually fine entrance porch. All this is dignified enough, but somehow the overall effect is perversely (if appealingly) humorous. This is a building with a serious weight problem. It looks as if it's trying to waddle its way into the Graben but has been eating too much strudel and has gotten too fat to squeeze through. Inside the church, the Baroque decoration is elaborate, with some fine touches (particularly the glass-crowned galleries high on the walls to either side of the altar), but the lack of light and years of accumulated dirt create a prevailing gloom, and the much praised ceiling frescoes by J. M. Rottmayr are impossible to make out.

Proceed west on Milchgasse and turn left onto Tuchlauben. The lusciously painted building at **No. 5** was constructed in 1984, but it retains the 1719 facade of its predecessor; it wears its miscellany of Baroque window pediments like so many party hats, classical dignity be damned.

⑳ Tuchlauben leads back to the west end of the Graben and then continues on as **Kohlmarkt.** None of the buildings here are remarkable, although they do include an entertainingly ironic odd-couple pairing: **No. 11** (early 18th century) and **No. 9** (early 20th century). The mixture of architectural styles is similar to the Graben, but the general feel is low-key, as if the street were consciously deferring to its splendid view stopper, the dome over the Michaelerplatz entrance to the Imperial Palace (*see* Tour 4). Still, Kohlmarkt lingers in the memory when flashier streets have faded. In its conjunction with imperial pomp, it is self-assured without being self-conscious—exactly the right approach.

Time Out **Demel's** (Kohlmarkt 14), Vienna's best-known (and priciest)
㉑ pastry shop, offers a dizzying selection, and if you possess a sweet tooth, a visit will be worth every penny of the extra cost. Chocolate lovers will want to participate in the famous Viennese Sachertorte debate by sampling Demel's version and then comparing it with its rival at the Hotel Sacher (*see* Tour 5).

Tour 4: The Hofburg and the Ringstrasse

㉒ The Imperial Palace, known as the **Hofburg,** faces Kohlmarkt on the opposite side of Michaelerplatz. Until 1918 the Hofburg was the home of the Habsburgs, rulers of the Austro-Hungarian Empire; today it is a vast smorgasbord of sightseeing attractions: the Imperial Apartments, two Imperial treasuries, *six* museums, the National Library, and the famous Winter Riding School all vie for attention. The entire complex takes a minimum of a full day to explore in detail; if your time is limited (or if you want to save most of the interior sightseeing for a rainy day), you should omit the Imperial Apartments, the Court Silver and Tableware Treasury (now closed for renovation), and all the museums mentioned below except the Kunsthistorisches (the Museum of Art History). An excellent multilingual full-color booklet describing the palace in detail is on sale at most ticket counters within the complex; it gives a complete list of attractions and maps out the palace's complicated ground plan and building history wing by wing.

Architecturally, the Hofburg is (like St. Stephen's) far from refined. It grew up over a period of 700 years (its earliest mention in court documents is 1279, at the very beginning of Habsburg rule), and its spasmodic, haphazard growth kept it from attaining any sort of unified identity. But many of the bits and pieces are fine, and one interior (the National Library) is a tour de force.

The entrance on the Michaelerplatz leads to a domed rotunda; the **Silberkammer** (the Court Silver and Tableware Treasury) is to the right, while the **Imperial Apartments** are to the left. The former is much as might be expected, an extremely well stocked royal pantry turned royal museum, now closed for renovation. The latter, however, may come as a shock. The long, repetitive suite of conventionally luxurious rooms has a sad and poignant feel. The decoration (19th-century imitation of 18th-century Rococo) tries to look regal, but much like the Empire itself in its latter days, it is only going through the motions and ends up looking merely official. Among the few signs of genuine life are Emperor Franz Joseph's Spartan iron field bed, on which he slept every night, and the Empress Elizabeth's wooden gymnastics equipment, on which she exercised every morning. Amid all the tired splendor they look decidedly forlorn. *Silberkammer, tel. 0222/93424–099. Closed for renovation. Imperial Apartments, tel. 0222/587-5554–515. Admission: AS25; Open Mon.–Sat. 8:30–noon, 12:30–4; Sun. 8:30–12:30.*

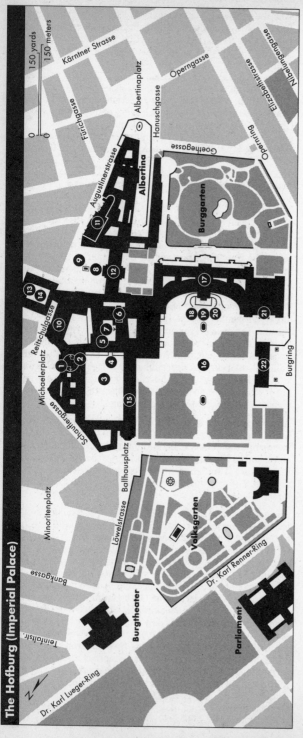

The Hofburg (Imperial Palace)

Augustinerkirche, 11
Burgtor, 22
Collection of Musical Instruments, 19
Collection of Weapons, 20
Emperor Joseph II monument, 9

Ephesus Museum, 18
Ethnological Museum, 21
Heldenplatz, 16
Hofbibliothek Prunksaal, 12
Hofburgkapelle, 6

Imperial Apartments, 2
In der Burg, 3
Josefsplatz, 8
Leopold Wing, 15
Neue Burg, 17
Schatzkammer, 7
Schweizertor, 4

Schweizer Hof, 5
Silberkammer, 1
Spanish (winter) Riding School, 10
Stallburg, 13
Stallburghof (courtyard), 14

On the far side of the rotunda is a large courtyard (known as In der Burg); set into the far left-hand wall is the **Schweizertor,** or Swiss Gate (dating from 1552 and decorated with some of the earliest classical motifs in the city), which leads through to the oldest section of the palace, a small courtyard known as the **Schweizer Hof.** In the southeast corner (at the top of the steps) is the entrance to the **Hofburgkapelle,** or Imperial Chapel, where the Vienna Boys' Choir sings Mass on Sundays and holidays from September to June (*see* Music in the Arts and Nightlife, below). At ground level is the entrance to the **Schatzkammer,** or Imperial Treasury, with its 1,000 years' of treasures. The display here is a welcome antidote to the monotony of the Imperial Apartments, for the entire Treasury was completely renovated in 1983–87, and the crowns and relics and vestments fairly glow in their new surroundings. *Schweizer Hof, tel. 0222/533–7931. Admission: AS60. Open Apr.–Oct., Mon. and Wed.–Fri. 10–6.*

A covered passageway leads from the Schweizer Hof into **Josefsplatz,** the most imposing of the Hofburg courtyards, with an equestrian monument (1807) to Emperor Joseph II in the center. To the left is the entrance to the **Spanische Reitschule,** the famous Spanish Riding School. Tickets to performances must be ordered in writing many weeks in advance, but daily practice is usually open to the public. The line starts forming at 9:30 for the opening at 10, but most sightseers are unaware that visitors may come and go as they please between 10 and noon, so it is often possible to walk right in between 11 and noon. The interior, the work of Fischer von Erlach the younger, is itself an attraction—surely Europe's most elegant sports arena— and if the prancing horses begin to pall, move up to the top balcony and examine the ceiling. *Josefsplatz 6, tel. 0222/533–9031. Admission: AS60 adults, AS15 children. Open mid-Feb.–June and Sept.–mid-Dec. (tour weeks excluded), Tues.–Sat. 10– noon.*

Across the square from the Riding School is the entrance to the **Augustinerkirche** (Church of the Augustinian Order), built during the 14th century and possessing the most unified Gothic interior in the city. But the church is something of a fraud; the interior, it turns out, dates from the late 18th century, not the early 14th. During the 1600s the old Gothic interior was completely remodeled in the Baroque style; then, at the beginning of the Gothic Revival in 1784, it was gutted and "restored" by the architect Ferdinand von Hohenberg.

A historical fraud the church may be, but a spiritual fraud it is not. The view from the entrance doorway is a stunner: a soaring harmony of vertical piers, ribbed vaults, and hanging chandeliers that makes Vienna's other Gothic interiors look earthbound by comparison. Farther inside, however, the effect is marred by a sculptural set piece against the right-hand wall: the memorial to the Archduchess Maria Christina (daughter of the Empress Maria Theresa), designed by Antonio Canova in 1798.

Back out on the square, a left turn from the Augustinerkirche exit leads to the entrance to the **Hofbibliothek Prunksaal** (the Gala Hall of the National Library), and a greater contrast between two interiors would be hard to imagine. The Augustinerkirche is one of the city's most restrained compositions; the

National Library is one of its most ornate. Designed by Fischer von Erlach the elder just before his death in 1723 and completed by his son, the Gala Hall is full-blown High Baroque, with trompe l'oeil ceiling frescoes by Daniel Gran taking over where the architecture flags. As usual, the frescoes are elaborately allegorical, the side ceilings are devoted to personifications of the sciences of peace and war, and the dome is devoted to a complicated symbolic glorification of the Emperor Charles VI, pictured in a medallion as supported by Apollo and Hercules.

The library may not be to everyone's taste. Certainly it is open to the charge of bombast, for only the central-oval balcony (with its elegantly squared and tapered supporting piers) suggests the special lightness and grace that serves, elsewhere in the city, as a counterbalance to conventional Baroque rhetoric. In the end it is the books themselves that come to the rescue. They are as lovingly displayed as the gilding and the frescoes, and they give the hall a warmth and humanity that the rest of the palace decidedly lacks. *Josefsplatz 1 (at the top of the stairs inside), tel. 0222/53410–397. Admission: AS15. Open May–Oct., Mon.–Sat. 10–4, Sun. 10–1; Nov.–Apr., Mon.–Sat. 10:30–noon.*

Walking back through the Schweizertor, turn left and walk under the Leopold Wing and out into the vast Heldenplatz. The long wing on the left is the youngest section of the palace, called the **Neue Burg.** It houses no less than four specialty museums: the **Ephesus Museum,** containing Roman antiquities unearthed by Austrian archaeologists in Turkey at the turn of the century; the **Collection of Musical Instruments,** including pianos that belonged to Beethoven, Brahms, Schumann, and Mahler; the **Collection of Weapons,** one of the most extensive arms-and-armor collections in the world; and the **Ethnological Museum,** devoted to anthropology (Montezuma's feathered headdress is a highlight of its collection). The first three museums are entered at the triumphal arch set into the middle of the curved portion of the facade; the Ethnological Museum is entered farther along, at the end pavilion. *Heldenplatz, tel. 0222/934541. Admission to Ephesus, Musical Instrument, and Weapons Museums on one ticket: AS30. Open Wed.–Mon. 10–4. Admission to Ethnological Museum: AS30. Open Mon. and Thurs.–Sat. 10–1, Wed. 10–5, Sun. 9–1.*

The Neue Burg stands today as a symbol of architectural overconfidence. Designed for Emperor Franz Joseph in 1869, it was part of a much larger scheme that was meant to make the Hofburg rival the Louvre, if not Versailles. The German architect Gottfried Semper planned a twin of the present Neue Burg on the opposite side of the Heldenplatz, with arches connecting the Neue Burg and its twin with the other pair of twins on the Ringstrasse, the Kunsthistorisches Museum (Museum of Art History) and the Naturhistorisches Museum (Museum of Natural History). But World War I intervened, and with the Empire's collapse the Neue Burg became merely the last in a long series of failed attempts to bring architectural order to the Hofburg.

The failure to complete the Hofburg building program left the Heldenplatz without a discernible shape, and today it's an amorphous sea of parked cars, with the Burgtor (the old main palace gate) stranded in the middle. On the other side of the Burgtor, across the Ringstrasse, is a much more successfully organized space, the **Maria-Theresien-Platz,** laid out in the 1870s around a matronly centerpiece monument to the matronly Empress Maria Theresa. To the west is the **Naturhistorisches Museum,** or Natural History Museum, home of, among other artifacts, the famous Venus of Willendorf, a tiny statuette thought to be some 20,000 years old. *Maria-Theresien-Platz tel. 0222/934541. Admission: AS30. Open Wed.–Mon. 9–6; in winter, ground floor only, 9–3.*

㉓ To the east is the **Kunsthistorisches Museum,** or Museum of Art History, housing one of the finest art collections in Europe. The collection was assembled by the ruling Habsburgs over several hundred years, and even a cursory description would run on for pages. Most of the great European old masters are represented, although many of the masterpieces are disgracefully dirty. Even the shortest list of highlights must include Rogier van der Weyden's *Crucifixion Triptych,* Raphael's *Madonna in the Meadow,* Holbein's *Portrait of Jane Seymour, Queen of England,* Titian's *Portrait of the Elector Johann Friedrich of Saxony,* the world-famous roomful of masterworks by Brueghel, Caravaggio's *Madonna of the Rosary,* a fine selection of Rembrandt portraits, and Vermeer's peerless *Allegory of the Art of Painting.* Benvenuto Cellini's famous gold saltcellar—certainly one of the most sumptuous pieces of tableware ever created—is on display amid the treasures of the applied-arts wing. *Maria-Theresien-Platz, tel. 0222/934541. Admission: AS45. Open Tues.–Sun. 10–6; Egyptian, antiques, and coin collections open Nov.–Mar., Tues.–Sun. 10–4; Apr.–Oct., Tues.–Sun. 10–6. Picture gallery open Tues. and Fri. evenings 7–9 (Mar.–Oct., 6–9).*

One block northwest of Maria-Theresien-Platz, walk west on Burggasse. The engaging 18th-century survivors at **Nos. 11 and 13** are adorned with religious and secular decorative sculpture, the latter with a niche statue of St. Joseph, the former with cherubic work-and-play bas reliefs. For several blocks around—walk down Gutenberggasse and back up Spittelberggasse—the 18th-century houses in the area have been beautifully restored (the entire area was scheduled for demolition in the 1970s but was saved by student protest). The sequence from **No. 5 to No. 19 Spittelberggasse** is an especially fine array of Viennese plain and fancy.

The huge, ominous concrete tower beyond the wall at the far end of Gutenberggasse is a grim reminder of World War II. It is **㉔** one of six **Flaktürme** (flak-towers) built in pairs around the city: concrete bunkers designed to withstand direct bombing hits and meant to serve as the Nazis' bastion of last resort against Allied attack. The towers remain standing because the only cost-effective means of demolishing them is dynamite, but any explosion powerful enough to do the job would damage the surrounding buildings.

Time Out Stop for a typical Viennese lunch at **Witwe Bolte** (Gutenberggasse 13), where in 1778, as noted on the arch just inside the entrance, the management unknowingly ejected Emperor Joseph II (apparently he was out for an incognito night on the town and was acting a bit strange). Good unpretentious Viennese food can also be found at **Boheme** (Spittelberggasse 19) and downstairs at **Zu ebener Erde und im ersten Stock** (Burg-gasse 13).

After continuing north from Spittelberggasse, take a right on Neustiftgasse and then cross Museumstrasse to Volksgar-tenstrasse; Volksgartenstrasse leads to the **Volksgarten,** on the east side of Dr.-Karl-Renner-Ring. The beautifully planted garden contains a little 19th-century Greek temple that offers an appropriate spot to sit for a few minutes and consider Vienna's most ambitious piece of 19th-century city planning: the famous **Ringstrasse.**

On December 20, 1857, Emperor Franz Josef issued a decree announcing the most ambitious piece of urban redevelopment Vienna had ever seen. The inner city's centuries-old walls were to be torn down, and the glacis—the wide expanse of open field that acted as a protective buffer between inner city and outer suburbs—was to be filled in. In their place was to rise a wide, tree-lined boulevard, upon which would stand an imposing collection of new buildings that would reflect Vienna's special status as the political, economic, and cultural heart of the Austro-Hungarian Empire.

During the 50 years of building that followed, many factors combined to produce the Ringstrasse as it now stands, but the most important was the gradual rise of liberalism after the failed Revolution of 1848. By the latter half of the Ringstrasse era, support for constitutional government, democracy, and equality—for all the concepts that liberalism traditionally equates with progress—was steadily increasing. As the turn of the century approached, the emperor's subjects were slowly but surely doing away with the Empire's long-standing tradi-tion of absolute imperial power, and it looked as if the transition from absolute to constitutional monarchy would be peaceful and unchallenged. Liberal Viennese voters could point with pride to a number of important civic improvements: The Dan-ube was controlled and canalized, a comprehensive municipal water-supply system was constructed, a public-health system was established, and the countryside bordering the city (in-cluding the Vienna Woods) was protected by new zoning laws. As it went up, the Ringstrasse stood as the definitive symbol of this liberal progress; as Carl E. Schorske put it in his *Fin-de-Siècle Vienna*, it celebrated "the triumph of constitutional *Recht* right over Imperial *Macht* might, of secular culture over religious faith. Not palaces, garrisons, and churches, but cen-ters of constitutional government and higher culture domi-nated the Ring."

But what should these centers of culture look like? The answer was the result of a new passion among the intelligentsia: archi-tectural Historicism. Greek temples, it was argued, reminded the viewer of the cradle of democracy; what could be more ap-propriate than a Parliament building designed in Greek Revi-val style? Gothic architecture, on the other hand, betokened the rule of the church and the rise of the great medieval city-states; the new Votive Church and the new City Hall would therefore be Gothic Revival. And the Renaissance Era, which produced the unprecedented flowering of learning and creativi-ty that put an end to the Middle Ages, was most admired of all; therefore, the new centers of high culture—the museums, the theaters, and the university—would be Renaissance Revival.

In building after building, architectural style was dictated by historical association, and gradually the Ringstrasse of today took shape.

The highest concentration of public building occurred in the area around the Volksgarten, where are clustered (moving from south to north, from Burgring to Schottenring) the **Museum of Art History,** the **Museum of Natural History,** the **26 27 Justizpalast** (Palace of Justice), the **Parlament** (Parliament), **28 29** the **Rathaus** (City Hall), the **Burgtheater** (National Theater), **30 31** the **Universität** (University of Vienna), and the **Votivkirche.** As an ensemble, the collection is astonishing in its architectural presumption: It is nothing less than an attempt to assimilate and summarize the entire architectural history of Europe. As critics were quick to notice, however, the complex suffers from a serious organizational flaw: Most of the buildings lack effective context. Rather than being the focal points of an organized overall plan, they are plunked haphazardly down on an avenue that is itself too wide to possess a unified, visually comprehensible character. In such surroundings, the buildings' monumental size works against them, and they end up looking like so many beached whales washed up on the inner-city shore.

The individual buildings, too, came in for immediate criticism. The Gothic Revival design of the City Hall, for instance, produced an interior so dark that large parts of it had to be fully lit all day long; the National Theater auditorium was so incompetently designed (bad sight lines and worse acoustics) that it had to be thoroughly reworked a few years later. And the Greek Revival Parliament building emerged looking monolithic and ponderous—traits more characteristic of bad bureaucracy than good government. The City Hall and the National Theater present the best face; they, at least, are sensibly placed, nodding soberly to each other across the Rathausplatz. But it is hard, when exploring the avenue, not to be oppressed by the overbearing monumentality of it all.

Exploring the Ringstrasse complex requires a considerable amount of time, but two attractions beyond the Votive Church at the Schottenring end deserve mention: Sigmund Freud's apartment (now a museum) and the Museum of Modern Art.

32 **Freud's Apartment** at Berggasse 19 (Apt. 6, one flight up; ring the bell and push the door simultaneously) was his residence from 1891 to 1938. The three-room collection of memorabilia is mostly a photographic record of Freud's life, with some documents, publications, and a portion of his collection of antiquities also on display. The waiting-room furniture is authentic, but the consulting-room and study furniture (including the famous couch) can be seen only in photographs. *Berggasse 19, tel. 0222/311596. Admission: AS30. Open daily 9–3.*

33 The **Museum Moderner Kunst** (Museum of Modern Art) is at Fürstengasse 1, three blocks north of Freud's apartment. The large 18th-century mansion was originally the Liechtenstein Summer Palace; today it houses the national collection of 20th-century art. Artists from Gustav Klimt to Robert Rauschenberg and Nam June Paik are represented, and a more inappropriate environment for modern art would be hard to imagine. Twentieth-century art and 18th-century architecture here declare war on each other and fight to an uneasy draw. Still, if you can shut out the architecture (or the art, depending on your taste), the museum is well worth a visit. *Fürsten-gasse 1, tel. 0222/341259. Admission: AS30. Open Wed.–Mon. 10–6.*

Tour 5: From St. Stephen's to the Opera

From the tall south tower of St. Stephen's Cathedral, the short Churhausgasse leads south to Singerstrasse. Two 18th-century palaces on this street are worth noting: the **Neupauer-Breuner Palace,** at No. 16 (1715, architect unknown), with its monumental entranceway and inventively delicate windows, and the **Rottal Palace,** at No. 17 (1750, attributed to Hilde-brandt), with its wealth of classical wall-motifs. For a contrast, turn up the narrow Blutgasse, with its simple 18th-century fa-cades. The little building at No. 3 is especially appealing, for it looks as if it's being bullied by the buildings on either side and has buckled under the pressure.

Blutgasse ends at Domgasse; at No. 5 is the **Figarohaus,** one of Mozart's 11 rented Viennese residences. It was here that he wrote *The Marriage of Figaro* and the six quartets dedicated to Joseph Haydn; the apartment he occupied now contains a small commemorative museum. *Domgasse 5, tel. 0222/513–6294. Admission: AS15. Open Tues.–Sun. 10–12:15 and 1–4:30.*

At the east end of Singerstrasse the 19th century takes over and the 18th-century interplay between strength and delicacy disappears. Monumentality has won out, as can be seen at the **Coburg Palace** (1843) on Seilerstätte. The Coburg facade lacks all sense of play compared to the Neupauer-Breuner and Rottal palaces. Its garden side, however, boasts a fine historical curi-osity: a section of the ancient Viennese city walls, one of the few that managed to escape demolition during the construction of the Ringstrasse.

Two blocks south of the Coburg Palace, turn west on Himmel-pfortgasse. The modest house at **No. 15** possesses a curlicued gable that derives from the facade of the Dominikanerkirche (*see* Tour 1); the interior passageway remains much as it was 150 years ago—woodpile, communal water basin, Biedermeier carriage, and all. Next door, at No. 13, the **Erdödy-Fürstenberg Palace** (1724) has design motifs mostly lifted from the Neupauer-Breuner Palace. The beautiful yellow-and-cream paint job gives the facade a finish that the architecturally more sophisticated Neupauer-Breuner lacks.

Also sporting a fine painted (and in places gilded) exterior is the **Ministry of Finance** at No. 8. Designed by Fischer von Erlach in 1697 and later expanded by Hildebrandt, the building was originally the town palace of Prince Eugene of Savoy, who, as commander-in-chief of the Imperial Army in the War of the Spanish Succession, led Austrian forces (alongside the English under the Duke of Marlborough) to victory over the French at the Battle of Blenheim in 1704. The Baroque details here are among the most inventively conceived and beautifully executed in the city. The large windows carry elegantly crafted pedi-ments that are more like top hats than eyebrows, and all the decorative motifs are so softly carved that they appear to have been freshly squeezed from a pastry tube. The Viennese are lovers of the baroque in both their architecture and their pas-try, and here the two passions seem visibly merged.

From Himmelpfortgasse, turn right onto Rauhensteingasse and then immediately right on Ballgasse, which winds to the left and then dwindles down to a short arched passageway leading into Franziskanerplatz. The **Moses Fountain** in the center of the square dates from 1798; the small **Franziskanerkirche** on the east side is an international hybrid, with a facade (1603) that imitates German churches of the early Renaissance and a later interior that imitates Italian churches of the Baroque. The small shopping arcade at the garishly painted No. 6 is worth exploring for its disturbingly surreal decoration.

From Franziskanerplatz, Weihburggasse leads west to **Kärntner Strasse,** Vienna's premier shopping street. These days Kärntner Strasse is much maligned. Too commercial, too crowded, too many tasteless signs, too much gaudy neon—the complaints go on and on. Nevertheless, the Viennese continue to arrive regularly for their evening promenade, and it is easy to see why. Vulgar the street may be, but it is also alive and vital, possessing an energy that the more tasteful Graben and the impeccable Kohlmarkt lack. For the sightseer beginning to suffer from art-history overdose, a Kärntner Strasse window-shopping break will be welcome.

The short Donnergasse (across Kärntner Strasse from Himmelpfortgasse) leads into Neuer Markt. The square's centerpiece, Georg Raphael Donner's **Providence Fountain,** has not had a happy life. Put up in 1739, it was at the time the very latest word in civic improvements, with elegantly mannered nude statuary meant to personify the Danube and four of its tributaries. The Empress Maria Theresa, however, was offended; despite having had 16 children, she disapproved of nudity in art. The figures were removed and stored away and later nearly melted down for munitions. They were finally restored in 1801, but were once again moved away (to be replaced by the present copies) in 1873. The original figures can be studied in quiet at the Lower Belvedere Palace (*see* Tour 6).

The church at the southwest corner of the Neuer Markt is the Kapuzinerkirche; in its basement (entrance to the left of the church) is the **Kaisergruft,** or Imperial Burial Vault. The crypts contain the partial remains of some 140 Habsburgs (the hearts are in the Augustinerkirche and the entrails in St. Stephen's) plus one non-Habsburg governess ("She was always with us in life," said Maria Theresa, "why not in death?"). The sarcophagi are often elaborate and occasionally bizarre: Maria Theresa is shown in bed with her husband awaking to the Last Judgment as if it were just another weekday morning, while the remains of her son (the ascetic Joseph II) lie in a simple casket at the foot of the bed as if he were the family dog. *Neuer Markt, tel. 0222/ 512-6853-12. Admission: AS30. Open daily 9:30-4.*

From the southwest corner of Neuer Markt, walk south on Tegetthofstrasse to Albertinaplatz. On the square's west side the **Albertina Museum** houses a vast collection of drawings and prints dating to the 15th century. Because of their fragility, only a very small selection of the more than 200,000 pieces of art is on view at any one time, and most of the famous works (for example, Albrecht Durer's *Praying Hands*) must usually be viewed in reproduction. *Augustinerstr. 1, tel. 0222/53483. Admission: AS30. Open Mon., Tues., Thurs. 10-4; Wed. 10-6; Fri. 10-2; Sat. and Sun. 10-1; closed Sun. July and Aug.*

Time Out Take a coffee break at one of three nearby cafés. The **Café Sacher,** in the Hotel Sacher on Philharmonikerstrasse—the street leading east from the south end of Albertinaplatz—is the most formal of the three (no shorts allowed inside during the summer); its famous Sachertorte can also be purchased at a small Kärntner Strasse shop on the hotel's east side. The **Café Mozart,** on the hotel's west side, opposite the Albertina, is almost as elegant as the Sacher, while the **Café Tirolerhof,** on the north side of Albertinaplatz, is a less upscale (but more typically Viennese) alternative.

From the north end of Albertinaplatz, Führichgasse leads east across Kärntner Strasse to Annagasse. The small neighborhood church at No. 2, the **Annakirche,** possesses a fine bulbous dome atop its tower and an unusually consistent Baroque decorative scheme inside, but the main attraction is the curved street itself, with its fine collection of unpretentious facades. The high point, undoubtedly, is **No. 14,** with its carved frieze of impish, gossiping cherubs. The poses here are conventional, but the execution is not, for the frieze achieves with ease the spontaneity that Baroque sculpture always sought but too often failed to find.

Return to Kärntner Strasse, and follow it south to the Ringstrasse. The building on the right, facing Opernring, is the famous Vienna **Opera House.** The first of the Ringstrasse projects to be completed (in 1869), it suffered severe bomb damage during World War II (only the front facade and the main staircase area behind it survived). Though it was rebuilt, it remains something of a shell, for the cost of fully restoring the 19th-century interior decor was prohibitive. Tours of the Opera are given regularly, but starting times vary according to opera rehearsals; the current schedule is usually posted at the west side entrance, where the tours begin.

The construction of the Opera is the stuff of legend. When the foundation was laid, the plans for Opernring were not yet complete, and in the end the avenue turned out to be several feet higher than originally planned. As a result, the Opera lacked the commanding prospect that its architects, Eduard van der Nüll and August Sicard von Sicardsburg, had intended, and even Emperor Franz Josef pronounced the building a bit low to the ground. For the sensitive van der Nüll (and here the story becomes a bit suspect), failing his beloved emperor was the last straw. In disgrace and despair, he committed suicide. Sicardsburg died of grief shortly thereafter. And the emperor, horrified at the deaths his innocuous remark had caused, limited all his future artistic pronouncements to a single immutable formula: *Es war sehr schön, es hat mich sehr gefreut* ("It was very nice, it pleased me very much").

Tour 6: South of the Ring to the Belvedere

Two blocks southwest of the Opera, facing the Schillerplatz, the **Academy of Fine Arts** was built in the later 19th century to house an institution founded in 1692. The academy's Renaissance Revival architecture was meant to instill in its students an appreciation of the past; traditional standards were staunchly maintained here in the face of the artistic rebellions of the early 20th century. In 1907 and again in 1908, an aspiring artist named Adolf Hitler was refused admission on the grounds of insufficient talent. Today the academy contains an old-master art collection that will be of interest mostly to specialists, the one exception being Hieronymus Bosch's famous *Last Judgment* triptych, which more than makes up in horrific imagination what it lacks in painterly sophistication. *Schillerplatz 3, tel. 0222/58816. Admission: AS15. Open Tues., Thurs., Fri. 10–2; Wed. 10–1, 3–6; weekends 9–1.*

If the Academy of Fine Arts represents the conservative attitude of the arts in the late 1800s, then its antithesis can be **42** found immediately behind it to the southeast: the **Secession Building.** Restored in the mid-1980s after years of neglect, the Secession Building is one of Vienna's preeminent symbols of artistic rebellion; rather than look to the architecture of the past like the revivalist Ringstrasse, it looked to a new anti-Historicist future. It was, in its day, a riveting trumpetblast of a building, today considered by many to be Europe's first piece of full-blown 20th-century architecture.

The Secession movement began in 1897 when 20 dissatisfied Viennese artists headed by Gustav Klimt "seceded" from the Künstlerhausgenossenschaft, the conservative artists' society associated with the Academy of Fine Arts. The movement promoted the radically new kind of art known as Jugendstil, which found its inspiration in both the organic, fluid designs of Art Nouveau and the related but more geometric designs of the English Arts and Crafts movement. (The Secessionists founded an arts-and-crafts workshop of their own, the famous Wiener Werkstätte, in an effort to embrace the applied arts.) The Secession Building was the movement's exhibition hall, designed by the architect Joseph Olbrich and completed in 1898. The lower story, crowned by the entrance motto *Der Zeit Ihre Kunst, Der Kunst Ihre Freiheit* (To Every Age Its Art, To Art Its Freedom), is classic Jugendstil: The restrained but assured decoration (by Koloman Moser) beautifully complements the facade's pristine flat expanses of cream-colored wall. Above the entrance motto sits the building's most famous feature, the gilded openwork dome that the Viennese were quick to christen "the golden cabbage" (Olbrich wanted it to be seen as a dome of laurel, a subtle classical reference meant to celebrate the triumph of art). The plain white interior—"shining and chaste," in Olbrich's words—was also revolutionary; its most unusual feature was movable walls, allowing the galleries to be reshaped and redesigned for every show. One early show, in 1902, was an exhibition devoted to art celebrating the genius of Beethoven; Gustav Klimt's *Beethoven Frieze*, painted for the occasion, has now been restored and is permanently installed in the building's basement. *Friedrichstr. 12, tel. 0222/587–5307. Admission: AS40, Beethoven Frieze only: AS15. Open Tues.– Fri. 10–6, weekends 10–4.*

To the south of the Secession Building run two parallel streets, the Linke (left) and Rechte (right) Wienzeile. Farther to the south, the River Wien, a tributary of the Danube, runs between them, but here the river was covered over at the turn of the century. The site is now home to the Naschmarkt, Vienna's main outdoor produce market.

Time Out Explore the **Naschmarkt** and pick up a meal as you go. The stands marked *Imbisse* (Snack) will sell you a *Hühnerschnitzel-Semmel* (chicken schnitzel inside a Viennese roll), the **Meeres-**

Buffet offers a vast array of seafood, **Heindl & Co. Palat-schinkenkuch'l** (pancake kitchen) sells a wide variety of meat and dessert crepes, and the **Naschmarkt Bäckerei** can supply the necessary pastry. If you want a more leisurely sit-down meal, try **Sopherl**, a favorite hangout of Naschmarkt vendors, on Linke Wienzeile on the market's west side.

The Ringstrasse-style apartment houses that line Linke Wienzeile are mostly an undistinguished lot, but four blocks south of the Secession Building, two unexpectedly stand out: **Nos. 38 and 40,** designed (1898–99) by the grand old man of Viennese fin-de-siècle architecture, Otto Wagner, during his Secessionist phase.

A good example of what Wagner was rebelling against can be seen next door, at **No. 42,** where Baroque decorative enthusiasm has degenerated into Baroque Revival decorative hysteria, and the overwrought facade seems to drown in a jumble of classical motifs. Wagner had come to believe that this sort of display was nothing but empty pretense and sham; modern apartment houses, he wrote in his pioneering text *Modern Architecture*, are entirely different from 18th-century town palaces, and architects should not pretend otherwise. Accordingly, Wagner banished classical decoration and introduced a new architectural simplicity, with flat exterior walls and plain, regular window treatments meant to reflect the orderly layout of the apartments behind them. For decoration, he turned to his younger Secessionist cohorts Joseph Olbrich and Koloman Moser, who designed the ornate Jugendstil patterns of red majolica-tile roses and gold stucco medallions that brighten the facades of Nos. 38 and 40. The crisp facades that resulted make the huffing-and-puffing classicism next door look tired and dowdy.

More of Wagner's secessionist work can be seen two blocks east of the Secession Building on the northern edge of Karlsplatz. In 1893 Wagner was appointed architectural supervisor of the new Vienna City Railway, and the matched **pair of small pavilions** he designed for the Karlsplatz station in 1898 are among the city's most ingratiating buildings. Their structural framework is frankly exposed (in keeping with Wagner's belief in architectural honesty), but they are also lovingly decorated (in keeping with the Viennese love of architectural finery). And Wagner's chronic failing—a pretentious desire to impress—is entirely absent. The result is Jugendstil at its very best, melding plain and fancy with grace and insouciance.

Like the space now occupied by the Naschmarkt, the Karlsplatz was formed when the River Wien was covered over at the turn of the century. At the time Wagner expressed his frustration with the result—too large a space for a formal square and too small a space for an informal park—and the awkwardness persists to this day. The buildings surrounding the Karlsplatz, on the other hand, are quite sure of themselves: on the south side the **Technical University** (1816–18) and on the north side the **Kunstlerhaus** (the exhibition hall in which the Secessionists refused to exhibit, built in 1881 and still in use) and the **Musikverein** (finished in 1869, now home to the Vienna Philharmonic). Much the most important building, however, is the oldest: the Church of Saint Charles Borromeo, familiarly known as **43** the **Karlskirche,** built in the early 18th century on what was then the bank of the River Wien and is now the Karlsplatz's southeast corner.

The church had its beginnings in a disaster. In 1713, Vienna was hit by a brutal plague outbreak, and Emperor Charles VI made a vow: If the plague abated, he would build a church dedicated to his namesake Saint Charles Borromeo, the 16th-century Italian bishop who was famous for his ministrations to Milanese plague victims. In 1715 construction began, using an the ambitious design by Johann Bernhard Fischer von Erlach that combined architectural elements from ancient Greece (the columned entrance porch), ancient Rome (the freestanding columns, modeled after Trajan's Column), contemporary Rome (the Baroque dome), and contemporary Vienna (the Baroque towers at either end). When it was finished, the church received (and continues to receive) a decidedly mixed press. Some critics view the facade as an unqualified success, a masterpiece that fuses its disparate elements into a triumphantly unified whole. Others think it a failure, contending that the visual weight of the Baroque dome seems to crush the Greek-temple porch below, and that the freestanding columns cut off the end towers, setting them uncomfortably adrift. History, incidentally, delivered a negative verdict: In its day the Karlskirche spawned no imitations, and it went on to become one of European architecture's most famous curiosities.

The main interior of the church utilizes only the area under the dome, and is surprisingly conventional given the unorthodox facade. The space and architectural detailing are typical High Baroque; the fine vault frescoes, by J. M. Rottmayr (1725-1730), depict Saint Charles Borromeo imploring the Holy Trinity to end the plague.

44 Finally, one last Karlsplatz building remains: the **Historisches Museum der Stadt Wien** (Museum of Viennese History), hidden away at the east end of the square next to the Karlskirche. The museum possesses a dazzling array of Viennese historical artifacts and treasures, all beautifully organized and displayed: models, maps, documents, photographs, antiquities, stained glass, paintings, sculpture, crafts, mementos, reconstructed rooms. For once, urban history is lovingly and comprehensively served. This is, it turns out, one of the finest museums in Europe, and the most woefully undervisited attraction in all Vienna. *Karlsplatz, tel. 0222/505–8747. Admission: AS30. Open Tues.–Sun. 9–4:30.*

Beyond the Karlsplatz to the east is the **French Embassy,** built in 1909 in an Art Nouveau style that offers a clear contrast to the more geometric Austrian Jugendstil. Beyond the embassy lies **Schwarzenbergplatz.** The militant monument occupying the south end of the square is the **Russian War Memorial,** set up at the end of World War II by the Soviets; the Viennese, remembering the Soviet occupation, call its unknown soldier "the unknown plunderer." South of the memorial is the formidable **Schwarzenberg Palace,** designed by Johann Lukas von Hildebrandt in 1697 and now (in part) a luxury hotel.

45 Hildebrandt's most important Viennese work is farther along, at Rennweg 6A: the **Belvedere Palace.** In fact the Belvedere is two palaces with extensive gardens between. Built just outside the city fortifications between 1714 and 1722, the complex originally served as the summer palace of Prince Eugene of Savoy;

much later it became the home of Archduke Franz Ferdinand, whose assassination in 1914 precipitated World War I. Though the lower palace is impressive in its own right (it served as Prince Eugene's living quarters), it is the much larger upper palace, used for state receptions, banquets, and balls, that is Hildebrandt's acknowledged masterpiece.

Best approached through the gardens, the upper palace displays a remarkable wealth of architectural invention in its facade. The main design problem—common to all palaces because of their excessive size—is to avoid monotony on the one hand and pomposity on the other. Hildebrandt's solution is inspired. To ward off monotony, he has varied the building's upper story and roof line so as to create seven separate compositions, all variations on the same central theme and all arranged in a gradual *diminuendo* from the center outward, with accented ends to supply the coda. To ward off pomposity, he has created an overall decorative scheme that possesses both variety and balance: Each section of the facade is given its own set of decorative motifs, but in all cases the decoration grows more complex with each story, with the upper story given less height so that its decorative complexity does not overwhelm the simpler stories below.

Hildebrandt's decoration here approaches the Rococo, that final style of the Baroque era when traditional classical motifs all but disappeared in a whirlwind of seductive asymmetric fancy. The main interiors of the palace go even further: Columns are transformed into muscle-bound giants, pilasters grow torsos, capitals sprout great piles of symbolic Imperial paraphernalia, and the ceilings are set aswirl with ornately molded stucco. The result is the finest Rococo interior in the city.

One other architectural detail is especially worthy of notice, on the facade of the south side of the palace (actually the front, facing away from the center city). Hildebrandt here added an extra fillip: an exuberantly decorated entrance porch topped with a luscious dollop-of-whipped-cream pediment. It was a motif he clearly loved, for he used it repeatedly, and today it is considered his architectural signature.

Today both the upper and lower palaces are museums devoted to Austrian painting. **The Austrian Museum of Baroque Art,** in the lower palace, displays Austrian art of the 18th century (including the original figures from Georg Raphael Donner's *Providence Fountain* in the Neuer Markt). Next to the Baroque Museum (outside the west end) is the converted Orangerie, devoted to works of the medieval period. The main attraction, however, is the upper palace's collection of **19th- and 20th-century Austrian paintings,** centering on the work of Vienna's three preeminent early 20th-century artists: Gustav Klimt, Egon Schiele, and Oskar Kokoschka. Klimt was the oldest, and by the time he helped found the Secession movement, he had forged a highly idiosyncratic painting style that combined realistic and decorative elements in a way that was completely revolutionary. Schiele and Kokoschka went even further; rejecting the decorative appeal of Klimt's glittering abstract designs and producing works that completely ignored conventional ideas of beauty. Today they are considered the fathers of modern art in Vienna. (The Kokoschka collection has recently been moved to the Lower Belvedere Stables, reached through the Baroque Museum; one hopes that this quarantine is only temporary.) *Tel. 0222/784158. Admission: AS30. Open Tues.–Sun. 10–5.*

Tour 7: Schönbrunn Palace

Schönbrunn Palace, the huge Habsburg summer palace laid out by Johann Bernhard Fischer von Erlach in 1696, lies well within the city limits, just a few subway stops west of Karlsplatz on line U4. The vast and elegantly planted gardens are open daily from dawn till dusk, and multilingual guided tours of the palace interior take place daily. The **Wagenburg** (Imperial Coach Collection) can be seen in the west wing, entered at the far end of the small courtyard off the southwest corner of the main courtyard, and the **Tiergarten** (the Imperial Menagerie, now the Vienna Zoo), founded in 1752 during the reign of Maria Theresa, is on the west side of the gardens.

The best approach to the palace and its gardens is through the front gate, located on Schönbrunner Schloss-Strasse halfway between the Schönbrunn and Hietzing subway stations. The vast main courtyard is ruled by a formal design of impeccable order and rigorous symmetry: Wing nods at wing, facade mirrors facade, and every part stylistically complements every other. The courtyard, however, turns out to be merely appetizer; the feast lies beyond. The breathtaking view that unfolds on the other side of the palace is one of the finest set pieces in all Europe and one of the supreme achievements of Baroque planning. Formal *allées* (garden promenades) shoot off diagonally, the one on the right toward the Zoo, the one on the left toward a rock-mounted obelisk and a fine false Roman ruin. But these, and the woods beyond, are merely a frame for the astonishing composition in the center: the sculpted fountain, the carefully planted screen of trees behind, the sudden almost vertical rise of the grass-covered hill beyond. And at the crest of the hill, topping it all off, sits a Baroque masterstroke: Johann Ferdinand von Hohenberg's incomparable **Gloriette.** Perfectly scaled for its setting, the Gloriette holds the whole vast garden composition together, and at the same time crowns the ensemble with a brilliant architectural tiara.

The 18th century was the Age of Reason, and its obsession with order produced elaborately formal gardens all over Europe. But Schönbrunn is exceptional, for here architecture combines with nature—man puts his stamp on God's design—with an assurance and an elegance that the 18th century rarely, if ever, surpassed.

After the superb gardens, the palace interior comes as something of an anticlimax. Of the 1,400 rooms, 45 are open to the public, and two are of special note: the Hall of Mirrors, where the six-year-old Mozart performed for the Empress Maria Theresa in 1762, and the Grand Gallery, where the Congress of Vienna (1815) danced at night after carving up Napoleon's collapsed empire during the day. The most unusual interior at Schönbrunn, however, is not within the palace at all. It is the newly restored Imperial subway station, known as the **Hofpavillon,** located just outside the palace grounds (at the northwest corner, a few yards east of the Hietzing subway station). Designed by Otto Wagner in conjunction with Joseph Olbrich and Leopold Bauer, the Hofpavillon was built in 1899 for the exclusive use of the Emperor Franz Josef and his entourage. The exterior, with its proud architectural crown, is Wagner at his best, and the lustrous interior is one of the finest examples of Jugendstil decoration in the city. The building is little more than a single enclosed room, but it is a true gem. *Schönbrunner Schloss-Str., subway stop Schönbrunn, tel. 0222/81113–238. Guided tours of palace interior AS50. Open Apr.–June and Oct., daily 8:30–5; July–Sept., daily 8:30–5:30; Nov.–Mar., daily 9–4. Gloriette roof admission: AS10. Open May–Oct., daily 8–6. Wagenburg, tel. 0222/823244. Admission: AS30. Open Tues.–Sun., Oct.–Apr., 10–4; May–Sept. 10–5. Tiergarten subway stop Hietzing, tel. 0222/837–1206. Admission: AS35, children AS10. Open daily 9–dusk, 6 PM the latest. Hofpavillon, Schönbrunner Schloss-Str. 13, tel. 0222/877–1571. Admission: AS15. Open Tues.–Sun. 9–12:15, 1–4:30.*

The vast **Technical Museum,** located close by though not within the Schönbrunn grounds, houses the world's first sewing machine, the first typewriter (and later models), the first gasoline-powered car, early airplanes, an outstanding collection of steam locomotives and railroad cars, a coal mine you can go through, and many other technical exhibits that include aluminum smelting and a collection of musical instruments. History and circumstances intervened in 1918, just as the museum opened to showcase Austrian industry, so that in some industries—papermaking, for example—models that were up to date then are now fascinating relics of the past. Changing shows supplement the fixed exhibits. *Mariahilfer Str. 212, tel. 0222/891010. Admission: AS30 adults, AS15 children. Open Sun.–Fri. 9–4:30. Subway stop Schönbrunn, or No. 52 or 58 streetcar to Technisches Museum.*

Vienna for Free

Vienna is not famous for its sightseeing generosity—there is even an admission charge when the Vienna Boys' Choir sings Mass at the Hofburgkapelle (in fairness, however, it should be noted that the musical masses at the nearby Augustinerkirche are free). The city's many public parks are the main no-cost attraction, notably the **Schönbrunn Gardens** (*see* Tour 7), the **Volksgarten** (*see* Tour 4), and the **Belvedere Gardens** (*see* Tour 6). In addition, the **Stadtpark** (on the Ringstrasse near its east end) offers early-evening band concerts in the summer; it also contains some fine turn-of-the-century architecture and a frothy monument to Johann Strauss. The beautifully planted **Burggarten** (on the east side of the Neue Burg) is flanked at its north end by the Imperial greenhouses, built in 1905. The famed **Wienerwald** (Vienna Woods) is not a park but a series of low wooded hills west of the city, actually the easternmost foothills of the Alps. Exploring the woods in fine weather is a time-honored Viennese pastime; the view of the city and the Danube from the Leopoldsberg Hill is especially beloved.

What to See and Do with Children

Vienna's main attraction for children is the famous **Wurstelprater** (or Volksprater), Vienna's foremost amusement park (at the Prater's north end; take the U1 subway line to Praterstern). It has all the traditional modern amusementpark rides plus a number of less innocent indoor, sex-oriented attractions and a museum devoted to the Wurstelprater's long history. The best-known attraction is the giant Ferris wheel that figured so prominently in the 1949 film *The Third Man*. One of three built in Europe at the end of the last century (the others were in England and France but have long since been dismantled), the wheel was badly damaged during World War II and restored shortly thereafter. Its progress is slow and stately, the views from its cars magnificent.

The **Vienna Zoo** will also appeal and possesses the added advantage of being located in the Schönbrunn Gardens (*see* Tour 7). In the basement of the **Theater Museum** is a children's museum that is reached by a slide (Lobkowitzpl., tel. 0222/512–3705). Also see the specialty museums, below. Lesser attractions include the **Museum of Natural History** (*see* Tour 4) and a notably bizarre **aquarium,** grotesquely housed in a World War II flak-tower in the middle of the tiny Esterhazy Park between Mariahilfer Strasse and Gumpendorferstrasse (tel. 0222/587–1417; admission: AS15; open daily 9–6). Finally, the climb to the top of the **south tower of St. Stephen's Cathedral** (*see* Tour 1) should work up an appetite for a visit, if the pocketbook allows, to **Demel's** (Kohlmarkt 14), Vienna's most famous pastry shop, where all children should at least once in their lives be allowed to eat themselves sick.

Off the Beaten Track

Vienna's most exalted piece of Jugendstil architecture is not in the inner city but in the suburbs to the west: the **Am Steinhof Church,** designed by Otto Wagner in 1904 during his Secessionist phase. Built on the grounds of the Lower Austrian State Asylum (now the Vienna City Psychiatric Hospital), Wagner's design united mundane functional details (rounded edges on the pews to prevent injury to the patients and a slightly sloped tile floor to facilitate cleaning) with a soaring, airy dome and glittering Jugendstil decoration (mosaics by Remigius Geyling and stained glass by Koloman Moser). The church is open once a week for guided tours (in German). *Baumgartner Höhe 1, tel. 0222/949060–2391. Admission free. Open Sat. 3–4. Subway stop: Unter-St.-Veit, then No. 47A bus to Psychiatrisches Krankenhaus.*

Music lovers will want to make a pilgrimage to the **Zentralfriedhof** (Central Cemetery, in the 11th District on Simmeringer Hauptstrasse), which contains the graves of most of Vienna's great composers, some moved here from other cemeteries: Ludwig van Beethoven, Franz Schubert, Johannes Brahms, the Johann Strausses (father and son), and Arnold Schönberg, among others. The monument to Wolfgang Amadeus Mozart is a memorial only; the approximate location of his actual burial, in an unmarked grave, can be seen at the now deconsecrated St. Marx-Friedhof at Leberstrasse 6–8; *streetcar 71.*

Musical residences abound as well. Schubert—a native to the city, unlike most of Vienna's other famous composers—was born at Nussdorferstrasse 54 (tel 0222/345–9924), in the Ninth District, and died in the Fourth District at Kettenbrückengasse 6 (tel. 0222/573–9072). Joseph Haydn's house is at Haydngasse 19 (tel. 0222/596–1307) in the Sixth District; Beethoven's Heiligenstadt residence, where at age 32 he wrote

the "Heiligenstadt Testament," an anguished cry of pain and
protest against his ever-increasing deafness, is at Probusgasse
6 in the 19th District (tel. 0222/375–408). Finally, the home of
the most popular composer of all, waltz king Johann Strauss
the younger, can be visited at Praterstrasse 54 (tel. 0222/240–
121), in the Second District; he lived here when he composed
"The Blue Danube Waltz" in 1867. All the above houses contain
commemorative museums (Admission: AS15. Open Tues.–
Sun. 9–12:15 and 1–4:30).

Two museums not covered on the walking tours are of special
note: the **Museum of Applied Arts** (on the Ring at Stubenring 5;
tel. 0222/71136; admission AS30; open Wed.–Mon. 11–6) contains a large collection of Austrian furniture and art objects;
the Jugendstil display devoted to Josef Hoffman and his follow-
ers at the Wiener Werkstätte is particularly fine. And the **Museum of Military History** (south of the Belvedere on Ghegastr.;
tel. 0222/782303; admission AS30; open Sat.–Thurs. 10–4) contains a vast array of Austro-Hungarian military relics and mementos, including the car in which Archduke Franz Ferdinand
was riding when he was assassinated in 1914 at Sarajevo.

Sightseeing Checklists

This list includes both attractions that were covered in the pre-
ceding tours and additional ones that are described here for the
first time.

Historic Buildings and Sights

Beethoven Heiligenstadt residence (*see* Off the Beaten Track).
*Subway stop: Heiligenstadt, then No. 38A bus to Armbrust-
ergasse.*
Café Central (*see* Tour 2). *Subway stop: Stephansplatz.*
Café Hawelka (*see* Tour 3). *Subway stop: Stephansplatz.*
City Hall (*see* Tour 4). *Subway stop: Rathaus.*
Dorotheum (Auction House; *see* Tour 3). *Subway stop: Steph-
ansplatz.*
Figarohaus (Mozart Residence; *see* Tour 5). *Subway stop:
Stephansplatz.*
Freud's Apartment (*see* Tour 4). *Subway stop: Schottentor.*
Haydn Residence (*see* Off the Beaten Track). *Subway stop:
Pilgramgasse.*
Hofburg (Habsburg Imperial Palace; *see* Tour 4). *Subway stop:
Herrengasse.*
Hofpavillon (*see* Tour 7). *Subway stop: Hietzing.*
Hundertwasserhaus. A 50-apartment public-housing complex,
designed by Friedrich Hundertwasser, Austria's best-known
living painter. Looking as if it was painted by a crew of mischie-
vous circus clowns wielding giant crayons, the building caused
a sensation when it went up in 1985. It remains a tourist attrac-
tion not to be missed. *Corner of Kegelgasse and Löwengasse.
Subway stop: Schwedenplatz, then streetcar N to Hetzgasse.*
Imperial Burial Vault (*see* Tour 5). *Subway stop: Stephans-
platz.*
Looshaus (House Without Eyebrows; *see* Tour 3). *Subway stop:
Herrengasse.*
National Library (in the Hofburg; *see* Tour 4). *Subway stop:
Herrengasse.*
National Theater (*see* Tour 4). *Subway stop: Rathaus.*

Opera House (*see* Tour 5). *Subway stop: Karlsplatz.*
Palace of Justice (*see* Tour 4). *Subway stop: Volkstheater.*
Parliament (*see* Tour 4). *Subway stop: Lerchenfelder Strasse.*
Pasqualatihaus (Beethoven's residence; *see* Tour 2). *Subway stop: Schottentor.*
Schönbrunn Palace (*see* Tour 7). *Subway stop: Schönbrunn.*
Schubert's Birthplace. (*see* Off the Beaten Track). *Subway stop: Schottentor, then No. 37 or No. 38 tram to Nussdorfer Strasse/Canisiusgasse.* **The house where he died.** *Subway stop: Kettenbrückengasse.*
Strauss Residence (*see* Off the Beaten Track). *Subway stop: Nestroyplatz.*
University of Vienna (*see* Tour 4). *Subway stop: Schottentor.*
Virgilkapelle. An old and mysterious chapel, uncovered during excavations for the subway system in the 1970s. It was probably constructed in the 13th century by hollowing out the ground underneath the charnel house next to St. Stephen's; no trace of an entrance door was found, its only possible means of access apparently being a trap door in the ceiling. Visible from the first underground level of the Stephansplatz subway station. *Subway stop: Stephansplatz.*
Winter Riding School (Hofburg; *see* Tour 4). *Subway stop: Herrengasse.*

Museums and Galleries

Academy of Fine Arts (*see* Tour 6). *Subway stop: Karlsplatz.*
Albertina Museum (*see* Tour 5). *Subway stop: Stephansplatz.*
Belvedere Palace (*see* Tour 6). *Subway stop: Karlsplatz.*
Cathedral and Diocese Museum (*see* Tour 1). *Subway stop: Stephansplatz.*
Clock Museum (*see* Tour 2). *Subway stop: Stephansplatz.*
Collection of Musical Instruments (Hofburg; *see* Tour 4). *Subway stop: Mariahilfer Strasse.*
Collection of Weapons (Hofburg; *see* Tour 4). *Subway stop: Mariahilfer Strasse.*
Court Silver and Tableware Treasury (Hofburg; *see* Tour 4). *Subway stop: Herrengasse.*
Ephesus Museum (Hofburg; *see* Tour 4). *Subway stop: Mariahilfer Strasse.*
Ethnological Museum (Hofburg; *see* Tour 4). *Subway stop: Mariahilfer Strasse.*
Imperial Apartments (Hofburg; *see* Tour 4). *Subway stop: Herrengasse.*
Imperial Coach Collection (Schönbrunn; *see* Tour 7). *Subway stop: Schönbrunn.*
Imperial Treasuries (Hofburg; *see* Tour 4). *Subway stop: Herrengasse.*
Museum of Applied Arts (*see* Off the Beaten Track) *Subway stop: Stubentor.*
Museum of Art History (*see* Tour 4). *Subway stop: Mariahilfer Strasse.*
Museum of Military History (*see* Off the Beaten Track). *Subway stop: Süd-Tiroler-Platz.*
Museum of Modern Art (*see* Tour 4). *Subway stop: Rossauer-Lände.*
Museum of Natural History (*see* Tour 4). *Subway stop: Volkstheater.*
Museum of Viennese History (*see* Tour 6). *Subway stop: Karlsplatz.*

Secession Building (*see* Tour 6). *Subway stop: Karlsplatz.*

In addition to the above, which are mentioned in the walking tours, Vienna possesses an astonishing array of little specialty museums, some of which are free, most of which have small admission fees.

Bell Museum. Troststr. 38, tel. 0222/604–3460. Open Wed. 2–5. *Subway stop: Reumannplatz.*

Circus and Clown Museum. Karmelitergasse 9, tel. 0222/21106–229. Open Wed. 5:30–7 PM, Sat. 2:30–5 PM, Sun. 10–noon. *Subway stop: Schwedenplatz.*

Doll and Toy Museum. Schulhof 4, tel. 0222/535–6860. Admission: AS60 adults, AS30 children. Open Tues.–Sun. 10–6. *Subway stop: Stephansplatz.*

Esperanto Museum. Hofburg (Michaelerplatz entrance), tel. 0222/535–5145. Open Mon., Wed., Fri. 9–3:30. *Subway stop: Herrengasse.*

Film Museum. Augustinerstr. 1, tel. 0222/533–7054. Film showings Oct.–May, Mon.–Sat. 6 and 8 PM. *Subway stop: Karlsplatz.*

Firefighting Museum. Am Hof 10, tel. 0222/53199. Open Sat. 10–noon, Sun. 9–noon. *Subway stop: Herrengasse.*

Folk Art Museum. Laudongasse 15–19, tel. 0222/438905. Closed for renovation. *Subway stop: Rathaus.*

Folk Art Museum (Religious). Johannesgasse 8, tel. 0222/512–1337. Open Wed. 9–4, Sun. 9–1. *Subway stop: Stephansplatz.*

Football (Soccer) Museum. Meiereistr. (in the Praterstadium), tel. 0222/21718. Open Mon., Fri. 10–1, Tues., Thurs. 2–6. Closed July–mid-Aug. *Subway stop: Praterstern, then streetcar 21.*

Glass Museum. Kärntner Str. 26 (Lobmeyr Store), tel. 0222/512–0508. Open weekdays 10–6, Sat. 10–1. *Subway stop: Stephansplatz.*

Globe Museum. Josefsplatz (National Library, 3rd floor), tel. 0222/53410–297. Open Mon.–Wed., Fri. 11–noon; Thurs. 2–3 PM. *Subway stop: Herrengasse.*

Heating Technology Museum. Längenfeldgasse 13–15 (Berufschule), tel. 0222/4000–93231 or 0222/4000–93319. Open Tues. 1–6 PM. *Subway stop: Längenfeldgasse.*

Horsedrawn Cab Museum. Veronikagasse 12, tel. 0222/432607. Open first Wed. of every month 10–noon. *Subway stop: Josefstädter Strasse.*

Horseshoeing, Harnessing and Saddling Museum. Linke Bahngasse 11, tel. 0222/71155–372. Open Mon.–Thurs. 1:30–3:30 PM by arrangement. *Subway stop: Rochusgasse.*

Medical History Museum. Währinger Str. 25/1 (in the Josephinum), tel. 0222/432154. Open weekdays 9–3. *Subway stop: Schottentor.*

Pathological Anatomy Museum. Spitalgasse 2 (in the Allgemeines Krankenhaus), tel. 0222/438672. Open Thurs. 8–11 AM, first Sat. each month 11–2; closed Aug. *Subway stop: Schottentor.*

Period Furniture Museum. Mariahilfer Str. 88, tel. 0222/934240. Open Tues.–Fri. 9–4, Sat. 9–noon. *Subway stop: Mariahilfer Strasse.*

Postal and Telegraph Services Museum. Mariahilfer Str. 212, tel. 0222/89101. Open Sun.–Fri. 9–4:30. *Subway stop: Schönbrunn.*

Railway Museum. Mariahilfer Str. 212, tel. 0222/89101. Open Sun.–Fri. 9–4:30. *Subway stop: Schönbrunn.*

Streetcar Museum. Erdbergstr. 109, tel. 0222/587–3186. Open May 7–Oct. 7, weekends and holidays 9–4. *Subway stop: Schlachthausgasse.*

Technology Museum. Mariahilfer Str. 212, tel. 0222/89101. Open Sun.–Fri. 9–4:30. *Subway stop: Schönbrunn.*

Theater Museum. Lobkowitzplatz 2, tel. 0222/512–3705. *Subway stop: Stephansplatz.*

Tobacco Museum (smoking allowed). Mariahilfer Str. 2 (Messepalast), tel. 0222/961716. Open Tues. 10–7; Wed.–Fri. 10–3; weekends 9–1. *Subway stop: Mariahilfer Strasse.*

Treasury of the Order of Teutonic Knights. Singerstr. 7, tel. 0222/512–1065–6. Open Mon., Thurs., Sat., Sun. 10–noon, Wed., Fri., Sat. 3–5; Closed Sun. Nov.–Apr. *Subway stop: Stephansplatz.*

Undertaker's Museum. Goldeggasse 19, tel. 0222/50195–227. Open weekdays noon–3 by prior arrangement only. *Subway stop: Südtiroler-Platz.*

Viticultural Museum. Döblinger Hauptstr. 96, tel. 0222/361–0042. Open Sat. 3:30–6 PM, Sun. 10–noon. *Subway stop: Heiligenstadt.*

Churches and Temples

Am Steinhof Kirche (*see* Off the Beaten Track). *Subway stop: Unter St. Veit, then No. 47A bus to Psychiatrisches Krankenhaus.*

Annakirche (*see* Tour 5). *Subway stop: Stephansplatz.*

Augustinerkirche (Hofburg; *see* Tour 4). *Subway stop: Herrengasse.*

Dominikanerkirche (*see* Tour 1). *Subway stop: Stephansplatz.*

Franziskanerkirche (*see* Tour 5). *Subway stop: Stephansplatz.*

Jesuitenkirche (*see* Tour 1). *Subway stop: Stephansplatz.*

Karlskirche (*see* Tour 6). *Subway stop: Karlsplatz.*

Kirche Am Hof (*see* Tour 2). *Subway stop: Stephansplatz.*

Maria am Gestade (*see* Tour 1). *Subway stop: Stephansplatz.*

Michaelerkirche (*see* Tour 3). *Subway stop: Herrengasse.*

Minoritenkirche (*see* Tour 2). *Subway stop: Herrengasse.*

Peterskirche (*see* Tour 3). *Subway stop: Stephansplatz.*

Ruprechtskirche (*see* Tour 1). *Subway stop: Schwedenplatz.*

Schottenhof (*see* Tour 2). *Subway stop: Schottentor.*

St. Stephen's Cathedral (*see* Tour 1). *Subway stop: Stephansplatz.*

Synagogue (*see* Tour 1). *Subway stop: Schwedenplatz.*

Votivkirche (*see* Tour 4). *Subway stop: Schottentor.*

Parks and Gardens

Burggarten (*see* Vienna for Free). *Subway stop: Mariahilfer Strasse.*

Prater In 1766, to the dismay of the aristocracy, the emperor Joseph II decreed that the vast expanse of imperial parklands known as the Prater would henceforth be open to the public. East of the inner city between the Danube Canal and the Danube proper, the Prater is a public park to this day, notable for its long promenade (the Hauptallee, over 3 miles in length), its sports facilities (a golf course, a stadium, a race track, and a swimming pool, for starters), and the Wurstelprater. *Subway stop: Praterstern.*

Schönbrunn Gardens (*see* Tour 7). *Subway stop: Schönbrunn.*

Stadtpark (*see* Vienna for Free). *Subway stop: Stadtpark.*

Volksgarten (*see* Tour 4). *Subway stop: Lerchenfelder Strasse.*
Wurstelprater (*see* What to See and Do with Children). *Subway stop: Praterstern.*

Other Places of Interest

Aquarium (*see* What to See and Do with Children). *Subway stop: Kettenbrückengasse.*
Central Cemetery (*see* Off the Beaten Track). *Subway stop: Karlsplatz.*
Danube Tower: In the middle of the Danube Park (a reclaimed garbage dump), 827 feet high with two revolving restaurants and fine views. Tel. 0222/235368. *Subway stop: Kaisermühlen.*
Flea Market: Held on Saturday (except public holidays), just south of the Naschmarkt on Linke Wienzeile. *Subway stop: Kettenbrückengasse.*
Naschmarkt (*see* Tour 6). *Subway stop: Karlsplatz.*
Roman ruins (Hoher Markt, Tour 1). *Subway stop: Stephansplatz.*
Vienna Zoo (Schönbrunn gardens; *see* Tour 7). *Subway stop: Hietzing.*

Shopping

Shopping Districts The **Kärntner Strasse, Graben,** and **Kohlmarkt** pedestrian areas claim to have the best shops in Vienna, and for some items, such as jewelry, some of the best anywhere, although you must expect high prices. The side streets within this area have developed their own character, with shops offering antiques, art, clocks, jewelry, and period furniture. Outside the center, concentrations of stores are on the **Mariahilfer Strasse** straddling the Sixth and Seventh districts; the **Landstrasser Hauptstrasse** in the Third District; and, still farther out, the **Favoritenstrasse** in the 10th District.

A collection of attractive small boutiques has sprung up in the **Sonnhof** passage between Landstrasser Hauptstrasse 28 and Ungargasse 13 in the Third District. The **Spittelberg** market, on the Spittelberggasse between Burggasse and Siebensterngasse in the Seventh District, has drawn small galleries and handicrafts shops and is particularly popular in the weeks before Christmas. That is the time also for the tinselly **Christkindlmarkt** on Rathausplatz in front of city hall; in protest over its commercialization, smaller markets specializing in handicrafts have sprung up on such traditional spots as Am Hof (First District).

Vienna's **Naschmarkt** (between Linke and Rechte Wienzeile, starting at Getreidemarkt) is one of Europe's great and most colorful food and produce markets. Stalls open at 5 or 6 AM, and the pace is lively until 1 or 2 PM. Saturday is the big day, when farmers come into the city to sell at the back end of the market. It's closed Sunday.

Department Stores The department stores are concentrated in the Mariahilfer Strasse. By far the best is **Herzmansky** (Mariahilfer Str. 26–30, tel. 0222/931–6360), definitely upmarket; outstanding gourmet shops and restaurants are in the basement. Farther up the street you will find slightly cheaper goods at **Gerngross** (Mariahilfer Str. and Kirchengasse, tel. 0222/932–5250) and **Stafa** (Mariahilfer Str. 120, tel. 0222/938621).

Flea Markets Every Saturday (except holidays) rain or shine, from about 7:30 AM to 5 or 6, the **Flohmarkt** in back of the Naschmarkt, stretching along the Linke Wienzeile from the Kettenbrücken subway station, offers a staggering collection of stuff ranging from serious antiques to plain junk. Haggle over prices.

Saturday and Sunday in summer from 2 to about 7:30 PM an outdoor **Art and Antiques** market takes place along the Danube Canal, stretching from the Schwedenbrücke to beyond the Salztorbrücke. Lots of books are sold, some in English, plus generally better goods than at the Saturday flea market. Bargain over prices all the same.

Auctions The **Dorotheum** (Dorotheergasse 17, tel. 0222/515600) is a state institution dating to 1707, when Emperor Josef I determined that he didn't want his people being taken advantage of by pawnbrokers. The place is intriguing, with goods ranging from furs to furniture auctioned almost daily. The special sections for fine art and postage stamps (at Dorotheergasse 11) are worth a visit just to look. Information on how to bid is available in English.

Specialty Stores You will find the best antiques shops located in the First District, many clustered close to the Dorotheum auction house, in
Antiques the **Dorotheergasse, Stallburggasse, Plankengasse,** and **Spiegelgasse.** And you'll also find interesting shops in the **Josefstadt** (Eighth) district, with prices considerably lower than those in the center of town. Wander up Florianigasse and back down the Josefstädter Strasse, not overlooking the narrow side streets.

D & S (Plankengasse 6, tel. 0222/512–2972) specializes in old Viennese clocks. Look in at **Galerie Kovacek** (Stallburg 2, tel. 0222/512–9954) to see a remarkable collection of glass paperweights and other glass objects; you'll also find paintings and furniture here. **Peter Feldbacher** (Annagasse 6, tel. 0222/512–2408) has items ranging from glass to ceramics to furniture. For art deco, look to **Galerie Metropol** (Dortheergasse 12, tel. 0222/513–2208) or **Galerie bei der Albertina** (Lobkowitzplatz 1, tel. 0222/513–1416).

Books Several good stores with books in English as well are on the Graben and Kärntner Strasse in the First District. For bookstores specializing in English-language books, *see* Important Addresses and Numbers, above.

Men's Clothing Clothing in Vienna is far from cheap but usually of better quality for the money than in the United States. The best shops are in the First District.

Sir Anthony (Kärntner Str. 21–23, tel. 0222/512–6835).
E. Braun (Graben 8, tel. 0222/512–5505).
House of Gentlemen (Kohlmarkt 12, tel. 0222/533–3258).
ITA (Graben 18, tel. 0222/533–6004).
Malowan (Opernring 23, tel. 0222/587–6296).
Silbernagel (Kärntner Str. 15, tel. 0222/512–5312).
Teller (Landstrasser Hauptstr. 88–90, tel. 0222/712–6397) for particularly good value.
Venturini (Spiegelgasse 9, tel. 0222/512–8845) for custom-made shirts.

For men's *Trachten,* or typical Austrian clothing, including lederhosen, try **Loden-Plankl** (Michaelerplatz 6, tel. 0222/533–8032), and go to **Collins Hüte** (Opernpassage, tel. 0222/587–1305) to get the appropriate hat.

A. E. Köchert, **36**
A. Heldwein, **12**
Albin Denk, **13**
Adlmüller, **49**
Arcadia, **56**
Art and Antiques Market, **3**
Augarten, **17**
Bakalowits, **18**
Berger, **33**
Berta Smejkal, **61**
Burgenland, **60**
Carius & Binder, **37**
Carola, **58**
da Caruso, **53**
Collins Hüte, **62**
Columbia, **48**
D & S, **32**
Dorotheum, **41**
E. Braun, **15**
Elfi Müller, **59**
Flohmarkt/Naschmarkt, **66**
Flamm, **31**
Galerie bei der Albertina, **46**
Galerie Kovacek, **26**
Galerie Metropol, **23**
Gerngross, **64**
Haban, **19**
Havlicek, **11**
Hemerle, **51**
Herzmansky, **63**
House of Gentlemen, **10**
Humanic, **57**
ITA, **6**
Kunz, **39**
Lanz, **30**
Liska, **5, 25**
Lobmeyr, **47**
Loden-Plankl, **14**
Maldone, **4, 21, 44**
Malowan, **55**
Niederösterreichisches Heimatwerk, **7**
Nigst, **43**
Österreichische Werkstätten, **24**
Pawlata, **38**
Peter Feldbacher, **50**
Plessgott, **29**
Popp & Kretschmer, **54**
Rasper & Söhne, **9**
Resi Hammerer, **45**
Rosenthal, **40**
Schullin, **8**
Silbernagel, **34**
Sir Anthony, **42**

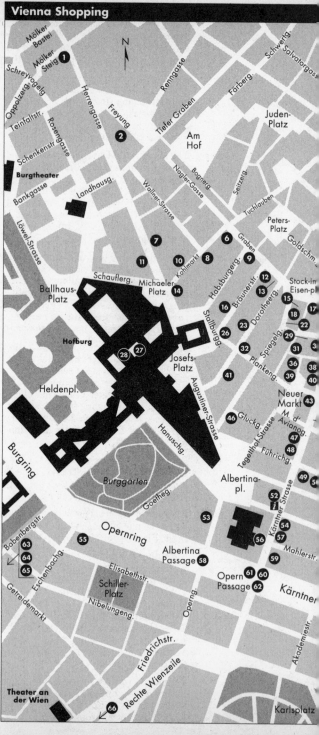

Vienna Shopping

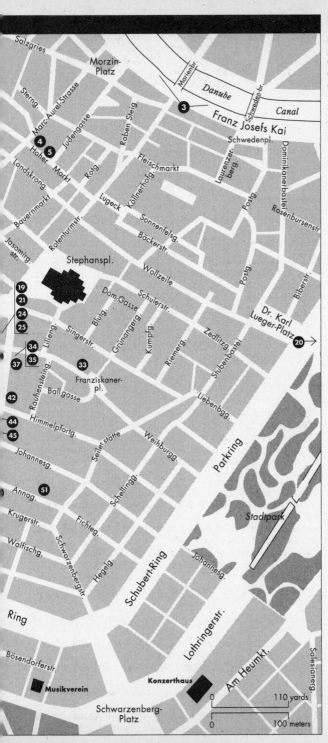

Women's Clothing The couturier to Vienna is **Adlmüller** (Kärntner Str. 41, tel. 0222/512–6661). Check also **Flamm** (Neuer Markt 12, tel. 0222/512–2889, **Braun, ITA,** or **Malowan** (*see* Men's Clothing, above). You'll find modern young styling at **Maldone** (Kärntner Str. 4, tel. 0222/512–2761; Kärntner Str. 12, tel. 0222/512–2234; Graben 29, tel. 0222/533–6091; and Hoher Markt 8, tel. 0222/533–2555).

Check out the selection of dirndls and women's *Trachten*, the typical Austrian costume with white blouse, print skirt, and apron, at **Lanz** (Kärntner Str. 10, tel. 0222/512–2456), **Niederösterreichisches Heimatwerk** (Herrengasse 6–8, tel. 0222/533–3495), **Resi Hammerer** (Kärntner Str. 29–31, tel. 0222/512–6952), and **Tostmann** (Schottengasse 3a, tel. 0222/533–5331). (*See* also **Loden-Plankl** under Men's Clothing, above.)

The best shop for furs is **Liska** (Kärntner Str. 8, tel. 0222/512–4120; Hoher Markt 8, tel. 0222/533–2211). Be sure to arrange to get the value-added tax (VAT) returned on your purchase.

Ceramics and Porcelain Ceramics are anything but dull at **Berger** (Weihburggasse 17, tel. 0222/512–1434); the more standard patterns of Gmunden ceramics are at **Pawlata** (Kärntner Str. 14, tel. 0222/512–1764) and around the corner at **Plessgott** (Kärntnerdurchgang, tel. 0222/512–5824). Check out Viennese porcelain patterns at **Augarten** (Graben/Stock-im-Eisen-Platz 3, tel. 0222/512–1494) and **Albin Denk** (Graben 13, tel. 0222/512–4439), **Rosenthal** (Kärntner Str. 16, tel. 0222/512–3994), and **Wahliss** (Kärntner Str. 17, tel. 0222/512–3856).

Crystal and Glass Select famous Vienna glassware at **Bakalowits** (Spiegelgasse 3, tel. 0222/512–6351) and **Lobmeyr** (Kärntner Str. 26, tel. 0222/512–0508), which also has a small museum of its creations upstairs; the firm supplied the crystal chandeliers for the Metropolitan Opera in New York City, a gift from Austria. **Tabletop** (Passage, Freyung 2, tel. 0222/535–4256) has the exquisite Riedl glass (though readers have reported that goods were never received), as does **Rasper & Söhne** (Graben 15, tel. 0222/534330).

Gift Items **Österreichische Werkstätten** (Kärntner Str. 6, tel. 0222/512–2418) offers handmade handicrafts, gifts, and souvenirs ranging from jewelry to textiles.
Souvenir in der Hofburg (Hofburgpassage 1 and 7, tel. 0222/533–5053) is another source of gifts.
Niederösterreichisches Heimatwerk (*see* Women's Clothing, above) has handmade folk objects and textiles.
Elfi Müller (Kärntner Str. 53, tel. 0222/512–6996) has a nice selection, but problems have been reported when goods were shipped.

Jewelry **Carius & Binder** (Kärntner Str. 17, tel. 0222/512–6750) is good for watches.
Haban (Kärntner Str. 2, tel. 0222/512–6730; Graben 12, tel. 0222/512–1220), has a fine selection of watches and jewelry.
A. Heldwein (Graben 13, tel. 0222/512–5781) sells elegant jewelry, silverware, and watches.
A. E. Köchert (Neuer Markt 15, tel. 0222/512–5828) has original creations.
Kunz (Neuer Markt 13, tel. 0222/512–7112) sells stunning modern pieces for men and women.

Schullin (Kohlmarkt 7, tel. 0222/533–9007) is known for some of the most original work to be found anywhere.

Jade Discover interesting pieces of Austrian jade at **Burgenland** (Opernpassage, tel. 0222/587–6266).

Needlework For Vienna's famous petit-point, head for **Berta Smejkal** (in the Opernpassage, tel. 0222/587–2102) or **Stransky** (Hofburgpassage 2, tel. 0222/533–6098).

Records Look for records and tapes at **Arcadia** (Kärntner Str. 40, in the Staatsoper Passage, tel. 0222/513–9568), which also features books and music-related souvenirs.

Carola is best for pop LPs and CDs (Albertinapassage, by the Opera, tel. 0222/564114).
Columbia (Kärntner Str. 30, tel. 0222/512–3675) and **da Caruso** (Operngasse 4, tel. 0222/513–1326) specialize in classics, with an emphasis on opera.
Havlicek (Herrengasse 5, tel. 0222/533–1964) features classics and is particularly knowledgeable and helpful.

Shoes and Leather Goods Try **Humanic** (Kärntner Str. 51, tel. 0222/512–5892 or Singerstr. 2, tel. 0222/512–9101). For exclusive styles, go to **Zak** (Kärntner Str. 36, tel. 0222/512–7257), **Popp & Kretschmer** (Kärntner Str. 51, tel. 0222/512–7801), and **Nigst** (Neuer Markt 4, tel. 0222/512–4303).

Wrought Iron *Weinhebers* (wine dispensers with pear-shape glass containers) and other iron items can be found at **Hemerle** (Annagasse 7, tel. 0222/512–4746) or **Zach** (Bräunerstr. 8, tel. 0222/533–9939).

Sports and Fitness

Participant Sports

Bicycling Vienna has more than 300 km (nearly 190 mi) of cycling paths, including specially marked routes through the center of the city; look for the special pathways either in red brick or marked with a stylized cyclist in yellow. Note and observe the special traffic signals at some intersections. Excellent paved cycling trails run along the Danube, the Danube Canal, and through the *Donauinsel*, the artificial island on the north bank of the Danube. You can take a bike on the subway (except during rush hours) for half fare, but only in cars with a blue shield on the door, and only on stairs or elevators with the "bike" shield, not the escalators. At most bookstores you can purchase a cycling map of Vienna put out by ARGUS (Frankenberggasse 11, tel. 0222/505–8435). You can rent a bike for about AS30 per hour, leaving your passport or other identification as a deposit. Pick up a bike at **Cooperative Fahrrad** from April to mid-October (Franz-Josefskai at Salztorbrücke, by the canal, tel. 0222/460–6072); at **Radverleih Hochschaubahn,** mid-March through October (in the Prater amusement park, by the Hochschaubahn, bear slightly right after you pass the Big Wheel, tel. 0222/260165); at **Radverleih Praterstern,** April–October (on the street level under Praterstern North rail station, tel. 0222/268557); or at **Fahrradstadl Semmering,** March–November (Ravelinstr., under the railroad bridge, tel. 0222/748859).

Boating Both the **Alte Donau** (Old Danube), a series of lakes to the north of the main stream, and the **Neue Donau,** on the north side of the Donauinsel (the artificial island in the river), offer good waters for paddleboats, rowboats, kayaks, sailboats, and windsurfing. The Danube itself is somewhat fast-moving for anything but kayaks. Rent boats from **Auzinger Boote** (Laberlweg 22, tel. 0222/235788), **Karl Hofbauer** (Obere Alte Donau 186, tel. 0222/236733), **Eppel** (Wagramer Str. 48, tel. 0222/235168), **Irzl** (Florian Berndl-Gasse 33 and 34, tel. 0222/236743), and **Newrkla** (An der Obere Alte Donau, tel. 0222/366105). For details about sailing and sailing events, check with **Haus des Sports** (Prinz-Eugen-Str. 12, tel. 0222/505–3742).

Golf The one in-town golf course is at **Freudenau** in the Prater (tel. 0222/218–9564). But the 18-hole par-70 course is so popular from April to November, even with the AS450 fee, that you'll probably need to be invited or have an introduction from a member to play. The alternative is **Föhrenwald,** an 18-hole par-72 course about 43 km (27 mi) away, at Wiener Neustadt (tel. 02622/27438 or 02622/29171), but this, too, is generally overbooked. Weekdays, of course, will be best for either course.

Health and Fitness Clubs Try **Gym and Art** (in Kursalon, Johannesgasse 33, tel. 0222/757775), **Fitness Center Harris** (Niebelungengasse 7, tel. 0222/587–3710, and in the Plaza Hotel, Schottenring 11, tel. 0222/31390–640), or **Zimmermann Fitness** (Linke Bahngasse 9, tel. 0222/753212; Kaiserstr. 43, tel. 0222/528–2000; and Kreuzgasse 18, tel. 0222/434625, women only).

Hiking The city has eight *Stadt-Wander-Wege*, marked routes whose starting points are reachable from a streetcar stop. Get route maps and information at the information office in City Hall (Friedrich Schmidt-Platz, tel. 0222/4000–2938). You can easily strike out on your own, city map in hand, taking a route through the vineyards up and around Kahlenberg/Leopoldsberg, starting either from the end station of the No. 38 streetcar (Grinzing) or from the Kahlenberg stop of the No. 38A bus and heading back down to Nussdorf (streetcar D). Another possibility is to wander the Lainzer Tiergarten, an enormous nature preserve with deer, wild boar, and other fauna within the city; reach it via the No. 60 streetcar from Kennedybrücke/Hietzing on the U4 subway, then the No. 60B bus.

Ice Skating The **Wiener Eislaufverein** (Lothringer Str. 22, behind the InterContinental Hotel, tel. 0222/713–6353) has public outdoor skating with skate rentals, October through March. Weekends are crowded. For indoor skating, check the **Donaupark-Eishalle** (Wagramerstr. 1; U1 subway to Kaisermühlen, tel. 0222/234596).

Jogging Jogging paths run alongside the Danube Canal, and runners also frequent the Stadtpark and the tree-lined route along the Ring, particularly the Parkring stretch. Farther afield, in the Second District, the Prater Hauptallee, from Praterstern to the Lusthaus, is a favorite.

Riding Splendid bridle paths crisscross the Prater park. To hire a mount, contact the **Reitclub Donauhof** (Hafenzufahrtstr. 63, tel. 0222/218–3646 or 0222/218–9716).

Skiing Nearby slopes such as **Hohe Wand** (take No. 49B bus from the Hütteldorf stop of the U4 subway), west of the city in the 14th District offer limited skiing, with a ski lift and man-made snow when the heavens refuse, but serious Viennese skiers (that includes nearly everybody) will head out to nearby Niederösterreich (Lower Austria), with the area around the **Semmering** (about an hour from the city) one of the favorite locations for a quick outing. You can take a train or bus to get there.

Swimming Vienna has at least one pool for every one of the 23 districts; most are indoor pools, but some locations have an outdoor pool as well. If you prefer a less formal environment, head for the swimming areas of the **Alte Donau** or the **Donauinsel**. The pools and the Alte Donau (paid admission) will be filled on hot summer weekends, so the informal Donauinsel can be a surer bet. Some beach areas are shallow and suitable for children, but the Donauinsel has no lifeguards, though there are rescue stations for emergencies. Changing areas are few, lockers nonexistent, so don't take valuables. And don't be tempted to jump into the Danube Canal; the water is definitely not for swimming, nor is the Danube itself, because of heavy undertows and a powerful current.

The city has information on all places to swim; contact City Hall (Rathaus, Friedrich Schmidt-Platz, tel. 0222/40005). Ask for directions on reaching the following:

Donauinsel Nord: a huge recreation area with a children's section and nude bathing.

Donauinsel Süd: good swimming and boating and a nude bathing area. Harder to get to and less crowded than other areas, but food facilities are limited.

Gänsehäufel: a bathing island in the Alte Donau (tel. 0222/235392), with lockers, changing rooms, children's wading pools, topless and nude areas, and restaurants; likely to be full by 11 AM or earlier.

Krapfenwaldbad: an outdoor pool tucked among the trees on the edge of the Vienna Woods (tel. 0222/321501). Full of Vienna's beautiful people, topless females, and singles. But get there early on sunny Sundays or you won't get in.

Stadionbad: a huge sports complex, popular with the younger crowd; go early. There is no direct transportation; take the No. 80B bus from Stadionbrücke in the Third District to the "Hauptallee" stop, or for the fun of it as well, ride the miniature railway (*Liliputbahn*) from behind the big wheel in the Prater amusement park to the "Stadion" station and walk the rest of the way (Prater, Marathonweg, tel. 0222/262102).

Tennis Though Vienna has plenty of courts close to wherever you'll be, they'll be booked solid. Try anyway; your hotel may have good connections, but you'll have to book at least a few days in advance. **Sportservice Wien-Sport** (Bacherplatz 14, tel. 0222/543131) operates a central court-booking service (100 courts in summer, four halls in winter) and **Vereinigte Tennisanlagen** (Prater Hauptallee, tel. 0222/218–1811) has courts in other locations as well. Or you can try **Tennisplätze Arsenal** (58 sand courts; Arsenalstr. 1, by the Südbahnhof, tel. 0222/782132; Faradaygasse 4, tel. 0222/787265; Gudrunstr. 31, tel. 0222/621521), **Tennisplätze Stadionbad** (Prater Hauptallee, tel. 0222/248261), or **Wiener Eislaufverein** (Lothringer Str. 22, behind the InterContinental Hotel, tel. 0222/713–6353).

Spectator Sports

Football (Soccer) Matches are played mainly in the **Vienna Stadium** in the Prater (Meiereistr., tel. 0222/218–0854) and the **West Stadium** (Keisslergasse 6, tel. 0222/945519). Indoor soccer takes place in the **Stadthalle** (Vogelweidplatz 14, tel. 0222/95490). **Cosmos** (Karntner Ring 15, A-1010, tel. 0222/51533). **Vienna Ticket Service** (Postfach 160, A-1060, tel. 0222/587–9843), tickets must be ordered a month in advance. **Kartenbüro Flamm** (Kärntner Ring 3, A-1010, tel 0222/512–4225). Tickets can usually be bought at the gate, but the better seats are available through ticket agencies.

Horse Racing The race track (both flat and sulky racing) is in the Prater (Trabbrennplatz, tel. 0222/218–9535), and the season runs April–November. The highlight is the Derby, which takes place the third Sunday in June.

Tennis Professional matches are played either in the Prater or in the Stadthalle (*see* above). Ticket agencies will have details.

Dining

In recent years Vienna, once a culinary backwater, has produced a new generation of chefs willing to slaughter sacred cows and create a New Vienna Cuisine. The movement is well past the "less is more" stage that nouvelle cuisine traditionally demands (and to which most Viennese vociferously objected), relying now on lighter versions of the old standbys and clever combinations of such traditional ingredients as liver pâtés and sour cream.

In a first-class restaurant you will pay as much as in most other Western European capitals. But you can still find good food at refreshingly low prices in the simpler restaurants, particularly at neighborhood *Gasthäuser* in the suburbs. If you eat your main meal at noon (as the Viennese do), you can take advantage of the luncheon specials.

Many restaurants are closed one or two days a week (often Saturday and Sunday), and most serve meals only 11:30–2:30 and 6–10. An increasing number now serve after-theater dinners, but reserve in advance. *Wien wie es isst* (in German; from almost any bookstore) gives up-to-date information on the restaurant, café, and bar scene.

Vienna's restaurant fare ranges from Arabic to Yugoslav, but assuming you've come for what makes Vienna unique, our listings focus not on the exotic but on places where you'll meet the Viennese and experience Vienna. Highly recommended restaurants are indicated by a star ★.

Category	Cost*
Very Expensive	over AS500
Expensive	AS300–AS500
Moderate	AS150–AS300
Inexpensive	under AS150

*per person, excluding drinks but including service (usually 10%) and sales tax (10%)

Very Expensive

★ **Korso.** Vienna's top restaurant, in the Bristol Hotel, surrounds you with subdued dark-paneled and gold elegance; tables are set with fine linen, glassware, and silver. The food matches the setting; chef Reinhard Gerer is one of Austria's great creative cooks. Try such specialties as scallops in white tomato butter or *Rehnüsschen*, tiny venison fillets. Ask sommelier Leopold Doppler to recommend an appropriate wine. *Mahlerstr. 2, tel. 0222/515–16–546. Reservations required. Jacket and tie required. AE, DC, MC, V. Closed Sat. lunch.*

★ **Palais Schwarzenberg.** This restaurant, in a former private palace, has one of the most impressive settings in Vienna, but be sure to book a table on the glassed-in terrace. You'll be surrounded inside by greenery, with a view out over the formal gardens. The food is a notch or two below Korso's (above), but still extremely good. The service may lag if the restaurant is full, so be prepared to relax and enjoy the setting. You can't go wrong with the fillet of beef in red wine sauce or the delicate pike. The wine list is excellent but the prices exaggerated; the house wines are a fully acceptable substitute. *Schwarzenbergplatz 9, tel. 0222/784515. Reservations required. Jacket and tie required. AE, DC, MC, V.*

★ **Rotisserie Prinz Eugen.** The setting, in the Hilton Hotel, is resplendent with dark woods, crystal and silver place-settings, and fresh flower arrangements on the tables. Chef Eduard Mitsche, who produces some of the finest food in town, is a master of the delicate touch, even with such dishes as *Kaninchenragout* (rabbit stew). Sample the roast young lamb with thyme or the exquisite scallops in orange sauce. The wine list is extensive, with excellent Austrian varieties as well as imports. *Am Stadtpark, tel. 0222/717–000–355. Reservations required. Jacket and tie required. AE, DC, MC, V. Closed Sat. and Sun. lunch.*

Steirer Eck. Some argue that this is Austria's top restaurant; others say it is overpriced. In any case, you can dine handsomely in classical elegance, among businesspeople at noon, amid politicians and personalities at night. Tables are set with flower arrangements and elegant crystal, with a flair that matches the food. Chef Helmut Österreicher is a genius at combining ideas and tastes; artichoke with lobster is a successful example, rack of wild boar with tiny sausages, another. The house wine list is overwhelming; you can ask for advice with the assurance that it will be good. *Rasumofskygasse 2, tel. 0222/713–3168. Reservations required. Jacket and tie required. AE. Closed weekends.*

Vier Jahreszeiten. The InterContinental's restaurant is an excellent if conservative choice for both the ample noontime buffet and evening dining. The atmosphere is elegant without being overdone. Service, too, is attentive but discreet, the wine list impressive but not overwhelming. The delicate roast lamb is consistently delicious; so is the fillet of beef with raw mushrooms. For dessert, ask for a *Mohr im Hemd*, literally, a moor in a shirt, a chocolate sponge-cake confection with chocolate sauce and whipped cream. *Johannesgasse 28, tel. 0222/ 71122–143. Reservations advised. Jacket and tie required. AE, DC, MC, V.*

Zu den Drei Husaren. The Three Hussars was for years Vienna's gourmet temple; like a culinary Dorian Gray, the house remains embalmed in its draped red velvet and gold. If you don't mind the heavy hand (which occasionally carries over to the

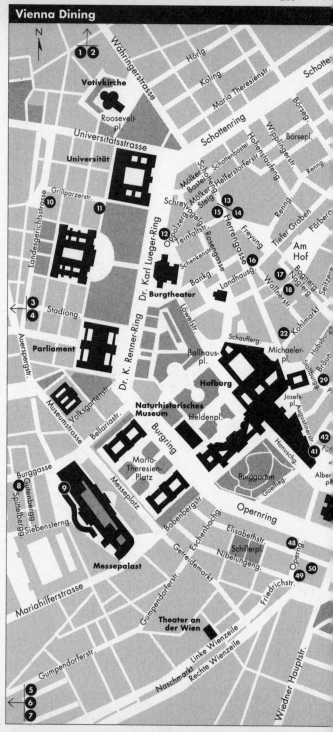

Vienna Dining

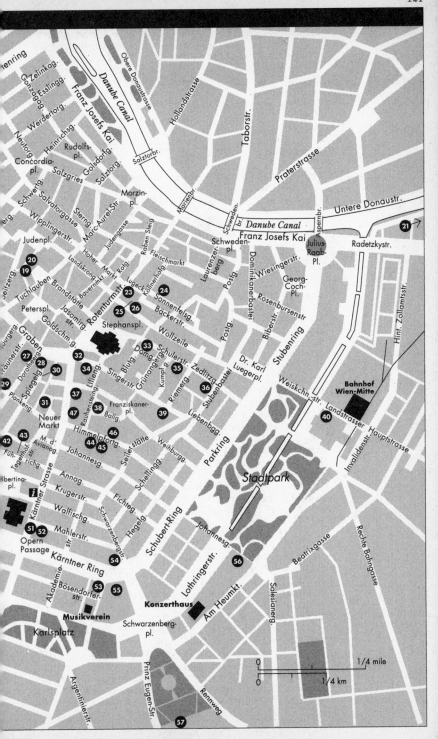

food and service), you may enjoy this touch of "old" Vienna, evening piano music included. Celebrities still celebrate evenings here, lunchtime is for business, and both are for tourists. Beware the enticing but unpriced hors d'oeuvre trolley; a single dip here can double your bill. The Husaren does best with standards: *Leberknödelsuppe* (liver-dumpling soup), Wiener schnitzel, roast beef, and the like. *Weihburggasse 4, tel. 0222/ 512–1092. Reservations advised at lunch, required in the evening. Jacket and tie required. AE, DC, MC, V. Closed mid-July–mid-Aug.*

Expensive

Hauswirth. Following a change in management and chefs, Hauswirth is struggling with some success to defend its former excellent reputation. The turn-of-the-century ambience remains friendly without being overbearing. Emphasis is now more toward basic Viennese cuisine, although some of the offerings—such as chicken liver parfait, bacon of wild boar, and guinea hen in morel sauce—are exotic and tasty. Ample open wines are available as accompaniment. *Otto-Bauer-Gasse 20, tel. 0222/587–1261. Reservations recommended. Closed weekends.*

★ **Imperial Café.** In the Imperial Hotel, the café is much more than just a (very good) meeting spot for coffee or *Torte;* both lunch and after-concert supper are popular and reasonably priced. The rooms are understated by local standards; crystal and velvet are evident but not overdone. The city's politicians, attorneys, and business types gather here for solid Viennese fare, selecting either from the choice daily specialties, which generally include a superb cream soup, or relying on such standards as *Leberknödelsuppe* and *Tafelspitz,* Viennese boiled beef. In summer, the terrace outside is pleasant but noisy. The wine list includes French and German selections, but many prefer an open wine by the glass. *Kärntner Ring 16, tel. 0222/ 501–10389. Reservations recommended. Jacket and tie advised. AE, DC, MC, V.*

König von Ungarn. In the hotel of the same name, the wood-paneled restaurant, with its comfortable atmosphere, is jammed at noon with businesspeople who come to deal and to sample the roast meats from the carvery trolley. When the relatively small space is packed, service can get lax. *Schulerstr. 10, tel. 0222/512–5319. Reservations required at lunch, advised in the evening. Jacket and tie advised. MC. Closed Sat.*

★ **Sirk.** This comfortable restaurant in traditional style is ideal for a light lunch or an evening snack. The sidewalk terrace is perfect for afternoon coffee and dessert, but for more privacy, take a table upstairs; those overlooking the Opera are best, but you'll have to fight Vienna's power brokers for one of them at noon. The daily menu is excellent value, or you might choose the rare roast beef with black-mushroom sauce. The post-opera menu is consistently good. *Kärntner Str. 53, tel. 0222/51516– 552. Reservations required at lunch, recommended at dinner. Jacket and tie advised. AE, DC, MC, V.*

★ **Steinerne Eule.** The Stone Owl, with its elegant but warm surroundings, is an outstanding choice for an evening out. Try the turbot in a saffron cream sauce or the breast of duck in honey-pepper sauce. Don't overlook the house-baked bread. *Halbgasse 30, tel. 0222/932250. Reservations required. Jacket and tie advised. MC. Closed Sun. and Mon.*

Zum Kuckuck. This intimate, wood-paneled restaurant, in a building many hundreds of years old, draws its clientele from the ministries in the neighborhood at noon. The kitchen does such variations on regional themes as fillet of pork Hungarian style (with a cabbage-tomato sauce) and fillet of venison in puff pastry. Try the outstanding whiskey-honey parfait for dessert. *Himmelpfortgasse 15, tel. 0222/512–8470. Reservations required. Jacket and tie advised. MC. Closed weekends.*

Moderate

Am Lugeck. At lunchtime you'll mingle with lawyers and businesspeople who appreciate the central location and the choice of Viennese food in an architecturally mixed but pleasant atmosphere. The modern grill-bar with a spiral stair is good for a quick snack; the great arched *Keller* rooms downstairs are more suited to a relaxed lunch or dinner. At the outdoor tables the generally good service tends to suffer. If you have the chance, choose any of the game dishes; the *Rehragout* (venison stew) is outstanding. The spareribs are more than ample. *Lugeck 7, tel. 0222/512–7979. Reservations advised. Jacket and tie advised; dress, outdoors: casual but neat. AE, DC, MC, V.*

Bastei Beisl. You'll find good basic Viennese cuisine in this unpretentious, friendly, pine-paneled restaurant. Try the *Zwiebelrostbraten*, a rump steak smothered in fried onions. The tables outside in summer add to the pleasure at noon or in the evening. *Stubenbastei 10, tel. 0222/512–4319. Reservations advised. Dress: casual but neat. AE, DC, MC. Closed Sun. and holidays; also Sat. during July and Aug.*

★ **Glacis-Beisl.** This restaurant, tucked beneath a section of the old city wall, is no longer the secret it once was, but the charm of the indoor rooms is still appealing, and its garden under grape arbors is unique. Alas, a proposed rebuilding of the Messepalast into a museum threatens the existence of this fascinating corner of Vienna. The menu is long; ask the waiter for help. You'll find most of the Viennese standards, but the place seems right for grilled chicken (*Brathendl*) and a mug of wine. *Messepalast (follow signs to the rear right corner), Messeplatz 1, tel. 0222/930–7374. Reservations required for the garden in summer. Dress: informal but neat. Closed Sat. lunch, Sun., and Jan.–Mar.*

Gösser Bierklinik. The rooms go on and on in this upstairs (more formal) and downstairs (preferred) complex that dates back four centuries. The fare is as solid as the house; you know the Wiener schnitzel here will be first class. The salad bar is new. And there's a menu in English. The beer, of course, is Austrian, from the Gösser brewery in Styria. You certainly may have wine if you prefer, although it is not in the same class with the beer. *Steindlgasse 4, tel. 0222/535–6897. Reservations advised, particularly at lunch. Jacket and tie advised upstairs; downstairs dress, casual but neat. AE, DC, MC, V. Closed Sun.*

★ **Gösser Brau.** This vast *Keller* with a (dummy) copper brewing vat is a noontime hangout of businesspeople from the city center who appreciate the good food and generally prompt service. Go for the game when it's available. *Rehrücken* (rack of venison) is a specialty. The appropriate accompaniment is Gösser beer, of course. *Elisabethstr. 3, tel. 0222/587–4750. Reserva-*

tions suggested at noon. Jacket and tie advised. AE, DC, MC, V.

★ **Martinkovits.** If you have time, head out to this typical "old Vienna" wine restaurant in the shadow of the Sievering vineyards, for grilled chicken of a quality and flavor you'll not soon forget. And the wines are excellent. The rooms inside are pleasant, but the garden is sheer delight. *Bellevuestr. 4, No. 39A bus from U2/U4 Heiligenstadt, Windhabergasse stop, tel. 0222/321546. Reservations advised on weekends. Dress: casual but neat. Closed Mon. and Tues. Closed Wed.–Fri. lunch. Check for winter closing months.*

★ **Ofenloch.** Unique for its turn-of-the-century ambience, this restaurant features waitresses in costume and the menu in miniature newspaper form. The fare is based on original recipes. A garlic fan will find the *Vanillerostbraten*, a rump steak prepared not with vanilla but with garlic, delicious. The misleading name came about because in early days, no one would admit to ordering anything with garlic. *Kurrentgasse 8, tel. 0222/533–8844. Reservations required. Jacket and tie advised. AE, MC, V.*

★ **Römischer Kaiser.** Spending a summer evening overlooking the Danube and part of the city in this idyllic garden setting under huge old trees is what Vienna is all about. Service is attentive, and you'll want to stay forever. The Beefsteak Tartare is excellent; if you don't like beef raw, choose one of the meats or fish from the outdoor charcoal grill. *Neustift am Walde 2, tel. 0222/441104. Reservations advised. Jacket suggested. MC, V. Closed Tues. and Wed.*

Stadtbeisl. The smallish dark-paneled rooms are packed at noon, as is the summer "garden" amid the ivy outside. Take the game in season, otherwise try one of the good Viennese standards. *Naglergasse 21, tel. 0222/533–3323. Reservations advised. Jacket advised inside, casual but neat outside. V.*

Zu den Drei Hacken. This is one of the last of the old *Gasthäuser* in the center of town; Schubert, among other luminaries of the past, is alleged to have dined here. You will find excellent Viennese fare, from schnitzel to Tafelspitz. The outdoor "garden" is attractive, but jammed in summer. *Singerstr. 28, tel. 0222/512–5895. Reservations advised. Dress: casual but neat. AE, DC, Closed Sat. evening, Sun.*

Zu ebener Erde und im ersten Stock. This gem of a historic house has an upstairs/downstairs combination: In the tiny room upstairs, done in old Vienna decor, the cuisine is adventurous, with such dishes as breast of duck with julienne zucchini and stuffed leg of hare, but you'll find old Viennese favorites as well. There's simpler (and cheaper) fare on the ground floor. *Burggasse 13, tel. 0222/936254. Reservations required. Jacket and tie required. AE, DC, V. Closed Sun. and Mon.*

Zum Laterndl. The atmosphere in the sidewalk "garden" is magical at night; the wood-paneled rooms inside comfortably carry the patina of the years. The food is good standard Viennese, with game in season. The venison is excellent; so, too, are the open wines. *Landesgerichstr. 12, tel. 0222/434358. Reservations advised. Dress: informal but neat. Closed weekends, holidays.*

Inexpensive

★ **Figlmüller.** If you'll accept the style of the house (you sit at a series of benches elbow-to-elbow with the other guests), this is *the* spot for Wiener schnitzel—one that overhangs the plate. (Waiters understand the doggie-bag principle.) Other choices are somewhat limited, and you'll have to take wine or mineral water with your meal because no beer or coffee is served. But Figlmüller is an experience you'll want to repeat. *Wollzeile 5, tel. 0222/512–6177. Reservations advised. Dress: casual but neat. No credit cards. Closed weekends.*

Gigerl. This charming and original wine restaurant offers a hot and cold buffet, specializing in vegetable and pasta dishes; try the macaroni salad or the *Schinkenfleckerl*, a baked noodle and ham dish. They go remarkably well with the light wines that the costumed waitresses keep pouring into your glass. In winter the rooms can get smoky and stuffy; in summer, the outside tables are delightful. *Rauhensteingasse 3/Blumenstockgasse 2, tel. 0222/513–4431. Reservations advised. Dress: casual but neat. AE, DC, MC, V. Evenings begin at 4 PM.*

★ **Göttweiger Stiftskeller.** In this traditional, basic restaurant, look for grilled and fried chicken, for schnitzel variants, tasty liver dishes such as Leberknödelsuppe, plus occasional surprises like oxtail soup. The food helps compensate for the rather unexciting rooms. The wines, on the other hand, are outstanding. *Spiegelgasse 9, tel. 0222/512–7817. Reservations not required. Dress: casual but neat. No credit cards. Closed weekends.*

★ **Gulaschmuseum.** The original idea behind this modern restaurant is literally dozens of tasty variants on the theme of goulash. They're just right for an in-between-meals snack, although most of the goulashes served are filling enough for a complete meal. *Schulerstr. 20, tel. 0222/512–1017. Reservations not required. Dress: casual but neat. AE.*

Naschmarkt. In this attractive cafeteria the food is good, of excellent value, and of far more variety than at the next-door McDonald's. Look for the daily specials on the blackboard. You'll also find good soups (chilled gazpacho on hot summer days), sandwiches, a salad bar, and a nonsmoking area. *Schwarzenbergplatz 16, tel. 0222/505–3115. Reservations not required. Dress: casual. No credit cards. Also at Schottengasse 1, tel. 0222/533–5186. Schottengasse is closed Sun. evening.*

Reinthaler. The atmosphere is thick enough to cut in this convenient "neighborhood" establishment, full of regulars. The fare is genuine Viennese: schnitzel, chicken, roast pork with *Knödel* (bread dumpling), and such. The ivy-fenced tables outside in summer are particularly popular. *Glückgasse 5, tel. 0222/512–3366. Reservations not required. Dress: casual. No credit cards. Closed Fri. evening and weekends.*

Stadtkeller. This self-service basement cafeteria offers good value in plain surroundings. The Wiener schnitzel is one of the cheapest in town, but you may fare better with the grilled chicken. *Singerstr. 6, tel. 0222/512–1269. Reservations not required. Dress: casual. No credit cards.*

★ **Trzesniewski.** "Unpronounceably good" is the (correct) motto of this tiny sandwich shop, a Viennese tradition for decades. If a quick snack will suffice, three or four of the open sandwiches and a *Pfiff* (⅛ liter) of beer, or a vodka, may be just the needed pickup. Share one of the few tables, or stand up at one of the counters. You'll be surprised at the elegance of many of the customers. *Dorotheergasse 1, tel. 0222/512–3291. Reservations not required. Dress: casual. No credit cards. Closed Sat. evening and Sun.*

Wine Taverns

In-town wine restaurants cannot properly be called *Heurige*, since they are not run by the vintner, so the term is "wine restaurant," or "cellar" (*Keller*). Many of them extend a number of levels underground, particularly in the older part of the city. Mainly open in the evening, they are intended primarily for drinking, though you can always get something to eat from a buffet, and increasingly, full dinners are available. Some of the better wine restaurants follow: no credit cards except where noted.

Antiquitäten-Keller. The fare is authentic Viennese cuisine, surrounded by authentic antiques and the strains of classical music. *Magdalenenstr. 32, tel. 0222/566–9533. Reservations advised. Jacket and tie required. AE, DC, MC, V. Moderate.*

★ **Esterhazykeller.** This maze of rooms offers some of the best Keller wines in town plus a hot-and-cold buffet. *Haarhof 1, tel. 0222/533–3482. Reservations advised on weekends. Jacket recommended. Stüberl closed Sat., Sun. lunch; Keller closed weekends. Moderate.*

★ **Melker Stiftskeller.** Down and down you go, into one of the friendliest Kellers in town, where *Stelze* (roast knuckle of pork) is a popular feature, along with outstanding wines by the glass. *Schottengasse 3, tel. 0222/533–5530. Reservations advised. Jacket recommended. Evenings only, closed Sun. Moderate.*

Piaristen Keller. The atmosphere, with live music, is sufficiently genuine that you can overlook the occasionally lax service. This is a dining Keller; the food is good and the house wines are excellent. *Piaristengasse 45, tel. 0222/429152. Reservations advised. Jacket and tie suggested. AE, DC, MC, V. Evenings only. Moderate.*

Augustinerkeller. This upstairs Keller is open at noontime as well. The grilled chicken is excellent. *Augustinerstr. 1/Albertinerplatz, tel. 0222/533–1026. Reservations not required. Dress: casual but neat. Inexpensive.*

Zwölf Apostel-Keller. You pass a huge wood statue of St. Peter on the way down to the two underground floors in this cellar in the oldest part of Vienna. The young crowd comes for the good wines and the atmosphere, and there's buffet food as well. *Sonnenfelsgasse 3, tel. 512–6777. Reservations advised on weekends. Dress: casual but neat. Inexpensive.*

Heurige

These taverns in the wine-growing districts on the outskirts of the city vary from the simple front room of a vintner's house to ornate establishments. (The name means "new wine," and that's what is chiefly served.) The true Heuriger is open for only a few weeks a year to allow the vintner to sell a certain quantity of his production tax-free for consumption on his own premises. The commercial establishments keep to a somewhat more regular season, but still sell only wine from their own vines.

The choice is usually between a "new" and an "old" white wine and a red, but you can also ask for a milder or sharper wine according to your taste. Most Heurige are happy to let you sample the wines before ordering. You can also order a *Gespritzter*, half wine and half soda water. The waitress will bring you the wine, usually in quarter-liter mugs, but you collect your own

food from the buffet. The wine tastes as mild as lemonade, but
it packs a punch. If it isn't of good quality, you will know by a
raging headache the next day.

Summer and fall are the seasons for visiting the *Heurige*,
though often the more elegant and expensive establishments,
called *Noble-Heuriger*, stay open year-round. No credit cards
except where noted.

Heurige are concentrated in several outskirts of Vienna:
Stammersdorf, Grinzing, Sievering, Nussdorf, Neustift, and a
corner of Ottakring. Perchtoldsdorf, just outside Vienna, is
also well known for its wine taverns.

Our favorite district is Stammersdorf, across the Danube. Try
Robert Helm. *Stammersdorfer Str. 121, tel. 0222/391244. Reservations advised on weekends and in winter. Dress: casual
but neat.*

The Grinzing district today is mainly for tourists, with a very
few exceptions; one is **Zum Martin Sepp**, where the wine, food,
service, and ambience are excellent. *Cobenzlgasse 32, tel. 0222/
323233. Reservations suggested on weekends. Jacket advised.
DC.*

In Sievering try **Haslinger**. *Agnesgasse 3, tel. 0222/441347.
Reservations advised on weekends. Dress: casual but neat.*

In Neustift, **Wolff** has a gorgeous garden and outstanding food,
as well as good wine. *Rathstr. 46, tel. 0222/442335. Reservations advised. Jacket suggested.*

In Nussdorf seek out **Schübl-Auer**. *Kahlenberger Str. 22, tel.
0222/372222. Reservations not required. Dress: casual but
neat. Closed Jan., July.* In good weather, try **Stift Schotten**,
with a superb garden under huge old trees. *Hackhofergasse 17,
tel. 0222/371575. Reservations not required. Dress: casual but
neat. Closed Jan., Feb.*

Cafés

The typical Viennese café, with polished brass or marble-
topped tables, bentwood chairs, supplies of newspapers, and
tables outside in good weather, is a fixed institution of which
there are literally thousands. Many people take breakfast in
the cafés, students do homework, businesspeople conclude
deals, billiards is played, and bridge clubs meet. Everybody
has his favorite; some people even have a regular table that is
reserved for them every day. All cafés serve pastries and light
snacks in addition to beverages. Many offer a menu or fixed
lunch at noon, but be aware that some can get rather expensive.
No credit cards except where noted.

When you want a quick (but excellent) coffee and dessert, look
for an **Aida** café; they are scattered throughout the city. Here's
a sampling of the best of the traditional cafés: **Alte Backstübe,**
(Lange Gasse 34, tel. 0222/431101; MC, V; closed Mon.), in a
gorgeous Baroque house, once a bakery, now a museum up
front, and a café in back; **Bräunerhof** (Stallburggasse 2, tel.
0222/512–3893) has music on some afternoons; **Café Central**
(Herrengasse 14, tel. 0222/535–4176; AE, DC, MC, V; closed
Sun.) is where Stalin and Trotsky played chess; **Frauenhuber**
(Himmelpfortgasse 6, tel. 0222/512–4323; closed Sat. evening
and Sun.) has its original turn-of-the-century interior and a

good choice of desserts; **Haag** (Schottengasse 2, tel. 0222/533–1810; closed Sun., June–Aug.), with crystal chandeliers and a shaded courtyard garden in summer, serves snacks and desserts; **Landtmann** (Dr. Karl Lueger-Ring 4, tel. 0222/630621; AE, DC, MC, V) is where government officials gather; **Museum** (Friedrichstr. 6, tel. 0222/565202), original interior by the architect Adolf Loos, draws a mixed crowd and has lots of newspapers; **Schwarzenberg** (Kärntner Ring 17, tel. 0222/512–7393), with piano music in late afternoons, is highly popular, particularly its sidewalk tables in summer; **Tirolerhof** (Tegetthofstr. 8/Albertinaplatz, tel. 0222/512–7833), with its excellent desserts, is popular with students.

Café Hawelka (Dorotheergasse 12, tel. 0222/512–8230; closed Mon., Sun. noon) deserves special mention; whole books have been written here and about this gathering place. Its international clientele ranges from artists to politicians; Hawelka is jammed any time of day, so you share a table (and the smoky atmosphere).

Pastry Shops

Viennese pastries are said to be the best in the world. In all shops you can buy them to eat on the premises as well as to take out. **Kurkonditorei Oberlaa** (Neuer Markt 16, tel. 0222/513–2936) has irresistible confections, cakes, and bonbons, as well as light lunches and salad plates, served outdoors in summer. Traditionalists and tourists with fat pocketbooks still go to **Demel** (Kohlmarkt 14, tel. 0222/533–5516), where the value is arguable but turn-of-the-century atmosphere prevails among velvet and polished brass. **Gerstner** (Kärntner Str. 15, tel. 0222/512–4963) is also recommended, and **Heiner** (Kärntner Str. 21–23, tel. 0222/512–6863, and Wollzeile 9, tel. 0222/512–4838) is dazzling for its crystal chandeliers as well as for its pastries. **Sluka** (Rathausplatz 8, tel. 0222/427172) has special dietetic desserts, snacks, and an appetizer buffet and serves outdoors in summer.

Lodging

In Vienna's best hotels the staff seems to anticipate your wishes almost before you have expressed them. Such service of course has its price, and if you wish, you can stay in Vienna in profound luxury. For those with more modest requirements, ample rooms are available in less expensive but entirely adequate hotels. Pensions, mainly bed-and-breakfast establishments often managed by the owner, generally represent good value. A number of student hostels are run as hotels in summer, offering about the most reasonable quarters of all. And several apartment hotels accommodate those who want to stay longer.

When you have only a short time to spend in Vienna, you will probably want to stay in the inner city (the 1010 postal code) or fairly close to it, within walking distance of the most important sights, restaurants, and shops. Although most of the hotels there are in the upper categories, excellent and reasonable accommodations can be found in the Eighth District, which borders the First and puts you close to the major museums. You'll also find a group of moderate and inexpensive hotels in the

Mariahilfer Strasse–Westbahnhof area, within easy reach of the city center by streetcar.

For the high season, Easter through October, and around the Christmas–New Year holidays, make reservations a month or more in advance. Vienna is continually the site of some international convention or other, and in March and September, when the semiannual trade fair is on, the city fills up quickly.

Our hotel categories correspond more or less to the official Austrian rating system, with five stars the equivalent to our Very Expensive category. All rooms have bath or shower unless otherwise stated; color television is usual in the top two categories; breakfast is included with all *except* the highest category. Highly recommended lodgings are indicated by a star ★.

Category	Cost*
Very Expensive	over AS2,200
Expensive	AS1,200–AS2,200
Moderate	AS850–AS1,200
Inexpensive	under AS850

All prices are for a standard double room for two, including local taxes (usually 10%) and service (15%).

Very Expensive

Ambassador. This superbly located dowager (from 1866) wears well. An air of decadent elegance radiates from the red velvet and crystal chandeliers in the high-ceiling guest rooms. The trade-off is room air conditioners and rather stuffy period furniture. But what was once good enough for Mark Twain—yes, he stayed here, but long before the renovations of 1990–91—is still very good, and you will know instantly that you are in Vienna. Unless you want the excitement of a direct view into the lively pedestrian Kärntner Strasse, ask for one of the quieter rooms on the Neuer Markt side. *Neuer Markt 5/Kärntner Str. 22, A–1010, tel. 0222/514660. 107 rooms. Facilities: restaurant, bar, TV on request. AE, DC, MC, V.*

★ **Bristol.** This hotel has one of the finest locations in Europe, on the Ring next to the opera house. The accent here is on tradition, from the brocaded walls to the Biedermeier period furnishings in the public rooms and many of the bedrooms. The house dates to 1896; renovations have left no trace of the fact that the Bristol was the U.S. military headquarters during the 1945–55 occupation. Like an old shoe, the hotel is seductively comfortable from the moment you arrive. The rooms on the Mahlerstrasse (back) side of the house are quieter, but the view isn't as spectacular as from rooms in front. *Kärntner Ring 1, A–1010, tel. 0222/515160. 152 rooms. Facilities: Korso, one of the 2 restaurants, is rated Vienna's best; American bar, sauna, exercise room. AE, DC, MC, V.*

de France. From the glass-fanned canopy entrance, the decor speaks of friendly efficiency. After the chic 1988 renovations, you'd never guess from the inside that the de France building dates to 1873. Some of the older rooms, with their characteristic red velvet, crystal, and Oriental carpets, are in clever con-

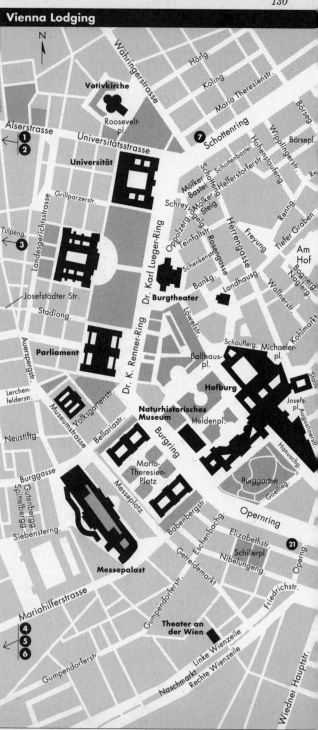

Vienna Lodging

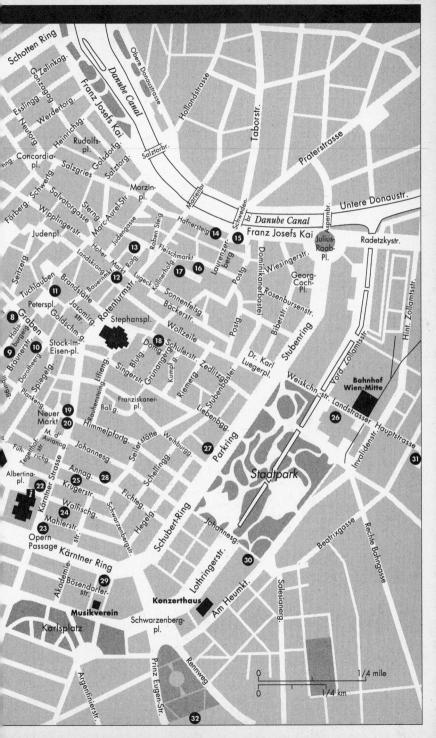

trast to the crisp blues and fresh white of the new design. And some of the traditional high ceilings have been retained. If you prefer modern, ask for a room in the new wing, added in 1988. The lofty maisonette (duplex) suites are sensational, with their living area and bathroom downstairs, sleeping area and toilet on a balcony. *Schottenring 3, A–1010, tel. 0222/345610. 183 rooms. Facilities: 2 restaurants (the Bistro is excellent for a light lunch), bar, sauna, theater-ticket office. AE, DC, MC, V.*

Hilton. The Art Deco public areas re-created for the opening in 1975 now look a bit dated, but the bedrooms are contemporary and a cut above the usual Hilton standard in size and individuality of decor. The suites are particularly spacious; who could resist breakfast on a suite balcony, with a 180-degree view of the city? The upper rooms are quietest; the no-smoking floor is so popular that you need to book at least a week in advance. The airport bus terminal is next door to the Hilton; the U3 and U4 subway lines, trains, and buses stop at the terminal across the street, yet you're within an easy walk of city center. *Am Stadtpark, A–1030, tel. 0222/717000. 620 rooms. Facilities: 2 restaurants (Rotisserie Prinz Eugen is outstanding), café, wine keller, Klimt lobby bar, sauna, fitness center. AE, DC, MC, V.*

Imperial. The hotel is as much a palace today as when it was completed in 1869. The emphasis is on "old Vienna" elegance and privacy; heads of state stay here when they're in town. Service is deferential; the rooms have high ceilings and are furnished in classic antiques and Oriental carpets. The bath areas, in contrast, are modern and inviting; many are as large as guest rooms in lesser hotels. The staff will adjust the hardness (or softness) of the beds to your specific wants. Don't overlook the ornate reception rooms to the rear or the formal marble staircase to the right of the lobby. *Kärntner Ring 16, A–1010, tel. 0222/501100. 158 rooms (nonsmoking rooms available). Facilities: 2 restaurants (the Café is excellent), piano bar. AE, DC, MC, V.*

InterContinental. This "first" among Vienna's modern hostelries (1964) has taken on the Viennese patina, and its public rooms, with glittering crystal and red carpets, suggest luxurious comfort. The guest rooms lean more toward the chain's norm, adequate though unexciting, but you will get either a view over the city park across the street (preferred) or over the city itself. The higher you go, the more dramatic the perspective. *Johannesgasse 28, A–1030, tel. 0222/711220. 498 rooms (nonsmoking rooms available). Facilities: 2 restaurants (Vier Jahreszeiten is recommended), 2 bars, sauna. AE, DC, MC, V.*

★ **Palais Schwarzenberg.** You will know from your first glimpse of the elegant facade that this is no ordinary hotel. Set in a vast formal park, the palace, built in the early 1700s, seems like a country estate, and you can even jog in the formal garden. Your room will be furnished in genuine (but surprisingly comfortable) antiques, with some of the Schwarzenberg family's art on the walls. The baths are modern, although you might miss a shower curtain. Each room is individual; duplex suites 24 and 25 have upstairs bedrooms and views over the park; Room 26 has exquisite furniture, gorgeous draperies, and a winding stair leading up to the bedroom. If you have any reason to celebrate, do it here; this is the genuine "old Vienna" at its most elegant. *Schwarzenbergplatz 9, A–1030, tel. 0222/784515. 38 rooms. Facilities: restaurant, bar, AE, DC, MC, V.*

Sacher. Few hotels in the world have featured so often in films or in history; you'll sense the musty atmosphere of tradition when you arrive. This is the house where the legendary cigar-smoking Frau Sacher reigned; Emperor Franz Josef was a regular patron. The Sacher dates to 1876; the patina remains (Room 329 exudes a sense of well-being) despite the elegant new baths installed in 1990. The corridors are a veritable art gallery, and the location directly behind the Opera House could hardly be more central. The staff is particularly accommodating; it has long been an open secret that the concierge at the Sacher could miraculously produce concert and opera tickets when all other possibilities were exhausted. The restaurant remains the great disappointment. *Philharmonikerstr. 4, A–1010, tel. 0222/514560. 125 rooms, 117 with bath (nonsmoking rooms available). Facilities: restaurant, café, 2 bars (the Blue is recommended). AE, MC, DC, V.*

Vienna Marriott. The metal-and-glass exterior gives the impression of a giant greenhouse, borne out by the inviting mini-jungle of green trees and plants in the vast atrium lobby. Some guests object to the perpetual waterfall in the bar/café area, but for Vienna the effect is certainly original. Despite the size, a friendly atmosphere pervades. For a hotel built in 1984, the rooms and suites are unusually spacious and furnished with extra attention to detail; the corner suites (number 24 on each floor) give a superb view out over the city park opposite. The upper rooms in back offer a panorama of the inner city; these and the rooms on the inner court are the quietest. You're an easy stroll from the city center. *Parkring 12a, A–1010, tel. 0222/51518. 304 rooms (nonsmoking rooms available). Facilities: 2 restaurants, café, 2 bars, sauna, pool, fitness room. AE, DC, MC, V.*

Expensive

Biedermeier im Sünnhof. This jewel of a hotel is tucked into a renovated 1820s house that even with all modern facilities still conveys a feeling of old Vienna. The rooms are compact but efficient, the public areas tastefully done in the Biedermeier style, and the service is friendly. The courtyard passageway around which the hotel is built has attracted a number of interesting boutiques and handicrafts shops, but at times there is an excess of coming and going as tour groups are accommodated. It's about a 20-minute walk or a six-minute subway ride to the center of the city. *Landstrasser Hauptstr. 28, A–1030, tel. 0222/755575. 204 rooms. Facilities: restaurant, bar. AE, DC, MC, V.*

Capricorno. In these intimate quarters on the four lowest floors of what is basically an office/apartment building, the mood is definitely Vienna, if not luxurious: The rooms have period furniture, and most overlook the Danube Canal. It's an ideal location, five minutes on foot from Stephansplatz, with subway and streetcar stops outside the door. The Danube city sightseeing boats dock across the street. Hotel services are limited (breakfast only), but the staff is unusually helpful, and good restaurants are nearby (even a McDonald's in the house). *Schwedenplatz 3–4, A–1010, tel. 0222/533–3104. 46 rooms. AE, DC, MC, V.*

Europa. The Europa had a face-lift in 1989, which almost worked, but the hotel cannot quite hide its 1957 birth year, and the garish blue-and-pink entry canopies don't help. But the rooms are comfortable without being luxurious and the baths are modern. You can't find a more central location. Rooms on the Neuer Markt side are quieter than those on Kärntner Strasse, and the best rooms are those on the corners. *Neuer Markt 3/Kärntner Str. 18, A–1010, tel. 0222/515940. 102 rooms. Facilities: restaurant, café, bar. AE, DC, MC, V.*

★ **König von Ungarn.** In a 16th-century house in the shadow of St. Stephen's cathedral, this hotel began catering to court nobility in 1815. (Mozart lived in the house next door when he wrote *The Marriage of Figaro*). A superb redesign has turned it into a modern hotel, and you could hardly hope for a happier result. The hotel radiates charm, from the greenery in the wood-paneled atrium lobby to the antiques of various periods and the pine country furnishings in the bedrooms. The rooms are not overly large, but each is individually and appealingly decorated. Those in back are somewhat quieter. *Schulerstr. 10, A–1010, tel. 0222/515840. 32 rooms. Facilities: restaurant, lobby bar. DC, MC, V.*

★ **Mailberger Hof.** This 14th-century house on a pedestrian street just off the Kärntner Strasse was once a Baroque town palace. In 1976 it was turned into an intimate family-run hotel with great success and is a favorite of stars at the nearby state opera. The rooms are so attractively decorated it's hard to imagine you're in a hotel; colors and furniture have been coordinated without fussiness to create a setting you won't want to leave. You'll have to book about a month ahead to get a room. *Annagasse 7, A–1010, tel. 0222/512–0641. 40 rooms. Apartments with kitchenettes are available by the month. Facilities: restaurant. AE, DC, V.*

★ **Opernringhof.** This establishment's spacious, comfortable rooms, furnished with real antiques of the mid-19th century, are only one reason why guests come back. The unusually friendly, personal attention of the owner, Susie Riedl, makes you feel as though you're the only guest. The hotel has Best Western affiliation. The rooms on the inner courtyard are quieter but have a dreary outlook; disregard the traffic noise (there's no air-conditioning, so you may want the windows open) and enjoy the extraordinary view of the Opera, diagonally across the Ring. *Opernring 11, A–1010, tel. 0222/587–5518. 35 rooms. AE, MC, DC, V.*

Moderate

★ **Austria.** This older house, tucked away on a tiny cul-de-sac, offers the ultimate in quiet and is only five minutes' walk from the heart of the city. The high-ceiling rooms are pleasing in their combination of dark wood and lighter walls; the decor is mixed, with Oriental carpets on many floors. You'll feel at home here, and the staff will help you find your way around town or get opera or concert tickets. *Wolfengasse 3 (Fleischmarkt). A–1010, tel. 0222/515230. 51 rooms, 40 with bath or shower. AE, DC, MC, V.*

Fürstenhof. This turn-of-the-century block, directly across from the Westbahnhof, describes its large rooms as "old-fashioned comfortable," and you reach them via a marvelous hydraulic elevator. Furnishings are a mixed bag. The side rooms are quieter than those in front. *Neubaugürtel 4, A–1070, tel. 0222/933267. 60 rooms. AE, DC, MC, V.*

Ibis Wien. About an eight-minute walk from the Westbahnhof and easily identifiable by its bronze metal exterior, the Ibis offers its standard chain accommodations in contemporary rooms that are compact, complete, and very good value. The blue and blue-gray accents are refreshing against the white room walls. The rooms on the shady Wallgasse side are more comfortable; those on the upper floors have a superb panoramic view. You may have to contend with some tour groups. *Mariahilfer Gürtel 22–24/Wallgasse 33. A–1060, tel. 0222/565626. 341 rooms. Facilities: restaurant, Weinstube, garage. AE, DC, MC, V.*

★ **Kärntnerhof.** Behind the "Schönbrunn yellow" facade of this elegant 100-year-old house on a quiet cul-de-sac lies one of the friendliest small hotels in the center of the city. Don't let the dated and uninteresting lobby put you off; take the gorgeously restored Art Deco elevator to the rooms upstairs. They have just been done over in either brown or white reproduction furniture, and the baths are modern. Room 205, in its combination of blue and white, is stunning. The staff is adept at getting theater and concert tickets for "sold out" performances and happily puts together special outing programs for guests. For a small fee, parking can be arranged in the abbey courtyard next door. *Grashofgasse 4, A–1010, tel. 0222/512–1923. 43 rooms. AE, DC, MC, V.*

Pension Christine. This quiet pension, just steps from Schwedenplatz and the Danube Canal, offers mainly smallish modern rooms, warmly decorated with attractive dark-wood furniture set off against beige walls. Room 524 is particularly spacious and inviting. *Hafnersteig 7, A–1010, tel. 0222/533–2961. 33 rooms. MC.*

★ **Pension Pertschy.** Housed in a former town palace just off the Graben, this pension is as central as you can get. A massive arched portal leads to a yellow courtyard, around which the house is built. Anybody who has stayed in Room 220 with its stylish old blue ceramic stove (just for show) would be happy again with nothing less. Most rooms are spacious with antique furniture of mixed periods, but even the small single rooms are charming. Baths are good. Use the elevator, but don't overlook the palatial grand staircase. *Habsburgergasse 5, A–1010, tel. 0222/533–7094. 43 rooms. MC.*

★ **Pension Zipser.** This 1904 house, with an ornate facade and gilt-trimmed coat of arms, is one of the city's very best hotel values. It's in a fascinating district of small cafés, shops, jazz clubs, and excellent restaurants, yet within steps of the *J* streetcar line direct to the city center. The rooms are newly redone in browns and beige, with modern furniture to match; the baths are elegant and well lit. The balconies of some of the back rooms overlook tree-filled neighborhood courtyards. The friendly staff will help get theater and concert tickets. Book ahead a month or two to be sure of a room. *Lange Gasse 49, A–1080, tel. 0222/420828. 47 rooms. Facilities: coffee bar. AE, DC, MC, V.*

Schweizerhof. Occupying Floors 4, 5, and 6 of an Art Deco building in the heart of the city, this hotel will make you feel comfortably at home with its pleasantly mixed decor, parquet floors, and Oriental carpets. Ask for Room 527, with unusual and valuable handcarved pine country furniture. Corner Room 523 gives you a look at the Anker Clock; from corner Room 508, you can glimpse the spires of St. Stephen's Cathedral. *Bauernmarkt 22, A–1010, tel. 0222/533–1931. 55 rooms. AE, V.*

Wandl. The colorful facade (newly restored) identifies a 300-year-old house that has been in family hands as a hotel since 1854. You couldn't find a better location, tucked behind St. Peter's church, just off the Graben. The hallways are punctuated by cheerful, bright openings along the glassed-in inner court. The rooms are modern, but some are a bit plain and charmless, despite parquet flooring and red accents. Ask for one of the rooms done in period furniture, with decorated ceilings and gilt mirrors; they're palatial, if a bit overdone. *Petersplatz 9, A–1010, tel. 0222/534550. 138 rooms. Facilities: bar. No credit cards.*

Zur Wiener Staatsoper. The hotel's florid facade, with oversize torsos supporting its upper bays, is pure 19th-century Ringstrasse style. The rooms are less well defined in style, small yet comfortable. The baths are adequate. And you'll find yourself within steps of the Opera and the Kärntner Strasse. *Krugerstr. 11, A–1010, tel. 0222/513–1274. 22 rooms. AE, V.*

Inexpensive

★ **Hospiz.** This hotel, run by the Austrian YMCA, is two short blocks and four minutes from the Westbahnhof. Fully renovated in 1988, the house still shows some of its 1912 Art Deco origins. There's no elevator, baths and toilets are mainly "down the hall," but there is parking space. The rooms are compact and somewhat Spartan but utterly clean and a real bargain. *Kenyongasse 15, A–1070, tel. 0222/931304. 25 rooms. MC, V.*

Pension Aclon. On the third floor of a gray but gracious older building just off the Graben (with the famous Café Hawelka downstairs), this family-run hostelry (complete with sheepdog) is attractively done up in "old Vienna" style, with lots of plants, 19th-century furniture, dark woods, and elegant marble baths. Rooms on the inner court are quieter, though the street in front carries no through traffic. *Dorotheergasse 6–8, A–1010, tel. 0222/512–7949. 22 rooms. AE, DC, V.*

★ **Pension City.** You'll be on historic ground here: In 1791 the playwright Franz Grillparzer was born in the house that then stood here; a bust and plaques in the entryway commemorate him. On the second floor (the Viennese call it the mezzanine) of the present 100-year-old house about three minutes away from St. Stephen's Cathedral, the pension's rooms are newly outfitted in a successful mix of modern and 19th-century antique furniture against white walls. The baths are small but complete, and the amenities (minibars, TV, telephones) are remarkable at the price. *Bauernmarkt 10, A–1010, tel 0222/639521. 19 rooms. AE, DC, MC, V.*

Pension Edelweiss. One flight up, behind the drab facade of this turn-of-the-century apartment house, are comfortable rooms with contemporary furnishings, many quite spacious and many completely renovated in 1990. The front rooms are noisy, but the nearby streetcar is a convenience. It's under the same management as pensions Pertschy and Christine. *Lange Gasse 61, A–1080, tel. 0222/422306. 20 rooms. No credit cards.*

Pension Nossek. This family-run establishment on the upper floors of a 19th-century office and apartment building lies at the heart of the pedestrian and shopping area. The rooms have high ceilings and are eclectically but comfortably furnished; those on the front have a magnificent view of the Graben. *Graben 17, A–1010, tel. 0222/533–7041. 26 rooms, 16 with bath or shower. No credit cards.*

★ **Pension Suzanne.** This 1950s building on a side street is just steps away from the Opera. The rooms are smallish but comfortably furnished in 19th-century Viennese style; baths are modern, although short on shelf space. Suzanne has regular guests who book months in advance, so you'd be well advised to do the same. *Walfischgasse 4, A–1010, tel. 0222/513–2507. 24 rooms, 7 apartments with kitchenette. No credit cards.*

★ **Rathaus.** This friendly hotel, under the same management as the nearby Zipser, is in a 1908 building that has been attractively renovated: The spacious rooms have contemporary furnishings. You'll be within an easy walk of the main museums and close to public transportation. *Lange Gasse 13, A–1080, tel. 0222/434302. 40 rooms. No credit cards.*

Seasonal Hotels (Inexpensive–Moderate)

Student residences, which operate as hotels July–September, are an excellent bargain. They have single or double rooms, all, unless noted, with bath or shower. You can book any of the Rosenhotels by phoning 0222/597–0680. Credit cards in general are not accepted; exceptions are noted.

Academia (fairly luxurious). *Pfeilgasse 3A, A–1080, tel. 0222/ 431661–55. 368 rooms. Facilities: restaurant, bar. AE, MC, V.*

Alsergrund. *Alser Str. 33, A–1080, tel. 0222/4332–317 or 0222/ 512–7493. 58 rooms without bath.*

Auersperg (very inexpensive). *Auerspergstr. 9, A–1080, tel. 0222/4325490. 76 rooms. MC.*

Avis. *Pfeilgasse 4, A–1080, tel. 0222/426374. 72 rooms. Facilities: restaurant, bar. AE, MC, V.*

Haus Döbling (very inexpensive). *Gymnasiumstr. 85, A-1190, tel. 0222/347631 or 0222/344545. 308 rooms without bath.*

Josefstadt. *Buchfeldgasse 16, A–1080, tel. 0222/435211 or 0222/ 512–7493. 40 rooms without bath. MC, V.*

Panorama (slightly farther than most from the city center). *Brigittenauer Lände 224, A–1200, tel. 0222/351541. 270 rooms, 136 with shower. Facilities: restaurant, bar, sauna, parking.*

Rosenhotel Burgenland 1. *Wilhelm-Exner-Gasse 4, A–1090, tel. 0222/439122. 71 rooms. Facilities: restaurant, bar, garage. AE, MC, V.*

Rosenhotel Burgenland 2. *Mittelgasse 18, A–1060, tel. 0222/ 596–1247. 150 rooms. Facilities: restaurant, bar, garage. AE, MC, V.*

Rosenhotel Burgenland 3. *Bürgerspitalgasse 19, A–1060, tel. 0222/597–9475. 130 rooms. Facilities: restaurant, bar, garage. AE, MC, V.*

Rosenhotel Europahaus (well outside the center but clean, and with a lovely garden). *Linzer Str. 429, A–1140, tel. 0222/ 972536. 26 rooms. Facilities: parking.*

Rosenhotel Niederösterreich. *Untere Augartenstr. 31, A–1020, tel. 0222/353526. 100 rooms. Facilities: restaurant. AE, MC, V.*

The Arts and Nightlife

The Arts

Vienna is one of the main music centers of the world. Theater is good, although recent tendencies to experiment have taken even the traditional houses somewhat far afield: for example, a German version of Shakespeare barely identifiable with the original. Contemporary music gets its hearing, but it's the "hometown" standards—the works of Beethoven, Brahms, Haydn, Mozart, Schubert—that draw the Viennese public. A monthly program, put out by the city tourist board and available at any travel agency or hotel, gives a general overview of what's going on in opera, concerts, jazz, theater, and galleries, and similar information is posted on billboards and fat advertising columns around the city.

Most theaters now reserve tickets by telephone against a credit card; you pick up your ticket at the box office with no surcharge. The same applies to concert tickets. Ticket agencies charge a minimum 20% markup and generally deal in the more expensive seats. Expect to pay (or tip) a hotel porter or concierge at least as much as a ticket agency. You might try **Vienna Ticket Service** (Postfach 160, A-1060, tel. 0222/587–9843), **Kartenbüro Flamm** (Kärntner Ring 3, A-1010, tel. 0222/512–4225), or **Cosmos** (Kärntner Ring 15, A-1010, tel. 0222/515330).

Tickets to the state theaters (Opera, Volksoper, Burgtheater, or Akademietheater) can be charged against your credit card (AE, DC, MC, V). You can order them by phone up to six days before the performance (tel. 0222/513–1513) or buy them in person up to seven days in advance at the central box office. *Theaterkassen, back of the Opera, Hanuschgasse 3, in the courtyard, tel. 0222/514440. AE, DC, MC, V. Open weekdays 8–6, Sat. 9–2, Sun. 9–noon.*

You can also write ahead for tickets. The nearest Austrian National Tourist Office can provide you with a schedule of performances and a special ticket order form. Send the form (no payment is required) to the ticket office (Kartenvorverkauf Bundestheaterverband, Goethegasse 1, A–1010 Vienna), which will mail you a reservation card; when you get to Vienna, take the card to the main box office to pick up and pay for your tickets.

Opera The **Staatsoper,** one of the world's great houses, has been the scene of countless musical triumphs and a center of unending controversies over how it should be run and by whom. (When Lorin Maazel was unceremoniously dumped as head of the opera not many years ago, he pointed out that the same house had done the same thing to Gustav Mahler a few decades earlier.) A performance takes place virtually every night from September through June, drawing on the vast repertoire of the house, with emphasis on Mozart and Verdi. (Opera here is nearly always performed in the original language, even Russian.) Check for possible out-of-(opera)-season performances by the Volksoper company in "the big house on the Ring" in July and August. And guided tours of the opera house are held year-round. The opera in Vienna is a dressy event. Evening dress and black tie, though not compulsory, are recommended for first-night performances and in the better seats. Jeans, even designer jeans, are frowned upon, even in standing room.

Light opera and operetta are performed at the **Volksoper,** outside the city center at Währingerstrasse and Währinger Gürtel (third streetcar stop on No. 41, 42, or 43 from "downstairs" at Schottentor on the Ring). Prices here are significantly lower than in the main opera, and performances can be every bit as rewarding. Mozart is sung here, too, but in German, the language of the house. If *Kiss Me, Kate* is on, it too is sung in German, and it's a good romp at that.

You'll find musicals and operetta also at the **Theater an der Wien** (Linke Wienzeile 6, tel. 0222/588300), the recently renovated **Raimundtheater** (Wallgasse 18, tel. 0222/599770), and **Ronacher** (Seilerstätte/Himmelpfortgasse, tel. 0222/513–8565). Opera and operetta are performed on an irregular schedule at the **Kammeroper** (Fleischmarkt 24, tel. 0222/512–0100–31).

In summer, chamber opera performances by the Kammeroper ensemble are given in the exquisite **Schlosstheater** at Schönbrunn Castle. Ticket agencies will have details.

Music Vienna is the home of four full symphony orchestras: the great Vienna Philharmonic and the Vienna Symphony, the broadcasting service's ORF Symphony Orchestra, and the Niederösterreichische Tonkünstler. There are also hundreds of smaller groups, from world-famous trios to chamber orchestras.

The most important concert halls are in the buildings of the Gesellschaft der Musikfreunde, called the **Musikverein** (*Dumbastr. 3; ticket office at Karlsplatz 6, tel. 0222/505–8190. AE, DC, MC, V. Open weekdays 9–6, Sat. 9–noon*) and the **Konzerthaus** (*Lothringerstr. 20, tel. 0222/712–1211. AE, DC, MC, V. Open weekdays 9–6, Sat. 9–1*). Both houses contain several halls; tickets bear their names: **Grosser Musikvereinssaal, Brahmssaal,** or **Kammersaal** in the Musikverein; **Grosser Konzerthaussaal, Mozartsaal,** or **Schubertsaal** in the Konzerthaus.

Concerts are also given in the small **Figarosaal** of Palais Palffy (Josefsplatz 6, tel. 0222/512–5681), the concert studio of the broadcasting station (Argentinierstr. 30a, tel. 0222/50101–881), and the **Bösendorfersaal** (Graf Starhemberg-Gasse 14, tel. 0222/656651).

Although the **Vienna Festival** (late May to mid-June) wraps up the primary season, the summer musical scene is bright, with something going on every day. Outdoor symphony concerts are given twice weekly in the vast arcaded courtyard of the Rathaus (entrance on Friedrich Schmidt-Platz). You can catch musical events in the Volksgarten and in the Schwarzenberg, Rasumofsky, and Trautson palaces; at Schönbrunn they're part of an evening guided tour.

Mozart concerts are performed in 18th-century costumes and powdered wigs in the Mozartsaal of the Konzerthaus; operetta concerts are held in the Musikverein and the Hofburg; tickets are available through hotels and travel and ticket agencies.

Church music, the Mass sung in Latin, can be heard on Sunday morning during the main season at **St. Stephen's;** in the **Franciscan church, St. Michael's;** and, above all, in the **Augustinerkirche.** At the latter, the schedule is posted on the door. The Friday and Saturday newspapers carry details. St. Stephen's also has organ concerts most Wednesday evenings from early May to late November.

The **Vienna Choirboys** sing at 9:15 AM Mass in the **Hofburgkapelle** from mid-September to late June. Written requests for seats (standing room is free but limited) should be made at least eight weeks in advance to Hofmusikkapelle Hofburg, A–1010 Vienna. You will be sent a reservation card, which you exchange at the box office (in the Hofburg courtyard) for your tickets. Tickets are also sold at ticket agencies and at the box office every Friday at 5 PM, but you should be in line by 4:30. Each person is allowed a maximum of two tickets.

Theater Vienna's **Burgtheater** (Dr. Karl Lueger-Ring 2, A–1010 Vienna; *see* above for ticket details) is the leading German-language theater of the world; for an actor to play the Burg means supreme achievement. It specializes in classical works: Goethe, Schiller, Grillparzer, Nestroy, plus translations of Shakespeare, Congreve, Wilde, Molière, and others. The Burg's smaller house, the **Akademietheater** (Lisztstr. 1) draws on much the same group of actors, for classical and modern plays. Both houses are closed during July and August.

The **Theater in der Josefstadt** (Josefstädterstr. 26, tel. 0222/ 402–5127) stages classical and modern works year-round in the house once run by the great producer and teacher Max Reinhardt. **Volkstheater** (Neustiftgasse 1, tel. 0222/932776) gives dramas, comedies, and folk plays; **Kammerspiele** (Rotenturmstr. 20, tel. 0222/533–2833) does modern plays.

For theater in English (mainly standard plays), head for **Vienna's English Theater** (Josefsgasse 12, tel. 0222/402–1260) or the equally good **International Theater** (Porzellangasse 8, tel. 0222/316272).

Dance Other than the ballet companies in the opera and Volksoper, Vienna offers nothing in the way of regular dance. The ballet evenings that are on the opera-house schedules are more of a fill-in than a serious attempt to offer good dance. Efforts to get an annual dance festival under way are making progress, so check schedules; the situation can only get better.

Film Film has enjoyed a recent renaissance, with viewers seeking original rather than German-dubbed versions. Look for films in English at **Burgkino** (Opernring 19, tel. 0222/587–8406)—in summer, Carol Reed's classic *The Third Man* with Orson Welles is a regular feature; **de France** (Hessgasse 7, tel. 0222/ 345236); and **Top-Kino** (Rahlgasse 1, tel. 0222/587–5557). In the film listings, *OmU* means original language with German subtitles.

The **Filmmuseum** in the Albertina (Augustinerstr. 1, tel. 0222/ 533–7054; screenings Mon.–Sat. 6 and 8 PM; AS 45) shows original-version classics like *Birth of a Nation, A Night at the Opera,* and *Harvey* and organizes retrospectives of the works of artists, directors, and producers. The monthly program is posted outside, and guest memberships for a week are available. It is closed July, August, and September.

Nightlife

Bars and Lounges Vienna has blossomed in recent years with delightful and sophisticated bars. Head for the Bermuda Triangle, an area in the First District roughly defined by Judengasse, Seitenstättengasse, Rabensteig, and Franz-Josefs-Kai. Here you will find dozens of bars, both intimate and large, like **Salzamt, Krah-Krah,** and **Ma Pitom.** Around Concordiaplatz and in the Heinrichsgasse, **Puerto** and **Domicil** are highly popular. Back toward Stephansplatz, on the Bäckerstrasse, check out **Weinorgel, Oswald & Kalb;** on Blutgasse, **Chamäleon;** on Singerstrasse, the **Galerie Bar. The American Bar** on Kärntner Durchgang has an original Adolf Loos turn-of-the-century interior.

Cabaret Cabaret has a long tradition in Vienna. **Simpl** (Wollzeile 36, tel. 0222/512–4742) continues earning its reputation for barbed political wit but has had to give way to some newcomers at **K&K** (Linke Wienzeile 4, tel. 0222/587–2275) and **Kabarett Niedermair** (Lenaugasse 1A, tel. 0222/408–4492). To get much from any of these, you'll need good German plus knowledge of local affairs and dialects.

Casinos Try your luck at the casino **Cercle Wien** (Kärntner Str. 41, tel. 0222/512–4836) in a former town palace. The Austrian casinos are state operated, so you'll get as fair a chance as anywhere.

Discos The disco scene is big in Vienna, and the crowd seems to follow the leader from one "in" spot to the next. A few continually draw full houses. Try **Atrium** (Schwarzenbergplatz 10, tel. 0222/505–3594); **Queen Anne,** still very much "in" (Johannesgasse 12, tel. 0222/512–0203); and **U–4,** popular with a mixed group, early thirties and under (Schönbrunner Str. 222, tel. 0222/858307).

Jazz Clubs Vienna is increasingly good for jazz, and though places where it can be heard tend to come and go, each seems to be known to the other. Nothing gets going before 9 PM. Try **Duke's** (Gumpendorferstr. 9, tel. 0222/568710); **Jazzland** (Franz-Josefs-Kai 29, tel. 0222/533–2575); **Miles Smiles** (Lange Gasse 51, tel. 0222/428–4814); **Opus One** (Mahlerstr. 11, tel. 0222/513–2075); **Papa's Tapas** Schwarzenbergplatz 10, tel. 0222/505–0311); and **Roter Engel** (Rabensteig 5, tel. 0222/535–4105).

Nightclubs Vienna has no real nightclub tradition, although there are a number of clubs in town. Most of the ones with floor shows are horribly expensive and not very good. The two where you run the least risk are **Casanova,** where singles can sit reasonably peacefully at the upstairs bar (Dorotheergasse 6, tel. 0222/512–9845; open daily till 4 AM), and **Moulin Rouge** (Walfischgasse 11, tel. 0222/512–2130; open Mon.–Sat. 10 PM–6AM).

The leading night spots for dancing are the **Eden Bar,** which always has a live band and is for the well-heeled mature crowd (Liliengasse 2, tel. 0222/512–7450; open 10 PM–4 AM); the **Splendid Bar,** which draws a mixed crowd (Jasomirgottstr. 3, tel. 0222/533–3430, open to 4 AM); **Chattanooga,** which often has a live band and has a younger crowd (Graben 29, tel. 0222/533–5000); and **Volksgarten** (in the Volksgarten, Burgring 1, tel. 0222/630518), where a mixed younger set comes, particularly in summer, for outdoor dancing.

Excursions from Vienna

Baden

This short tour takes you to Baden through the band of rolling wooded hills called the Vienna Woods (Wienerwald) that border Vienna on the west. The hills are skirted by vineyards forming a "wine belt," which also follows the valleys south of Vienna. You can visit this area easily in a day's outing, either by car or by public transportation, or you can spend the night in Baden, Mödling, or Alland for a more leisurely tour, visiting Mayerling, Heiligenkreuz, and a few other sights in the area.

Tourist Information Get information in Vienna before you start out, at the tourist office of Lower Austria (Heidenschuss 2, tel. 0222/533–4773).

Other tourist offices are for Perchtoldsdorf (tel. 0222/8676–3434); Mödling (tel. 02236/26727); Gumpoldskirchen (tel. 02252/62421); Baden (tel. 02252/8680–0310).

Escorted Tours This is one of the standard routes offered by the sightseeing-bus tour operators in Vienna, and it usually includes a boat ride through the "underground sea" grotto near Mödling. For details, check with your hotel or **Cityrama** (tel. 0222/534130) or **Vienna Sightseeing Tours** (tel. 0222/712–4683).

Getting Around You can get to Baden directly from Vienna by bus or, far more
By Bus or Train fun, interurban streetcar in about 40 minutes; the bus departs from the Ring directly opposite the Opera; the streetcar, from the Ring across from the Bristol Hotel. It is possible, with advance planning, to go on to Mayerling and Heiligenstadt on post office buses (tel. 0222/71101), but schedules are infrequent, and driving is preferable.

By Car Head for Liesing (23rd District), then take the Wiener Strasse to Perchtoldsdorf; from there, follow the signs south to Mödling and Baden. From Baden, take Route 210 (marked "Helen-ental") to Mayerling and on to Alland; return to Vienna via route 11, stopping in Heiligenkreuz en route.

Exploring *Numbers in the margin correspond with points of interest on the Vienna Excursions map.*

1 Just over the Vienna city line is **Perchtoldsdorf,** a picturesque market town with many wine taverns; a 13th-century Gothic parish church; and the symbol of the town, an imposing stone defense tower completed in 1511. Locally known as Pedersdorf, this is a favorite excursion spot for the Viennese, who come mainly for the good local wines. Continue south 8 km (5 mi) to
2 **Mödling,** founded in the 10th century, where you'll find another Gothic parish church; a Romanesque 12th-century charnel house (where the bones of the dead were kept); and the town hall, which has a Renaissance loggia.

A few km east of Mödling—about 16 km (10 mi) south of Vien-
3 na—is **Schloss Laxenburg,** a complex consisting of a large Baroque Neues Schloss (New Castle), a small 14th-century Altes Schloss (Old Castle), and an early 19th-century neo-Gothic castle set into the sizable lake. The large park is full of birds and small game, such as roe deer and hare, and is decorated with statues, cascades, imitation temples, and other follies. The Altes Schloss was built in 1381 by Duke Albrecht III as his summer residence, and several Habsburg emperors spent summers in the Neues Schloss, which now houses the International Institute of Applied Systems Analysis. Opposite is the large Baroque Convent of the Charitable Sisters.

4 West of Mödling on Route 11 is the **Seegrotte Hinterbrühl,** a fascinating but now somewhat commercialized underground sea, created years ago when a mine filled up with water (Grutschg. 2, tel. 02236/26364). You can take a motorboat trip on the lake and look at the reflections through the arched caverns of the mine. Not far is the "Höldrichsmühle," a mill that's now a restaurant, made famous by Franz Schubert's song about the linden tree.

Back in Mödling, we follow the "wine road" through the lush vineyard country to the famous wine-producing village of
5 **Gumpoldskirchen,** the home of one of Europe's pleasantest white wines. Vintners' houses line the main street, many of

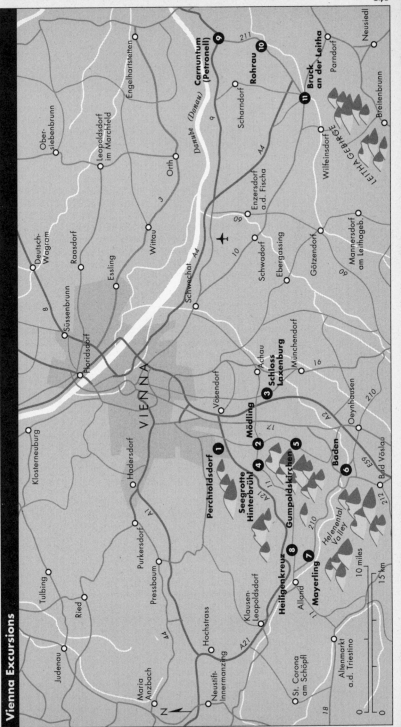

Vienna Excursions

them with the typical large wooden gates that lead to the vine-covered courtyards where the Heuriger (wine of the latest vintage) is served by the owner and his family at simple wooden tables with benches. Gumpoldskirchen also has an arcaded Renaissance town hall, a market fountain made from a Roman sarcophagus, and the castle of the Teutonic knights, whose descendants still own some of the best vineyard sites in the area.

Continuing on the wine road brings you to the famous spa of **❻ Baden.** Since antiquity, Baden's sulphuric thermal baths have attracted the ailing and the fashionable from all over the world. When the Romans came across the springs, they dubbed the town *Aquae;* the Babenbergs revived it in the 10th century, and when the Russian Czar Peter the Great visited in 1698, Baden's golden age began. Austrian Emperor Franz II spent the summers here; every year for 12 years before his death in 1835, the royal entourage moved from Vienna for the season. In Baden, Mozart composed his "Ave Verum"; Beethoven spent 15 summers here and wrote large sections of his Ninth Symphony and *Missa Solemnis;* here Franz Grillparzer wrote his historical dramas; and Josef Lanner, both Johann Strausses (father and son), Carl Michael Ziehrer, and Karl Millöcker composed and directed many of their waltzes, marches, and operettas in Baden.

The loveliest spot in Baden, and the main reason for a visit, is the huge and beautiful **Kurpark,** where many outdoor public concerts still take place. Operetta is given under the skies in the Summer Arena (the roof closes if it rains); in winter, it is performed in the Stadttheater. People sit quietly under the old trees or walk through the upper sections of the Kurpark for a view of the town from above. The old Kurhaus, now enlarged and renovated, incorporates a convention hall. The ornate casino, with its 19th-century decor, is a marvelous sight.

The six spa buildings are built directly over the 15 springs, which pour forth 8 million liters (1.76 million gallons) of the water every day. The water is about body temperature and is considered a particularly good cure for rheumatic diseases. Outdoors there are two thermal-water swimming complexes, the larger with five pools and a water temperature of 32° C (just under 90° F).

Route 210 takes you through the quiet Helenental Valley west **❼** of Baden to **Mayerling,** scene of a suicide pact in 1889 between the 30-year-old Habsburg heir, Crown Prince Rudolf, Emperor Franz Josef's only son, and his 17-year-old mistress, Baroness Marie Vetsera. The mystery surrounding the tragedy is still a juicy subject for speculation. In an attempt to suppress the scandal—the full details are not known to this day—the baroness's body was smuggled back into the city by carriage, propped up between two uncles. The Mayerling story surfaces regularly in books, films, and tabloid-newspaper gossip. The hunting lodge is no longer there; it was replaced by a Carmelite convent, built by the bereaved emperor.

About 4 km (2.5 mi) northeast of Mayerling, in the heart of the **❽** southern section of the Vienna Woods is **Heiligenkreuz,** a magnificent Cistercian abbey with a famous Romanesque and Gothic church, founded in 1135 by Leopold III. The church itself is lofty and serene, with beautifully carved choir stalls (the Cistercians are a singing order) surmounted by busts of Cistercian saints. The cloisters are interesting for the Chapel of the Dead, where the brothers lie in state guarded by four gesticulating skeletons holding candelabra. The chapterhouse contains the tombs of Babenberg rulers.

Dining and Lodging
Alland

Marienhof. Close to both Mayerling and Heiligenkreuz, this stylish building set in a beautiful park has simple but immaculate rooms. The **Kronprinz** restaurant serves outstanding, adventuresome fare, and there's a simpler and cheaper restaurant as well. *A–2534, tel. 02258/2378. 25 rooms. Facilities: restaurant (reservations not required, jacket and tie advised). No credit cards. Closed Sun. evening and Mon. Expensive.*

Baden

Sauerhof. "Schönbrunn yellow" marks this appealing country house that's been elegantly renovated, with rooms in "old Vienna" style. The hotel caters to seminars and group activities. Nevertheless, the restaurant is excellent (try the veal steak with mushrooms, or for dessert, the famous house crêpes). *Weilburgstr. 11–13, A–2500, tel. 02252/41251. 83 rooms. Facilities: restaurant (reservations not required, jacket and tie advised, open for lunch Sun. only), bar, indoor pool, tennis. AE, DC, MC, V. Very Expensive.*

Krainerhütte. This friendly house, in typical alpine style, with balconies and lots of natural wood, is family run. The rooms are attractively furnished in country style. *Helenental, A–2500, tel. 02252/4451. 60 rooms. Facilities: restaurant, indoor pool, sauna, solarium, tennis, DC, MC, V. Expensive.*

Mödling

Rosenhotel. The inside of this modern block, with its rustic decor, is far pleasanter than you'd expect from the plain outside. The rooms are simple but comfortable. *Guntramsdorferstr. 10a, A–2340, tel. 02236/85123. 50 rooms. Facilities: restaurant, bar. Moderate.*

Perchtoldsdorf

Jahreszeiten. This elegant, formal restaurant is now in the capable hands of Günter Winter, who achieved an excellent reputation with Hauswirth in Vienna. The menu offers international cuisine with an Austrian flair. Beyond the kitchen, the atmosphere, like the tables, is set to perfection, and the menu is supplemented by wines from an outstanding cellar, international as well as local. *Hochstr. 17, tel. 0222/864763. Reservations required. Jacket and tie advised. AE, DC, MC, V. Closed Mon. and early Aug. Very Expensive.*

Carnuntum and Rohrau

As the Romans moved up the Danube, they set up installations and fortresses along the way, mainly on the south side of the river. The Roman ruins in Vienna have long since been covered by later generations of buildings and can now be seen only in the handful of underground museums in the First District. But about 20 km (12 mi) east of the airport, one of the more impressive Roman camps, Carnuntum, has been extensively excavated, and in an easy day trip by car or public transportation, you can see this ancient community and the nearby towns of Rohrau and Bruck an der Leitha.

Escorted Tours With the opening of Czechoslovakia, more tours may be offered to the eastern part of Lower Austria, but for the moment this is one area you'll probably have to explore on your own.

Getting Around
By Train or Bus

The suburban rail line from Wien-Mitte (Landstrasser Hauptstr.) stops at Petronell, with service about once an hour.

Carnuntum is about a 10-minute walk from the Petronell station. You can also take a post office bus, from the Wien-Mitte bus station, which drops you right at the ruins. From Petronell, a bus runs to Rohrau (check schedules), and from Rohrau, you can either return to Petronell or take a bus on to Bruck an der Leitha and from there a bus or train back to Vienna.

By Car In leaving the city, follow signs to "Airport/Bratislava" (A–4). Leave the divided highway at the airport for the more scenic Route 9, which will be marked to Hainburg. At Petronell, you will have to take a sharp right off the new road, but signs are clear for the Roman ruins (Carnuntum). From Petronell, take Route 211 to Rohrau and on to Bruck an der Leitha; from there, Route 10 takes you back to Vienna.

Exploring The Roman town and military camp of **Carnuntum** was the larg-
9 est garrison on the Roman "Amber Road" leading south from the Baltic Sea. At its peak it had a civilian population of 30,000 and boasted two amphitheaters. The settlement collapsed following a defeat by the Germans in the third century. You can take a guided tour (tel. 02165/2480; admission: AS25 adults, AS15 children; open Apr.–Oct., daily 9–5) or you can wander through the excavations, arranged as an open-air museum, with the remains of Roman houses, the amphitheater that once held 25,000 people, and the Heidentor (Heathen Gate), in a nearby field. New buildings are being completed to house the artifacts found in the course of the diggings, many of which are now on display in the Museum Carnuntinium in Bad Deutsch-Altenburg, 4½ km (2.8 mi) east. The Danube Museum in the great castle at Petronell contains some relics from the excavations (it is the only part of the castle open to visitors).

10 About 8 km (5 mi) south of Petronell is **Rohrau,** the birthplace of the composers Franz Josef (1732–1809) and Michael (1737–1806) Haydn. The compact straw-roofed house in which the family with 12 children lived is now a museum that gives a good idea of country life of the time (tel. 02164/2268; admission: AS20 adults, AS10 children; open Tues.–Sun. 10–5). Down the road is the 16th-century **Harrach Castle,** with an entry bridge (over the former moat) and a lake at the back. The art gallery contains the largest private collection in Austria (dating to 1668) with works by Rubens, Van Dyck, Breughel, and many Spanish and Italian artists. Haydn's mother was a cook at the castle, and Count Harrach became one of Haydn's first patrons. *Tel. 02164/22530. Admission: AS40 adults, AS20 children. Open Apr.–Oct., Tues–Sun. 10–5.*

Time Out **Schlosstaverne.** The restaurant tucked into the front corner of the castle serves substantial portions of good country food and wines from the region. Service slows somewhat when tour groups appear. The terrace is particularly inviting on a warm, sunny day. *Tel. 02164/2487. Reservations advised on weekends. Dress: casual but neat. No credit cards. Closed Mon., in winter. Inexpensive.*

11 If you return to Vienna via **Bruck an der Leitha,** take time to look around this walled community, which until 1921 marked the border with Hungary. Note the town square, with the 15th-century Holy Trinity church and the town hall with its arcaded court and Rococo balcony. The 17th-century Prugg castle (once moated) is not open to the public, but you can wander under tall trees in the surrounding park.

The Waldviertel

The "Forest District" north of the Danube and to the northwest of Vienna was long dormant, out of the mainstream and cut off from neighboring Czechoslovakia by a sealed border. Today, with the collapse of communism in Czechoslovakia and the reopening of many crossing points, the Waldviertel has reawakened. Here gentle hills bearing stands of tall pine and oak are interspersed with small farms and friendly country villages. The region can be seen in a couple of days, longer when you pause to explore the museums, castles, and other attractions. Zwettl and Raabs an der Thaya make good bases for discovering this area away from the major tourism routes, where facilities are more modest and much less expensive.

Tourist Information The tourist office for Lower Austria in Vienna (Heidenschuss 2, tel. 0222/533–4773) has ample material on the Waldviertel. Other tourist offices within the region are those at Gars am Kamp (tel. 02985/2680), Horn (tel. 02982/265614), Zwettl (tel. 02822/2233), Gmünd (tel. 02852/53212), Waidhofen an der Thaya (tel. 02842/233117), and Raabs an der Thaya (tel. 02846/365).

Escorted Tours The Waldviertel remains undiscovered for organized tourism; for the time being, visitors are on their own.

Getting Around
By Bus or Train The main rail line from Vienna to Prague passes through the Waldviertel, making the region accessible by train. In addition, post office buses cover the area fairly well and with reasonable frequency. Bus hubs are Horn, Waidhofen, and Zwettl. An express bus service runs between Vienna and Heidenreichstein via Waidhofen an der Thaya.

By Car Signs for Prague will head you in the right direction out of Vienna. At Stockerau take Route 4 to Horn, Route 38 west to Zwettl, an unnumbered road to Weitra, Route 41 to Gmünd and Schrems, Route 30 north to Heidenreichstein, Route 5 to Waidhofen an der Thaya, an unnumbered road via Gross Siegharts to Raabs an der Thaya, Route 30 to Riegersburg, an unnumbered road to Hardegg. Return on Route 30 to Geras, Route 4 to Horn, Route 34 down the Kamp valley past Langenlois, and Route 3 back to Vienna.

Exploring The successful Austrian field marshall Radetzky (1766–1858) is buried at Heldenberg in the tiny village of **Kleinwetzdorf,** in elegant but lugubrious surroundings. His tomb, arranged for by a wealthy uniform supplier, is set in a park studded with dozens of larger-than-life busts of Austrian royalty and nobility. The small castle has a Radetzky museum. *Tel. 02956/2619. Admission: AS30 adults, AS60 family. Open May–Oct., weekends 10–5.*

Time Out **Restaurant Naderer** at the top of the hill above Maissau is an ideal stop for coffee: The house cakes are particularly good. A full meal can be enjoyed in summer on the terrace overlooking the valley.

At **Horn** are remnants of the impressive fortification walls built in 1532 as a defense against the invading Turks. Note the painted Renaissance facade on the house (1583) at Kirchenplatz 3.

About 5 km (3 mi) outside Horn, at **Altenburg** on Route 38, **Altenburg abbey** was built in 1144 and rebuilt in 1645–1740 after its destruction by the Swedes. The library and the frescoed ceilings are glorious. *Tel. 02982/3451. Admission: AS35 adults, AS15 children. Open (with guided tours) Easter–Oct., daily 9–noon and 1–5.*

Almost 25 km (15 m) west of Altenburg, the castle at **Ottenstein,** now a hotel-restaurant, has a number of impressive reception rooms and parts dating to 1178. Ottenstein defied the Swedes only to be devastated by the Russians in 1945. Sports enthusiasts will find boating and swimming in the reservoir-lake and golf at Niedergrünbach. The ruined **Lichtenfels castle** nearby can be explored.

Zwettl is known for the vast **Cistercian abbey** dating to 1138 about 2¼ km (1½ mi) west of the town. Later renovations added the glorious Baroque touches. *Tel. 02822/531–8117. Admission: AS35 adults, AS20 children. Open (with guided tours) May–Oct., Mon.–Sat. 10–noon and 2–4, Sun. 11–noon and 2–4.*

About 2 km (1 mi) north of Zwettl on Route 36, a fascinating **museum of medicine and meteorology** is housed in a cloister chapel built in 1294. Exhibits follow the development of medicine from earliest times to the present, and the courtyard garden of medicinal herbs adds another dimension to the history. *Tel. 02822/53180. Admission: AS40 adults, AS15 children. Open May–early Nov., Tues.–Sun. 10–6.*

Time Out In the Zwettl abbey the **Stiftsrestaurant,** a spacious tavern complex, serves good Austrian country fare such as grilled chicken and roast pork with bread dumpling. The beer is fresh from the nearby brewery.

About 7½ km (almost 5 mi) west of Zwettl (follow signs to Rosenau), **Rosenau castle** is an impressive renaissance structure built in 1590 with later Baroque additions. The castle was ravaged by the Soviets in 1945, then rebuilt as a hotel and museum complex housing the unique **Freemasonry museum,** with a secret room once used for lodge ceremonies that was discovered during the renovations. Displays show the ties of Haydn and Mozart to freemasonry, and many exhibit labels are in English, reflecting the origins of the brotherhood. *Tel. 02822/8221. Admission: AS40 adults, AS30 senior citizens, AS20 children. Open mid-Apr.–mid-Nov., daily 9–5.*

On the main road, turn west 20 km (12½ mi) to **Weitra,** a small town stunning for its ornate painted houses (Sgraffiti) dating from the 17th and 18th centuries. A charming small brewery here has been in business since 1321! And the tradition is well founded: in 1645, 33 citizens held the right to operate a brewery.

Gmünd lies 16 km (10 mi) north of Weitra on Route 41, a town that was divided when the border with Czechoslovakia was established. The actual line passes through a few houses and backyards, but with the barbed-wire defenses removed, the border is now a harmless affair. Railroad fans have a field day here; the Czechs still use some steam locomotives for switching, and on the Austrian side Gmünd is one of the main points on the narrow-gauge Waldviertler Bahn, which runs occasional steam excursions (tel. 02852/4120 or 02852/4386). The nature park to the northeast of the center, open to the public all year, includes a geological open-air museum and a stone marking the 15th meridian east of Greenwich.

North of Schrems a detour west from Route 30, on Route 303, leads to Neunagelberg, a center of glassmaking since 1740. Among the glassworks you can visit is *Glasstudio Zalto* (tel. 02859/237). Another, *Stölzle Kristall* (tel. 02859/531), has a showroom and factory outlet.

At **Heidenreichstein** on Route 30, the massive moated **castle** with its corner towers has never been captured since it was built in the 15th century; some of the walls, 3 meters (10 ft) thick, went up in the 13th century. *Tel. 02862/2336. Admission (with guided tour): AS30 adults, AS15 children. Open mid-Apr.–mid-Oct., Tues.–Sun. 9–noon and 2–5.*

Route 5 leads east to **Waidhofen an der Thaya,** a three-sided walled defense city typical of the 13th century. Fires destroyed much of the early character of the town, but the town square, rebuilt at the end of the 19th century, has a pleasing unity of character. The town is dominated by its Baroque parish church; the Rococo chapel to Mary includes a madonna of 1440 and distinguished portraits marking the stations of the cross. Outside the city walls, the **Bürgerspitalkapelle** has a side altar with a Gothic carved-wood relief of Mary and child and 13 assistants, from about 1500.

An unnumbered road continues east 21 km (13 mi) via Gross-Siegharts to **Raabs an der Thaya,** an attractive village watched over by an 11th-century castle perched dramatically on a rock outcropping and reflected in the river below. *Tel. 02846/659. Admission AS20. Open May–Oct., daily 9–noon and 1–4.*

The intriguing ruins of the Kollmitz castle to the southeast of Raabs can be explored, and a bit farther along are the ruins of Eibenstein castle, another link in the defense chain along the border with Bohemia.

Route 30 leads to Drosendorf, with a castle built in 1100 and a town center typical of a small walled community. Farther along—27 km (17 mi) from Raabs—**Riegersburg castle** was originally moated, then the substantial edifice was given a Baroque rebuilding in 1731 and restored again after heavy damage inflicted by the Russians in 1945. Note the window variations and the figures that ornament the roofline. *Tel. 02916/332. Admission (on guided tour only): AS58 adults, AS27 children. Combination ticket with Hardegg: AS95. Open Apr.–June, Sept.–Oct., daily 9–5; July–Aug., daily 9–7.*

About 6 km (4 mi) east of Riegersburg on an unnumbered road, **Hardegg castle** stands mightily on a rock promontory high above the Thaya river, challenging Czechoslovakia. (The river midstream marks the boundary; as recently as 1990, the pedestrian bridge was unpassable, the border sealed, and Czech border defenses concealed in the woods opposite.) The earliest parts of the castle date to 1140. The armory and armament collection, chapel, and the museum's exhibits on the emperor Maximilian in Mexico are alone worth the visit. In addition, the kitchen and other working rooms of the castle give a real feeling of the daily life of an earlier era. *Tel. 02949/8225. Admission: AS50 adults, AS45 senior citizens, AS27 children. Open Apr.– June, Sept.–Nov., daily 9–5; July–Aug., daily 9–6.*

From Hardegg, retrace your steps on Route 30 to Geras, where the impressive abbey has a marvelous Baroque interior. Continue south on Route 4 to Horn and take Route 34 south to Rosenburg and on through the Kamp river valley.

The castle at **Rosenburg** dates to 1200 and dominates the north entrance to the valley. Its interesting features include the jousting field, the reception rooms, and the Renaissance balconies and small courtyards incorporated into the design. *Tel. 02982/2911. Admission (with guided tour): AS50 adults, AS35 children. Falconry demonstration daily at 11 and 3; combination ticket AS80 adults, AS60 children. Open Apr.–mid-Nov., daily 9–5.*

The scenic Kamp valley technically belongs to the Waldviertel, though for the amount of wine produced here, it might as well be a part of the Weinviertel, the wine district to the east. The villages along the route—Gars am Kamp, Schönberg am Kamp, Zöbing, and Langenlois—are all known for excellent wines, mainly varietal whites. Castle ruins dot the hilltops above the vineyards; the area has been populated since well before 900 BC.

Route 34 takes you through more vineyards to Kollersdorf, where Route 3 east will return you to Vienna.

Dining and Lodging

Grafenegg

★

Schlosstaverne Grafenegg. Behind the golden facade of the elegant tavern waits a friendly and welcoming atmosphere. Rooms are comfortably furnished in beiges and reds. The restaurant offers game in season and local cuisine with international touches. The strawberries in early summer taste even better outdoors on the sunny dining terrace. *A–3485 Haitzendorf, tel. 02735/2616. 6 rooms. Facilities: restaurant (reservations advised on weekends). No credit cards. Closed Jan.–Feb. Moderate.*

Kirchberg am Wagram

★

Gut Oberstockstall. A former cloister houses this country inn where the rustic setting indoors is charming and the courtyard garden idyllic in summer. The menu promises lamb, duck, game in season, and tempting desserts such as grilled apricots—all to the accompaniment of the house's own wines. *Tel. 02279/2335. Reservations advised. Dress: casual chic. No credit cards. Closed Sun.–Tues.; mid-Dec.–Feb., last 2 weeks in Aug. Expensive.*

Langenlois

Brundlmayer. This country Heuriger offers outstanding wines from one of Austria's top vintners as well as a tasty hot and cold buffet, all in a rustic setting or in the Renaissance courtyard. The simple but delicious fare includes *Schinkenfleckerl*, a baked dish of noodles and ham. *Walterst. 14, tel. 02734/2883. Reservations advised in winter. Dress: casual chic. No credit cards. Closed Mon.–Wed.; Jan.–Feb. Moderate.*

Raabs an der Thaya

★

Hotel Thaya. A family-run hotel directly on the river, the Thaya offers modern rooms in beiges and dark wood in the new annex. Rooms overlooking the river are the favorites. The restaurant prepares such solid local specialties as roast pork and veal. *Hauptstr. 14, A–3820 Raabs an der Thaya, tel. 02846/ 2020. 25 rooms. Facilities: restaurant, bar, beer garden, disco,* *sauna, solarium, fitness room, parking. No credit cards. Moderate.*

★ **Pension Schlossblick.** This small modern pension has a homey atmosphere in its spacious lounge and cheery breakfast room. The beige-and-red rooms on the town side looking through the trees to the castle are the nicest. *Eduard Breit-Str. 7, A–3820 Raabs an der Thaya, tel. 02846/437. 13 rooms. Facilities: restaurant for hotel guests, parking. No credit cards. Inexpensive.*

Rosenau **Schloss Rosenau.** Set in an elegant palace, this small hotel offers country quiet and modern rooms furnished in period style.
★ The wood-paneled restaurant is one of the best in the area, featuring garlic soup, bread soup, and lamb or game in season. In summer food seems to taste even better on the sunny outdoor terrace. *A–3924 Rosenau, tel. 02822/8221. 18 rooms. Facilities: restaurant (reservations advised on weekends), indoor pool, sauna, solarium, fishing. AE, DC, MC, V. Closed mid-Jan.–Feb. Moderate.*

The Weinviertel

The "Wine District," the rolling countryside north of Vienna, earns its name from the ideal terrain and climate here for wine. Both reds and whites come from the region, bounded by the Danube on the south, the Thaya river and the reopened Czech border on the north, the March river and Czechoslovakia to the east. No well-defined line separates the Weinviertel from the Waldviertel to the west; the Kamp river valley, officially part of the Waldviertel, is an important wine region. Whether wine, crops, or dairying, this is farming country, its broad expanses of vineyards and farm crops broken by patches of forest and neat villages. A tour by car, just for the scenery, can be made in a day; you may want two or three days to savor the region and its wines—generally on the medium-dry side. Don't expect to find here the elegant facilities you found elsewhere in Austria; prices are low by any standard, and village restaurants and accomodations are mainly *Gasthäuser* that meet local needs. This means that you'll rub shoulders over a glass of wine or a beer with country folk, a rugged specie different from that you find in most parts of the nation.

Tourist Information The tourist office for Lower Austria in Vienna (Heidenschuss 2, tel. 0222/533–4773) has basic information on the Weinviertel. Other tourist offices within the region are those at Poysdorf (Liechtensteinstr. 1, tel. 02552/3515), Retz (Herrenplatz 30, tel. 02942/2700), Laa an der Thaya (Rathaus, tel. 02522/5010), Mistelbach (Hauptplatz 6, tel. 02572/2787), Poysdorf (Singerstr. 2, tel. 02552/220017), and Gänserndorf (Rathausplatz 1, tel. 02282/26501).

Escorted Tours The Weinviertel has yet to be exploited by tour operators, and visitors are on their own.

Getting Around Bus service to and through the area is good, with direct ser-
By Bus or Train vices available between Vienna and Retz, Laa an der Thaya, and Poysdorf as well as buses between the region's larger towns. Trains run from Vienna to Mistelbach, and to Gänserndorf and beyond to Bernhardsthal on the Czech border.

By Car Roads are good and well marked. Head out of Vienna to Stockerau on Route 3 or the autobahn A22/E49/E59, following the signs to Prague. After Stockerau, turn north on Route 303 to beyond Hollabrun, then Routes 2 and 30 to Retz. From Retz, backtrack on Route 30 to Route 45 and head east to Laa an der Thaya. Then follow Route 46 to Staatz, Route 219 to Poysdorf, Route 7/E461 south beyond Gaweinstal, Route 220 to Gänserndorf, and Route 8 back to Vienna.

Exploring Like Linz, **Korneuburg** is a center of Austrian shipbuilding; many Danube passenger ships, including those under USSR and other flags, were built here. The massive Gothic-style town hall dominates the main square, though other buildings are far older. The Augustine church has a *Last Supper* (1770) by the Austrian painter Maulpertsch as part of the altar.

Schloss Schönborn at **Göllersdorf** was laid out in 1712 by that master of baroque architecture, Lukas von Hildebrandt. Today the castle is in private hands, but the harmony of design can be appreciated from the outside.

Retz, at the northwest corner of the Weinviertel, is known for its red wines. Here you can tour Austria's largest wine cellar, tunneled 20 m (65 ft) under the town, and at the same time taste wines of the area. Some of the tunnels go back to the 13th century, and at the end of the 15th century each citizen was permitted to deal in wines and was entitled to storage space in the town cellars. Efforts to use the cellars for armaments production during World War II failed because of the 88% humidity. The temperature remains constant at 8–10°C (47–50°F). Entrance to the cellars is at the Rathauskeller. *Tel. 02942/2700 or 02942/2379. Guided tour (includes a commemorative glass and a wine sample): AS40 adults, AS15 children. Tours Mon.–Sat. 2 PM, Sun. 10, 11, 2, 3.*

The Retz town square is an attractive mixture of Sgraffito (painted) facades, Biedermeier, and other styles. Most buildings date to 1660 or later; during the Thirty Years' War the Swedes occupied Retz and left only 28 buildings standing. The Dominican church (1295) at the southwest corner of the square survived, and it is interesting for its long, narrow design.

To the northwest of the center, outside the walls on a hillcrest at Kalvarienberg 1, the windmill—the town's emblem—dates to 1830 and was in commercial use to 1927 as a gristmill and is still operational.

Retrace your way south on Route 30 to Route 45 and turn east to **Laa an der Thaya,** once an isolated town but increasingly a commercial center for Czechoslovakian shoppers now that the border is open. (As long as you have your passport with you, you should be able to cross the border and return without complication.) Laa boasts a **Beer Museum,** located in the town fortress, that traces the history of beer (the nearby Hubertus brewery has been in business since 1454) and maintains an imposing collection of beer bottles. *Tel. 02522/5010. Admission: AS15 adults, AS10 children. Open May–Sept., weekends 2–4.*

Time Out If a coffee break seems in order, **Café Weiler,** upstairs on the main square at Stadtplatz 2, has outstanding cakes and pastries.

Driving Route 46 from Laa, you'll find that the impressive hilltop castle ruin at **Staatz** loses significance the closer you get. It's possible to wander through the ruin, but little is left of the onetime fortress other than a pile of stone and a strategic view of the countryside.

Route 219 leads to **Poysdorf** and the heart of the Weinviertel. Poysdorf vintages, mainly whites, rank with the best Austria has to offer. The town museum includes a section on viticulture and wine making. *Brunner Str. 9, tel. 02552/220025. Admission: AS20 adults. Open Easter–Nov., Sun. 10–noon and 2–4.*

South of **Gänserndorf,** the **auto safari park** allows visitors to drive through recreated natural habitats of live wild animals, many of which (lions and tigers) are hardly indigenous to Austria. The adventure takes five to six hours. *Siebenbrunner Str., tel. 02282/7261. Admission: AS135 adults, AS80 children. Open Palm Sunday–Nov., weekdays 9:30–4:30, weekends 9–5.*

Nearby at **Strasshof** the **Heizhaus** is a fascinating private collection of dozens of steam locomotives and railroad cars stored in a vast engine house. Enthusiasts have painstakingly rebuilt and restored many of the engines, which are operated on weekends. The complex includes transfer table, water towers, and coaling station, and visitors can climb around among many of the locomotives awaiting restoration. *Sillerstr. 123, tel. 02287/3027. Admission (with parking and guided tour): AS50 adults, AS25 children. Open Apr.–Sept., Sun. 10–4.*

Route 8 returns you to Vienna, passing through one of Austria's few oil fields, where operating pumps patiently pull up crude to be piped to the refinery about 20 km (12½ mi) south.

Dining and Lodging *Deutsch Wagram*	**Marchfelderhof.** This sprawling complex with its eclectic series of rooms decorated with everything from antiques to hunting trophies has been undergoing renovation, but its character is unlikely to change. Nor is the menu, which pretends to grander things. The standards—Wiener Schnitzel, roast pork, lamb—are more successful than the more expensive efforts at innovation. *Tel. 02247/2243. Reservations advised. Jacket and tie advised. AE, DC, MC, V. Closed late Dec.–early Feb. Expensive.*

Laa an der Thaya
★

Restaurant Weiler. Light woods and country accessories set the tone in this family-run restaurant, and in summer dinner is served in the outdoor garden. The delicate cream of garlic soup is worth a visit, and a house specialty is game in season. For dessert, the cakes of the house are displayed in a showcase. *Staatsbahnstr. 60, tel. 02522/379. Reservations advised on weekends. Dress: casual neat. No credit cards. Closed Mon. and late June–mid-July. Moderate.*

Mistelbach

Zur Linde. This friendly restaurant with the rustic decor is setting higher standards for such traditional fare as roast pork, flank steak, and fresh game in season. But the major attraction here is the remarkable range of wines from the neighborhood at altogether reasonable prices. *Bahnhofstr. 49, tel. 02572/2409. Dress: casual but neat. AE, MC, V. Closed Mon. dinner; mid-Jan.–mid-Feb. Moderate.*

Gasthof Goldene Krone. This friendly, traditional house offers simple but adequate accommodation. Rooms are quaintly old-fashioned yet comfortable, and guests are in the heart of the Weinviertel for excursions. *Oberhofer Str. 15, A–2130, tel. 02572/27295. 22 rooms. Facilities: restaurant, bar, garage. No credit cards. Inexpensive.*

Poysdorf

Schreiber. Choose the shaded garden under huge trees or the country rustic decor indoors. The typical Austrian fare—roast

pork, stuffed breast of veal, boiled beef, filet steak with garlic—is commendable, as is the house-made ice cream. The wine
card lists more than 60 area labels. *Bahnst. 2, tel. 02552/2348.*
Dress: casual but neat. No credit cards. Closed Wed. lunch,
Thurs.; mid-Jan.–mid-Feb. Moderate.

Winzerstadl. Local wines and such specialties as roast pork
with caraway, and smoked ham, are the fixtures at wine restaurants. This is a typical Weinviertel house, where in summer
diners relax in the garden under huge chestnut trees. *Brunner*
Str. 7, tel. 02552/2772. Dress: casual but neat. No credit cards.
Closed Mon., Tues.; Nov.–Apr. Moderate.

4 Eastern Austria

*by Earl
Steinbicker*

*Earl Steinbicker is
the author of
several guidebooks
to Europe.*

No part of the nation offers a greater range of scenery than what is loosely defined as Eastern Austria, yet despite its proximity to Vienna it is largely overlooked by foreign tourists. Not that the region lacks visitors—it has long been a favorite of the Austrians themselves and is becoming increasingly popular with the neighboring Hungarians and other Eastern Europeans as border restrictions are relaxed. This fact alone ensures that prices will remain lower here than in other parts of the country for some time, since most of the visitors are cost conscious and demand value for their money.

There are no singularly great sights in the region—no Schönbrunn Palace, no towering Alps, and no not-to-be-missed three-star attractions. What you'll find instead is a largely unspoiled land of lakes, farms, castles, villages, and vineyards. It's also a sports lover's paradise, rich in history, with a distinguished musical past and—yes—one genuine city, Graz, whose sophistication and beauty may surprise you. In short, this is a destination for experienced travelers who have already explored Vienna, Salzburg, the Tirol, and other better-known parts of Austria. It is a place to relax and mingle with Austrians who have not yet been overwhelmed by mass tourism.

Eastern Austria, as it is defined here, consists of Burgenland, most of Styria (*Steiermark*), and a small section of Lower Austria (*Niederösterreich*)—three distinctly different provinces with little in common. Its geography varies from the haunting steppes and the mysterious Lake Neusiedl in the east to the low, forested mountains of the south; the industrial valleys of the center and west; and the more rugged mountains of the north where Austrian skiing began. Culturally, Eastern Austria is strongly influenced by neighboring Hungary and Yugoslavia, especially in its earthy and flavorful cuisines. Along with hearty food, the region is noted for its wines, many of which never travel beyond the borders and are best enjoyed right where they were made.

Because the main centers of Eastern Austria are so easily reached from Vienna, it is possible to explore the region one bit at a time, in segments as short as a day or two. For more thorough coverage, however, you should allow at least four days to a week, spending some nights at country inns or castles instead of at regular hotels.

Essential Information

Important Addresses and Numbers

Tourist Information The regional tourist information office for Burgenland province is the **Landesfremdenverkehrsverband für das Burgenland** (Schloss Esterhazy, A–7000 Eisenstadt, tel. 02682/3384). For Styria, the provincial tourist office is the **Steiermärkischer Landesfremdenverkehrsverband** (Herrengasse 16, Landhaus, A–8010 Graz, tel. 0316/835241). Lower Austria has a tourist office in Vienna, the **Niederösterreichisches Landesreisebüro** (Heidenschuss 2, A–1010 Vienna, tel. 0222/533–4773). Among the many local tourist offices, the most important are:

Bruck an der Mur (Reisebüro der Stadt Bruck, Koloman-Wallisch-Platz 24, A–8600, tel. 03862/51811).
Eisenstadt (Fremdenverkehrsamt, Hauptstr. 35, A–7000, tel. 02682/2710).
Graz (Graz-Steiermark-Information, Herrengasse 16, A–8010, tel. 0316/835241, and Platform 1 of the main train station, tel. 0316/916837).
Judenburg (Bezirkshauptmannschaft Judenburg, Kapellenweg 11, A–8750, tel. 03572/320–1208).
Köflach (Fremdenverkehrsbüro, Bahnhofstr. 24, A–8580, tel. 03144/252070).
Mariazell (Fremdenverkehrsverband, Hauptplatz 13, A–8630, tel. 03882/2366).
Neusiedl am See (Fremdenverkehrsbüro, Hauptplatz 1, A–7100, tel. 02167/2229).
Wiener Neustadt (Fremdenverkehrsverein, Herzog-Leopold-Str. 17, A–2700, tel. 02622/29551).

Emergencies **Police,** tel. 133; **Fire,** tel. 122; **Ambulance,** tel. 144; in Graz, **Medical Service,** tel. 190, **Late-night Pharmacies,** tel. 18.

Car Rental **Avis** (Schlögelgrasse 10, Graz, and airport, tel. 0316/812920).
Budget (Bahnhofgürtel 73, Graz, tel. 0316/916966; airport 0316/292506).
Europcar (Raubergasse 20, Graz, tel. 0316/824308).
Hertz (Andreas-Hofer-Platz, Graz, tel. 0316/825007).

Arriving and Departing

By Plane Eastern Austria is served primarily by Vienna's International Airport at Schwechat, 19 km (12 mi) southeast of the city center (*see* Arriving and Departing in Chapter 1).

Graz has its own international airport at Thalerhof, just south of the city, with flights to and from Vienna, Innsbruck, Klagenfurt, Athens, Munich, Frankfurt, and Zurich. **Austrian Airlines** is the major carrier. For information, tel. 0316/291541.

By Car Driving is the best way to enter and explore Eastern Austria, especially if you're visiting the smaller towns and villages or if your time is limited. Route 10 from Vienna to Lake Neusiedl in Burgenland is adequate, and the new A–4 autobahn is under construction. Graz is connected to Vienna by both A–2 and a more scenic mountain road, Route S–6 over the Semmering Pass to Bruck an der Mur, then south through the Mur Valley.

By Train Trains depart from Vienna's Südbahnhof (South Station) hourly for the one-hour ride to Neusiedl am See, where Tour 1 begins. Connections can be made there for Eisenstadt and Pamhagen. There is also fairly frequent express service from the same station in Vienna to Graz, 2½ hours away, with intermediate stops at Wiener Neustadt, Mürzzuschlag, and Bruck an der Mur, and connections to Puchberg am Schneeberg, Semmering, and points west. Trains for Mariazell depart from Vienna's Westbahnhof (West Station), with a change at St. Pölten. For information about all departures from Vienna, tel. 0222/1717; for Graz's main station, tel. 0316/1717. The clerks speak English.

Eastern Austria is served by luxurious **EuroCity** trains from Munich, Salzburg, Linz, and Klagenfurt, as well as from neighboring countries. Nearly all long-distance trains going through

this region meet at Bruck an der Mur, where connections can
be made.

By Bus The major bus services connecting Vienna to towns in Eastern
Austria are **Bundesbus** (tel. 0222/71101), **Austrobus** (tel. 0222/
534110), **Blaguss Reisen** (tel. 0222/501800), and **Dr. Richard**
(tel. 0222/331000). There is good service to Neusiedl am See,
Eisenstadt, and Güssing in Burgenland; Mariazell in Styria;
and Wiener Neustadt in Lower Austria. Direct express service
to Graz is infrequent. Most buses leave Vienna from the Wien
Mitte Bus Station on Landstrasser Hauptstrasse, opposite the
Air Terminal and Hilton Hotel, but be sure to check first.

Guided Tours

Relatively few guided tours visit Eastern Austria, and those
that do are conducted in German, although English may be
available on request. Enquire when booking. General orientation tours, departing from Vienna and lasting one to four days,
are offered by the following reputable operators: **Vienna Sightseeing Tours** (Stelzhammergasse 4/11, Vienna, tel. 0222/712–
4683), **Cityrama Sightseeing** (Börsegasse 1, Vienna, tel. 0222/
534130), **Blaguss Reisen** (Wiedner Hauptstr. 15, Vienna, tel.
0222/501800), and **Austrobus** (*see* above). The one-day tours are
usually to Lake Neusiedl and include a boat ride or to the
Semmering mountain region with a cable-car ride.

Minibus sightseeing tours of Graz are conducted on weekdays
from May through October. **Guided walking tours** of the Old
Town, in English and German, are held on Saturday year-round
and on Tuesday, Friday, and Sunday from late April until late
October. Guided tours of the Schlossberg are conducted daily
except in winter, departing hourly 8–5 from the Glockenturm
near the upper station of the Schlossberg funicular. For prices,
bookings, and current schedules of all tours, contact the tourist
offices listed above.

Exploring Eastern Austria

This chapter describes a circular route through Eastern Austria, beginning and ending at Vienna. It is divided into four
connecting tours, each of which could be taken independently.
By making a few adjustments, visitors coming from Salzburg
or other parts of Austria can adapt the tours to fit their own
itinerary.

Tour 1 takes you from Vienna to Lake Neusiedl, Europe's
strangest lake, and its vineyards, with a possible side trip into
the steppes (*puszta*) along the Hungarian frontier. It then goes
on to Eisenstadt, the provincial capital of Burgenland, a small
town renowned for its memories of Joseph Haydn. From there
it heads south, visiting Burgenland's medieval castles along
the way, then west to Graz. **Tour 2** begins by exploring this university city, which is steeped in Old World atmosphere mixed
with youthful vitality. Graz is a good base for excursions into
southern Styria before turning north. **Tour 3** brings you to the
old crossroads town of Bruck an der Mur, from which you can
continue southwest along the Mur Valley, perhaps as far as
Murau, or northwest to Admont, through the spectacular
Gesäuse Ravine and back again via Eisenerz. Once again in
Bruck, you can head north to Mariazell, an ancient place of pil-

grimage, and perhaps continue through the mountains to Vienna. You can also return to Bruck and take **Tour 4,** which goes to Vienna by way of the famous Semmering Pass and Wiener Neustadt, with side trips into the Höllental and up the Schneeberg mountain.

Travelers with only a day at their disposal could take Tour 1 as far as Eisenstadt, then return to Vienna via Wiener Neustadt. Another good one-day excursion is to Mariazell, described in Tour 3, or to the Schneeberg, easily reached from Vienna by car or train.

Highlights for First-time Visitors

Admont and the Gesäuse Ravine (*see* Tour 3: Through Styria to Vienna)

Austrian Open-Air Museum (*see* Tour 2: Graz and Environs)

Graz Old Town (*see* Tour 2: Graz and Environs)

Lake Neusiedl, especially Rust and Mörbisch (*see* Tour 1: Through Burgenland to Graz)

Mariazell (*see* Tour 3: Through Styria to Vienna)

Schneeberg and the Höllental Gorge (*see* Tour 4: The Mountain Route to Vienna)

Tour 1: Through Burgenland to Graz

Numbers in the margin correspond with points of interest on the Burgenland map.

This tour demonstrates that there's more to Austria than the Alps, as it travels the length of Burgenland from the flat *puszta* of the north to the rolling castle-capped hills of the south before turning west to Styria, ending at Austria's second city, Graz. While it is possible to cover the entire route of about 300 km (185 mi) in a single day, doing so is certainly not recommended. A leisurely countryside calls for a leisurely pace.

Burgenland, a region of castles, corn, and wine, is a narrow fertile belt of vineyards and rich agricultural land stretching some 170 km (106 mi) from the Czech border, along the Hungarian frontier, and south to Yugoslavia. Only 65 km (40 mi) across at its widest point, its waist narrows to a mere 4 km (2½ mi).

The name Burgenland, meaning land of castles, dates only from 1921; prior to World War I this area was a part of Hungary. Throughout its long history it has been a battleground between east and west, which accounts for the many ruined fortifications and strongholds. It was part of the ancient Roman province of Pannonia, occupied by Celts, Roman settlers, Ostrogoths, and Slavs. After them came the Bavarians, Hungarians, and Austrians, followed by the invading Turks. This legacy of conflict has continued into the late 20th century, with the tensions of the Iron Curtain being, until recently, a stark fact of life. The opening of the Hungarian border has again brought change and increased Burgenland's appeal to tourists.

From Vienna it is only 52 km (32 mi) southeast by car, train, or bus to Neusiedl am See, but driving is by far the best way to travel in these parts. Leave Vienna via the A–4 autobahn or the more scenic Route 10, past Schwechat Airport and Bruck an der Leitha, then turn south on Route 50 at Parndorf to Neusiedl am See.

This short ride brings you into a strange world that is completely alien to the rest of Austria. **Lake Neusiedl** (Neusiedler See) is one of the largest lakes in Europe and the Continent's only true steppe lake—a bizarre body of water, indeed. Its sole tributary is far too small to replenish the water lost through evaporation, and there is no outflow at all. Underground springs feed it, but when they fail it dries up, which last happened in the 1860s. At times strong winds drive the warm, slightly salty water to one shore, leaving the other high and dry. At present the water is nowhere more than about 7 feet deep, and it is possible (but dangerous) to walk across the lake; its depth has varied dramatically, however, at times nearly engulfing the villages on its banks. Most of its 320-square-km (124-square-mi) surface area is in Austria, but the southern reaches extend into Hungary.

But what really sets Lake Neusiedl apart is the thick belt of tall reeds—in some places more than a mile wide—that almost completely encircles it. This is the habitat of a large variety of birds (more than 250 species) that nest near the water's edge. The lake is also a paradise for anglers, boaters, and windsurfers; other activities include swimming and bicycling.

1 The first town you come to is **Neusiedl am See,** a pleasant resort with good facilities. Direct hourly commuter trains from Vienna have made it very popular, so you won't be alone here. Follow the main street for three blocks east of the Hauptplatz and turn right on Seestrasse, a mile-long causeway that leads through the reeds to the lake, where you can rent small boats, swim, or just lie on the beach. Near the water's edge is the **Seemuseum,** which has a well-rounded exhibit of local flora and fauna. *Seebad, tel. 02167/2207. Admission: AS10 adults, AS5 senior citizens, students, and children. Open Easter–Oct., daily 9–noon and 1–5.*

Time Out Enjoy snacks, drinks, or even complete meals indoors or out at the modern, inexpensive **Seerestaurant** overlooking the beach and lake, near the boat harbor. It's closed in winter.

Back in town, if you have an hour to kill, visit the ruins of a 13th-century hill fortress (*Ruine Tabor*), a 15th-century parish church near the town hall, and the **Pannonisches Heimatmuseum** (museum of local Pannonian life), which displays room settings, tools, and crafts of the last few centuries. *Kalvarienbergstr. 40, tel. 02167/8173. Admission: contribution. Open May–Oct., Tues.–Sat. 2:30–6:30, Sun. and holidays 10–noon and 2:30–6:30.*

The region east of the lake is the beginning of the unusual Hungarian *puszta,* the great flat steppe marked with occasional windmills and characteristic wells with long wooden poles for drawing up the water. A circular tour of about 70 km (44 mi) by car (or bicycle) would cover nearly everything of interest before returning you to Neusiedl am See. Begin by following the local
2 road south to **Podersdorf,** which has the best beach on the lake. Some of the houses have thatched roofs, and their chimneys are often adorned in summer with storks nesting after wintering in Egypt. Podersdorf has excellent swimming, and among its other attractions are the **Heimatmuseum** (museum of local life)

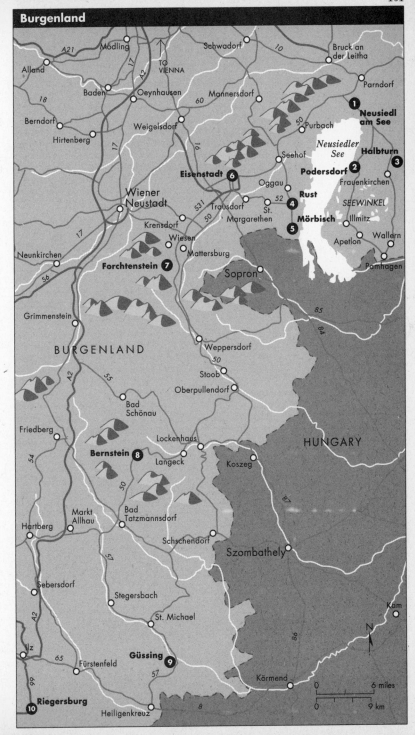

Burgenland

(Weinberggasse 1a, tel. 02177/2258) and the **Natur- und Tierlehrpfad** (nature learning trail). There is also a **windmill** that you can visit. *Mühlstr. 26, tel. 02177/2227. Admission: AS20 adults, AS10 senior citizens, students, and children. Open mid-May–mid-Sept., daily 5–7 PM.*

Continue south into the **Seewinkel**, a flat marshy area dotted with small lakes and ponds, much of which is a wildlife sanctuary. The village of **Illmitz** has a noted **biological station** and a nature trail (tel. 02175/2383). Beyond this, the road goes through Apetlon to **Pamhagen**, a border hamlet with a zoo exhibiting animals and birds of the Hungarian steppes. Now head north through Wallern and St. Andrä to **Frauenkirchen**, a village famous for its **Pilgrimage Church**, rebuilt in 1702 after its 14th-century predecessor was destroyed by invading Turks. The Baroque interior has a much-venerated wooden statue of the Virgin, from the 13th century.

❸ Just northeast of Frauenkirchen, **Halbturn** has a Baroque **imperial hunting lodge** built in 1710 by Johann Lukas von Hildebrandt, the great architect of the Baroque. It was once used by Empress Maria Theresa as a summer residence and is especially noted for its ceiling frescoes. It now houses temporary art exhibitions and is surrounded by a large and lovely park. From here, it is only a short drive back to Neusiedl am See. *Schloss Halbturn, tel. 02172/8577. Admission: AS25 adults, AS15 senior citizens, students, and children. Open May–Oct., daily 9–6.*

The road down the west side of the lake takes you through the old wine villages of Breitenbrunn, Purbach, and Donnerskirchen, all of which retain traces of their medieval fortifications. Leave Route 50 at Seehof and follow the local road past ❹ Oggau to **Rust**, the most popular village on the lake. It is some 30 km (19 mi) southwest of Neusiedl am See, and tourists flock here in summer to see the famous storks that nest atop the Renaissance and Baroque houses in the town's well-preserved historic center. Be sure to visit the Gothic **Fischerkirche** (Fishermen's Church) off the west end of the Rathausplatz. Built between the 12th and 16th centuries, it is surrounded by a defensive wall and is noted for its 15th-century frescoes and an organ from 1705. *Open daily 10–noon and 2–6.*

Time Out You can sample the excellent local vintages, along with a light lunch, in a number of friendly cafés, cellars, and the typical *Heurige*, where young wines are served by their own makers. A favorite spot is the **Rathauskeller** on Rathausplatz, open daily except Wednesday at 11:30 AM. The Ruster Blaufränkisch red wine is particularly good, resembling a well-rounded Burgundy.

A causeway leads through nearly a mile of reeds to the **Seebad** beach and boat landing, where you can rent boats, swim, or enjoy a waterside drink or snack at an outdoor table of the Seerestaurant Rust.

❺ The road continues south for 5½ km (3½ mi) to **Mörbisch**, the last lakeside village before the Hungarian border. Considered by many to be the most attractive settlement on the lake, Mörbisch is famous for its low, whitewashed Magyar-style houses, whose open galleries are colorfully decorated with flowers and bunches of corn. The local vineyards produce some

superb white wines, especially the fresh-tasting Welschriesling and the full-bodied Muscat-Ottonel. Here, too, a causeway
leads to a beach on the lake, where an international operetta
festival is held each summer. Ask at the tourist office about
trips through the nearby countryside in horse-drawn wagons
and about the old wine house that you can visit.

❻ Return to Rust and take Route 52 west past St. Margarethen
and Trausdorf to Burgenland's provincial capital, **Eisenstadt.**
Scarcely more than a village, this small town has an illustrious
history and enough sights to keep you busy for half a day. It is
connected to Neusiedl am See by train and to Vienna and places
throughout Burgenland by bus.

Although the town has existed since at least the 12th century,
it was not of any importance until the 17th, when it became the
seat of the Esterhazys, a princely Hungarian family that traced
its roots to Attila the Hun. Esterhazy support was largely responsible for the Habsburg reign in Hungary under the Dual
Monarchy. The composer Joseph Haydn lived in Eisenstadt for
some 30 years in the service of the Esterhazys. When Burgenland was ceded to Austria after World War I, its major city,
Sopron, elected to remain a part of Hungary, and so in 1925 tiny
Eisenstadt was made the capital of the new Austrian province.

Begin your tour in the center of town at **Schloss Esterhazy,** the
former palace of the ruling princes. Built in the Baroque style
between 1663 and 1672 on the foundations of a medieval castle,
it was later modified and is still owned by the Esterhazy family,
who lease it to the provincial government for use mostly as offices. Its lavishly decorated **Haydn Room,** an impressive concert hall where the composer conducted his own works from
1761 until 1790, is still used for presentations of Haydn's works,
with musicians often dressed in period costumes. Along with
several other rooms, it can be seen on guided tours (in English
on request) lasting about 30 minutes. *Tel. 02682/3384. Admission: AS20 adults, AS10 senior citizens, students, and children. Open Easter–Oct., daily 9–4:30; Nov.–Easter, weekdays
9–4:30; conducted tours hourly.*

The park behind the *Schloss* is a pleasant place for a stroll or a
picnic; in August it is the site of the Festival of a Thousand
Wines.

Time Out The **Schlosscafé,** opposite the west end of the palace at
Gloriettealle 1, is open daily until 2 AM and is a handy place for
refreshments.

A slightly uphill walk on Esterhazystrasse brings you to the
Bergkirche, an ornate Baroque church that includes the
strange *Kalvarienberg,* an indoor Calvary Hill representing
the Way of the Cross with life-size figures placed in cavelike
rooms along an elaborate path. At its highest point, the trail
reaches the platform of the belfry, offering a view over the
town and this section of Burgenland. The magnificent wooden
figures were carved and painted by Franciscan monks more
than 250 years ago. The main part of the church contains the
tomb of Joseph Haydn, who died in 1809 but whose body minus
its head was not moved here until 1932 (the head, stolen by ad-
mirers and kept in Vienna, was returned in 1954!). *Kalvarien-
bergplatz, tel. 02682/52553. Admission: AS15 adults, AS10*

senior citizens, students, and children. Open Apr.–Oct., daily 9–noon and 2–5.

Return down the hill and turn left on Wertheimergasse to Unterbergstrasse, where there was a barred Jewish ghetto from 1671 until 1938. During that time, Eisenstadt had a considerable Jewish population; today the **Austrian Jewish Museum** (Österreichisches Jüdisches Museum) recalls the experience of all Austrian Jews throughout history. A reconstructed Jewish cemetery is nearby. *Unterbergstr. 6, tel. 02682/5145. Admission: AS25 adults, AS20 senior citizens, students, and children. Open late May–late Oct., Tues.–Sun. 10–5.*

Not far away is the **Landesmuseum** (Burgenland provincial museum), which brings the history of the region to life with displays on such subjects as Roman culture and the development of vineyards. *Museumgasse 5, tel. 02682/2652. Admission: AS20 adults, AS10 senior citizens, students, and children. Open Tues.–Sun. 9–noon and 1–5.*

Pass the Esterhazy palace and turn left to Haydn Gasse. The simple house at No. 21 is where Haydn lived from 1766 until 1778. Now the **Haydn Museum**, it contains several of the composer's original manuscripts and other memorabilia. The house itself, and especially its flower-filled courtyard, is unpretentious but quite delightful. *Tel. 02682/2652. Admission: AS15 adults, AS8 senior citizens, students, and children. Open Easter–Oct., daily 9–noon and 1–5.*

Eisenstadt has a few other attractions that its tourist office can tell you about, including the Museum of Austrian Culture, the Diocesan Museum, the Fire Fighters Museum, Haydn's little garden house, and some churches.

Heading southwest from Eisenstadt brings you into the narrow waist of Burgenland, squeezed between Lower Austria and Hungary. Take Route S–31 for 20 km (12½ mi) to Mattersburg, then a local road 3 km (2 mi) west to **Forchtenstein.** This small village, noted for its strawberries, is dominated by its medieval hilltop castle. **Burg Forchtenstein,** a formidable fortress, was built in the early 14th century, enlarged by the Esterhazys around 1635, and twice defended Austria against the invading Turks. Captured enemy soldiers were put to work digging the castle's 466-foot-deep well, which has a famous echo. As befits a military stronghold, there is a fine collection of weapons in the armory and booty taken from the Turks; also an exhibition of stately carriages. *Burgplatz 1, tel. 02626/81212. Admission: AS34 adults, AS17 senior citizens, students, and children. Open Apr.–Oct., daily 8–noon and 1–4.*

Return to the highway and take S–31 and Route 50 south past Weppersdorf and Stoob, the latter famous for its pottery. The road then goes through Oberpullendorf and close to Lockenhaus, where a renowned music festival is held each summer in the 13th-century castle. The next stop is at **Bernstein,** 58 km (36 mi) from Forchtenstein. This small village is one of the only sources of *Edelserpentin*, a dark green serpentine stone also known as Bernstein jade. Much of this stone is made locally into jewelry and objets d'art on display in the **Felsenmuseum** (stone museum). *Potsch, Hauptplatz 5, tel. 03354/6620. Admission: AS40 adults, AS25 senior citizens, students, and children. Open Mar.–Dec., daily 9–noon and 1:30–5.*

Overlooking the village is **Burg Bernstein,** a 12th-century fortress that was rebuilt in the 17th century. Part of it is now a romantic castle-hotel, but the rest may be visited. *Tel. 03354/ 6520. By appointment only. Admission: AS20 adults, AS10 children. Open Apr.–Oct., daily 8–noon and 1–5.*

Continue south on Route 50 past Bad Tatzmannsdorf, home of the South Burgenland Open-Air Museum (tel. 03353/8314), then follow Route 57 to **Güssing,** another castle-dominated village, some 52 km (32 mi) south of Bernstein. Güssing has express bus service to Vienna and Graz. Its classic 12th-century fortress, **Burg Güssing,** perched high on a solitary volcanic outcrop, has wonderful views of the surrounding countryside. It also has a fine collection of Old Master paintings, weapons and armor, and a Gothic chapel with a rare 17th-century cabinet organ. *Tel. 03322/2491. Admission: AS25 adults, AS15 senior citizens, students, and children. Open Apr.–Oct., Tues.–Sun. 9– noon and 1–5.*

Stay on Route 57 to the frontier village of Heiligenkreuz-im-Laftnitztal, then take Route 65 west to Fürstenfeld, leaving Burgenland and crossing into Styria. Continue on to Ilz, then turn south on Route 66 to Riegersburg, a total distance of 57 km (35 mi) southwest of Güssing.

Rising some 600 feet above the valley is the mighty **Riegersburg Castle,** one of the great defensive bastions of Austria. Originally built in the 11th century on the site of Celtic and Roman strongholds, it has never been humbled in battle, not even in 1945, when its German occupants held out against the Russians. The present structure dates from the 17th century and is entered by way of a heavily defended, rocky path. The well restored castle has rooms with period furnishings, weapon displays, and even a museum of witchcraft and magic. Guided tours are offered, and the views are magnificent. *Tel. 03153/ 2130. Combination admission including museum: AS70 adults, AS40 students, children. Open Apr.–Oct., daily 9–5.*

From here, it is 56 km (35 mi) west via Route 65 or A–2 to Graz, the site of our next tour.

Tour 2: Graz and Environs

Numbers in the margin correspond with points of interest on the Eastern Styria and Lower Austria and Graz maps.

Although **Graz,** the capital of Styria and the second-largest city in Austria, lies in a somewhat remote corner of the country and is often overlooked by tourists, it is easily reached from Vienna or Salzburg and provides the urban highlight of an itinerary through southeastern Austria. Its Old Town quarter is remarkably well preserved, with narrow pedestrian lanes connecting several first-rate attractions, some outstanding examples of Baroque architecture, a palace, and the remnants of an ancient fortress atop a midtown hill. Graz is also a lively cultural center, the seat of two universities, and a city of gardens and parks. Once a favorite retirement center for civil servants, it has long since outgrown its reputation for staidness.

The name Graz derives from the Slavic *gradec,* meaning small castle; there was probably a fortress atop the Schlossberg hill as early as the 9th century. This strategic spot guarded the southern end of the narrow Mur Valley, an important approach

Eastern Styria and Lower Austria

LOWER AUSTRIA

Arzberg

Weyer-Markt

121

115

UPPER
AUSTRIA

Altenmarkt
b. St. Gallen

Wildalpen

24

117

Hieflau

146

Gesäuse Ravine

Polster
Mountain

Aflen
Kuro

Eisenerz 33

115

Thörl 3

Pyhrnpass

112

32 **Admont**

Vordernberg

Kap

Trieben

Kalwang

113

E57

Trofaiach

Seiz

Leoben 28

St. Michael

Gleinalm-
tunnel

Möderbrugg

S T Y R I A

Seckau Abbey 29

5.6

Pöls

Knittelfeld

96

Zeltweg

30

Judenburg

Scheifling

Piber

22

Bärn

31 **Murau**

Köflach

V

83

Mühlen

92

78

C A R I N T H I A

Pack
Sattel

Twimberg

70

93

Pöckstein

Mösel

Wolfsberg

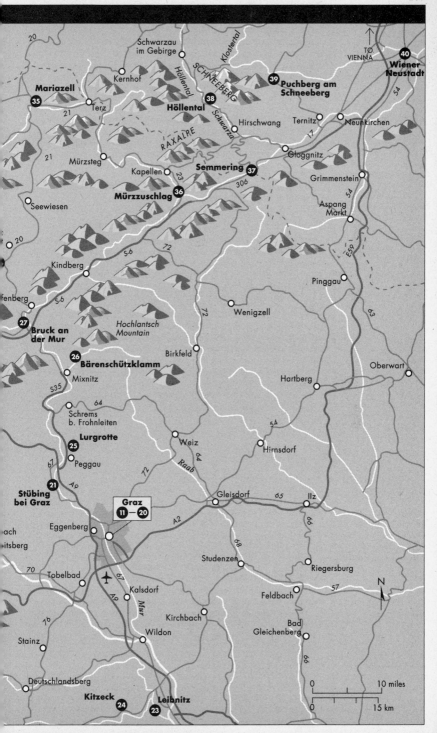

to Vienna, from invasion by the Turks. By the 12th century, a town developed at the foot of the hill, which in time became an imperial city of the ruling Habsburgs. Graz's glory faded in the 17th century when the court moved to Vienna, but the city continued to prosper as a provincial capital, especially under the enlightened 19th-century rule of Archduke Johann.

Streetcars and buses are an excellent way of traveling within the city. Single tickets (fare: AS15) can be bought from the driver, and one-day and multiple-ride tickets are also available. All six streetcar routes converge at Jakominiplatz near the south end of the Old Town. One fare may combine streetcars and buses as long as you take a direct route to your destination. For more detailed information, tel. 0316/887445.

Taxis can be ordered by phone (tel. 0316/983 or 0316/2801). Driving in the Old Town quarter is not advisable, since there are many narrow, one-way, and pedestrian streets and few places to park.

Nearly all tourist attractions in Graz are conveniently located in the compact **Old Town** quarter, which can easily be explored on foot in an hour or so, not including any visits. Begin at the ⑫ **Hauptplatz** (main square), a triangular area first laid out in 1164 and used today as a lively open-air produce market. In its center stands the **Erzherzog Johann Brunnen** (Archduke Johann Fountain), dedicated to the popular 19th-century patron whose enlightened policies did much to develop Graz as a cultural and scientific center. The four female figures represent what were then the four main rivers of Styria; today only the Mur and the Enns are within the province. Behind the statue, to the north, rises the **Schlossberg** (Castle Hill) with its 16th-century **Uhrturm** (clock tower), the very symbol of Graz. Take a careful look at the richly ornamented 17th-century **Luegg House** at the corner of Sporgasse, noted for its Baroque stucco facade, and at the Gothic and Renaissance houses on the west side of the square. The late-19th-century **Rathaus** (city hall) totally dominates the south side.

A short stroll down the narrow Franziskanergasse brings you to the **Franziskanerkirche** (Franciscan church), which has a 14th-century choir, a 16th-century nave, and a 17th-century tower. The tiny streets of this former butchers' quarter retain much of their medieval atmosphere and are well worth exploring.

Continue on Neue-Welt-Gasse and Schmiedgasse, from which you get a superb view of the Hauptplatz. A short side trip can ⑬ be made to the **Landesmuseum Joanneum,** the oldest public museum in Austria, founded by Archduke Johann in 1811. Actually, this is part of a large complex of museums on different subjects, several of which are in other parts of town. The entrance at Raubergasse 10 is for the natural-history departments, while that at Neutorgasse 45 leads into the applied-arts department and the **Alte Galerie** (Old Gallery), a world-famous collection of art from the Middle Ages through the Baroque period. Among its treasures are works by Pieter Brueghel the Younger and both Hans and Lucas Cranach, the noted *Admont Madonna* wood carving from 1400, and a medieval altarpiece depicting the murder of Thomas à Becket. *Admission to each section: AS25 adults, AS10 senior citizens. Natural-history section, tel. 0316/8770. Open weekdays 9–4, weekends and holi-*

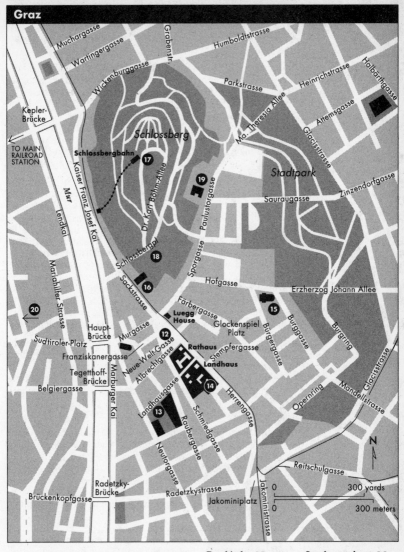

Graz

Domkirche, **15**
Glockenturm, **17**
Hauptplatz, **12**
Herberstein
Palace, **16**
Landesmuseum
Joanneum, **13**

Landeszeughaus, **14**
Schloss Eggenberg, **20**
Steirisches
Volkskunde-
museum, **19**
Uhrturm, **18**

days 9–noon. Applied-arts section, tel. 0316/877–2458. Open Mon. and Wed.–Fri. 10–5, weekends and holidays 10–1. Alte Galerie, tel. 0316/877–2457. Open Tues.–Fri. 10–5, weekends and holidays 10–1.

Return via Landhausgasse to Herrengasse, the main business street of Graz. To the left at No. 3 is the 15th-century **Gemalte Haus** (Painted House), a former ducal residence decorated with frescoes from 1742. Along the west side of the street stands the massive **Landhaus** (Styrian Provincial Parliament), built between 1557 and 1565 by Domenico dell' Allio in the Italian Renaissance style. Its arcaded courtyard is magnificently proportioned and features a 16th-century fountain that is an unusually fine example of old Styrian wrought-iron work.

⑭ Just adjacent is the most noted attraction of Graz, the **Landeszeughaus** (provincial arsenal). Virtually unchanged since it was built in the mid-17th century, this four-story armory still contains the original 16th- and 17th-century weapons intended for use by Styrian mercenaries in fighting off the Turks. Nearly 30,000 items are on display, including more than 3,000 suits of armor (some of which are beautifully engraved), thousands of halberds, swords, firearms, cannons, and mortars. Probably the most important collection of its type in the world, it is still arranged exactly as it was three centuries ago, still ready for an enemy attack. *Herrengasse 16, tel. 0316/877–3639. Admission: AS25 adults, AS10 senior citizens. Open Apr.–Oct., weekdays 9–5, weekends and holidays 9–1.*

Farther down Herrengasse, on the left, is the **Stadtpfarrkirche** (town parish church), built early in the 16th century, to which was added a Baroque facade and 18th-century spire. Tintoretto's *Assumption of the Virgin* decorates the altar. Across the street begins a narrow lane named after Johann Bernhard Fischer von Erlach, the great architect of the Austrian Baroque, who was born in one of the houses here in 1656.

Walk up the narrow Stempfergasse and turn left on Enge Gasse to the delightful **Glockenspielplatz,** where wooden figures emerge from a wall above a café, dancing to an old folk tune at 11 AM and 6 PM and at other times as well. Look into the courtyard at No. 5, which has an impressive 17th-century open staircase. The house at No. 7 has an arcaded Renaissance courtyard. Practically adjacent to the square is the **Mehlplatz,** lined with historic houses.

Time Out   You can wait for the musical show right under the glockenspiel itself, at the trendy **Glockenspiel Café.** The coffee, sandwiches, and pastries are all excellent, and there are plenty of outdoor tables from which to enjoy the passing parade. *Glockenspielplatz 4. Open weekdays 7:30–6, Sat. 8–2; closed Sun.*

⑮ Now follow Abraham-a-Santa-Clara-Gasse and turn left on Bürgergasse. An open staircase on the right leads to the 15th-century late-Gothic **Domkirche** (cathedral). On its south exterior wall, near the steps, is a rather faded 15th-century fresco called the *Landplagenbild*, which graphically depicts the local torments of those times—the plague, the locusts, and the Turks. Step inside to see the outstanding high altar made of colored marble, the choir stalls, Raphael Donner's 1741 tomb of Count Cobenzl, and Konrad Laib's *Crucifixion* of 1457. The 15th-century reliquaries on either side of the triumphal arch leading to the choir were originally the hope chests of Paola Gonzaga, daughter of Ludwig II of Mantua.

Adjoining the cathedral, to the south, is the Baroque **Mausoleum** of emperor Ferdinand II, who died in 1637. Its sumptuous interior is partly an early design by native son Fischer von Erlach and the only work of his to be seen in Graz. *Burggasse 3, tel. 0316/821683. Admission free. Open Mon.–Sat. Guided tours at 11; closed other times.*

Just north of the cathedral, across Hofgasse, are the scanty remains of a former imperial palace known as the **Burg.** Now housing government offices, most of this uninspired structure is from the 19th and 20th centuries, but two noteworthy vestiges of the original 15th-century stronghold remain: the **Burgtor** (palace gate), which opens into the sprawling **Stadtpark** (municipal park), and the double-spiral **Gothic staircase** of 1499 at the far end of the grand courtyard.

Continue west on Hofgasse and turn left into the narrow, winding Sporgasse. One of the oldest streets in Graz, it is lined with boutiques and cafés and leads downhill to the Hauptplatz. Turn right at the bottom and follow Sackstrasse. The 17th-century **Herberstein Palace,** a former city residence of the ruling princes, houses the **Neue Galerie** (New Gallery). Its collection of paintings, graphics, and sculpture from the 19th century to the present includes works by such Austrian artists as Egon Schiele, along with the latest in Styrian art. *Sackstr. 16, tel. 0316/829155. Admission: AS25 adults, AS10 senior citizens. Open weekdays 10–6, weekends and holidays 10–1.*

The nearby **Palais Khuenburg** was the birthplace in 1863 of Archduke Franz Ferdinand, heir to the throne of the Austro-Hungarian empire. His assassination at Sarajevo in 1914 led directly to the outbreak of World War I. The palace now houses the **Stadtmuseum** (city museum), whose exhibits trace the history of Graz. *Sackstr. 18, tel. 0316/822580. Admission free. Open Tues. 10–9, Wed.–Sat. 10–6, Sun. and holidays 10–1.*

Farther along is the Schlossbergplatz, at the east end of which is a stone staircase leading to the top of Graz's midtown mountain. The view from the summit takes in all of the city and much of central Styria, but since it is a 395-foot climb, you may prefer to use the **Schlossbergbahn** funicular railway (fare: AS15). To reach it, just continue down Sackstrasse to Kaiser-Franz-Josef-Kai 38.

As its name implies, the **Schlossberg** (Castle Hill) was once a defensive fortification, whose ramparts were built to prevent the invading Turks from marching up the Mur Valley toward Vienna. The ramparts remained in place until 1809, when a victorious Napoleon had them dismantled after defeating the Austrians. The town paid a large ransom to preserve two of the castle's towers, but the rest was torn down and is today a well-manicured and very popular park.

Time Out   The **Schlossberg Café,** at the top of the funicular railway, has garden tables with a sweeping view across Graz. Among its specialties are *Germknödel* (a sweet dumpling in poppyseed sauce) and *Most* (a light nonalcoholic wine)—or you could just have coffee or beer while resting your feet.

17 A few steps east of the funicular station is the **Glockenturm** (bell tower), an octagonal structure from 1588 containing Liesl, the famous 4-ton bell, the largest in Styria. This is also the departure point for guided walking tours of the Schlossberg, conducted daily except in winter, every hour from 8 to 5. The **Open-Air Theater,** just yards to the north, is built into the old casemates of the castle and has a sliding roof in case of rain. Both opera and theater performances are held in summer.

A downhill walk toward the Old Town brings you to the 16th-
18 century **Uhrturm** (clock tower), the most notable landmark of Graz. Its 18th-century clock mechanism has four giant faces that might at first confuse you—until you realize that the *big* hands tell the hour and the *small* hands, the minutes. This was thought to be easier to read at a distance.

Continue downhill on Dr. Karl Böhm-Allee, named for the fa-
mous conductor who was born in Graz in 1894 and died in 1981. Returning to the Old Town, you might want to see one more
19 sight before ending the tour. The nearby **Steirisches Volks-kundemuseum** (Styrian folklore museum) occupies parts of a former monastery and displays regional costumes, period room settings, and other items of local interest. *Paulustorgasse 13, tel. 0316/830416. Admission: AS25 adults, AS10 senior citizens. Open Apr.–Oct., weekdays 9–4, weekends and holidays 9–noon.*

Another major attraction of Graz, which requires at least a few
20 hours to enjoy, is **Schloss Eggenberg,** a 17th-century palace sur-rounded by a large deer park on the very edge of the city. Take streetcar No. 1 from the Hauptplatz or elsewhere to Schloss Strasse, then walk two blocks south past a sports stadium to the entrance.

Built around an arcaded courtyard lined with antlers, this fine example of the high Baroque style contains gorgeous **state apartments** (Prunkräume), noted for their elaborate stucco decorations and frescoes, as well as three branch museums of the Joanneum. The largest is the **hunting museum** (*Jagd-museum*) on the first floor, which displays antique weapons, paintings, and realistic dioramas. The **museum of pre- and early history** (Abteilung für Vor- und Frühgeschichte), on the ground floor, has a remarkable collection of Styrian archaeo-logical finds, including the small and rather strange **Strettweg Ritual Chariot** dating from the 7th century BC. The **numismatic museum** (Münzensammlung) is tucked away in a corner on the ground floor.

Time Out The attractive outdoor café in the park surrounding Schloss Eggenberg is the perfect place to fortify yourself before or af-ter visiting the museums. It's just north of the main entrance.

During the summer, candlelit chamber concerts are held in the palace. *Eggenberger Allee 90, tel. 0316/5326411. Combination admission to park, state apartments, and museums: AS35 adults, AS20 senior citizens, students, and children. Park open daily 8–7; state apartments Apr.–Oct., daily 10–1 and 2–5; hunting and numismatic museums Feb.–Nov., daily 9–1 and 2–5.*

Short Excursions from Graz If you're staying in the city for more than a day, you might want to make a short excursion or two into the countryside. Here are three favorites; each can be done in a few hours.

The major attraction in the area is the Open-Air Museum, which can be reached on a guided bus tour from Graz every Tuesday afternoon from April through October or by municipal bus from Lendplatz, a 40-minute ride. By car, the museum is 15 km (9½ mi) northwest of Graz via Route 67 to Gratkorn, or you can take a 15-minute train ride to Stübing and walk from there 2 km (1¼ mi) to the entrance.

㉑ Northwest of Graz, in **Stübing bei Graz**, the **Austrian Open-Air Museum** (Österreichisches Freilichtmuseum) covers some 100 acres of hilly woodland. Here is an interesting collection of about 80 authentic farmhouses, barns, alpine huts, working water mills, forges, and other rural structures dating from the 16th century through the early 20th century, moved to this site from every province of Austria. Buildings that otherwise would have been lost in the rush to progress have been preserved for posterity, complete with their original furnishings. Most of the buildings are open to visitors, and in several there are craftsmen at work, sometimes in costume. No refreshments are available within the museum grounds, but there is a restaurant and outdoor café by the entrance. *Stübing bei Graz, tel. 03124/22431. Admission: AS35 adults, AS20 senior citizens, students, children. Open Apr.–Oct., Tues.–Sun. 9–5, last admission at 4.*

A second excursion might include a visit to a stud farm at Piber, with stops at a small museum in Köflach and a modern church in Bärnbach. Guided tours from Graz to the stud farm are conducted on Friday afternoon, April through October. By car, take Route 70 from Graz west to Köflach, a distance of 41 km (25 mi). Piber is 3 km (2 mi) northeast of Köflach. The train from Graz to Köflach takes an hour (the bus 75 minutes), with departures every hour or two. Some trains split en route; be sure to board the correct car. You'll have to walk or take a taxi between Köflach and Piber.

㉒ The hamlet of **Piber** is devoted to raising horses, and from the **Lippizaner Stud Farm** come the world-famous stallions that perform at the Spanish Riding School in Vienna. These snow-white horses trace their lineage back to 1580 when Archduke Karl of Styria established a stud farm at Lipiza near Trieste, using stallions from Arabia and mares from Spain. Born black, the steeds gradually turn white between the ages of two and seven. After World War I, when Austria lost Lipiza, the farm was transferred to Piber. *Bundesgestüt Piber, tel. 03144/3323. Admission: AS40 adults, AS20 children. Open Easter–Oct., guided tours, lasting about 70 minutes, start between 9 and 10 AM and 2 and 3 PM. No afternoon tours on special horse-show days.*

The museum in **Köflach** has interesting exhibits of local life. *Museum der Stadt Köflach, Hause des Dichters Dr. Hans Kloepfer, Bahnhofstr. 24, tel. 03144/251971. Contribution requested. Open Mon., Tues., Thurs., Fri., and holidays, 9–4.*

On the way back to Graz, a 3-km (2-mi) detour east brings you to **Bärnbach**, whose Church of St. Barbara is an amazing sight. Completely redone in 1988 by the contemporary Austrian painter Friedensreich Hundertwasser, its exterior is a fantasy of abstract religious symbols in brilliant colors and shapes. From here you can turn south to Voitsberg and get a bus back to Graz.

For the third excursion, to the Styrian wine country south of Graz near the Yugoslav border, you'll need a car and a good road map. There are several possible routes; the following one is especially recommended. Public transportation through the area is severely limited, although you might ask the Graz tourist office if any guided tours are being offered.

㉓ Drive south from Graz on either Route 67 or A–9. About 32 km (20 mi) from the city is the exit for **Leibnitz,** a center of the local wine trade. The small town is dominated by Seggau Castle (tel. 03452/24350); from the 9th century, it was a stronghold of the Salzburg prince-bishops and later the Styrian bishops of Seckau. Leibnitz stands on the site of the Roman town *Flavia Solva,* founded about AD 70, and a collection of Roman stone reliefs is displayed in the castle. More Roman remains can be seen at Frauenberg near Seggau, where a temple of Isis once existed and a pilgrimage church stands today.

Drive south on the local road to **Ehrenhausen,** the beginning of the South Styrian Wine Road. This road leads across undulating hills to the Yugoslav border, which the road straddles, half its width in Austria and the other half in Yugoslavia! The scenery here is spectacular; some of the steepest vineyards in the world—so steep they must be worked by hand—cling to the hills on either side. A feature common to the area is the wind-operated scarecrow, always made of cherry wood, whose noise is supposed to scare the birds away. Numerous little wine taverns, called *Buschenschanks,* offer the local vintage along with cold cuts and bread.

㉔ Take Route 69 to Leutschach and continue west to Arnfels, then head north through St. Johann im Saggautal, Gündorf, Grossklein, and Fresing to **Kitzeck,** the highest wine village in Europe. This tiny hamlet has a small **wine museum** (Steinriegel 11, tel. 03456/2243) that is well worth a visit, since it manages to capture much of the local flavor.

Time Out On a hill northwest of Kitzeck sits **Steirerland** (*see* Dining and Lodging, below), a country inn famous for its cooking. For wine and snacks, there are several attractive taverns in the area, including the **Buschenschank Küahmüller,** which sells its own wines. *Near the wine museum. Open after 2 PM. Closed Mon.*

The area west of Kitzeck is home to the unique *Blauer Wildbacher* grape, grown nowhere else on Earth, from which comes the tangy, almost sour *Schilcher* rosé wine, an acquired taste beloved by many. Continue on to Neudorf and make your way back to Graz.

Tour 3: Through Styria to Vienna

The route from Graz to Vienna allows opportunities for jaunts into the mountainous green heartland of Styria. After a scenic ride north through the Mur Valley to the historic crossroads of Bruck an der Mur, you can head southwest to Judenburg and possibly Murau and even continue into Salzburg province. Another option is to start toward Judenburg but turn northwest beyond Leoben to the abbey at Admont and then either return to Bruck via Eisenerz or continue north through Upper Austria to Linz on the Danube. Back at Bruck an der Mur, where several highways and rail lines converge, you can head north to Mariazell and then continue on one of the country's most scenic mountain drives (or rail trips) back to the Danube Valley.

Head north from Graz on Route 67, driving through the heavily forested, narrow Mur Valley toward Bruck an der Mur. (A rail line parallels the road, with trains every hour or two making local stops near the points of interest.) Along the way you will pass the Austrian Open-Air Museum (*see* above). Just north of the industrial town of **Peggau** (rail stop: Peggau-Deutsch-feistritz) is the famous **Lurgrotte,** the largest stalactite and stalagmite cave in Austria. Conducted tours lasting one or two hours follow a subterranean stream past illuminated sights, and there is a small restaurant at the entrance. *Tel. 03127/2580. Admission, 1-hr tour: AS40 adults, AS25 children under 15; 2-hr tour: AS60 adults, AS30 children. Open Apr.–Oct., Tues.–Sun. 9–4.*

Still farther north is **Mixnitz,** the starting point for a rugged 4½-hour hike through the wild **Bärenschützklamm,** a savage gorge that can be negotiated only on steps and ladders but should nevertheless be visited for its spectacular foaming waterfalls. Beyond it are peaceful mountain meadows and finally the 5,650-foot **Hochlantsch** mountain with its sweeping views.

Bruck an der Mur is known primarily as the major traffic junction of Styria, a point where four valleys and two rivers converge and where several highways and main rail lines come together. Although most of the busy town is devoted to industry, its historic center, dating partially from the 13th century, is compact and well worth a short visit. The architecturally distinguished main square, Koloman-Wallisch-Platz, is four blocks west of the train station. On its northeast corner stands the late-15th-century **Kornmesserhaus,** a magnificent example of secular architecture in the Flamboyant Gothic style, noted especially for its elaborate loggia and arcades.

Another attraction, just across the square, is the famous **Eiserner Brunnen.** This 17th-century wrought-iron well housing is considered to be the best piece of ironwork in Styria, a province noted for its metalwork. The **Rathaus** (town hall) facing it is also attractive and houses a small museum of local life (Heimatmuseum, tel. 0382/51521). On the hill behind is the **Pfarrkirche,** built between the 13th and 15th centuries, which has an interesting late-Gothic sacristy door of wrought iron.

Overlooking the town, just two blocks northeast of its center, are the remains of **Burg Landskron,** a 13th-century fortress that once defended the confluence of the Mur and Mürz rivers. Today only its clock tower remains intact, but the view is worth the short climb.

Time Out   The small park surrounding the Landskron ruins, on the Schlossberg hill, makes a wonderful spot for a picnic. Buy your supplies at one of the shops in the streets below.

Interesting side trips fan out in several directions from Bruck. One takes you southwest for 16 km (10 mi) by car (Rte. S-6), train, or bus to **Leoben,** the largest town in central Styria and the center of an important mining and heavy-industry region.

Most of the attractions in the Old Town are near the Hauptplatz, six blocks south of the train station. There you will find the **Altes Rathaus** of 1568, the **Plague Column** (Pestsäule) of 1717, and the handsome 17th-century **Hacklhaus** with its incredibly decorated Baroque facade. Walking one block west brings you to the **Museum der Stadt Leoben,** a municipal museum of local history, industry, art, and nature (Kirchgasse 6, tel. 03842/43581). Next to it is the **Stadtpfarrkirche** (city parish church) of 1660 and a block to the south, the **Mautturm** (custom tower) of 1615, locally called the *Schwammerl* because it looks more or less like a mushroom.

Across the river from here is the **Maria-am-Wasser Kirche,** a Gothic church with outstanding 15th-century stained-glass windows. The suburb of **Göss,** 2 km (1¼ mi) south, is where the famous Gösser beer is made in a former monastery founded in 1020. The small beer museum may be seen by prior arrangement (tel. 03842/22621).

Continue southwest on Route S-6 along the Upper Mur Valley past St. Michael and on to Knittelfeld. About 16 km (10 mi) **❷❾** north of this small industrial town is the famed **Seckau Abbey,** founded in 1140. The original Romanesque style of its church is visible despite later additions, and it contains several outstanding features of various periods, from the late-Renaissance mausoleum of Archduke Karl II to the strikingly modern apocalyptic frescoes in the Angels' Chapel by the 20th-century painter Herbert Boeckl. For 550 years Seckau was the episcopal center of Styria, and the whole complex of buildings bears rich testimony to the wealth that was lavished on it. The stained-glass windows, wrought-iron fittings, paintings, and sculptures make it well worth the slight detour. *For information regarding visits, tel. 03514/234 or contact the tourist office in Knittelfeld, tel. 03512/6464.*

❸⓿ Farther west along the Upper Mur Valley is **Judenburg,** an ancient and attractive hill town overlooking the steelworks along the river. Its origins date to prehistoric times—the famous Strettweg Ritual Chariot (now on display at Schloss Eggenberg in Graz) was found here—but its name derives from a medieval colony of Jewish merchants. From its Hauptplatz rises the lofty **Stadtturm,** a 240-foot-high watch tower built between 1449 and 1520, which you can climb. The early 16th-century **Pfarrkirche** next to it has some excellent sculptures, especially of the Virgin. The small **Stadtmuseum** around the corner offers dioramas depicting local history and a display of minerals from nearby mines. *Kaserngasse 27, tel. 3572/5053. Contribution requested. Open Tues.–Fri. 9–noon.*

Just across the river, on Feldgasse, stands the 12th-century **Magdalenenkirche,** a Romanesque church with 14th-century frescoes and medieval stained-glass windows.

❸❶ Route 96 continues west for 45 km (28 mi) to **Murau** (train and bus riders change at Unzmarkt), a well-preserved medieval town with some unusual attractions. If you ever dreamed of becoming a steam-locomotive engineer (*Lokführer*)—or just enjoy riding behind the beasts—this is your place. The narrow-gauge **Murtalbahn** (Mur Valley Railroad), operated by the *Steiermärkischen Landesbahnen* (Styrian Provincial Railways) gives engine-driving lessons on Thursday from mid-July until early September, ranging from a quarter-hour on just a locomotive to longer periods with passenger cars attached; bring your friends, stock the bar car, and hire the local brass band to provide inspiration while you shovel the coal! The steam line also provides regular passenger service between Murau and Tamsweg several days a week from mid-July to early September. *For current information, tel. 03532/2231 or 03532/2233.*

In Murau you can see stretches of the medieval **town wall;** the **Pfarrkirche** from 1296 with its ancient frescoes and late-Gothic "lantern of the dead" in the churchyard; the dominating **Schloss Obermurau,** a 13th-century castle that was rebuilt in the 17th century; and the **Altes Rathaus,** the old town hall that was once a part of the fortifications.

Another itinerary from Bruck an der Mur through western Styria crosses mountainous country to the renowned Benedictine Abbey of Admont. You can get there directly by taking Routes S-6, 113, and A-9 west and northwest almost to Liezen, then turning east on Route 117. The total distance is 100 km (62 mi); both trains and a limited bus service operate over the entire route, with changes required. If you prefer picturesque back roads, follow the itinerary previously described to a point 6 km (4 mi) west of Judenburg, take the steep but scenic Hohentauern Pass Road (Route 114) north to Trieben, and then continue as above.

32 The small market town of **Admont** is dominated by its famous **Benedictine Abbey,** founded in the 11th century but almost entirely rebuilt after a disastrous fire in 1865. Of the earlier structures, only the magnificent Baroque **library** survived intact. Fortunately, its treasures were also saved and are on view, including a Bible belonging to Martin Luther and a *New Testament* edited by Erasmus. The large building, 236 feet long, contains some 150,000 volumes and is noted for its 18th-century ceiling frescoes by Bartholomeo Altomonte as well as for its statues of *The Four Last Things* (Death, Judgment, Hell, and Heaven). There is also an extensive natural-history museum with lots of insects, an art museum, and a museum of local life. *Tel. 0316/23120. Admission: AS25 adults, AS15 children. Open May–Sept., daily 10–1 and 2–5; Apr. and Oct., 10–noon and 2–4; Nov.–Mar., 11–noon and 2–3. Closed Mon. Oct.– Mar.*

The tour now continues east and follows Route 146 through the spectacular **Gesäuse Ravine** where the Enns River surges through limestone formations. The 7,770-foot Hochtor peak can be seen on the right. This is among the wildest scenery to be found anywhere in the Alps, and it's a favorite challenge for rock climbers. At Hieflau, turn southeast on Route 115 into the somewhat more subdued Erzbach Valley. Make a slight detour to a hidden mountain lake of great beauty, the **Leopoldsteiner See,** and continue on to Eisenerz, 40 km (25 mi) from Admont. Rail service over the same route is limited and requires a change at Hieflau. There are no through buses.

33 The old mining town of **Eisenerz** is of considerable interest, not only for its own attractions but for the mountain of iron ore next to it. The community huddles around the Gothic **Parish Church of St. Oswald,** first built in 1282 and fortified as a defensive bastion against the invading Turks in 1532. Its fantastically embellished interior is well worth seeing. West of the church stands the famous **Schichtturm,** an old tower whose bell once signaled the change of shifts at the mines. The **Stadtmuseum Eisenerz** is devoted to mining and ironworking, as well as to local life and culture. *Tel. 03848/3615. Admission: AS20 adults, AS15 senior citizens, AS10 students, children, and the handicapped. Open May–Oct., daily 9–5; Nov.–Apr., Tues.–Fri. 9–noon.*

Just south of the town is its reason for being: the rust-colored, towering **Erzberg.** This mountain of iron ore has been worked since ancient times and still yields an ore that is 34% pure iron. Its present height is about 4,800 feet, although it was once much higher. Strip mining has given it a steplike appearance, similar to a ziggurat. Guided tours lasting about 1½ hours are conducted through the workings. *Schau Bergwerke, lower station of the cableway near the road from Präbichl, tel. 03848/ 453–1470 or 03848/3700. Admission: AS90 adults, AS45 children and students. Open May–Oct., daily; tours at 10 and 2:30.*

Drive southeast on Route 115, past the **Polster,** a 6,250-foot mountain that can be ascended by chair lift, and continue to the ancient mining town of **Vordernberg,** where Romans once worked with iron. There is no rail service between here and Eisenerz, but a few buses go through daily. The route soon returns to Leoben, 30 km (18½ miles) from Eisenerz and 16 km (10 mi) southwest of Bruck an der Mur.

A third excursion from Bruck takes you north 61 km (38 mi) to Mariazell, known for its pilgrimage church and gingerbread. Leave Bruck an der Mur on Route 20, heading north to the village of **Thörl,** which is dominated by the ruined 15th-century stronghold of Schloss Schachenstein. Nearby stands a curious roadside chapel with an unusually carved Calvary from 1530. Just north is the popular mountain resort of **Aflenz Kurort,** from which a chair lift ascends the 5,110-foot Bürgeralm. It operates daily during the ski season, but only Friday through Monday and on holidays the rest of the year. The village church, dating partially from the 12th century, is noted for its rustic stonework.

Route 20 continues north, soon climbing to over 4,000 feet as it crosses the Seeberg Pass, from which you can see the surrounding mountain ranges of Hochschwab and Veitschalpe. A descent to the valley is followed by another rise to **Mariazell,** a place of pilgrimage since 1157, when the Benedictines established a priory here. After Louis I, King of Hungary, attributed his victory over the Turks in 1377 to the intervention of its Virgin, Mariazell's reputation for miracles began to spread.

A visit to the town begins with the **basilica,** which replaced the original church during the 14th century and was itself enlarged in the late 17th century by the Italian architect Domenico Sciassia. Its exterior is unusual, with the original Gothic spire and porch flanked by squat, bulbous Baroque towers. Step inside to see the incredibly elaborate plasterwork and paintings. In the **Gnadenkapelle,** or Chapel of Miracles, in the nave, is the main object of pilgrimage: the 12th-century statue of the Virgin of Mariazell. It stands under a silver baldachin designed in 1727 by the younger Fischer von Erlach and behind a silver grille donated by Empress Maria Theresa.

The **high altar** of 1704, by the elder Fischer von Erlach—the leading architect of the Austrian Baroque—is in the east end of the nave. Don't miss seeing the **Schatzkammer** (Treasury) for its collection of votive offerings from medieval times to the present. *Treasury admission: AS20. Open May–Oct., daily 10–noon and 2–3.*

As a year-round resort, Mariazell offers a wide range of sports and recreation; in winter there's a good ski school for beginners and young people. The 1,266-meter (4,150-foot) **Bürgeralpe** is quickly reached by cable car from a lower station just two blocks north of the basilica. Paths from the upper station fan out in several directions for country walks in summer. *Bürgeralpebahn, Wienerstr. 28, tel. 03882/2555. Round-trip fare: AS70 adults, AS45 children under 15. Operates daily 9–5 in summer, 9–4 in winter.*

Time Out On top of the Bürgeralpe, just beyond the observation tower, a few minutes' walk from the upper cable car station, you can have drinks or such simple meals as thick pea soup and sausages at the rustic **Edelweiss Mountain Hut.**

Back in Mariazell, pay a visit to the **Heimatmuseum,** or Regional Museum of Local Life, at Wienerstrasse 35, and the **mechanical Nativity figurines** at the **Stations of the Cross** on Calvary Hill (Kalvarienberg 1, tel. 03882/2108).

From here, you can continue on to Tour 4 by returning south on Route 20 in the direction of Bruck an der Mur and joining S–6 at Kapfenberg or by taking Routes 21 and 23 southeast to Mürzzuschlag, the first stop of Tour 4. If you prefer to head directly to the **Danube Valley** and **Vienna,** however, your best route is north via Route 20 over the Ötscher Massif to St. Pölten. This exceptionally scenic drive is paralleled by a narrow-gauge rail line offering one of the most spectacular train rides in Austria, with at least five runs a day in each direction. St. Pölten is on the main east–west express line.

Tour 4: The Mountain Route to Vienna

The most direct route from Bruck an der Mur back to Vienna is also in some ways the most interesting. It takes you through the cradle of Austrian skiing, past several popular resorts, and over the scenic Semmering Pass and offers an opportunity to ride a 19th-century steam cog-wheel train to the top of the highest mountain in this part of the country, a peak that often remains snowcapped into the summer. It also takes you to Wiener Neustadt, a small, historic city. This area's proximity to Vienna makes day trips or weekend excursions from the capital practical.

Rail service along the route is excellent, with frequent expresses linking the main towns to Vienna. The trains follow Europe's first alpine rail line, a bold feat of engineering that was completed in 1854. You can still take this thrilling ride, which will, unfortunately, be less so after a new tunnel under the mountain pass is opened. Local buses connect all the towns, but few direct express buses go as far as Vienna.

Leave Bruck an der Mur on S–6, northeast past the industrial 36 town of Kapfenberg, and take the exit for **Mürzzuschlag,** 42 km (26 mi) away. This lively resort town is popular for both winter and summer sports. It is regarded as the birthplace of Austrian skiing and, in a sense, of the Winter Olympics, since the first Nordic Games were held here in 1904. The main focus of ski activity has long since moved west to the Tirol, but Mürzzuschlag is still a favorite of the Viennese and preserves its past glories in the excellent **Winter Sports Museum,** which displays equipment past and present from around the world. *Wiener Str. 3, tel. 03852/2555. Contribution requested. Open Tues.–Sun. 9– noon and 2–5.*

The road continues as Route 306, climbing to the Semmering Pass, the boundary between Styria and Lower Austria, at a height of 3,230 feet. A bridle path has existed on this mountainous route since at least the 12th century, but the first road was not built until 1728. Fourteen km (8½ mi) northeast of Mürzzuschlag is **Semmering,** the first town in Lower Austria, a resort on a south-facing slope overlooking the pass. Sheltered by pine forests and built on terraces reaching as high as 4,250 feet, it's considered to have a healthy atmosphere and has several spa-type hotels and pensions.

A delightful side trip can be made from Semmering into the **Höllental** (Valley of Hell), an extremely narrow and romantic gorge cut by the Schwarza stream between two high mountains, the Raxalpe and the Schneeberg (Snow Mountain). Follow local roads north 22 km (13½ mi) to Hirschwang, the beginning of the valley. From here you can ride the **Raxbahn cable car** to a plateau on the Raxalpe at 5,075 feet. *Tel. 02666/ 2497. Round-trip fare: AS135 adults, AS70 children. Operates daily at half-hour intervals, 8–6 or 9–4:30, depending on the season.*

From Höllental, continue north into the valley for another 18 km (11 mi), passing through the wildest section, to Schwarzau im Gebirge. Then circle around the north slope of the Schneeberg via the Klostertal to **Puchberg am Schneeberg.**

People flock to this quiet mountain resort largely to ride the marvelous old narrow-gauge **cog-wheel steam train** to a plateau near the top of the Schneeberg. Allow the better part of a day for this trip, since the ride takes 1⅓ hours each way and the trains are none too frequent, some running on a schedule and others according to demand. This excursion to Lower Austria's highest peak is very popular, so make seat reservations as soon as you get to the Puchberg station, from which there are also regular trains to Wiener Neustadt and Vienna.

Bring along a light sweater or jacket even in summer. Ordinary walking shoes are sufficient unless you wander off the main trails, in which case you'll need hiking boots, along with some mountain experience.

The steam engines, dating from the 1890s, are built at a peculiar angle to the ground so that their fireboxes remain level while climbing. The wooden cars they haul are of equal vintage, with hard seats, but for relief, a rest stop is made at the **Baumgartner Haus,** where you can get refreshments before continuing up past the timberline and through two tunnels (close the windows or suffocate!). When you reach the upper station (5,892 feet), you should immediately make reservations for the return trip. Near the station hut is the small **Elizabeth Chapel** and the **Berghaus Hochschneeberg,** a simple lodge with a restaurant and overnight guest facilities. From here, you can walk to the **Kaiserstein** for a panoramic view and to the **Klosterwappen,** the highest peak, at 6,811 feet above sea level.

Allow about 2–3 hours for these walks. Maps are available at the lodge.

Time Out   Real stick-to-your-ribs mountain food, draft beer, and plenty of *Gemütlichkeit* are served up at the inexpensive **Damböck Haus,** a rustic hut operated by the Austrian Touring Club (*ÖTK*). It's only a 15-minute walk from the upper station, following a wide trail with green blazes.

The last train down usually leaves about 4:30 or 5:30, although later runs are made if traffic warrants. *Schneeberg Bahn, Bahnhof Puchberg, tel. 02636/22250. Round-trip fare: AS154 adults, AS77 children. Eurailpass and Rabbit Card holders travel free but need seat reservations. Operates late Apr.–early Nov.*

40   When you've come down from the mountains, one attraction remains before you return to Vienna. Although today's **Wiener Neustadt** is a busy industrial center built on the ashes of its prewar self, just enough of its past glories survived World War II's bombings to make a visit worthwhile. The small city was established in 1194 as a fortress protecting Vienna from the Hungarians. During the mid-15th century it was an imperial residence, and in 1752 it became, and still is, the seat of the Austrian Military Academy.

Begin your exploration of the Old Town at the **Hauptplatz** (largely closed to traffic), which contains several rebuilt medieval houses with Gothic arcades standing opposite the 16th-century **Rathaus.**

Time Out   The nicest place in town for pastries, ice cream, snacks, or even light meals is the **Café Witetschka,** located on a delightful and historic little square just half a block from the southwest corner of the Hauptplatz. You can sit at tables in the garden in good weather. *Allerheiligenplatz 1. Closed Sun.*

Take Böheimgasse north to the Domplatz, in the center of which stands the **Stadtpfarrkirche** (town parish church), also known as the Liebfrauenkirche. Begun in the 13th century, it had cathedral status from 1468 until 1784. The interior is attractive, with painted wooden figures of the Apostles, a mural of the *Last Judgment,* and the splendid tomb of Cardinal Khlesl with a bust carved in 1630 by Giovanni Bernini, the master of the Italian Baroque.

A narrow lane called the Puchheimgasse brings you to the 12th-century **Reckturm,** a defensive tower said to have been paid for with part of Richard the Lionheart's ransom money. Follow Baumkirchnerring to Wiener Strasse. At the corner is the 14th-century **Church of St. Peter-an-der-Sperr,** now an exhibition gallery. Continue north on Wiener Strasse to the **Stadtmuseum,** whose greatest treasure is the *Corvinusbecher,* a goblet from 1487, a gift from the Hungarian king who conquered the town.

Return to the Old Town via Grazer Strasse. To the east of the Hauptplatz, on Neuklostergasse, is the **Neukloster Church,** part of a Cistercian convent founded in 1250. Behind the high altar in the richly Baroque interior is the tomb of Eleanor of Portugal (died 1467), wife of the emperor Frederick III.

Two blocks farther south on Grazer Strasse stands the massive **Burg,** a castle begun in the 13th century, rebuilt as an imperial residence in the 15th century, and made the Austrian Military Academy by order of Empress Maria Theresa in 1752. The Nazis took it over in 1938, and its first German commandant was none other than General Erwin Rommel, the Desert Fox. Enter its grounds to visit the famous 15th-century **Church of St. George,** whose gable is decorated with, among others, 14 Habsburg coats of arms. Beneath the gable is a statue of Frederick III curiously inscribed "A.E.I.O.U.," which some believe stand for the Latin words that mean, "Austria will rule the world." Inside the church, under the steps of the high altar, are buried the remains of the Emperor Maximilian I.

From here, it is about 50 km (31 mi) north to Vienna via A–2, Route 17, or an express train.

What to See and Do with Children

Children adore knights in shining armor, and **Graz** has just the place to let their imaginations run wild—the **Landeszeughaus** armory. While in the area, you might also take them to the **Austrian Open-Air Museum** to experience rural life in centuries past or to the **Lippizaner Stud Farm** to see how the great stallions are raised (*see* Tour 2, above).

Lake Neusiedl (*see* Tour 1, above) has as many attractions for children as it has for adults. Besides the beaches and nature preserves, there are wonderful opportunities for easy bicycling, boating, and a variety of water sports (*see* Sports and Fitness, below). A more leisurely activity, suitable for even the youngest, is to tour the countryside in a **horse-drawn wagon.** Operators in several lakeside villages will arrange this, including Johann Mad (Ruster Str. 14, Mörbisch, tel. 02685/8250).

Austrian parents traditionally bring their children to **Mariazell** (*see* Tour 3, above) in winter to learn skiing on the safe and gentle slopes. There are organized programs for young beginners that the local tourist office can tell you about.

The old steam trains at **Murau** are a treat for children of all ages (*see* Tour 3, above). Call ahead for current schedules.

Another steam-train ride, this to the top of a high mountain, is offered at **Puchberg am Schneeberg** (*see* Tour 4, above).

Of all the castles in Eastern Austria, **Riegersburg,** with its theatrical displays, is the most suitable for children (*see* Tour 1, above).

Off the Beaten Track

In a sense, everything in Eastern Austria is off the beaten track, at least for overseas visitors, but if you'd like to depart even farther from the obvious, you might try some of these. They are given in tour sequence, beginning in northern Burgenland.

Kittsee, in the northeast corner of Burgenland, practically touching Bratislava in Czechoslovakia, is noted for its fine **ethnographic museum** in the Altes Schloss, a 17th-century horseshoe-shaped castle. The museum specializes in folk art from eastern and southern Europe. *Tel. 02143/2304. Admission:*

*AS20 adults, AS10 senior citizens and children. Open daily
10–4.*

One of the strangest sights in Burgenland is the ancient Roman
quarry (Römer Steinbruch) at **St. Margarethen,** just west of
Rust on the road to Eisenstadt. Its limestone was used to build
Roman strongholds, as well as much of Vienna, including the
cathedral. Today it provides the raw material for modern sculp-
tors who work on the site, creating an ever-changing sculpture
garden. A Passion play is performed here each summer (tel.
02680/2234 or 02680/2100).

Another composer from this part of Austria was Franz Liszt
(1811–1886), who was born some 50 km (31 mi) south of
Eisenstadt, in the tiny village of **Raiding.** The modest family
house is now the **Franz-Liszt Museum** (Liszt Geburtshaus), displaying various mementos of his life, including a church organ
he used to play. *Tel. 02619/7220. Admission: AS15 adults, AS8
senior citizens, students, and children. Open Apr.–Oct., daily
9–4.*

Besides being the major spa of Burgenland, **Bad Tatzmannsdorf,** on the road between Bernstein and Güssing, is home to
the recently opened **South Burgenland Open-Air Museum**
(Freilichtmuseum), which displays restored old barns, farmhouses, and stables from the region. *Tel. 03353/8314. Admission: AS10 adults, AS5 senior citizens, students, and children.
Open daily 8–6.*

If you stop in Güssing to explore its castle, consider a visit to
the **Güssing Game Park** (Naturpark Güssing). A variety of wild
animals live in more than a square mile of open space, with observation posts scattered throughout. *1 km (⅗ mi) northeast of
Güssing, tel. 03322/2444. Admission: AS15 adults, AS5 children. Open Apr.–Oct., daily during daylight hours.*

Nearly all the tourist attractions of **Graz** are in its Old Town,
but just across the river stands the **Mariahilferkirche** (Church
of Our Lady of Succor), built in 1611, with Baroque towers
added in 1744. It is famous for its 17th-century painting, the
Madonna of Graz, an object of pilgrimage. The adjacent Minorite Cloisters are noted for their architecture. *Mariahilferplatz
3, tel. 0316/913170. Open weekdays 8–noon and 2–6.*

The world's oldest **steam tramway** operates between Mariazell
and the Erlaufsee, for a ride of about 3½ km (2 mi) to a lovely
lake. Ask the local tourist office for details. *Museumtramway,
Bahnhof Mariazell. Operates July–Sept., weekends and holidays, hourly from 9:30 until late afternoon.*

Shopping

Traditional handicrafts still thrive in Burgenland, and you can
buy good-quality mementos of your trip without the usual tourist hype. Look for pottery and ceramic ware, particularly in the
potters' village of Stoob (which has a small ceramics museum at
Hauptstrasse 85); woven baskets from the Lake Neusiedl area
and, especially, from the basket weavers' hamlet of Pirings-
dorf; and jewelry and objets d'art made of Bernstein jade from
Bernstein. These three craftsmen's villages are all on Route 50
in the center of the province. Visitors to Eisenstadt can find

crafts from all over Burgenland in local stores, such as the **Trachten Tack** shop at Hauptstrasse 8.

In Styria, be on the lookout for traditional skirts, trousers, and jackets of gray loden cloth; dirndls; modern sportswear and ski equipment; handwoven garments; and objects of wrought iron. The **Heimatwerk** shop at Paulustorgasse 4 in Graz is associated with the local folklore museum and stocks a good variety of regional crafts and products. For a wide selection of more conventional goods, try the leading department store, **Kastner & Öhler,** at Sackstrasse 7, just off the Hauptplatz, and the many smart boutiques in the surrounding streets.

Sports and Fitness

Bicycling The flat plains around **Lake Neusiedl,** with their tiny hamlets and unspoiled scenery, are perfect for leisurely bicycling. Practically every village has a bike rental (Radverleih) shop. Neusiedl am See: **Bahnhof** (train station, tel. 02167/2437) and **Hotel Wende** (Seestr. 40, tel. 02167/8111); Podersdorf: **Strandhotel** (Strandplatz 1, tel. 02177/2204), and **Hlousek** (Campingstr. 18, tel. 02177/2452); Illmitz: **Polay** (Floriangasse 5, tel. 02175/24192); Rust: **Johannes Schreiner** (Kirchengasse 4, tel. 02685/436); and Mörbisch: **Posch** (Blumentalgasse 9, tel. 02685/8242). There's a circular bike route around the lake, with a short ferry ride near the southern end. In 1992 you will be able to go completely by land, using a new path through Hungary. This and many other routes are described in a map/brochure called "Radlerland Burgenland" that you can pick up free at tourist offices. The brochure also has an extensive list of rental and service shops throughout the province, most of which is level enough for easy riding.

Styria has a much hillier terrain, so you might want to confine your bicycling to urban areas. The **Graz** tourist office (tel. 0316/835241) at Herrengasse 16 will lend you free a "white bicycle" for use in town, or you can rent one at the main train station (tel. 0316/913500) and at numerous other places. Nearly all other towns in the province have bike-rental shops, among them **Admont, Leibnitz,** and **Mariazell** (at the train stations).

In the small part of Lower Austria covered in this chapter, you can rent bikes in the train stations at **Puchberg am Schneeberg** and **Wiener Neustadt.**

Guided group bicycle tours through parts of Eastern Austria, including overnight accommodations, are offered by several independent operators. Contact the national or regional tourist office for current details.

Boating All kinds of small craft—rowboats, pedal boats, electric boats, and sailboats—can be rented along the shores of Lake Neusiedl, by the hour or by the day. Some rental places (*Bootsvermietung*) are **Baumgartner** (Neusiedl am See, tel. 02167/2782), **Knoll** (Podersdorf, tel. 02177/2431), **Gangl** (Illmitz, tel. 02175/2158), **Freizeitcenter** (Rust, tel. 02685/595), and **Lang** (Mörbisch, tel. 02685/8374). Expect to pay about AS30 per hour for a rowboat, AS60 for a pedal boat, and AS90 for an electric boat. Sailboat prices vary widely.

Golf You can play golf on an excellent 18-hole course at the **Golfclub Murhof** (Frohnleiten, Styria, tel. 03127/2101), in the Mur Valley between Graz and Bruck an der Mur, from April through October. Another major course is the **Wiener Neustadt Golf Club** (Föhrenwald, Lower Austria, tel. 02622/27438), 10 km (6 mi) south of the city on Route 54. It is open year-round. There's also an 18-hole course at **Donnerskirchen** in Burgenland.

Hiking　Eastern Austria is prime hiking country, and most tourist centers have marked trails. You'll need a local hiking map (*Wanderkarte*), which you can usually buy at the town's tourist office, whose staff can also suggest routes for short rambles in the vicinity. Some particularly good places for walks are around **Lake Neusiedl** and **Güssing** in Burgenland; in the **Mur Valley** of Styria, especially the Bärenschützklamm at **Mixnitz** (*see* Tour 3, above); around **Mariazell;** and atop the **Schneeberg** in Lower Austria (*see* Tour 4, above).

For the truly ambitious, several long-distance trails cut through this region, among them the **Nordalpen-Weitwanderweg** past the Raxalpe to Rust and the **Oststeiermärkischer Hauptwanderweg** from western Austria to Riegersburg. There's no need to carry either food or a tent because you stay overnight in staffed huts. Camping is highly discouraged for both safety and environmental reasons.

Horseback Riding　The *puszta* (steppe) to the east of **Lake Neusiedl** is a perfect place for riding (*Reiten*), and horses (*Pferde*) can be hired in several of the villages. Ask at the local tourist office. One livery stable near the lake is **Reitercsárda** at Obere Wiesen 1 in Neusiedl am See (tel. 02167/8659).

Skiing　When you think of skiing in Austria, you naturally think of the western and central parts of the country. The east has neither the tall mountains nor the highly developed facilities, yet real alpine skiing in Austria first began around **Mürzzuschlag** in Styria. The town is still popular with Viennese skiers and has a fine museum of the sport's history. In the nearby regions of **Schneeberg, Rax,** and **Semmering,** all in Lower Austria, there's pleasant (if not too exciting) skiing within easy reach of Vienna. Austrian children have traditionally learned to ski on the gentle slopes near **Mariazell** in Styria. All the eastern ski areas share a casual *Gemütlichkeit*. The resorts mentioned have cross-country as well as downhill skiing and plenty of lifts, hotels, inns, restaurants, and so on. Contact the regional tourist offices for more complete details.

Water Sports　The best swimming on Lake Neusiedl is at **Podersdorf,** whose 5-km (3-mi)-long beach (*Strand*) is virtually free of reeds. Neusiedl am See and Rust also have good beaches. Most towns in Eastern Austria have at least one public indoor swimming pool (*Hallenbad*), and many have outdoor pools (*Freibad*). Ask at the local tourist office about conditions of use and fees.

Lake Neusiedl is also excellent for windsurfing. You can take lessons and rent sailboards at most lakeside villages.

Dining and Lodging

Dining

When choosing a restaurant, it's good to keep in mind that each of the three provinces of Eastern Austria has its own cooking style. In Burgenland, the local Pannonian cooking, strongly influenced by neighboring Hungary, features spicy dishes, like *Gulyas* (goulash), flavored with paprika. You'll also find fish from Lake Neusiedl, goose specialties, game, and fresh local vegetables. Styria, bordering on Yugoslavia, has a hearty cuisine with Serbian overtones. A typical dish of the region is *Steirisches Brathuhn* (roast chicken turned on a spit), and *Kernöl*, a strange but very tasty greenish-black pumpkinseed oil is used as a dressing. Such Balkan specialties as *cevapcici* (spicy meatballs) are often found on Styrian menus. You are most likely to encounter the lighter and more urbane Viennese cooking in Lower Austria, where you can get Wiener schnitzel nearly everywhere.

Eastern Austria is also wine country, with all three provinces being major producers. Excellent white wines predominate, although there are a few decent reds and rosés as well. Burgenland's vineyards, mostly around Lake Neusiedl, produce wines that tend to be slightly on the sweet side, with perhaps the best examples coming from the village of Rust. In Styria, the wines from south of Graz along the Yugoslav border and near Leibnitz are superb, especially the tangy *Schilcher* rosé.

Although beer is made all over Austria, the most renowned are produced in Styria. They are *Gösser*, from Leoben, and *Puntigamer* and *Reininghaus*, both from Graz.

Many of the restaurants described below are actually country inns that provide overnight accommodations as well as meals, as noted in the reviews.

Restaurant prices include taxes and a service charge, but it is customary to give the waiter an additional tip of up to 10%.

Highly recommended restaurants are indicated by a star ★.

Category	Cost*
Very Expensive	over AS500
Expensive	AS300–AS500
Moderate	AS200–AS300
Inexpensive	under AS200

**per person for a typical 3-course meal, excluding drinks and additional tip*

Lodging

Accommodations in Eastern Austria range from luxury city hotels to mountain and lakeside resorts to castles and romantic country inns, and all are substantially lower in price than those in Vienna or Salzburg. There are also guest houses in every town and village, which give good value as long as you don't expect a private bath. These bargains are usually identified by signs reading *Zimmer frei* (room available) or *Frühstückspension* (bed-and-breakfast).

The tourist information office (*Verkehrsverein* or a similar word) in virtually every town can usually find you a decent place to sleep if you haven't made a reservation (*see* Essential Information, above).

Hotel room rates include taxes and service, and frequently breakfast—although you should always ask about the latter. It is customary to leave an additional tip, say AS20 per day, for the maid in larger city hotels for longer stays.

Highly recommended lodgings are indicated by a star ★.

Category	Cost*
Very Expensive	over AS2,000
Expensive	AS1,000–AS2,000
Moderate	AS600–AS1,000
Inexpensive	under AS600

All prices are for a standard double room for two, including taxes and service charge.

The following abbreviations are used after the town names to indicate which province they are in: (B.), Burgenland; (L.A.), Lower Austria; and (St.), Styria.

Bernstein (B.)

Lodging
★
Burg Bernstein. This medieval hilltop castle, built in the 12th century, was converted into a hotel in 1953. It is just west of the village of Bernstein, overlooking the peaceful Tauchen valley. The rooms tend to be huge and are furnished with antiques and heated with traditional ceramic stoves. Meals are served, with regional wines, in a baronial hall decorated in the Baroque style. *Schlossweg 1, A–7434, tel. 03354/6382. 10 rooms with private bath. Facilities: outdoor pool, sauna, private trout pond, private hunting preserve. AE, DC, V. Closed Oct.–Easter. Expensive.*

Bruck an der Mur (St.)

Dining
★
Zur Schnepf'n. This comfortably elegant country inn is well regarded locally for its imaginative variations on Austrian cuisine. It is on the western edge of town, in the hamlet of Unteraich along the Mur river. Among the dishes you might expect to find are a parfait of goose liver with leafy salad, fillet of beef with horseradish sauce served with asparagus and corn, and strawberries with seasonal sherbet. *Unteraich 23, tel. 03862/51474. Reservations advised. Jacket and tie advised. AE, DC, MC, V. Closed Tues. Expensive.*

Dining and Lodging
Bayer. This family-operated small-town hotel-restaurant is noted for serving simple Styrian dishes. The building, which dates from 1608, stands opposite the famous fountain on the town's main square. The 33 rooms (16 with bath or shower) are all soundproof and in the Moderate category. Some of the dishes offered are *Rohschinken* (a ham appetizer), cheese soup, mixed sausages with sauerkraut, and homemade strudel. *Hauptplatz 24, A–8600, tel. 03862/51218. Reservations not required. Dress: casual. AE, DC, MC, V. Moderate.*

Eisenstadt (B.)

Dining
★
G'würzstöckl. Some of the best cooking in Burgenland can be found at this light-filled and spacious modern restaurant in the

Hotel Burgenland. The creative cuisine features lighter versions of Austrian specialties, with distinct Hungarian overtones. The menu varies, but might include calves' liver with apples and walnuts, fillet of lamb baked with goat cheese, and fruit soup. There's a superb choice of Burgenland wines. *Hotel Burgenland, Schubertplatz 1, tel. 02682/5521. Reservations advised. Dress: casual. AE, DC, MC, V. Closed Sat. lunch, Sun. dinner, and early July–early Aug. Expensive.*

Schlosstaverne. Gypsy music and candlelight accompany the food at the Schlosstaverne, housed in the former stables of Schloss Esterhazy. This is a rather touristy place, but friendly and enjoyable nonetheless. Its cuisine is a satisfactory blend of Viennese and Hungarian styles, and its location just across from the princely palace couldn't be more convenient. You'll find old favorites like Wiener schnitzel and goulash on the menu, as well as a good choice of local wines. *Esterhazyplatz 5, tel. 02682/3102. Reservations advised. Dress: casual. AE. Closed Sun. and Mon. in winter. Moderate.*

Lodging **Hotel Burgenland.** This recently built, strikingly contempo-
★ rary hotel has everything you'd expect in a first-class establishment and is often considered the best hotel in the province. It's near the town center, within walking distance of all the tourist attractions, and the large rooms are bright and airy. *Schubertplatz 1, A–7000, tel. 02682/5521; fax 02682/5531. 88 rooms with bath. Facilities: G'würzstöckl restaurant, café, bar, sauna, indoor pool, conference room. AE, DC, MC, V. Expensive.*

Parkhotel Mikschi. Although rather small, this modern four-story hotel in the town center provides accommodations of exceptionally high quality. Many of the large rooms have balconies, some overlooking the hotel's private garden, and the public areas are pleasantly contemporary. *Joseph-Haydn-Gasse 38, A–7000, tel. 02682/4361. 28 rooms with bath. Facilities: café, conference room. DC, MC, V. Moderate.*

Hotel Eder-Fröhlich (Goldener Adler). The same family has run this cozy old-fashioned guest house in the center of town since 1772. Its bedrooms are spartan but clean, and the public areas are rustically furnished. *Hauptstr. 25, A–7000, tel. 02682/ 2645. 25 rooms, a few with bath or shower. Facilities: restaurant with garden terrace. AE, DC, MC, V. Closed Jan. Inexpensive.*

Forchtenstein (B.)

Dining **Reisner.** The delicately prepared traditional food served at this popular place attracts people from all over the region. You can eat in the somewhat formal dining room or in a rustic tavern favored by the locals. The restaurant is on the main road at the eastern end of the village. Some typical dishes are trout with a ragout of fresh vegetables; excellent steaks; and, for dessert, a rhubarb tart or poppyseed parfait. *Hauptstr. 141, tel. 02626/ 63139. Reservations advised. Dress: casual. AE, DC, MC. Closed Wed. Expensive.*

Lodging **Gasthof Sauerzapf.** This simple country inn on the main road just five minutes west of the castle has recently modernized its rooms. *Rosalienstr. 9, A–7212, tel. 02626/81217. 14 rooms, some with shower. Facilities: restaurant serving local wines, garden. No credit cards. Inexpensive.*

Graz (St.)

Dining **Restaurant Wiesler.** In Graz's leading hotel, on the banks of the
★ Mur, there's a sophisticated restaurant where the ambience is
fairly formal but still festive, and well-dressed guests dine on
nouvelle Styrian cuisine. The meat, poultry, venison, vegetables, fruit, and wines are all from the region surrounding Graz,
and for those who would rather not experiment with such deli-
cacies as beef bouillon with quails' eggs, or calves' sweetbreads
with cream dressing, classic international dishes are also
served. *Grieskai 4, tel. 0316/913–2410. Reservations recommended. Jacket and tie advised. AE, DC, MC, V. Open until
late evening. Very Expensive.*

★ **Hofkeller.** This former wine and beer cellar in the heart of the
Old Town, one block west of the cathedral, has been transformed into a most elegant restaurant. It's done in an attractive
traditional style, with heavy wood paneling and elaborate table
settings. Both Austrian and international specialties are
served, along with a good choice of Austrian wines. Some of the
dishes you might encounter are seafood salad in walnut oil, delicately browned asparagus with chicken-liver mousse, salmon
trout in lemon butter, and artichoke hearts with goose liver
and mushrooms. *Hofgasse 8, tel. 0316/832439. Reservations advised. Jacket and tie advised. AE, DC, MC, V. Closed Sun. Expensive.*

Stündl. An unprepossessing facade on a simple corner building
belies the sophisticated up-to-date cuisine served in this slightly out-of-the-way restaurant. It's just beyond the university,
1½ km (1 mi) northeast of the Hauptplatz, and it can be reached
by taxi or by bus No. 58. Meals are served in the garden during
the warm months. Among the inventive, Italian-inspired
dishes might be a terrine of fresh vegetables with herb sauce or
lamb cutlets with oyster mushrooms in puff pastry. Local
Styrian wines are featured. *Heinrichstr. 55, tel. 0316/33413.
Reservations advised. Jacket and tie recommended. AE, DC,
MC, V. Closed Sat. and Sun. Expensive.*

★ **Keplerkeller.** The astronomer Johannes Kepler is supposed to
have lived here at the end of the 16th century, but, alas, there's
no proof of this. It is, nevertheless, an atmospheric old wine
cellar with heavy paneling and rustic decor, between the
Landeszeughaus and the Glockenspielplatz in the pedestrian
zone of the Old Town. There is a lovely Renaissance courtyard
for alfresco dining and live music after 9 PM. The menu features
local specialties like wurst in vinegar and pumpkinseed oil, a
Styrian farmers' cutlet, and locally made strudel, along with a
few more exotic items and the usual schnitzels. The
Keplerkeller is especially popular for its selection of local wines
in open carafes. *Stempfergasse 6, tel. 0316/822449. Reservations advised. Dress: casual. AE, DC, MC, V. Closed Sun.
Dinner only. Moderate.*

Milchmariandl. An artistic crowd favors this unassuming little
restaurant on the edge of town, especially on warm summer
evenings when the quiet garden terrace provides welcome relief. It is 1.6 km (1 mi) northeast of the Hauptplatz, by car, or
you can take bus No. 31. The mostly Styrian cooking is simple
and hearty, and the menu features such local items as *Stainzer
Rohschinken* (a local ham dish) and country sausages with wine
and poppyseed noodles. *Richard Wagner-Gasse 31, tel. 0316/
34400. Reservations advised. Dress: casual. AE, DC, MC, V.
Closed Sun. Moderate.*

Graz Dining and Lodging

Dining

Gambrinuskeller, **12**

Hofkeller, **11**

Keplerkeller, **14**

Landhauskeller, **16**

Milchmariandl, **1**

Restaurant Wiesler, **10**

Stadtheuriger, **15**

Stainzerbauer, **13**

Stündl, **2**

Lodging

Alba-Wiesler, **10**

Hotel Daniel, **6**

Hotel Erzherzog
Johann, **8**

Hotel Europa, **5**

Hotel Gollner, **17**

Hotel Mariahilf, **7**

Hotel Pfeifer, **18**

Hotel Strasser, **9**

Rosenhotel
Steiermark, **3**

Schlossberg Hotel, **4**

Rich. Wagner-Gasse

Kreuzgasse

Bergmanngasse

Grillparzerstrasse

Körblergasse

Grabenstrasse

Franckstrasse

Rosenberggürtel

Max Mell-Allee

Heinrichstrasse

Schubertstrasse

Auersperggasse

nburggasse

Humboldtstrasse

Heinrichstrasse

Herdergasse

Parkstrasse

Universität

Leechgasse

lossberg

Max Theresia Allee

Attemsgasse

Halbärthgasse

Geidorfgürtel

Liebiggasse

Dr. Karl Böhm-Allee

Stadtpark

Glacisstrasse

Zinzendorfgasse

Elizabethstrasse

Paulustorgasse

Sauraugasse

Beethovenstrasse

Leonhardstrasse

gpl

Hofgasse

Erzherzog Johann Allee

Merangasse

asse

Spoorgasse

Färbergasse

Burggasse

Burgring

Schillerstrasse

gasse

Herrengasse

Burggergasse

Rechbauerstrasse

Naglergasse

Hans Sachs G.

Opernring

Glacisstrasse

Mandellstrasse

N

Raubergasse

Schmiedgasse

Neutorgasse

Reitschulgasse

Jakominiplatz

0   600 yards

0   600 meters

Stadtheuriger. This colorful *Weinstube* (wine cellar) is hidden away in 400-year-old vaults in the Old Town, two blocks from the Landeszeughaus. Styrian dishes are featured, and salads, cold and warm meats, steaks, seafood, and desserts may be selected from either the buffet or from a daily menu. A good variety of local wines is sold by the glass or by the bottle. *Hans-Sachs-Gasse 8, tel. 0316/832482. Reservations suggested. Jacket and tie advised. No credit cards. Closed Sun. and Aug. Dinner only. Moderate.*

★ **Stainzerbauer.** This cheerful restaurant, one block south of the cathedral, is popular with local residents, who return again and again to their regular tables. Its Styrian specialties may include such hearty dishes as pork chops on a wooden plank with garlic bread, *Semmelknödel* (bread-and-meat dumplings) in cream sauce, and a variety of crisp salads. Quick ready-made platters are served at lunch. *Bürgergasse 4, tel. 0316/821106. Reservations suggested. Jacket and tie advised. AE, DC, MC, V. Closed Sun. Moderate.*

★ **Gambrinuskeller.** This large, popular place in the heart of the Old Town is known for its grilled meat, salads, and unusual dishes from such places as the Balkans and Brazil. The interior is comfortably rustic, and there's a garden with tables overlooking a quiet square. Among the dishes are Serbian bean soup, a copious mixed grill, cevapcici (spicy meatballs), kebabs, and pastas. Local wines and beers are featured. *Färbergasse 6–8, tel. 0316/810181. Reservations not required. Dress: casual. No credit cards. Closed Sat. dinner, Sun., holidays. Inexpensive.*

Landhauskeller. The Landhaus complex, which includes the provincial parliament and the armory, is also home to a favorite traditional Weinstube that serves a variety of Styrian dishes in its rustic dining rooms and in its courtyard. Such hearty fare as cheese dumplings and sauerkraut with meat will be found on the extensive menu. *Schmiedgasse 9, tel. 0316/830276. Reservations not required. Dress: casual. DC, MC, V. Closed Sun., holidays. Inexpensive.*

Lodging **Alba-Wiesler.** This five-star hotel, just across the Mur from the
★ Old Town, is undoubtedly the best in Graz. It dates from the turn of the century, as evidenced by high ceilings and large spaces, and was totally renovated in 1986. The decoration of both the public areas and the rooms is predominantly updated art nouveau, with much pale marble, cherry wood, and brass. *Grieskai 4, A–8010, tel. 0316/913241. 98 rooms with bath. Facilities: Restaurant Wiesler, bistro, bar, sauna, 3 conference rooms. AE, DC, MC, V. Very Expensive.*

Hotel Daniel. A 1960s-style modern Best Western hotel, the Daniel was once plagued by its noisy location. Clever soundproofing has solved that problem and, with its smart contemporary decor, it is again a favorite among business travelers, who like the easy highway access, the adjacent main train station, and the fact that the in-town airline terminal is in the building. The Old Town is 1.6 km (1 mi) east, on the streetcar line. *Europaplatz 1, A–8021, tel. 0316/911080; fax 0316/911085. 100 rooms with bath. Facilities: restaurant, bar, 4 conference rooms. AE, DC, MC, V. Expensive.*

Hotel Erzherzog Johann. Travelers preferring a traditionally elegant city hotel will be happy with this Old World establishment in a 16th-century building. Its location, just steps from the Hauptplatz in the Old Town, is perfect for tourists. Try to book one of the recently renovated rooms that open onto a charming atrium; the older ones to the rear are less desirable. *Sackstr. 3–5, A–8011, tel. 0316/811616; fax 0316/811515. 70 rooms with bath. Facilities: restaurant, bar, café, 2 conference rooms. AE, DC, MC, V. Expensive.*

Hotel Europa. Graz's newest hotel, opened in 1986, is directly across from the main train station, 1.6 km (1 mi) west of the Old Town. Its thoroughly contemporary design and interiors and its ease of access make it popular with both business executives and tourists. A new underground shopping mall connects it directly with the station and air terminal. *Bahnhofgürtel 89, A–8020, tel. 0316/916601; fax 0316/916–601–606. 114 rooms, 4 suites, all with bath. Facilities: restaurant, café, bar, sauna, 5 conference rooms. AE, DC, MC, V. Expensive.*

Hotel Gollner. A friendly, atmospheric, older hotel near the opera house on the edge of the Old Town, the Gollner has long been a favorite of the theatrical and operatic crowd. Its soundproof rooms are comfortably large and have been recently renovated; those without a private bath are less expensive and rate in the Moderate category. *Schlögelgasse 14, A–8010, tel. 0316/ 822521; fax 0316/822–5217. 56 rooms, 37 with bath or shower. Facilities: bar, sauna, solarium, conference room. AE, DC, MC, V. Expensive.*

★ **Schlossberg Hotel.** This old inn, overlooking the Mur River at the foot of the Schlossberg, was completely rebuilt in 1982 and is a superb example of quiet good taste in a casually refined atmosphere. Each room is individually decorated and furnished with provincial antiques, although the creature comforts are thoroughly modern. *Kaiser-Franz-Josef-Kai 30, A–8010, tel. 0316/80700; fax 0316/807–0160. 43 rooms with bath. Facilities: bar, outdoor swimming pool, terrace garden, 2 conference rooms. AE, DC, MC, V. Expensive.*

Hotel Mariahilf. A comfortable old hotel in the center of things, just across the river from the Old Town. Although the location is fairly busy, the rooms have been soundproofed. Those without private bath rate in the Inexpensive category. *Mariahilferstr. 9, A–8010, tel. 0316/913163; fax 0361/917652. 44 rooms, 38 with private bath or shower. Facilities: restaurant. DC, V. Moderate.*

★ **Hotel Pfeifer.** This typically Austrian country inn, surrounded by plenty of trees, is in the suburbs of Graz, about 5½ km (3½ mi) northeast of the Old Town. It offers a quiet alternative to staying in a city hotel, has a modern and comfortable interior, and can be reached easily by taking streetcar No. 1 to the end of the line in the direction of Mariatrost. *Kirchplatz 9, A–8044, Graz-Mariatrost, tel. 0316/391112. 60 rooms with bath. Facilities: restaurant, sauna, solarium, conference room. No credit cards. Moderate.*

Rosenhotel Steiermark. An exceptional value, this recently built and very modern student accommodation, two blocks northeast of the university, functions as a hotel from early July until late September. Naturally, it attracts a young crowd and has an institutional feel about it, but if you want a clean, contemporary room with a private bath at a low price, this is a good choice. *Liebiggasse 4, A–8010, tel. 0316/340410; fax 0316/ 38–150–362. 112 rooms with bath. Facilities: restaurant, bar, sauna. No credit cards. Closed Oct.–June. Moderate.*

★ **Gasthof Zum Kreuz.** It's a bit far out of town, 7 km (4½ mi) southwest of the Hauptplatz, but those who like small country inns will appreciate this guest house for both its charm and its low prices. If you don't have a car, you can get here by taking bus No. 32 from Jakominiplatz in the Old Town. The same family has operated Zum Kreuz for over a century and has always been noted for its traditional cooking. *Kärntnerstr. 451 at Strassgang, A–8054, tel. 0316/283436. 12 rooms with bath or shower. Facilities: restaurant. MC. Inexpensive.*

Hotel Strasser. This friendly budget hotel, just two blocks south of the main train station, offers acceptable accommodations at rock-bottom prices. There is no elevator, the toilets are down the hall, and it is a bit noisy, but the clean rooms are large and comfortable and the cozy restaurant is a good value. *Eggenberger Gürtel 11, A–8020, tel. 0316/913977. 30 rooms, most with showers. Facilities: restaurant. No credit cards. Inexpensive.*

Heiligenkreuz (B.)

Dining and Lodging **Gasthof Gibiser.** Its proximity to Hungary has inspired the creative dishes served at this classical white villa-styled country inn. The Pannonian cuisine combines the best of the Austrian and Hungarian culinary traditions to produce such specialties as cabbage soup and steak stuffed with goose liver. For overnight guests there are 12 quiet rooms plus a few rustic cottages in the garden. *Heiligenkreuz 81, A–7561, tel. 03325/216. Reservations advised. Dress: casual. AE, DC, MC. Closed Mon. Dec.–Feb. Moderate.*

Judenburg (St.)

Dining
★ **Lindenwirt.** A pleasant country restaurant considered by many to be the best in the area, Lindenwirt is as famous for its international specialties as for its Styrian cuisine. It's in the hamlet of Wöllmersdorf, some 3 km (2 mi) east of Judenburg's Hauptplatz via Weisskirchner Strasse. There's outdoor dining when the weather permits. Some typical dishes are fillet of beef with asparagus salad, roast shoulder of lamb in thyme, and cold strawberry soup with tiny cheese dumplings. *Wöllmersdorf 12, tel. 03572/2306. Reservations advised. Dress: casual. No credit cards. Closed Mon. Moderate.*

Lodging **Rasthaus Grünhübl.** A modern version of a traditional Austrian inn, the two-story Grünhübl is on the main street at the western edge of town. Its cheerful, simple rooms overlook an outdoor café and tennis courts. *Burggasse 132, A–8750, tel. 03572/2437. 14 rooms with bath. Facilities: restaurant, bar, 2 private tennis courts. No credit cards. Moderate.*

Kitzeck (St.)

Dining **Steirerland.** This country inn atop a hill overlooking the heart of the Styrian wine country is reached by a steep, narrow, twisting road. It is well known for its regional cooking and has 12 comfortable guest rooms. It is 4 km (2½ mi) northwest of Kitzeck, not far from the Yugoslav border. The menu includes such dishes as wine soup with eggs and cream; roast lamb served with leeks and potatoes and with other vegetables cooked in bacon fat; and pancakes with ricotta cheese and bilberries. *Höch 10, tel. 03456/2328. Reservations advised. Dress: casual but neat. No credit cards. Closed Wed. in winter and Jan.–mid-Feb. Moderate.*

Köflach (St.)

Dining **Zum Kleinhapl.** This is one of the best restaurants in Austria,
★ and it's up on all the latest trends in Styrian cuisine. Although
part of a simple village guest house, its unpretentious dining
room attracts knowledgeable diners from all over the region,
including Graz—41 km (25 mi) east. Among the ever-changing
specialties are such dishes as homemade jellied meats with
pumpkinseed oil, sliced breast of duck with fresh vegetables
and noodles, and elderberry sherbet. *Judenburgstr. 6, tel.
03144/3494. Reservations required. Jacket and tie advised. No
credit cards. Closed Sun. dinner, Mon. Expensive.*

Mariazell (St.)

Dining **Jägerwirt.** In what is basically a tourist town, this restaurant,
★ directly across from the basilica, offers traditional country atmosphere and solid Austrian cuisine at fair prices. Besides the
usual steaks and Wiener schnitzels, the menu includes such
items as boiled pork with grated horseradish and breast of veal
with dumplings. *Hauptplatz 2, tel. 03882/2362. Reservations
not required. Dress: casual. No credit cards. Closed Mon. and
most of Dec. Moderate.*

Lodging **Hotel Feichtegger.** Although this is a boxy modern city-type hotel of five stories, near the basilica and the cable car, its ambience is one of quiet, understated luxury, and the well-equipped
guest rooms have balconies. *Wienerstr. 6, A–8630, tel. 03882/
2416. 55 rooms with bath. Facilities: restaurant, bar, indoor
pool, fitness center, conference room, terrace. AE, DC, MC, V.
Closed Apr. and Nov. Moderate–Expensive.*
Mariazellerhof. This small, cheerfully modern chalet-style hotel one block west of the basilica is known for its gingerbread;
the spicy aroma fills the house. Its comfortable rooms have balconies. *Grazerstr. 10, A–8630, tel. 03882/2179; fax 03882/
217951. 10 rooms with bath, 4 with shower. Facilities: café. AE,
DC, MC, V. Closed mid-Feb.–mid-Mar. Moderate.*

Mörbisch (B.)

Lodging **Hotel Steiner.** Though in the center of the village, the Steiner is
close to the vineyards and Lake Neusiedl. It offers rustically
styled accommodations with many modern conveniences.
*Hauerstr. 1, A–7072, tel. 02685/8444. 50 rooms with bath. Fa-
cilities: restaurant, indoor swimming pool, sauna, solarium,
terrace. No credit cards. Closed Dec.–Mar. Moderate.*

Neusiedl am See (B.)

Dining **Barth-Stuben.** The pretty and cheerfully decorated Barth-
★ Stuben regularly attracts diners from Vienna as well as vacationers at the resort. Considered the best restaurant in town, it
serves inventive variations on Austrian cuisine, sometimes
with Hungarian overtones, and is well known for its fish dishes.
It's on a back street in the town center, is quiet, and in warm
weather tables are set up in the garden. You might find on the
menu fillet of pike in wine sauce, and gnocchi with mussels.
The fresh vegetables are locally grown, and much of the wine
comes from nearby vineyards. *Franz-Liszt-Gasse 37, tel.*

02167/2625. Reservations advised. Dress: casual. AE, DC, MC, V. Closed Mon. Expensive.

Lodging **Hotel Wende.** This sprawling new three-story hotel complex is close to the lake and has many standard amenities, but don't expect the charm of a country inn. The comfortable rooms with balconies are of adequate size, and the restaurant is well regarded. Most facilities are included in the price. *Seestr. 40, A–7100, tel. 02167/8111; fax 02167/822–3649. 105 rooms with bath. Facilities: restaurant, bar, fitness center, indoor pool, sauna, private tennis courts, terrace garden, bicycle rentals, conference rooms. DC, MC, V. Closed early Feb. Expensive.*

Podersdorf (B.)

Lodging **Haus Attila.** In this small, simple family-run lakefront hotel, the rooms facing the lake are especially cozy. *Strandplatz 1, A–7141, tel. 02177/2415. 21 rooms with bath. AE. Closed Nov.–Mar. Moderate.*

Puchberg am Schneeberg (L.A.)

Lodging **Puchbergerhof.** This charming old country inn, with shuttered
★ windows and gabled roof, is set in a large garden near the village center and train station. The rooms are old-fashioned but equipped with phones; some have balconies, and those facing the garden are exceptionally peaceful. *Wiener-Neustädter-Str. 29, A–2734, tel. 02636/2278. 20 rooms with bath. Facilities: fitness room, sauna. No credit cards. Moderate.*
Berghaus Hochschneeberg. The only way to reach this simple mountaintop lodge, other than by climbing, is by the famous old steam cog railway from Puchberg. You arrive to find panoramic views and a sturdy stone hotel, as old as the railway (1898), set in peaceful surroundings. Although there are few modern conveniences (one bathroom per floor, running water in rooms, TV only in the reception room), staying here is an invigorating experience. There are wonderful places to hike. *Hochschneeberg, A–2734, tel. 02636/2257. 25 rooms without bath. Facilities: restaurant, sauna, solarium. No credit cards. Closed Nov.–Apr. Inexpensive.*

Purbach (B.)

Dining **Nikolauszeche.** This is one of the best restaurants in the Lake Neusiedl region, noted for its elegant Baroque decor as well as for its regional cuisine. Its location in a tiny village between Neusiedl-am-See and Rust is convenient for travelers staying in Eisenstadt. Among the specialties are local goat cheese with olive oil, and a pink fillet of pork with tomato and basil sauce served with a noodle soufflé. There is an excellent selection of local wines. *Purbach, tel. 02683/5514. Reservations advised. Jacket and tie advised. AE, DC. Closed mid-Nov.–Mar. Expensive.*

Dining and **Am Spitz.** A rustic country inn, famous for its local Burgenland
Lodging and Pannonian cooking, Am Spitz is near Lake Neusiedl, at the end of an attractive lane of wine cellars. The menu might include a spicy Hungarian fish soup, a cassoulet of lake fish in basil cream, and roast veal steak. All 17 guest rooms have baths. *Waldsiedlung 2, A–7083, tel. 02683/5519. Reservations*

advised. Dress: casual. No credit cards. Closed Mon. and late Dec.–Apr. Moderate.

Riegersburg (St.)

Dining and **Zur Riegersburg.** This old country inn near the foot of a castle is
Lodging adorned with flower boxes and shutters. Its large paneled din-
★ ing room with ceiling beams is bright and airy, and there's dining in the garden in season. The Austrian cuisine is hearty,
with such dishes as bratwurst with sauerkraut and dumplings,
and roast beef with corn meal. A fine selection of Styrian wines
is offered. 33 inexpensive rooms are available for overnight
guests. *Riegersburg 29, A–8333, tel. 03153/216. Reservations
not required. Dress: casual. AE, DC, MC, V. Closed Tues.
Oct.–Apr. Moderate.*

Rust (B.)

Lodging **Seehotel.** Set on the very edge of Lake Neusiedl, the luxuriously modern Seehotel is in striking contrast to the historic village
it borders. The comfortable guest rooms are in contemporary
Scandinavian style; ask for one facing the lake. *Am Seekanal
2–4, A–7071, tel. 02685/381. 89 rooms with bath. Facilities: restaurant, bar, indoor pool, sauna, private beach, terrace garden, 3 conference rooms. AE, DC, MC, V. Expensive.*

Semmering (L.A.)

Dining **Kaiser Karl.** The noted restaurant in the grand 19th-century
Hotel Panhans has refurbished Art Nouveau decor and great
mountain views from its window tables. The ambitious menu
features such Austrian dishes as a blood-sausage soufflé with
potato rolls served with a bacon-and-cabbage salad, roast venison, and fruit pancakes with yogurt ice cream. The comprehensive wine list covers all of Austria. *Hochstr. 32, tel. 02664/8181.
Reservations advised. Jacket and tie suggested. AE, DC, V.
Expensive.*

Dining and **Hotel Panhans.** This classic mountain lodge in the grand tradi-
Lodging tion is set near the center of town. It was built in 1888, thoroughly renovated in 1982, and has retained its characteristic
Art Nouveau ambience despite the modernization. It's a popular resort hotel that is frequently booked for conventions.
*Hochstr. 32, A–2680, tel. 02264/8181. 70 rooms with bath. Fa-
cilities: Kaiser Karl restaurant, café, bar, disco, fitness center,
indoor pool, sauna, conference rooms. AE, DC, V. Very Expensive.*
Belvedere. Recently renovated, this old mountain inn in a heavy
alpine style is well known for its hearty Austrian food. Though
located in town, it has a garden for outdoor dining in fine weather. Expect to find on the menu such dishes as fresh cream of
asparagus soup, pork chops, and bilberry dumplings. There
are 19 bedrooms for overnight guests, who are free to use the
indoor pool and sauna. *Hochstr. 60, A–2680, tel. 02664/270.
Reservations advised. Dress: casual but neat. AE, DC, MC, V.
Closed Nov. Moderate.*

Wiener Neustadt (L.A.)

Dining and   **Hotel Corvinus.** A low, modern, and exceptionally pleasant ho-
Lodging   tel next to the city park, the recently built Corvinus is two
★   blocks east of the train station and only a few minutes' stroll
from the main square. It caters primarily to business travelers,
and the restaurant is recommended. *Bahngasse 29–33, A–
2700, tel. 02622/24134; fax 02622/24139. 68 rooms with bath. Facilities: restaurant, bar, sauna, whirlpool, steam bath, terrace, 2 conference rooms. AE, DC, MC, V. Expensive.*

The Arts and Nightlife

The Arts

Several important music festivals featuring internationally
known musicians are held annually in Burgenland. The Styrian
capital of Graz is noted for its avant-garde theater and outstanding opera, concerts, and jazz. A free comprehensive list
(in German) of events for Burgenland, called "Was-Wer-Wo?,"
is generally available at local tourist offices. The Graz tourist
office distributes the "Graz Stadtanzeiger" (City Informer), a
free monthly guide in German, and a seasonal brochure in English called "Arts in the Old Town."

The annual **Styrian Autumn Festival** *(Steirische Herbst),* a
sometimes shocking celebration of the avant-garde in experimental theater, music, opera, dance, jazz, film, video, and other performing arts, is held in Graz from mid-October to late
November. Contact the tourist office for current details.

Theater   Graz, a major university town, has a lively theater scene known
especially for its experimental productions. Its **Schau-
spielhaus,** built in 1825, is the leading playhouse, although
there are smaller theaters scattered around town. Contact the
tourist office for current offerings.

Music   In early September, Eisenstadt plays host to the annual **Haydn
Festival** in the Esterhazy Palace. Many of the concerts are by
world-famous performers and orchestras, and admission prices
vary with the event. For further information, contact the
Haydnfestspiele office in Schloss Esterhazy (tel. 02682/61866)
or the local tourist office.

Eisenstadt's **Haydn Quartet,** dressed in 18th-century costumes, plays short matinee concerts of the master's works at 11
AM on Tuesday and Friday, mid-May to mid-October, at the
Esterhazy Palace. Admission: AS50. Call for further information (tel. 02682/3384).

Among the most popular concerts in Graz are those held by candlelight in the **Eggenberg Palace** on Monday evening in summer
at 8:30. Also popular are the organ recitals in the **cathedral** on
Sunday at 8 PM, when unusual works are often played. Ask the
Graz tourist office for details.

The **International Chamber Music Festival** (Kammermusikfest)
of Lockenhaus, in central Burgenland, takes place annually in
the 13th-century castle during the first half of July. World-famous musicians are invited, and an intimate relationship is
formed between performers and audience, who also may attend

morning rehearsals. Call for information, reservations, and accommodations (tel. 02616/2224).

The **Wiesen Jazz Festival** attracts top-name performers from America and around the world. It is held during early July in Wiesen, Burgenland, 12 km (7½ mi) southeast of Wiener Neustadt. Current information is available from the Jazz Pub in Wiesen (tel. 02626/81648 or 02626/81769).

Opera The 19th-century **Graz Opera House,** with its resplendent rococo interior, was completely renovated in 1984. Famed as a showcase for young talent and experimental productions, as well as more conventional works, it stages three to five performances a week from late September through June. Tickets are generally available until shortly before the performances; call for information (tel. 0316/826451).

At the **Mörbisch Lake Festival,** held on weekends from mid-July through August on Burgenland's Lake Neusiedl, operettas are performed outdoors on a floating stage. Special buses run from Vienna on the days of performance. For current information, contact the Mörbisch tourist office or the festival office in Schloss Esterhazy in Eisenstadt (tel. 02682/66210).

Nightlife

A clever postcard sold in the area has the picture side completely black, with the words *"Graz bei Nacht."* Well, **Graz** by night isn't quite that dead, as the nocturnal visitor soon finds out.

Casinos The **Casino Graz,** at the corner of Landhausgasse and Schmiedgasse in the Old Town, is open daily from 3 PM until the wee hours. Besides the slots, it offers both French and American roulette along with blackjack, baccarat, and punto banco. The entrance fee of AS170 gets you AS200 worth of chips. A passport is required, you must be at least 21, and men are expected to wear a jacket and tie.

Visitors to the Eisenstadt and Wiener Neustadt areas may want to use the casino in nearby **Baden** (*see* Chapter 3) or cross the border to Sopron in Hungary.

Jazz Clubs With its large student population, Graz has many late-night jazz clubs. Among the best are the **Royal Garden** at Bürgergasse 4 and **Jazz** at Mondscheingasse 9. The scene is constantly changing, so check with the tourist office first.

5 The Danube Valley

Vienna to Linz

Introduction

by George W.
Hamilton

In this chapter we follow the course of the Danube upstream from Vienna as it winds through Lower Austria (Niederöster-reich) and a bit of Upper Austria (Oberösterreich) to Linz, past castles and industrial towns, the vineyards of the Weinviertel, and apricot and apple orchards. This is a wonderful trip in early spring, when the fruit trees are in bloom, or in fall after the grape harvest, when the hillside vineyards turn reddish blue and a crisp autumn chill settles over the Danube at dusk. This is where Lorelei lured sailors to the shoals, where Richard the Lionheart was locked in a dungeon for years, where marvelous castles suddenly appear at a turn in the road.

Linz, Austria's third-largest city (and perhaps its most under-rated) is a key industrial center. It's a fine town for shopping; the stores are good, prices more reasonable than in Vienna or the big resorts, and it's fun just to wander the narrow streets of the old city. Concerts and opera at Linz's modern *Bruck-nerhaus* can be every bit as good as those in Vienna or Salz-burg. From Linz, we explore several nearby towns and return along the Danube's south bank, visiting the great abbey at Melk (setting for the historical novel and film *The Name of the Rose*), the Göttweig abbey above the river opposite Krems, and the abbey at Klosterneuburg.

The Danube, rising in Germany's Black Forest and emptying into the Black Sea, is our focal point: The route that brought the Romans to the area and contributed to its development re-mains one of Europe's important waterways, with three na-tional capitals on its banks—Vienna, Budapest, and Belgrade. Many of the hilltop castles along the route were built to give an overview of this vital channel; the cities developed as ports for the salt, wood, ores, and other cargo it carried; and the rail-roads and highways of today largely parallel its course. (The Danube, not the latitudes, determines the names: Upper Aus-tria is upstream, Lower Austria is downstream.)

Essential Information

Important Addresses and Numbers

Tourist
Information

For general information on the area, check with the district tourist offices for **Lower Austria** (Heidenschuss 2, A–1010 Vi-enna, tel. 0222/533–4773), **Upper Austria** (Schillerstr. 50, A–4010 Linz, tel. 0732/663021), and **Styria** (Herrengasse 16, A–8010 Graz, tel. 0316/835–2410). Tourist offices for the towns are:

Bad Hall (Kurhaus, A–4540, tel. 07258/20310)
Dürnstein (Parkplatz Ost, A–3601, tel. 02711/360, 02711/200)
Eferding (A–4070 Eferding, tel. 07272/555520)
Freistadt (Hauptplatz 12, A–4240, tel. 07942/2974)
Grein (Hauptstr. 3, A–4360, tel. 07268/680)
Klosterneuburg (Niedermarkt, A–3400, tel. 02243/2038)
Krems/Stein (Undstr. 6, A–3500, tel. 02732/82676)
Melk (Linzer Str. 3–5, A–3390, tel. 02752/2307)
Pöchlarn (Regensburger Str. 11, A–3380, tel. 02757/231040)
St. Polten (Rathausplatz 1, A–3100, tel. 02742/53354)
Steyr (Stadtplatz 27, A–4400, tel. 07252/23229)

Tulln (Stadtgemeinde, Nussallee 4, A–3430, tel. 02272/42850)
Wachau (Undstr. 6, A–3500 Krems, tel. 02732/85620)
Waidhofen an der Ybbs (Obere Stadtplatz 28, A–3340, tel. 07442/251–1165)
Weissenkirchen (Gemeinde Weissenkirchen, A–3610, tel. 02715/2232.

Arriving and Departing

You can travel to and from Vienna from most parts of the world (*see* Chapter 3, Vienna, Arriving and Departing by Plane). Linz is served mainly by Austrian Airlines, plus Lufthansa, KLM, Swissair, and Air France. Regular flights connect it with Vienna, Amsterdam, Düsseldorf, Frankfurt, London, Milan, Paris, and Zurich. The Linz airport (tel. 07221/72700–0) is in Hörsching, about 12 km (7.5 mi) southwest of the city. *See also* Chapter 3, Vienna: Arriving and Departing by Car, Train, Boat and Bus.

Getting Around

By Car   A car is certainly the pleasantest way to make this trip. Roads are good and well marked, and if at any point you should be in a hurry, you can switch over to the A-1 autobahn, which parallels the general east–west course of the route. (*See* Chapter 1, Renting and Leasing Cars.)

By Train   Every larger town and city on this tour can be reached by train—assuming you have the time—but the train misses the Wachau valley along the Danube's south bank. The rail line on the north side of the river literally clings to the bank in places, but service on that line is infrequent. You can combine rail and boat transportation along this route and have the best of both, taking the train upstream and crisscrossing your way back on the river. From Linz, the delightful LILO interurban line (tel. 0732/54376) makes the run up to Eferding, and you can also get to Bad Hall by train.

By Bus   If you link them together, bus routes will get you to the main points of this trip and even to the hilltop castles and monasteries, assuming you have the time. If you coordinate your schedule to arrive at a point by train or boat, you can usually make reasonable bus connections to outlying destinations. In Vienna you can book bus tours (*see* Guided Tours, below); in Linz, ask at the municipal bus station (Bahnhofplatz 12, tel. 0732/1671.)

By Boat   Taking the heart of this tour by boat is one of the highlights of an Austrian trip. Large river boats with sleeping accommodations ply the route between Vienna and Linz and on to Passau on the German border. Smaller day boats go between Vienna and the Wachau valley, and there you can change to local boats that crisscross the river between the colorful towns. Bridges across the river are few along this stretch, so boats are essential transportation; service is frequent enough that you can cross the river, visit a town, catch a bus or the next boat to the next town, and cross the river farther up- or downstream. You can take a day trip from Vienna and explore one of the stops, such as Krems, Dürnstein, or Melk. Boats run from May to late September. For information on boat schedules, contact DDSG/ Danube Steamship Company (Handelskai 265, A–1020 Vienna, tel. 0222/217100 or Regensburger Str. 9, A–4010 Linz, tel. 0732/770–01115).

By Bicycle A bicycle trail parallels the Danube from considerably southeast of Vienna to Passau. The tourist offices of the towns along the way (*see* Tourist Information, above) have information, maps, and recommendations for sightseeing and overnight and mealtime stops.

Guided Tours

Tours out of Vienna take you to Melk and back by bus and boat in eight hours, with a stop at Dürnstein. Bus tours operate year-round, but the boat runs only April–October. **Cityrama/ Gray Line**, *Börsegasse 1, tel. 0222/534130; adults AS690, children AS300, lunch not included;* **Vienna Sightseeing Tours**, *Stelzhammergasse 4/11, tel. 0222/712–4683); adults AS870, children AS480, lunch and hotel transfer included.*

Day boat trips with loudspeaker announcements in English run daily from mid-April to late October. Contact the DDSG/ Danube Steamship Co. (Handelskai 265, tel. 0222/217100).

In Linz two-hour guided city sightseeing tours leave the DDSG/Danube Steamship Co. landing quay (Niebelungenbrücke) daily, May–October, at 2:15. For information and tickets, check with Tourist Information (Hauptplatz 34, Linz, tel. 0732/2393–1777).

Exploring the Danube Valley and Linz

This trip can be done in as little as three days, allowing one day along the north Danube side (Tour 1), a day in Linz and surroundings (Tours 2 and 3), and a day to return along the south shore (Tour 4). You could also happily spend six or more days: adding time in Eferding and Freistadt, a day in Kremsmünster and Steyr, a day for Waidhofen an der Ybbs, and perhaps returning by ship.

Highlights for First-time Visitors

Burg Kreuzenstein (*see* Tour 1)
Dürnstein castle ruins (*see* Tour 1)
Freistadt (*see* Tour 3)
Carved wood altar at Kefermarkt (*see* Tour 3)
The library at the great abbey at Melk (*see* Tour 4)
100-year-old open streetcars in Linz (*see* Tour 2)
Stift Göttweig (*see* Tour 4)
Town square in Steyr (*see* Tour 3)
Weinkolleg Kloster Und (*see* Tour 1)

Tour 1: The North Bank of the Danube, the Wachau

Numbers in the margin correspond with points of interest on the Danube Valley maps.

If you're taking the tour by train, take streetcar D to the Franz Jozefs Bahnhof. If you're driving, the trickiest part may be getting out of Vienna. Follow signs to Prague to get across the

Danube. Avoid the right-hand exit marked Prague, which
leads to the autobahn, and continue ahead, following signs for
Prager Strasse and turning left at the traffic light. Prager
Strasse (Route 3) heads you toward Langenzersdorf and
Korneuburg.

Korneuburg is a center of Austrian shipbuilding, where river
passenger ships and barges and transfer cranes are built for the
Soviet Union. Stop for a look at the imposing neo-Gothic city
hall (1864), which dominates the central square and towers over
the town.

Continue on Route 3 about 3 km (2 mi) beyond Korneuburg, and
❶ atop a hillside to your right you'll spot **Burg Kreuzenstein,** a
fairyland castle with turrets and towers. Using old elements
and Gothic and Romanesque bits and pieces brought here for
the purpose, Count Wilczek built Kreuzenstein, from 1879 to
1908, on the site of a destroyed castle, to house his Late Gothic
collection. You wouldn't suspect the building wasn't absolutely
authentic if the tour guides weren't so honest. You'll see rooms
full of armaments, the festival and banquet halls, library, chapel, even the kitchens. You can also reach Kreuzenstein via the
suburban train *(S-Bahn)* to Leobendorf and a ¾ hour hike up to
the castle. *Leobendorf bei Korneuburg, tel. 02262/66102. Admission: AS50 adults, AS30 children. Open for guided tours
Mar.–Nov., Tues.–Sun. 9–5 (last tour at 4).*

Route 3 continues past Stockerau, through a lush meadow and
woodland area, and after about 33 km (21 mi), at Grafenwörth,
❷ you'll see signs pointing to your right to **Schloss Grafenegg.** The
moated Renaissance castle dating to 1533 was stormed by the
Swedes in 1645 and rebuilt from 1840 to 1873 in the English
Gothic Revival style. Greatly damaged during the 1945–55 occupation, it was extensively restored in the 1980s. Look for
such fascinating detail as the gargoyle waterspouts, and don't
miss the chapel. *Haitzendorf, tel. 02735/220527. Admission:
AS50 adults, AS15 children. Open May–Oct., Tues., Thurs.
1–5, weekends and holidays 10–5, depending on scheduled exhibitions.*

Time Out   The **Schlosstaverne** in Haitzendorf (tel. 02735/2616) offers excellent food in a delightful setting, either in the Biedermeier
dining room or under an umbrella in the garden. In season,
you'll find game; otherwise, turn to the excellent Austrian
standards such as *Tafelspitz.*

❸ Return to Route 3 or follow signs over the back roads to **Krems.**
This Renaissance town is closely tied to Austrian history; here
the ruling Babenbergs set up a dukedom in 1120, and the earliest Austrian coin was struck in 1130. In the Middle Ages,
Krems looked after the iron trade, while neighboring Stein
traded in salt and wine. Today the area is the center of a thriving wine production. Krems over the years became a center of
culture and art, and today it is an attractive city to wander
through, with narrow streets and irregular squares in a pedestrian zone.

Among the sights of Krems–Stein is the **Steiner Tor,** the massive square gate protected by two stubby round towers, once
set into the wall of the moated city. The oldest part of town is to
the east. Follow along the Obere and Untere Landstrasse, and
you'll spot dozens of eye-catching buildings in styles ranging

from Gothic to Renaissance to Baroque. It's easy to pick out the heavy Gothic **Piaristenkirche,** begun in 1470, with its distinctive square tower and central peak and minitowers at each corner. The main altar and most of the side altars incorporate paintings by the local artist Martin Johann Schmidt (1718–1801), popularly known as Kremser Schmidt, whose translucent works you will repeatedly come across in the course of this trip. Close by is the parish church of **St. Veit,** completed in 1630. The interior is surprisingly spacious; Kremser Schmidt did the ceiling frescoes.

The 14th-century former Dominican cloister, farther along the street, now serves as the **city museum,** with a wine museum that holds tastings; notice the arcade with its variety of pillars. *Tel. 02732/801338. Admission: AS20 adults, AS10 children. Open Easter–late Oct., Tues.–Sat. 9–noon and 2–5; Sun., holidays 9–noon.*

On the entry portal of the **Bürgerspitalkirche** at Obere Landstrasse 15, you'll see Friedrich III's legend *AEIOU*, standing for *Austria Erit In Orbe Ultima*, literally, "Austria extends to the ends of the earth."

Between Krems and Stein, in a beautifully restored Capucin cloister in the tiny town of **Und,** is the **Weinkolleg Kloster Und.** The building also houses the tourist office and a small wine museum, where you can taste (and buy) more than 100 Austrian wines. *Undstr. 6, Krems–Stein, tel. 02732/73073. Admission (with tasting): AS120. Open daily 11–7.*

In **Stein,** the former 14th-century **Minoritenkirche,** just off the main street in the pedestrian zone, now serves as a museum with changing displays. A few steps farther on, an imposing square Gothic tower identifies the 15th-century St. Nicholas parish church, whose altar painting and ceiling frescoes were done by Kremser Schmidt. The upper part of the Gothic charnel house (1462), squeezed between the church and the hillside, has been converted to housing. Notice, too, the many architecturally interesting houses in Stein, among them the former tollhouse, with rich Renaissance frescoes. Stein was the birthplace of Ludwig Köchel, the cataloguer of Mozart's works, which are referred to by their "Köchel number" from the index.

Moving along Route 3, you'll see **Dürnstein** ahead, distinguished by its prominent Baroque church and castle ruin on the hill overlooking the town. In the tower of this castle Richard I of England, was imprisoned (1192–93), until he was rescued by Blondel, the faithful minnesinger. It's said that Blondel, while wandering the area trying to find where his king was imprisoned, heard the sound of his master's voice completing the verse of a song he was singing. The town is small; leave the car at one end and walk the narrow streets. A 30-minute rather steep climb to the ruins will earn you a breathtaking view up and down the Danube valley and over the hills to the south. The gloriously Baroque former **Stiftskirche,** from the early 1700s, sits on a cliff overlooking the river. More than 100 tiny angels decorate the heavens of its ceiling, and couples come from near and far to be married in the romantic setting.

Tucked among vineyards, just around the bend in the Danube, is **Weissenkirchen,** a picturesque town that was fortified against the Turks in 1531. A fire in 1793 laid waste to much of the town, but the 15th-century parish church of **Maria**

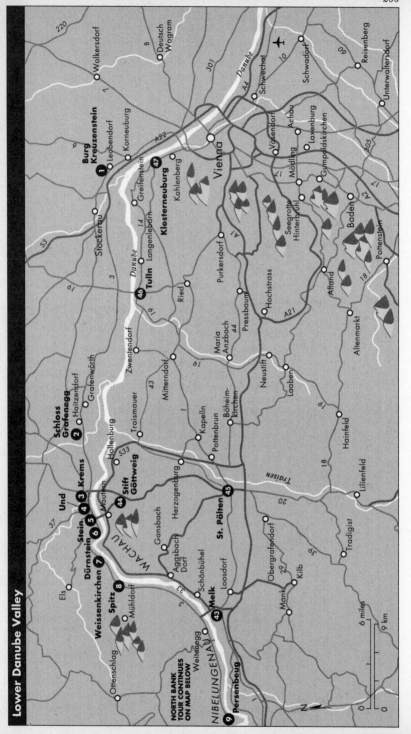

Lower Danube Valley

220

Wolkersdorf

Deutsch Wagram

8

7

Burg
Kreuzenstein
1

Leobendorf

Korneuburg

9

Stockerau

Greifenstein

Klosterneuburg
47

Kahlenberg

Schwechat

Schwadorf

10

Reisenberg

Unterwaltersdorf

Achau
Vösendorf

Laxenburg

Mödling

Gumpoldskirchen

60

301

Danube

A22

Vienna

A4

17

A2

305

Baden

Pottenstein

Langenlebarn

Tulln
46

Ried

Purkersdorf

A1

Hochstrass

A21

Pressbaum

Seegrotte
Hinterbrühl

Altland

18

Allenmarkt

14

S3

Danube

3

19

Grafenwörth

Haitzendorf

Schloss
Grafenegg
2

Krems
4 3
Und

Stein
5
6
Dürnstein
7
Weissenkirchen
Spitz
8

Els

Ottenschlag

37

Mautern

Stift
Göttweig
44

WACHAU

Gansbach

Aggsbach
Dorf

Mühldorf

Hollenburg

S33

Traismauer

43

Mitterndorf

Zwentendorf

Kapelln

Pottenbrun

Böheim-
kirchen

Maria
Anzbach
44

61

Neustift

Laaben

19

Hainfeld

18

Lilienfeld

Tradigist

Herzogenburg

St. Pölten
45

Traisen

20

Obergrafendorf

29

Kilb

39

Mank

Schönbühel

Loosdorf

Melk
43

33

3

Weitenegg

NIBELUNGENGAU

Persenbeug
9

1

NORTH BANK
TOUR CONTINUES
ON MAP BELOW

6 miles

9 km

0

0

N

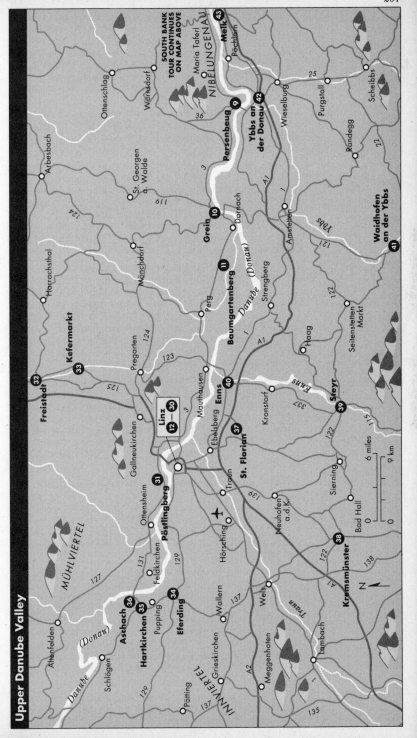

Upper Danube Valley

MÜHLVIERTEL

INNVIERTEL

NIBELUNGENAU

SOUTH BANK
TOUR CONTINUES
ON MAP ABOVE

Danube (Donau)

Melk **43**

Maria Taferl

Pöchlarn

Wieselburg

Purgstall

Scheibbs

Randegg

Persenbeug **9**

Ybbs an
der Donau **42**

Wörnsdorf

Ottenschlag

St. Georgen
a. Walde

Arbesbach

Harrachsthal

Mönchdorf

Grein **10**

Dornach

Amstetten

Waidhofen
an der Ybbs **41**

Baumgartenberg **11**

Strengberg

Perg

Haag

Steyr **39**

Pregarten

Kefermarkt **33**

Freistadt **32**

Mauthausen

Enns **40**

Kronstorf

Seitenstetten
Markt

Gallneukirchen

Linz **12 — 30**

Ebelsberg

St. Florian **37**

Sierning

Bad Hall

Ottensheim

Pösslingberg **31**

Traun

Neuhofen
a.d.K.

Kremsmünster **38**

Altenfelden

Aschach **36**

Harrkirchen **35**

Pupping

Feldkirchen

Eferding **34**

Hörsching

Wallern

Wels

Lambach

Meggenhofen

Grieskirchen

Schlägen

Pötting

Danube (Donau)

Traun

Ybbs

Enns

N

6 miles
9 km
0

Himmelfahrt, built on earlier foundations, largely survived the conflagration. You can compare styles and eras here: The south nave dates to 1300, the middle nave to 1439, the chapel to 1460. The madonna on the triumphal arch goes back to the Danube school of about 1520; the Baroque touches date to 1736; and to complete the picture, the Rococo organ was installed in 1777. On the Marktplatz, check out the 15th-century *Teisenhoferhof,* which has a charming Renaissance arcaded courtyard. The building now houses the Wachau museum and contains many paintings by Kremser Schmidt. *Tel. 02715/2268. Admission: AS20 adults, AS10 children. Open Apr.–Oct., Tues.–Sun. 10–5.*

About 4 km (2½ mi) farther along Route 3 is **St. Michael** at Wösendorf, noted for the Late Gothic parish church dating to 1500, with its choir roof ridge ornamented by curious ceramic deer, horses, and hares. They are copies; the originals are in the museum in Krems. The church's Baroque interior has traces of late 16th-century frescoes. The charnel house contains mummified remains from 1150 to 1300 and a rather grotesque altar made of skulls.

Less than 1 km (½ mi) farther, a road swings off to the right ❽ into **Spitz,** set like a jewel in the surrounding vineyards and hills. One vineyard, the "thousand bucket" hill, is said to produce a thousand buckets of wine in a good year. A number of interesting houses in Spitz go back to the 16th and 17th centuries. The Late Gothic 15th-century parish church contains Kremser Schmidt's altar painting of the martyrdom of St. Mauritius. Note the carved wood statues of Christ and the 12 apostles dating to 1380, on the organ loft.

Just beyond Spitz and above the road is the ruin of the castle Hinterhaus, to which you can climb. A side road here marked to Ottenschlag (Route 217) leads up the hill, and about 4 km (2½ mi) farther on, to **Burg Ranna,** a well-preserved castle surrounded by a double wall and dry moat. The original structure dates to 1114–25, the St. George chapel possibly even earlier. *Ober-Ranna 1, Mühldorf, tel. 02713/8221. Admission: AS19. Open May–Nov., Sat. 3–5, Sun. and holidays 2–6.*

You can return on a back road to Route 3 at Aggsbach. The views are now mainly of the other side of the Danube, as you look across at Schönbühel and Melk. Shortly after Weitenegg the Wachau ends, and you come into that part of the Danube valley known as the Niebelungenau, where the mystical race of dwarfs, the Niebelungen of legend, are supposed to have settled for a while.

Crowning a hill on the north bank is the two-towered **Maria Taferl,** a pilgrimage church with a spectacular outlook. It's a bit touristy, but the church and the view are worth the side trip. About 4 km (2½ mi) up a back road is **Schloss Artstetten,** a massive square castle with four round defense towers at the corners. This is the burial place of Archduke Franz Ferdinand and his wife Sophie, whose double assassination in 1914 in Sarajevo was one of the triggers that set off World War I. *Tel. 07413/8302. Admission: AS50 adults, AS 26 children. Open Apr.–Nov., daily 9–5:30.*

❾ The Niebelungenau ends at **Persenbeug,** a small town with an important castle (viewable only from the outside) and a number of attractive Biedermeier houses. The castle, which sits directly over the Danube, was the birthplace in 1887 of Austria's last emperor and still belongs to the Habsburg family.

⑩ About 19 km (12 mi) upstream you'll come to **Grein,** a picturesque town with a castle set above the Danube. The river bend below, known for years as "the place where death resides," was one of the most dangerous stretches of the river until the reefs were blasted away in the late 1700s. In Grein, take time to see the intimate Rococo **Stadttheater** in the town hall, built in 1790 by the populace and still occasionally used for concerts or plays. *Rathaus. Admission: AS10 adults, AS5 children. Tours Apr.–late Oct., daily 9, 10:30, 2:30.*

Time Out **Café Blumensträussl** (Stadtplatz 6) is a lovely spot for coffee and cake, amid the Viennese Biedermeier decor in winter or outdoors in the garden in summer. The *Mozarttorte* is renowned, as are the delicious goodies served during strawberry season. You can also get soup and snacks.

At Dornach the road leaves the Danube, and about 6 km (just
⑪ under 4 mi) farther you'll find **Baumgartenberg,** which is worth a visit for its ornate Baroque parish church and the unusual chancel supported by a tree trunk.

Just before **Mauthausen** the road and the river again come together, and from the south the Enns river, one of six main tributaries, joins the Danube. Mauthausen, which has some interesting 16th-century houses, is better known today as the location of the Nazi concentration camp *KZ Lager,* northwest of the town. It has been preserved as a memorial to those who died here and in other such camps. Seventeen countries, including the United Kingdom, the Soviet Union, and France, have given monuments. There's a map and booklet in English. *Marbach 38, tel. 07238/2269. Admission: AS15 adults, AS5 children. Open Feb.–Mar., daily 8–3; Apr.–Sept., daily 8–5; Oct.–mid-Dec., daily 8–3; closed mid-Dec.–Jan.*

⑫ From Mauthausen it's 27 km (17 mi) to **Linz.** Route 3 takes you across the Danube south of the city and then into the center.

Tour 2: Linz

Numbers in the margin correspond with points of interest on the Linz map.

The capital of Upper Austria, set where the Traun river flows into the Danube, has a fascinating old city core and an active cultural life. In 1832 it had a horse-drawn train to Czechoslovakia that was the first rail line on the Continent. It is also the center of Austrian steel and chemical production, both started by the Germans in 1938. In the past, these industries made Linz a dirty city; with pollution controls now in place, Linz has been proclaimed cleaner than Vienna or Graz.

The heart of the city has been turned into a pedestrian zone; either leave the car at your hotel or use the huge new parking garage under the main square in the center of town. Streets in the center are narrow and mostly one-way, but distances are not great, and you can take in the highlights in the course of a two-hour walking tour.

Start at the Tourist Information Office (Hauptplatz 34, tel. 0732/2393–1777) and pick up the "Linz from A–Z" booklet in

⓭ English. Here you're on the main square at the **Altes Rathaus,** the Old City Hall. Although the original 1513 building was mainly destroyed by fire and replaced in 1658–59, its octagonal corner turret and lunar clock, as well as some vaulted rooms, remain, and you can detect traces of the original Renaissance structure on the Rathausgasse facade. The present exterior dates from 1824. The approach from Rathausgasse 5, opposite the Keplerhaus, leads through a fine arcaded courtyard. On the facade here you'll spot portraits of Emperor Friedrich III, the mayors Hoffmandl and Prunner, the astronomer Johannes Kepler, and the composer Anton Bruckner.

One of the symbols of Linz is the 20-meter (65-ft) Baroque ⓮ **Pillar to the Holy Trinity** in the center of the square. Completed in 1723 of white Salzburg marble, the column offers thanks by an earthly trinity, the provincial estates, city council, and citizens, for deliverance from the threat of war (1704), fire (1712), and plague (1713).

Turn right on the west side of the square into the Kloster-⓯ strasse. On your left at the end of the block is the **Minorite Church,** once part of a monastery. The present building dates to 1752–58 and has a delightful Rococo interior with side altar paintings by Kremser Schmidt and the main altar by Bartolomeo Altomonte. (Open Oct.–June, Mon.–Sat. 7:30–11, Sun. 7:30–noon; July–Sept., daily 7:30–4.) The adjoining early Renaissance monastery buildings with the distinctive tower ⓰ are now the **Landhaus,** seat of the provincial government. Look inside to see the inner arcaded courtyard with the 1852 Planet Fountain and the Hall of Stone on the first floor, above the barrel-vaulted hall on the ground floor. The beautiful Renaissance doorway (1570) is made of red marble. Around the corner at ⓱ Altstadt 17 is the three-story Renaissance **Mozart Haus,** with a later Baroque facade and portal, where Mozart wrote his *Linz* symphony in 1783. Inside is a fine 17th-century three-story arcaded courtyard.

Headed down Altstadt toward the river, you'll pass the ⓲ **Waaghaus,** bought by the city in 1524, at one time the public weighing office and now an indoor market. Emperor Friedrich ⓳ III is said to have died in the **Kremsmünstererhaus** (Altstadt 10) in 1493. The building was done over in Renaissance style in 1578–80, and a story was added in 1616, with two turrets and onion domes. There's a memorial room to the emperor here; his heart is entombed in the Linz parish church, but the rest of him is in St. Stephen's cathedral in Vienna. *Tel. 0732/2393–1912. Open by appointment.*

Just around the corner to your left, in Tummelplatz, you come to a massive four-story building with two inner courtyards, the ⓴ **Linz Castle,** rebuilt by Friedrich III about 1477 (and much restored since), literally on top of a castle that dates to 799. Note the **Friedrichstor,** the Friedrich gate, with the same AEIOU monogram we saw earlier in Krems. The castle houses the Upper Austrian provincial museum, with weapons, musical instruments, nativity scenes, Upper Austrian art, and prehistoric and Roman relics. *Tummelplatz 10, tel. 0732/774419. Admission: AS25. Open Tues.–Fri. 9–5, weekends and holidays 10–4.*

Up the Herrenstrasse, at the corner of Bischofstrasse, you'll ㉑ find the **Bischofshof** (1721), with its fine wrought-iron gate-

Linz

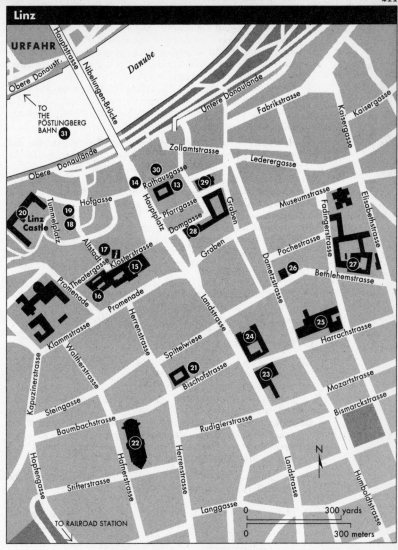

URFAHR

Danube

TO THE PÖSTLINGBERG BAHN **31**

Linz Castle

TO RAILROAD STATION

N

| 0 | 300 yards |
| 0 | 300 meters |

Alter Dom, **28**

Altes Rathaus (Old City Hall), **13**

Bischofshof, **21**

Carmelite Church, **23**

Deutschordens-kirche, **25**

Elisabethinen-kirche, **27**

Johannes Kepler House, **30**

Kremsmünsterer-haus, **19**

Landhaus, **16**

Linz Castle, **20**

Minorite Church, **15**

Mozart Haus, **17**

Neuer Dom, **22**

Nordico (City Museum), **26**

Pillar to the Holy Trinity, **14**

Pöstlingbergbahn, **31**

Stadtpfarrkirche, **29**

Ursuline Church, **24**

Waaghaus, **18**

㉒ way. The massive **Neuer Dom** (New Cathedral) in Baumbach-
strasse is to your right diagonally across Herrenstrasse. The
bishop of Linz in 1862 engaged one of the architects of the Cologne cathedral to develop a design in neo-Gothic French-ca-
thedral style and ordered that its tower not be higher than that
of St. Stephen's in Vienna. At 134 meters (440 ft), it is shorter
by a scant 2 meters. The 1633 statues of Saint Peter and Saint
Paul on the high altar came from the parish church in nearby
Eferding. The crypt contains a large nativity scene. *Open daily
7:30–7.*

From Herrenstrasse, cross left through Rudigierstrasse and
walk north one block in the pedestrian Landstrasse to the
Harrachstrasse, where magnificent Baroque churches sit on
㉓ either side: the **Carmelite Church,** modeled on St. Joseph's in
㉔ Prague (open daily 7–noon, 3–6:30), and the **Ursuline Church,**
with double-figured towers, one of the identifying symbols of
Linz (open daily 8–6). Go down the Harrachstrasse to see the
㉕ former **Deutschordenskirche** (Seminary Church, 1723), a beautiful yellow and white Baroque treasure with an elliptical
dome, designed by Johann Lukas von Hildebrandt, who also
designed its high altar. *Open May–Sept., daily 7–6; Oct.–
Apr., daily 7–5.*

Down the Dametzstrasse, at the corner of Bethlehemstrasse,
㉖ you'll find the **Nordico,** the city museum (1610), whose collection follows local history from pre-Roman times to the mid-
1880s. *Bethlehemstr. 7, tel. 0732/2393–1912. Admission free.
Open weekdays 9–6, weekends 1–5.*

㉗ Farther up the Bethlehemstrasse is the **Elisabethinenkirche,**
built in the mid-18th century. Note the unusually dynamic
colors in the dome fresco by Altomonte. Turn down the Elisabethstrasse and head west along the Museumstrasse into Graben (straight ahead, don't turn right, although that's also
㉘ called Graben) to reach the Baroque **Alter Dom,** the old cathedral (1669–78), whose striking feature is the single nave, together with the side altars. Anton Bruckner was organist here
from 1856 to 1868. *Open daily 7–noon and 3–7.*

Continue around the corner in the Domgasse to come to the
㉙ **Stadtpfarrkirche** (city parish church), which dates to 1286 and
was rebuilt in Baroque style in 1648. The tomb in the right wall
of the chancel contains Friedrich III's heart. The ceiling frescoes are by Altomonte, the figure of Johann Nepomuk (a local
saint) in the chancel is by Georg Raphael Donner, in a setting
by Hildebrandt. *Open Mon.–Sat. 8–7, Sun. 9–7.*

Head back toward the main square via the Rathausgasse. At
㉚ No. 5, the astronomer **Johannes Kepler** lived from 1622 to 1626;
Linz's first printing shop was established in this house in 1745.

For a splendid view over Linz and the Danube, take the run up
㉛ the **Pöstlingberg** on the electric **Pöstlingbergbahn.** To reach the
base station for the railway, take streetcar line 3 across the river to Urfahr, Linz's left bank. The cars take 16 minutes for the
2.9-km (nearly 2-mi) trip, making a 255-meter (840-ft) climb in
the process. When it was built in 1898, it boasted the steepest
incline of any noncog railway in Europe. In summer, the old
open-bench cars are used. *Tel. 0732/28010. Round-trip fare:
AS28 adults, AS14 children 6–15, two children under 6 free.
Service daily all year, every 20 min, 5:30 AM–8:20 PM.*

A treat at the top for children is the fairy-tale-grotto railroad, which runs through a colorfully illuminated imaginary world. *Admission: AS25 adults, AS12 children under 15. Open Sat. before Easter–Nov., daily 9–5:45.*

The twin-towered Baroque pilgrimage church (1748) at the summit is another Linz landmark. The zoo on Pöstlingberg is still in the development stage, but it has some 600 animals. *Windflachweg 19, tel. 0732/237180. Admission: AS15 adults, AS5 children. Open Oct.–Mar., daily 10–4; Apr.–Sept., daily 10–6; closed Dec. 24–26, 31, and Jan. 1.*

Also in Urfahr is the exceptional **Neue Galerie,** one of Austria's best modern-art museums, which has a fine, well-balanced collection, mainly by contemporary artists. *Blütenstr. 15, Urfahr, tel. 0732/2393–3600. Admission: AS30 adults, AS10 children. Open Mon.–Wed., Fri., Sat. 10–6, Thurs. 10–10, Sun. 10–1.*

Tour 3: Short Excursions from Linz

Numbers in the margin correspond with points of interest on the Danube Valley maps.

The **Mühlviertel** (mill district in the agricultural, not industrial, sense) north of Linz to the Czechoslovak border is made up of meadows and gentle wooded hills interspersed with towns whose appearance has changed little since the Middle Ages. To the west of Linz, south of the Danube, lies the **Innviertel,** named for the Inn river (which forms the border with Germany before it joins the Danube), a region of broad fields and meadows, of enormous woodland tracts, ideal for cycling, hiking, and riding. To the south, the hilly landscape with its many streams and forested areas begins the foothills of the Austrian Alps, also a countryside for fishing, hiking, and riding.

㉜ To get to **Freistadt,** a beautifully preserved walled city in the eastern part of the Mühlviertel, cross the Danube to Linz–Urfahr and turn right onto Freistädter Strasse (Route 125/E55).

Freistadt developed as a border defense city on the salt route into Bohemia (now Czechoslovakia), which accounts for the wall, towers, and gates. Look at the Late Gothic **Linzertor,** the Linz gate, with its steep wedge-shaped roof, and the **Böhmertor,** on the opposite side, leading to Bohemia. If you have the time, walk around the wall to get an impression of how a city in the Middle Ages was conceived and defended; it will take you about a half hour. The city's central square, aglow with pastel facades, is virtually the same as that of 400 years ago, with no jarring modern buildings; only the parked cars intrude into the picture.

Wander through the side streets and alleys back of the central square and note the architectural details; many of the arcades contain interesting small shops. The 15th-century parish church of St. Catherine's was redone in Baroque style in the 17th century but retains its slender tower with the unusual balconies with railings on all four sides. The Late Gothic castle to the northeast of the square now houses the Mühlviertel district museum (Heimathaus); the display of painted glass (for which the nearby town of Sandl is famous) in the chapel and the hand tools in the tower are especially interesting. *Tel. 07942/2274.*

*Admission: AS10 adults, children free. Guided tours only.
May–Oct., Tues.–Sat. 10 and 2; Sun., holidays, 10; Nov.–
Apr., Tues.–Fri. 10; Tues. and Thurs. also at 2.*

㉝ On the way back from Freistadt, detour slightly east to
Kefermarkt, about 10½ km (6½ mi) south. Here in the Late
Gothic St. Wolfgang's church is one of Europe's great anony-
mous art treasures, a 13-meter- (42-ft-) high winged altar intricately carved from linden wood.

㉞ About 26 km (16¼ mi) west of Linz on Route 129 lies **Eferding,** a
centuries-old community with an attractive town square. The
double door in the south wall of the 15th-century church of St.
Hippolyte is a gem of Late Gothic stonecutting, with the madonna and child above flanked by Saints Hippolyte and Agyd.
Inside, note the Gothic altar with its five reliefs and the statues
of Saints Wolfgang and Martin. Several of the gravestones in
the church have unusual motifs from the Bible. Also visit the
Spitalskirche (originally built in 1325) and note the Gothic frescoes in the Magdalen chapel, which date to about 1430.

㉟ Take Route 130 north from Eferding to Pupping, and if you like
to explore ruins, follow signs for the turnoff on the left to
Schaunberg's castle ruin. Otherwise, continue 3 km (2 mi) up
the road from Pupping to the parish church at **Hartkirchen,** to
see fine Baroque wall and ceiling frescoes that create the illusion of space and depth. And 2 km (1 mi) farther (Route 131), on
㊱ the Danube, is **Aschach,** a small village that was once a river toll
station, with gabled-roof burgher houses, a castle, and a Late
Gothic church.

㊲ Southeast of Linz lies **St. Florian,** best known for the great abbey where Anton Bruckner (1824–96) was organist for 10 years
and where he is buried. Take the road south to Kleinmünchen
and Ebelsberg, or for a most romantic approach, try the
Florianer Bahn, a resurrected electric interurban tram line,
which runs museum streetcars on Sunday and holidays 6 km
(nearly 4 mi) from Pichling to St. Florian (tel. 0732/485323,
821722, or 07435/4075). You enter the abbey complex via a magnificent figured gate that encompasses all three stories. A
large and elegant staircase leads to the upper floors, and the
major rooms are grouped around the inner courtyard. Guided
tours include these and the imperial suite. In the splendid abbey church, where the ornate decor is somewhat in contrast to
much of Bruckner's music, the Krismann organ (1770–74) is
one of the largest and best of its period. *Tel. 07224/89030. Admission: AS40 adults, AS15 children. Guided tours only, 1½
hrs. Apr.–Oct., daily at 10, 11, 2, 3, 4.*

㊳ Take Route 139 southwest (or the train) from Linz to the vast
Benedictine abbey at **Kremsmünster,** established in 777, one of
the most important cloisters in Austria. Inside the church is
the Gothic memorial tomb of Gunther, killed by a wild boar,
whose father, Tassilo, duke of Bavaria, vowed to build the abbey on the site. Note the Baroque decor added in the 18th century and the frescoes and paintings. There are magnificent
rooms: the **Kaisersaal** and the frescoed library with more than
100,000 volumes, many of them manuscripts. On one side of the
Prälatenhof courtyard are four elegant fish basins amid splendid Baroque statuary, and opposite is the **Abteitrakt,** whose art
collection includes the Tassilo chalice, from about 765. The
eight-story observatory houses an early museum of science.

The "mosque" garden house from 1640 has Oriental decoration. *Tel. 07583/275216. Admission: AS35 adults, AS15 children. Guided tours only when 5 or more are interested; tours are run Easter–Nov., daily at 9, 10, 11, 1, 2, 3, and 4, including observatory May–Nov.; tours Nov.–Easter by prior arrangement.*

Where Route 139 joins Route 122, cut south to **Bad Hall,** known for its saline-iodine curative springs. Tassilo, who founded Kremsmünster, gave the springs to the abbey in 777, but the town is now an independent spa.

㊴ About 17 km (10½ mi) farther along Route 122, at the confluence of the Steyr and Enns rivers, you'll come to **Steyr,** a stunning Gothic market town. Today the main square is lined with pastel facades, many with Baroque and Rococo trim, all complemented by the castle that sits above. On the Enns side, steps and narrow passageways lead down to the river. So many of the houses are worthy of attention that you have to take your time and explore. The **Bummerlhaus** at No. 32, in its present form dating to 1497, has a Late Gothic three-story effect. The Steyrertalbahn, a narrow-gauge museum railroad, wanders 17 km (10½ mi) from Steyr through the countryside. (For information, tel. 07252/26569).

Tour 4: The South Bank of the Danube, the Wachau

South of the Danube is a district of gentle countryside crossed by the valleys of rivers that rise in the Alps and eventually feed the Danube. Little evidence remains today, in this prosperous country of small-industry and agriculture, that the area was heavily fought over in the final days of World War II. Neither mass tourism nor commerce has spoiled its tranquil life.

㊵ The return trip east starts at **Enns.** A settlement has existed continuously here at least since AD 50; the Romans set up a major encampment shortly after that date. From 1945 to 1955, the Enns river east of the city marked the border between the Soviet occupation zone and the U.S. zone.

Enns is dominated by the 56-meter (184-ft) square city tower (1565–68) that stands in the town square. A number of Gothic buildings in the center have Renaissance or Baroque facades. Visit the **St. Laurence basilica,** built on the foundations of a far earlier church, west of the town center, to see the glass-enclosed layers of earlier civilizations that the archaeologists discovered as they uncovered a part of the floor. And outside, look for the Baroque carved-wood Pontius Pilate disguised as a Turk, alongside a hand-bound Christ, on the balcony of the old reliquary.

Take the A1 autobahn or Route 1 east from Enns to just before Amstetten, where Route 121 cuts south paralleling the Ybbs river and the branch rail line for about 25 km (16 mi) to **㊶ Waidhofen an der Ybbs.** This appealing river town developed early as an industrial center, turning Styrian iron ore into swords, knives, sickles, and scythes. These weapons proved successful in the defense against the Turks in 1532; in remembrance, the hands on the north side of the town tower clock remain at 12:45 (your watch is right and the clock isn't). In 1871, Baron Rothschild bought the collapsing castle and assigned Friedrich Schmidt, architect of the Vienna city hall, to rebuild it in neo-Gothic style. Stroll around the two squares in the

Altstadt to see the Gothic and Baroque houses, and to the Graben on the edge of the old city, for the delightful Biedermeier houses and the churches and chapels.

Make your way back to the Danube via Routes 31 and 22 east, then Route 25 north through the beer-brewing town of **42** Wieselburg to **Ybbs an der Donau.** Or retrace your steps up Route 121 and take the autobahn. Floods and fires have left their mark here, but many 16th-century and Renaissance houses remain, their courtyards vine covered and shaded. Look particularly at the houses around the main square. The parish church of St. Laurence has interesting old tombstones, a gorgeous gilded organ, and a Mount of Olives scene with clay figures dating to 1450. Note, too, that Ybbs boasts one of Austria's finer restaurants, Villa Nowotni (*see* Dining and Lodging, below).

From Ybbs, backtrack about 2 km (1 mi) on Route 25 to Route 1, then head northeast for about 1½ km (1 mi) until you come to a road on the left marked to Sarling and Sausenstein. Follow that road to **Pöchlarn,** the birthplace of the artist Oskar Kokoschka, whose dramatic and colorful oils are in museums around the world. His birthplace is now a museum that has special exhibits every year. *Regensburger Str. 39, tel. 02757/7656. Admission: AS30. Open mid-June–mid-Sept., Wed.–Sun. 10–noon and 2–5.*

Continuing eastward through Pöchlarn brings you back to Route 1. About 4 km (2½ mi) on, you'll glimpse the magnificent **43** **Melk** abbey ahead, on its promontory above the river, one of the great views in all Austria. The ideal time for this approach is mid- to late afternoon, when the sun sets the abbey's ornate yellow facade aglow.

Melk by any standard is a Baroque masterpiece. Here the story of *The Name of the Rose* took place, and in fact as in fiction, the monastery did burn in 1297, in 1683, and again in 1735. The Benedictine abbey was established in 1089; the building you see today dates to 1736, although earlier elements are incorporated. A tour of the building will include the main public rooms: the magnificent library, with more than 70,000 books and 2,000 manuscripts and a superb ceiling fresco by the master Paul Troger; the marble hall, whose windows on three sides enhance the ceiling frescoes; the glorious spiral staircase; and the church of Saints Peter and Paul, an exquisite example of Baroque. Note the side altars and the portraits of the saints; the artist Paul Troger was active here, too. The pulpit and even the confessionals are glorious; the organ loft is breathtaking. *Abt. Berthold Dietmayr-Str. 1, tel. 02752/23120. Admission: AS50 adults, AS30 children. Open Mar.–Oct., daily 9–noon, 1–4; June–Sept., daily 9–5; guided tours hourly last about 50 min.*

Time Out   The **Stiftsrestaurant** here offers standard fare, but the abbey's excellent wines elevate a simple meal to an experience—particularly on a sunny day on the terrace. The roast chicken is good and combines superbly with the dry white wines. *Closed Nov.–May.*

From Melk, take Route 33 along the south bank, and you're back in the Wachau again. About 4 km (2½ mi) along, you'll come to **Schönbühel an der Donau,** whose unbelievably picturesque castle, perched on a cliff overlooking the Danube, is unfortunately not open to visitors.

Past **Aggsbach Dorf** you'll spot, on a hill to your right, the romantic ruin of 13th-century Aggstein castle, reportedly the lair of pirates who preyed on river traffic. As you continue northeast, you'll have lovely views of the towns across the river.

Mautern, opposite Krems, was a Roman encampment mentioned in the tales of the Niebelungen. The old houses and the castle are attractive, but contemporary Mautern is known for one of Austria's top restaurants, in an inn run by Lisl Bacher; in nearby Klein-Wien there's another—also superb—run by her sister (*see* Dining and Lodging, below).

44 You're bound to have seen **Stift Göttweig** as you came along the riverside road: The vast Benedictine abbey high above the Danube valley watches over the gateway to the Wachau. To reach it, go along Route 33, turn right into the highway south (marked to Stift Göttweig and St. Pölten), and turn right again (marked to Stift Göttweig) at the crest of the hill. Göttweig was redone outside in the mid-1700s in classic style, which you'll note from the columns and balcony and relatively plain side towers. Inside, it is a monument to Baroque art, with marvelous ornate decoration against the gold, brown, and blue. The stained-glass windows behind the high altar date to the mid-1400s. The public rooms of the abbey are splendid, particularly the Kaiserzimmer (Emperor's rooms), in which Napoleon stayed in 1809, reached via the elegant Emperor's staircase. Depending on the schedule of exhibitions, rooms may or may not be open to view. In postwar years, surprising treasures turned up in the Göttweig library, including original musical scores by Haydn and Mozart. *Furth bei Göttweig, tel. 02732/855810. Admission:AS30 adults, AS15 children. Guided tours only, Easter-Oct., daily at 10, 11AM and 2, 3, 4PM.*

Time Out | The terrace of the **Stiftsrestaurant** on the abbey grounds offers not only good local cuisine but, on a good day, a spectacular view. It's a great spot for lunch, coffee, or a drink. You might try—and buy by the bottle—the excellent wines produced by the abbey.

45 You may want to make a detour 20 km (12½ mi) south to **St. Pölten,** Lower Austria's capital. The old center of the city, now mainly a pedestrian zone, shows a distinctly Baroque face: The originally Romanesque cathedral on Domplatz has a rich Baroque interior; the Rococo Franciscan church at the north end of the Rathausplatz has four altar paintings by Kremser Schmidt. The Institute of English Maidens (a former convent) in nearby Linzer Strasse is one of the finest Baroque buildings in the city. The church contains frescoes by master Paul Troger.

Take the Wiener Strasse (Route 1) out of St. Pölten headed east for 12 km (8 mi) to Kapelln, then turn left to **Herzogenburg.** In the great Augustine cloister here, the buildings date mainly to the mid-1700s. Fischer von Erlach was among the architects who designed the abbey. The church, dedicated to Saints George and Stephen, is ornate Baroque; the organ loft is a beauty. *Tel. 02782/3112. Admission: AS30 adults, AS10 chil-*

dren. Open Apr.–Oct. Guided tours only (about 1 hr) 9–noon and 1–5.

Head north on Route S33 or the parallel road, marked to Traismauer, and pick up Route 43 east. If you're ready for back roads (too well marked for you to get lost), cut off to the left to Oberbierbaum (Upper Beer Tree) and then on to Zwentendorf (there's a fascinating black madonna in the side chapel of the parish church here). If you follow Route 43, it will land you on Route 1 at Mitterndorf; drive east and after 4 km (2½ mi), turn left off Route 1 onto Route 19, marked for Tulln.

46 At **Tulln,** you'll spot a number of charming Baroque touches in the attractive main square. There's a new museum to honor the artist Egon Schiele (1890–1918) who was born here, although you'll find his best works in Vienna. *Donaulände 26, tel. 02272/ 4570. Admission: AS30 adults, AS15 children. Open Tues.– Sun. 9–noon and 2–6.*

The Romanesque parish church of St. Stephen on the Wiener Strasse is noteworthy for its west door and the six figures carved in relief circles on each side (presumably the 12 apostles). Beside the church, the unusual combined chapel (upstairs) and charnel house (below) is in a structure that successfully combines late Romanesque and early Gothic.

Drive east on Route 14 and turn left at St. Andrä-Wördern to hug the Danube shoreline en route to **Greifenstein.** Atop the hill there, another castle with a spectacular view looks up the Danube and across to Stockerau. Its earliest parts date to 1135, but most of what you see stems from a thorough but romantic renovation in 1818. The view is worth the climb, even when the castle is closed. *Kostersitzgasse 5, tel. 02242/2353. Currently closed.*

47 As you come down into **Klosterneuburg,** the great Augustine abbey dominates the scene. It has changed many times since it was established in 1114, most recently in 1892, when Friedrich Schmidt, architect of Vienna's city hall, added neo-Gothic features to its two identifying towers. Klosterneuburg was unusual in that until 1568 it had both men's and women's orders in the same abbey.

In the abbey church, look for the carved wood choir and oratory and the large 17th-century organ. Among Klosterneuburg's treasures are the beautifully enameled 1181 Verdun Altar in the Leopold chapel, stained-glass windows from the 14th and 15th centuries, Romanesque candelabra from the 12th century, and gorgeous ceiling frescoes, in the great marble hall. In the wine cellar there's a huge cask over which people slide. The exercise, called *Fasslrutsch'n,* is indulged in during the *Leopoldiweinkost,* the wine tasting around Saint Leopold's day, November 15. The abbey foundation owns vast properties in Austria, including many vineyards whose wines are excellent. *Stiftsplatz 1, tel. 02243/621–0212. Admission: AS30 adults, AS10 children; guided tours only (about 1 hour) every half-hour, Mon.–Sat. 9–11 and 1:30–5; Sun. and holidays 11, 1:30–5.*

Time Out   Stop at **Café Veit** (Niedermarkt 13) for a light snack, coffee (house roasted), or tea (25 varieties). Try the potato soup or the semolina dumpling soup and finish off with an excellent apple strudel.

About 3 km (2 mi) down the road, off to the right tucked under Leopoldsberg, is the charming small vintner's village of **Kahlenberg,** an excellent spot to stop and sample the local wines. And you're now on the outskirts of Vienna, where our trip began.

What to See and Do with Children

Burg Kreuzenstein (*see* Tour 1, above).

The trip up the **Pöstlingberg** (*see* Tour 2, above) the fairytale grotto and the zoo.

The museum at **Schloss Ebelsberg** in Linz (take the Wiener Strasse from Blumauerplatz near the main rail station, or Streetcar 1 to Simonystrasse and change to Bus 11 to Ebelsberg) shows weapons, from the breech loader to the automatic rifle, and has a collection of old-time cars and motorcycles. *Schlossweg 7, Ebelsberg, tel. 0732/307632. Admission: AS38 adults, AS20 children. Open June–Sept., weekends and holidays 10–noon, 1–5.*

The **Florianer Bahn** from Pichling to St. Florian (*see* Tour 3, above).

The **Steyrertalbahn** (*see* Tour 3, above).

The castle at **Kremsegg,** on Route 139 near Kremsmunster, has a collection of old-fashioned cars and motorcycles. *Tel. 07583/247. Admission: AS50 adults, AS20 children. Open Sat. 1–5, Sun., holidays 10–noon, 1–5; July–Aug., daily 10–noon, 1–5.*

In a moated castle north of **Pottenbrunn,** 6½ km (4 mi) east of St. Pölten, there's a museum (*Zinnfigurenmuseum*) of tin soldiers. Imagine a bird's-eye view of entire armies in battle; you'll see thousands of soldiers, at their places in the battles of Leipzig (1813), Berg Isel (Innsbruck, 1809), Vienna (1683), and World War I. *Pottenbrunner Hauptstr. 77, tel. 02785/2337. Admission: AS35 adults, AS10 children. Open Apr.–Oct., Tues.–Sun. 9–5.*

The **Feuerwehrmuseum** (Firefighters' Museum) in St. Florian displays equipment from the Baroque era to the present day. Saint Florian, the patron saint of firefighters and the guardian against fire, is easily recognized in Austrian churches as a figure pouring water from a bucket over a blazing house. *Stiftstr. 3, tel. 07224/219. Admission: AS20 adults, AS10 children. Open May–Oct., Tues.–Sun. 9–noon, 2–4.*

Off the Beaten Track

There's a marvelous *Heuriger* (wine garden) at Hollenburg, 1 km (½ mi) up the hill after the Routes 33 and S33 intersection, southeast of Krems, then about 5½ km (3½ mi) east—the turnoff is marked to Thallern. The setting is on a hill above the Danube, and there's even a castle ruin. The **Ruinenheuriger** is one of those seasonal places that's open when it's open, so call ahead. The wines come from the Geymüller vineyards; nearly everybody in the town appears to be a vintner. *Tel. 02732/2229.*

Steyr has an intriguing section of abandoned industrial buildings along the Steyr river (take Gaswerkgasse and turn down to
the river). In the same area, you'll see workers' housing of 100
years ago; it was provided by the employer and was probably
better than that which the workers would otherwise have had.

Shopping

If you want to shop for wine, you're in the ideal area. St. Pölten
has a large selection of more standard items, and you will find
good local souvenirs in Krems and Enns. Linz is a good place to
shop; prices are generally lower than those in resorts and other
large cities, and selections are good. The major shops are found
in the main square and the adjoining side streets, in the Old
Quarter to the west of the main square, in the pedestrian zone
of the Landstrasse and its side streets, and in the Haupstrasse
of Urfahr, over the Niebelungen bridge across the Danube. For
local handmade items and good-quality souvenirs, try **Ö.Ö.
Heimatwerk** (Landstr. 31, Linz, tel. 0732/773–3760), where
you'll find silver, pewter, ceramics, fabrics, and some clothing.
All kinds of stuff, from clothing to china, is sold (March–mid-
November, Saturday 7–2) on the Hauptplatz (main square). In
winter the **Flea Market** moves across the river next to the new
city hall, left just over the bridge. The state-run "Dorotheum"
auction house is at Fabrikstrasse 26 (tel. 0732/773132).

For antiques go to the old city, on the side streets around the
main square. Try **Otto Buchinger** (Bethlehemstr. 5, tel. 0732/
770117), **Richard Kirchmayr** (Bischofstr. 3a, tel. 0732/276–
9843), **Kunsthandlung Kirchmayr** (Herrenstr. 23, tel. 0732/
774667), **Ute Pastl** (Wischerstr. 26, Urfahr, tel. 0732/237306),
and **Heinz Roland** (Khevenhüllerstr. 25, tel. 0732/663003). For
jewelry, try **Pfaffenberger** (Landstr. 42, tel. 0732/772495) or
Wild (Landstr. 49, tel. 0732/774105).

Sports and Fitness

Participant Sports

Bicycling The trail along the Danube must be one of the great bicycle
routes of the world. For much of the way (the exception being
the Korneuburg–Krems stretch) you can take this trip by bike
on both sides of the river. For details and information, *see* Getting Around, By Bicycle, above. Get the folder "Danube Cycle
Track" (in English, from Niederösterreich-Information, Heidenschuss 2, A–1010 Vienna, tel. 0222/533–4773) for hints on
what to see and where you'll find "cyclist friendly" accommodations, repairs, and other services. Some small hotels will even
pick up you and your bike from the cycle path. You'll find bicycle
rentals at Aggsbach–Markt, Dürnstein, Grein, Krems,
Mautern, Melk, Persenbeug–Gottsdorf, Pöchlarn, Schönbühel/
Aggsbach Dorf, Spitz, Weissenkirchen, and Ybbs.

The landscape around Linz is relatively level, and within the
city there are 89 km (55 mi) of marked cycle routes. Get the brochure "Cycling in Linz" from the tourist office. You can rent a
bike through the city (tel. 0732/239–31777; AS20 per day) and
at Verein Arbeitsloseninitiative (Bischofstr. 7, tel. 0732/
771986). In the areas of Eferding, St. Florian, through the

Enns river valley, and around Steyr, the territory is generally good for cycling, with gentle hills and special routes. Bicycles can be rented at the railroad stations in Freistadt (tel. 07942/ 2319), Kremsmünster (tel. 07583/218), and Steyr (tel. 07252/ 1700 or 07252/233210).

Canoeing The Danube in general is fast and tricky, so you're best off to stick to the calmer waters back of the power dams (at Pöchlarn, above Melk, and near Grein). You can rent a canoe at Pöchlarn. You can also canoe on an arm of the Danube near Ottensheim, about 8 km (5 mi) west of Linz. For information call Ruderverein Donau (tel. 0732/236250) or Ruderverein Ister-Sparkasse (tel. 0732/774888).

Fishing This is splendid fishing country. Check with the town tourist offices about licenses and fishing rights for river trolling and fly-casting in Aggsbach–Markt, Dürnstein, Emmersdorf, Grein, Kleinpöchlarn, Krems, Mautern, Mauthausen, Persen-beug–Gottsdorf, Pöchlarn, Schönbühel/Aggsbach Dorf, Spitz, Waidhofen/Ybbs, and Ybbs. In Linz, check **Fischereiverband** (Kärntnerstr. 12, tel. 0732/50507) or **Weitgasser** (Figulystr. 5, tel. 0732/56566).

In the streams and lakes of the area around Linz, you can fly-cast for rainbow and brook trout and troll for pike and carp. For details, contact the tourist offices or the numbers listed below: Aschach (Dreihann-Harrach'sche Gutsverwaltung, tel. 07273/ 6312), Bad Hall (Pfarrkirchen, Schloss Feyregg, tel. 07258/ 2591; Gasthof Schröck "Hofwirt," hotel guests only, tel. 07258/ 2274), Freistadt (Sportgeschäft Gutenbrunner, tel. 07942/ 2720; Sportgeschäft Juch, tel. 07942/2532), Kremsmünster (Gerhard Fleck, tel. 07583/6103), Steyr (Angelsportverein Steyr, tel. 07252/615443).

Golf An 18-hole, par-72 course at **Tillysburg,** near St. Florian, is open April to November, but you'll have to caddy for yourself. *Tillysburg, St. Florian bei Linz, tel. 07223/2873. Greens fee: AS300 weekdays, AS400 weekends.*

Health and Fitness Clubs To keep fit in Linz, try **Olympic** (Mozartkreuzung, tel. 0732/ 776156; open weekdays 10–9, Sat. 2–6, Sun. 10–2) or **Sport-studio California** (Landwiedstr. 119, tel. 0732/41157; open weekdays 10–9, weekends 10–2).

Hiking You could hardly ask for better hiking country: From the level ground of the Danube valley, hills rise on both sides, giving great views when you reach the upper levels. There are *Wanderwege* (marked hiking paths) virtually everywhere; local tourist offices have maps and route details, and in Linz you can get the booklet "Urban Hiking Paths in Linz." Around the city you might retrace the route of the Linz–Budweis horse-drawn tramway, continental Europe's first railway, or wander from one castle to another. You can arrange to hike in the Mühlviertel from Freistadt to Grein (information: tel. 0732/ 235020) and even get your pack transferred from hotel to hotel.

Jogging Runners also use the bicycle trail along the Danube. The place to jog in Linz is along the river bank on the far side of the Danube (Urfahr).

Skating Linz is an ice-skating city; from late October to late February, there's outdoor skating daily 2–5 and 6–9 (no evening skating on Thurs.), weekends and holidays also 9–noon, and indoors from late September to late April, Wednesday 9–noon, Saturday 2–5, Sunday 10–noon, 2–5, 6–9. Untere Donaulände 11, tel. 0732/778513.

Tennis   You'll find tennis courts—indoors and out—throughout this area in nearly every town. Ask at the tourist offices in Aggsbach–Markt, Dürnstein, Grein, Krems, Maria Taferl, Mautern, Persenbeug–Gottsdorf, Pöchlarn, Spitz, Waidhofen/Ybbs, and Weissenkirchen. In Linz, contact the Upper Austrian Tennis Association (Waldeggstr. 16, tel. 0732/51250). The Novotel also has two clay courts (Wankmüllerhofstr. 37, tel. 0732/47281).

In the country around Linz, there are courts in Bad Hall (Kurverwaltung, tel. 07258/20310), Freistadt (Turn- und Sport-Union, tel. 07942/2570), Kremsmünster (Tennishallenbe-trib, tel. 07583/395 and Tennis-Center Stadlhuber, tel. 07583/7498), and Steyr (Tennishof Rottenbrunner, tel. 07252/61219).

Water Sports and Swimming   All along the Danube there are many water sports available (check with the tourist offices in Krems, Mautern, and Pöchlarn), but the Danube is not for swimming. Virtually every town has an outdoor pool, and some have them indoors as well. You'll find large pools at Artstetten, Dürnstein, Grein, Krems, Maria Taferl, Mauthausen, Melk, Pöchlarn, Schönbühel/Aggs-bach–Dorf, Spitz, and Waidhofen/Ybbs. All are family facilities, with changing rooms and lockers; most have snack bars or restaurants, too. In Linz, the Kral Waterskiing School offers waterskiing and other water sports (Talgasse 14, 0732/231494). The closest swimming is at the Pleschinger lake; to get there, take the No. 1 tram to Urfahr/Reindlstrasse and the No. 32 bus to the lake. This is a pleasant spot for family swimming, although it tends to be crowded on sunny, warm weekends.

Spectator Sports

Soccer matches are played in Linz in the **Stadion** (Roseggerstr. 41, tel. 0732/56055 or 0732/660670). Tennis matches and other sports events are held at the adjacent **Stadthalle** (tel. 0732/57311). Hockey and skating competitions are held in the **Eishalle.** Buy tickets for sports events at Kartenbüro Ruefa (Landstr. 67, tel. 0732/662–6810. Open weekdays 8:30–noon, 2–6; Sat. 8:30–noon).

Dining and Lodging

Dining

The restaurants in this chapter are varied; there are sophisti-cated and stylish ones, as well as the plain and peasant type. Everywhere they capitalize on the river view, and outdoor din-ing is common. Many of the towns along both sides of the Dan-ube will have country inns with dining rooms rather than separate restaurants. Prices include tax and a service charge, but you may want to leave a small additional tip.

Highly recommended restaurants are indicated by a star ★.

Category	Cost*
Very Expensive	over AS500
Expensive	AS300–AS500
Moderate	AS200–AS300
Inexpensive	under AS200

per person for a typical three-course meal with a glass of house wine

Lodging

On this trip you might stay in a castle hotel, a standard city hotel, or a country inn. Distances are short between tours, so you can easily stay in one place and drive to another to try a different restaurant. Room rates include taxes and service and almost always breakfast (except in the most expensive hotels), but it is wise to ask. It is customary to leave a small (AS20) additional tip for the chambermaid.

Highly recommended lodgings are indicated by a star ★.

Category	Cost*
Very Expensive	over AS1,500
Expensive	AS1,000–AS1,500
Moderate	AS700–AS1,000
Inexpensive	under AS700

All prices are for a standard double room, including tax and service.

Aschach/Feldkirchen

Dining and Lodging ★

Faust Schlössl. Once a toll-collection station belonging to the Schaunberg family (ruins of the family castle are nearby), this castle, on the river directly across from Aschach, is said to be haunted and to have been built by the Devil in a single night for Dr. Faustus. Ignore the tale and enjoy simple but modern comfort in the converted castle among the towers and turrets. *Oberlandshaag 2, A–4082 Feldkirchen, tel. 07233/7402. 25 rooms. Facilities: restaurant (closed Tues.), outdoor pool, bicycle rental, fishing. No credit cards. Moderate.*

Zur Sonne. The welcome of the bright yellow facade carries over to the comfortable traditional decor inside. You're right on the Danube here, and the best rooms have a river view. The popular restaurant offers regional and traditional specialties and, of course, fish, including fresh trout. *Kurzwernhartplatz 5, A–4082 Aschach/Donau, tel. 07273/6308. 12 rooms, 6 with bath. Facilities: restaurant (closed Fri., Oct.–Easter), sauna. No credit cards. Moderate.*

Bad Hall

Dining and Lodging ★

Schlosshotel Feyregg. You'll be in an exclusive setting in this Baroque castle just outside town, the elegant summer residence of an abbot. The comfortable, spacious guest rooms on the ground floor are furnished in period style. *A–4540 Bad Hall/*

Feyregg-Pfarrkirchen, tel. 07258/2591. 14 rooms. Facilities: restaurant, bar, garage. No credit cards. Very Expensive.

Gasthof Mitter. In this traditional family-run *Gasthof*, you're in the heart of town, convenient to the train station and the spa facilities. The rooms are in a pleasant country style in light colors. The hotel restaurant offers local dishes, including lamb, and game in season. *Hauptplatz 1, A–4540, tel. 07258/23630. 20 rooms, 16 with bath. Facilities: restaurant (closed Mon.), bar, garage. No credit cards. Closed Jan. Moderate.*

Dürnstein

Dining   **Loibnerhof.** Here, in an idyllic setting on the banks of the Danube, you'll dine on interesting variations on Austrian themes: ravioli with blood-sausage filling and various grilled fish or lamb specialties. The wines come from the restaurant's own vineyards. *Unterloiben 7, tel. 02732/82890. Reservations advised on weekends. Dress: casual. No credit cards. Closed mid-Jan.–mid-Feb. and Mon.–Tues. Expensive.*

Zum Goldenen Strauss. A onetime post station, long a simple *Gasthaus*, now has ambitions to be something more. You'll be offered enormous portions of very good Austrian fare, with a flair that helps compensate for the occasionally slow service. Try the garlic soup followed by *Tafelspitz*. The rooms inside are cozy, the terrace a delight. *Tel. 02711/267. No reservations. Dress: casual but neat. No credit cards. Closed Tues. and mid-Jan.–mid-Mar. Moderate.*

Lodging   **Richard Löwenherz.** The superb vaulted reception and dining rooms of this former convent are beautifully furnished with antiques. Though spacious and comfortable, the balconied guest rooms in the newer part of the house are more modern in decor and furnishings. The restaurant is known for its regional specialties and local wines. *A–3601, tel. 02711/222. 40 rooms. Facilities: restaurant, bar, outdoor pool. AE, DC, MC, V. Closed Nov.–Feb. Very Expensive.*

★ **Schlosshotel Dürnstein.** If there's to be one big fling on your trip, it might well be here. This 17th-century early Baroque castle, on a rocky terrace with exquisite views over the Danube, offers dream accommodations, surrounds you with genuine elegance and comfort, and has a particularly friendly and helpful staff. The best rooms look onto the river, but all are unusually bright and attractive; of moderate size, they have pillows, comfortable chairs, and country antiques throughout. The kitchen has a good reputation and wines are from the area. Dining on the terrace is a memorable experience. *A–3601, tel. 02711/212. 37 rooms. Facilities: restaurant (reservations advised, jacket and tie advised), bar, outdoor pool, sauna, solarium, garage. AE, MC. Closed Nov.–Mar. Very Expensive.*

Sänger Blondel. Behind the yellow facade is a very friendly, typical, traditional family hotel, with elegant country rooms of medium size that have attractive paneling and antique decorations. The staff is particularly helpful and can suggest several excursions in the area. The hotel is known for its restaurant, which features local specialties and a wide range of salads and lighter dishes. You can even buy a loaf of the house bread or a jar of the apricot marmalade. *A–3601, tel. 02711/253. 16 rooms. Facilities: restaurant (reservations advised on weekends, jacket advised, closed Sun.) bicycle rental, garage. No credit cards. Restaurant and hotel closed mid-Dec.–Feb. Moderate.*

Eferding

Dining   **Dannerbauer.** Two km (1¼ mi) north of Eferding on the road to Aschach, right on the Danube, is one of the area's best restaurants. It serves species of fish you probably never heard of, poached, grilled, broiled, or fried. Many of the fish come from the river; some are kept in the house tanks, to ensure freshness. There are meat dishes, too, and game (delicious wild hare) in season, and the soups (try the nettle soup) are excellent. The place has a pleasant outlook with lots of windows. *Brandstatt bei Eferding, tel. 07272/2471. Reservations advised. Jacket suggested. DC. Closed Mon., Tues., and Feb. Expensive.*

Dining and **Zum Goldenen Kreuz.** The golden facade indicates a typical
Lodging   country-style hotel, simple but with the charm of a family-run establishment. You'll sleep on fluffy feather beds. The restaurant is known for its good regional cuisine, and there are occasional specialty weeks. *Schmiedstr. 29, A–4070, tel. 07272/ 42470. 21 rooms. Facilities: restaurant (closed Sun. night). AE, DC, MC. Closed a few days at Christmas. Moderate.*

Enns

Dining and **Lauriacum.** You might overlook this plain contemporary build-
Lodging   ing, set as it is among Baroque gems in the center of town, but it's the best place to stay. The bright rooms offer modern comfort, and the quiet garden is a welcoming spot. *Wiener Str. 5–7, A–4470, tel. 07223/2315. 30 rooms. Facilities: restaurant, bar, sauna, tennis, garage. MC, V. Very Expensive.*

Freistadt

Dining and **Deim/Zum Goldenen Hirschen.** This romantic 600-year-old
Lodging   house full of atmosphere fits perfectly into the old city and is a
★   wonderful place to stay. The rooms are up to date and attractive. The stone-arched ceiling adds to the elegance of the dining room, where you'll find international and local specialties and game in season (closed Fri. in winter). *Böhmergasse 8, A– 4240, tel. 07942/2258, 07942/2111. 23 rooms, 19 with bath. Facilities: restaurant. DC. Expensive.*

★   **Zum Goldenen Adler.** Here you'll be in another 600-year-old house; it has been run by the same family since 1807, so tradition runs strong. The medium-size rooms are modern and full of country charm; the service is exceptionally accommodating. The newly renovated garden, with a piece of the old city wall as background, is a delightful oasis. The restaurant is known for such excellent regional specialties as *Böhmisches Bierfleisch,* a cut of beef cooked in beer. The desserts are outstanding. *Salzgasse 1, A–4240, tel. 07942/2112, 07942/2556. 30 rooms. Facilities: restaurant (closed Tues. Apr.–Oct.), pub, outdoor pool, solarium, sauna, fitness room. MC. Moderate.*

Göttweig/Klein Wien

Dining   **Schickh.** This restaurant, tucked away among lovely old trees
★   below the north side of the Göttweig abbey, is worth looking for. The variety of dishes, from lamb to lobster, is astonishing for a small place, and the creative ideas that come out of the kitchen have made it a draw for knowledgeable diners. (It's in

friendly competition with Bacher in nearby Mautern; the two are run by a pair of sisters.) In summer you'll dine in the garden, probably rubbing elbows with the prominent of Vienna. There's a handful of guest rooms available for overnights. *Avastr. 2, A–3511 Klein-Wien/Furth bei Göttweig, tel. 02736/ 218. Reservations required. Jacket and tie advised. No credit cards. Closed Wed., Thurs. Very Expensive.*

Klosterneuburg

Dining **Stiftskeller.** These atmospheric underground rooms in a historic part of the abbey are an authentic cellar in every sense of the word: Some of the fine wines carry the Klosterneuburg label. You can sample them along with standard Austrian fare, from Wiener schnitzel to rumpsteak with onions. *Albrechtsberggasse 1, tel. 02243/2070. Dress: casual but neat. Reservations advised on weekends. No credit cards. Moderate.*

Korneuburg

Dining **Tuttendörfl.** This rustic-modern restaurant is attractive, if just for the terrace right on the Danube. The kitchen turns out standard Viennese fare, good but unexciting, and there's game in season. To get here, look sharp for the turnoff left from Route 3 (*not* the A–22 autobahn) marked "Tuttendörfl," about 1½ km (1 mi) west of the Bisamberg intersection and traffic light. *Tuttendörfl 6, tel. 02262/2485. Reservations suggested on weekends. Jacket advised. No credit cards. Closed Sun., Mon., and Jan. Expensive.*

Krems/Stein

Dining and Lodging ★ **Alte Post.** You're allowed to drive into the pedestrian zone to this romantic old house in the heart of the old town, next to the Steinener Tor (west gate). The rooms are in comfortable country style, but the real feature here is dining on regional specialties or having a glass of local wine in the arcaded Renaissance courtyard. The staff is particularly friendly, and cyclists are welcome. *Obere Landstr. 32, A–3500 Krems, tel. 02732/82276. 25 rooms, 5 with bath. Facilities: restaurant, bicycle rental, garage. No credit cards. Moderate.*

Am Förthof. An inn has existed on the riverside site of this modern hotel for hundreds of years. The rooms are comfortable and balconied; those on the front have a view of the Danube and Göttweig abbey across the river—and the sounds of the traffic. The dining room offers good regional cuisine, and breakfasts are particularly recommended. *Förthofer Donaulände 8, A–3500, tel. 02732/83345, 02732/81348. 22 rooms. Facilities: restaurant, outdoor pool, sauna, solarium, bicycle rental. DC, MC. Moderate.*

Langenlebarn

Dining ★ **Zum Roten Wolf.** In an unpretentious but attractive rustic restaurant (one of Austria's top three dozen), the stylishly elegant table settings complement the outstanding food. Try any of the lamb variations or the breast of duck. The service is especially friendly; ask for advice on the wines. You can get here by local train from Vienna; the station is virtually at the door. *Bahnstr.*

*58, tel. 02272/2567. Reservations required. Jacket and tie rec-
ommended. AE, DC, MC, V. Closed Mon., Tues. Expensive.*

Linz

Dining　**Allegro.** Upstairs here in Linz's top restaurant, you'll find dis-
★　　　tinctive table settings and outstanding cuisine and service in a
modern-elegant wood and rose-colored setting. Many of the
dishes emphasize the careful treatment of local and regional
fare; the lentil soup with sour cream garnished with grilled
frankfurter bits is an example. The fish dishes and lamb are
particularly praiseworthy—but you can hardly go wrong. Ask
for advice on the food as well as the wines. The abundant cheese
tray is excellent. *Schillerstr. 68, tel. 0732/669800. Reservations
required. Jacket and tie required. AE. Closed Sat., Sun., except Sat. evening in Oct.–Apr.; closed early Aug. Very Expensive.*

★　**Kremsmünsterer Stuben.** In a beautifully restored house in the
heart of the old city you'll find an attractive wood-paneled restaurant offering everything from regional specialties to a sev-
en-course dinner. You might choose from saddle of hare or fillet
of venison as a main course as you relax in the comfortable, traditional ambience. *Altstadt 10, tel. 0732/782111. Reservations
advised. Jacket and tie required. AE, DC. Closed Mon., two
weeks in Jan., two weeks in Aug. Very Expensive.*

Vogelkäfig. This excellent restaurant across the river, on the
edge of the city, gives the impression of a country estate; with
its many bird cages, the atmosphere is a bit exotic. The intriguing variations on local specialties are surprising, but they do
work; how about onion soup garnished with an apple dumpling?
*Neulichtenberg 13, tel. 0732/234037. Reservations recom-
mended. Jacket and tie advised. AE, DC, MC, V. Closed Sun.
eve., Mon. Expensive.*

Wolfinger. Upstairs in this house that's been beautifully restored to expose the old timbers is a restaurant that features
both local dishes (excellent soups and a renowned Tafelspitz)
and Italian fare. This is a favorite gathering place for Linz businesspeople. *Hauptplatz 19, tel. 0732/773–2910. Reservations
advised. Jacket and tie recommended. AE, DC, MC, V. Closed
Sun. Expensive.*

Tautermann. Downstairs you can choose from the café's
prizewinning cakes and pastries and enjoy them with coffee at
the wrought-iron tables upstairs. *Klammstr. 14, tel. 0732/
779686. No reservations. Dress: casual but neat. No credit
cards. Closed Tues. Moderate.*

★　**Traxlmayr.** This is one of Austria's great coffeehouses in the
old tradition, with the patina of age, where you can linger all
day over one cup of coffee, reading the papers in their bentwood
holders, and then have a light meal. All Linz gathers on the terrace in summer. Ask for the specialty, *Linzer Torte*, with your
coffee. *Promenade 16, tel. 0732/773353. Reservations unneces-
sary. Dress: casual but neat. No credit cards. Closed Sun.
Moderate.*

Zum Klosterhof. This complex in the former Kremsmünster abbey gives you a choice of upstairs and downstairs rooms that
range from fairly formal to rustic-country to completely informal. The fare is traditional Austrian, and the beverage of
choice is Salzburger Stiegl beer. *Landstr. 30, tel. 0732/773–
3730. Reservations usually not necessary. Dress: jackets or casual, depending on the room. AE, DC, MC, V. Moderate.*

Dining and Lodging

Schillerpark. This very modern complex (glass outside, marble inside) puts you close to the south end of the pedestrian zone but still reasonably near the center and the sights. The casino is in the same building. The rooms have clean lines, with contemporary furnishings. *Rainerstr. 2–4, tel. 0732/554050. 111 rooms. Nonsmoking floor. Facilities: 2 restaurants (1 in the casino), 2 bars (1 in the casino), café, sauna, solarium, garage. AE, DC, MC, V. Very Expensive.*

Dom-Hotel. Behind the plain facade on a quiet side street near the new cathedral and the city center is a modern hotel with its own garden. The rooms are compact but attractive, in natural woods and shades of blue. *Baumbachstr. 17, tel. 0732/778441. 44 rooms. Facilities: restaurant, bar, sauna, solarium, parking. AE, DC, MC, V. Expensive.*

Spitz. This ultramodern neo–Art Deco hotel in Urfahr is an easy walk across the bridge from the city center. The rooms are smallish but comfortable, and some have a view over the new city hall to the main city. *Paladino*, its restaurant, is earning a good reputation. *Karl-Fiedler-Str. 6, tel. 0732/236–4410. 56 rooms. Facilities: restaurant (closed Sun.), bar, sauna, solarium, garage. AE, DC, MC, V. Expensive.*

Trend. You'll be directly on the Danube in this multistory modern hotel, next to the Brucknerhaus concert hall and within reasonable walking distance of the center. The rooms are compact-modern and attractively decorated; ask for an upper room on the river side for the superb views. The excellent restaurant is packed with businesspeople at lunchtime. *Untere Donaulände 9, tel. 0732/76260. 176 rooms. Facilities: restaurant, bar, nightclub, café, indoor pool, sauna, solarium, fitness room, garage. AE, DC, MC, V. Expensive.*

Drei Mohren. This has been an inn since 1595, and the rooms are well worn, but they have up-to-date baths. It's all in the heart of the old city within a block of the pedestrian zone. *Promenade 17, tel. 0732/772626. 27 rooms, 24 with bath. Facilities: restaurant, bar. AE, DC, V. Moderate.*

Prielmayerhof. This attractive, traditional house is not central, but bus No. 21 will take you the eight blocks to the pedestrian zone or the main rail station. The Oriental-carpeted rooms are larger than those in the newer hotels, and the baths are fully up to standard. *Weissenwolfstr. 33, tel. 0732/774131. 32 rooms, 30 with bath. Facilities: restaurant, bar. AE, DC, MC, V. Moderate.*

★ **Wolfinger.** This charming, traditional hotel in an old building in the heart of the city is a favorite of regular guests, certainly, in part, because of the friendly staff. You couldn't be more central. The medium-size rooms have been recently modernized, with comfortable new furniture and bright fabrics. Those on the front are less quiet but give you a first-hand view of city activities. The restaurant is excellent (*see* Dining, above). *Hauptplatz 19, tel. 0732/773–2910. 27 rooms, 23 with bath. Facilities: restaurant, wine stube. AE, DC, MC, V. Moderate.*

Zum Schwarzen Bären. This fine, traditional house near the center of the old city, a block from the pedestrian zone, was the birthplace of the tenor Richard Tauber (1891–1948). The rooms are smallish and well worn, but the baths (mostly with shower) are modern, if compact. *Herrenstr. 9–11, tel. 0732/772–4770. 36 rooms, 29 with bath. Facilities: restaurant, bar, wine stube. AE, DC, MC, V. Moderate.*

Maria Taferl

Dining and Lodging **Krone–Kaiserhof.** Two hotels under the same family management share each other's luxurious facilities. The Krone looks out over the Danube valley, the Kaiserhof has views of the nearby Baroque pilgrimage church. The rooms are done a bit slickly in a country style in both houses. Every Sunday in July and August there's a buffet with live dance music, on Wednesdays a *Heuriger* buffet (new wine and cold dishes) with zither music. *A–3672 Maria Taferl, tel. 07413/63550, 07413/3250. 65 rooms. Facilities: 2 restaurants, bar, indoor and outdoor pools, sauna, solarium, fitness room, minigolf, garage. No credit cards. Expensive.*

Mautern

Dining ★ **Landhaus Bacher.** Lisl Bacher's creative, light cuisine here has elevated this attractive country restaurant to one of the top dozen in the country. The light-flooded rooms are elegant but not stiff, and there's an attractive garden. A recent menu offered crabmeat salad, breast of pigeon, and spring lamb. Ask for advice on wines; the choice is wide. You can buy a copy of Mrs. Bacher's cookbook, although it costs about as much as a meal. Note that there are a few small and cozy rooms for overnight guests in an adjoining guest house. *Südtirolerplatz 208, tel. 02732/829370 or 02732/85429. Reservations required. Jacket and tie advised. DC, V. Closed Mon., Tues. and mid-Jan.–mid-Feb. Very Expensive.*

Melk

Dining and Lodging **Stadt Melk.** This traditional hotel in the heart of town offers plain but adequate accommodations in smallish rooms, but the main feature here is the excellent and attractive restaurant. The cuisine ranges from regional traditional to creative light; try one of the cream soups and stuffed chicken breast to enjoy the contrasts; dishes here are individually prepared. *Hauptplatz 1, A–3390, tel. 02752/2475. 16 rooms. Facilities: restaurant (reservations advised, jacket advised) garage. AE, V. Expensive.*

Goldener Ochs. Here in the center of town you're in a typical village *Gasthof* with the traditional friendliness of a family management. The rather small rooms were renovated in 1990, and the restaurant offers solid standard fare. *Linzer Str. 18, A–3390, tel. 02752/2367. 35 rooms, 25 with bath. Facilities: restaurant (closed Sat., Sun. Nov.–Apr.) wine cellar, sauna. AE, DC, MC, V. Moderate.*

Persenbeug

Dining **Donaurast.** You look through lots of glass over the Danube, about 2 km (1 mi) below Persenbeug, as you dine. Various river fish are specialties here, and interesting meat dishes such as wild boar, roast chicken, or Tafelspitz. Finish up with any of the excellent desserts or the selection of Austrian cheese. There are rooms as well, should you decide to stay overnight. *Wachaustr. 28, Persenbeug/Metzling, tel. 07412/2438. Dress: informal. Reservations not required. No credit cards. Closed Tues. in Nov., Dec., also Wed. in Mar.–May, Oct.; closed mid-Jan.–end Feb. Moderate.*

St. Pölten

Dining **Galerie.** Stock from the antique shop next door flows over to lend atmosphere to this stylish small restaurant. In contrast to the antiques, the kitchen strives to do new things—generally successfully—with Austrian standards like pork fillet. *Fuhrmanngasse 1, tel. 02742/51305. Reservations advised. Jacket and tie advised. AE, DC, MC. Closed Sun., Mon. Expensive.*

Spitz

Dining **Mühlenkeller.** You're really in an old mill here, and the cellar rooms go back to the 11th century. This is as much a *Heuriger* as it is a restaurant, open mainly in late afternoon and evening; wines come from neighboring vineyards. In summer you've the choice of the inside courtyard or the garden. Huge portions are served of local specialties like roast pork and Tafelspitz. *Auf der Wehr 1, tel. 02713/2352. No reservations. Dress: informal. No credit cards. Closed Wed., mid-Dec.–mid-Jan. Moderate.*

Dining and Lodging **Wachauer Hof.** This appealing traditional house, set near the vineyards, has been under family management for generations. You can enjoy the wines in the *Gaststube*, the shaded garden, or the restaurant, which offers basic Austrian fare. The medium-size rooms have comfortable chairs, ample pillows, and rustic decor in reds and browns. *Hauptstr. 15, A-3620, tel. 02713/2303. 32 rooms, 15 with bath. Facilities: restaurant. AE, MC. Closed mid-Nov.–Palm Sunday. Moderate.*

Steyr

Dining **Rahofer.** You'll have to search out this attractive intimate Italian restaurant in one of the passageways off the main square down toward the river. The choice is limited but of excellent quality; try the Saltimbocca. Soups and desserts are praiseworthy. *Stadtplatz 9, tel. 07252/24606. Reservations advised. Dress: casual but neat. AE, DC, MC, V. Closed Sun., Mon. Moderate.*

Dining and Lodging ★ **Minichmayr.** From this traditional hotel the view alone—out over the confluence of the Enns and Steyr rivers, up and across to Schloss Lamberg—will make your stay memorable. Add to that the especially homey rooms, a friendly staff, and an excellent restaurant offering creative, light cuisine and regional specialties, and there's little more to want, except easier parking. Ask for rooms on the river side. *Haratzmüllerstr. 1–3, A-4400, tel. 07252/23410. 51 rooms. Facilities: restaurant, sauna, solarium. AE, DC, MC, V. Expensive.*

★ **Mader/Zu den Drei Rosen.** In this very old family-run hotel with small but pleasant modern rooms, you're right on the picturesque town square. The restaurant offers solid local and traditional fare, with outdoor dining in a delightful garden in the ancient courtyard. *Stadtplatz 36, A-4400, tel. 07252/23358. 53 rooms. Facilities: restaurant (closed Sun.), garage. MC, V. Moderate.*

Tulln

Dining and Lodging ★ **Zur Rossmühle.** Starting with the cheerful yellow facade, elegance is the byword in this attractively renovated hotel on the town square. From the abundant greenery of the reception area to the table settings in the dining room, you'll find pleasing little touches. The rooms are in modern Baroque decor. For sheer pleasure, take lunch in the courtyard garden; here, as in the more formal dining room, you'll find Austrian standards and ambitious creations by the aspiring young chef. You'd do well with any of the excellent open wines on the list. *Hauptplatz 12–13, A-3430, tel. 02272/2411. 55 rooms. Facilities: restaurant (reservations advised, jacket and tie advised), bar, sauna, riding. AE, DC, MC, V. Closed Mon. and Jan. Expensive.*

Waidhofen an der Ybbs

Dining **Türkenpfeiferl.** "Family atmosphere" is served at this attractive, family-run restaurant, along with excellent creative, light cuisine and regional standards. Try the breast of chicken or lamb in a spiced crust. Note the attention to details: The bread is house baked. The garden is particularly pleasant for summer dining, and children are welcome. *Hoher Markt 23, tel. 07442/3507. Reservations recommended. Jacket advised. DC, MC. Closed Mon. and first week in July. Moderate.*

Weissenkirchen

Dining **Jamek.** Josef Jamek is known for his outstanding wines, his
★ wife Edeltraud for what she and her chefs turn out in the kitchen of this excellent restaurant, which is, in fact, their home. The combination makes for memorable dining in a rustic-elegant atmosphere. You dine in a succession of tastefully decorated rooms with 18th-century touches. Creative variations on typical Austrian specialties are emphasized; lamb and game in season are highlights. *Joching 45, tel. 02715/2235, 02715/2414. Reservations required. Jacket and tie advised. No credit cards. Closed Sun., Mon.; mid-Dec.–mid-Feb.; first week in July. Very Expensive.*

Florianihof. This is one of those restaurants that's packed on pleasant weekends; come during the week if possible. The dark-wood paneling in the succession of rooms is imposing and lends an illusion of elegance to this simple place. Check the *Rostbraten* (rumpsteak), roast pork, or grilled chicken. *Wösendorf 74, tel. 02715/2212. Reservations advised. Dress: casual but neat. No credit cards. Closed Thurs. and Jan.–Feb. Expensive.*

Kirchenwirt. The fare here is dependably Austrian: You'll find Tafelspitz, roast pork, *Kaiserfleisch* (corned pork), and other standards, all well prepared and served in the cozy rooms done in dark wood. *Weissenkirchen 17, tel. 02715/2332. Reservations advised on weekends. Dress: casual but neat. No credit cards. Closed Mon., Tues. in winter; closed mid-Dec.–mid-Jan. Expensive.*

Prandtauerhof. The Baroque facade is the work of Jakob Prandtauer, the architect responsible for many buildings in the area. Ornate details are carried over into the cozy guest rooms and the inner court; a sense of history pervades the house. The kitchen delivers excellent traditional cuisine with such creative touches as pork medallions in a light Gorgonzola sauce. You'll find fish and game in season, and the wines come from the house vineyards. *Joching 36, tel. 02715/2310. Reservations recommended. Jacket and tie advised. MC. Closed Tues., Wed. and mid-Feb.–mid-Mar. Expensive.*

Lodging **Raffelsbergerhof.** This stunning Renaissance building (1574),
★ once a shipmaster's house, has been tastefully converted into a
hotel with every comfort. The rooms are attractively decorated
without being overdone. The family management is particularly friendly, and there's a quiet garden to complement the *gemütlich* public lounge. *A-3610 Weissenkirchen, tel. 02715/2201.
12 rooms. MC. Closed Nov.–Apr. Expensive.*

Ybbs an der Donau

Dining **Villa Nowotni.** Dining in this gorgeous Art Deco house makes
★ you feel almost as though you'd been personally invited.
Evelyn Nowotni looks after the attractive rooms while her husband, Franz, handles the kitchen. The cuisine is basically Austrian with imaginative touches, such as the steamed corned leg
of venison or breast of duck stuffed with fillet of beef. Six open
wines are offered in addition to a wide range of bottled wines.
And children are welcome in this gourmet temple; there's a
great meadow playground behind the villa. *Trewaldstr. 3, tel.
07412/2620. Reservations required. Jacket and tie advised.
AE, DC, MC, V. Closed Sun. eve. Oct.–May and Mon. year-
round. Expensive.*

The Arts and Nightlife

In the smaller towns and cities covered in this chapter, the arts
tend to come to life in summer. Nightlife is not bad in Linz and
St. Pölten, and each town or group of towns has a hangout
where the crowd gathers, but this is family country for vacationers, and nightlife will usually consist of sitting around a table with a glass of wine.

The Arts

In Linz, the tourist office's monthly booklet "Was ist los in Linz
und Oberösterreich" (What's On in Linz and Upper Austria)
will give you details of theater and concerts. Two ticket agencies are **Linzer Kartenbüro** (Herrenstr. 4, tel. 0732/776127) and
Ruefa (Landstr. 67, tel. 0732/662–6810).

Music Summer concerts are held in June and July at the abbeys at
Kremsmünster and St. Florian (tel. 0732/775230). A chamber-
music festival takes place at Schloss Tillysburg in July (tel.
0732/778800). From June to September, a series of concerts on
the Bruckner organ is given on six Sunday afternoons at 4 in
the church at St. Florian (tel. 07224/8903). Melk also offers a
series of concerts around Pentecost, and concerts are held at
Grafenegg during the summer. Get details and dates from the
town or regional tourist offices.

In Linz, concerts and recitals are held in the **Brucknerhaus,** the
modern hall on the banks of the Danube. From mid-September
to early October, it's the center of the International Bruckner
Festival. *Untere Donaulände 7, tel. 0732/775230. Box office
open weekdays 10–6.*

Opera During July, the operetta festival in **Bad Hall** presents a different work each week (tel. 07258/2255–35).

The **Linz** opera company is excellent and often more willing to
mount venturesome works and productions than those in Vien-

na or even Graz. Most performances are in the **Landestheater** (tel. 0732/777655), some in the Brucknerhaus.

The **Stadttheater** (tel. 02742/520260 or 02742/541830) in **St. Pölten** includes operetta and occasionally opera in its repertoire. Check with the tourist office for schedules and times.

Theater   In **Linz,** plays (in German) in the classical tradition and some operas are performed at the **Landestheater;** in the **Kammerspiele** you'll find more contemporary plays. Several smaller "cellar" theaters also offer drama; the tourist office will have information. *Landestheater: Promenade 39, tel. 0732/777655. Box office open Tues.–Fri. 10–12:30 and 4½ hrs before performances; Sat. 10:30–12:30; Mon., weekends, and holidays, 6 PM to performance; Kammerspiele: Promenade 39, tel. 0732/ 777855. Box office open same hours as Landestheater.*

The theater in **St. Pölten** is quite good for a provincial house; classical and contemporary plays in German are presented. *Stadttheater, Rathausplatz 11, tel. 02742/520260 or 02742/ 541830. Box office open Tues.–Sun. 11–1, 5–6:30.*

Summer theater is held on the grounds next to the abbey in **Melk** during July and August, and **Grein** puts on a summer festival; call the tourist office for details.

Nightlife

Linz is a far livelier town than most Austrians realize, and the local population is friendlier than in Vienna or Salzburg and much less cliquish than in the top resort towns.

Cabaret   Linz has no cabaret in the Viennese tradition, but there's strip-tease at **Bambi-Diele** (Landwiedstr. 140, tel. 0732/84516) from 9 PM on.

Casinos   The Linz casino, with roulette, blackjack, poker, and slot machines, is in the **Hotel Schillerpark,** and the casino complex includes a bar and the **Rouge et Noir** restaurant. *Rainerstr. 2–4, tel. 0732/54487. Open daily except Good Friday, Nov. 1, and Dec. 24, 3 PM–3 AM. Admission: AS170, includes four AS50 tokens. Passport required. Jacket and tie advised.*

Bars and Lounges   Linz has not lagged behind other Austrian cities in developing its own "Bermuda triangle." Around the narrow streets of the old city (Klosterstrasse, Altstadt, Hofgasse) are dozens of fascinating small bars and lounges, and as you explore, you'll probably meet some Linzers who can direct you to the current "in" location. In St. Pölten, try the **New York Pub & Steakhouse** (Kugelgasse 6, tel. 02742/52829) for a start.

Discos   St. Pölten is the place for disco activity, and the **Fabrik,** with its bars and pizzeria, continues to pack in crowds from as far away as Vienna (Radlberger Hauptstr. 60, tel. 02742/65521, nightly from 9). You might also try **Bellini** (Mühlweg 67, tel. 02746/ 66407). The vast Fabrik is a perennial favorite, but otherwise the mortality rate of St. Pölten's clubs and discos is high.

6   The Lake District

Introduction

by George W. Hamilton

This trip touches heights material and spiritual. From the Schafberg, above St. Wolfgang, you can see forever, and in the pilgrimage church below, Michael Pacher's winged altar, 10 years in the making, rises like a prayer. The Lake District of Upper Austria centers on the region known as the *Salzkammergut* (literally, "salt estates"), an area with mountain peaks and year-round glaciers rising above tranquil mountain lakes and valleys dotted with villages. Most of the Salzkammergut is in Upper Austria, but it extends into adjacent areas of Salzburg province and Styria and has no defined borders. In summer, vacationers flock to the lakes, streams, meadows, and woods for hiking, boating, fishing, and swimming; in winter, they come to ski in the mountains of Salzburg province and Styria. Amid this pastoral perfection, many sophisticated restaurants have sprung up; you can stay in age-old *Schloss* hotels or modern mansions; and shoppers come to buy the linens and ceramics, wood carvings, and painted glass of the region.

Below the unspoiled landscapes lie vast salt mines that have played a large role in the history of the area. Today when salt is one of the cheapest and most common commodities around, we forget how important it was in the not-too-distant past. Since it was essential for food preservation, salt was usually a government monopoly. To prevent smuggling, visitors were not allowed into the Salzkammergut and peasants were confined to their valleys. This situation continued until the late 19th century, when Emperor Franz Josef established his summer residence in Bad Ischl. The court and aristocracy flocked to the region, thus ending the Salzkammergut's isolation.

Essential Information

Important Addresses and Numbers

Tourist Information

The main tourist offices for the provinces covered in this chapter are:

Land Salzburg (Mozartplatz 1, A–5020 Salzburg, tel. 0662/8042–2232)
Styria (Herrengasse 16, A–8010 Graz, tel. 0316/835241)
Upper Austria (Schillerstr. 50, A–4010 Linz, tel. 0732/663021)

Offices for the individual towns in the Salzkammergut:

Altaussee (Kurhaus, A–8992, tel. 06152/71643)
Bad Aussee (Hauptstr. 48, A–8990, tel. 06152/4720 or 06152/2323)
Bad Ischl (Bahnhofstr. 6, A–4820, tel. 06132/3520)
Gmunden (Am Graben 2, A–4810, tel. 07612/4305 or 07612/338–1246)
Hallstatt (Seestr. 169, A–4830, tel. 06134/208)
Mondsee (Dr.-Muller-Str. 3, A–5310, tel. 06232/2270)
St. Gilgen (Mozartpl. 1, A–5340 tel. 06227/348)
St. Wolfgang (Markt 28, A–5360, tel. 06138/2239)

Arriving and Departing

By Plane The Lake District is closer to Salzburg than to Linz, but ground transportation is such that there is little preference. The **Salzburg** airport is about 53 km (33 mi) from Bad Ischl, heart of the Salzkammergut; the **Linz** airport (Hörsching) is about 75 km (47 mi). **Austrian Airlines** flies to both cities from Vienna; **Lufthansa** serves Linz from Frankfurt. A number of charter lines fly into Salzburg, including some from the United Kingdom.

By Car Driving is by far the easiest and most convenient way to reach the Lake District. From **Salzburg,** you can take Route 158 east to Fuschl, St. Gilgen, and Bad Ischl or the A–1 autobahn to Mondsee. Coming from **Vienna** or **Linz,** A–1 passes through the north part of the Salzkammergut; get off at the Steyrermühl exit or the Regau exit and head south on Route 144/145 to Gmunden, Bad Ischl, Bad Goisern, and Bad Aussee. From the Seewalchen exit, take Route 152 down the east side of the Attersee, instead of the far less scenic Route 151 down the west side.

By Train The geography of the area means that rail lines run mainly north–south. Trains run from Vöcklabruck to Seewalchen at the top end of the Attersee and from Attnang-Puchheim to Gmunden, Bad Ischl, Hallstatt, Bad Aussee, and beyond. Both starting points are on the main east–west line between Salzburg and Linz.

Getting Around

By Car For sheer flexibility—plus being able to stop when you want to admire the view—travel by car is the most satisfactory way to see the Salzkammergut. Roads are good and traffic is excessive only on weekends (although it can be slow on some narrow lakeside stretches).

By Train and Bus As long as the railroad goes where you want to, train travel is a possibility in the region. Service is fairly good, but you won't get off the beaten path. Where the trains don't go, the post office or railroad buses do, so if you allow enough time, you can cover virtually all the area by public transport.

Guided Tours

You can take day-long tours of the Salzkammergut from Salzburg. Full-day tours to Salzburg from Vienna pass through the Salzkammergut via Gmunden and the Traunsee, Bad Ischl, the Wolfgangsee, St. Gilgen, and Fuschlsee, but these are such appealing areas it seems a shame to see them only briefly from a bus window. Of the tours from Vienna, the one run by **Cityrama/Gray Line** (Börsegasse 1, A–1010 Vienna, tel. 0222/534130) is by far the cheapest.

Special-interest Tours At Bad Ischl you can arrange excursions to nearby glaciers or a tour of a salt mine, and the working mines in the Sandling mountains are also open to the public.

Exploring the Salzkammergut

With Bad Ischl as the starting point, two circuit tours cover most of this colorful part of Austria. One tour swings west (Wolfgangsee, Fuschlsee), then north (Mondsee, Attersee), and finally south (Traunsee) back to Bad Ischl. The second takes you south to the Hallstättersee, then to Bad Aussee and Altaussee, returning via the Pötschen mountain pass.

Highlights for First-time Visitors

Carved Gothic altar, St. Wolfgang (*see* Tour 1)
Dachstein ice caves (*see* Tour 2)
Double castle Schloss Ort in the Traunsee (*see* Tour 1)
Emperor Franz Josef's summer villa, Bad Ischl (*see* Tour 1)
Lake steamer Gisela on Traunsee (*see* Tour 1)
The White Horse Inn, St. Wolfgang (*see* Tour 1)

Tour 1: Bad Ischl, Wolfgangsee, and Beyond

Numbers in the margin correspond with points of interest on the Lake District/Salzkammergut map.

❶ The town of **Bad Ischl** grew up around the curative mineral springs that are still the raison d'être of the 19th-century classic yellow *Kurhaus* (spa) and the baths in the adjoining new buildings. But the arrival of the royal entourage from Vienna in the late 1800s really brought Bad Ischl to life. Take the short walk to the *Kaiservilla*, the colorful Imperial residence rather like a miniature Schönbrunn. Markus von Habsburg, great-grandson of Franz Josef II, still lives here, but you can tour parts of the building to see the suprisingly modest residential quarters and ornate reception rooms. *Kaiserpark, tel. 06132/ 3241. Admission to grounds: AS20, children AS15; combination tickets, including tour of villa: AS59 adults, AS28 children. Open May–mid-Oct., daily 9–noon and 1–5.*

Don't overlook the small but elegant "marble palace" built nearby for Empress Elisabeth; it now houses the Austrian photography museum. (The marriage of Franz Josef and Elisabeth was not a happy one. A number of houses in Bad Ischl bearing women's names are said to have been quietly given by the emperor to his various lady friends around town.) *Kaiserpark, tel. 06132/4422. Admission: AS15 adults, AS10 children, AS30 family. (You'll need a ticket to enter the park grounds.) Open Apr.–Oct., daily 9:30–5.*

Composers followed the aristocracy and the court to Bad Ischl. Bruckner, Brahms, Johann Strauss the younger, and Oscar Straus all spent summers here, but it was Franz Lehar, composer of *The Merry Widow*, who left the most lasting musical impression. The operetta festival in summer always includes one Lehar work. Lehar's villa is now a museum, open for guided tours. *Pfarrgasse 11, tel. 06132/6992. Admission: AS30 adults, AS15 children. Open Easter and May–Sept., daily 9– noon and 2–5; last tours at 11:30 and 4:30.*

❷ Heading west from Bad Ischl on Route 158, you can bear right on a country road to **St. Wolfgang** on the Wolfgangsee or contin-

The Lake District/Salzkammergut

UPPER AUSTRIA

STYRIA

SALZBURG

GERMANY

Traunsee

Traun

Attersee

Mondsee

Zellersee

Wallersee

Salzach

Traunsee

Altaussee *See*

Grundlsee

Hallstätter *See*

Königssee

Fuschlsee

Wolfgangsee

7 Gmunden

Almünster

Traunkirchen

Roith

145

Weyregg a. Attersee

Steinbach

152

153

Abtsdorf

151

Unterach

Pölmberg

154

151

Mondsee

6 Mondsee

Henndorf

Plainfeld

Plomberg

5 Fuschl

St. Gilgen 4

3 Schafberg

2 St. Wolfgang

158

Strobl

1 Bad Ischl

Bad Goisern

166

Gosau

160

Hallstatt 8

9 Obertraun

10 Bad Aussee

11 Altaussee

145

TO DACHSTEINEISHÖHLE

Pichl

Abtenau

Kuchl

159

Golling

162

Torren

Hallein

E55

150

Anif

Grödig

Berchtesgaden

305

20

Pidng

Bad Reichenhall

Freilassing

304

20

156

Obertrum

Burgheim

158

Salzburg

A1

Leobendorf

N

6 miles

9 km

ue on Route 158 to Strobl, where a smaller road to the right will take you there. Alternatively, you can leave your car at Strobl and take the lake steamer to St. Wolfgang, which is really the right way to approach this picturebook town. The view of St. Wolfgang, against the dramatic mountain backdrop, is one you'll see again and again on posters and postcards.

The tower of the pilgrimage church rises behind the five connected buildings of the wonderful **Weisses Rössl**, the inn made famous in a hit comedy of the 1890s and a later musical and film. The White Horse Inn's dining terraces are on stilts over the water, and fresh lake fish is served to the sound of zither music.

Aside from immersing yourself in the sheer romance of St. Wolfgang, you shouldn't miss seeing **Michael Pacher's great carved altar** (1481) in the 16th-century parish church, one of the finest examples of Gothic woodcarving to be found anywhere. The crowning of the Virgin is depicted in detail so exact that you can see the stitches in her clothing. Surrounding her are various saints, including the local patron, the hermit Saint Wolfgang. Since the 15th century, St. Wolfgang has been a place of pilgrimage. *Open May–Sept., daily 9–5; Oct.–Apr., daily 10–4.*

From May to October the cog-railway trip from St. Wolfgang to ❸ the 1,783-meter (about 5,800-ft.) peak of the **Schafberg** offers a great chance to survey the surrounding countryside from "the belvedere of the Salzkammergut Lakes." On a clear day, you can see the German mountains west of Salzburg. Allow at least a good half day for the outing, which costs AS168 for adults, half that for children. (tel. 06138/22320).

From St. Wolfgang, backtrack along the lake shore to Strobl and head west again on Route 158. At the top of the lake you ❹ will come to **St. Gilgen,** whose proximity to Salzburg makes it less appealing than St. Wolfgang. The town is pleasant enough, with a nice beach, but it has been rather overrun and overbuilt; society forgathers here at Salzburg Festival time. St. Gilgen has indirect musical ties: A Mozart fountain in the town square commemorates the fact that Mozart's mother was born here and his sister Nannerl later settled here.

❺ From St. Gilgen, take a detour on Route 158 to **Fuschl,** on the Fuschlsee, a gem of a small lake surrounded by a nature preserve. This area, too, has become a weekend playground for the Salzburgers, and it has produced many good places to eat and spend the night.

❻ Head north from St. Gilgen on Route 154 to **Mondsee,** a town rich in fine restaurants (*see* Dining, below). As you go up the west side of the lake, you'll pass Plomberg, where Karl Eschelböck's restaurant draws gourmets from all over Austria. In Mondsee there's the Weisses Kreuz, and a bit farther along Route 154 is Schlössl, home of La Farandole. Whichever your choice, you won't be disappointed—unless you've failed to reserve in advance.

First visit the **Mondseer Freilichtmuseum,** an outdoor museum that shows how people in the area lived 100 years or more ago. The *Rauchhaus* focuses on the smokehouse technology of preserving meats. *Tel. 06232/2270. Admission: AS25 adults, AS12 children. Open Apr.–May, Sat., Sun., holidays 9–6; June–mid-Oct., daily 8–6.*

Look, too, at the town square and visit the marvelously Baroque twin-tower abbey church; if it looks familiar, you may have seen it in *The Sound of Music.*

Proceed south from Mondsee via Route 151 south along the east shore of the lake. Continue north on Route 151 and do a circuit of the Attersee, the largest lake of the region and pleasantly quieter than the others. (If you prefer to skip the Attersee circuit, at Unterach bear right on Route 152 and drive around the bottom of the lake to Steinbach.)

Time Out   **Obendorfer.** This low-slung hotel on the Attersee, with its own beach, is ideal for a stop. It has a stunning view of the Höllen mountains across the lake and a good restaurant as well (closed in November, January, and February).

At Seewalchen at the top of the lake, head south on Route 152 to Steinbach. Turn east at Steinbach, following signs to Gmunden; the scenic route takes you over high mountain passes.

❼ Gmunden, at the top of the Traunsee, is an attractive town to wander in. It was an administrative center and the gateway city that sealed off the salt-producing areas beyond. Note the ornate, arcaded **town hall,** with ceramic carillon bells made from local clay.

The tree-lined Esplanade along the lake is reminiscent of past days of the idle aristocracy. You can easily walk to the **Strandbad,** the swimming area, from the center of town. The beaches are good, and you can sail, waterski, or windsurf.

Take time to look at, or visit, **Schloss Ort,** a double castle with a beautiful arcaded courtyard, whose two parts (one on land, one on Roman foundations in the lake) are connected by a wooden bridge. *Admission free. Open Apr.–Sept., daily 8 AM–dusk.*

From Gmunden, take a lake trip on *Gisela,* built in 1872, the oldest coal-fired steam side-wheeler running anywhere. It carried Emperor Franz Josef 100 years ago and is now restored. For departure times, check with **Traunschiffahrt Eder** (tel. 07612/5215 or 07612/66700). Boat lines crisscross and traverse the whole 11-km (7-mi) length of the lake.

From beyond the railroad station, take the 12-minute cable car ride to the top of **Grünberg.** From here you will have a superb view out over the Traunsee, with the Dachstein glacier forming the backdrop. In winter, the Grünberg area offers good skiing. *Freygasse 4, tel. 07612/49770. Fare: AS95 round-trip, AS65 up only; children AS63 round-trip, AS42 up only. May–Oct., daily 8:15–6; Dec., daily 9–4:30; Jan–Mar., daily 9–6. Closed Nov. and Apr.*

From Gmunden, Route 145 takes you first along the lake shore and then along the Traun river, back to Bad Ischl.

Tour 2: Hallstatt and Bad Aussee

From Bad Ischl, head south on Route 145 to Bad Goisern, which also has curative mineral springs, but never achieved the cachet of Bad Ischl. Just south of town, watch the signs for the turnoff
❽ to the exquisite little town of **Hallstatt.** Since the lake is

squeezed between two sharply rising mountain ranges, the road parallels the shore, with spectacular views.

The Hallstatt railroad station is on the opposite side of the lake; if you arrive by train, a boat (tel. 06124/294 or 06124/228) will take you across to the town, which clings precariously to the mountainside above the lake.

Salt mining in the area has been known for at least 2,800 years, and the Hallstatt mines are the oldest in the world. From 800 to 500 BC the town flourished, giving its name to an era of the early Iron Age. Take the cable car up and tour the mines above town; after a 10-minute walk, you enter the mines, either via stairs or a wooden chute the miners used. There you'll see a subterranean lake and ride on the mile-long underground train. *Cable car round-trip: AS80 adults, AS45 children; one way AS45 adults, AS30 children. Mine admission and tour: AS110 adults, AS55 children. Open May and mid-Sept.–Oct., daily 9:30–4:30.*

Most of the early relics of the Hallstatt era are in Vienna, but some are in the **Hallstätter Museum**. *Admission: AS30 adults, AS20 children. Open May–Sept., daily 10–6; Oct., daily 10–4; hours at other seasons from tourist office (tel. 06134/208).*

The market square, now a pedestrian area, is bordered with colorful 16th-century houses. The charnel house beside the parish church by the lake is a rather morbid but regularly visited spot. Because there was little space to bury the dead, the custom developed of digging up the bodies after 12 or 15 years, piling the bones in the sun, and painting the skulls: ivy and oak-leaf wreaths for the men, alpine flowers for the women, plus names, dates, and often the cause of death!

In Gasthof Hallberg (Seestr. 113, tel. 06134/286) there is a curious **war museum** containing Nazi gold, and propaganda materials that were to be air-dropped on Britain, discovered by the owner, Gerhard Zauner, on diving expeditions in nearby lakes.

9 From Hallstatt, take the scenic road around the bottom of the lake to **Obertraun**. From here, you can visit the Dachstein giant ice caves (follow signs to *"Dachsteineishöhle"*) via cable car, the *Dachsteinseilbahn*. The vast ice caverns, many hundreds of years old, contain ice stalactites and stalagmites and are filled with an eerie light. Guided tours run from May to mid-October. The cave entrance is at about 2,000 meters (6,500 ft), still well below the 3,000 meters (9,750 ft) of the Dachstein peak farther to the south. Be sure to wear warm, weatherproof clothing; inside the caves it's cold, and outside, the slopes can be swept by chill winds.

10 Continue along the road marked to **Bad Aussee**. You'll find yourself in company with the railroad and Traun river, but watch out for the precipitous 23-degree gradient at one point. In Bad Aussee the salt and mineral springs have been developed into a modern spa complex, yet the town retains much of its 15th- and 16th-century character, in the narrow streets and older buildings, particularly in the upper reaches. The 1827 marriage of Archduke Johann to the daughter of the local postmaster brought attention and a burst of new construction, including some lovely 19th-century villas. Bad Aussee is a good base for hiking in the surrounding countryside in summer and for excellent skiing in winter.

Time Out Those "on the cure" can undo all the good in a quick visit to
Kurhauskonditorei Lewandofsky, where the pastries—particularly the honeycakes—are irresistibly tempting, especially
when served in the summer garden with its overview of the central square, next to the Bad Aussee city park.

⑪ About 4 km (2.5 mi) north up a fairly steep road from Bad
Aussee, you'll find **Altaussee** tucked away at the end of a lake
cradled by the mountains that form it. The town is completely
unspoiled, perfect for those who simply want an Alpine idyll, to
do nothing, or to hike in the meadows, climb the slopes, or row
on the lake. Over the years the romantic setting has attracted a
number of artists and writers. Springtime, when the field flowers burst forth and the town holds its annual narcissus festival,
is perhaps the best time to visit.

Salt is still dug in the nearby Sandling mountains, and the
mines are open to visitors. Check with the tourist office or
phone 06152/71332 for details of guided tours. *Admission:
AS95 adults, AS50 children. Open mid-May–mid-Sept.,
Mon.–Sat. 10–4.*

The mines deep in the mountains have a more recent notoriety.
During World War II, the Nazi leaders stored stolen art in the
underground caverns above Altaussee. In their hurry to get
the job done, they overlooked a few details; one story has it that
a famous painting from Vienna, a Rubens or a Rembrandt, was
forgotten and spent the remaining war years well packed but
out in the open on the porch of a house near the entrance to the
mines. At the end of the war, Allied forces were directed to the
mines by the local populace, and once unsealed, the caverns released such a treasure as has probably never been (or ever again
will be) assembled in one place.

To get back to Bad Ischl, your best bet is to return to Bad
Aussee and then take Route 145 north. It's only 28 km (18 mi),
but a great deal of this is up and down, the highest point being
at 992 meters (3,200 ft) before you head down through the
Pötschen pass. Not surprisingly, the views are spectacular;
don't miss the lookout point at a hairpin turn at **Unter,** far above
the Hallstätter lake.

What to See and Do with Children

The salt mines of Hallstatt, the Nazis' treasure caves at Aussee, and the ice caves of Dachstein (*see* Tour 2).

The Mondseer Freilichtmuseum and boat rides on any of the
lakes (*see* Tour 1).

Off the Beaten Track

About 4½ km (3 mi) north of Ebensee on Route 145 you'll come
to **Traunkirchen;** stop for a look at the "fishermen's pulpit" in
the parish church. This 17th-century Baroque marvel, carved
from wood decorated with silver and gold, portrays the astonished fishermen of the Sea of Galilee pulling in their suddenly
full nets at Jesus's direction.

Shopping

Bad Ischl and Gmunden offer the best selection of general goods. You'll find souvenirs and handicrafts in most communities along the way. The **Gmunden Keramik** shop (Keramikstr. 24, tel. 07612/5441) sells the green-decorated white country ceramics for which the town is famous. The ware is also decorated with blue and with yellow.

Sports and Fitness

Bicycling Much of this tour is rather hilly for biking, but you'll find reasonably good cycling country around the lakes, particularly the Traunsee and Attersee. You can cycle the 14 km (nearly 9 mi) from Bad Ischl to St. Wolfgang on back roads. Bicycle rentals are available at the railroad station in St. Wolfgang (tel. 06138/22320) and at sports shops throughout the area; local tourist offices can head you to the right place.

Canoeing The lakes of the Salzkammergut are excellent for canoeing because most prohibit or limit power boats. Try kayaking on the Hallstätter See (for information, call 06135/8254) or white-water kayaking on the Traun river (contact **Intersport Steinkogler**, Salzburgerstr. 3, Bad Ischl, tel. 06132/3655).

Fishing This is superb fishing country for casting or trolling, but you'll need a license. Check in **Altaussee** and **Bad Aussee** with the local tourist offices; **Attersee:** Franz Zotter (Hauptstr. 16, tel. 07666/334); **Bad Ischl:** Ischler Waffen, Ferdinand Zeitler (Schröpferplatz 4, tel. 06132/3351 or 68–714); **Ebensee:** Sportgeschäft Steinkogler (Marktgasse 9, tel. 06133/53500), Gasthaus in der Kreh (Langbathsee 1, tel. 06133/8944); **Gmunden:** Forstverwaltung Traunstein (Klosterplatz 1, tel. 07612/4529), Höller-Eisen (Kammerhofgasse 6, tel. 07612/33000, Gasthof Steinmaurer (Traunsteinstr. 23, tel. 07612/4239); **Mondsee:** J. Engelharts Nachf. (Marktplazt 15, tel. 06232/2229), Drogerie Maritsch (Rainerstr. 1, tel. 06232/3436); **St. Wolfgang:** Fischerhaus Höplinger (Markt 79, tel. 06138/2241). A number of hotels in the Altaussee/Bad Aussee area have packages that combine a week's stay with the fishing license; for details and booking, contact **Steiermark-Graz-Information** (Herrengasse 16, A–8010 Graz, tel. 0316/835–2410); the main season runs from June through September.

Golf There are two golf courses in the area:

Bad Ischl. Salzkammergut Golfclub. *Tel. 06132/6340. 18 holes, par 71. Greens fees: AS250 on weekdays, AS350 weekends. Open Apr.–Nov.*

Hof bei Salzburg. Golf- und Jagdclub Schloss Fuschl. *Tel. 06229/2390. 9 holes. Greens fees: AS200 weekdays, AS250 weekends. Open Apr.–Oct.*

Hiking Local tourist offices will have details and route maps of the many hiking paths throughout this region. Bad Ischl alone has more than 100 km (62½ mi) of trails. There are long-distance hiking trails in the Attersee area; one 35-km (22-mi) course takes about 7½ hours to complete. The mountains in the Hallstatt and Altaussee/BadAussee areas are good for mountain hiking; Bad Aussee has about 150 km (93 mi) of trails.

Rafting There's white-water rafting in the Traun river at Bad Ischl (check **Intersport Steinkogler,** *see* Canoeing, above) and over the 14-km (nearly 9-mi) stretch between Hallstätter See and Bad Ischl and from Bad Aussee to Obertraun. Contact **Sport Zopf** (Hauptstr. 327, Bad Goisern, tel. 06135/8254).

Skiing You're on the edge of good ski country here, with good downhill slopes in the Altaussee/Bad Aussee region, in the mountains south of Bad Ischl, and on the slopes bordering the lakes, particularly around St. Gilgen and Hallstatt.

Tennis This is great tennis country, with courts in almost every town. In Bad Ischl, the **Tennisclub Bad Ischl** has indoor and outdoor courts, ball-throwing machines, and equipment rental (tel. 06132/3458 or 06132/4432.)

Water Sports and Swimming There's every kind of water sport in this region, from windsurfing to sailing yachts. You can water ski at Strobl and St. Wolfgang on the Wolfgangsee, and at most towns on the Attersee and Traunsee. At Ebensee, check with **Diving School Gigl** (Strandbadstr. 12, tel. 06133/77155), which also offers skin diving; in Gmunden, contact **Wasserskischule** (tel. 07612/3602). A "round" will cost you about AS100.

Swimming is excellent in the clear, cool waters of the lakes. On the Wolfgangsee, Strobl has the best beach, but most of the small towns have public beaches safe enough for small children.

Dining and Lodging

In many of the towns of the Salzkammergut, you'll find country inns that have dining rooms but few, if any, separate restaurants. Prices for meals include taxes and a service charge, but not the customary small additional tip.

Highly recommended restaurants are indicated by a star ★.

Category	Cost*
Very Expensive	over AS500
Expensive	AS300–AS500
Moderate	AS200–AS300
Inexpensive	under AS200

per person for a typical three-course meal, with a glass of house wine

The accommodations will range from luxurious lakeside resorts to small country inns or even guest houses without private baths. In peak summer season St. Wolfgang is packed, and you may find slightly less crowding and the same magnificent settings 3 km (2 mi) up the lake at Ried or back at Strobl. Room rates include taxes and service and almost always breakfast, except in the most expensive hotels, but it is wise to ask. It is customary to leave a small (AS20) additional tip for the chambermaid.

Highly recommended lodgings are indicated by a star ★ .

Category	Cost*
Very Expensive	over AS1,500
Expensive	AS1,000–AS1,500
Moderate	AS700–AS1,000
Inexpensive	under AS700

All prices are for a standard double room for two, including local taxes (usually 10%) and service (15%).

Altaussee

Dining and Lodging
★

Seevilla. This elegant, multistory, rustic-style house sits amid great trees directly on the lake. The balconied rooms upstairs, reached by a stone staircase, are spacious and furnished in modern country style; baths are elegantly modern. *Fischerndorf 60, A–8992, tel. 06152/71302. 30 rooms. Facilities: restaurant (closed Thurs. in winter), bar, indoor pool, sauna, solarium, garage. AE, DC. Closed Apr. Expensive.*

Zum Loser. The rooms are simple but inviting in this attractive hostelry. The restaurant specializing in fish, game, and pork, offers excellent local dishes. *Fischerndorf 80, A–8992, tel. 06152/71373. 8 rooms. Facilities: restaurant (reservations advised). AE, DC, MC, V. Closed Oct.–mid-Dec., late Jan., mid-Mar.–mid-Apr. Moderate.*

Bad Aussee

Dining and Lodging
★

Alpenhof. This modern establishment in rustic Alpine style with an attractive garden, central to activities, offers modest but spacious and cheerful rooms, some large enough to be suites. *Altausseer Str. 337, A–8990, tel. 06152/2777. 10 rooms. MC. Expensive.*

★ **Erzherzog Johann.** A golden yellow facade identifies this traditional house, which is in the center of town but quiet. A direct passageway connects the hotel to a spa next door, with a swimming pool and cure facilities. The hotel rooms are modern and immaculate in their country decor. The restaurant on the first floor serves the best creative cooking in the area in an elegant ambience that is intimate nevertheless. *Kurhausplatz 62, A–8990, tel. 06152/2507. 62 rooms. Facilities: restaurant, bar, indoor pool, sauna, solarium, fitness room, spa, garage. MC. Expensive.*

★ **Kristina.** Set in a lovely wooded park, this hotel is decorated in the style of a hunting lodge, with antlers and trophies; its rooms are appropriately outfitted in older furniture. *Altausser Str. 54, A–8990, tel. 06152/2017. 12 rooms. Facilities: restaurant for guests only. AE, DC, MC, V. Closed mid-Nov.–mid-Dec. Moderate.*

Wasnerin. This Styrian-style chalet above town offers magnificent views of the Dachstein peak. The rooms are simple but adequate, and the management is especially friendly. *Sommersbergseestr. 19, A–8990, tel. 06152/2108. 30 rooms. Facilities: limited restaurant for guests, tennis. No credit cards. Moderate.*

Bad Ischl

Dining
★ **Café Zauner.** Unless you've been to Zauner, you haven't been to Bad Ischl. The desserts—particularly the house creation, *Zaunerstollen*, a chocolate-covered confection of sugar, hazelnuts, and nougat—have made this one of Austria's best-known pastry shops. The other possibilities include lunch or early dinner in the courtyard garden. *Pfarrgasse 7, tel. 06132/3522. Reservations suggested. Jacket and tie advised. No credit cards. Closed Tues. in winter. Expensive.*

★ **Weinhaus Attwenger.** This restaurant is set under massive trees overlooking the river. In summer the garden alone is worth a visit; the cheery service and the food just add more. Ask for seasonal recommendations, but the fish and game dishes are particularly good. In the cozy wood-paneled rooms inside, the environment is rustic. *Leharkai 12, tel. 06132/3327. Reservations advised. Dress: informal but neat. No credit cards. Closed Sun. eve., Mon., mid-Jan.–early Mar. Expensive.*

Goldener Ochs. This typical country *Gasthof* offers the standards—Wiener schnitzel, boiled beef, roast pork—in good quality and quantity in attractive rustic surroundings. *Grazer Str. 4, tel. 06132/35290. Reservations not required. Dress: informal but neat. No credit cards. Moderate.*

Lodging
Kurhotel. This fairly new and, for Bad Ischl, high-rise hotel, within a two-minute walk of the railroad station, serves as a training institute for the regional hotel school, so you're sure to get good, enthusiastic service. The rooms are modern in dark browns and beige, and many have magnificent views of the mountains around the city. An underground passageway leads to the nearby mineral baths; use of the pool and sauna is free. The hotel restaurant is good, specializing in regional dishes and game in season. *Vogelhuberstr. 10, A–4820, tel. 06132/4271. 115 rooms. Facilities: restaurant (jacket and tie advised), bar, pool, sauna, garage. AE, DC, MC, V. Expensive.*

★ **Zum Goldenen Schiff.** This traditional older house, overlooking the river, offers typical country comfort. Rooms with a balcony on the river side are preferred, but all are charming, with lots of natural wood in evidence. The restaurant specializes in fish. *Adelbert-Stifter-Kai 3, A–4820, tel. 06132/4241. 56 rooms. Facilities: restaurant (jacket and tie advised), bar. AE, DC, MC, V. Moderate.*

Fuschl

Dining
★ **Brunnwirt.** You'll have to knock to be admitted, but once inside, you'll find elegantly set tables in this atmospheric 15th-century house. Frau Brandstätter presides over a kitchen that turns out good-size portions of excellent Austrian and regional dishes. You might be offered game or roast lamb, but they always have a light touch. Fish fresh from the lake is a regular specialty. *Tel. 06226/236. Reservations essential. Jacket and tie required. AE, DC, MC, V. Closed Sun. and last three weeks of Jan. Very Expensive.*

Dining and Lodging
★ **Hotel Schloss Fuschl.** This noble hotel up the lake, built in 1450, was once the hunting castle of the prince-bishops of Salzburg. Now tastefully adapted and modernized, the blockhouse-style main building enjoys a setting about as perfect as you could imagine. Fireplaces and timbered ceilings abound amid the stonework. The hotel's Imperial restaurant overlooking the

lake is one of Austria's best. Tables are elegantly set with Wedgwood china. You can expect such regional specialties as rack of venison and lake fish. It's a member of Leading Hotels of the World. *A–5322 Hof bei Salzburg, tel. 06229/22530. 84 rooms. Facilities: restaurant (reservations required, jacket and tie required), bar, indoor and outdoor pools, sauna, solarium, fitness room, tennis, golf, bowling, garage. AE, DC, MC, V. Very Expensive.*

Parkhotel Waldhof. This alpine chalet, with bright red geraniums on the balconies, seems perfect in its setting against the lake and mountains. You'll feel comfortable in the paneled public rooms with an open fireplace; the bedrooms are individually furnished. The restaurant emphasizes local duck and game dishes and variations with fish from the lake. *See promenade, A–5330, tel. 06226/264. 70 rooms. Facilities: restaurant (reservations advised, jacket and tie advised), bar, indoor pool, shooting gallery, sauna, fitness room, solarium, tennis, sailing, windsurfing, lake swimming. No credit cards. Closed mid-Jan.–Mar. Expensive.*

Gmunden

Dining and Lodging
★

Parkhotel am See. This traditional house, separated from the lake by the promenade, is about a five-minute walk from the town center. Although the house has had recent renovations, antique furnishings continue to set the scene. There's a private pier for swimming. *Schiffslände 17, A–4810, tel. 07612/4230. 50 rooms. Facilities: restaurant, bar, swimming pier, tennis, solarium, garage. MC, V. Closed Oct.–mid-May. Expensive.*

Schlosshotel Freisitz Roith. On a hill overlooking the lake, this architectural amusement, a mixed-up Victorian wonder, now houses a modern hotel, but it has kept many of the old details, such as the arched ceilings. *Traunsteinstr. 87, A–4810, tel. 07612/4905. 26 rooms. Facilities: restaurant, bar, sauna, fitness room, garage. AE, DC, MC, V. Closed Jan.–Feb. Expensive.*

Hallstatt

Dining and Lodging
★

Grüner Baum. This friendly house, directly on the lake, in the typical yellow with white trim, dates from 1760. The simple but comfortable rooms overlook the lake, yet you're right in the center of town. The restaurant is known for its fish specialties. *Markplatz 104, A–4830, tel. 06134/263. 34 rooms. Facilities: restaurant, bar, lake swimming. No credit cards. Moderate.*

Mondsee

Dining
★

Eschlböck. Karl Eschlböck, who apprenticed at Troisgros in France, is ranked among Austria's top chefs. He has developed his 300-year-old alpine chalet overlooking the lake south of Mondsee into a point of pilgrimage for gourmets; you can even spend the night if you wish. What's offered in the individual dining rooms is what's fresh in the market that day; it could be anything from calf's tongue in mustard sauce to terrine of lake fish. The long menu offers many variations on classical Austrian dishes. *Plomberg-Mondsee, tel. 06232/3572. Reservations required. Jacket and tie advised. AE, V. Sept.–Apr., closed Mon. Very Expensive.*

★ **La Farandole.** Just above Mondsee on Route 154, you'll find an intimate restaurant offering creative French-Swiss-Austrian cuisine. Specialties change with the season, but you may be offered a delicate cream of potato soup or crisp roast duck with panfried potatoes. The applecake dessert is superb. Wines come from France and Austria. The bistro menu at noon is unusually reasonable. *Schlössl 150/Tiefgraben, tel. 06232/3475. Reservations required. Jacket and tie advised. Sept.–June, closed Sun. and Mon. Very Expensive.*

★ **Weisses Kreuz.** Another outstanding restaurant in Mondsee is combined with a comfortable hotel in the center of town. In elegant white dining rooms, you'll select from the light variations on classical Austrian cuisine; they could range from fresh perch in mushroom sauce to baby lamb with rosemary. Desserts, such as steamed figs in cassis, are especially imaginative. Wines are mainly from the Austrian Wachau, but French and Italian vintages are available as well. Ask for recommendations. *Herzog-Odilo-Str. 13, tel. 06232/2254. Reservations advised. Jacket and tie advised. AE. Sept.–July, closed Wed. Very Expensive.*

St. Gilgen

Dining **Timbale.** Don't look for haute cuisine in St. Gilgen, but if you'd like something a bit different from the usual rustic atmosphere, this tiny restaurant may offer a pleasant surprise. Ask about the specials not shown on the menu. You might find roast lamb or grilled shrimp. *Salzburger Str. 2, tel. 06227/7587. Reservations advised. Jacket and tie suggested. No credit cards. Nov.–May, closed Thurs. Expensive.*

Lodging **Parkhotel Billroth.** This elegant villa, in turn-of-the-century style, is set in a huge park directly on the lake. The house is pleasantly worn at the edges, yet spaciously arranged and luxuriously appointed. The sun terraces are particularly inviting. *A–5340, tel. 06227/217. 44 rooms. Facilities: restaurant, private beach. AE, V. Closed Oct.–May. Expensive.*

Zur Post. This house, one of the most attractive in town, dates to 1415. The rooms now are comfortable and complete with modern baths. The restaurant, with a new chef, emphasizes regional fare; try the cream of garlic soup or the boiled beef. *Mozartplatz 8, A–5340, tel. 06227/239. 26 rooms. Facilities: restaurant (jacket and tie advised, closed Tues.). No credit cards. Closed Oct.–Apr. Moderate.*

St. Wolfgang

Dining and **Im Weissen Rössl.** The White Horse Inn is really the *only* place
Lodging to stay in St. Wolfgang. Not that there aren't other excellent
★ *Gasthäuser* in town, but the golden yellow house that has been featured in films and theater over the years has kept its reputation for outstanding accommodations and service. Despite the busloads that come "to have a look," the hotel maintains a personal charm toward its regular guests. As you'd expect, the rooms are comfortable country-rustic; the ones on the lake side have antique furnishings and canopy beds. The restaurant overlooking the lake is excellent; fish, of course, is in order. *A–5360, tel. 06138/23060. 68 rooms. Facilities: restaurant (reservations advised, jacket and tie advised), bar, indoor pool, sau-*

na, sailing, windsurfing, tennis. AE, DC, MC, V. Closed mid-Nov.–mid-Dec. Expensive.

The Arts and Nightlife

The Arts

Music   The main musical events of the year in this area are the July and August operetta weeks in **Bad Ischl.** Performances of at least two operettas (*The Merry Widow* is a standard favorite) take place at 8 in the Kurhaus (tel. 06132/3766), where tickets are sold.

The area is full of spontaneous musical events during the summer. **Strobl** holds a Day of Popular Music and Tradition in early July—"popular" meaning brass band, and "tradition" being local costume. **St. Wolfgang** arranges concerts every Monday from June to September, band concerts every Wednesday and Saturday at 8:30. Ask at the tourist offices in the individual towns to find out what is going on; the folk events are usually well publicized with posters.

Nightlife

Bars and Lounges   You're in a quiet region here, so nighttime activity tends more toward locally organized folk-music evenings than bar-hopping. Most of the large hotels have bars, and frequently one of them will be a local gathering spot.

7 Salzburg

Introduction

*by Delia
Meth-Cohn*

*A freelance
journalist based in
Vienna, Delia
Meth-Cohn writes
about Austria and
Eastern Europe.*

Salzburg has all the attributes of a capital city—grandeur, culture, and a fascinating history—in the setting of a small town in the mountains. The city is majestically beautiful, arranged around the banks of the river Salzach, squeezed between two cliff outcrops, and surrounded by alpine peaks. The only real problem with visiting the place is that the whole world seems to be here, too.

Although summer is the best time to visit when you want to find everything open or if you're headed for the Salzburg Festival (July–August), the city is packed with tourists then, and hotel prices are high. If this bothers you, go out of high season; there's much to offer musically year-round, and the city has its own particular charms in every season.

Finding your way around Salzburg is no problem. The old center is very small and bursting with historic sights—from the remnants of the Roman city, Juvavum, to the churches, palaces, and squares constructed during Salzburg's thousand years under the powerful prince-archbishops. Towering over the city is the medieval fortress, symbol of the power politics and religion that ruled the town. The other element that has shaped Salzburg is music, and there is music everywhere: in the churches, castles, palaces, and concert halls. The bicentennial of Mozart's death brought a surfeit of activities in 1991—and encouraged some needed attention to tourist sites.

Essential Information

Important Addresses and Numbers

Tourist Information The **Salzburg City Tourist Office** (Auerspergstr. 7, A–5024 Salzburg, tel. 0662/889870), handles written and telephone requests for information. You can get maps, brochures, and information in person from **Information Mozartplatz** in the center of the old city (Mozartplatz 5, tel. 0662/847568, open daily 9–9) and from the **Railway Station** (Platform 10, tel. 0662/71712, open daily 8:30–8).

All the major highways into town have their own well-marked information centers: **Salzburg-Mitte** (Münchner Bundesstr. 1, tel. 0662/32228), at the AGIP service station, is open daily 9–7; **Salzburg-Süd** (Alpenstr. 67, tel. 0662/20966) is open daily 9–6; **Salzburg-West-Airport** (Innsbrucker Bundesstr. 95, tel. 0662/852451), at the BP service station, is open April to November, daily 9–9; **Salzburg-Nord** (Autobahn, Kasern service facility, tel. 0662/663220) is open April to November, daily 9–7.

Consulates The United States consular office (Giselakai 51, tel. 0662/28601) is open weekdays 9–11 and 2–4; that of the United Kingdom (Alter Markt 4, tel. 0662/848133) is open weekdays 9–noon.

Emergencies The emergency numbers are 133 for the **police**, 144 for an **ambulance**, 122 for the **fire department**. The main hospital is **St. Johanns Spital** (Müllner Hauptstr. 48, tel. 0662/31581), just past the Augustiner monastery heading out of town. If you need a doctor or dentist, call the **Ärtztekammer fur Salzburg** (Schrannengasse 2, tel. 0662/71327); for emergency service on weekends and holidays, call the **Ärtzenotdienst-Zentrale** (Paris Lodron Str. 8A, tel. 0662/141).

English-language Bookstores **American Discount** (Alter Markt 1, tel. 0662/843–8932), the only English-language bookstore in Salzburg, concentrates on popular paperbacks and magazines. You can, however, find some books in English in most good bookstores. **Hintermeyer** (Imbergstr. 23, tel. 0662/757541), across the footbridge from Mozartplatz, sells discount paperbacks in English.

Pharmacies In general, pharmacies are open weekdays 8 AM–12:30 PM and 2:30–6, Saturday 8–noon. When they're closed, the name and location of a pharmacy that's open are posted on the door.

Travel Agencies **American Express** (tel. 0662/842501) is next to the tourist office in Mozartplatz. **Thomas Cook** can be found under the name **Wagons-Lits** (Münzgasse 1, tel. 0662/842755) in the old city.

Arriving and Departing

By Plane **Salzburg Airport** (Innsbrucker Bundesstr. 96, tel. 0662/851223; for flight information, tel. 0662/852091), 4 km (2½ mi) west of the city center, is Austria's second largest international airport. There are direct flights from London and other European cities, but not from the United States. Americans can fly to Munich and take the 90-minute train ride to Salzburg.

Taxis are the easiest way to get downtown; the ride costs around AS120 and takes about 20 minutes. The No. 77 city bus, which goes by the airport every 15 minutes, takes you to the train station (about 20 minutes), where you change to the No. 1, 5, 6, 51, or 55 for the city center. The bus stop is a few minutes' walk from the terminal (turn right out of the airport, follow the small road up to the highway, and turn right past the BP gas station). Alternatively, you can take the No. 77 four stops to Aiglhof (look for a Mobil gas station on the corner), cross the road, and take the No. 29 (every 10–15 minutes) to the center of town.

By Car The fastest routes to Salzburg are the autobahns. From Vienna, take A–1; from Munich, A–8 (in Germany it's also E–11); from Italy, A–10. The only advantage to having a car in Salzburg is that you can get out of the city for short excursions or for cheaper accommodations. The old city is a pedestrian zone (except for taxis), and the rest of the city, with its narrow, one-way streets, is a driver's nightmare. A park/ride system covering the major freeway exits is being developed, and there are several underground garages throughout the city.

By Train You can get to Salzburg by rail from most European cities, arriving at **Salzburg Hauptbahnhof** (the main station, Südtirolerplatz, tel. 0662/71541), a 20-minute walk from the center of town in the direction of Mirabellplatz. A taxi should take about 10 minutes and cost AS75. Train information is available by phone (tel. 0662/1717); don't be put off by the recorded message in German—eventually, you will be put through to a real person who should be able to speak English. You can buy tickets at any travel agency or at the station. The bus station and the local railroad station are across the street.

By Bus **American Express** (Kärntnerstr. 21–23, 1010 Vienna, tel. 0222/514400) and **Vienna Sightseeing Tours** (Stelzhammergasse 4/11, 1030 Vienna, tel. 0222/712–4683) run one-day bus trips to Salzburg from Vienna, which include a tour of the city and lunch, for AS1,500. **Cityrama/Gray Line** (Börsegasse 1, 1010 Vienna, tel. 0222/534130) offers a similar tour, without lunch, that is considerably cheaper.

Getting Around

The old city, composed of several interconnecting squares and narrow streets, is best seen on foot. An excellent bus service covers the rest of the city. A tourist map (available free from tourist offices in Mozartplatz and the train station) shows all bus routes but is vague on stops; if you use the map in conjunction with the public transport network map (also free), you should have no problem getting around.

By Bus Single tickets bought from the driver cost AS18. Special multiple-use tickets, available at tobacconists (Tabaktrafik), ticket offices, and tourist offices, are usually much cheaper. You can buy five single tickets for AS12 each (not available at tourist offices); five transferable 24-hour tickets at AS23 each; a nontransferable 24-hour ticket for AS48 that's good on buses, the funicular railway to the castle, the lift to the Mönchsberg, and the tramway to Bergheim; and a 72-hour ticket for AS96. These last two tickets are worthwhile only if you use the extras. Note that the small city-center buses do not take tickets—you put AS7 in the machine as you enter.

By Taxi There are taxi stands all over the city; for a radio cab, call 0662/8111. Limousines can be hired for AS600 per hour from Salzburg Panorama Tours (tel. 0662/74029).

By Horse-drawn Carriage *Fiakers*, carrying up to four people, will show you around the old city for AS320 for 20 minutes and AS620 for 50 minutes. They are stationed on the Residenzplatz.

By Bicycle Salzburg is fast developing a network of bike paths as part of its effort to get cars out of the city. From April to November, bikes can be rented at the **Railway Station** (Desk 3, tel. 0662/7154-1337) for AS90 per day (AS45 if you have a train ticket for that day). You can rent a bike year-round, by the day (AS80) or the week (AS400) from **Veloclub** (Franz Josef Str. 15, tel. 0662/882788), where mountain bikes are also available. You can also rent bikes from **Walter Egger** (Willibald-Hauthaler-Str. 4, tel. 0662/31682). It's best to call and reserve in advance; you will need to leave your passport or a deposit.

Opening and Closing Times

Banks are open weekdays 8–noon and 2–4:30. You can change money at the railway station 7 AM–10 PM every day and at the Mozartplatz tourist information office on summer weekends, noon–4 on Saturday, 10–4:30 on Sunday.

Guided Tours

Because the old city is largely a pedestrian zone, bus tours do little more than take you past the major sights. You would do better seeing the city on foot unless your time is really short.

Orientation **Salzburg Sightseeing Tours** (Am Mirabellplatz 2, tel. 0662/881615) conducts 1- and 2-hour city tours. The desk clerks at most hotels will book for you and arrange hotel pickup. Depending on the number of people, the tour will be in either a bus or a minibus; if it's the former, a short walking tour is included, since large buses can't enter the old city. Both tours briefly cover the major sights in Salzburg, including Mozart's house, the Festival Houses, the major squares, the churches; the longer tour also goes out to the castles at Hellbrunn and Leopoldskron. Tours leave daily at 9:30 and 11 AM and at 2 PM and cost AS180.

Special-interest The Sound of Music tour has been a staple of visits to Salzburg for the past 20 years and is still a special experience. All tour operators conduct one, but the most personal (corny but nice) is that run by **Bob's Special Tours** (Dreifaltigkeitsgasse 3, tel. 0662/72484 or 06246/3377). The four-hour minibus tour (AS250) begins with the major city sights, takes in outlying Leopoldskron and the Nonnberg convent, and explores the surrounding mountains, accompanied by music from the film. The twice-daily tour includes a stop at a lead-crystal workshop and water-slide rides in summer.

Bob's Special Tours also runs a four-hour minibus tour (AS250) into the Bavarian Mountains for a view of Hitler's Eagle's Nest, a one-hour stop in Berchtesgaden, and a picnic in Untersberg Nature Park. It begins at 9 AM and also at 2 PM in summer.

Personal Guides The **Salzburg City Tourist Office** (Auerspergstr. 7, tel. 0662/889870) will arrange personal tours of 2–3 hours in English for individuals and groups of up to 30 people at a cost per tour of AS1,320, not including entry fees. A special Mozart Walk tour covers his birthplace, the palaces where he played, and the Magic Flute Cottage in the Mozarteum.

Walking The tourist office's general booklet "Salzburg—A City that Keeps Its Looks" describes a self-guided one-day walking tour that's marked out on a map.

Exploring Salzburg

The old city, where most of the major sights are concentrated, is a very compact area between the jutting outcrop of the Mönchsberg and the Salzach river. The cathedral and interconnecting squares surrounding it form what used to be the religious center, around which the major churches and the old archbishops' residence are arranged. The rest of the old city belonged to the wealthy burghers: the Getreidegasse, the Alter Markt (Old Market), the town hall, and the tall, plain burgher houses (like Mozart's birthplace). The Mönchsberg cliffs emerge unexpectedly behind the old city, crowned to the east by the Hohensalzburg Fortress. Across the river, in the small area between the cliffs of the Kapuzinerberg and the riverbank, is Steingasse, a narrow medieval street where the working people lived. Northwest of the Kapuzinerberg lies Mirabell Palace and its gardens, now an integral part of the city, but formerly a country estate on the outskirts of Salzburg.

Tour 1 will cover the architectural and cultural riches of the old city. Tour 2 will start at the fortress and then cross the river to explore the other bank. Ideally you should take one day for each tour; if you have only one day, you can get a good overview of the city by combining the tours, but you will have very little time to spend in any one place. An alternative, if you enjoy ex-

ploring churches and castles, is to stop Tour 1 after the first
Time Out and go directly up to the fortress, either on foot or by
returning through the cemetery to the funicular railway. You
can also pick and choose among sights without getting too far
away from your next one.

Tour 3 is a selection of short excursions from Salzburg.

Highlights for First-time Visitors

Dom (Cathedral) (*see* Tour 1)

Fortress Hohensalzburg (*see* Tour 2)

Franciscan Church (*see* Tour 1)

Hellbrunn (*see* Tour 3)

Mirabell Palace and Gardens (*see* Tour 2)

Mozart's birthplace (*see* Tour 1)

St. Peter's Cemetery and Catacombs (*see* Tour 1)

St. Peter's Church (*see* Tour 1)

St. Sebastian's Cemetery (*see* Tour 2)

Steingasse (*see* Tour 2)

Tour 1: The Old City

*Numbers in the margin correspond with points of interest on
the Salzburg map.*

❶ The tour begins at **Mozartplatz;** here you will find the main
tourist information office, where you can get a free city map.
The statue of Mozart, erected in 1842, was the first recognition
the great composer received from his birth-town since his
death as a pauper in Vienna in 1791. As you will notice, the Mozart memorial industry has grown considerably since then.
While the statue's pedestal was being constructed, a mosaic
with the words "Here Dwells Happiness—May Nothing Evil
Enter" was uncovered, from the time when Salzburg was the
Roman city of Juvavum.

Walk past the Glockenspiel café into the next square,
Residenzplatz, the heart of the Baroque city laid out around
1600 by Archbishop Wolf Dietrich. An admirer of the Italian
Renaissance, Wolf Dietrich hired an Italian architect, Sca-
mozzi, who fervently believed that the perfect city required
five squares. A cemetery and 55 old houses were demolished to
make way for them, giving the old city its characteristic spacious feel. On the left is the famous carillon tower, the
❷ **Glockenspiel,** perched on top of the **"Neubau,"** Wolf Dietrich's
government palace and his first attempt at the Baroque. The
carillon was a later addition, brought from the Netherlands in
1688 and finally put in working order in 1702. The 35 bells play
classical tunes at 7 AM, 11 AM, and 6 PM, with a charming lack of
concern for musical accuracy. From Easter to October, they
are immediately followed by a resounding retort from the 200-
pipe "bull" organ housed in the fortress. Details of the music
are listed on a notice board across the square on the corner of
❸ the **Residenz** building.

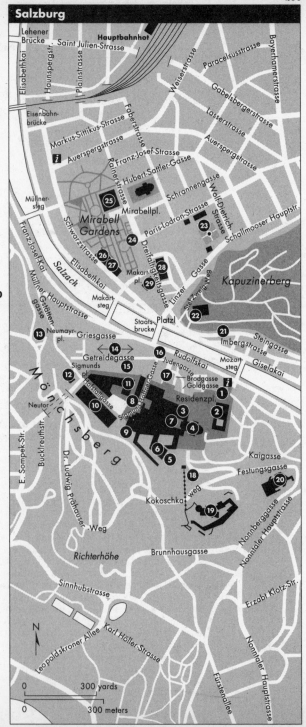

Salzburg

The Residenz was built between 1600 and 1619 as the home of
the prince-archbishops. Until the year 987, the prince-arch-
bishop had also served as abbot of St. Peter's monastery, but as
successive prelates assumed more secular roles, they developed grander living styles. The Residenz now houses an excellent small art museum, the **Residenzgalerie,** which is strong on
17th-century Dutch and Flemish art (Rembrandt, Brouwer,
Rubens) and paintings of Salzburg. The Rittersaal (Knight's
Hall), often used for concerts, can be seen with the rest of the
state rooms on a guided tour. *Residenzplatz 1, tel. 0662/8042–
2690. Admission: AS30 adults, AS20 senior citizens. Guided
tours: July and Aug., every 20 minutes daily 10–4:40; Sept.–
June, weekdays 10, 11, 2, and 3, weekends and holidays 10, 11,
and 12. Art museum admission: AS35 adults, AS20 senior citizens. Combined tickets: AS40 adults. Open Mar.–Jan., daily
10–5.*

From the Residenzplatz, walk through the arches into
Domplatz. During the summer festival, this is the stage for the
annual production of Hugo von Hofmannsthal's *Jedermann*
❹ (Everyman). There has been a **Dom** (cathedral) in this spot
since the 8th century, but the present structure stems from the
17th. Archbishop Wolf Dietrich took advantage of (some say he
caused) the old Romanesque-Gothic cathedral's destruction by
fire in 1598 to demolish the remains and make plans for a huge
new building facing onto the Residenzplatz. But the townspeo-
ple revolted against his excesses and in 1612 imprisoned him in
the fortress. His successor, Markus Sitticus, and the new court
architect, Santino Solari, built the Renaissance-style cathedral, which was consecrated with great ceremony in 1628. Four
statues at the front of the cathedral depict the two founders of
the church in Salzburg, Saint Rupert and Saint Virgil, at the
ends and the two founders of the church universal, Saint Peter
and Saint Paul, in the middle. Above these statues are the four
evangelists, then Moses and Elijah, crowned finally by Christ.
The simple gray and white interior of the church, a peaceful
counterpoint to the usual Baroque splendor, dates from a later
renovation. Mozart was christened in the 13th-century font inside the cathedral, where he was organist in 1779–81. Some of
his compositions, such as the Coronation Mass, were written
for the cathedral, and many were performed there for the first
time. Don't miss the three bronze doors, built in 1957–58, that
symbolize the three virtues: faith, hope and charity. The
Dommuseum, beside the main doors, displays the cathedral's
treasures, along with an odd collection of "arts and wonders"
from the 17th century. *Tel. 0662/844189 or 0662/842591–125.
Admission: AS25 adults, AS15 senior citizens, AS5 children.
Open mid-May–mid-Oct., daily 10–5.*

Walk into the Kapitelplatz through the arches across the
square and go through two wrought-iron gateways into the
❺ eerie but intimate **St. Peter's Cemetery.** Just before you reach
the fountain in the center, look to your right: Here lies Harry J.
Collins, the only American to be buried in St. Peter's. He was
in charge of the liberation of Salzburg in 1945 and subsequently
married an Austrian woman who is buried with him. In crypt
XXXI is the grave of Santino Solari, architect of the cathedral;
in XXXIX that of Sigmund Haffner, for whom Mozart's
Haffner serenade is named. The final communal crypt contains
the body of Mozart's sister, Nannerl, and the torso of Joseph
Haydn's brother, Michael (his head is inside an urn in St. Pe-

ter's church). This grave leads to the **Catacombs** built into the cliffs; two tiny chapels are hewn out of the rock, dating from the 3rd century when Christianized Romans held secret Masses here. *Tel. 0662/844–5780. Admission: AS10 adults, AS7 senior citizens and children. Guided tours: May–Sept., hourly 10–5; Oct.–Apr., 11, noon, 1:30, 2:30, and 3:30. Check times on noticeboard.*

⑥ St. Peter's Abbey is the most luxurious church in Salzburg. This is the final burial place of Saint Rupert, who founded a monastery here in 696 and so created the new bishopric and city of Salzburg on the ruins of Roman Juvavum. The porch has beautiful Romanesque vaulted arches from the original structure built in the 12th century, but the interior was decorated in the characteristically voluptuous late-Baroque style when additions were made in the 1770s.

⑦ As you leave the church, look up to your right: Rising above the monastery buildings is the thin Gothic spire of the **Franciscan Church.** Leave the courtyard in this direction, cross the road, and enter the church by the side entrance, which will bring you directly into the semicircular Gothic apse crowned by an ornate red marble and gilt altar designed by Austria's most famous architect of the Baroque, Fischer von Erlach.

⑧ Go down the aisle and leave the church by the front entrance, which opens on Sigmund-Haffner Gasse. Opposite is the back entrance to the **Rupertinum,** Salzburg's museum of 20th-century art, with permanent and changing shows. *Tel. 0662/804– 22336. Admission: AS35 adults, AS20 senior citizens. Open Tues. 10–5, Wed. 10–9, Thurs.–Sun. 10–5.*

Time Out You don't have to visit the gallery to eat in the **Rupertinum café,** which serves excellent food and drinks. Here you get a slice of Salzburg's art scene and a worm's-eye view of the elegant arcaded mansion in which the museum is housed.

⑨ Turn left around the corner into **Toscaninihof,** the square cut into the dramatic Mönchsberg cliffs. On the left through the archway is the school for Benedictine monks built in 1926. If you are interested in 20th-century expressionist art, you must see Jakob Adlhart's wooden crucifix from 1925. The crucified figure bends painfully forward, his body crying out with anguish. *Open weekdays 8–11 and 2–5.*

⑩ The wall on the other side of the Toscaninihof, with its harp-shaped organ pipes, is part of the **Festspielhaus** (Festival Hall). The carved steps going up the Mönchsberg are named for Clemens Holzmeister, the architect of the Festival Halls. If you climb them, you get an intimate view of the Salzburg churches at the level of their spires, rather than from above, and if you climb a little farther to the right, you can look down into the open-air festival hall, cut into the cliffs. (From here you can walk to the Fortress along the top of the Mönchsberg in about 20 minutes.)

The festival hall complex is made up of three theaters: the small hall, originally built in 1937 and nowadays known as the Mozart Stage; the large hall, built into the solid rock of the Mönchsberg in 1960 and, because of its width, known as the Wagner Stage; and an open-air theater, the old summer riding school, which was cut into the cliffs around 1600 and adapted for the festival when it began in 1926. The theaters are linked by tunnel to an enormous parking space hidden inside the hill and are decorated with works of modern art by Oscar Kokoschka, Rudolf Hoflehner, and Anton Feistauer, among others. Unless you go to a concert, you can see inside only on a guided tour. *Hofstallgasse 1, tel. 0662/8045. Admission: AS30 adults, AS15 senior citizens and children. Tours (rehearsal schedule permitting) weekdays, May, June, and Sept. at 11 and 3; Oct.–Feb. at 3; Mar. and Apr. at 2; Sat. usually at 11. Closed July and Aug.*

From Hofstallgasse, you can either walk directly up to Sigmundsplatz or walk around by the Universitätsplatz to take a look at one of Fischer von Erlach's Baroque masterpieces, the **❶ Kollegienkirche,** built 1696–1707. Despite its relatively small area, the interior has a liberating feeling of space and light, unusual for this style of architecture.

In Sigmundsplatz is another point at which building and cliff **❷** meet: the **Pferdeschwemme,** a royal horse trough, decorated with wild and romantic horse paintings. To the left is **Neutor,** the impressive road tunnel blasted through the Mönchsberg in 1764. Looking back toward Universitätsplatz you'll see the famous hotel and restaurant **Goldener Hirsch,** its two buildings painted pink and blue.

Pass by the tiny Gothic church of **St. Blasius,** built in 1350, which has a special entrance for patients from the old hospital next door. Follow the road on through the **Gstättentor,** a street lined with 15th-century houses clinging to the cliffs. At **❸** Neumayrplatz you'll find the **Mönchsberg elevator,** which takes you up through solid rock to Café Winkler; turn right out of the lift onto the terrace. *Gstättengasse 13. Round-trip fare: AS19 adults, AS10 children. Open daily 7–3.*

Time Out **Café Winkler** is one of Salzburg's most popular (and most expensive) restaurants, with a simply magnificent view over the churches and the fortress. You can have afternoon coffee or tea Tuesday–Sunday from 2 to 7 at fairly normal prices.

After you descend from the heights, walk back toward the Blasius church, which stands at the beginning of the old city's **❹** major shopping street, **Getreidegasse.** The name means "grain street," and in summer it's as closely packed with people as a corncob is with kernels. You can always escape for a while through one of the numerous passageways—some with flower-bedecked arcaded courtyards—that link the Getreidegasse to the river and to the Universitätsplatz; try the one at Getreidegasse 3.

❺ Getreidegasse 9 is **Mozart's Birthplace,** now a museum. The third floor, where the Mozart family lived until 1773, is furnished much as it was then. Mozart's first violin and piano are on display, along with portraits of the family, letters, and other belongings. Downstairs, several rooms are devoted to miniature stage models from various productions of Mozart operas. (The **Stranz & Scio** delicatessen and the adjoining **Hagenauer** café in the same building serve excellent food.) *Getreidegasse 9, tel. 0662/844313. Admission: AS50 adults, AS35 senior citizens, AS10 children. Combined tickets for the Birthplace and the Mozart Residence (Note that the Residence is included on the guided tour of the Mozarteum, Tour 2) cost AS70, AS45, and AS15. Open Oct.–Apr., daily 9–6; May–Oct., daily 9–7.*

⑯ If you continue down Getreidegasse, you will pass the **Rathaus** (town hall) on your left, a remarkably insignificant building in the Salzburg skyline, no doubt reflecting the historical weakness of the burghers vis-à-vis the Church. A little farther on, to

⑰ the right, is the **Alter Markt,** the old marketplace and the center of secular life over the past few centuries. The square is lined with sober 17th-century middle-class houses. The old royal pharmacy, the **Hofapotheke,** still functioning today, has an incredibly ornate black and gold Rococo interior built in 1760 and a curious apothecarial smell. Across the square, next to the **Tomaselli** café, is the smallest house in Salzburg, now an optician's. The slanting roof is decorated with a dragon gargoyle. In the center of the square, surrounded by flower stalls, the marble **St. Florian's Fountain** was dedicated in 1734 to the patron saint of firefighters. From here you can return to the Mozartplatz.

Tour 2: The Fortress and the New Town

⑱ We begin this tour at the entrance to the **funicular railway** (Festungsbahn) by St. Peter's Cemetery. If it is not running, you can walk up the zigzag path that begins a little farther up Festungsgasse; it's steep in parts but gives a better impression of the majesty of the fortress. *Festungsgasse, tel. 0662/842682. Round-trip AS27 adults, AS14 children; one way AS17. Every 10 min.; hours vary from 9–5 in winter to 8AM–9PM July and Aug. Closed Nov.–mid-Dec.*

⑲ The **Fortress Hohensalzburg,** founded in 1077, is the largest preserved medieval fortress in central Europe. It was originally built by Salzburg's Archbishop Gebhard, who had thrown his support behind the Pope in the political struggle against the Holy Roman Emperor. Over the centuries, the archbishops gradually enlarged the castle and used it at first as a residence and then as a siege-proof haven against invaders and the rebellions of their own subjects. Don't miss the 40-minute guided tour, which takes you inside to the state rooms and torture chamber and up 100 tiny steps to the lookout post with a sweeping view of Salzburg and the mountains. Lines can be long, so come early. *Mönchsberg 34, tel. 0662/8042–2123. Admission plus 40-min. guided tour: AS45 adults, AS40 senior citizens, AS25 children. Admission only: AS20 adults, AS10 children. Open Apr.–Sept., daily 8–7; Oct.–Mar., daily 8–6. Tours every ½ hr. from 10 AM.*

Leave the fortress by the footpath but turn right toward the

⑳ **Nonnberg Convent,** rather than taking the steps into town. The convent was founded around 700 by Saint Rupert, and his niece, Saint Erentrudis, was the first abbess. It's more famous these days as Maria's convent—both the one in *The Sound of Music* and that of the real Maria. The Gothic church dates from the late 1400s but contains 12th-century frescoes from the earlier Romanesque building. Each evening in May at 6:45, the nuns sing a 15-minute service called *Maiandacht.* Their beautiful singing can be heard also at midnight mass on December 24.

Return along the path to the first set of steps, walk down them into Kaigasse, and continue on to the Mozartplatz. From here you can cross the Salzach River over the footbridge, Mozartsteg. Cross the road and walk west a minute or two along Imbergstrasse until you see a bookstore on the corner. Here a

㉑ little street leads into **Steingasse.** This narrow medieval street, walled in on one side by the bare cliffs of the Kapuzinerberg, backed right on to the waterfront before the Salzach was controlled. While the burghers lived on the other side of the river, this was where the tradespeople lived: dyers, tanners, potters, and so on. Nowadays it's a fascinating mixture of artists' workshops, unfashionable antiques shops, trendy nightclubs, and brothels, but with its high tumbledown houses the street still manages to convey an idea of how life used to be in the Middle Ages. Walk through the **Steintor** gate into the oldest section of the street; here on summer afternoons the light can be particularly striking. No. 23 on the right still has deep, slanted peep-windows for guarding the gate.

Time Out **Schmied,** at Steingasse 17, is primarily a place to taste and buy Austrian wines, but you can also nibble cheese and pâté while sipping a cup of tea.

A little farther up the street, at Steingasse 9, is the house where Josef Mohr, who wrote the words to "Silent Night, Holy Night," was born in 1792. Climb the adjacent stone stairway, which leads up the Kapuzinerberg, through a maze of medieval doorways. At the top of the first flight of steps is a tiny, newly renovated chapel, **St. Johann am Imberg,** built in 1681. Farther **㉒** up you'll see a signpost and gate to the **Hettwer Bastion,** part of the old city walls, which is one of the most spectacular viewpoints in Salzburg. Continue up the path to the simple **Kapuzinerkloster,** the monastery where Pope John Paul II stayed on a visit to Salzburg in 1988. From here, follow the winding road down past the Stations of the Cross along either side. This road is called Stefan-Zweig Weg, for the Austrian Jewish writer, who lived on this mountain until 1935, when he realized that Hitler would soon be crossing the border.

Turn right at the bottom of the road into Linzer Gasse, the new town's answer to the Getreidegasse, less chic but less crowded. Continue up this street until you come to St. Sebastian's church on the left. Shortly before the church is an archway that leads **㉓** behind the church into **St. Sebastian's Cemetery,** one of the most peaceful spots in Salzburg. Archbishop Wolf Dietrich commissioned the cemetery at the end of the 16th century to replace the old cathedral graveyard, which he planned to demolish. It was built in the style of an Italian *Campo santo*, with arcades on four sides, and in the center of the square he had an unusual, brightly tiled Mannerist mausoleum built for himself, where he was buried in 1617. Several famous Salzburgers are buried here, including the physician and philosopher Paracelsus (by the church door); Mozart's wife, Constanze; and his father, Leopold (by the central path leading to the mausoleum). *Open daily dawn until 6. If the gate is closed, try going through the church.*

When you leave the cemetery, walk north through a passageway until you reach Paris-Lodron-Strasse. To the left as you walk west down this street is the **Loreto Church** (1633). At Mirabellplatz, cross the road to the **Mirabell Gardens,** where a small entrance takes you into the orangery. Opposite is the **㉔** **Baroque Museum,** which features a collection of late 17th- and 18th-century paintings, sketches, and models, illustrating the development of the extravagant Baroque vision of life. *Orangeriegarten, tel. 0662/877432. Admission: AS30 adults,*

AS15 senior citizens. Open Tues.–Sat. 9–noon and 2–5, Sun. 9–noon.

The Baroque section of the gardens was laid out partly by Fischer von Erlach. Another section is devoted to 15 grotesque marble statues of dwarfs; the sculptor is unknown, but they were modeled after the archbishop's court dwarfs. In another section is a theater made out of hedges.

㉕ Wolf Dietrich built the gardens in 1606, along with the **Mirabell Palace,** for his mistress, Salome Alt, and their 10 children; it was originally called Altenau in her honor. (The story that Wolf Dietrich was imprisoned for violating his vow of celibacy is not true: He was the victim of an alliance between his nephew and successor, Markus Sittikus, and Duke Maximilian of Bavaria.) In the palace itself, now the town hall, you'll find the Angel Staircase, romantically draped with sleepy cupids, leading to the Marble Hall, which is used for weddings and concerts. *No phone. Admission free. Open weekdays except holidays 8–6.*

Turn left out of the park on the busy Schwarzstrasse. Along
㉖ this road you will find the **Mozarteum,** the Academy of Music and Performing Arts and the home of the enormous Mozart archive. The **Zauberflötenhäuschen,** the little summerhouse where Mozart is said to have composed his opera *The Magic Flute*, is in the Mozarteum garden, having been dismantled and transported here from its original location in Vienna in 1877 (it moved several times before finding its final resting place). The guided tour, which lasts over an hour, includes the Mozart family residence around the corner (*see* below). *Schwarzstr. 26, tel. 0662/844313. Cost: AS60 adults, AS30 senior citizens, AS10 children. Guided tours: July–Aug., weekdays 11:15.*

㉗ Next door is the **Marionetten Theater,** an outstanding puppet theater that specializes in opera performances. The theater company travels all over the world, but it will be in Salzburg around Christmas, during the late January Mozart Week, and from May to September (schedule subject to change). The repertoire is heavy on Mozart operas, which seem particularly suited to the skilled puppetry; a delightful new production of *Cosi fan tutte* captures the humor of the work better than most stage versions. *Schwarzstrasse 24, tel. 0662/872406. Tickets: AS250–AS400.*

Turn left at the corner, around the **Landestheater** (1775), and continue into Makartplatz, which is dominated at the far end by Fischer von Erlach's first architectural work in Salzburg, the
㉘ **Dreifaltigkeitskirche** (Church of the Holy Trinity) built 1694–1707. It was patterned after a church by Borromini in Rome and prefigures von Ehrlach's Karlskirche in Vienna. Across
㉙ from the Hotel Bristol is **Mozart's Residence,** where he lived with his family from 1773 until his abrupt departure from Salzburg in 1781, following a dispute with the archbishop. The house was partially destroyed during World War II and has none of the atmosphere of his birthplace, but there's a collection of old musical instruments and an informative film in English about Mozart's life and work. *Makartplatz 8, tel. 0662/ 871776. Admission: AS35 adults, AS25 senior citizens, AS5 children. Combined tickets for Birthplace (Tour 1) and Residence: AS70, AS45, AS15. Open May–Sept., Mon.–Sat. 10–6; Oct.–Apr., Mon.–Sat. 10–4.*

Tour 3: Short Excursions from Salzburg

Lustschloss Hellbrunn, 6.5 km (4 mi) south of Salzburg, was the pleasure palace of the prince-archbishops. It was built in the early 17th century by Santino Solari for Markus Sittikus, after he'd imprisoned his uncle, Wolf Dietrich, in the fortress. The castle has some fascinating rooms, including an octagonal music room and a banquet hall with a trompe l'oeil ceiling. In the formal Baroque gardens, one corner is reserved for a joke: the **Wasserspiele,** or trick fountains. Some of the exotic and humorous fountains spurt water from strange places at unexpected times—you will probably get wet! The **Monatsschlösschen,** the old hunting lodge, now contains an excellent folklore museum; the palace deer park now sports a zoo (*see* What to See and Do with Children, below). You can get to Hellbrunn by bus No. 55, by car on Route 159, or by bike or foot along the beautiful Hellbrunner Allee past several 17th-century princely mansions. The restaurant in the castle serves good food. *Tel. 0662/ 820372. Guided tour of the castle, trick fountains, and museum. Admission: AS48 adults, AS24 children. The park is free. Open Apr. and Oct., daily 9–4:30; May and Sept., daily 9–5; June–Aug., daily 9–6.*

Oberndorf, a little village 21 km (13 mi) north of Salzburg, has just one claim to fame; it is where, on Christmas Eve, 1818, the organist and schoolteacher Franz Gruber composed "Silent Night, Holy Night" to a lyric by the local priest, Josef Mohr. The church where the masterpiece was created was demolished and replaced in 1936 by a tiny memorial chapel containing a copy of the original composition; stained-glass windows representing the two men; and a nativity scene, donated by the Noppinger Brewery (one of the best places in town to eat). The nativity scene has a certain grisly aspect: Mohr's skull, separated from his body so a sculptor could use it as a model, was embedded "accidentally" in the wood below the crib, rather than being returned to his grave. (The sculpture is now in the new St. Nicholas Church.) The local **Heimatmuseum** documents the history of the carol. You can get to Oberndorf by the local train (opposite the main train station) or by car on the Oberndorferstrasse. *Memorial Chapel open daily 8–5. Heimatmuseum, Salzburgerstr. 88, tel. 06272/7569 for admission and opening hours when renovation is completed.*

Hallein, 16 km (10 mi) south of Salzburg and easily reached by car or train, was an active salt-mining center from the early Stone Age until 1988. You can get to the Dürrnberg mines by cable car or on foot, and a 1½-hour tour takes you by electric train to the caverns and by slide down through the different levels. You won't need your passport, but at one point deep under the surface, you'll cross the subterranean border from Austria into Germany and back. *Tel. 06245/3511. Admission: AS95 adults, AS50 children. Combined ticket with cable car: AS155 adults, AS80 children. Open late April–mid-Oct., daily 9–5.*

Take a bus from the train station to the town of Grossgmain, about 10 km (6 mi) southwest of Salzburg, to visit the **Freilichtmuseum** (Open Air Museum). Under a program to preserve authentic rural architecture and building methods, the government has bought, dismantled, trucked in from all over Austria, and reconstructed 33 houses and about 25 other buildings on a 125-acre site. Some of the buildings are more than 300

years old, and whenever possible, they contain furnishings of
their period. *Hasenweg, A–5084 Grossgmain, tel. 0662/851018
or 0662/850–0110. Admission: AS40 adults, AS30 senior citizens, AS20 children, AS90 family. Open Mar.–Nov., Tues.–
Sun. 9–6; Nov.–Dec., Sat.–Sun. 10–4.*

You can take bus No. 55 from Salzburg to the **Untersberg** and
ascend the mountain by a daringly constructed aerial cable car.
And you might visit the spa town of Berchtesgaden/Königsee,
over the border in Germany, and the Eagle's Nest, Hitler's retreat nearby on top of a mountain.

Salzburg for Free

Salzburg is an expensive city, but much of what makes the place
so compelling is free: the sweeping views, the Baroque gardens, haunting cemeteries, and a multitude of churches.

The Dom (Tour 1)

Franciscan Church (Tour 1)

Hellbrunn gardens (Tour 3)

Mirabell Palace and gardens (Tour 2)

Silent Night Chapel and museum (Tour 3)

St. Peter's Cemetery and church (Tour 1)

St. Sebastian's Cemetery (Tour 2)

Steingasse-Kapuzinerberg (Tour 2)

There are several delightful hill walks in the city (if you are on
your own, try taking a Mozart tape along on a Walkman); the
Mönchsberg is covered with trails. Look on the map for the
Richterhöhe, a view point at the southwest tip of Mönchsberg
from which you can see the fortress, the Leopoldskron Palace,
and the mountains beyond Salzburg. A pathway nearby leads
down the hillside, across a field empty but for one house (the
hangman used to live here) and out south past Leopoldskron.
And an interesting nature trail leads up to the top of the
Kapuzinerberg from the Steingasse. Schloss Leopoldskron itself, now owned by Harvard University, is not open to the public.

What to See and Do with Children

Hellbrunn (*see* Tour 3) is probably the number-one attraction
for children. Apart from the trick fountains, it has a well-designed **zoo** featuring free-flying vultures and alpine creatures
that largely roam unhindered, contained by moats. *Schloss
Hellbrunn, tel. 0662/820176. Admission: AS35 adults, AS15
children. Open Apr.–Sept., daily 8:30–6; Oct.–Mar., daily
9–5.*

The natural history museum, the **Haus der Natur,** is always full
of children. It has the usual dinosaur skeletons and models and
an aquarium, a reptile house, and a motley but interesting exhibit on human decoration: headdresses, body-painting, earrings, nose rings, and the like. *Museumsplatz 5, tel. 0662/
842653. Admission: AS35 adults, AS20 children. Open daily
9–5.*

Although children may not enjoy the nostalgic thrill of looking at old dolls and rocking horses, the **toy museum** has taken good care to appeal to them, with play areas and modeling corners; a learn-by-doing technical section, with lots of knobs to push; and a puppet show every Wednesday and Friday afternoon at 3. *Spielzeugmuseum, Burgerspitalgasse 2, tel. 0662/847560. Admission: AS25 adults, AS20 senior citizens, AS10 children. Open Tues.–Sun. 9–5.*

Unfortunately, there are no boat rides on the Salzach River, but a **fiaker ride** might make up for it (*see* Getting Around Salzburg, above). And in the Christmas season, large decorated horse-drawn carts take people around the Christmas markets. *Residenzplatz. AS320 per fiaker (4 people) for 20 min.*

The **funicular** up to the fortress (*see* Tour 2) is a must for children, and the fortress itself has plenty of diversions: cannon, armor, and ancient torture instruments, as well as eerie narrow passages and long spiral staircases.

If you want to give older children a treat, try an evening at the puppet opera in the **Marionetten Theater** (*see* Tour 2).

Off the Beaten Track

Erwin Markl, the owner of the leather-goods store **Jahn-Markl**, has built up a small museum of the leather trade in a building that was a tannery hundreds of years ago. His collection includes lederhosen from all over, a tanners guild banner from 1781, and original leather riding pants from the Spanish Riding School in Vienna. Herr Markl will take you around personally if the store is not too busy. *Jahn-Markl, Residenzplatz 3, tel. 0662/842610. Open weekdays 8–6.*

Shopping

For a small city, Salzburg has a wide range of stores. The specialties are traditional clothing, like lederhosen and loden coats, jewelry; glassware; handicrafts; confectionery; dolls in native costume; Christmas decorations; sports equipment; silk flowers; and *Gewürzsträussl*, a group of whole spices bunched and arranged to look like a bouquet of flowers.

Stores are open weekdays 8–6:30 and Saturday 8–noon. Many stores stay open until 5 on the first Saturday of the month and on Saturdays during the festival and before Christmas. Some stores stay open until 8 on Thursday or Friday. Only shops in the railway station are open on Sunday.

Shopping Streets

The most fashionable specialty stores and gift shops will be found along the Getreidegasse, the Judengasse, and around the Residenzplatz. Linzer Gasse, across the river, is less crowded and good for more practical items. There are also interesting antiques shops and jewelry workshops along Steingasse in the medieval buildings.

Specialty Stores

Antiques   Along Gstättengasse you'll find, among others, **Kirchmayer** (No. 3, tel. 0662/842219), **Peter Paul Burges** (No. 31, tel. 0662/848115), and **Gerhard Schöppl** (No. 5, tel. 0662/842154). For inexpensive secondhand curiosities, try **Trödlerstube** (Linzer Gasse 50, tel. 0662/71453). An annual antiques fair is held shortly before Easter in the state room of the Residenz.

Confectionery   If you're looking for the kind of *Mozart Kugeln* (chocolate marzipan confections) you can't buy at home, try the two stores that claim to have discovered them: **Konditorei Schatz** (Getreidegasse 3, tel. 0662/842792) and **Konditorei Fürst** (Brodgasse 13, tel. 0662/843759).

Galleries   Salzburg is a good place to buy modern paintings, and there are several galleries on Sigmund-Haffner-Gasse. One of the best known, which also has an exhibition gallery, is **Galerie Welz** (Sigmund-Haffner-Gasse 16, tel. 0662/841771).

Glass   **Fritz Kreis** (Sigmund-Haffner-Gasse 14, tel. 0662/841323) sells everything you can imagine: dirndls, ceramics, wood carvings, fabric, candles, jewelry, and so on. The markets around the Alter Markt and the Domplatz sell *Gewürzsträussl* and other decorations, especially before Christmas.

Jewelry   For exquisite costume jewelry and antique pieces, go to **Anton Koppenwallner** (Klampferergasse 2, tel. 0662/841298), **Paul Koppenwallner** (Alter Markt 7, tel. 0662/842617), or **Gerhard Lährm** (Universitätsplatz 5, tel. 0662/843477), which is somewhat more expensive.

Men's Clothing   Men's outfitters are everywhere; the best are **Antonino** (Münzgasse 2, tel. 0662/841109), **Peter's Peter Bayer** (Griesgasse 27, tel. 0662/842213), and **Resmann M Exclusiv** (Getreidegasse 25, tel. 0662/843214).

Traditional Clothing   **Lanz** (Schwarzstr. 4, tel. 0662/74272) has a wide selection of long dirndls, silk costumes, and loden coats. A more specialized place, selling wool and silk shawls and chamois-leather skirts and vests, is **Wacht** (Griesgasse 7, tel. 0662/841622). For an enormous range of leather goods, some made to order, try **Jahn-Markl** (Residenzplatz 3, tel. 0662/842610).

Women's Clothing   If dirndls are not your style, try **Lady Boss** (Schwarzstr. 4, tel. 0662/71247), **Peter's Peter Bayer** (Griesgasse 27, tel. 0662/842213), and **Sine Tempore** (Goldgasse 11, tel. 0662/841276).

Sports and Fitness

Bicycling   Getting Around Salzburg, above, lists rental shops. The tourist office has maps of cycle paths; for more detailed information contact **Velobüro** (Franz-Josef-Str. 15, tel. 0662/882788). The Hellbrunner Allee out to Hellbrunn castle and the Almkanal path out past Leopoldskron castle are two of the pleasantest and least strenuous routes.

Fishing   There is plenty of fishing around Salzburg, largely for trout, carp, and pike. The season runs from May to December. Day licenses are available for around AS200 from the sports department of the **Forum** department store, opposite the station.

Golf The **Golf and Country Club Salzburg** (Schloss Klessheim, Salzburg-Wals, tel. 0662/850851), just west of the city, is a 9-hole course at Klessheim castle. Take the A-1 freeway to the Klessheim exit.

Hiking Footpaths and trails of varying degrees of difficulty will be found all around Salzburg and the surrounding mountains. The simpler walks are on the Kapuzinerberg, the Mönchsberg, the Hellbrunner Allee, along the Almkanal (take bus No. 5 to the last stop and walk back), from the Gaisberg (bus marked "Gaisberg" to the top from Mirabellplatz), and along the Untersberg mountain trail (bus No. 60 to Grödig). The city map from the tourist office outlines two long-distance paths crossing Salzburg. For more detailed information, contact the **Österreichischer Alpenverein** (Nonntaler Hauptstr. 86, tel. 0662/822692).

Horseback Riding Contact **Reiterhof** (Moosstr. 135, tel. 0662/825024) or **Reitzentrum Doktorbauer** (Eberlinggasse 5, tel. 0662/822056).

Skiing Within Salzburg, the Gaisberg and the Untersberg have good ski slopes. Cross-country skiing is possible on the Hellbrunner Allee and around the Gaisberg (Rauchenbühelhütte). The tourist office at Mozartplatz will inform you about skiing facilities farther afield. Skis can be rented at **Sporthaus Markus Maier** (Rainerstr. 2, tel. 0662/71441) and **Hintner** (Getreidegasse 22, tel. 0662/842662–12). For snow reports (in German) call 0662/1584.

Swimming The **Paracelsus-Kurhaus** (Auerspergstr. 2, tel. 0662/73200) has a large swimming pool with a sauna and Turkish bath. There are several outdoor pools: Try **Freibad Alpenstrasse** (tel. 0662/20832; bus No. 3) or **Freibad Leopoldskron** (Leopoldskronerstr. 50, tel. 0662/843252).

Tennis Salzburg has plenty of courts, although not in the center of town. The best tennis clubs are **Salzburger Tennis Club** (Ignaz-Rieder-Kai 3, tel. 0662/22403; bus No. 6 or No. 7) and **Salzburger Tenniscourts-Süd** (Berchtesgadener Str. 35, tel. 0662/820326; bus No. 5). The cheapest is **Tenniscenter Kunsteisbahn** (Hermann-Bahr-Promenade 2, tel. 0662/23411; bus No. 6 or No. 7; open Apr.–Aug.).

Dining

The prices in Salzburg's excellent restaurants are certainly higher than in the rest of Austria, including Vienna, but the food is consistently better. Most restaurants lean toward new Austrian cuisine, a lighter version of the traditional, somewhat heavy specialties, but with more substance than nouvelle cuisine. The only truly indigenous Salzburg dish is *Salzburger Nockerln*, a snowy meringue of sweetened whisked egg whites. But the Salzburgers have a better way with fish than do chefs in most places in Austria, particularly with salmon and smoked trout.

The categories below should serve as a rough guide to relative prices. In the more expensive places, the set menus give you an opportunity to sample the chef's best; in the less expensive ones, they're a way of keeping costs down.

Many restaurants are open all day; otherwise, lunchtime is from approximately 11 to 2 and dinner from 6 to 10. During the festival season and in summer, you'd be well advised to make reservations.

Highly recommended restaurants are indicated by a star ★.

Category	Cost*
Very Expensive	over AS500
Expensive	AS300–AS500
Moderate	AS200–AS350
Inexpensive	under AS250

per person, for a three-course meal including house wine, 10% service, and VAT, but excluding extra tip

Very Expensive

★ **Café Winkler.** This modern glass-front restaurant is something of an eyesore from down below, but once you've eaten here, you'll look at it with a tolerant smile. Even without Manfred Brugger's wonderful food and original menus—mustard-seed soup with oat-and-sausage dumplings, pickled lamb in its own juices—and the elegant but relaxed service, the view would make the meal memorable. The decor is gray and red. The best tables to reserve are by the tall windows, but no matter where you sit, at night Salzburg's floodlit beauty is hard to miss. And there are a few very inexpensive dishes on the menu. *Mönchsberg 32, tel. 0662/841215. Reservations advised. Jacket and tie suggested. AE, DC, MC, V. Closed Mon. and Tues. noon except during the festival.*

Goldener Hirsch. When you seek a very special night out in an atmosphere of relaxed and simple elegance, this hotel restaurant may be the place. The food is not especially innovative, but the chef, Herbert Pöckelhofer, is a master of traditional Austrian cooking: liver-dumpling soup, fillet of lamb with thyme, smoked trout. Everything is beautifully prepared and served. If you want food from the same kitchen that's cheaper but less sophisticated, try the little **s'Herzl**, next door. *Getreidegasse 37, tel. 0662/848511. Reservations required. Jacket and tie advised. AE, DC, MC, V.*

Paris Lodron. The restaurant in the Schloss Mönchstein is a retreat into Old World elegance. Antique furniture, beautiful porcelain, and heavy plated cutlery provide a wonderful contrast to the modern Austrian cuisine: cream of red-onion soup with cheese croutons, lamb wrapped in light pastry. The food is not the best Salzburg has to offer, but the quietly efficient service and sophisticated ambience make the place quite delightful. *Mönchsberg 26, tel. 0662/848555–18. Reservations required. Jacket and tie required. DC, MC, V.*

Expensive

★ **Brandstätter.** Despite its unlikely location just off the freeway (Autobahn-Mitte) exit, this chalet-style restaurant has managed to create a cozy *Gasthaus* atmosphere. The menu, carefully prepared by the chef Gustav Esshuettner, contains a selection of reasonably priced traditional Austrian dishes, such as veal lungs with dumplings, and more expensive dishes like roast pheasant breast with a cranberry and bacon sauce. The desserts are light, the soups creamy and delicate, and the service solicitous. The restaurant, in Liefering, northwest of the city, is less than half an hour away by bus (by cab, 20 minutes). Take bus No. 29 from the center to the Fischergasse stop. *Münchner Bundestr. 69, tel. 0662/32217. Reservations advised. Dress: neat but casual. AE, MC, V. Closed Dec. 22–Jan. 12.*

Hagenauer Stuben. You wouldn't expect a restaurant in the same building as Mozart's birthplace to be either good or reasonable, but this little place is both. A small snack bar downstairs serves excellent food but can be uncomfortably crowded. Upstairs is a peaceful haven, with an elegant, traditional decor enlivened by a changing exhibition of modern paintings. The house specialty is smoked trout, which, apart from being excellent value, is about the best you're likely to taste; or you may like the pheasant breasts stuffed with chicken liver. There is always a daily menu with a choice of starters and a set main course. *Universitätsplatz 14, tel. 0662/842657. Reservations advised. Jacket and tie suggested. AE, DC, MC, V. Closed for dinner. Closed Sun. and holidays.*

★ **Zum Eulenspiegel.** Salzburgers claim that the food here is not as good as elsewhere and that the place is too full of tourists. They're right, but the restaurant, on four floors of a narrow old house, has numerous intimate corners, a winding staircase, and delicately elegant decor and is one of the most romantic places around. It's right in the middle of town, the friendly staff speaks English, and the food is certainly nothing to complain about. With dishes such as suckling pig with potato strudel, and pickled salmon trout with honey-mustard sauce, it should be on your agenda. *Hagenauerplatz 2, tel. 0662/843180. Reservations advised. Jacket suggested. AE, MC, V. Closed Sun. except during the Festival; closed Jan.–Feb.*

Moderate

★ **Auerhahn.** This find serves a lighter version of Austrian cuisine in an unassuming modern building in a desolate area five minutes by taxi north of the train station. The atmosphere is cozy but undistinguished—the food and service, however, are close to perfect. Try the pink-roasted breast of duck with orange-zest sauce (not your typical duck à l'orange) or the fillet of salmon in a Riesling dill sauce. *Bahnhofstr. 15, tel. 0662/51052. Reservations advised. Jacket suggested. AE. Closed Tues., Wed. evening, and Nov.*

Brasserie zur Bastey. A strange but successful mixture: a French creperie, Salzburg style. This small restaurant, just off the Mozartplatz, serves crepes stuffed with game, or cheese and ham, or fruit, along with a traditional Austrian menu of schnitzel and boiled beef with horseradish. Although it's a little dark and cramped, the decor is cozy and approaches elegance. *Kaigasse 7, tel. 0662/841180. Reservations advised. Jacket suggested. AE, DC, MC, V. Closed Sun.*

G'würzmühl. There is nothing special about the "Spice Mill," but the place has a warm atmosphere, and the food is reliably good. The kitchen serves excellent schnitzels and some unusual seafood dishes, such as a mixture of lobster and crab with a dill sauce. The restaurant, about 10 minutes from the center of town, specializes in catering to groups. *Leopoldskronstr. 1, tel. 0662/846356. Reservations advised. Dress: casual. AE, DC, MC, V. Closed Sun. and mid-June–early July.*

Dining
Auerhahn, **2**
Augustinerbräu, **5**
Brandstätter, **1**
Brasserie zur
Bastey, **26**
Café Winkler, **15**
Fasties, **7**
Goldener Hirsch, **20**
G'würzmühl, **17**
Hagenauer Stuben, **22**
König Ludwig, **30**
Paris Lodron, **6**
Sternbräu, **18**
Zum Eulenspiegel, **21**
Zum Fidelen Affen, **12**
Zum Mohren, **24**

Lodging
Auersperg, **8**
Bayrischer Hof, **3**
Blaue Gans, **19**
Bristol, **14**
Elefant, **23**
Eva Maria, **29**
Gablerbräu, **13**
Goldene Krone, **10**
Goldener Hirsch, **20**
Kasererbräu, **28**
Schloss Mönchstein, **6**
Sheraton, **4**
Trumer Stube, **11**
Wartenberg, **16**
Weisse Taube, **27**
Wolf, **25**
Wolf Dietrich, **9**

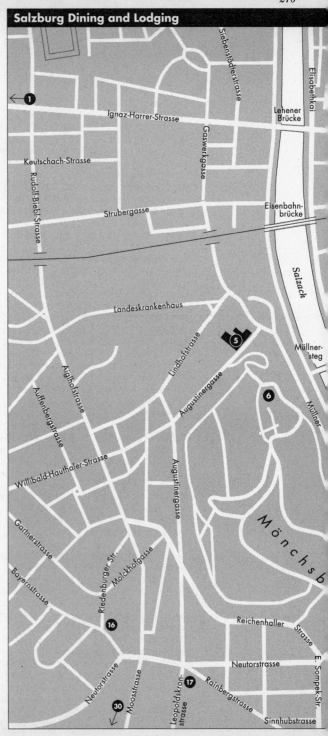

Salzburg Dining and Lodging

Stauffenstrasse

Plainstrasse

Elisabethstrasse

③

②

Hauptbahnhof

Last enstrasse

Breitenfelderstrasse

0   300 yards

0   300 meters

Merianstrasse

Bayerhamerstrasse

N

St. Julien-Strasse

Haunspergstrasse

Rainerstrasse

Weiserstrasse

Gabelsbergerstrasse

Sterneckstrasse

Faberstrasse

Markus-Sittikus-Strasse

Auerspergstrasse

Franz-Josef-Strasse

Paracelsusstrasse

Lasserstrasse

⑦

Auerspergstrasse

⑧

Rupertgasse

i

④

Hubert-Sattler-Gasse

Schrannengasse

Wolf-Dietrich-Strasse

Schallmooser Hauptstrasse

Rainerstrasse

Mirabell Gardens

Paris-Lodron-Strasse

⑨

Schwarzstrasse

Dreifaltigkeitsgasse

Priesterh.

Bergstrasse

Stef. Zweig Weg

St. Linzer Gasse

⑩

Kapuzinerberg

Franz-Josef-Kai

Elisabethkai

⑭

Makartplatz

⑪

⑫

⑬

Makartsteg

Platzl

Staatsbrucke

Salzach

Imberg strasse

Steingasse

Hauptstrasse

Gstättengasse

Neumayr-pl.

⑮

Griesgasse

⑱

⑳

Getreidegasse

②①

②②

②③

Judengasse

②④

Rudolfskai

Mozartsteg

Giselakai

⑲

⑳

Sigmundspl.

Universitätsplatz

Sigmund-Haffner-Gasse

Hofstallgasse

Brodgasse

Goldgasse

i

Residenzplatz

②⑤ ②⑥

②⑦

Kaigasse

berg

Dr. Ludwig Prahauser-Weg

Bucklreuthstr.

②⑧

Nonntaler Brücke

②⑨

Herrengasse

Kaigasse

Festungsgasse

König Ludwig. This large, old-fashioned restaurant is a favorite destination for locals on a special night out, and it has a correspondingly formal but festive atmosphere. The food, if not top-notch, is hearty and imaginative, with such dishes as fillet of hare served with a sour-cherry and peppercorn sauce and piquant leg of lamb cooked with olives, artichokes, and pepper. On weekdays there's a choice of three-course business lunches. The restaurant is on the marshland southwest of Salzburg and can be reached by bus No. 60 (Firmianstrasse stop) in about 15 minutes. *Moosstr. 72, tel. 0662/824605. Reservations advised. Jacket suggested. AE, DC, MC, V. Closed Mon. and 2 weeks in Jan.*

Zum Mohren. Good food, a central location by the river, a welcoming atmosphere, friendly service, and reasonable prices have made Zum Mohren a favorite with both Salzburgers and tourists. The restaurant is in the basement of a 15th-century house: atmospheric but a little cramped and smoky. If this bothers you, try for a table in the room to the right as you enter. The menu always offers at least one vegetarian item and several fish dishes among a selection of Austrian specialties like sautéed veal liver and roast hare. *Judengasse 9/Rudolfskai 20, tel. 0662/842387. Reservations required. Dress: neat but casual. No credit cards. Closed Sun. and holidays; June; and 1 week in Nov.*

Inexpensive

Augustinerbräu. Salzburg's homegrown version of a Munich beer house is located at the north end of the Mönchsberg. You can bring your own food; pick up a stone jug of strong, frothy (not fizzy) beer; and sit down in the gardens or at a dark-wood table in one of the large halls. Shops in the huge monastery complex sell so-so salads, sausage, and fried chicken, and a little stall has tasty spirals of salted radish. If you don't feel up to cold beer, there's an old copper beer warmer in the main hall. *Augustinergasse 4, tel. 0662/31246. No reservations. Dress: casual. No credit cards. Open daily 3–11.*

Fasties. A fast-food restaurant that serves excellent food is always useful. This informal neighborhood place not far from the Mirabell gardens is decorated in a bright, cheerful style; you sit on high stools at long tables by the window. The menu consists of soups, quiches, pâtés, and one or two larger dishes, prepared by a chef who used to specialize in sauces. The wine list is small but well chosen, and you can have the food packed to go. *Lasserstr. 19, tel. 06222/873876. No reservations. Dress: casual. No credit cards. Closed Sat., Sun., and after 7:30 PM.*

Sternbräu. This is a place to come on summer evenings, to sit in the gardens, drink beer, and listen to folk music, usually on Friday and Sunday. The food outside is from a self-service buffet; inside, typical Austrian specialties, like sausages or boiled beef with horseradish, are served. *Griesgasse 23, tel. 0662/842140. No reservations. Dress: casual. No credit cards.*

★ **Zum Fidelen Affen.** The name means "To the Jolly Monkey," which explains the monkey motifs in what is otherwise a traditional Austrian Gasthaus. The place is dominated by a large circular bar surrounded by tables, and the menu is not unusual for Austria: beef salad with pumpkinseed oil, a wide variety of goulashes. What *is* unusual is the excellent quality of the food, particularly at these prices. Because half Salzburg knows this, the place is always packed. *Priesterhausgasse 8, tel. 0662/*

877361. Reservations advised. Dress: casual. No credit cards. Closed Sun.

Lodging

The old city has a wide variety of hotels and pensions, some with surprising locations and considerable atmosphere, but there are few bargains. In high season, and particularly during the festival (July and August), some prices soar and rooms are very difficult to find, so try to reserve at least two months in advance. If you don't have a reservation, go to one of the Tourist Information offices or the accommodations service *(Zimmernachweis)* on the ground floor of the railway station. If you're looking for something very cheap (below AS400 for a double), clean, and comfortable, stay in a private home, though the good ones are all a little way from downtown. The tourist information offices don't list private rooms; try calling Eveline Truhlar of Bob's Special Tours (tel. 0662/872484 or 06246/3377), who runs a private-accommodations service.

Highly recommended lodgings are indicated by a star ★.

Category	Low Season*	High Season*
Very Expensive	over AS2,000	over AS2,500
Expensive	AS1,300–AS2,000	AS1,500–AS2,500
Moderate	AS900–AS1,300	AS1,200–AS1,800
Inexpensive	under AS900	under AS1,200

All prices are for a standard double room for two, with bath, including breakfast, except where noted, and VAT.

Very Expensive

Bristol. This is the large, old deluxe hotel at its best: elegant surroundings, friendly and efficient service, spacious corridors. Standardization is an unknown concept here; every room is different. Some are newly renovated, with pine furniture and light colors; others are dark and rich, with Persian carpets and armchairs. Views vary from park to street to courtyard, and the rooms are different sizes, so be sure to express your preferences when reserving. The hotel is centrally located in the new town, opposite one of Mozart's houses and next to the theater. *Makartplatz 4, tel. 0662/873557. 85 rooms. Facilities: restaurant, bar. AE, DC, MC, V. Closed Jan.–Mar.*

★ **Goldener Hirsch.** The Golden Stag is a jewel among Salzburg's top hotels. The 800-year-old pink and blue houses, overlooking Getreidegasse on one side and Sigmundsplatz on the other, offer a variety of rooms furnished with antiques. The service is second to none—discreet, friendly, and incredibly polite. The hotel has recently acquired a new house across the road on Getreidegasse, where the rooms are larger and are furnished in a slightly more modern style. If you want to be in the old building, specify it when reserving. Breakfast is not included in the room price. *Getreidegasse 37, tel. 0662/848511. 71 rooms. Facilities: restaurant, bar, tavern. AE, DC, MC, V.*

Schloss Mönchstein. If you are a romantic with money to spend, look no further. This ancient ivy-covered, fairy-tale castle, hidden in the woods at the top of the Mönchsberg, is a dream. The rooms are very uneven in size and decor, but the best are luxurious. Service is formal and discreet, and the restaurant is a sea of bow ties and flowing silk. The castle has its own wedding chapel, which is particularly popular with American and Japanese couples! Getting in and out of town calls for a car or taxi, unless you are willing to negotiate steps or take the nearby casino elevator. *Mönchsberg 26, tel. 0662/848-5550. 17 rooms. Facilities: restaurant, café, bar, terrace, tennis court, chapel. DC, MC, V.*

Sheraton. You won't have any surprises at the Sheraton. A newly built hotel, looking onto the Mirabell gardens, the hotel is decorated in a quiet style somewhere between modern and traditional. The rooms are luxurious if a little bland. There are a limited number of nonsmoking rooms and a limited number of double beds as opposed to twin beds. Be sure to ask for a room overlooking the gardens. Guests have a private entrance to the adjacent swimming pool and sauna *(Kurhaus)*, but these facilities cost extra. *Auerspergstr. 4, tel. 0662/793210. 165 rooms. Facilities: restaurant, café, bar. AE, DC, MC, V.*

Expensive

Bayrischer Hof. No one would call this a beautiful hotel, but the rooms, after substantial renovation, are comfortable. The staff is efficient and helpful, the restaurant excellent. The advantage of being only a few minutes' walk from the train station is offset by the ugliness of the station area; still, all the windows are soundproof, and if you are looking for a one-night stay before going on by train, this hotel would be a good choice. *Kaiserschützenstr. 1, tel. 0662/541700. 60 rooms. Facilities: restaurant. AE, MC, V.*

Kasererbräu. A variety of tastes went into designing this hotel, resulting in a curious mixture of kitsch and elegance in the hallways and reception areas, with plain but adequate rooms. Apart from the friendly staff, the hotel has two big advantages: It's right next to Mozartplatz, and it has pleasant sauna and steambath facilities included in the price; a massage costs extra. *Kaigasse 33, tel. 0662/842406. 43 rooms. Facilities: sauna, steambath. AE, DC, MC, V.*

★ **Wolf Dietrich.** Don't be put off by the dreary exterior and lobby. This hotel is peaceful, central, and one of the few city hotels with a pool-and-sauna complex—a small and intimate one, decorated with wall-to-wall mirrors and sea-green tiles depicting Neptune. All the rooms are cheerful, if a little small, but by far the best are those at the back, looking out on St. Sebastian's *campo santo* cemetery and over the old city. The newly renovated rooms have balconies and look more like colorful modern bedrooms in a private house than in a hotel. Although it doesn't take groups, the hotel is very popular, so reserve well in advance. *Wolf-Dietrich-Str. 7, tel. 0662/871275. 30 rooms. Facilities: restaurant, bar, indoor pool, sauna (AS80) and solarium (AS40). AE, DC, V. Closed Feb.–mid-Mar.*

Moderate

Blaue Gans. Reasonable rates in a 500-year-old building in the heart of the old city make the Blue Goose an extremely popular choice. Despite the building's undeniable atmosphere of a medieval inn, the rooms are unimaginative—some are even a little dingy—and the service is nothing special. But stepping straight out onto Getreidegasse gives the hotel all the advantage it needs, so make reservations early. *Getreidegasse 43, tel. 0662/841317. 45 rooms, 29 with bath. Facilities: restaurant. AE, DC, MC, V.*

★ **Elefant.** Four hundred years as a hotel in a 12th-century building, bang in the middle of the old city, have given Elefant an atmosphere of traditional comfort rather than merely old age. The public areas, including a quiet writing room, and the high-ceiling private rooms are well decorated with Persian carpets and Biedermeier furniture in dark woods. Double rooms are of three sizes. *Sigmund-Haffner-Gasse 4, tel. 0662/843397. 36 rooms. Facilities: 2 restaurants, private dining room for parties. AE, DC, MC, V.*

Gablerbräu. This centrally located five-story hotel, built, according to the management, in 1408 (despite the "1553" painted on the roof) and completely renovated in 1979, has a younger, livelier clientele than do most other Salzburg hotels and is often host to private parties. The rooms are bright and large, simply decorated with elegant carpets; the lobby is attractive; and the adjoining restaurant serves good, hearty food. Although the staff is friendly, service can be erratic. *Linzer Gasse 9, tel. 0662/873441. 52 rooms. Facilities: restaurant, private dining room. AE, DC, MC, V.*

Weisse Taube. A traditional family-run hotel, close to the Mozartplatz, the White Dove is always heavily booked, though it does not take groups. The 14th-century house, with its uneven floors and strange nooks and crannies, is a listed property, which forced the owners to find original solutions to modern problems, such as bathrooms encapsulated in plastic, to protect the building from water. The parts of the building that were bombed during World War II have been entirely renovated. The rooms are a little dark and are decorated with heavy patterned wallpaper and carpet. The pleasant breakfast room is only for nonsmokers; smokers are relegated to a dreary back room. *Kaigasse 9, tel. 0662/842404. 33 rooms, 29 with bath. Facilities: bar. AE, DC, MC, V.*

Wolf. The embodiment of Austrian *gemutlichkeit*, just off the Mozartplatz, the Wolf offers spotlessly clean and cozy rooms at reasonable prices. The rooms in this small family-run hotel are idiosyncratically arranged on several upper floors, connected by narrow, winding stairs, and are decorated with a pleasing Salzburg mix of Persian carpets and rural furniture. The staff is friendly and helpful; the only problem is getting a room here. *Kaigasse 7, tel. 0662/843453. 12 rooms. AE.*

Inexpensive

Auersperg. A good price and spacious rooms are the main reasons for choosing the Auersperg. The building is drab; the hotel caters mainly to large gróups; and though the location is convenient, between the station and the river, it's not attractive. Rooms with a tub are more expensive than are those with a shower. *Auerspergstr. 61, tel. 0662/88944. 63 rooms. Facilities: bar. AE, DC, MC, V.*

Eva Maria. Almost every room in this little chalet/guest house, close to the Leopoldskron castle, has a balcony and looks out across moorland to lovely alpine scenery. The rooms are bright and cheerful, and the reception area is welcoming, with comfortable chairs and tables. Unless you like walking, you'll need a car or taxi to get into town. *Sinnhubstr. 25, tel. 0662/845960. 7 rooms. AE, DC, MC, V.*

Goldene Krone. This is the kind of place that people come back to; the building has a solid, comfortable feel, the service is friendly and informal, and the rooms come in all shapes and sizes (with a few large ones for families). The rooms are homey, if a little worn, and you step out the door into the busy Linzer Gasse. *Linzer Gasse 48, tel. 0662/872300. 27 rooms. No credit cards.*

★ **Trumer Stube.** Readers repeatedly recommend this family-run pension, mentioning in particular its friendly atmosphere and helpful staff. It's in a well-kept old building in a narrow, winding street near Mirabellplatz and is scrupulously clean. It has a bright and cheerful breakfast room and simply decorated, pleasant rooms that are renovated every four years. *Bergstr. 6, tel. 0662/874776. 22 rooms. No phones or TVs in rooms. No credit cards.*

Wartenberg. If you're looking for perfection, this is not the place to come. But it is one of the best values in Salzburg, with spacious double rooms at a reasonable price and tiny singles and doubles without bath at a steal. It's a rambling old house, a 10-minute walk from the town center, and all the rooms are furnished with antique peasant furniture; the family also runs an excellent restaurant on the premises. *Riedenburger Str. 2, tel. 0662/844284. 20 rooms, 7 with bath. Facilities: restaurant. No phones or TV in rooms. No credit cards. Closed last 2 weeks in Jan.*

The Arts and Nightlife

The Arts

Information and tickets for the main Salzburg Festival (July 26–August 31), the Easter Festival (March 23–31), and the Pentecost Concerts (mid-May) can be obtained from **Salzburger Festspiele** (Hofstallgasse 1, A–5020 Salzburg, tel. 0662/842541). You must reserve well in advance. Tourist Information provides schedules for all arts performances, and you can find listings in the daily newspaper *Salzburger Nachrichten.* Tickets can be purchased directly at the box office, at your hotel, or at a ticket agency like **Polzer** (Residenzplatz 4, tel. 0662/846500) or **American Express** (Mozartplatz 5, tel. 0662/842501).

Theater The season at the **Landestheater** (Schwarzstr. 22, tel. 0662/715120) runs from September to June; in 1992, it offers new productions of *Lohengrin* (in the Festival Hall) and *The Merry Widow.*

The **Salzburg Festival** performs Hugo von Hofmannsthal's morality play *Jedermann* (in German) annually in the forecourt of the cathedral—one of the few festival traditions not connected with Mozart.

Music There is no shortage of concerts in this most musical of cities. The **Salzburg Palace Concerts,** the **Fortress Concerts,** and the **Mozart Serenades** take place year-round. In addition, there is the **Easter Festival,** the **Pentecost Concerts, Mozart Week** (Jan. 24–Feb. 2), and the **Salzburg Cultural Days** (October).

Opera The great operatic event of the year is, of course, the **Salzburg Festival,** which will remain heavy on Mozart operas this year.

The **Easter Festival** will also feature operas (by Mozart), and the **Salzburg Cultural Days** will present two operas (including Rimsky-Korsakov's *Mozart and Salieri*). The **Marionettentheater** is also devoted to opera, with an acclaimed new production of *Cosi fan tutte*, giving puppet performances the first week of January, during Mozart Week, May–September, and after Christmas.

Film Salzburg has very few movie theaters, and these few, frustratingly, dub English-language films into German.

Nightlife

Salzburg is not famous for its nightlife; after 10 PM the streets are pretty empty. The tourist office will tell you where there's folk dancing and singing. The more exclusive night spots are around the Steingasse; bars and discos for a young crowd are around the Gstättengasse.

Bars/Nightclubs **Chez Roland** (Giselakai 15, tel. 0662/74335) is the haunt of "Loden-preppies," or the wealthy and stylish young, and is open Monday–Saturday 7 PM–1 AM. **Bazillus** (Imbergstr. 2a, tel. 0662/71631), on the other hand, is small, scruffy, and makeshift, but very cool; it's open daily 7PM–1AM. **Flip** (Gstättengasse 7, tel. 0662/843643), near the Mönchsberg elevator, is a 1950s neon bar, open daily 11 AM–3 AM. **Saitensprung** (Steingasse 11, tel. 0662/881377) is an elegant cocktail bar with food, open daily 8 PM–3 AM.

If you would prefer something more indigenous, try the **Paracelsus Stub'n** (Kaigasse 8, tel. 0662/843277), or have a drink at **Zum Fidelen Affen** (Priesterhausgasse 8, tel. 0662/77361) or the larger **Bacchus Weinstuben** (Rudolfskai 16, tel. 0662/842275), which has live music until 4 AM.

Discos **Disco Seven** (Gstättengasse 7, tel. 0662/844181) is large, has a youngish crowd, and goes for the American market; it's open daily 9 PM–3 AM. The **Half Moon** (Gstättengasse 4–6, tel. 0662/841670) caters to a mixed crowd and is open daily 9 PM–3AM. The **Old Grenadier** (Ursulinenplatz 2, tel. 0662/843718) is an English-style disco pub with a small dance floor; open Monday–Saturday 8 PM–4 AM.

Casino **Salzburg's casino** is in the same building on top of the Mönchsberg as the Café Winkler; even if you're losing, the floodlit view over Salzburg is a consolation. The casino is reached by the elevator from Gstättengasse, and admission costs AS170, for which you will receive gaming tokens for AS200. Remember to take your passport.

Cabaret The **Casanova Bar** (Linzer Gasse 23, tel. 0662/75031) offers a cabaret and striptease show, daily 9 PM–6 AM.

8 Carinthia

Introduction

by George W. Hamilton

In 1877 the German composer Johannes Brahms described an unexpected holiday he spent in Carinthia: ". . . the first day was so lovely that I determined to stay for a second, and the second was so lovely that I have decided to stay here for the time being." Little has changed since; just mention Carinthia (*Kärnten*) to most Austrians, and they'll start to describe either superb but little-known ski slopes or their favorite lake.

The province itself is nestled among mountains; to the south is the sharp Karawanken range, which defines the Italian border, and other ranges lie east, west, and north. To the northwest rise the peaks of the Höhe Tauern, crowned by the Grossglockner at 3,797 meters (12,457 ft), tallest of the Austrian Alps. From the top of Pyramidenkogel above the Wörther See or from the Kanzelhöhe and Gerlitzen above Ossiacher See, you can look out over great sweeps of terrain laid out like a huge arena.

The Drau, Gurk, and Glan rivers wind their way through, passing the Gothic and Baroque steeples of countless village churches. Between the low forested hills lie blue-green lakes, reflecting golden light from the rocky faces of the Karawanken and Carnic Alps.

Carinthia is slightly warmer in winter than other parts of Austria, slightly cooler in summer. The province is known for sunshine, which draws skiers to its slopes and warms the lakes in summer.

In the last week before Lent, when the spirit of Carnival captivates all of Austria, the Villach Carnival is the hub of it all. Its costume parades, floats, parodies, and cabarets are now televised annually for international consumption. The "Carinthian Summer" festival is held in July and August, with performances in Villach and Ossiach.

People settled here as early as the Bronze Age. Various Illyrian tribes came during the Hallstatt period; Alpine Celts ruled until the Romans moved in, and when the Romans departed, about AD 600, they left the area to the Slovenes, then known as Carinthians, thus giving the region its name. The Habsburgs took over in 1335, and most of Carinthia has been Austrian ever since. Numerous Celtic and Slovene traditions have survived, and a Slovene minority still lives in Carinthia.

Klagenfurt is the official seat of the government, but over the course of time, Villach, an equally attractive and interesting small city, has emerged as the "secret" capital.

Essential Information

Important Addresses and Numbers

Tourist Information The official tourist office for the province is Kärntner Tourismus in **Krumpendorf** (Hallegger Str. 1, A–9201, tel. 04229/2224). Other offices (Fremdenverkehrsamt) are:

Bad Kleinkirchheim (A–9546, tel. 04240/8212)
Gmünd (A–9853, tel. 04732/2197)
Klagenfurt (Rathaus, A–9010, tel. 0463/537223)

Maria Wörth (Verkehrsamt, A–9081, tel. 04273/2240)
Millstatt (Kurverwaltung, A–9872, tel. 04766/2022)
Ossiach Lake area (A–9570 Ossiach, tel. 04243/497)
Pörtschach (Kurverwaltung, A–9210, tel. 04272/2354 or 04272/281015)
Spittal an der Drau (Burgplatz 1, A–9800, tel. 04762/3420)
Velden (Kurverwaltung, Box 91, A–9220, tel. 04274/2103)
Villach (Europaplatz 2, A–9500, tel. 04242/244440).

Arriving and Departing

By Plane Carinthia is served—mainly by Austrian Airlines—through the Klagenfurt-Wörther See Airport just northeast of Klagenfurt. Several flights daily connect the provincial capital and Vienna. In summer, service is also available from Zurich, Rome, and Frankfurt. For flight information, call 0463/415000.

By Car The most direct route from Vienna is via the Semmering mountain pass, through Styria, entering Carinthia on Route 83 just above Friesach and going on to Klagenfurt. Route 95 leads into central Carinthia over the Turracher Höhe pass, a particularly scenic route. From Salzburg, the A–10 autobahn tunnels beneath the Tauern range and the Katschberghöhe to make a dramatic entry into Carinthia, although the parallel Route 99, which runs "over the top," is the scenic route. Several mountain roads cross over from Italy, but the most traveled is Route 83 from Tarvisio.

By Train The main rail line south from Vienna parallels Route 83, entering Carinthia north of Friesach and continuing on to Klagenfurt and Villach. From Salzburg, a line runs south, tunneling under the Tauern mountains and then tracing the Möll and Drau river valleys to Villach. A line from Italy comes into the Drau valley from Lienz in East Tirol. The main line north from Udine in Italy runs through Tarvisio and up to Villach; other rail lines tie Yugoslavia with Klagenfurt.

Getting Around

By Car Highways in Carinthia are good, although you can hit some stretches as steep as the 23-degree gradient on the Turracher pass road (Route 95), for example. Hauling trailers is not recommended (or is forbidden). The north–south passes are kept open in winter as far as possible, but the tunnels under the Tauern and Katschberg mountains ensure that Route A–10 is now passable all year.

By Train Much of Carinthia's attractive central basin is missed by the rail routes. Though you can get into and through Carinthia fairly easily by train, to see the province, you'll need to rely on a car or the network of buses.

By Bus As in all of Austria, the post office or railroad (Bundesbahn) buses go virtually everywhere, but you'll have to allow plenty of time and coordinate schedules carefully so as not to get stranded in some out-of-the-way location.

Exploring Carinthia

Carinthia's biggest draw is its chain of narrow lakes that run from east to west across the southern half of the province. We'll explore them, along with their cities and towns; venture into the underpopulated regions; visit ruins and resorts; and make detours for wonderful food and serene views. On Tour 1 we'll visit Villach, drive along the Ossiacher See and through the Gurktal up to the medieval town of Friesach, taking in a Disneyesque castle and a Roman excavation on our way to Klagenfurt. Tour 2 begins in Klagenfurt, then shows us a bit of both sides of the fashionable Wörther See, and makes a loop by the Faakersee and the Feistritzer-Stausee back to Klagenfurt. Tour 3 starts in Villach and goes northwest to Spittal and the walled town of Gmünd, takes in the Millstätter See, and detours to a lively ski resort and spa.

Highlights for First-time Visitors

Brauerei Hirt (Tour 1)
Hochosterwitz Castle (Tour 1)
The view from the Pyramidenkogel (Off the Beaten Track)
16th-century Gmünd (Tour 3)
Swimming, fishing, boating on the Faaker See (Tour 2)

Tour 1: From Villach through the Gurktal to Klagenfurt

Numbers in the margin correspond with points of interest on the Carinthia map.

① **Villach,** Carinthia's "other" capital (Klagenfurt is the real one), sits astride the Drau River. The Romans may have been the first to bridge the river here for their settlement of Bilachium, from which the present Villach is derived. The city is compact, with narrow, twisting lanes (restricted to pedestrians) winding through the old city south of the river. Attractive small shops are tucked into arcaded buildings, and each corner brings a fresh and surprising perspective.

Renaissance houses surround the main square, which has a Baroque column in honor of the Trinity. At **Hauptplatz 14** lived the 16th-century alchemist and physician Theophrastus Bombastus von Hohenheim Paracelsus (best known simply as Paracelsus); his father was the town physician. Curiously, the Late Gothic 14th-century **parish church of St. Jacob** was Protestant during the mid-1500s, making it Austria's first Protestant church. Its marble pulpit dates to 1555; the ornate Baroque high altar contrasts grandly with the Gothic crucifix. If the stair entry is open and you don't mind the rather steep climb, the view from the 95-meter (310-ft) tower is marvelous. Near the river, at the intersection of Ossiacher Zeile and Peraustrasse, the pinkish **Heiligenkreuz parish church,** with two towers and cupola, is a splendid example of fully integrated Baroque.

On the southern outskirts of the city lies **Warmbad Villach,** its name reflecting the hot springs of radioactive water, which is believed to combat aging. Many hotels have been built around the *Kurpark,* the wooded grounds of the spa.

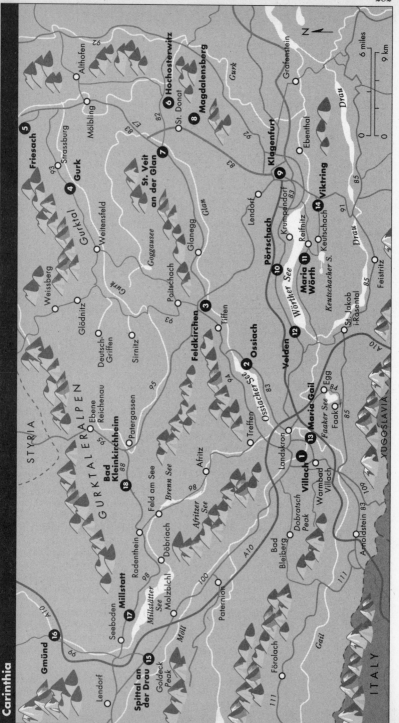

Carinthia

A few kilometers northeast of Villach on Route 83 (the road to Ossiach), the ruined castle atop the hill at **Landskron** makes an interesting stopping point. The first castle here dated from 1351, was destroyed by fire in 1861, and parts since have been rebuilt. The views out over Villach, the Ossiach lake, and the Karawanken mountain range to the south are magnificent.

2 Follow the road about 10 km (6 mi) along the south side of the Ossiacher See to reach the resort town of **Ossiach,** now the center of the Carinthian Summer festival. In season the town is afflicted with wall-to-wall tourists. Look instead at the 11th-century former monastery, a typical square building around an inner court, with a chapel at the side. The abbey is now an apartment hotel, and rooms could be available in this magnificent building overlooking the lake (tel. 04243/497 for information).

From June through August the office of the summer festival is located in the monastery complex. The chapel, for all of its stern, conservative look, is wonderfully Baroque inside. Legend has it that in the 11th century the Polish king Boleslav II lived incognito in the abbey for eight years, pretending to be mute, in penance for murdering the bishop of Cracow. A tombstone and a fresco on the church wall facing the cemetery commemorate the story.

Time Out At the east end of the Ossiacher See, Route 83 makes a sharp turn to the left to reach Route 94 en route to Feldkirchen. Ignore the turn and take the first dirt side road to the left. You'll see immediately on your right a small dark-stained wood cabin with colorful umbrellas outside, next to a pond. You're at **Forellenstation Niederbichler.** Stop here and order trout—*bleu,* grilled, or breaded and fried. It comes fresh from the pond and, accompanied by a *G'spritzter* (wine with soda water), makes a memorable meal at a bargain price.

At **Tiffen,** a few minutes past Ossiach on Route 94 toward Feldkirchen, the walled church stands guard on the hill to your left; you can wander through the churchyard.

3 Some relics of the ancient wall around **Feldkirchen** remain (the town dates to 888). In the pedestrian zone and around the main square, the colorful facades from the Middle Ages are worth a stop. At the north end of town (Kirchgasse), look at the parish church in early Romanesque style, with a Gothic choir and Baroque decor.

Take Route 93 north out of Feldkirchen. Stretches of the road offer marvelous views to the west. All along the route are small roads to the left and right that lead to colorful villages: **Goggau** on the right, with its small but charming lake; **Sirnitz** farther along to the left; also on the left, **Deutch-Griffen** and its picturesque defense church; and then **Glödnitz** and beyond on a scenic road.

Weitensfeld is the focus of a local festival over the Pentecost weekend. The plague decimated the population in the 16th century leaving, it's said, only three young men and a noblewoman who lived in nearby Thurnhof castle. A race was proposed to determine which of them should win her in marriage, and though history failed to record the outcome, the tradition of the race continues. The winner now kisses the noblewoman's statue plus any other attractive female within reach, and the celebration goes on. Thurnhof castle is up on the left after you leave Weitensfeld.

❹ The massive Romanesque cathedral at **Gurk** has an interesting history: In the 11th century, Hemma, a wealthy woman, devoted her life to building convents and churches, including the convent at Gurk. About 100 years after Hemma's death in 1045, the bishop of that time began the cathedral in her honor; it was consecrated in 1200. Hemma was canonized in 1938. Her crypt is surrounded by 100 marble columns, and the small green slate chair from which she personally supervised her building construction is also there. The high altar is one of the most important examples of early Baroque in Austria; note the cast *Pietà* by George Rafael Donner. The 900-square-foot Lenten altar cloth of 1458, showing 98 scenes from the Old and New Testaments, is displayed from Ash Wednesday to Good Friday. The guidebook in English is helpful. *Tel. 04266/8236. Contributions requested. Open daily 9–6. Tours (AS30) mid-Apr.–Sept., daily 9:30, 11, 2:30, and 4:15, church services permitting.*

In **Strassburg,** the seat of the Gurk bishopric until 1787, the episcopal palace, now restored, houses small museums covering the history of the valley and of the diocese. The Gothic parish church, one of the most beautiful in Carinthia, has stained-glass windows dating from 1340.

At the intersection of Route 93 with Route 83/E–7, the impressive yellow building you'll see is the 18th-century Pöckstein castle, belonging to the Carinthian bishops. Just across the highway is the northern terminal of a small narrow-gauge railway, the **Gurktaler Museumbahn,** which meanders under steam power down to Treibach on weekends and holidays, June through September. *Tel. 0463/25601. Fare: AS40 adults, AS20 children. Departures Sat. 2 and 4, Sun. and holidays 10, 2, 4.*

Time Out Head north on Route 83/E–7 toward Friesach, and you'll come to **Brauerei Hirt,** a brewery since 1270. You might have a draft beer under the huge tree in the side garden or in one of the paneled rooms. The food is good, standard Austrian; service tends to lag on crowded weekends.

❺ The medieval town of **Friesach,** about 8 km (5 mi) north of the intersection, is great for relaxed wandering. You'll find the main square with its picturesque facades immediately, and as you stroll you'll discover parts of the old double wall and the moat, towers, and gates. Look into the churches; the 12th-century Romanesque parish church has some excellent stained glass in the choir. The 13th-century Dominican church was the first of its order in Austria and contains a wonderful Early Gothic choir. Take the easy 20-minute climb up to the ruins of Petersburg castle, where you can see 12th- and 13th-century frescoes.

From Friesach, retrace your steps south on Route 83/E–7. After you've passed Pöckstein castle, in the distance off to the left you'll notice a castle on a hilltop, which you can see close up by turning left at Mölbling on a road marked "Treibach/Althofen." The castle is actually in **Ober Markt,** an unusually picturesque town with 15th-century decorated houses.

6 Continue south on the back road about 12 km (7.5 mi) from Treibach or on Route 83/E–7 to 13th-century **Hochosterwitz,** a dramatic castle complex perched atop an isolated mountain, absolutely out of a fairy tale. You can hardly overlook the Disneyland effect, but this one is original. The most recent fortifications were added in the late 1500s against the invading Turks; each of the 14 towered gates is a small fortress unto itself. Inside there's an impressive collection of armor and weapons and a café-restaurant in the inner courtyard. Views are great in all directions. *Tel. 04213/2010. Admission: AS40 adults, AS20 children. Open Easter–June, Sept., Oct., daily 9–5; July and Aug., daily 8–6; closed Nov.–Easter.*

7 Cross on Route 82 to **St. Veit an der Glan,** until 1518 the capital of Carinthia. The old ducal city remains largely unchanged, with the town hall's Baroque facade and ancient patrician houses forming the main square. Be sure to walk into the 15th-century town hall's arcaded Renaissance courtyard, overflowing with flowers in summer. The 12th-century Romanesque parish church was later given Gothic overtones; note the attractive entry. The ducal palace at the north end of town now houses a small medieval collection; the building itself has a marvelous arcaded stairway in the courtyard.

8 Continue south of St. Veit on Route 83, and after about five minutes, below St. Donat, you'll see on the left signs for **Magdalensberg,** a Celtic-Roman settlement, now being excavated. Among the sights are the remains of a Roman villa that had central heating, public baths, and temple foundations. The marble *Youth from Magdalensberg,* now in the Museum of Art History in Vienna, was found here in 1502; a small museum displays other discoveries. *Tel. 04224/2255. Admission: AS20 adults, AS10 children. Open May–Oct., daily 8–6.*

Continue south on Route 83 to Klagenfurt.

Tour 2: Klagenfurt and the Southern Lakes

9 **Klagenfurt** lay in ruins in 1518, when it became the provincial capital, so most of what you see today is 16th century or later. And while Klagenfurt itself may not pulse with excitement, it's an excellent base for excursions to surrounding parts of Carinthia. The nearby Wörther See is sometimes called Austria's Riviera for its abundance of resorts, beautiful people, and emphasis on dawn-to-dawn pleasure. But the region also has exquisite scenery; small, peaceful lakes; and picturesque towns outside the major resorts.

You can hardly overlook the *Lindwurm,* Klagenfurt's famous emblematic dragon with a twice-curled tail, which adorns the fountain on Neuer Platz (new square). The oldest part of the city, north of the fountain, has a pleasant pedestrian area with tiny streets and alleys. Look at the **Landhaus** (district government headquarters), with its towers and court with arcaded stairways. It was completed in 1591 and at the time formed a corner of the city wall. The building's dramatic Wappensaal (Hall of Arms) contains 665 coats of arms of the communities of Carinthia. South of the Neuer Platz is the Domkirche, or cathedral, completed as a Protestant church in 1591, given over to the Jesuits and reconsecrated in 1604. The 18th-century side-altar painting of Saint Ignatius by Paul Troger is typical of his transparent style.

From Klagenfurt, take the Villacher Strasse (Route 83) rather than the autobahn to the **Wörther See,** Austria's great summer-resort area. The Wörther See is 17 km (10½ mi) long and the warmest of Carinthia's large lakes; people swim here beginning in early May. A great way to see the lake is on one of the boats that run from one end to the other, making frequent stops along the way. One of them, the SS *Thalia,* built in 1908, has been beautifully restored.

You can follow the crowded north shore to Velden by way of Pörtschach, bubbling with celebrities and excitement, or swing south and take the less traveled, scenic route; in any case, you should visit Maria Wörth on the south shore.

The first town on the north side is **Krumpendorf,** less chic and far less pretentious than the other resorts, but pleasant all the same, particularly for families seeking to escape the higher prices and singles crowds of other areas. Midway along is ⑩ **Pörtschach,** where the nightlife is as varied as the daytime activities. You'll find dozens of places to stay, including private rooms; most people book for a week.

⑪ On the southern side of the lake, in the beautiful town of **Maria Wörth,** the spired chapel on the peninsula reflected in the lake is one of Austria's most photographed sights. The present two churches date from the 12th century. The smaller "Winter," or "Rosary," church is basically Romanesque with later Gothic additions; the interior has a Romanesque choir with fragments of 12th-century frescoes of the apostles, a stained-glass Madonna window from 1420, and Gothic carved-wood figures. The larger parish church, despite its Romanesque portal, is mainly Gothic, with a Baroque interior. Skulls and bones can still be seen in the round Romanesque charnel house in the cemetery.

⑫ **Velden,** the most fashionable resort on the lake, sits at the west end of the Wörther See. The atmosphere here is definitely international chic—classy and lively—and the summer carnival in August adds to the action. If you're looking for a quiet holiday, Velden may be too exuberant, but the town is a good (if expensive) base for trips around the area.

You can take a back route (Villacher Strasse, Route 83) out of ⑬ Velden toward Villach to **Maria Gail.** The Romanesque parish church here has an unusually good 14th-century Gothic winged triptych altar. At Maria Gail, take Route 84 east 4 km (2.5 mi) to the **Faaker See.** This small lake is popular yet less crowded than other resort areas. The setting at the foot of the mountains is idyllic.

You can continue on Route 84 via Egg am Faaker See or go around the other side of the lake to Faak am See, and then south to scenic Route 85. This brings you into the Rosental, the attractive and fertile "Rose Valley," of which **St. Jakob,** a summer and winter resort, is the largest community.

Follow the valley on Route 85 until you come to the junction with Route 91 and turn north toward Klagenfurt. Stop at ⑭ **Viktring,** about 7 km (4½ mi) up the road, to see its Cistercian convent, established in 1142; you can still see parts of the moat. Don't miss the convent's arcaded cloisters, and look for the 14th- to 16th-century stained glass in the choir of the church, behind the Baroque high altar.

From Viktring it's 6½ km (4 mi) back to Klagenfurt.

Tour 3: North of Villach

Take Route 86 north from Villach to reach Route 100/E–14 and
⑮ head west. Follow the Drau valley to **Spittal an der Drau,** known
for its 16th-century Porcia castle, a beautiful Renaissance
building set in an attractive park. You've seen its graceful Italianate courtyard stairways and open corridors pictured often
in tourist literature. In summer it becomes the setting for classical plays, often Shakespeare. The upper floors house the local
museum (AS35, open May–mid-Oct., daily 9–6). Don't overlook
the Gothic parish church, with traces of earlier Romanesque, to
your left as you come into town. The **Goldeckbahn,** the aerial
tramway that leaves from behind the tennis hall on Ortenbur-
gerstrasse (tel. 04762/2864), will take you up to the 2,142-meter
(6,960-ft) peak of the Goldeck mountain, from which you get a
splendid panoramic view to the north and east.

From Spittal take Route 99 (Gmündner Strasse) 19 km (12 mi)
⑯ north to **Gmünd.** This little 16th-century town with medieval
walls has been carefully restored; the bright colors of the building facades on the oval central square stand in contrast to the
dark green of the forested hills. The new castle (1651) is
watched over by the old castle, in ruins above the town. Take a
look at the parish church and the ancient fresco on the outside
wall, which shows the town as it was in the 17th century, little
different from the way it looks today, except that the castle is
complete. The town museum in the lower gate tower seems always to be closed, but try it anyway. The automobile designer
Ferry Porsche was born and worked in Gmünd; a museum
shows a series of the cars he designed and built. *Tel. 04732/
2471. Admission: AS45 adults, AS25 children. Open mid-
May–mid-Oct., daily 9–6; mid-Oct.–mid-May, daily 10–4.* In
summer you can head up the scenic Malta valley to see the massive hydroelectric dam and lake at the top; in winter Gmünd
makes an ideal base for skiing the nearby slopes.

Tempting as it is to continue north along scenic Route 99, retrace your steps and turn east onto Route 98 to **Seeboden** at the
north end of the Millstätter See, a popular family summer re-
⑰ sort. About 5 km (3 mi) farther along you come to **Millstatt,** the
largest resort on the lake. The Benedictine abbey, with its imposing towers, many courtyards, and centuries-old linden
trees, was founded in the 11th century but secularized in the
18th. Parts can be seen only on conducted tours. The twin-tower Romanesque church of the same period was partially rebuilt
in Gothic style and later given some Baroque ornamentation,
but its 12th-century Romanesque portal remains its outstanding feature. Note also the *Kreuzgang*, the arcaded courtyard
between the church and the monastery, with its complicated
pillar ornaments. The abbey is scene of a music festival in summer months.

From Millstatt, continue along scenic Route 98 to reach
Radenthein. You'll skirt Döbriach, at the southern end of the
Millstätter See, another resort with a sandy shoreline and
warm water, mainly for summer tourists.

Radenthein is now the center of magnesite mining. Garnets,
said to be the petrified blood of giants, used to be found here in
some quantity. This is a good, inexpensive base for both winter
and summer vacations.

Heading north on Route 88, after about 6 km (4 mi), you come to
⓲ the booming town of **Bad Kleinkirchheim,** a stylish resort barely known 25 years ago. Although it's popular in summer, Bad
Kleinkirchheim really comes to life in the ski season. After a
day on the slopes you can plunge into the (re-created) Roman
baths, fed by thermal mineral springs. Nearby, the *Kathari-
nenkapelle* (St. Catherine's chapel) marks the location of one of
the springs; it has an organ loft with carved-wood reliefs and a
Late Gothic winged altar. Stop at **St. Oswald,** north of town, to
look at the unusual iron hinges on the doors of the Late Gothic
church and to see its frescoes of 1514.

Return on Route 88 to Radenthein, and head south on Route 98.
The first significant town is **Feld am See,** on the Feldsee, a little-known region of Carinthia, that appeals to those who want a
quiet resort. The Feldsee and the Afritzer See, just below, are
said to have once been one long lake until the legendary local
dragon swished his tail, knocking off the top of the Mirnock
mountain, which tumbled down and split the lake in two. Even
minus its crown, the mountain, at 2,110 meters (6,860 ft), is still
the highest peak around. Farther south, just below the two
lakes, is Afritz, a year-round resort whose onion dome on the
Gothic church was a later addition.

Just as the valley opens out, you'll come to **Treffen,** with a Baroque castle dating to 1691. A turn to your right on Route 94
brings you back to Villach.

What to See and Do with Children

Hochosterwitz castle (*see* Tour 1).

The **Minimundus** park, between Klagenfurt and the Wörther
See (*see* Tour 2) is a great place for children, with its 1:25-scale
models of such buildings as the Eiffel tower and St. Peter's cathedral. *Villacher Str. 241, tel. 0463/21194. Admission: AS60
adults, AS18 children. Open May–June and Sept.–mid-Oct.,
daily 8:30–6; July–Aug., daily 8:30–8. Closed mid-Oct.–April. Check for folklore performances on Wed. evenings in summer.*

The **Porsche automobile museum** in Gmünd (*see* Tour 3).

The **Puppen museum,** displaying 630 dolls made by dollmaker
Elli Riehl, is off Route 98 between Afritz and Treffen (*see* Tour
3); the turn is marked to *"Puppenmuseum." Winklern 14, tel.
04248/2395. Admission: AS35 adults, AS15 children. Open
mid-Apr.–June and late Sept.–mid-Oct., daily 2–6 PM; June–
late Sept., daily 9–noon and 2–6. Closed late Sept.–mid-Apr.*

Off the Beaten Track

In summer the MS *Villach* cruises the Drau River from Villach;
watching the sun set over the mountains while you dine on
board makes a memorable evening. For schedule and details,
check with the tourist office or **Drau-Schiffahrt** (Neubaugasse
32, tel. 04242/58071).

Southwest of Villach, the extremely scenic Villach alpine highway climbs the mountain ridge to about 1,540 meters (5,000 ft).
From there, a lift gets you up to Hohenrain, and a trail runs up
to the peak of the **Dobratsch mountain,** at 2,166 meters (7,040

ft), well above the rest of the surroundings, where you'll be rewarded by a spectacular view.

From Reifnitz, a quiet resort about 8 km (5 mi) west of Klagenfurt on the south side of the Wörther See, take a short side road to the small emerald-green Keutschacher lake and the town of **Keutschach,** with the Romanesque church of St. George, a Baroque castle, and an 800-year-old linden tree. A winding 5-km (3-mi) road ascends to the observation tower atop the 850-meter (2,790-ft) Pyramidenkogel; on a clear day you can see out over half of Carinthia.

Shopping

Carinthia is a good place to shop for fine hunting rifles, souvenirs, dolls, and regional clothing. The pedestrian zone of Villach has excellent shops selling a wide range of goods.

Sports and Fitness

Bicycling The area around the Ossiacher See (*see* Tour 1, above) is excellent for cycling, and many of the main roads have parallel cycling paths. You can rent a bicycle at the **Ossiach-Bodensdorf railroad station** (tel. 04243/2218), where there's also a dock; you can put the bike on the boat, get off and cycle to the next boat landing, and return by boat when you run out of energy.

Bicycles can be rented in the larger resort towns around the Wörther See and at several railroad stations along the route of Tour 2: at **Faak am See** (tel. 04254/2149), **Klagenfurt main station** (tel. 0463/1700), and **Velden** (tel. 04274/2115).

The area around the Millstätter See is about the only area good for cycling on Tour 3. You can rent bicycles at the **Spittal-Millstätter See railroad station** (tel. 04762/397–6390).

Fishing The Ossiacher See, Wörther See, and Faaker See all have excellent fishing. You'll need a license, which is issued by the tourist office. Some lakeside hotels offer fishing packages and allow you to fish in reserved waters. The booklet *Kärnten Fischen* from Kärnten Information (Box 15, A–9021 Krumpendorf) gives details of fishing waters, season, possible catch, bait, and local license-issuing authorities. Check also with boat-rental shops (*Bootsverleih*); often they can assist, and some can issue licenses.

Golf The courses around the southern lakes are:

Kärntner Golf Club at Dellach/Maria Wörth. *18 holes, par 70. Tel. 04273/2515. Greens fee: AS500. Open Apr.–Oct.*

Golfclub Klopeiner See at St. Kanzian/Grabelsdorf. *18 holes, par 72. Tel. 04239/3800. Greens fee: AS450. Open late-Mar.– early Nov.*

Golfanlage Moosburg-Pörtschach. *18 holes, par 72. Tel. 04272/ 83486. Greens fee: AS450. Open Apr.–Nov.*

Golfanlagen Velden-Köstenberg. *18 holes, par 72. Tel. 04724/ 7045. Greens fee: AS500. Open Apr.–Nov.*

The 18-hole, par-72 course of **Golfclub Bad Kleinkirchheim** is challenging for beginners and advanced golfers alike. *Tel. 04275/594. Greens fee: AS450. Open May–Oct.*

Hiking   Trails crisscross the hills and mountains of the Ossiacher See
               area, and hiking is also good around Friesach and Hochost-
               erwitz. From every community around the southern lakes,
               marked paths radiate out over mountains and through valleys.
               There's unusually good hiking starting from Spittal, and even
               better from Gmünd, Seeboden, Millstatt, Bad Kleinkirchheim,
               Feld am See, and Afritz. Local information offices will have
               suggestions for routes and for combining a hike with a return
               by local bus.

Riding   Carinthia offers superb riding terrain, from mountains to
               woodlands. In nearly 30 towns you'll find stables and a number
               of hotels that offer riding package holidays. Otherwise a day's
               outing will cost you AS600–AS900. The brochure *Reiten*, from
               Kärnten Information, has details.

Skiing   Friesach is developing as a ski area, particularly for cross coun-
               try, but **Bad Kleinkirchheim** is unquestionably Carinthia's top
               ski resort. In Gmünd, Feld am See, and Afritz, costs are far
               lower but après-ski entertainment is sparse.

Swimming and   All communities along the major lakes have public beaches.
Water Sports   The water in the Carinthian lakes is pure enough to drink, and
               by late summer water temperatures can reach 25°C (75° F).
               Most of the swimming beaches also have wading or supervised
               areas for small children. To avoid the crowds, book at a hotel
               that has its own private beach (most do), or try one of the small-
               er lakes. Pörtschach and Velden on the Wörther See are the
               centers of activity for windsurfing, parasurfing, and sail-
               ing. Check **Herbert Schweiger** (10-Oktober-Str. 33, Pörtschach,
               tel. 04272/2655) or **Segel-u. Surfschule Wörthersee/Berger**
               (Seecorso 40, Velden, tel. 04274/2691 or 2956). Several hotels on
               the Wörther See offer sailing and surfing packages. You can
               also rent boats at Seeboden, Millstatt, Dobriach, and Feld am
               See.

Tennis   Most of the large towns have public courts, but you'll either
               have to book in advance or wait your turn. In the Villach area,
               try **Tennisplätze ASKÖ** (Süduferstr., tel. 04242/41879) or
               Tenniscenter Warmbad (Villach-Warmbad Villach, tel. 04242/
               300–1393). Many hotels around the southern lakes have their
               own courts, some of them indoors. In Klagenfurt, check
               Tenniscenter Allround (Welzeneggerstr., tel. 0463/31571) or
               Tennisplätze M. Schoklitsch (Feschnigstr. 209, tel. 0463/
               41140). In Feld am See, the **Hotel Alte Post** specializes in tennis
               packages (*see* Dining and Lodging, below).

Dining and Lodging

Dining

In many of the towns of Carinthia you'll find country inns that
have dining rooms, but few, if any, separate restaurants.
Prices for meals include taxes and a service charge but not the
customary small additional tip.

Highly recommended restaurants are indicated by a star ★.

Category	Cost*
Very Expensive	over AS500
Expensive	AS300–AS500
Moderate	AS200–AS300
Inexpensive	under AS200

per person for a typical 3-course meal, with a glass of house wine

Lodging

The accommodations will range from luxurious lakeside resorts to small country inns or even guest houses without private baths. Room rates include taxes and service and almost always breakfast, except in the most expensive hotels, but it is wise to ask. It is customary to leave a small (AS20) additional tip for the chambermaid.

Highly recommended lodgings are indicated by a star ★.

Category	Cost*
Very Expensive	over AS1,500
Expensive	AS1,000–AS1,500
Moderate	AS700–AS1,000
Inexpensive	under AS700

per person for a standard double room with bath, including service and tax

Bad Kleinkirchheim

Dining and Lodging **Römerbad.** This family-run chalet-style hotel, tucked away behind fir trees, is a bit east of the center, but the Roman bath is just down the hall and sports facilities a short walk away. Public rooms are spacious, balconied guest rooms slightly less so, and the warmth of the rustic decor with lots of wood creates a comfortable atmosphere. Rooms on the south side have a view of the mountains. The restaurant is the best in the area, with creative cuisine based on Austrian and regional specialties. Seasonal salads, lamb, and game are recommended favorites. *Zirkitzen 69, A-9546, tel. 04240/8234. 37 rooms. Facilities: restaurant (reservations required, jacket advised), sauna, solarium, fitness room. AE, DC, MC. Closed mid-Apr.–mid-May. Expensive (hotel)–Very Expensive (restaurant).*

Lodging **Pulverer.** This friendly hotel, in a group of interconnected chalet-style buildings, is not only in the center of town but is one of the centers of activity. You can take a cure with the medicinal thermal waters and undo the good work at the enticing buffets: breakfast, salad, strudel, and hors d'oeuvre. The reception area has a cathedral ceiling; the guest rooms are done in elegant country-rustic decor, with lots of wood. *Bach 1, A-9546, tel. 04240/744. 100 rooms. Facilities: restaurant, indoor and outdoor pools, sauna, solarium, spa with therapeutic thermal* *water treatment. No credit cards. Closed Nov.–mid-Dec. Very Expensive.*

Ronacher. You can easily spoil yourself at this combination sports and cure facility, with its in-house thermal baths and luxurious balconied rooms in modern rustic decor. The large hotel, in a typical country design—dark wood against white— is off the main road in the middle of town. It organizes many activities for those who dislike planning. *Bach 8, A–9546, tel. 04240/282. 92 rooms. Facilities: restaurant, indoor and out- door pools, sauna, solarium, medicinal spa with thermal- water treatment. AE, DC, MC, V. Closed Apr. and late Oct.– mid-Dec. Very Expensive.*

Egg am Faaker See

Dining and
Lodging
★

Karnerhof. A chalet with a long, low extension, in a style that suits the dramatic landscape, is set in a garden on the lake with the mountain range as a backdrop. This affiliate of the Silencehotel group offers attractive rustic rooms and an excel- lent restaurant to complement the sensational setting. The food alone is worth a visit; all dishes are freshly prepared, and the fish is particularly good. *A–9580, tel. 04254/2188. 105 rooms. Facilities: restaurant (reservations advised, jacket ad- vised), indoor pool, sauna, solarium, fitness room, tennis. No credit cards. Closed Nov.–Apr. Expensive.*

Feld am See

Dining and
Lodging

Lindenhof. The location is quiet, but the friendly family man- agement runs an active program at this modern house, with a bar for dancing and entertainment. The rooms are warmly fur- nished with country charm and much attention to detail. The restaurant offers Austrian and area specialties; soups are par- ticularly good. *Dorfstr. 8, A–9544, tel. 04246/2274. 27 rooms. Facilities: restaurant (DC, MC; closed in winter), bar, sauna, boating, tennis. No credit cards in hotel. Closed Nov. and Mar.–Easter. Expensive.*

Alte Post. This typical country hotel contrasts rustic wood against sparkling white and overflows in summer with red ge- raniums. The balconied rooms are equally friendly. But sports are featured at this family-run resort hotel; you can play tennis to your heart's content or learn windsurfing or sailing. *Kirchenplatz 1, A–9544, tel. 04246/2276. 45 rooms. Facilities: restaurant, outdoor pool, sailing, windsurfing, tennis, riding. No credit cards. Closed Nov. Moderate.*

Friesach

Lodging
★

Friesacherhof. This comfortable hotel is incorporated into a centuries-old building on the main square. The rooms in the front look out over the square and the Renaissance fountain and are somewhat noisy. *Hauptplatz 4, A–9360, tel. 04268/2123. 22 rooms. Facilities: restaurant, café. AE, DC, MC, V. Moderate.*

Gmünd

Dining

Stadtschänke zu den Grafen Lodron. No matter what kind of decor you like, you'll find it in this attractive 14th-century house tucked against the town wall. There's an elegant dining room upstairs; a rustic one on the ground floor; and a few steps down, a vaulted stone Keller. The food is mostly local specialties; try the lamb or ask for suggestions. For dessert you might ask for the Salzburger Nockerln, a delicious baked meringue that's done to perfection. *Hauptplatz 27, tel. 04732/2218. Reservations advised. Jacket and tie required upstairs; jacket advised elsewhere. AE, DC, MC, V. Moderate.*

Dining and Lodging
Kohlmayr. Behind the pinkish facade of this family-run hotel on the town square you'll find a particularly friendly staff and modern, attractive rooms in rustic decor. Up the stone steps is a large reception room furnished with country antiques (including a spinning wheel). The rooms in front have a stunning view over the square. The whole town gathers in the *Bierstube* in the late afternoon and on Sunday morning. The restaurant offers good standard Austrian country fare. *Hauptplatz 7, A-9853, tel. 04732/2149. 24 rooms. Facilities: restaurant, bierstube. No credit cards. Closed Nov. Moderate.*

Klagenfurt

Dining
★
Lido am See. Your choice here is either the inexpensive but very good bistro or the outstanding small restaurant (preferred). Both overlook the end of the Wörther See, and fish is featured in the top-rated restaurant. Try the mousse of smoked eel or lake perch with thyme butter or the beef fillet in shallot–red-wine sauce. The wine list is good. *Friedelstrand 1, tel. 0463/261723. Reservations recommended in restaurant; jacket and tie advised. Dress in bistro: casual but neat. AE, DC, MC, V. Closed Tues. Oct.–June. Expensive.*

★
Peterwirt. In Walddorf, about 6 km (4 mi) north of Klagenfurt on Route 83, you'll find one of the better-kept restaurant secrets. This is country cooking at its best, with no pretension. Ask for recommendations, then choose from such Austrian standards as roast chicken, beef roulade, or Carinthian cheese noodles (a local form of ravioli with cream-cheese filling); everything is freshly prepared. *Klagenfurt/Walddorf 1, tel. 0463/42646. Reservations not required. Dress: jacket advised. No credit cards. Moderate.*

Weinstube Kanzian. The atmosphere is plain in this friendly courtyard, but the wines are good and the food, mainly local specialties, includes huge Wiener schnitzels that are bigger than the plate. *Kardinalplatz 2, tel. 0463/512233. Reservations not required. Jacket advised. No credit cards. Moderate.*

Dining and Lodging
Dermuth. On the outskirts of the city at the edge of a wood, this recently renovated mansion-chalet now has all amenities. Try to get a room on the woods side—they're gloriously peaceful. *Kohldorferstr. 52, A-9020, tel. 0463/21247. 55 rooms. Facilities: restaurant, indoor pool, sauna, solarium. AE, MC, V. Closed late Dec.–mid-Jan. Expensive.*

Europapark. At this small hotel out of the center of town, toward the lake, you'll be a five-minute walk from Minimundus park and its models of famous buildings. The rooms are comfortable, and the decor is abstract modern with contemporary furnishings. The garden café-restaurant under the chestnut trees is particularly inviting. *Villacher Str. 222, A-9020, tel. 0463/21137. 21 rooms. Facilities: restaurant, garage. AE, DC, MC, V. Expensive.*

Kurhotel. This modern beige-and-brown block is in the middle of the city. The rooms are standard contemporary; those on the inside are quieter. *8.-Mai-Str. 41, A-9010, tel. 0463/511645. 28* *rooms. Facilities: restaurant, sauna. AE, DC, MC, V. Expensive.*

★ **Moser-Verdino.** Renovations have kept pace with the times at this striking pink-and-white hostelry, the city's leading hotel for 100 years. The Art Deco design carries over into some of the rooms, no two of which are alike. The café is nearly always full and is a good spot for a snack. *Domgasse 2, A–9010, tel. 0463/ 57878. 73 rooms. Facilities: restaurant, bar, café. AE, DC, MC, V. Expensive.*

★ **Musil.** Modern hotel amenities have been tastefully incorporated into a 15th-century nobleman's palace in the center of town, and the elegance is beautifully preserved. The style is personal and intimate, and each room is different. Decor ranges from overblown Baroque to fussy Biedermeier and simple Austrian rural. Rooms open onto a series of interior balconies. The popular café serves cakes from the hotel's own bakery. The candlelit restaurant is good; try the game in season. The hotel is a member of the Romantik Hotel group. You'll need to book a couple of months ahead. *10.-Oktober-Str. 14, A– 9010, tel. 0463/511660. 13 rooms. Facilities: restaurant (reservations advised, jacket and tie advised), sauna, café. AE, DC, MC, V. Hotel closed last 2 weeks Dec. Expensive.*

★ **Wörthersee.** At the end of the lake, on its own beach, this glowing yellow mansion with fancy woodwork, towers, and balconies will remind you of the era of the grand hotels. The rooms are modern and comfortable; the preferred ones overlook the lake. The restaurant, featuring regional dishes, is one of the best in the area. Try any of the lamb specialties. *Villacher Str. 338, A–9010, tel. 0463/21158. 41 rooms. Facilities: restaurant (reservations advised; jacket advised at lunch and required at dinner; closed Sun., Mon. lunch), lake swimming. DC, V. Closed Jan. Expensive.*

★ **Sandwirt.** This centrally located hotel, incorporated into a 17th-century town house, preserves its large rooms and high ceilings and has traditional, comfortable furnishings. The family management is hospitable and friendly. The hotel is now part of the Best Western group. *Pernhartgasse 9, A–9010, tel. 0463/56209. 40 rooms. Facilities: restaurant, garage. AE, DC, MC, V. Moderate.*

Krumpendorf

Lodging **Schloss Hallegg.** Just east of Krumpendorf, a small road head-
★ ing north leads to an early 13th-century castle above the lake, tucked away on the edge of a nature preserve. Now adapted as a hotel, its rooms are spacious and comfortable. You'll get breakfast only, but there are restaurants in town. There's a small lake for swimming and fishing, and ample grounds for hunting and riding. *Hallegger Str. 131, A–9201, tel. 0463/ 49311. 15 rooms. Facilities: swimming, fishing, tennis, riding. No credit cards. Closed Oct.–mid-May. Moderate.*

Maria Wörth

Lodging **Astoria.** This massive, comfortable villa on the lake is just 2 km from the 18-hole, par-70 Kärntner Golf Club course at Dellach (*see* Sports, above); the hotel offers golf-holiday packages. The rooms are attractively furnished; those overlooking the lake are preferred. *A–9082, tel. 04273/2279. 46 rooms. Facilities: restaurant, Bierstube, indoor pool, lake swimming, sailing,* *sauna, garage. No credit cards. Closed mid-Oct.–mid-May. Expensive.*

Millstatt

**Dining and
Lodging**

Alpenrose. This attractive house advertises itself as Austria's first "bio-hotel"—it is constructed entirely of natural materials (primarily wood and brick) and uses no plastic or anything artificial in either the structure or the rooms, which are particularly inviting in their rustic design. The excellent restaurant carries on with only natural ingredients; many of the vegetables are organically grown in the side garden. Try the cabbage soup or the Carinthian cheese noodles to start, and follow with the lake trout or pepper steak. *Obermillstatt 84, A–9872, tel. 04766/2500. 27 rooms. Facilities: restaurant (reservations advised, jacket advised, closed Tues.), outdoor pool, sauna, spa facilities. No credit cards. Expensive.*

Die Forelle. This four-story balconied house sprawls along the lake, its tree-shaded terrace directly over the water. The public rooms are elegant but comfortable, the guest rooms bright and welcoming. The hotel has its own stretch of fishing water. The restaurant is good and improving; fish is featured here, but ask for recommendations. *Fischergasse 65, A–9872, tel. 04766/2050. 68 rooms. Facilities: restaurant (reservations not required, dress casual but neat at lunch, jacket advised at dinner), outdoor pool, lake swimming, sailing, sauna, solarium, fishing. No credit cards. Closed Nov.–Apr. Expensive.*

Post. This is a spot for family relaxation; the hotel will happily look after the children. Many of the spacious newer rooms have small kitchenettes and extra sleeping space for children. You're in the center of town here, but guests can use the huge lawn and large bathing beach of the nearby Postillion am See, which is under the same management. Fishing can be arranged. *Mirnockstr. 38, A–9872, tel. 04766/2108. 31 rooms. Facilities: restaurant, lake swimming. No credit cards. Closed Nov.–May. Moderate.*

Ossiach

Lodging

Schlosswirt Pribernig. Rooms in this wood-paneled chalet-style house are compact, but it's close to the lake and the restaurant is good. The terrace is particularly pleasant, and the staff is friendly if sometimes overworked. *A–9570, tel. 04243/347. 8 rooms. No credit cards. Closed Nov.–May. Inexpensive.*

Pörtschach

Dining

Casa Rossa. This Italian restaurant has long been one of the in spots in Pörtschach. It serves fish and some unusual dishes with an Italian flair, such as gnocchi in spinach cream sauce, spaghetti with asparagus, or saltimbocca. Wines are Italian. *Hauptstr. 211, tel. 04272/2410. Reservations advised. Dress: jacket and tie. No credit cards. Closed for lunch. Closed Oct.–May. Moderate.*

**Dining and
Lodging**

Schloss Seefels. At Töschling, about 3 km (2 mi) west of Pörtschach, this hotel attracts a prominent international clientele. The sprawling, interconnected buildings are set in a huge park on the lake, the staff is friendly, and the elegantly furnished rooms are in the *Grand Hotel* tradition. You can go by boat directly to Klagenfurt and to the Kärntner golf course across the lake (*see* Sports and Fitness, above). Relax in the wicker-furnished café-restaurant or indulge in any of a dozen sports. *A–9210, Pörtschach/Töschling 1, tel. 04272/2377. 80 rooms. Facilities: restaurant, indoor and outdoor pools, sailing, sauna, solarium, fitness room, tennis, golf. AE, DC, MC, V. Very Expensive.*

Europa. This modern hotel, rather uninspired on the outside, stands directly on the water. Ask for a room on the lake side and enjoy the sunniest corner of the lake. The water view is wonderful from the excellent restaurant. Fish is the best choice here: for example, the grilled lake perch, with just a touch of garlic. *Augustenstr. 24, A–9210, tel. 04272/2244. 40 rooms. Facilities: restaurant (reservations advised, jacket advised), swimming, sailing, cycling, golf. AE, DC, MC, V. Closed Oct.–May. Expensive.*

Parkhotel. The hotel's setting—on a peninsula jutting into the lake—is the feature here, rather than its cubist modern style. The rooms are comfortably contemporary, and you'll have a great view of the lake and mountains from your balcony. There are special programs for children. *Elisabethstr. 22, A–9210, tel. 04272/2621. 199 rooms. Facilities: restaurant, indoor pool, swimming, sailing, sauna, solarium, tennis, putting green, golf. AE, DC, V. Expensive.*

★ **Schloss Leonstain.** This appealing 500-year-old castle, complete with tower and antique furnishings, is unfortunately between the railroad and the highway. Quiet is hard to find, but other distractions help compensate for the drawback. The restaurant is rated the best in town and is well worth a visit on its own. In summer tables are set in the courtyard as well as in the historic rooms. You might try the pepper steak, veal in cream sauce, or the unusually good Austrian boiled beef. The wine list is excellent, and service is outstanding. *Hauptstr. 228, A–9210, tel. 04272/2816. 35 rooms. Facilities: restaurant (reservations advised, jacket and tie advised), swimming, sailing, sauna, solarium, tennis, golf. AE, DC, MC, V. Closed mid-Oct.–early May. Expensive.*

Werzer-Astoria. This complex offers the choice of a room in one of the villas or in the (less appealing) hotel block, with perhaps greater comfort but less charm. The setting, in a park on a small peninsula, is splendid, and the family management has succeeded in blending the traditional with the new. The charming 19th-century boathouse contains a restaurant. *Werzerpromenade 8, A–9210, tel. 04272/2231. 132 rooms. Facilities: restaurant, indoor and outdoor pools, lake swimming, sailing, sauna, solarium, fitness room, tennis, golf, squash, riding, cycling. AE, DC, MC, V. Closed Oct.–Apr. Expensive.*

Radenthein

Dining and Lodging **Metzgerwirt.** Looking at first like little more than a mauve cube, the inside of this modern house offers friendly comfort in a rustic atmosphere. For hikers, the location is fine, and it's close to ski slopes, but note that it's some miles from the nearest swimming, in the Millstätter See. The house has its own butcher, which usually guarantees the quality of the meat; indeed, the restaurant has a fairly good reputation. Try the baked meringue Salzburger Nockerl for dessert. The service is fine, and the wine list is up to par. *Hauptstr. 22, A–9545, tel.*

04246/2052. 18 rooms. Reservations not required in restaurant. Dress: casual but neat. AE, DC, MC, V. Moderate.

St. Veit an der Glan

Dining ★

Pukelsheim. Despite its enlargement, this restaurant remains crowded—which testifies to its good reputation. You'll find variations on Austrian themes, such as veal tongue with vegetables, or stuffed roast chicken. But Pukelsheim is best known for its desserts: superb cakes and pies made with whatever fruit is in season. The open wines are excellent. *Erlgasse 11, tel. 04212/2473. Reservations advised; jacket and tie advised. AE, MC, V. Closed Mon., 1 week in Feb., first week of Sept. Expensive.*

Spittal an der Drau

Dining and Lodging

Alte Post. This traditional, friendly house in the center of town has comfortable modern rooms, a good restaurant, and the bonus of fishing rights on a reserved stretch of the Drau river. *Hauptplatz 13, A–9800, tel. 04762/22170. 42 rooms. Facilities: restaurant, bar, garage. No credit cards. Closed Jan. Expensive.*

Ertl. You can't miss this red-fronted family-run hotel; it's just steps from the railroad station but away from heavy traffic. If you're touring by train, this is your choice; the rooms are large and attractively decorated. *Bahnhofstr. 26, A–9800, tel. 04762/2048. 40 rooms. Facilities: restaurant, outdoor pool, mini-golf, garage. No credit cards. Closed Nov. Expensive.*

Velden

Dining and Lodging

Parkhotel. This exclusive turn-of-the-century mansion, set in a park amid a stand of huge old trees, has been renovated to offer every comfort. From the spacious lobby to the guest rooms, you'll find elegance and attentive service. The restaurant is rated best in the area; try such specialties as the potato–sour cream soup, the trout, and the excellent desserts. The menu changes frequently, with the season. The wine list is good; ask for advice in selection. *Seecorso 68, A–9220, tel. 04274/2298. 88 rooms. Facilities: restaurant (reservations advised; jacket and tie suggested), bar, indoor pool, lake swimming, sailing, tennis. AE. Closed Oct.–May. Very Expensive.*

Hubertushof. Two typical resort houses from the turn of the century comprise this family-run complex directly on the lake. A touch of the original Art Deco carries over into some of the rooms, most of which have balconies. The best rooms face the lake. *Europaplatz 1, A–9220, tel. 04274/2676. 48 rooms. Facilities: restaurant, indoor pool, lake swimming, sailing, sauna, solarium. DC, V. Closed Nov.–Apr. Expensive.*

Seehotel Engstler. This newly renovated hotel is in the center of town, but its design cleverly protects its peaceful lakeside beach. Rooms in the new wing or on the lake side of the older house are preferred. *Am Korso, A–9220, tel. 04274/2644. 46 rooms. Facilities: restaurant, bar, lake swimming, sailing, sauna, solarium, putting green. No credit cards. Closed mid-Oct.–late Apr. Expensive.*

Villach

Dining
★
If you head north out of Villach on Route 86, you'll come to Untere Fellach, with a turnoff to the left marked to "Bleiberg" (there's also bus service out of Villach). About 13 km (8 mi) up this scenic country road, Bad Bleiberg is the site of the **Bleibergerhof,** one of Austria's dozen best restaurants. You'll dine in elegant but unpretentious splendor on Carinthian specialties that vary with the season, with a choice of exquisite soups or light first courses. The service is impeccable; ask for advice on wines. The Bleibergerhof also has spa facilities, drawing on the hot mineral springs that flow from the mountain behind it. *A–9530, tel. 04244/2205. Reservations required for lunch and dinner. Jacket required at lunch, jacket and tie at dinner. AE, DC, V. Closed Sun. dinner through Tues. lunch; closed Nov. to just before Christmas. Very Expensive.*

Dining and
Lodging
★
Post. This beautifully adapted Renaissance palace, which dates to 1500, is in the pedestrian zone in the heart of the old city. Architects have cleverly created an elegant, modern hotel while preserving the vaulting and other original features of the building and its arcaded inner court. Service is personal and friendly. The ocher tones in the restaurant, with its arched ceiling, create a warm, inviting atmosphere; dishes range from the "light" health and diet food of the new Austrian cuisine to such traditional Carinthian specialties as cheese noodles and other Austrian standards. It is a member of the Romantik Hotel group. *Hauptplatz 26, A–9500, tel. 04242/26101. 77 rooms. Facilities: restaurant, bar, sauna, solarium, fitness room, garage. AE, DC, MC, V. Expensive.*

Lodging
Europa. You'll be across the river from the old city but just two minutes from the main rail station in this attractive yellow-and-white hostelry. The rooms are done with 19th-century reproduction furnishings; those on the inner side are quieter. The house is associated with the Best Western group. *Bahnhofstr. 10, A–9500, tel. 04242/26766. 44 rooms. Facilities: café, bar, sauna, fitness room, garage. AE, DC, MC, V. Moderate.*

Warmbad Villach

Dining and
Lodging
★
Warmbaderhof. The cure's the thing here, with the tranquil setting in the park seducing you into relaxation. The feeling of quiet comfort in this meandering house carries over into the guest rooms. Ask for one of the modern, balconied rooms overlooking "Napoleon's meadow." The Kleines Restaurant, with its wood and brass decor, is one of the best in the area; you can expect delicious lamb and game in season. *A–9504, tel. 04242/ 30010. 128 rooms. Facilities: restaurant (reservations suggested, jacket and tie advised), connecting indoor and outdoor pools, sauna, solarium, fitness room, tennis, riding, garage. AE, DC, MC. Very Expensive.*

Lodging
Karawankenhof. The larger rooms in this recently rebuilt hotel will appeal to those who want to take the cure or use this as a base for further excursions in Carinthia. Children are particularly welcome. An underground passageway leads to the spa, with its water slide and pools. The glassed-in terrace restaurant is a delight, but the kitchen does not live up to it. *A–9504, tel. 04242/3002. 80 rooms, 9 apartments. Facilities: restau-*

rant, indoor and outdoor pools, sauna, tennis. AE, DC, V. Expensive.

Josephinenhof. Modern without being impersonal, this newish hotel is set in the comfortable isolation of the Kurpark. The restaurant is unexciting, but ample other possibilities are close by. *A–9504, tel. 04242/3003. 61 rooms. Facilities: restaurant, indoor and outdoor pools, spa, sauna, tennis. AE, V. Closed late Nov.–mid-Dec. Moderate.*

The Arts and Nightlife

The Arts

Music and Opera During the Carinthian Summer festival in July and August, performances are given in Villach and Ossiach. Emphasis is on the classics, but jazz and pop are heard, too. Chamber concerts are all the more attractive for their setting in the Baroque chapel in Ossiach. For a schedule or tickets, contact **Carinthischen Sommer** (Stift Ossiach, A–9570 Ossiach, tel. 04243/2510, June–Aug., and at Gumpendorfer Str. 76, A–1060 Vienna, tel. 0222/568198 the rest of the year). Opera and operetta are given at the Stadttheater in Klagenfurt year round. For details and tickets, contact **Stadttheater Klagenfurt** (Theaterplatz 4, A–9020 Klagenfurt, tel. 0463/548910. Box office open Sept.–June, Tues.–Sat. 9–noon, 4–6; July–Aug., Tues.–Sat. 9–noon, 5–7). In Millstatt there's something going on much of the year: **Musical Spring** runs from April through June; **International Music Weeks** take over during July and August, followed by **Musical Autumn** in September. Most events take place in the Benedictine abbey. For program details and ticket reservations, contact the secretariat (Stiftgasse 1, A–9872 Millstatt, tel. 04766/2165).

Theater From late June to mid-August there's open-air theater at **Friesach,** in German. Check with the local tourist office for details and tickets. In **Spittal an der Drau,** from mid-July through August, three or four plays are presented in the marvelous setting of **Schloss Porcia.** The experience is exciting, even if the productions in German are not always as polished as you might expect. For program information and ticket details, call 04762/3420.

Nightlife

In resort centers, such as Ossiach and Bad Kleinkirchheim, you'll find regular evenings of **folk music and dancing,** some of them organized by the hotels. The local tourist offices will have details, and notices are often posted around the area. Après-ski life in Bad Kleinkirchheim centers on the hotels, **Ronacher** and **Pulverer** being the current favorites.

In Pörtschach the crowd at **Rainer's** is young, and the nights, lively, loud, and long. The restaurant, already earning a good reputation, is a recent addition to this popular watering hole. *Monte-Carlo-Platz 1, tel. 04272/3046. AE, DC, MC, V. Open May–Sept., nightly.*

The chic Klagenfurt crowd gathers at **Scotch Club,** currently the city's best disco. *Pfarrplatz 20, tel. 0463/54097. No credit cards. Open daily from 8 PM.*

The casino in the center of **Velden** is a focal point in the evening, but you must be 19 or over. Along with the gambling tables and slot machines, the complex contains a disco, bars, and a restaurant, whose terrace overlooks the lake. *Am Corso 17, tel. 04274/2064. Passport required. Jacket and tie required; no tennis shoes. Open nightly 3 PM–3 or 4 AM.*

9 Eastern Alps

East Tirol,
Salzburg Province,
West Styria

Introduction

by George W. Hamilton

The Eastern Alpine region of Austria is marked by long river valleys and majestic peaks, many well over 3,000 meters (9,750 ft.) high. The broad valleys (many with the suffix "au," meaning marsh meadow) are the basins of rivers that cross the region between mountain ranges, sometimes meandering, sometimes plunging. The land is full of ice caves and salt mines, deep gorges, and hot springs. Higher up, slow-drifting glaciers give way to sweeping alpine meadows, in spring and summer ablaze with wildflowers. This is dramatic countryside, with breathtaking scenery and great winter sports equal to those in Switzerland, but it is for most tourists almost unknown. Most of the tourism is concentrated in relatively few towns, but wherever you go you'll find good lodging, solid local food, and friendly folk. Don't look for anything too fancy here; this isn't where the beautiful people go to see and be seen. Rather, it's countryside to drive and hike and ski through, where people live simply, from and close to the land.

The Hohe Tauern national park stretches across the southern extreme of Salzburg province and into parts of East Tirol and Carinthia—a beautiful and largely undeveloped area. At its heart is an alpine wilderness, with a unique plant and animal world that includes chamois and ibex. The park's easiest approach is from Heiligenblut or Grosskirchen/Döllach.

Essential Information

Important Addresses and Numbers

Tourist Information For information about **Carinthia** (C.), contact Kärnten Information (Hallegger Str. 1, A–9201 Krumpendorf, tel. 04229/2224); for **East Tirol** (E.T.): Tirol-Information (Bozner Platz 6, A–6010 Innsbruck, tel. 0512/53200); for **Salzburg Province** (S.P.): Salzburger Land Tourismus (Alpenstr. 96, A–5033 Salzburg, tel. 0662/20506); for **Styria** (S.): Landesfremdenverkehrsverband Steiermark (Herrengasse 16, A–8010 Graz, tel. 0316/835241).

Tourist offices (*Fremdenverkehrsamt*) in the individual towns are:

Heiligenblut (Verkehrsbüro, A–9844, C., tel. 04824/200122).

Hermagor (Wulfeniaplatz 1, A–9620, C., tel. 04282/2043).

Kötschach–Mauthen (Kurverwaltung, Kötschach 390, A–9640, C., tel. 04715/8516).

Lienz (Albin-Egger-Str. 17, A–9900, E.T., tel. 04852/65265).

Matrei (Rauterplatz 1, A–9971, E.T., tel. 04875/6709, 04875/6527).

Radstadt (Stadtplatz 17, A–5550 Radstadt, S.P., tel. 06452/305, 06452/7472).

Ramsau am Dachstein (Kulm 40, A–8972, S., tel. 03687/81925, 03687/81500, 03687/81833).

Saalbach-Hinterglemm (A–5753, S.P., tel. 06541/7272).

Saalfelden (Bahnhofstr. 10, A–5760, S.P., tel. 06582/3195, 06582/2513).

St. Jakob in Defereggen (Unterrotte 75, A–9963, E.T., tel. 04873/5265, 04873/5228, 04873/5484, 04873/5485).

St. Johann im Pongau (Hauptstr. 41, A–5600, S.P., tel. 06412/465, 06412/6036).

Schladming (Hauptplatz 18, A–8970, S., tel. 03687/222680).

Zell am See (A–5700, S.P., tel. 06542/26000).

Arriving and Departing

By Plane The closest airport is at Klagenfurt, 50 km (31 mi) from Villach, where the tour begins. It is served by Austrian Airlines, Lufthansa, KLM, Swissair, and Cross Air. The tour ends near Salzburg, which has its own airport (*see* Chapter 7). Both have frequent connections to other Austrian cities and other points in Europe; neither airport has scheduled overseas connections.

By Car Coming from northern Italy, you get to Villach on the E-56 autobahn; from Klagenfurt, about 35 km (23 mi) away, taking the A-2 autobahn is quickest.

By Train The starting and ending points, Villach and Salzburg, are both served by frequent main-line rail service from Vienna; Villach is also connected to Italy, and Salzburg, to Germany and beyond.

Getting Around

By Car A car is by far the preferred means of seeing this area; the roads are good, and you can stop for picnics or just to marvel at the scenery. Be aware that the Grossglockner mountain road is closed from mid-November or possibly earlier (the first heavy snow) to mid-May or early June, and though many of the other high mountain roads are kept open in winter, driving them is nevertheless tricky.

By Train You can reach most of the towns on this tour by train, but highlights such as the Grossglockner and the Dachstein mountains are reachable in a practical sense only by road. If you follow the tours by train, you can go from Villach to Hermagor, to Lienz, and northward (north of Spittal an der Drau) via Mallnitz and Badgastein to the main line at Schwarzach. You can cut back westward to Zell am See or continue onward to Bischofshofen, connecting there via Radstadt to Schladming, in the Dachstein area. Back at Bischofshofen, the main line continues north to Salzburg.

By Bus As is typical throughout Austria, where trains don't go, the post office and railroad buses do, though some of the side routes are less frequently covered. You'll need to coordinate your schedule with that of the buses, not as difficult as it may sound; the Austrian travel offices are unusually helpful in this regard. In Villach, call 04242/23666 or 04242/206–3305; in Salzburg, 0662/517–2238 or 0622/72150 for bus information.

Guided Tours

Day-long guided bus tours from Salzburg include the Grossglocker mountain highway (*see* Guided Tours in Chapter 7 for details).

Exploring the Eastern Alps

Tour 1 takes us from Villach, in Carinthia, to Lienz, in East Tirol, then into the Defereggental, north to Matrei and back to Lienz. Tour 2 goes north over the Grossglockner mountain pass (only in summer), through Salzburg province to the charming Zell am See and beyond. Tour 3 heads east along the Salzach river valley from Zell am See, with a side trip to Badgastein, then on to Radstadt and Schladming, just over into Styria. Tour 4 takes in the magnificent Dachstein mountain complex and retraces our steps to go up through the Salzburg Dolomite range, ending about 40 km (25 mi) from Salzburg. You can do it all in a rather full three days, or you could take a leisurely week, exploring the smaller towns and byways.

Highlights for First-time Visitors

Dachstein Glacier (*see* Tour 4)
Geo-Trail near Hermagor (*see* Tour 1)
Grossglockner mountain pass (*see* Tour 2)
Zell am See (*see* Tour 2)

Tour 1: To Lienz, into the Defereggental, and Back

Numbers in the margin correspond with points of interest on the Eastern Alps map.

Take Route 86 south out of Villach, through Warmbad Villach, and then Route 83 to Arnoldstein, about 10 km (6 mi) away. You're in the Gail river valley here, with the magnificent Karawanken mountains rising in Yugoslavia on your left. Just beyond Arnoldstein, turn right onto Route 111, marked for Hermagor. On the way up, the views now will be on the right, the dramatic Gailtal Alps in the background as you head west.

❶ **Hermagor** is best known as a summer resort, with hiking and climbing and swimming in the nearby Pressegger lake, but there's also skiing in winter. The Late Gothic church, dating to 1484, is interesting for its intricately carved and painted winged altar in the south Wolkenstein chapel and for the decorated keystones in the long nave. It is clear from the paintings (1485) in the parish church that in the Middle Ages, these keystones were taken to symbolize Jesus Christ holding the framework of the church together.

Did the creation of the earth take place in this area? Geologists from all over the world are fascinated by the possible answers that are believed to lie within the nearby Gartnerkofel mountain south of Hermagor off Route 90. You can follow the "Geo-Trail," tracing 50 million years of geological history, on a map (from the tourist office), gathering fossils as you go. Botanists are equally intrigued by the blue *wulfenia*, which flowers in June in the Nassfeld mountain area, slightly farther along Route 90 on the Italian border; this protected species grows only here and in the Himalayas.

From Hermagor, the choice is tough: Both Route 87, running northwest to Greifenburg, and Route 111 up to Kötschach–Mauthen offer gorgeous views, and the distances to Lienz are both about 55 km (35 mi). If you choose Route 87, shortly before Greifenburg, you can turn right for a detour to the blue–green **Weissensee,** a virtually undeveloped narrow lake 11 km (almost 7 mi) long, tucked in between high mountain ridges, where there's excellent fishing and boating. Then, at Greifenburg, turn west onto Route 100 up the Drau river valley toward Lienz.

❷ Kötschach–Mauthen, just off Route 111 about 25 km (16 mi) from Hermagor, is a year-round resort, a good base for excursions via the Plöcken pass over the border into Italy or up the picturesque Lesach valley through the Austrian (Lienzer) Dolomites. The 1527 parish church in Kötschach has a highly ornate and unusual decorated arched ceiling and some early frescoes. The town is the site of Kellerwand, one of Austria's top restaurants (*see* Dining, below).

The scenic Route 110 north over the Gailberg will bring you, after about 8 km (5 mi) and some dramatic twists and turns, to Route 100 at Oberdrauburg. From here to Lienz (20 km, or 12 mi) the highway follows the Drau river valley, with splendid views up into the Kreuzeck mountain range on your right. The Romans recognized the strategic importance of the region and about AD 50 established **Aguntum** here. About 5 km (3 mi) before you reach Lienz, you'll come to the excavations; stop and take a closer look.

Just beyond Oberdrauburg you cross the provincial border from Carinthia into that political anomaly, East Tirol (Östtirol), the state that has to trespass to get to its capital. In 1918, after World War I, South Tirol was ceded to Italy, leaving East Tirol completely cut off by a small northward jut of Italy from the rest of Tirol and the administrative capital in Innsbruck. Furthermore, the mountains along the Italian border and those of the Höhe Tauern, to the north, geographically isolate East Tirol, which has consequently been neglected by tourists.

❸ Tucked in at the confluence of the Drau and Isel rivers, with the Dolomites a dramatic backdrop to the south, **Lienz,** a summer and winter resort, is now the capital of this curiously isolated Austrian semiprovince. The awe-inspiring peaks rising around the town might make your first impression one of human insignificance in the face of overwhelming power and glory. Such feelings of reverence may account for the number of notable churches in Lienz; at least five are worth a visit, particularly the parish church of **St. Andreas,** which you can reach by walking up the Muchar Gasse and Schweizergasse or by following the Rechter Iselweg along the river. Completed in 1457, the present-day Gothic edifice shows traces of the earlier Romanesque church (1204); look for the Romanesque lion doorway. And don't overlook the Baroque winged high altar or the wood crucifix from 1500 on the right side altar. The ceiling fresco (1761) is particularly vivid in its colors and expression. Note the ornate marble tombstones of the noble Görz family.

Three short blocks away (cross the Pfarrbrücke into Beda Weber Gasse and turn left into Patriasdorferstrasse) is the **war memorial chapel** designed by the late Clemens Holzmeister, the architect responsible for Salzburg's Festspielhaus and

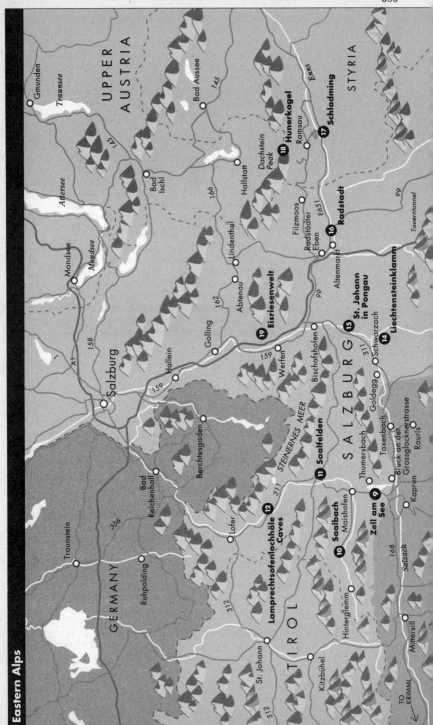

Eastern Alps

UPPER AUSTRIA

Gmunden

Traunsee

145

Attersee

125

166

Bad Aussee

145

STYRIA

Ems

Schladming **17**

18 Dachstein Peak

Ramsau

Hunerkogel **17**

Bad Ischl

Hallstatt

99

E651

16 **Radstadt**

Filzmoos

Radstädter Eben

Mondsee

Mondsee

158

Lindenthal

162

Abtenau

Golling

19 Eisriesenwelt

Altenmarkt

99

15 St. Johann in Pongau

Salzburg

Hallein

159

Werfen

159

Bischofshofen

14 Liechtensteinklamm

Tauerntunnel

99

A1

Bad Reichenhall

Berchtesgaden

STEINERNES MEER

311

11 Saalfelden

SALZBURG

Goldegg

311

Schwarzach

Traunstein

306

Lofer

312

12 Lamprechtsofenlochhöle Caves

Thumersbach

Taxenbach

Bruck an der Grossglocknerstrasse

Ruhpolding

10 Saalbach

Maishofen

9 Zell am See

Kaprun

Rauris

GERMANY

312

Hinterglemm

168

Salzach

TIROL

St. Johann

Kitzbühel

TO KRIMML

Mittersill

Felsenreitschule (the festival theaters). The wall paintings are by Albin Egger-Lienz (1868–1926), from Lienz, who portrayed human strength and weakness with unusual ability, and who is buried here.

The **Franciscan church** close to the center of town was originally a Carmelite cloister, founded in 1349 by the Countess Euphemia of Görz (not vitally important, but isn't the name marvelous?), which was taken over by the Franciscans in 1785 and restored in 1947–48. It has a Gothic pietà from about 1400 on the left side altar at the back; its wall frescoes are from 1400 to 1500. The **Dominican church,** of 1243, subsequently rebuilt in Late Gothic style, holds a wooden statue to Saint Wolfgang (1510); **St. Michael's** on Michaeler Platz on the north side of the Isel was completed in 1530, but the north tower, with its onion dome, dates only to 1713. Note the fancy ceiling ornamentation, the 1683 high altar, and the gravestones. The Rococo **St. Joseph's** (Spitalskirche) by the Spitalsbrücke was badly damaged in 1945 and rebuilt in 1957. Just down Kärntner Strasse on the Hauptplatz is **St. Antonius,** dating to the 16th century. Also on the Hauptplatz you can hardly overlook the recently restored 16th-century **Lieburg palace,** with its two towers, now housing provincial government offices.

Just beyond Lienz atop a small hill on Route 108 (Iseltaler Strasse), you'll find **Schloss Bruck,** a battlemented residential castle that dates to 1280, which now serves as the city museum. The castle itself is remarkably well preserved; notice the massive tower and the Romanesque chapel's late-15th-century ceiling and wall frescoes. Works by Egger-Lienz and Franz Defregger (1835–1921), another Tirolean painter, are displayed here, along with Celtic and Roman relics from nearby excavations, including those at Aguntum. *Tel. 04852/62580. Admission: AS28 adults, AS9 children. Open Palm Sunday to late Oct., Tues.–Sun. 10–5; mid-June–mid-Sept., daily 10–6.*

Just before you reach the castle, there's a ski jump and a chair lift that will take you nearly to the crest of the 2,057-meter (6,685-ft) Hochstein mountain, from which you'll get a splendid panoramic view out over the city and to the east. You'll have to hike the last 1 km (½ mi).

Continue northwest on Route 108, following the Isel valley, and turn left at the village of Huben, about 20 km (12 mi) out of Lienz, onto a scenic side roadway that takes you up the Defereggental along the Schwarzach river. The route, overshadowed by an enormous mountain range to the north, is dotted with unspoiled villages, and **St. Jakob in Defereggen,** a small summer and winter resort, is one of the most charming in East Tirol. You'll encounter few tourists other than knowledgeable Austrians, and don't look for unusual excitement here. There are sulfur baths nearby at St. Leonhard and a waterfall at Mariahilf, but in summer it's hiking, climbing, or fishing; in winter it's skiing, skiing, or skiing.

On Route 108, about 10 km (6 mi) north of Huben, the town of **Matrei in Osttirol,** is a good place to stop. This, too, was once a Roman and later a Celtic settlement, chosen for its strategic location on the most secure north–south route over the Alps to Italy. On the eve of Saint Nicholas's day (December 6), weirdly dressed characters with furs and bells storm through the town in an old tradition called *Klaubaufgehen*. In the 13th-century

Romanesque St. Nicholas church you can see remarkably well-preserved frescoes of the 14th century on the outside walls. Inside are late-13th-century frescoes depicting Adam and Eve and an early-15th-century carved wood statue of Saint Nicholas himself. Just north of Matrei is Schloss Weissenstein, a 12th-century castle that underwent substantial rebuilding in the 1800s, now privately owned. From here return on Route 108 to Lienz.

Tour 2: Over the Grossglockner Pass to Zell am See

Winter travelers have no choice but to drive north out of Lienz on Route 108, arriving in Mittersill in Salzburg province via the 5,200-meter (3¼-mi) Felbertauern toll tunnel (AS180) under the Tauern mountains, and taking Route 168 east to Zell am See. But if the road is open, we'll go north over one of the absolute highlights of the Eastern Alps—the Grossglockner Mountain Highway. (The trip can be done by car or bus.) Leave Lienz via Route 107, but stop on the way up the hill outside Iselsberg–Stronach for a great panoramic view west and south out over the city. As you go over the ridge, you'll be entering Carinthia again. At Winklern the road follows the Möll river ❻ valley, and after about 11 km (about 7 mi) you'll come to **Döllach** (Grosskirchheim) im Mölltal, a summer and winter resort where gold was once mined. Stop to look at the Gothic St. Maria Cornach church, with its ornate Baroque interior, and the local museum in Schloss Grosskirchheim, which records the history of local gold mining. *Tel. 04825/226. Admission: AS25 adults, AS10 children. Open Apr.–Oct., daily 9–6, tours at 10, 11, 1:30, 3, 4:30.*

❼ As you approach **Heiligenblut** (about 17 km, or 10 mi), the scenery becomes even more dramatic, the contrasting blues and greens almost prismatic. Here you'll find the small but notable parish church of St. Vincent, its slender spire and narrow nave in harmony with nearby peaks. Completed in 1490 after more than a century of construction under the toughest conditions, it contains a beautifully carved Late Gothic double altar nearly 11 meters (36 ft) high. The central painting, of the crowning of Mary, imparts a feeling of quiet power in this spare, high church.

From Heiligenblut the climb begins up the Carinthian side of the Grossglockner. You'll be tapped here for AS280 toll; if you ❽ continue on and return over the **Grossglockner highway** the same day, the return trip is free, so save the receipt. The peak itself—at 3,797 meters (12,470 ft) the highest point in Austria—is off to the west. You can get somewhat closer than the main road takes you by following the highly scenic but steep Gletscherstrasse highway westward up to the Gletscherbahn on the Franz-Josef-Plateau, where you'll be rewarded with absolutely breathtaking views out over the Austrian Alps and, on a clear day, into Italy as well.

The Grossglockner road twists and turns as it struggles to the 2,575-meter (8,370-ft) Hochtor. At this point you've crossed into Salzburg province, very much at the top of the world.

An unsolved mystery surrounds the Grossglockner highway. Before it was completed in 1935, there was no passage over the high mountain ranges anywhere between the Brenner pass and the Radstadt Tauern pass, which are 160 km (100 mi) apart. Nor was there any record that there had ever been a regularly traveled road over the mountains at this point. Yet when the engineers were blasting for the Hochtor tunnel, they found deep inside the mountain a Roman statuette of Hercules.

You're now on the Edelweiss-Strasse, where the rare white-starred edelweiss grows. The species is protected, but don't worry about the plants you get as souvenirs; they are cultivated from seed for the purpose. A stop at the Edelweissspitze will give you a view out over East Tirol, Carinthia, and Salzburg.

The views are sensational on the way down as well, this time looking more to the north. After the toll station on the north side, the highway finally exhausts its hairpin curves and continues to Bruck an der Grossglocknerstrasse. From here it's only about 8 km (5 mi) west on Route S11 and then north on **❾** Route 311 to **Zell am See,** directly on the Zeller lake. This is another of those idyllic Austrian towns that are so alluring as you go through on the train that you feel the urge just to get off and stay. Nevertheless, Zell am See is not overrun with tourists. In about 790, a monastery was established here, the monks' cells giving the town its name. In the splendid Romanesque parish church of Saint Hippolyte, built in 1217 and beautifully renovated in 1975, the statues of Saint George and Saint Florian on the west wall are unusually fine. Also visit the 17th-century Renaissance Rosenberg castle, now the town hall, and the city tower, originally a granary in around 1100.

The lake boasts excellent swimming and boating. If you take a boat ride to Thumersbach on the opposite shore, you get a wonderful reflected view of Zell am See. Take the cable lift virtually out of the center of town up to the Schmittenhöhe for a 180-degree panorama that takes in the peaks of the Glockner and Tauern granite ranges to the south and west and the very different limestone ranges to the north. The romantic narrow-gauge **Pinzgauer railroad** winds its way under steam power on a two-hour trip through the Pinzgau, following the Salzach river valley westward 54 km (34 mi) to Krimml. Nearby are the famous Krimmler waterfalls, with a 400-meter (1,300-ft) drop, which you can see from an observation platform or explore close at hand in about 3½–4 hours (take a raincoat and sneakers). *Trains leave Zell am See for Krimml at about 9:30 AM Tues. and Thurs. in July and Aug., Sat. in Sept. Round-trip fare: AS190 adults, AS130 children. For detailed information, call 06562/539140.*

When you finally manage to tear yourself away from Zell am See, continuing north on Route 311 brings you to Maishofen, where the Glemm valley opens to the west. About 14 km (nearly 9 mi) west along the scenic road is the famous skiing village of **❿** **Saalbach** and at the valley's head, Hinterglemm. These two towns have combined with Kaprun and Zell am See to form a recreational region that offers a wide range of sports in all seasons at varying prices.

⓫ About 10 km (6 mi) farther up Route 311 is **Saalfelden,** at the foot of the Steinernes Meer ("Sea of Stone"), the formidable ridge that divides Austria from Germany. Saalfelden is primarily a summer resort and mountaineering center, but the country is also good for skiing. Sights in Saalfelden include the 19th-century Romanesque parish church with a Late Gothic winged altar, the nearby 14th-century Farmach castle (now a retirement home), the 13th-century Lichtenberg castle (privately owned), and the Christmas-manger museum in Ritzen castle. *Tel. 06582/2759. Admission: AS20 adults, AS10 children. Open Jan.–Easter and mid-Sept.–Oct., Wed., weekends, holidays 2–4; mid-June–mid-Sept., daily 10–noon, 2–5; Dec., daily 2–4. Closed Easter–mid-June, Nov.*

Off at the edge of the Steinernes Meer, signs lead you to a Late Gothic chapel in a cave, containing a winged altarpiece near the stone pulpit and hermit's cell. The Sea of Stone is a climber's mecca, but don't attempt it unless you're experienced. This is especially true of the 2,941-meter (9,560-ft) Hochkönig, due east of Saalfelden.

If you continue on Route 311 toward the German border, in about 14 km (8 mi) you come to Weissbach bei Lofer, where you can visit the **Lamprechtsofenlochhöle caves,** with their great domes and waterfalls. *Tel. 06582/8343. Admission: AS30 adults, AS15 children. Open Apr.–mid-Oct., daily 8–6.*

Other well-marked attractions in the area are the Vorderkaserklamm gorge and the Hirschbichl pass, a strategic route where several battles were fought during the Napoleonic wars.

Tour 3: Along the Salzach, to Radstadt and Schladming

From Zell am See, turn east on Route 311 to pass Bruck again, continue through Taxenbach, and turn south at the intersection of Route 167 for a short side trip.

Badgastein, once one of Europe's leading spas, has fallen into a kind of trance. Its attraction is clear; this is a most unusual town in a stunning setting, with a mountain torrent rushing through it, yet all efforts to rejuvenate this turn-of-the-century jewel have foundered. Despite excellent facilities and good slopes in Sportgastein, some 9 km (5½ mi) south, other winter sports areas in Austria are more popular. But don't let this discourage you from trying Badgastein. To reach the wintersports region, turn right at Bockstein onto the Gasteiner Alpenstrasse toll road. *Toll: AS40 per person, children under 15 free. The winter ski pass includes the highway toll.*

Return to Route 311 and turn east toward Schwarzach in Pongau, where the road heads north. Between Schwarzach and St. Johann is the **Liechtensteinklamm,** the deepest (300 meters, or 1,000 ft), narrowest (fewer than 4 meters, or 12½ ft), and most spectacular gorge in the eastern Alps, with a 60-meter (200-ft) waterfall at the far end. The tour on a walkway crisscrossing the gorge takes about 45 minutes. *Tel. 06412/7278. Admission: AS25. Open May–Oct., daily 8–5.*

St. Johann im Pongau has developed into a full-fledged year-round resort. The area is favored by cross-country and intermediate skiers, since the gentle side slopes provide an almost endless variety of good downhill runs. The huge twin-spired parish church, built in 1861 in neo-Gothic style and locally known as the "Pongau cathedral," appears unnecessarily overbearing. Every four years on January 4 the population of St. Johann celebrates the *Pongauer Perchtenlauf,* wearing weird masks and costumes and ringing huge cow bells to drive away evil spirits.

Continue north on Route 311 to about 2½ km (1½ mi) beyond Bischofshofen, where Route 99/E14 cuts off east to Radstadt. The rail line that parallels the highway also ties in at Bischofshofen; the stretch from Eben in Pongau eastward is particularly scenic. **Altenmarkt,** halfway between Eben and Radstadt, is a popular resort in winter and summer, when there's good fishing in the nearby streams. The parish church of St. Mary's contains an outstanding statue of the Virgin, the *Schöne Madonna,* dating to before 1384.

Just before you reach Radstadt, look for **Schloss Tantalier,** built in 1450 for a noble family, reconstructed in 1569, and now serving as a youth hostel. The castle is unusual for its virtually square shape, with round towers on the south side, square on the north.

16 Despite wars and fires, the picturesque walled town of **Radstadt** still retains its 12th-century character. Radstadt, watching over one of the key north–south routes, was granted the right to warehouse goods and to trade in iron, wine, and salt. Today's prosperity is a reflection of tourism: The area is popular in winter for skiing and in summer for hiking. The town's north and west walls, dating to 1534, are well preserved, as are three of the towers that mark the corners of the old town. Most of the buildings around the square are also from the 16th century. The Late Romanesque parish church north of the square dominates the town, but reconstructions over the ages have destroyed much of its original character. The interior contains several Baroque altars.

17 From Radstadt, take scenic Route 146 east along the Enns river valley for 18 km (11 mi) over the provincial border (at Mandling) to **Schladming** in Styria. In the 14th and 15th centuries, Schladming was a thriving silver-mining town. But in 1525 the town was burned in an uprising of the miners and farmers, so most of what you see today dates to 1526, when reconstruction was begun. Traces of the earlier town wall are still here; look, too, at the old miners' houses. The St. Achaz parish church, with its Romanesque tower, stands out. Schladming is popular as a year-round resort. This is an area where sport is taken seriously; not only does it attract the world's best skiiers, but it also gives beginners ample scope. And in happy contrast to fashionable resorts in Tirol and Vorarlberg, Schladming and its surroundings are reasonably priced.

Tour 4: The Dachstein and the Salzburg Dolomites Highway

A breathtakingly gorgeous local road leads north out of Schladming to **Ramsau am Dachstein,** and about 4½ km (about 3 mi) west of Ramsau, a small road (toll: AS25 per person) turns north toward the Dachstein itself, a majestic craggy outcrop of 2,995 meters (9,826 ft). Take the impressive 20-minute cable car ride (round-trip: AS195 adults, AS127 children) to the **18** 2,694-meter (8,755-ft) **Hunerkogel;** you're at the top of the Alps here. (A phone call to 03687/81315 will tell you in German what the weather's like up there.) To the north lie the lakes of the Salzkammergut, to the west, the Tennen mountain range. South and east lie the lower Tauern mountains. A snowmobile ride will take you very close to the Dachstein peak, just to the west, or you can hike over. The glacier here can be skied year-round, although the summer snow conditions require considerable expertise. Marked trails lead down the north side and along the ridge to the northwest. In summer the south cliff at Hunerkogel is a favorite "jumping-off spot" for paragliders, who seem to fear nothing as they lunge out into space.

Back in the valley again, turn west through Filzmoos, a popular and not terribly expensive winter resort, to rejoin Rte. 99/E14 again at Eben im Pongau. Here you can take the A10 autobahn north to Salzburg, if you're in a hurry. But if you have time for more majestic scenery and an interesting detour, continue about 4 km (2½ mi) on Route 99/E14 and turn north on Route 166, the Salzburg Dolomites highway, for a 43-km (27-mi) swing around the Tennen mountains. Be careful, though, to catch the left turn onto Route 162 at Lindenthal; it will be marked to Golling. At **Abtenau,** stop for a look at the colorful town square and the 14th-century St. Blasius parish church, with its late Gothic frescoes and Baroque high altar. Salt-water springs here supply the local spa, and just outside town you'll find waterfalls and the Tricklfall caves.

As an alternative to the autobahn, take Route 159 north from Bischofshofen, stopping on the way north at Werfen to see the formidable castle that identifies the town. **Burg Hohenwerfen** dates to 1077, but fires, reconstructions, and renovations, most recently in 1948, have altered it over the centuries. *Tel. 06468/ 7603. Admission and tour: AS40 adults, AS20 children. Open Easter–Oct. Tours Apr. and Oct., daily 11, 1, 3; May, June, Sept., daily 11, 1, 2, 4; July, Aug., hourly 10–5. Birds of prey open to viewing daily Apr.–Oct. Flight performances, combination ticket with castle: AS80 adults, AS40 children. Performances early May–mid-Oct., daily 11 AM and 3 PM.*

⑲ Near Tenneck, north of Werfen, is the **Eisriesenwelt,** the World of the Ice Giants, the largest known complex of ice caves, domes, galleries, and halls in Europe. It extends for some 42 km (25 mi), with a fantastic collection of frozen waterfalls, natural formations suggesting statues, and other icy wonders. You drive to the resthouse about halfway up the hill, then walk 20 minutes to the cable car, which takes you to the cave entrance for the two-hour guided tour. You can also take a bus from Werfen, but be sure to leave at least an hour before the start of the next scheduled cave trip. The entire adventure will take about half a day. And remember, no matter how warm it is outside, it's below zero inside, so bundle up, and wear appropriate shoes. *Tel. 06468/248, 06468/291. Admission (including cable car): AS150 adults, AS75 children. July–Aug. tours begin hourly, 9:30–4:30; May–June and Sept–mid-Oct., 9:30, 11:30, 1:30 and 3:30.*

From here, you're about 40 km (25 mi) from Salzburg, the end of Tour 4.

What to See and Do with Children

Birds of prey (Tour 4).

Grossglockner glacier (Tour 2).

Krimmler waterfall (Tour 2).

Pinzgauer steam train (Tour 2).

Dachstein glacier (Tour 4).

The **Eisriesenwelt** (Tour 4).

You can pan for gold in the streams around **Heiligenblut** (*see* Tour 2) and in the **Rauris** valley in the town of the same name. Turn south off Route 311 near Taxenbach (*see* Tour 3). At the "gold digging" office, you buy a ticket for the excursion, which includes a picnic lunch, the necessary equipment, and a permit to take home your finds. Contact the tourist office for details (in Rauris, 06544/6237 or 06544/7049).

Take the teenagers to the 1,600-meter (1 mile) **summer toboggan run** at Saalfelden; with 63 curves, it is the longest such run in Europe.

Shopping

In Lienz, look for such **traditional Austrian clothing** as dirndls, the blouse, skirt, and apron combinations. Note also that there are summer and winter dirndls! Good ones are not cheap, but they last a lifetime. Near Ramsau am Dachstein in Styria (*see* Tour 4), in the village of Rössing, you'll find Richard Steiner's **Lodenwalker,** which, since 1434, has been turning out that highly practical feltlike fabric called loden. Here you can find various colors and textures at reasonable prices. *Tel. 03687/ 81930. Open weekdays.*

Sports and Fitness

Bicycling Not only is the gorgeous area around **Zell am See** good for bicycling, you can also cycle around the lake and up the valley to and around **Saalfelden.** Rent a bike at the railroad station (Zell am See, tel. 06542/365–1380; Saalfelden, tel. 06582/23440) for AS90; AS45, if you've a valid rail ticket. **Abtenau** is hilly, but the town has a program of mountain biking, with plenty of rental bikes.

Fishing **Zell am See** offers fine lake fishing, but for mountain fishing, try the streams around **Matrei** and **St. Jakob in Defereggen** in East Tirol or cast a fly for trout in the Enns river near **Schladming** from May to mid-September (contact Walter Dichtl, Hauptplatz 28, tel. 08687/22354) or around **Filzmoos** and **Altenmarkt,** where several hotels have fishing packages.

Golf Golfers have a choice of three courses in Salzburg province, in towns that offer golfing packages, and one in Badgastein. The courses at **Zell am See/Kaprun** are 18 holes (par 72) and 9 holes. Both are open May–November. *Golfstr. 25, tel. 06542/6161. Greens fee (18 holes): AS420 weekdays, AS530 weekends.*

At **Saalfelden** you'll find a tricky 18-hole, par 72 course, open April–mid-October, that crisscrosses the wild Saalach stream. *Hohlwegen 4, tel. 06582/217–6555. Greens fee: AS380 weekdays, AS430 weekends.*

The 9-hole, par 33 course at **Goldegg,** near Schwarzach in Pongau (off Route 311, between Bruck an der Grossglocknerstrasse and St. Johann im Pongau) is open May–November. *Box 6, tel. 06415/8585. Greens fee: AS340 weekdays, AS400 weekends.*

The attractive 9-hole, par-36 course in **Badgastein** is open mid-April–November. *Golfclub Gastein, tel. 06434/2775. Greens fee: AS350 weekdays, AS450 weekends.*

Hiking   You'll find miles of marked trails, and detailed maps are available (*see* Hiking in Chapter 1, Essential Information) that show mountain lodges and other facilities. If you want to learn to climb, contact Leo Baumgartner at the **Alpinschule Lienz/Osttirol** (Deffreggerstr. 11, A–9900 Lienz, tel. 04852/48932). Trails in Tirol are marked as easy, moderate, or difficult. In the difficult Dachstein area, contact the **Alpinschule Dachstein** (A–8972 Ramsau am Dachstein 233, tel. 03687/81223) or **Bergsteigerschule Dachstein Tauern** (A–8972 Ramsau am Dachstein 101, tel. 03687/81424).

Rafting   White-water rafting is possible on stretches of the Isel river from Matrei down to Lienz in East Tirol. Check the regional tourist offices or phone 04853/5231. It costs about AS300 per person, with a minimum of five people required for a run. Two clubs are active in Abtenau, where the runs on the Salzach and Lammer rivers cost AS420–AS590 per person. The Lammer, with its "Hell's run," is particularly wild. Call 06243/2939 or 06243/3069 for details.

Skiing   There's downhill skiing in Badgastein, St. Jakob in Defereggen, Matrei in Osttirol, Grosskirchheim/Döllach, Heiligenblut, Saalfelden, Saalbach, St. Johann in Pongau, Radstadt, Schladming, Ramsau am Dachstein, Filzmoos and Abtenau; Schladming is the most fashionable. The spots for advanced skiers are Heiligenblut and the Dachstein (Schladming and Ramsau am Dachstein). For cross-country, go to Abtenau, Zell am See, Saalfelden, and Radstadt.

Tennis   Many of the larger hotels in the resort centers have their own courts, and virtually every town has municipal courts that you can arrange to use. Call the tourist office for information. You'll find concentrations of courts around Saalbach (20 courts), Zell am See (19), Saalfelden (17), and St. Johann im Pongau (15 courts).

Water Sports   Boating—from paddleboats to sailboats—and swimming are excellent on the lakes of this tour. Try the uncrowded Weissensee in Carinthia or the Zeller See. Power boats are restricted on many Austrian lakes—Zeller See included—so you won't find much water skiing.

Dining and Lodging

Dining

In many small towns you'll find country inns that have dining rooms, not always separate restaurants. Some hotels open their best restaurants only in the peak season, and in resort areas you occasionally may be required to take half-pension. Prices for meals include taxes and a service charge but not the customary small additional tip.

Highly recommended restaurants are indicated by a star ★.

Category	Cost*
Very Expensive	over AS500
Expensive	AS300–AS500
Moderate	AS200–AS300
Inexpensive	under AS200

per person for a typical 3-course meal, with a glass of house wine

Lodging

This chapter covers relatively inexpensive areas of Austria, except for the top resort towns of Saalbach, Badgastein, and Zell am See. Even there, however, cheaper accommodations are available outside the center of town or in pensions. Prices out of season may be as low as half those of the high season. Room rates include taxes and service and almost always breakfast, except in the most expensive hotels, but it is wise to ask. It is customary to leave a small (AS20) additional tip for the chambermaid.

Highly recommended lodgings are indicated by a star ★.

Category	Top Resorts*	Other Towns*
Very Expensive	over AS2,200	over AS1,500
Expensive	AS1,500–AS2,200	AS1,000–AS1,500
Moderate	AS900–AS1,500	AS700–AS1,000
Inexpensive	under AS900	under AS700

for a standard double room with bath in high season

The four provinces covered in this chapter are abbreviated as follows: Carinthia (C.), East Tirol (E.T.), Salzburg province (S.P.), and Styria (S.).

Abtenau (S.P.)

Dining and Lodging

Moisl. This typical alpine chalet–style house in the center of town, with flower-laden balconies and overhanging eaves, dates back to 1764, but its services and facilities are absolutely up to date. The rooms are done in country decor. *Markt 26, A-5441, tel. 06243/22320. 75 rooms. Facilities: restaurant, bar, indoor pool, sauna, solarium, fitness room, bowling, tennis, garage. Closed Apr., mid-Oct.–mid-Dec. No credit cards. Expensive.*

Roter Ochs. Colorfully decorated white stucco walls and flowered balconies under spreading eaves mark this family-run hotel in the center of town. Inside, you'll find modern public rooms and rustic country-decor bedrooms. The restaurant has a good reputation for Austrian and international specialties; ask for the *Tafelspitz*. There's entertainment and folk dancing in the beer and wine *Stube. Markt 32, A-5541, tel. 06243/2259. 42 rooms. Facilities: restaurant, sauna, solarium, fitness room, children's program and facilities. MC, V. Expensive.*

Post. This older, centrally located hotel, decorated in rustic style, with much natural wood in evidence, has comfortable rooms with up-to-date facilities. And transportation is at the door; the Windhofer family also runs the town's taxi and bus service. The restaurant is good; try the Rumpsteak Tirol or any of the other beef dishes. *A–5541, tel. 06243/2209. 40 rooms. Facilities: restaurant, indoor pool, sauna, garage. DC. Closed Apr., Nov.–mid-Dec. Moderate.*

Altenmarkt (S.P.)

Dining
★
Lebzelter Stub'n. In this excellent family-run country restaurant, with paneling and lots of windows, you'll find about anything you want, from steaks to fish to cheese dishes to pizza, but the emphasis is on traditional fare. Prices are remarkably low for the quality and servings. *Tel. 06452/503. Reservations advised. Dress: casual but neat. AE, DC, MC, V. Moderate.*

Dining and Lodging
Markterwirt. This traditional house in the center of town goes back 900 years. The personal style of the family is reflected in the charming country decor, and the rooms are comfortable. The main dining room and the informal *Stube* are good. The hotel has its own lake for fishing. *A–5541, tel. 06452/420. 31 rooms. Facilities: 2 restaurants, café, sauna, solarium. MC, V. Closed Nov., Apr. Moderate (summer)–Expensive (winter).*

Badgastein (S.P.)

Dining and Lodging
Elisabethpark. The public rooms go on and on in this elegant but modern hotel of the traditional old school in the center of town. The atmosphere is underscored by the Oriental carpets, marble, and crystal chandeliers. The rooms are particularly comfortable, with period furnishings, and the service has a pleasantly personal touch. *A–5640, tel. 06434/25510. 115 rooms. Facilities: restaurant, café, bar, indoor pool, sauna, solarium, fitness room, health spa, garage. AE, DC, MC, V. Closed Apr.–early June, Oct.–mid-Dec. Very Expensive.*
Grüner Baum. You're out of the center of town here, in a relaxing, friendly hotel village set amid meadows and woodlands. The guest list has included Austrian Empress Elisabeth and Saudi King Saud. The five separate houses have comfortable rustic, wood-paneled rooms, giving the complex a feeling of intimacy and personality. Children are well looked after. The elegant restaurant has an excellent reputation; try the duck or game. *Kötschachtal, A–5640, tel. 06434/25160. 91 rooms. Facilities: restaurant (reservations advised, jacket and tie advised), bar, indoor and outdoor pools, sauna, solarium, fitness room, tennis, kindergarten, garage. AE, DC, MC, V. Closed Apr., Nov.–mid-Dec. Very Expensive.*
Villa Hiss. This is ranked as one of Austria's top restaurants. Jörg Wörther is an acknowledged master at basically Austrian cuisine, magnificently transformed by elegant sauces and other touches. You'll be offered lamb, possibly roast kid, trout, game in season, and a splendid range of accompaniments, along with one of Austria's best wine lists. The turn-of-the-century Art Nouveau house has elegant, balconied rooms. *Erzherzog-Johann-Promenade 1, A–5640, tel. 06434/38280. 12 rooms. Facilities: restaurant (reservations advised, jacket and tie advised, closed Mon., lunch Tues.), bar, health spa. AE, DC, MC, V. Closed June, Nov. Very Expensive.*
Krone. Most of the rooms in this in-town hotel have balconies,

and you're about three minutes from the cable car up the mountain. In addition, the thermal spa is next door. The rooms are pleasant and bright. *Bahnhofsplatz 8, A–5640, tel. 06434/2330. 55 rooms. Facilities: restaurant, bar, health spa, garage. MC. Closed Oct.–Nov. Inexpensive (summer)–Moderate (winter).*

Döllach (Grosskirchheim) (C.)

Dining and Lodging
★
Schlosswirt. The rooms range from somewhat spartan to elegant (four-poster beds) in this appealing chalet hotel at the base of the mountains on the fringe of the Grossglockner national park. You can climb, hike, and ski in season, and ride horseback in the gorgeous "hidden valley" of the Graden brook. The hotel has its own fishing streams and lake, and it organizes dinners and wine tastings in the local 500-year-old castle. The restaurant has slipped recently, but is still worth a try; ask for recommendations. *A–9843, tel. 04825/211 or 04825/411. 21 rooms. Facilities: restaurant (reservations advised, jacket advised), bar, outdoor pool, sauna, tennis, riding, garage. MC, V. Moderate (restaurant)–Very Expensive (hotel).*

Filzmoos (S.P.)

Dining and Lodging
Sporthotel Filzmooserhof. Minigolf and tennis are close by, as well as chair lifts and T-bars to the ski slopes. Inside, the chalet-style hotel is bright and cheerful; most rooms have balconies. There's live music and dancing until 3 AM in ski season. *Neuberg 85, A–5532, tel. 06453/232. 36 rooms. Facilities: restaurant, outdoor and indoor pools, sauna, solarium, fitness room, garage. AE, DC, MC. Closed Nov. Expensive (summer)–Very Expensive (winter).*

Unterhof. A member of the Silencehotel group, this collection of chalets with dark-wood balconies gives you comfortable accommodations in a modern-rustic, quiet but friendly atmosphere. The family-run hotel has its own fishing waters, stocked with brook and rainbow trout. *Neuberg 33, A–5532, tel. 06453/2250. 48 rooms. Facilities: restaurant (reservations advised, jacket required evenings), bar, terrace café, outdoor and indoor pools, sauna, solarium, fitness room, tennis, putting green, garage. No credit cards. Closed Apr., Nov. Expensive (summer)–Very Expensive (winter).*

Hanneshof. From a modest single room to a spacious apartment, all the rooms are attractively and comfortably furnished, if slightly on the plastic-modern side. The restaurant serves substantial but reasonably priced portions, and the meat is guaranteed to be good; it comes from the house butcher. Once a week in summer, the hotel puts on a "farmer's buffet" outdoor grill, with music. *A–5532, tel. 06453/275. 45 rooms. Facilities: restaurant, indoor pool, sauna, solarium, fitness room, garage. AE, DC, MC, V. Closed Nov. Moderate (summer)–Expensive (winter).*

★
Hubertus. In this highly personal hotel in the center of town, every last detail is attractive. Fishermen have 20 km (12 mi) of mountain streams and two small lakes at their disposal. The restaurant is the best in the area; try the potato cream soup with mushrooms, the medallions of venison, the beef tongue, or the house's own blood sausage and liverwurst, and finish with *Topfenknödel* (cream cheese dumpling), a house specialty. *A–5532, tel. 06453/204. 17 rooms. Facilities: restaurant (reservations advised, jacket suggested), bar, terrace café, sauna, so-*

larium, fitness room, garage. No credit cards. Closed Nov. Moderate (summer)–Expensive (winter).

Alpenkrone. From the balconies of this chalet complex, you'll have a great view of the surrounding mountains. The rooms are simple, with no particular style. The dance bar is popular. *A–5532, tel. 06453/280. 51 rooms. Facilities: restaurant, bar, indoor pool, hot whirlpool, sauna, solarium, fitness room. DC, MC, V. Closed Easter–early May, mid-Oct.–mid-Dec. Moderate.*

Heiligenblut (C.)

Dining and Lodging

Glocknerhof. This dark wooden chalet in the center of the village fits perfectly into the surroundings. You'll feel comfortable in its cozy, attractive rooms. It's close to climbing in summer and skiing in winter. Tour groups stop here on the way over the Grossglockner road, but the restaurant is good. *Hof 4, A–9844, tel. 04824/2244. 52 rooms. Facilities: restaurant, bar, indoor pool, sauna, solarium, garage. MC. Closed mid-Apr.–May, Oct.–mid-Dec. Very Expensive.*

Kärntner Hof. Several chalet-style houses set close together have been combined to make up this intimate, family-run complex on the edge of thick woods about 2 km (1¼ mi) from the center of town. There's entertainment twice weekly. *Winkl 3, A–9844, tel. 04824/2004. 43 rooms. Facilities: restaurant, bar, outdoor and indoor pools, sauna, solarium, fitness room, garage. DC. Closed 2 weeks at Easter, mid-Oct.–mid-Dec. Expensive.*

Senger. Weathered wood and flowered balconies mark this old farmhouse chalet, which has been cleverly enlarged and yet keeps its original rustic atmosphere. The rooms and romantic apartments, with lots of pillows and country prints, continue the attractive rural theme. *Glocknerstr. 23, A–9844, tel. 04824/22150. 5 rooms, 18 apartments. Facilities: restaurant, bar, sauna, solarium, fitness room, garage. AE, DC, MC, V. Closed 2 weeks after Easter–mid-June, Oct.–mid-Dec. Expensive.*

Kötschach–Mauthen (C.)

Dining and Lodging ★

Kellerwand. The restaurant, one of the top dozen in Austria, is the focal point here. Elegant tables in a quiet, luxurious atmosphere highlight the superb quality of the food. The cuisine that draws gourmets from all over the country is a pleasantly imaginative treatment of area specialties; recommendations include perch filet on crisp lettuce, a delicate calves' liver, and, among desserts, the rhubarb strudel, and a local farmer's cheese. The unpretentious residence includes a small hotel; the rooms and two apartments are simply but attractively decorated in a country style with tile floors. *Mauthen 24, A–9640, tel. 04715/269. 12 rooms. Facilities: restaurant (reservations required 3 weeks in advance; jacket and tie required; closed Mon., Tues. lunch), bar, garage. AE, DC, MC, V. Closed mid-Nov.–mid-Dec. Expensive (hotel)–Very Expensive (restaurant).*

Kürschner. Your health is important at this modern, pale yellow *Gesundheitshotel*, which offers massage, acupuncture, beauty care, and various diets. You must take half or full board, and the family management arranges hikes and social affairs, so there's plenty to do. *Kötschach 74, A–9640, tel. 04715/259 or 04715/239. 53 rooms. Facilities: restaurant, bar, outdoor pool,* *sauna, solarium, fitness room, tennis, garage. DC, MC. Closed 2 weeks in Apr., 2 weeks in Nov. Expensive.*

Post. This interesting house of eccentric design, with a cupola and a triangular garden, is in the center of town and offers excursions, riding, rafting, and fishing. The rooms are attractive and fresh. *Hauptplatz 66, A–9640, tel. 04715/221. 24 rooms. Facilities: restaurant, bar, outdoor pool, heated whirlpool, sauna, solarium, fitness room, garage. MC. Closed late Apr., mid-Nov.–mid-Dec. Moderate.*

Lienz (E.T.)

Dining and Lodging
★

Traube. This traditional central hotel has a red facade, and in summer striped awnings shade the cafés on the street and balcony. The atmosphere is elegant, with a mix of older furniture and antiques; the rooms are spacious and comfortable. The hotel has its own fishing waters and a rooftop swimming pool, with wonderful views of the surrounding mountains. The restaurant's new chef is doing his best to regain its excellent reputation, and it's still the best in town; the cellar disco offers evening entertainment. *Hauptplatz 14, A–9900, tel. 04852/644440. 54 rooms. Facilities: 2 restaurants, bar, café, disco, indoor pool, sauna, fitness room. DC, MC, V. Closed Nov.–mid-Dec. Very Expensive.*

Sonne. This hotel, with a design reminiscent of the grand hotels of the past, dominates the Südtirolerplatz in the center of town. Public areas, such as the bar with a fireplace, are spacious and welcoming; the rooms are compact and modern. There's a playroom for children. It's a member of the Best Western group. *Südtirolerplatz 7, A–9900, tel. 04852/63311. 56 rooms. Facilities: restaurant, bar, sauna, solarium, fitness room, garage. AE, DC, MC, V. Expensive.*

★ **Tristachersee.** A little more than 4 km (about 2½ mi) southeast of Lienz (take the road via Amlach marked to Tristacher See), you'll find a small lake hidden away up the hill—a magical setting for this diminutive, totally renovated country hotel, with dark paneled walls and lots of fabrics. A lakeside terrace provides opportunity for relaxation, and the hotel restaurant is good. *A–9900, tel. 04852/676660. 43 rooms. Facilities: restaurant, indoor pool, sauna. No credit cards. Closed Nov. Expensive.*

Matrei in Osttirol (E.T.)

Dining and Lodging
★

Rauter. Starting with the ultramodern facade, this fashionable house offers elegant comfort in stark contemporary contrast to the usual "alpine rustic" style: clean lines and slick surfaces. Here, too, are many diversions and the best restaurant in East Tirol. The fish comes from the hotel's own waters, the lamb from the nearby mountains; the house bakery supplies the café. A hotel bus brings you to and from the hiking areas in summer, ski slopes in winter. Riding is available nearby. *A–9971, tel. 04875/6611. 50 rooms. Facilities: restaurant, bar, café, outdoor and indoor pools, sauna, solarium, garage. No credit cards. Closed Nov.–mid-Dec. Very Expensive.*

Panzlwirt. "Genuine East Tirol" is the motto of this chalet-style traditional house, with a highly decorated facade and overflowing windowboxes. The rooms are well furnished and comfortable. *Tauerntalstr. 4, A–9971, tel. 04875/6518. 24* *rooms. Facilities: restaurant, café, bowling, garage. MC. Moderate.*

★ **Tauernhaus.** There's quiet comfort here in this simple rustic *Gasthof*, about 14 km (9 mi) up the Tauern valley at the base of the Felbertauern pass. The hotel began as a resthouse, founded in 1207 by the archbishops of Salzburg. It is a good starting point for hiking and skiing. *A–9971, tel. 04875/8811. 40 rooms, 27 with shower. Facilities: restaurant. No credit cards. Inexpensive.*

Radstadt (S.P.)

Dining and Lodging **Sporthotel Stegerbräu.** Emphasis here is on fish, and the sport is fishing; the hotel has its own lake and rights on the Enns river. The rooms are comfortable, and the restaurant features trout. *A–5550, tel. 06452/590. 30 rooms, 24 apartments. Facilities: restaurant, outdoor and indoor pools, sauna, solarium. No credit cards. Closed mid-Apr.–May, mid-Oct.–Dec. Moderate (summer)–Expensive (winter).*

Ramsau am Dachstein (S.)

Dining and Lodging **Edelweiss.** This elegant chalet-style hotel has family housekeeping apartments and diversions for those who don't want to tackle the mountains. The rooms are pleasantly decorated with lots of colorful fabrics and furniture in light woods. *A–8972, tel. 03687/819880. 50 rooms. Facilities: restaurant, bar, sauna, fitness room, tennis, garage. No credit cards. Closed early May, late June. Expensive.*

Sporthotel Matschner. This attractive twin chalet-style house specializes in hiking and tennis, and there's a program just for children. The rooms are amply large, and most have balconies. *A–8972, tel. 03687/817210. 60 rooms. Facilities: restaurant, bar, supervised children's playroom, indoor pool, sauna, solarium, fitness room, outdoor and indoor tennis, garage. No credit cards. Closed mid-Nov.–mid-Dec. Expensive.*

Lodging
★ **Peter Rosegger.** This rustic chalet in a quiet area on the forest's edge is decorated with homey touches that are mementos of the Styrian writer for whom it is named: framed letters, embroidered mottoes. This is the place to stay when you've come for climbing: Fritz Walcher heads the alpine school. The rooms are country comfortable. It has the best kitchen in the area, but the restaurant is only for hotel guests, who are treated to such local specialties as Styrian corned pork and stuffed breast of veal. *A–8972, tel. 03687/81223. 13 rooms. Facilities: restaurant, sauna, fitness room, garage. No credit cards. Closed mid-Apr.–mid-May, Nov. Expensive.*

Almfrieden. This modern chalet offers peaceful comfort, with nearby meadows and mountains; the fireplaces welcome you in winter. The rooms are in attractive country-modern style with dark wood and clean lines. *A–8972, tel. 03687/81021. 45 rooms, 42 with bath. Facilities: restaurant, sauna, solarium, fitness room, indoor rifle range, garage. MC. Closed mid-Apr.–mid-May, mid-Oct.–mid-Dec. Moderate (summer)–Expensive (winter).*

Pehab-Kirchenwirt. *Kirchenwirt* means "next to the church," which describes the location of this rustic family-run hotel. Many of the comfortable rooms have balconies; those in the back have the best mountain view. You're close to hiking trails in summer, the hotel-operated ski lift and ski runs in winter. The restaurant serves good local food. *A–8972, tel. 03687/ 81732. 40 rooms, 37 with bath. Facilities: restaurant, beer cellar, café. Closed one month after Easter, Nov. Moderate.*

Saalbach–Hinterglemm (S.P.)

Dining and Lodging
Alpenhotel Saalbach. The attentive family management at this great double chalet compensates for its impersonal size. The lobby is spacious, as are the comfortable rustic rooms and apartments. The rather good restaurant called Vitrine is open only in winter; the house restaurant is unexciting. But the *Kuhstall* and the other three cellar bars offer lively entertainment. *Dorfstr. 212, A–5753, tel. 06541/6660 or 06541/6670. 100 rooms. Facilities: 2 restaurants, 4 bars, indoor pool, sauna, solarium, fitness room, disco, garage. AE, DC, MC, V. Closed Nov. Expensive (summer)–Very Expensive (winter).*

Ingonda. There's an international flair to this chalet-style hotel near the center of town. It has golden wood paneling and flower-laden balconies; the comfortable rooms are a generous size, and the restaurant is good. *Dorfstr. 218, A–5753 Saal-bach, tel. 06541/262. 45 rooms. Facilities: restaurant, bar, hot whirlpool, sauna, solarium, fitness room, garage. AE, DC, MC, V. Closed last 2 weeks in Nov. Moderate (summer)–Very Expensive (winter).*

★ **Hinterhag.** This charming family-run hotel outside the center of town contains a small art gallery and paintings by the hostess. You'll find cozy details, such as four-posters and lots of paneling. Hinterhag-Alm restaurant, the best in the area, uses local ingredients (and herbs from the hotel garden) imaginatively in regional dishes. Try the beet soup, followed by veal nuggets, or lamb with rosemary sauce. *A–5753 Saalbach, tel. 06541/2910; restaurant tel. 06541/7212. 27 rooms. Facilities: restaurant (reservations advised, jacket and tie suggested), sauna. No credit cards. Closed Apr.–Dec. Expensive.*

Glemmtalerhof. This massive chalet is rather intimate inside, with pleasant paneled rooms in alpine style, most with balconies. It is mainly a winter resort, but there's still plenty to do in summer. *Glemmtaler Landstr. 150, A–5754 Hinterglemm, tel. 06541/7135. 62 rooms. Facilities: 2 restaurants, 2 bars, café, nightclub, indoor pool, sauna, solarium, fitness room, tennis, riding, supervised children's room, garage. AE, DC, MC, V. Closed mid-Apr.–mid-May, mid-Oct.–mid-Dec. Moderate (summer)–Expensive (winter).*

Saalbacher Hof. This family-run chalet in the center of town is identified by a rustic bell tower and overflowing red geraniums against weathered dark wood. Warm paneling and a large fireplace welcome you; the rooms are spacious and comfortable. *Dorfstr. 27, A–5753 Saalbach, tel. 06541/71110. 100 rooms. Facilities: 2 restaurants, bar, nightclub, outdoor pool, sauna, solarium, tennis. AE, DC, MC, V. Closed mid-Apr.–May, Oct.– Nov. Moderate (summer)–Expensive (winter).*

Saalfelden (S.P.)

Dining
★ **Schatzbichl.** The reputation of this simple Gasthaus, slightly east of Saalfelden draws guests from near and far. The pine-paneled interior is bright and cheerful, as is the (sometimes overworked) staff. Local dishes are simply prepared and presented; try the garlic soup, lamb chops, or any of the fish of-

fered. *Ramseiden 82, tel. 06582/3281. Reservations required. Dress: casual but neat, jacket required at dinner. No credit cards. Closed Nov. Moderate.*

Dining and Lodging **Sporthotel Gut Brandlhof.** This ranch, about 5 km (3 mi) outside town, is perfect for an active vacation; the vast complex provides all manner of sports. The 18-hole, par-72 Saalfelden golf course belongs to the hotel. The rooms are comfortable in alpine-country style, with exposed wood and lots of fabric. *Hohlwegen 4, A-5760, tel. 06582/21760. 150 rooms. Facilities: restaurant, bar, outdoor and indoor pools, sauna, solarium, fitness room, outdoor and indoor tennis, squash, riding, golf, bowling, fishing, hunting, supervised children's room, garage. AE, DC, MC, V. Expensive.*

Dick. The reception area here has impressive paneling and a collection of antiques. A new management may have made changes, but the choicest room of the house has 18th-century furnishings, while the other guest rooms are considerably more modern in decor. The restaurant features local dishes, especially freshwater fish. *Bahnhofstr. 106, A-5760, tel. 06582/2215. 30 rooms. Facilities: restaurant, bar, outdoor pool, garage. No credit cards. Moderate.*

St. Jakob in Defereggen (E.T.)

Dining and Lodging **Alpenhof.** A large chalet set against a velvet green hillside is an ideal starting point for summer hiking, and later for skiing. The comfortable rooms all have flowered balconies. The restaurant has a good reputation for local dishes; ask for recommendations. *Unterrotte 35, A-9963, tel. 04873/5351. 85 rooms. Facilities: restaurant, bar, nightclub, outdoor and indoor pools, sauna, solarium. No credit cards. Closed May–June, mid-Oct.–mid-Dec. Expensive.*

St. Johann im Pongau (S.P.)

Dining and Lodging **Sporthotel Alpenland.** The newest hotel in town has a somewhat more commercial approach to innkeeping than do the family-run chalets, but you get an attractive room, efficient service, and plenty of facilities. Three restaurants offer pizza, steaks, and such local specialties as lamb. *Hans-Kappacher-Str. 7–9, A-5600, tel. 06412/70210. 137 rooms. Facilities: restaurant, bar, indoor pool, hot whirlpool, sauna, solarium, fitness room, tennis, garage. AE, DC, MC, V. Very Expensive.*

Lodging **Silbergasser.** This balconied chalet in the center of town is managed by a friendly family. The rooms are cozy and comfortable, with attractive rustic decor. *Hauptstr. 49, A-5600, tel. 06412/421 or 06412/483. 22 rooms. Facilities: sauna, solarium, fitness room, garage. No credit cards. Closed Apr., Nov.–mid-Dec. Moderate.*

Schladming (S.)

Dining and Lodging **Sporthotel Royer.** There's enough activity at this contemporary complex to keep you going every minute. The rooms, though modern, efficient, and well furnished, are rather bare, without that extra luxurious touch you might expect, and some are noisy from nearby traffic. (Ask for a room on the quieter side.) The activities are set with children in mind; besides the pools, there are pony rides and playgrounds. *Europaplatz 583, A–8970, tel. 03687/23240. 130 rooms. Facilities: 2 restaurants, grill, bar, outdoor and indoor pools, sauna, solarium, fitness room, outdoor and indoor tennis, squash, bowling, pony riding, garage. AE, DC, MC, V. Closed May–mid-June. Expensive.*

★ **Alte Post.** This member of the Romantik Hotels group dates to 1618 and is notable for its particularly attractive *Stuben* and the older rooms with vaulted ceilings. Guest rooms are cozy and comfortable. The restaurants vary; the main dining room is noted for its outstanding cuisine in winter, but critics say it declines in summer. Even then, however, the quality remains first-rate and the atmosphere superb. The beefsteaks are excellent. *Hauptplatz 10, A–8970, tel. 03687/225710. 40 rooms. Facilities: 2 restaurants (reservations required, jacket and tie advised), bar. AE, DC, MC, V. Closed Nov. Moderate (summer)–Expensive (winter).*

Werfen (S.P.)

Dining **Lebzelter.** On the way back to Salzburg, the slight detour is
★ worth it to dine in one of Austria's top half-dozen restaurants. This *Landgasthaus* is a gourmet temple that draws people from the entire country. Reserve well in advance and allow plenty of time; this is fine cuisine. The menu is constantly changing to match the imagination of the chef; diners choose a fixed menu or select from the à la carte menu, where the fish entrées are particularly interesting. You can stay overnight here, too; the house has seven rooms (reserve in advance, for the season varies; Expensive). The nearby **Erzherzog Eugen,** under the same management, has 12 rooms (Expensive). *Hauptstr. 46, A–5450, tel. 06468/2120. Reservations required. Jacket and tie advised. AE. Closed 2 (varying) days a week. Very Expensive.*

Zell am See (S.P.)

Dining and **Mövenpick Grand.** In the style of the great turn-of-the-century
Lodging resort hotels, this totally renovated house is probably the grandest place to stay in Zell. Most of the accommodations are small apartments, complete with kitchenette and fireplace; some are duplex. You're right on the lake, and the best rooms are those farthest out on the small peninsula. One of the restaurants is set in a semicircular room overlooking the lake. A disappointing restaurant downstairs serving frozen fish has replaced the excellent one that started here. *Esplanade 4, A–5700, tel. 06542/23880. 111 rooms. Facilities: 2 restaurants, rooftop bar, disco, lake swimming, sailing, indoor pool, hot whirlpool, sauna, solarium, squash, garage. AE, DC, MC, V. Very Expensive.*

★ **Salzburgerhof.** This impressive family-managed chalet, not far from the lake and the ski lift, is the town's foremost hotel; comfort and personal service are the rule. Each of the attractive rooms and suites has a flower-bedecked balcony. The pleasant garden is used for barbecues and evenings of folkloric entertainment. Golfer guests get a 20% discount at the local club. *Auerspergstr. 11, A–5700, tel. 06542/28280. 36 rooms, 8 suites, 16 junior suites. Facilities: restaurant, bar, indoor pool, hot whirlpool, sauna, solarium, fitness room, garage. AE, DC. Closed Apr., Nov.–mid-Dec. Very Expensive.*

St. Georg. This chalet-style house, slightly above the center, away from the lake, has balconies with many of its rooms. The Salzburgerhof manages this hotel as well, where dark wood sets the tone with natural stone, and the antiques and hunting trophies create an elegant atmosphere. The rooms and one apartment are spacious and particularly comfortable. The restaurant is above average; try the lamb chops or T-bone steak. And golfers can get a 20% reduction at the local course. *Schillerstr. 32, A–5700, tel. 06542/3533 or 06542/3534. 38 rooms. Facilities: restaurant, bar, lake swimming, indoor pool, sauna, solarium, garage. AE, DC. Closed Apr., Nov.–mid-Dec. Expensive.*

Zum Hirschen. You'll be directly in the center of town here, close to shops and the lake. Wood paneling sets the elegant rustic style, in both the public areas and the comfortable guest rooms. The restaurant serves good standard Austrian fare, including *Zwiebelrostbraten* (rump steak with onions) and lamb fillet in pastry crust. Ask for advice on wines; the cellar holds some surprises. *Dreifaltigkeitsgasse 1, A–5700, tel. 06542/2447. 44 rooms. Facilities: restaurant, bar, indoor pool, hot whirlpool, sauna, solarium, garage. No credit cards. Closed mid-Apr.–mid-May, Nov.–mid-Dec. Expensive.*

Katharina. You're out of the center, at the south end of the lake here. The attractive wood facing on this hotel makes it look smaller than it really is; inside you'll find a spacious lobby and lounge bar, with beautiful wooden ceilings. The imaginative twin-bedded rooms with living areas can be cleverly combined into family apartments. *Kirchenweg 11, Schüttdorf, A–5700, tel. 06542/7310 or 06542/7311. 60 rooms. Facilities: restaurant, bar, terrace café, indoor pool, sauna, solarium. AE. Closed May, mid-Oct.–mid-Dec. Moderate (summer)–Expensive (winter).*

★ **Erlhof.** An 11th-century estate house with vaulting and beamed ceilings has been transformed into an inconspicuously modern and comfortable hotel. The location and view are exquisite, on a plateau above the east shore overlooking the lake. The hotel has its own beach and offers golfers a 20% discount on fees at the nearby club. The restaurant, the best in the area, offers attentive service and excellent food with no pretentiousness. Try the spring-onion soup or any of the freshwater fish dishes. *Erlberg 22, A–5700 Zell am See/Thumersbach, tel. 06542/6637 or 06542/6638. 19 rooms. Facilities: restaurant (reservations required, jacket advised, closed Tues., Wed. lunch), lake swimming, sauna, solarium, fitness rooms, tennis. MC, V. Closed mid-Apr.–early May, Nov.–mid-Dec. Moderate.*

St. Hubertushof. On the opposite side of the lake from town, this sprawling hotel complex offers a great view across and is done in rural style with paneling and antlers over the fireplace in the lounge. The dance bar draws a regular crowd, and the restaurant offers a wide range of international and local dishes. *Seeuferstr. 7, A–5700 Zell am See/Thumersbach, tel. 06542/31160. 112 rooms. Facilities: restaurant, bar, sauna, garage. AE, DC. Closed Nov. Moderate.*

The Arts and Nightlife

The Arts

On this trip the mountain regions offer little theater or music, but hotels in the main resort centers do put on folkloric evenings and other entertainments, some of which are open to other than hotel guests.

Nightlife

Nightlife centers in the hotels in the major resorts, such as Saalfelden and Zell am See. With the possible exception of Saalfelden, these are not slick, sophisticated bars and discos, but local hangouts where you can get to know the people. In Badgastein, the casino in the Grand Hotel de l'Europe has baccarat, blackjack, roulette, and slot machines. Entry is AS170, for which you get chips worth AS200. *Kaiser-Franz-Josef-Str. 14, tel. 06434/24650. Passport required. Jacket and tie advised. Open daily 5 PM–2 AM; closed Apr.–June, Nov.–mid.-Dec.*

Après Ski Saalbach has a number of places that crowd up quickly as the slopes are vacated. Try the **X-Lodge** disco in the Hotel Kristall (tel. 06541/377) or the disco in the **Hotel Panther** (tel. 06541/227), which also plays video clips. The **Alpenhotel** (tel. 06541/6660) and **Neuhaus** (tel. 06541/7151) have small local bands. Also check out the **Sporthotel Ellmau** (tel. 06541/72260) for disco or dance music.

In Zell am See, the in spot is the **Wunderbar** in the Grand Hotel (tel. 06542/23870). The emphasis in Zell is more on drinking than on disco or dancing, but the scene changes. Check out the action in the cellar of the **Sporthotel Lebzelter** (tel. 06542/24110).

10 Western Alps

Innsbruck, Tirol,
Vorarlberg

Introduction

by George W. Hamilton

The Western Alpine region of Austria—basically the two provinces of Vorarlberg and Tirol—is so different from the rest of the country that you might think you've crossed a border. In fact, you have.

The border between the provinces of Salzburg and Tirol is defined by mountains; four passes make traffic possible. The faster trains cut across Germany rather than agonizing through the Austrian Alps. To the west, Tirol and Vorarlberg are separated from each other by the Arlberg mountain range (from which Vorarlberg gets its name, "in front of the Arlberg"). Until a tunnel was cut through, the Arlberg was passable only in summer; in winter, Vorarlberg was effectively cut off from the rest of the country.

This has now changed, but the isolation of both provinces meant that their culture has been preserved. The Tiroleans are strong on tradition, but nowhere in Austria will you find such conservativism and determined adherence to old customs as in Vorarlberg. You'll see the folk costumes on the street, not in museums, and your chances are very good of running into a local celebration any time of year.

What you probably won't notice is that Austrians from the eastern part of the country feel out of water in Tirol and Vorarlberg. The spoken dialects in each of the two provinces are totally different from that of the eastern part of the country, as is the way of thinking. And while Austrians from the east may go skiing or take vacations in Tirol, and although they've probably been to the United States, Britain, and maybe even Sri Lanka, many never make it to Vorarlberg in the course of their lives.

After the collapse of the Habsburg monarchy following World War I, Vorarlberg came very close to becoming a part of Switzerland. In 1919, 80% of the populace voted in favor of negotiating with the Swiss to join the confederation, but the St. Germain peace conference put an end to such ideas, and Vorarlberg remained Austrian.

The Tiroleans are considerably more nationalistic than the Vorarlbergers. In 1809–10 Andreas Hofer led bands of local patriots against Napoleon to break free from Bavaria and rejoin Austria. After three successes, including the battle of Bergisel just outside Innsbruck, Hofer lost the fourth attempt against combined French and Bavarian forces, was executed in Mantua, and became a national hero. The spirit of Tirolean identity is strong to this day.

Nowadays, these two provinces are very much a part of Austria. The Viennese semiaffectionately refer to Vorarlberg as *Ländle,* meaning "the little province." Tirol looks to Vienna for political support in its perpetual dispute with Italy over the South Tirol, a large and prosperous wine-growing region that was ceded to Italy after World War I. Many Austrian Tiroleans still own property in South Tirol and consider it very much a part of their homeland. Yet even Austria's Tirol is physically divided: East Tirol, a small enclave of remarkable natural magnificence wedged between the provinces of Salzburg and Carinthia, definitely belongs to the basic Tirol, except that it can be reached from there only by trespassing through Italy or the province of Salzburg.

Innsbruck is the treasure house of the whole of Tirol, historically, culturally, and commercially. It is also a convenient base from which to explore. Even if you are staying at an area resort, spending a day or two in Innsbruck first will give you a far better perspective on the rest of the region.

Innsbruck

The capital of Tirol is one of the most beautiful towns of its size anywhere in the world, owing much of its fame and charm to its unique setting. To the north, the steep, sheer sides of the Alps of the northern chain rise like a shimmering blue-and-white wall, literally from the edge of the city, an impressive backdrop for the mellowed green domes and red roofs of the Baroque town tucked beneath. No matter where you look there are more mountains. To the south, the peaks of the Tuxer and Stubai ranges form a hazy purple sequence fading into the distance.

Innsbruck has been an important crossroads for hundreds of years. When it was chartered in 1239, it was already a key point on the north–south highways between Germany and Italy and the east–west axis tying eastern Austria and the lands beyond to Switzerland. Today Innsbruck is the transit point for road and rail traffic between the bordering countries.

The charming Old World aspect of Innsbruck has remained virtually intact, with ample evidence of its Baroque past. The skyline encircling the center suffers somewhat from high rises, but the heart, the old city, remains much as it was 400 years ago. The protective vaulted arcades along main thoroughfares, the tiny passageways giving way to noble squares, and the ornate restored houses all contribute to the unforgettable picture of Innsbruck.

Essential Information

Important Addresses and Numbers
Tourist Information

The city's main tourist office (Burggraben 3, tel. 0512/5356) is open daily 8 AM–7 PM. The main office for information on Tirol (Wilhelm-Greil-Str. 17, tel. 0512/532–0170) is open weekdays 8:30–6, Saturday 9–noon.

Travel Agencies

American Express. *Brixner Str. 3, tel. 0512/582491. Open weekdays 9–5:30, Sat. 9–noon.*

Wagons-Lits/Cook. *Brixner Str. 2, tel. 0512/52079. Open weekdays 8:30–12:30, 2–6, Sat. 9–noon.*

Accommodations

If you arrive in Innsbruck without a hotel room, check with the *Zimmernachweis* in the railroad station (Südtiroler Platz, tel. 0512/583766; open daily 9–9). The same organization also has offices on the incoming west autobahn (tel. 0512/573543), the east autobahn (tel. 0512/46474), and the Brenner (south) autobahn (tel. 0512/577933). For information on youth hostels, phone 0512/46179.

Emergencies

For emergency medical help, telephone 0512/144 or call the university clinic (Anichstr. 35, tel. 0512/504). If you need a doctor during a weekend or holiday, check with your hotel or call 0512/575544, the weekend hotline.

Exchange In addition to banks (open weekdays 8–12:30 and 2:15–4) and the American Express office, you can change money at the main train station (open daily 7:30–12:30, 12:45–6, and 6:30–8:15) and at the city tourist information office. But compare rates; you'll probably do best at a bank.

Late-night Pharmacies Several pharmacies stay open late on a rotational basis. The newspaper will give the names, addresses, and phone numbers of them. Otherwise, try phoning the university clinic.

Arriving and Departing By Plane The airport, 3 km (2 mi) west of the city, is served principally by **Austrian Airlines** and **Tyrolean.** For flight information, phone 0512/22220. Buses to the main train station take about 20 minutes. Get your ticket from the bus driver; it costs AS17. Taxis should take no more than 10 minutes into town, and the fare is about AS60–AS70.

By Car Exit from the east–west autobahn (Rte. A–12/E–60), or from the Brenner autobahn (Rte. A–13/E–45) running south to Italy. Since the heart of the old city is a pedestrian zone and much of the rest of the downtown area is paid parking only, you'll be best off leaving the car in a central garage, unless your hotel has parking.

By Train Direct trains serve Innsbruck from Munich, Vienna, Rome, and Zurich, and all arrive at the railroad station at Südtiroler Platz. For train information and reservations, phone 0512/1717.

By Bus Innsbruck is connected by bus to other parts of Austria, and the long-distance terminal (tel. 0512/1717 or 05012/585155) is beside the main train station.

Getting Around By Bus and Streetcar Most bus and streetcar routes begin or end at the main train station. Get your ticket on the bus or streetcar. Single fare is AS17, a block of four tickets AS42, and four 24-hour tickets good on the entire network AS88. You can transfer to another line with the same ticket as long as you continue in more or less the same direction in a single journey. The bus is also the most convenient way to reach the five major ski areas outside the city. A **Club-Innsbruck** pass (free from the tourist office or your hotel if you spend three nights or more) gives you free transportation to the ski areas; many hotels provide shuttle service to the special ski bus stop. The public ski buses leave from the Landestheater on Rennweg, across from the Hofburg. Check with your hotel or the tourist offices for schedules.

By Taxi Taxis are not much faster than is walking, particularly along the one-way streets and in the old city. Basic fare is AS25. To order a radio cab, phone 0512/5311 or 0512/45500.

By Horsecab Horse-drawn cabs, still a feature of Innsbruck life, can be hired at the stand in front of the Landestheater, but set the price before you head off.

By Car Private cars are not allowed in the old city, and parking anywhere near the center in Innsbruck requires vouchers, which you buy from tobacconists, the tourist office (Burggraben 3), post offices, or coin-operated dispensers. Each ½ hour costs AS5. Maximum parking time is 1½ hours in the areas marked off by blue/white lines. Large blue *P* signs direct you to parking garages. The bus is about as convenient as a car for reaching the ski areas if you have to cope with chains and other complications of winter driving.

Guided Tours Bus tours with English-speaking guides cover the city high-lights (1½ hours), leaving daily at noon, year-round, from the hotel information office at the Südtiroler Platz station and at 12:10 from the Hypobank, across from the Tiroler Landesreise-büro on Boznerplatz. In summer, additional buses are scheduled at 10 AM and 2 PM. Your hotel or one of the tourist offices will have tickets and details, or phone 0512/581145.

Exploring Innsbruck

Squeezed by the mountains and sharing the valley with the Inn river (Innsbruck means "bridge over the Inn"), the city is compact and very easy to explore on foot. As you tour Innsbruck, you'll find constant reminders of three historic figures: the local hero Andreas Hofer, whose band of patriots challenged Napoleon in 1809; Emperor Maximilian I (1459–1519); and Empress Maria Theresa (1717–80), the last two of whom were responsible for much of the city's architecture. Maximilian ruled the Holy Roman Empire from Innsbruck, and Maria Theresa, who was particularly fond of the city, spent much time here.

Note that a Club-Innsbruck pass entitles you to reduced-price admissions to the Olympic museum, Hofkirche, Volkskunst-museum, Landesmuseum (Ferdinandeum), Alpenverein museum, Bergisel museum, and the Alpine zoo.

Numbers in the margin correspond with points of interest on the Innsbruck map.

❶ A good starting point for a walking tour is the **Goldenes Dachl** (the Golden Roof), which made famous the Late Gothic mansion whose balcony it covers. In fact the roof is made of gilded copper tiles, and its recent refurbishment is said to have taken 14 kg (nearly 31 lbs) of gold. The house was built in 1420 for Duke Friedrich (otherwise known as Friedl the Penniless); the balcony was added in 1501 by Maximilian I as a sort of "royal box" for watching street performances in the square below. The original building was altered and expanded at the beginning of the 18th century, and now only the loggia and the alcove are identifiable as original. The magnificent coats of arms representing Austria, Hungary, Burgundy, Milan, the Holy Roman Empire, Styria, Tirol, and royal Germany are copies. You can see the originals (and up close, too) in the Ferdinandeum museum. The Goldenes Dachl building now houses an **Olympic Museum,** which features videotapes of past Innsbruck winter Olympics. The admission ticket gets you entry also to the ❷ **Stadtturm,** the nearby 15th-century city tower. *Museum, Herzog Friedrich-Str. 15, tel. 0512/53600. Admission: AS20. Open daily 10–5:30. City tower admission: AS16. Open Mar.–Oct., daily 10–5.*

❸ Across the street is the dramatic blue-and-white **Helbling House,** originally a Gothic building (1560) to which the obvious ornate Rococo decoration was added in 1730.

Around the corner, go north on the Pfarrgasse to the Baroque ❹ **Domkirche,** the cathedral, built in 1722 and dedicated to Saint Jacob. The main attraction here, aside from the ornate Baroque interior, is the high-altar painting by Lucas Cranach the Elder, dating to about 1520. *Open Sat.–Thurs. 6–noon and 2–5, Fri. 2–5.*

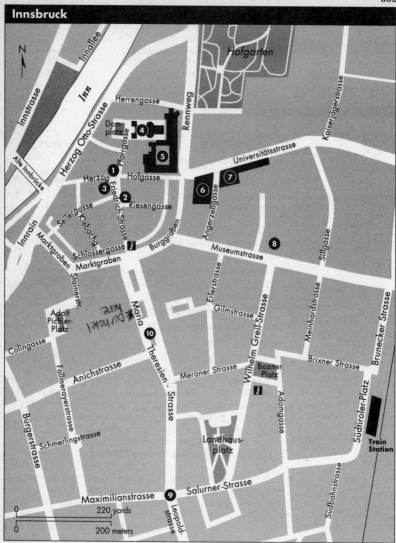

Innsbruck

Annasäule, **10**
Domkirche, **4**
Ferdinandeum, **8**
Goldenes Dachl, **1**
Helbling House, **3**
Hofburg, **5**
Hofkirche, **6**
Stadtturm, **2**
Tiroler
Volkskunstmuseum, **7**
Triumphpforte, **9**

5 Pass through the Herrengasse and turn right on the Rennweg to come to the **Hofburg,** the imperial palace built in the 14th–16th centuries for Maximilian I. The booklet (in English) at the ticket office will tell you more interesting tidbits about the palace than the tour guide will. The Rococo decor and the portraits of Habsburg ancestors in the ornate white-and-gold Great Reception Hall were added in the 18th century by Maria Theresa. *Rennweg 1, tel. 0512/587186. Admission: AS20. Visits by guided tour only, every hour on the hour. Open mid-May–mid-Oct., daily 9–4; mid-Oct.–mid-May, Mon.–Sat. 9–4.*

6 Close by is the **Hofkirche,** the imperial church, built as a mausoleum for Maximilian I (although he is actually buried in Wiener Neustadt, south of Vienna). The emperor's ornate black marble tomb is surrounded by 24 marble reliefs portraying his accomplishments, as well as 28 larger-than-life statues of his ancestors, including the legendary King Arthur of England. Andreas Hofer is also buried here. Don't miss the 16th-century "silver" chapel, up the stairs opposite the entrance, with its ornate altar and silver madonna. The chapel was built in 1578 to be the tomb of Archduke Ferdinand II and his wife, Philippine Welser, a commoner, the daughter of a rich and powerful merchant family. She was a superb cook and left behind an excellent cookbook. Visit the chapel in the morning to take pictures; the blinding afternoon sun comes in directly behind the altar. *Tel. 0512/584302. Admission: AS18; combined ticket with Volkskunstmuseum, AS25. Open May–Sept., daily 9–5; Oct.–Apr., daily 9–noon and 2–5.*

7 The **Tiroler Volkskunstmuseum** (Tirolean folk-art museum), in the same complex as the Hofkirche, exhibits Christmas mangers, costumes, rustic furniture, and entire rooms from old farmhouses and inns, decorated in styles ranging from Gothic to Rococo. Displays are somewhat static, and the information cards are in German. *Universitätsstr. 2, tel. 0512/584302. Admission: AS15. Volkskunstmuseum open Mon.–Sat. 9–noon and 2–5, Sun. 9–noon.*

8 Turn south into Angerzellgasse, then east on Museumstrasse to the **Ferdinandeum** (Landesmuseum), which houses Austria's largest collection of Gothic art, 19th- and 20th-century paintings, and medieval arms. The interesting industrial-arts collection, open only May–September, has exhibits on mining, woodworking, other area crafts and industries, clocks, musical instruments, old coaches, and locomotives. *Museumstr. 15, tel. 0512/594897. Admission: AS20. Open Oct.–Apr., Tues.–Sat. 10–noon and 2–5, Sun. 9–noon and 2–5; May–Sept., daily 10–5, Thurs. 7–9 PM.*

9 Walk south on Wilhelm Greil-Strasse and turn west on Salurner-Strasse to the **Triumphpforte** (Triumphal Arch), built in 1765 to commemorate both the marriage of emperor-to-be Leopold II and the death of Emperor Franz I, husband of Empress Maria Theresa. Then walk up Maria Theresien-Strasse **10** past the **Annasäule** (Anna Column), commemorating the withdrawal on St. Anna's day in 1703 of Bavarian forces in the war of the Spanish succession. Have your camera ready at this point to get the glorious classic view of Innsbruck, with the mountains in the background.

Excursions from Innsbruck

Hungerberg You're barely outside the city here, yet the combined funicular and cable cars will take you soaring above the skyline. Take the No. 1 streetcar or "C" bus to the base station (Rennweg 41, tel. 0512/586158). From here you take the funicular up to the Hungerberg (853 m, 2,800 ft), then a two-stage cable car to Seegrube at 1,904 meters (6,250 ft) and Hafelekar at the dizzying height of 2,286 meters (7,500 ft). The round-trip to Hungerberg costs AS52, children AS26; the round-trip to Hafelekar is AS243, children AS122. At all three stops you'll find hotels and restaurants commanding breathtaking views over the Tirolean Alps and Innsbruck.

When you're staying in Innsbruck for a few days, you may enjoy the exercise more if you take it one stage at a time. Start with Hungerberg and visit a different altitude and perspective each day, enjoying a leisurely lunch at each level.

A short walk from the Hungerberg station, the **Alpenzoo** has an unusual collection of alpine birds and animals, including endangered species. The zoo alone is worth the trip up the Hungerberg, and on top of that, if you buy your ticket for the zoo at the base station, the trip up and back is free. *Weiherburggasse 37a, tel. 0512/292323. Admission: AS32. Open daily 9–6.*

At the base station of the Hungerbergbahn you'll find the round building housing the **Riesengemälde,** or giant painting, a huge panorama depicting the 1809 battle of Bergisel, in which Andreas Hofer's Tirolean patriots fought the French; it may add to your perspective when you visit Bergisel. *Rennweg 39, tel. 0512/584434. Admission: AS15. Open Apr.–Oct., daily 9–4:45.*

Wilten and Bergisel South of the city beyond the rail line is the district of Wilten, even older than the city core. Wilten today is best known for its 18th-century Rococo parish church, which was made a basilica in 1958. Note the ornate painted ceilings. You can reach the church via the No. 1 streetcar to Stubaitalbahnhof/Bergisel. *Klostergasse 7, tel. 0512/583–0480. Open daily until about dusk.*

About a 15-minute walk from the Wilten Basilica (follow the signs) is the Bergisel park, with the Olympic ski jump. The winding walkway to the "landing area" is a bit steep but a pleasant hike; from there, you'll have a magnificent view out over all Innsbruck. It seems so close in perspective, you'd almost expect the ski jumpers to overfly the target and land in the middle of the city. The hill itself includes a field of remembrance to the soldiers who fought here in 1809 and a memorial to Andreas Hofer. The memorials and buildings of the Bergisel grounds are spaced widely apart amid woods and lawns. *Open daily in summer, 9–5; check winter hours.*

What to See and Do with Children

The **Alpine Zoo** in Hungerberg (*see* Excursions from Innsbruck, above) is ideal for a family outing. The tourist office has a booklet on Innsbruck for children.

Off the Beaten Track

In Amras, 3 km (2 mi) southeast of the city and easily reached by bus or streetcar, **Schloss Ambras** is one of the country's finest and best-preserved castles. The original building dating from the 11th century was rebuilt by Archduke Ferdinand in the late 16th century, adding the large Renaissance Spanish hall (ca 1573). His commoner wife Philippine Welser lived here. Most of the original art is now in the Kunsthistorisches Museum in Vienna, but there is still a large collection of pictures, weapons, armor, furniture, ingenious household gadgets, and other curiosities dating from medieval times to be seen. Look around the grounds as well to see the fencing field and a small cemetery to which have been brought samples of earth from 18 battlefields around the world. *Tel. 0512/41215. Admission: AS30. Open May–Sept., Wed.–Sun. 10–4.*

Shopping

The best shops are along the arcaded Herzog Friedrich-Strasse in the heart of the old city; along its extension, Maria Theresien-Strasse; and the cross street Maximilianstrasse in the newer part of town. Innsbruck is *the* place to buy native Tirolean dress, particularly Lederhosen, and you can comparison-shop within a relatively small area. Look also for cut crystal and wood carvings.

Tiroler Heimatwerk (Meraner Str. 2–4, tel. 0512/582320) is the first place to look for local clothing and souvenirs of good quality. The extremely attractive shop carries textiles and finished clothing, ceramics, carved wooden chests, and some furniture. You can also have clothing made to order.
Lanz (Wilhelm Greil-Str. 5, tel. 0512/583105), with shops throughout Austria, is an outstanding source of dirndls, those attractive country costumes for women, with the white blouse, dark skirt, and colorful apron. It also has other sportswear and children's clothing.
Rudolf Boschi (Kiebachgasse 8, tel. 0512/589224) turns out reproductions of old pewterware, using the original molds when possible. Among other items, he has locally produced hand-decorated beer mugs with pewter lids.
Galerie Bloch (Herzog Friedrich-Str. 5, tel. 0512/577402) sells graphics by the droll Tirolean artist Paul Flora; you'll find much to smile at here, and maybe even to take home.

Sports and Fitness

Gliding The mountains create updrafts, which makes Innsbruck a good place for sail gliding. Call Flugsportzentrum Innsbruck (tel. 0512/283157) for details.

Golf **Golfclub Innsbruck/Igls** in Lans, about 9 km (6 mi) outside the city, has two 9-hole courses, par 66 (tel. 0512/77165; open Apr.–Nov.); **Golfclub Innsbruck/Igls** in Rinn, about 12 km (7½ mi) away, has 18 holes, with a par 71 (tel. 05223/8177; open Apr.–Oct.). Both courses charge a AS240 greens fee on weekdays, AS350 on weekends. Several hotels—Alpenhof, Sporthotel Igls, and Gesundheitszentrum Lanserhof at Lans and the Geisler at Rinn—have special golfing arrangements.

Health and Fitness Clubs   In Innsbruck, try **Europ** (Salurner-Str. 15, tel. 0512/575382) and, for women, **Isabella** (Sonnenburgstr. 9, tel. 0512/588072).

Hiking   Both easy paths and extreme slopes await hikers and climbers. From June to September, members of Club-Innsbruck (*see* Getting Around, above) can take free daily guided mountain hikes. If you want to learn to climb, look to the **Alpine School Innsbruck** (Natters, In der Stille 1, tel. 0512/577122); if you already know how, to the **Österreichische Alpenverein** (Wilhelm Greil-Str. 15, tel. 0512/584107). If you'll be taking the cable-car lifts with any frequency, get a *Super-Bergbahnkarte* for a week's unlimited use on the Hungerburg, Nordketten, and Patscherkofel runs (AS1,680 adults, AS1,010 children over age 6). The card is available at the city office of the Innsbrucker Verkehrsbetriebe (Salurner-Str. 11), at the tourist office, and at any of the *Zimmernachweis* offices.

Riding   Horseback riding can be arranged through **Reitclub Innsbruck** (Langer Weg, tel. 0512/47174) or Hotel Astoria (tel. 0512/774810).

Skiing   In winter, check with the tourist office for information on snow conditions and how to get to the five ski areas. Your Club-Innsbruck membership card will get you free transportation to the areas and reductions on a number of ski lifts. If you're a summer skiier (and can take the altitudes), there's year-round skiing on the Stubai glacier, about 40 km (25 mi) from Innsbruck, via the "ST" bus from the train station. You can book with the **Schischule Innsbruck** (tel. 0512/582310) or at the hotel-information stand (tel. 0512/583766) in the station.

Swimming   Around Innsbruck there are plenty of lakes, but in town you have little choice other than pools, indoor and out. Outdoors, try the **Freischwimmbad Tivoli** (Purtschellerstr. 1, tel. 0512/42344); indoors, **Hallenbad Amraser Strasse** (Amraser Str. 3, tel. 0512/42585) or **Hallenbad Olympisches Dorf** (Kugelfangweg 46, tel. 0512/61342).

Tennis   Innsbruck has an abundance of courts, although they tend to be scattered and booked well ahead. Your hotel or the tourist office can be helpful. Try the **Olympia-Eissportzentrum** (Olympiastr. 10, tel. 0512/59838) or the **Tennisclub IEV** (Reichenauer Str. 144, tel. 0512/46229); your Club-Innsbruck card will get you a reduction at both.

Dining

All the hotels serve meals; the larger ones offer some of the best dining in Innsbruck. But the town also has some excellent restaurants, many of them new, with young and ambitious chefs. And as in most regions of Austria, local specialties are being rediscovered, adopted, and adapted to modern cuisine. Highly recommended restaurants are indicated by a star ★.

Category	Cost*
Very Expensive	over AS400
Expensive	AS250–AS400

Moderate	AS125–AS250

Inexpensive	under AS125

*per person, excluding drinks but including service (usually 10%) and sales tax (10%).

Very Expensive **Altstadtstüberl.** You'll find Tirolean specialties in this comfortable country environment. The kitchen has made recent efforts to achieve greater heights, not always with success, but a visit is worth the risk. Try the roast lamb, or game, if it's offered. *Riesengasse 13, tel. 0512/582347. Reservations advised. Jacket advised. AE, DC, MC, V. Closed Sun. and early June.*

★ **Europa-Stüberl.** Warm wood paneling sets the tone for this fairly formal, elegant restaurant, considered by many to be the city's best. You'll find interesting variations on regional themes, such as the sour cream/watercress sauce accompanying the veal schnitzel and the different treatments of lamb. The wine cellar offers a good choice of the best Austrian vintages, as well as international specialties. *Brixner Str. 6, in Hotel Europa, tel. 0512/5931. Reservations required. Jacket and tie advised. AE, DC, MC, V.*

Goldener Adler. In this 600-year-old hotel, the ancient rooms with their timbered ceilings create just the right setting for the local cuisine. Look for fresh trout and game in season, and ask for recommendations on specialties from both north and south Tirol. The upstairs restaurant is the more elegant, but the Goethe-Stube is pleasantly intimate. *Herzog Friedrich-Str. 6, tel. 0512/586334. Reservations advised. Jacket and tie suggested. AE, DC, MC, V.*

Kapeller. You'll find one of Innsbruck's best restaurants outside the center of town, in the Kapeller hotel in Amras (take the No. 3 streetcar). The atmosphere is elegant modern, the cuisine mainly on the light side. You might start with the cream of lobster soup with salmon dumplings or a bouillabaisse and follow with the fillet of wild hare. Ask for wine recommendations; the list is excellent. *Philippine-Welser-Str. 96, tel. 0512/43106. Reservations advised. Jacket and tie advised. AE, DC, MC, V. Closed Sun., Mon. lunch; Jan. and early Aug.*

Picnic. Don't let the name put you off; this is a sophisticated modern restaurant attractively done up in white with brick and red-tile accents. The city's power brokers gather here at noon to enjoy pepper steak or veal steak with lemon sauce, among the international offerings. The wine list is a bit weak, so ask for advice. *Fallmerayerstr. 12, tel. 0512/583859. Reservations advised. Jacket and tie advised. AE, DC, MC, V. Closed Sun.*

★ **Schwarzer Adler.** Of the comfortable restaurants in the Schwarzer Adler hotel, the preferred one is the intimate restaurant upstairs, with wood-paneled rooms and lead-paned windows, but the cellar rooms with light, vaulted ceilings are full of atmosphere: the "K. & K." room is furnished in period antiques, the other *Stube* rooms in Tirolean country style. You'll be offered local and national specialties, including roast duck and a good schnitzel, but go for the more adventurous-sounding dishes. The wine list includes mainly Austrian and South Tirolean vintages. *Kaiserjagerstr. 2, tel. 0512/587109. Reservations recommended, particularly for the Stuben. Jacket and tie advised. AE, DC, MC, V. Closed Sun. and mid-Jan.*

Expensive **Bistro.** This onetime simple *Gasthaus* is a bit outside the city center (take the No. 3 streetcar or *B* bus to Pradl), but you'll

Innsbruck Dining and Lodging

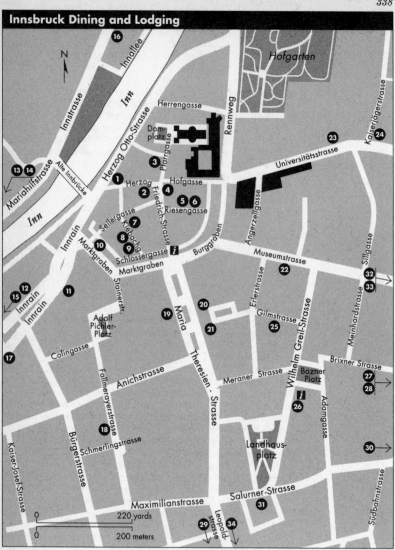

Dining
Alte Teestube, **6**
Altstadtstüberl, **5**
Bistro, **33**
Central, **25**
Dom Café-Bar, **3**
Europa-Stüberl, **27**
Gasthaus Engl, **16**
Goldener Adler, **2**

Grauer Bär, **23**
Hirschenstuben, **7**
Kapeller, **34**
Munding, **9**
Ottoburg, **1**
Picnic, **18**
Schwarzer Adler, **24**
Stieglbräu, **26**
Weisses Rössl, **8**
Wienerwald, **19, 22**

Lodging
Alpotel, **11**
Bergisel, **29**
Binder, **30**
City-Club Hotel, **13**
Europa, **28**
Goldener Adler, **2**
Goldene Krone, **21**
Grauer Bär, **23**
Innsbruck, **17**

Internationales
Studentenhaus, **15**
Kapeller, **34**
Leipziger Hof, **32**
Maria Theresia, **20**
Maximilian, **10**
Rössl in der Au, **14**
Royal, **12**
Scandic Crown, **31**
Schwarzer Adler, **24**
Weisses Kreuz, **4**

find a modern, cool restaurant, and if you order any of the fish dishes—starting with the fish soup—you'll be glad you took the short trip. Try also the veal schnitzel in parsley sauce. *Pradlerstr. 2, tel. 0512/46319. Reservations advised. Jacket and tie suggested. AE, DC, MC, V. Closed Sun.*

★ **Grauer Bär.** The large arcaded room is a bit old-fashioned, but the young kitchen staff brings imaginative lightness to the table. You might be surprised by the snails with roast potatoes and a garlic-herb sauce, or the tiny lamb sausages in paprika-eggplant sauce. The wine list includes nearly all of Austria's best; ask for recommendations. Finish with a coffee; it's superb. *Universitätsstr. 5, tel. 0512/5924. Jacket advised. Reservations not required. AE, DC, MC, V.*

Moderate **Hirschenstuben.** These rustic rooms are just right for the
★ game, trout, and other local specialties served in this ancient house. The Italian dishes such as osso buco are also excellent. *Kiebachgasse 5, tel. 0512/582979. Reservations not required. Dress: neat but casual. AE, DC, MC, V. Closed Sun.*

★ **Ottoburg.** It's fun just to explore the rabbit warren of paneled rustic rooms upstairs in this red-and-white shuttered house built in 1494. Several of the bay-window alcoves have great views toward the Goldenes Dachl square. Try the trout, if it's on the menu, but the chicken and duck dishes are also excellent. *Herzog Friedrich-Str. 1, tel. 0512/574652. Reservations not required. Jacket advised. AE, DC, MC, V. Closed Tues. Oct.–Apr.*

★ **Weisses Rössl.** In the authentically rustic rooms upstairs, an array of antlers adds to the decor. This is the right place for solid local standards, like roast pork with dumpling and venison goulash. *Kiebachgasse 8, tel. 0512/583057. Reservations not required. Dress: neat but casual. AE, DC, MC, V. Closed Sun., early Nov., mid-Apr.*

Inexpensive **Dom Café-Bar.** The former Domstuben restaurant has been transformed into a comfortable evening café-bar, with lighter foods, snacks, and salads at reasonable prices. *Pfarrgasse 3, tel. 0512/577931. Dress: casual. No credit cards. Closed for lunch.*

Gasthaus Engl. Here is a Gasthaus in the best sense of the word: a simple setting, moderately attentive but overworked personnel, and large servings of delicious food. It's a favorite with students from the nearby university. Look for pork and chicken dishes here, but check the daily specials as well. *Innstr. 22, tel. 0512/283112. No reservations. Dress: casual. AE, MC, V. Closed weekends.*

Stieglbräu. In this large and popular complex you'll find a long menu of standard Austrian fare, including liver-dumpling soup, roast meats, and chicken, egg, and pasta dishes. The usual accompaniment is beer (Stiegl is brewed in Salzburg). *Wilhelm Greil-Str. 25, tel. 0512/584338. No reservations. Dress: casual. No credit cards.*

Wienerwald. This chain started out on grilled chicken (and very good indeed) but now serves pastas as well as roast and grilled meats in a modern rustic environment. In summer, the gardens of both locations are particularly pleasant and are open to 12:30 AM. The wines sold by the glass are good. *Maria Theresien-Str. 12, tel. 0512/584165, and Museumstr. 24, tel. 0512/588994. No reservations. Dress: casual. AE, DC, MC, V.*

Cafés   **Alte Teestube.** In an intimate upstairs room, you'll be offered some four dozen kinds of tea, with a choice of pastry accompaniments. *Riesengasse 6, tel. 0512/582309. Reservations not required. Jacket advised. No credit cards. Closed Sun. and May–Oct.*

★ **Central.** Since 1878 this large traditional café in the Viennese style has been the place to relax over a coffee. Newspapers and magazines are available, as is a variety of food and pastries. *Gilmstr. 5, in the Central Hotel, tel. 0512/5920. No reservations. Dress: casual but neat. AE, DC, MC, V. Closed Nov.*

★ **Munding.** People literally stand in line to get into these small rooms for coffee and the house-made pastries. *Kiebachgasse 16, tel. 0512/584118. No reservations. Dress: neat but casual. No credit cards.*

Lodging

If you're driving, you may want to seek out a hotel that has parking, since cars must be left some distance from the city center. Hotel rates vary widely by season, with the off-peak periods being March–May and September–November. Highly recommended lodgings are indicated by a star ★.

Category	Cost*
Very Expensive	over AS1,500
Expensive	AS1,000–AS1,500
Moderate	AS700–AS1,000
Inexpensive	under AS700

*Prices are for a standard double room, including service charge and taxes, and with breakfast except in the Very Expensive category.

Very Expensive   **Europa.** Crystal chandeliers and red velvet convey the traditional elegance of this hotel opposite the railroad station yet
★ only a short walk from the old city. For more than 100 years the Europa has been *the* place to stay in Innsbruck and a social center as well. Rooms are furnished mainly in period style, but some are contemporary; those on the inner court are considerably quieter. The restaurant, Europa-Stüberl (*see* Dining, above), is one of Innsbruck's best. *Südtiroler Platz 2, A–6020, tel. 0512/5931. 130 rooms. Facilities: restaurant, sauna, solarium, garage. AE, DC, MC, V.*

★ **Goldener Adler.** This traditional hotel, a 600-year-old house with stone walls, winding staircases, and nooks and crannies, has spacious rooms with baths. It's in the heart of the old city, directly across from the Goldenes Dachl; dukes, princes, presidents, and ambassadors have stayed here over the years. The rooms are luxuriously furnished in period or elegant Tirolean style. *Herzog Friedrich-Str. 6, A–6020, tel. 0512/586334. 36 rooms. Facilities: restaurant, wine stube. AE, DC, MC, V.*

Innsbruck. Here, in one of the city's newest hotels, the mood is modern from the lobby to the efficient rooms with their touches of finished wood. From some of the rooms you'll get gorgeous views of the old city; from those on the river side, of the Nordkette mountains directly behind. *Innrain 3, A–6020, tel. 0512/59868. 91 rooms. Facilities: restaurant, indoor pool, sauna, garage. AE, DC, MC, V.*

Scandic Crown. This modern high-rise block close to the railroad station looks out of place but offers contemporary comfort in friendly Scandinavian style. The rooms are luxurious yet efficiently modern. Look for Scandinavian specialties in the restaurants; the Sunday noon smorgasbord is justifiably popular. Innsbruck's new casino is located in the hotel. *Salurner-Str. 15, A–6020, tel. 0512/59350. 176 rooms. Facilities: 2 restaurants, bar, indoor pool, sauna, solarium, garage. AE, DC, MC, V.*

Expensive ★

Alpotel. All rooms are quiet in this modern building tucked into a small square off the street, yet you're almost in the old city. Furnishings throughout are in warm colors and natural wood. The rooms are particularly light and welcoming; those on the upper floors on the city side have a truncated view of the distant mountains. *Innrain 13, A–6020, tel. 0512/577931. 75 rooms. Facilities: restaurant, sauna, solarium, garage. AE, DC, MC, V.*

Grauer Bär. Despite renovations that have added baths as well as color, the Gray Bear remains a family-run hotel in the old style, with vast public spaces and generous, comfortable rooms and spacious baths. The bar in rustic decor completes the picture, and it's just steps from the old city center. *Universitätsstr. 5, A–6020, tel. 0512/59240. 81 rooms. Facilities: restaurant, bar. AE, DC, MC, V.*

Kapeller. Outside the center in Amras (take the No. 3 streetcar), this friendly *Gasthof* offers cozy rooms and the advantage of an outstanding restaurant in-house (*see* Dining, above). *Philippine-Welser-Str. 96, A–6020, tel. 0512/43101. 36 rooms. Facilities: restaurant, parking. AE, DC, MC, V.*

Maria Theresia. Behind the elegant 1920s facade you'll find a freshly renovated hotel, now part of the Best Western chain. You couldn't be more central, but you have to choose between a room on the street overlooking the Anna Column and the active main thoroughfare or one on the inside where it's considerably quieter. The rooms are stylishly furnished in neo-Baroque. *Maria Theresien-Str. 31, A–6020, tel. 0512/5933. 105 rooms. Facilities: restaurant, garage. AE, DC, MC, V.*

Maximilian. From the pine-paneled lobby of this attractive hotel built in 1982 to the dark wood furnishings in the compact rooms, you'll feel at home. Tucked away in a peaceful corner of the old city, it's convenient to most of the sights and shops. You'll get the best view from the back, over the old city roofs. Meals are for hotel guests only. *Marktgraben 7–9, A–6020, tel. 0512/59967. 40 rooms. Facilities: dining room, parking. AE, DC, MC, V.*

Schwarzer Adler. This member of the Romantik Hotels group radiates tradition, and ongoing renovations have updated the rooms. The wood paneling, antique furniture, and other Old World touches in the lobby are repeated in the rooms, making them individual and unusually inviting. You're only a few steps from the heart of the old city. And the restaurants are excellent. *Kaiserjägerstr. 2, A–6020, tel. 0512/587109. 27 rooms. Facilities: 2 restaurants, garage. AE, DC, MC, V.*

Moderate

Goldene Krone. The colorful facade of this older house conceals a set of smallish rooms that are modern and clean, and you couldn't ask for a better location, overlooking the main square. *Maria Theresien-Str. 46, A–6020, tel. 0512/586160. 35 rooms. Facilities: parking. AE, MC, V.*

Leipziger Hof. In the Pradl district, but not too far behind the railroad station, this comfortable hotel with its rustic rooms is within walking distance of the center of town. *Defreggerstr. 13, A-6020, tel. 0512/43525. 45 rooms. Facilities: restaurant, garage. No credit cards.*

Royal. This modern hotel overlooks the river and is only steps from the old city. Rooms are simple but spacious and comfortable. *Innrain 16, A-6020, tel. 0512/586385. 20 rooms. Facilities: breakfast room, parking. AE, DC, MC, V.*

★ **Weisses Kreuz.** At first encounter, you'll fall in love with this hotel, set over the stone arcades in the heart of the old city. It has seen massive renovations since the first Gasthof stood on this site in 1465, and the rooms are simple but comfortable, with mainly rustic furniture and lots of light wood. The service is friendly and accommodating; there are special rooms on the ground floor in which you can keep your skis; hotel reception and a restaurant are upstairs. *Herzog Friedrich-Str. 31, A-6020, tel. 0512/594790. 32 rooms. Facilities: 2 restaurants, garage. AE, V.*

Inexpensive **Bergisel.** Take the No. 1 streetcar to get to this hotel, tucked under the Bergisel ski jump on the edge of the city. The rooms are a bit plain but adequate. *Bergisel 2, A-6020, tel. 0512/581912. 21 rooms, 5 with bath. Facilities: restaurant, parking. No credit cards.*

Binder. A short streetcar trip (No. 3) from the center of town brings you to the less costly comfort of this small, friendly hotel. Rooms are modest but modern and attractive. *Dr.-Glatz-Str. 20, A-6020, tel. 0512/42236. 32 rooms. Facilities: garage. DC, MC, V.*

Summer Hotels Student accommodations are turned into inexpensive hotels in summer and are extremely good value if you don't require the amenities of a full hotel. On the other hand, you may discover that Austrian university students don't live too badly! The best located and cheapest is the **Internationales Studentenhaus** (Innrain 64, A-6020, tel. 0512/59477. 275 rooms. Facilities: garage. No credit cards.) Across the Inn river and overlooking the city are the **City-Club Hotel** (Höttinger Au 84, A-6020, tel. 0512/42236. 42 rooms. Facilities: restaurant, parking. AE, DC, MC, V.) and **Rössl in der Au** (Höttinger Au 34, A-6020, tel. 0512/286846. 125 rooms. Facilities: garage, parking. AE, DC, MC, V).

The Arts and Nightlife

Theater and Opera Innsbruck's principal theater is the **Tiroler Landestheater** (Rennweg 2, tel. 0512/520-7401 for program information, 0512/520-7430 for bookings). Both opera and operetta are presented in the "large house," usually starting at 7:30; plays in the Kammerspiele start at 8. Get tickets at the box office or at the main tourist office.

Music Concerts take place in the modern Saal Tirol of the **Kongresshaus** (Rennweg 3, tel. 0512/5936). Each year at Pentecost the churches resound with organ music during the annual International Organ Week. In summer, concerts are held in various historic places around Innsbruck, including Schloss Ambras, and there are brass-band folk-music concerts in the public squares almost every day. (It's said that Tirol has more bandleaders than mayors.) Folk shows at the Hotel Europa and other spots around the city feature real Tirolean folk dancing, yodeling, and zither music. Your hotel will have details.

Nightlife One of the more intriguing of the night bars is **Café Toscana** (Adolf Pichler-Platz 10, tel. 0512/583985), where the chairs are Thonet bentwood and the walls are hung with an eclectic collection of amusing old prints and photographs.

Of the classic discos, the best is **Pascha** (Anichstr. 7, tel. 0512/582420), with Italian cuisine for that extra twist.

Along the nightclub circuit, start first at **Filou** (Stiftgasse 12, tel. 0512/580256), where in summer you can sit in an attractive garden until 10 PM, when things move indoors for the sake of neighborhood peace and quiet, or **Nofretete** (Hofgasse 12, tel. 0512/572157). **Lady O** (Brunecker Str. 2, tel. 0512/586432) is the traditional striptease nightclub; you can see a teaser program on the ground floor at 9 PM for an AS20 admission charge, but the first drink costs AS120.

Tirol

Many British visitors come to Tirol, particularly in summer; they first appeared in numbers in the late 1800s, and today they come by charter plane from London, Birmingham, and Glasgow. In fact, the British Kandahar Ski Club played an important part in the development of Tirol in the 1920s by hiring Hannes Schneider to teach his revolutionary ski technique, thus popularizing the sport and making Austrian skiing world-famous.

Americans discovered the area not long after the British. In 1906 the railroad millionaire J. Pierpont Morgan spent a holiday in Innsbruck, and from that point on, Tirol was promoted in the United States as a vacation playground.

As if the sheer splendor of Tirol (nature imitating art) weren't enough, the region can look back on a history filled with romance (life imitating operetta?). Up to the beginning of the 16th century, Tirol was a powerful state in its own right, under a long line of counts and dukes: personages of such varying fortunes as Friedl the Penniless and his son Sigmund the Wealthy. (On the whole, Tirolean rulers were considerably more wealthy than penniless.) The province reached the zenith of its power under Emperor Maximilian I (1459–1519), when Innsbruck was the seat of the Holy Roman Empire. Maximilian's tomb in Innsbruck gives ample evidence of this onetime far-reaching glory.

Essential Information

Tourist Most small-town tourist offices have no specific street address
Information and are accommodated in the village hall. Address letters to Tourist Information and include the postal code of the town. The main office for Tirol is in **Innsbruck** (Wilhelm Greil-Str. 17, tel. 0512/532–0170). Other offices (*Fremdenverkehrsamt* or *Fremdenverkehrsverband*) are:

Achenkirch (A–6215, tel. 05246/6270)
Brixlegg (Marktstr. 6b, A–6230, tel. 05337/2581)
Imst (Johannesplatz 4, A–6460, tel. 05412/2419)
Ischgl (A–6561, tel. 05444/5266 or 5620)

Jenbach (Achenseestr. 37, A–6200, tel. 05244/3901)
Kitzbühel (Hinterstadt 18, A–6370, tel. 05365/22720)
Kufstein (Münchner Str. 2, A–6330, tel. 05372/2207)
Landeck (Malserstr. 10, A–6500, tel. 04552/62344)
Mayrhofen (Dursterstr. 222, A–6290, tel. 05285/2305)
Obergurgl/Hochgurgl (A–6456, tel. 05256/258 or 353)
Rattenberg (Klostergasse 94, A–6240, tel. 05337/3321)
Schwaz (Franz-Josef-Str. 26, A–6130, tel. 05242/3240)
Seefeld (Klosterstr. 43, A–6100, tel. 05212/2316)
Sölden/Hochsölden (A–6450, tel. 05254/22120)
St. Anton am Arlberg (A–6580, tel. 05446/22690)
St. Johann in Tirol (Speckbacherstr. 11, A–6380, tel. 05352/2218)
Zell am Ziller (Dorfplatz 3a, A–6280, tel. 05282/2281)

Getting Around
By Car Driving is the best way to see Tirol, since it allows you to wander off the main routes at your pleasure or to stop and admire the view. Roads are good, but a detailed highway map is recommended. In winter, check with one of the automobile clubs for road information (tel. 0222/711997) before starting out. Watch your gas gauge, particularly on Sundays and holidays, when some stations may be closed.

The autobahns are fastest, but for views, you'll be best off on the byways. One important exception is the 1.8-km (6,000-ft) Europabridge on the Brenner autobahn running south into Italy, although, if you follow the parallel route from Patsch to Pfons, you'll have the views without the traffic. Roads with particularly attractive scenery are marked on highway maps with a parallel green line.

By Train The railroad follows nearly all the main routes in Tirol, with highways and tracks sharing the same narrow valleys. Some of the most fascinating and memorable side trips can be made by rail; two narrow-gauge lines steam out of Jenbach, for example, one up to the Achensee, the other down to Mayrhofen in the Zillertal. From Innsbruck, the narrow-gauge Stubaitalbahn runs south to Telfes and Fulpmes.

The main railway line of Tirol runs east–west, entering Tirol via the Griessen pass, then heading on to St. Johann and Kitzbühel before wandering over to Wörgl and onward to Jenbach, Hall i.T., and Innsbruck. From Innsbruck on, the line follows the Inn valley to Landeck, then to St. Anton, where it plunges into an 11-km (6.8-mi) tunnel under the Arlberg range, emerging at Langen in Vorarlberg. From Innsbruck, a line runs north into Germany to Garmish-Partenkirchen and onward back into Austria, to Ehrwald and Reutte in Tirol and beyond, into Germany again. A line from Innsbruck to the south goes over the dramatic Brenner pass (1,374 m, 4,465 ft) into Italy.

By Bus In Tirol, as throughout Austria, where the train doesn't go, the post office or railroad bus does, and except in the most remote areas, buses are frequent enough so that you can get around. But bus travel requires time and planning. In summer, tour-bus operators run many sightseeing trips through Tirol that often include East and South Tirol. Check with your travel agent or the nearest tourist office.

Exploring Tirol

Tirol's gorgeous geography precludes the convenient loop tour; you must go up into the valleys to discover the hundreds of charming villages and hotels, and a certain amount of back-tracking is necessary. We've outlined six tours over familiar routes, touching on the best of the towns and suggesting side trips and pleasures off the beaten track.

Tour 1 will take you east of Innsbruck through the lower Inn valley, then south into the Ziller and Tuxer valleys, with detours to the Achensee and to Gerlos. Tour 2, also east of Innsbruck, continues up the Inn valley to Kufstein on the German border and to the ski resorts of St. Johann and Kitzbühel. Tour 3 is a day trip south of Innsbruck into the Stubaital, and Tour 4, another day trip, takes you northwest from Innsbruck to Seefeld and then on past Reutte. Tour 5 explores the Inn valley west of Innsbruck to Imst, then goes south up the Ötz valley; Tour 6 heads west from Imst, takes in Landeck and the upper Inn valley, ending with St. Anton and the Arlberg.

If time is short, take Tour 3 to get the feeling of a remote valley; then, depending on where you're headed, take Tour 1 or Tour 5 to see a cross-section of Tirol's highlights: the old and the new, glossy resorts, medieval castles, and always that superlative scenery.

Highlights   The **Zillertalbahn** from **Jenbach** to **Mayrhofen** (*see* Tour 1)
Gauderfest in Zell am Ziller (*see* Tour 1)
An evening at **Tenne** in **Kitzbühel** (*see* Tour 2)

Tour 1: Around the Lower Inn Valley   Northeast of Innsbruck the Inn river valley broadens out and courses right through Tirol toward Kufstein and the German border. Route 171 along the valley is a much pleasanter route than the autobahn running parallel.

Numbers in the margin correspond with points of interest on the Tirol: Tours 1–3 map.

⓫ **Hall in Tirol** (Solbad Hall), a bare 9 km (5 mi) from Innsbruck, is an old city founded by salt miners. The picturesque old part of the town is made up of narrow lanes running east–west, interrupted by a few short cross alleys. Stop and look around; from the main road, you cannot get a proper perspective of the fine old buildings. The *Rathaus*, built in the mid-15th century, has ornately carved councillors' rooms and beautifully worked mosaics covering the walls. The mint tower, symbol of the town, and the 17th-century monastery church, the oldest Renaissance ecclesiastical building in Tirol, are all interesting examples of local craftsmanship. The mint was moved to Hall from Meran, and the first coins were struck here in 1477. Legend has it that Duke Sigmund the Wealthy, son of Friedl the Penniless, got his nickname by tossing handfuls of Hall-minted coins to the populace wherever he went. The Inntal (Inn valley) gave its name to the coin, known as the *Taler*, from which came the word "dollar."

Eight km (5 mi) farther on is the town of **Wattens,** home of the Swarovsky glass empire. Stop at the **Kristall** shop (Innstr. 1, tel. 05224/5886) not only to buy the famous crystal and glassware but to watch the glass-cutting and blowing and the cutting of precious stones upstairs.

Tirol: Tours 1–3

346

(12) Schwaz, on the south bank of the Inn, dates back to the 12th century. In the 15th century it was a rich and important mining center, with copper and silver mines dug deep under the towering Tuxer Alps. Those mines indeed may have been the reason for setting up the mint in nearby Hall. Many of the 15th- and 16th-century houses built during those prosperous times still stand, and the marketplace has kept its atmosphere. Look at the vast parish church, the largest Gothic hall-church in Tirol. The roof, dating to 1510, is covered with 15,000 copper shingles. The church was expanded in 1490 and divided into two parts (once they were separated by a wooden wall): the southern chancel for the miners, the northern, or the "Prince's chancel," for the upper classes. The organ dates to 1734. Also see the Franciscan cloister, whose murals and frescoes depict the history of Christ from the Last Supper to the Last Judgment.

Jenbach, another 8 km (5 mi) on, across the river, is notable mainly as a rail and highway junction; from here Route 169 follows the Ziller river valley (Zillertal) south, past the Gerlos valley (Route 165) and the Tuxer mountain range to Mayrhofen. The alpine lake Achensee lies on the plateau to the north, fed by the Achen river rising high in the mountains beyond, on the German border. Both regions have become immensely popular in summer and winter.

(13) From Jenbach, head first to the **Achensee.** If you're driving, take Route 181; the initial stretch involves hairpin turns and a steep climb, but the views back down over the Inn valley are exquisite. You could take a bus, too, but the most adventuresome and romantic way to reach the Achensee is on the steam-powered 100-year-old **Achenseerbahn,** built in 1889 as Tirol's first mountain cog railway (tel. 05244/2243). The line does its 400-meter (1,300-ft) climb in a nearly straight line over 7 km (4 mi) to the lower end of the Achensee (Seespitz), where you can get a lake steamer on to Buchau and Pertisau and to the north end.

The Achen valley has fine skiing in winter, but the lake in summer, with water sports and excellent fishing, is the main attraction. It is the largest and most beautiful in Tirol—10 km, over 6 mi, long—with the great mountains of the Karwendel and Sonnwend ranges rising from its blue-green waters. The lake steamer connects the villages strung out along its length.

Pertisau, a small, picturesque village set into the thick pine forest of a nature preserve, is the only community on the western shore of this undeveloped lake. It offers excellent swimming, sailing, tennis, fishing, and a golf course (tel. 05243/5377), all at budget prices. Although it's less popular, the eastern side of the lake enjoys at least two hours of sunshine more every day, and the water is consequently warmer.

Scenic Route 181 leads along the eastern shore of the lake through Buchau to the northern end, passing through Achenseehof and Scholastika, among various small settlements belonging to the community of Achenkirch.

Because this area is so close to Innsbruck, the lake is crowded on summer weekends; try to visit on a weekday.

The drive south from Jenbach on Route 169 follows the Ziller river, which rises high in the Alps to the south, in an area of perpetual glacier, then flows north. Route 169 parallels the narrow-gauge Ziller railway, **the Zillertalbahn,** which makes daily runs between Jenbach and Mayrhofen, some under steam power. If your childhood dream was to drive a train, check in Jenbach (tel. 05244/2311) about renting this one; you can take a crash course in railroad operations and play engineer of the steam locomotive, all for a modest fee.

The first part of the Zillertal is broad and shallow, and the scenery is not very inspiring. But from Stumm onward, where you pass through some pretty alpine villages, and particularly the stretch south of Zell am Ziller, the valley starts to live up to its reputation.

⑭ The big event in the valley is the traditional 400-year-old *Gauderfest,* on the first weekend in May, when thousands of tourists from far and wide pack the little market town of **Zell am Ziller** for the colorful skits, music, and singing—and great quantities of *Gauderbier,* a strong brew run up for the occasion. You can hear some of the country's best singing, by the valley residents, and listen to expert harp and zither playing, for which the valley is famous throughout Austria. This is a typical Tirolean country town, with alpine lodges and a round-domed pink village church (note the Baroque painting of the Holy Trinity); in winter it's a center of skiing and sports activity. A monument in front of the courthouse commemorates the 1816 visit of Emperor Franz I following the reunion of Tirol and Austria.

⑮ Ten km (6 mi) down the road you'll come to **Mayrhofen,** end of the line for the narrow-gauge railway. This is the valley's main tourist base and the favorite summer resort of the British for many years. Mayrhofen is the starting point for summer hiking into the highly scenic valleys that branch off to the southeast, south, and southwest and for excursions into the Ziller glacier areas at heights of 3,000 meters (9,750 ft) and above.

At Mayrhofen the valley splits into four parts. Three are called *Gründe* (grounds): the Zillergrund, Stillupgrund, and Zemmgrund, the latter threaded by Route 169 into the Zamser valley. They are prime examples of picture-postcard alpine areas, swept at the top with glittering pale blue glaciers.

⑯ The fourth arm is the **Tuxer valley,** highest of the four and a summer ski region, which ends at the foot of the massive Olperer and Rifflerspitz glaciers, nearly 3,350 meters (11,000 ft) high. Frequent buses leave Mayrhofen for **Lanersbach,** a small mountain village, and **Hintertux,** right at the doorstep of the great glaciers. Hintertux is a popular spa, with a small thermal swimming pool, and the center of an ancient woodcarving industry. Rubies (called Tirolean garnets) were once mined in this area, and you might run across local amethyst in the shops as well.

⑰ **Hainzenberg,** just outside Zell am Ziller, was once a gold-mining town. Stop at the pilgrimage church Maria Rast, built in 1739 by the prospectors, to see its stuccos and fine ceiling paintings. Don't look for the western transept wing of the church; it slid down the precipice in 1910.

The sensationally scenic Route 165 climbs east out of Zell am Ziller, past Gerlos, and finally achieves the 1,630-meter (5,300-ft) Gerlos pass and plunges into the province of Salzburg in a series of double-back hairpins close to the dramatic 400-meter

(1,300-ft) Krimmler waterfalls. You can complete the circuit back into Tirol by continuing east to Mittersill and cutting north to Kitzbühel via the Thurn pass.

⑱ If you don't want the glitz of Kitzbühel, **Gerlos,** somewhat to the northeast, is a splendid choice for a summer or winter holiday, with the 2,560-meter (8,300-ft) Kreuzjoch mountain prominent in the background. Scheduled buses make the run up from Zell am Ziller. The Gerlos ski slopes are varied, and in summer the same slopes offer excellent hiking. Check in advance about hotel arrangements; many of the better houses in Gerlos require a minimum of half-board (breakfast and one other meal a day).

Tour 2:
From Jenbach
to Kitzbühel
Starting again from Jenbach in the main Inn valley, continue northeast on Route 171. You'll come first to **Brixlegg,** a former copper-mining town with two famous castles, Schloss Kropfsberg, built to defend the approaches to the Ziller valley, and Schloss Matzen, a 12th-century structure on the mountainside. The radioactive sulfur waters of the Mehrn spa just outside town are said to be good for rheumatism.

Just up the road is **Rattenberg,** a quaint medieval town once famous for its silver mines. When the mines were exhausted, the town lapsed into a trance of centuries. Were it not for the constant procession of cars and trucks (which the residents are trying to ban), you might think you were back in the Middle Ages. The narrow old streets are full of relics of past glory, and the ruins of Emperor Maximilian's massive castle above the town are said to be haunted.

Kramsach, across the river, has been a glass-production center since the 17th century. At the glassworks' school (call 05337/ 2523 to arrange a visit) you can see etching, engraving, and painting on glassware.

Back on Route 171, the road leads to **Wörgl,** a rail junction where the main Austrian east–west line and the shortcut via the "German corner" come together. From Wörgl an extremely scenic road leads south to the small resort villages of **Niederau, Oberau,** and **Auffach.**

⑲ About 13 km (8 mi) farther along Route 171 is **Kufstein,** marking the border with Germany. The town was captured from Bavaria in 1504 by Emperor Maximilian I, who added it to the Habsburg domains. You'll immediately notice that Kufstein is dominated by a fortress, built in 1200 and since expanded and strengthened. The guided tour takes about an hour and covers the apartments and cells of the old castle. *Admission: AS25. Tours daily Apr.–Oct., 9:30, 11, 1:30, 3, and 4:30. Closed Nov.–Mar. and Mon. Apr.–June and Sept.–Oct.*

The center of town boasts a remarkable concentration of Art Nouveau buildings, both public and private. The **Burgher's Tower** houses the *Heldenorgel,* the world's largest outdoor organ, with 26 registers and 1,800 pipes. The instrument is played in summer at noon and 6 PM.

At Wörgl take Route 312 toward St. Johann, the world-famous winter and summer resort, about 30 km (19 mi) away. You can do the circuit of St. Johann and its more famous neighbor, Kitzbühel, by taking Route 161 10 km (6 mi) between the two resorts and returning to Wörgl via Route 170.

The towns of **Söll, Ellmau,** and **Going** along Route 312 have developed into attractive, small winter and summer resorts. Their altitude (and their snow) is about the same as that of Kitzbühel and St. Johann, but their prices are half as high, if that.

Time Out   In Söll you'll find a friendly restaurant, the **Schindlhaus** , which serves original variations on Austrian dishes in a modern environment. Try the lightly braised fillet of venison with red cabbage or one of the fish specialties, served with a delicate sauce.

② **St. Johann** for years lived in the shadow of Kitzbühel, but today the town, with its colorfully painted houses, has developed a personality of its own and for better or worse is equally mobbed, winter and summer. The facilities are similar to those in Kitz, and prices are still lower, although climbing. (The dark horse here could be **Kirchdorf,** 4 km (2 mi) north of St. Johann, where costs appear to be holding, or **Fieberbrunn,** 12 km/7 mi east on Route 164.) While in St. Johann, don't miss the magnificently decorated Baroque parish church or the Gothic *Spitalskirche,* with its fine late-medieval stained glass, just west of town in Weitau.

② Long before **Kitzbühel** became one of the fashionable winter resorts, the town had gained a reputation for its summer season. The accent now is almost completely on skiing, and the facilities are among the finest in the world. The famous Ski Circus, a carefully planned, clever combination of lifts, cable railways, and runs, lets you ski for over 80 km (50 mi) without having to climb a single foot under your own power.

Kitzbühel is in perpetual motion, packed with celebrities in December and again in February. But at any time during the season there's plenty to do, from sleigh rides to fancy-dress balls. Built in the 16th century with proceeds from copper and silver mining, the town itself is picturesque enough, but take time to check the churches: St. Andrew's parish church (1435–1506) has a lavishly Rococo chapel, the Rosakapelle, and the marvelously ornate tomb (1520) of the Kupferschmid family; the Church of St. Catherine, built about 1350, houses a Gothic winged altar dating to 1515.

In summer, get a Guest Card stamped by your hotel for substantial reductions on various activities (some of which are then free) like tennis, riding, and golf. The best swimming is in the nearby Schwarzsee (Black Lake). To see alpine flowers in their natural glory, take the cable car up the Kitzbühler Horn to the **Alpine Flower Garden Kitzbühel** at 2,000 meters (6,500 ft). It leaves every half hour.

Tour 3: South of Innsbruck into the Stubaital   The autobahn A–13/E–45 south is heavily traveled; Austria forbids heavy truck movement by night, so it all cuts loose in the daytime. Take Route 182 south if you're driving farther down the valley and you want to enjoy the scenery without the autobahn's traffic.

The delightful little Stubaital valley, less than 40 km (25 mi) long, is one of the showpieces of the Tirol, with no fewer than 80 glistening glaciers and more than 40 towering peaks. If you just want to look, you can see the whole Stubaital in a full day's excursion from Innsbruck. The narrow-gauge electric **Stubaitalbahn** (departure from the station just below the Bergisel ski jump in Innsbruck) goes as far as Fulpmes, partway up the valley. You can take the bus as far as Ranalt and back to Fulpmes, to see more of the valley, then return on the quaint rail line. Buses leave from Gate 1 of the Autobusbahnhof, just behind the rail station at Südtiroler Platz, about every hour (tel. 0512/ 5307).

Both Fulpmes and nearby Telfes on Route 183 are known as winter and summer resorts, but since they are so close to Innsbruck, they are crowded. In **Telfes,** take a look at the ceiling frescoes in the Baroque parish church (built 1344), and in **Fulpmes,** visit the church of St. Vitus of 1368, with beautifully overdone Rococo decoration added in 1747. A small museum in the center of Fulpmes with a fully equipped old smithy recalls the iron mining nearby and local tool industry of earlier days. *Tel. 05225/241124 or 05225/2240. Admission: AS20. Open Apr.–Sept., Wed. 2–5 and by appointment.*

At **Neustift** the paved road ends, but a beautifully scenic unimproved road continues upward to Ranalt, at 1,260 meters (4,100 ft), and into the glacial plain, up to 1,730 meters (5,600 ft). Neustift is an excellent starting point for hikers, with trails in many directions. Stop to look at the unusually large village church dedicated to St. George, reconstructed in 1764, with three shallow domes and lavish ceiling paintings.

Tour 4: Northwest from Innsbruck to Seefeld and past Reutte It's delightful and relaxing to take a train from Innsbruck on the Karwendel railway line, which winds in leisurely fashion, describing a huge "S" through stunning scenery, across the border into Bavaria and on to Reutte in the northwest corner of Tirol. Route 171 parallels the railroad at the outset; after leaving Innsbruck, both follow the Inn valley as far as Zirl, where Route 313 branches off. The train climbs steeply around the massive Solstein mountains, popping in and out of tunnels, until it reaches the great Seefeld plateau on the edge of the Wetterstein range.

Numbers in the margin correspond with points of interest on the Tirol: Tours 4–6 map.

Seefeld, one of the big three winter-sports centers, ranks with Kitzbühel and St. Anton for accommodations and atmosphere but concentrates more on cross-country skiing. Seefeld has been the site of numerous competitions, including the 1964 and 1976 Winter Olympics. In summer, too, Seefeld is popular, a useful base for exploring the countryside or neighboring Bavaria, yet only 26 km (16 mi) from Innsbruck. In summer the little **Wildmoos** lake, 4 km (2½ mi) from Seefeld, is good for swimming when it has water, but from time to time it dries up, leaving only a lush green meadow and a small bubbling spring to mark its location!

Friedl the Penniless and Sigmund the Wealthy were responsible for the Gothic stone church of St. Oswald in Seefeld. Duke Friedrich began the church in 1423 and his son completed it in 1474. Note the combined Austrian and Scots coats of arms inside and repeated over the main portal; Sigmund's wife was Eleanor of Scotland.

The rock in the area contains oil and was referred to as early as 1350 as "smelling stone." Once used as a popular medicine and lubricant, the oil today is extracted for commercial use as a pharmaceutical ingredient.

Tirol: Tours 4–6

N

6 miles

9 km

Innsbruck

Sill

A13

Brenner Pass

A22

ITALY

GERMANY

Mittenwald

Garmisch

Partenkirchen

2

Telfes

Fulpmes

Neustift

24

Griesen

Scharnitz

221

Zirl

Inn

25

Seefeld

Zugspitz

26

28

Telfs

St. Sigmund

Sölden

31

32

Obergurgl

Heiligenkreuz

Ehrwald

A12

171

186

Ötztal

Wildspitze

Nassereith

514

Lermoos

187

Plansee

189

Ötz

30

27

Reutte

Imst

29

T I R O L

Stausee-Gepatsch

Elmen

Lech

Ried

34

Tannheim

Inn

Serfaus

198

Bach

Landeck

33

Pians

315

Nauders

Sonthofen

Oberstdorf

Vinadi

SWITZERLAND

315

St. Anton am Arlberg

35

Paznaun Valley

Hittisau

Baad

Kl. Walsertal

Ischgl

188

Galtür

Lech

Zürs

St. Christoph

Arlberg Pass

316

188

Partenen

Bludenz

Schruns

VORARLBERG

SWITZERLAND

182

From Seefeld the road (Route 177) and the railroad wander north to cross into Germany via the Scharnitz pass. Both road (German Route 2) and railroad pass Garmisch-Partenkirchen and swing around the back side (Route 24) of the 2,963-meter (9,630-ft) **Zugspitz,** which marks the border. You can reach the peak via cog railway from Garmisch or by cable car on the German or the Austrian side. You'll need your passport if you want to make the round-trip via Germany and back. Just past Griesen you'll reenter Austria (Route 187/E–6), headed south to Ehrwald.

The cable car on the Austrian side of the Zugspitz runs 3,380 meters (10,990 ft, or just over 2 mi), reaching the top in 20 minutes. Service runs hourly 8–11 AM and 1–5 PM. From the restaurant at the top you can see the Grossglockner and Dachstein peaks and look out over the Bavarian range.

The region around **Ehrwald** and **Lermoos** was mined for galena, sphalerite, and silver until 1938. Stop to view the churches in the area, especially St. Catherine's in Lermoos, built in 1753. The Rococo structure you see is the original. Also notice the ornate wrought-iron crosses in the cemetery.

Railroad and highway (Route S–14) head northwest up the Grundbach valley to **Reutte,** mainly a summer resort area, although cross-country skiing is growing more popular. The 18th-century burghers' houses in Reutte, with their painted facades and wickerwork grilles for ventilation, are distinctive, as are the fancy inn signs. Nearby is the 6-km (nearly 4-mi)-long **Plansee,** Tirol's second largest lake, with mountains literally rising out of its emerald water. You can swim here, but the water is cold.

Southwest of Reutte, Route 198 takes in the long wandering Lech valley, following the course of the mountain stream through the Lech Alps right up to the Arlberg and the provincial frontier of Vorarlberg. In summer this rather out-of-the-way valley is a favorite base for mountaineering.

Tour 5: West from Innsbruck to Imst and the Ötz Valley The upper Inn valley from Innsbruck to the Swiss border is beautiful countryside, particularly the narrow valleys that branch off to the south. Take Route 171 west from Innsbruck along the banks of the Inn, rather than the autobahn, which hugs the cliffs along the way.

From Telfs you have a choice of taking a very scenic Route 189/E–6 to Nassereith and down to Imst or following the rail line along the river on Route 171. All three towns are attractive for their richly decorated 15th- and 16th-century buildings and churches.

In **Telfs** the traditional Carnival celebration of Schleicherlaufen takes place every five years (next in 1995) just before the start of Lent, with the whole population joining in the masked procession. Some of the grotesque masks can be seen in the local museum.

Schemenlaufen, a masked procession depicting the struggle between good and evil, takes place in **Imst** on Shrove Tuesday. The tradition is ancient, and here, too, you can see some of the 100-year-old carved masks in the local museum (Ballgasse 1); check with the tourist office for opening times. Don't overlook the 15th-century frescoed parish church in the upper part of Imst.

The Ötz (or Oetz) valley begins east of Imst, where you turn south off Route 171 onto Route 186. The valley climbs in a series of six great natural steps for nearly 42 km (26 mi) from the Inn river to the glaciers around Obergurgl, at 1,910 meters (6,200 ft) above sea level. The entire distance offers stunning scenery, with the most dramatic part beginning around Sölden, where the final rise begins to the 2,500-meter (8,100-ft) pass over the Timmel Alps and across the Italian border into South Tirol.

30 Ötz is a typical Tirolean mountain village, with some of its Gothic houses bearing colorful fresco decorations. The parish church of St. George and St. Nicholas, its tower once a charnel house, sits on a rock promontory above the village. The small St. Michael's chapel has a splendid altar dating to 1683.

31 From Ötz you'll drive about 28 km (18 mi) along the river to reach **Sölden,** the first of the famous villages in the valley. The area is acquiring an international reputation for its natural skiing conditions, and its chair lift up to **Hochsölden** (2,062 m, 6,800 ft) ensures excellent snow for the whole season. A modern cable car, the highest in Austria, takes you from Sölden over the glaciers to the permanent-snow area at almost 3,050 meters (9,910 ft) on Gaislacher Kogel, where you can ski all year.

32 Farther along Route 186 you'll come to Austria's highest village, tiny **Obergurgl,** famous for winter sports and as the place where the Swiss physicist Auguste Piccard landed his famous stratospheric balloon in the 1930s. And what a wonderful name for a town! In winter, a vast expanse of snow and ice shimmers all around you, and all year, the great peaks and glaciers of the Ötztal Alps appear deceptively close at hand. A high alpine road takes you from Obergurgl to the hotel settlement at **Hochgurgl,** another excellent skiing spot, and farther up to the Timmelsjoch pass through magnificent mountain scenery. From Hochgurgl, a three-stage chair lift brings you into an area of year-round skiing. In summer, ask at the tourist office about river rafting possibilities.

On your way back down the Ötz valley, before you get to Sölden, you might want to turn left on a road marked to Heiligenkreutz, to explore the Ventertal. This valley burrows still farther into the Ötztal Alps, finally ending at **Vent,** a tiny village at about the same elevation as Obergurgl. Vent, too, is a popular winter resort center and in summer is the base for serious mountain climbers, experienced in ice and rock climbing, who want to attempt the formidable **Wildspitze** (3,795 m, 12,450 ft) or other even more difficult neighboring peaks. Hiring a professional local guide is strongly advised.

Tour 6: To Landeck, the Upper Inn Valley, and on to St. Anton Back on Route 171, headed westward, you'll come to Landeck, 24 km (15 mi) from Imst, a popular place in summer and a good base from which to explore the Paznaun valley and the upper Inn valley, leading into Switzerland and Italy.

33 **Landeck** is known for an ancient and awe-inspiring rite that takes place on "Cheese Sunday," the first Sunday following Ash Wednesday. At dawn the young men set out to climb to the top of the great rocky crags that overshadow and hem in the old city on three sides. As dusk falls, they light huge bonfires that can be seen for miles around and then set fire to great discs of pinewood dipped in tar, which they roll ablaze down to the valley below. The sight of scores of these fiery wheels bounding down the steep slopes toward town is a fearsome spectacle worthy of Ezekiel.

The 13th-century Burg Landeck castle dominates from its position above the town. Climb up and catch the views from this vantage point. Also note the 16th-century winged altar in the 15th-century Gothic parish church of the Assumption.

At Landeck the Inn river turns southward along the edge of the Silvretta mountains. The valley, tucked between two dramatic **(34)** ranges, climbs toward the Italian border. In **Ried,** as you follow Route 315/S–15 beside the river, you'll come across Schloss Sigmundsried, a small castle built by Duke Sigmund the Wealthy about 1470 around an earlier tower; the castle holds worthwhile 16th-century coats-of-arms paintings. You can canoe or raft in the river here. At Ried, turn west off Route 315 for the scenic but steep climb up to **Serfaus,** on the plateau above the valley. This old village has taken on new class in recent years as an important winter-sports center. There are several ski lifts, and the Komperdell cable car takes you in summer, too, up to points from which you can either hike or just enjoy the views.

Backtrack to Landeck and take Route 316/S–16 west toward Vorarlberg. Tucked between the entrance to the Arlberg tun- **(35)** nel and the railway is **St. Anton am Arlberg,** one of the world's most famous ski centers—indeed, the cradle of modern skiing (*see* Sports and Fitness, below). At the height of the season the small town seethes with visitors. The wealthy, the prominent, and, occasionally, royalty appear regularly to see and be seen—some even to enjoy the winter sports. Their presence boosts prices into the very-expensive-to-outrageous category, but if you shop around, you can find accommodations outside the center of the action at a bearable price.

Two km higher up toward the pass is the hamlet of **St. Christoph,** where a hospice was founded as early as the 15th century to care for imperiled travelers stranded by the snows on the pass. St. Christoph today is another important but much smaller winter resort. The slopes and snows are good; the Austrian government holds its exacting courses for aspiring ski instructors here.

While St. Christoph hasn't the same social cachet as St. Anton, the skiing facilities are precisely the same (and even closer at hand). If you take your skiing seriously and are willing to forgo the high life as too distracting or too expensive, you may find winter sports per se more fun at St. Christoph.

What to See and Do with Children

Aside from skiing at towns both large and small throughout Tirol and the usual outdoor sports at the lakes and in the countryside in summer, try the narrow-gauge railroads such as the **Auchenseerbahn** and **Zillertalbahn** (Tour 1) and the **Stubaitalbahn** (Tour 3).

Off the Beaten Track

From Brixlegg (Tour 2) a small side road runs down a valley to the unspoiled picture-book village of **Alpbach.** The town is nominally a winter-sports center, but it takes the international spotlight once a year in spring when world leaders of government and industry gather at the European Forum to discuss global issues.

From Landeck (Tour 6), you can arrange an easy excursion by bus or car (Route 188) up the enchanting **Paznaun valley,** which runs southwest out of the village of Pians on the main east–west road. The valley follows the course of the Trisanna river for over 40 km (25 mi), into the heart of the Blue Silvretta mountains, named for the shimmering ice-blue effect of the great peaks and glaciers. They are dominated by the Fluchthorn (3,219 m, 10,462 ft) at the head of the valley near Galtür.

Ischgl, about halfway up the valley, is the largest town. It has excellent skiing, particularly in the small Fimber valley to the south, and in summer is a popular high-altitude health resort. You can get to the 2,307-meter (7,500-ft) Idalpe via the 4-km-long Silvretta cable-car run.

Slightly higher up the valley is **Galtür,** the best-known resort in the Paznaun, equally popular for winter sports, as a summer resort, and as a base for mountain climbing. Although Galtür is a starting point for practiced mountaineers, many of the climbs up the Blue Silvretta are very easy and lead to the half-dozen mountain huts belonging to the Alpenverein.

Sports and Fitness

Climbing For the adventuresome, Peter Habeler at the **Alpin-und Wanderschule Zillertal** (Tuxerstr. 716, A–6290 Mayrhofen, tel. 05285/2563 or 2829) gives instruction in ice-climbing.

Would-be climbers can take lessons by contacting Hugo Walter at the **Bergsteigerschule Piz Buin-Silvretta** (A–6563 Galtür, tel. 05443/260).

Those particularly interested in ice-climbing should contact Anton Tomann at the **Hochgebirgs-und Wanderschule Tuxertal** (Juns 424, A–6293 Lanersbach, tel. 05287/372).

Golf **Golfclub Kitzbühel** has 9 holes, par 72. *Tel. 05356/3007. Greens fees: AS350 weekdays, AS450 weekends. Open Apr.–Nov.*

Golf-Club Kitzbühel-Schwarzsee, has 18 holes, par 72. *Tel. 05356/71645. Greens fees: AS500 weekdays, AS600 weekends. Open May–Oct.*

Golfclub Seefeld-Wildmoos is an 18-hole, par-72 course. *Tel. 05212/3003 or 2313. Greens fees: AS520 weekdays, AS630 weekends. Open May–Oct.*

The Astoria, Klosterbräu, Lamm, Lärchenhof, Prachenskyhof, and Tümmlerhof hotels have one- and two-week golf packages that include greens fees.

Skiing In 1921 in St. Anton am Arlberg, Hannes Schneider (1890–1955), an unknown young ski instructor with advanced ideas, set up a ski school to teach his new technique, at the invitation of the just-founded Kandahar Ski Club. This "Arlberg School"

method, developed by Schneider in the '20s and '30s, laid down
the basic principles later followed by all skiing courses the
world over. St. Anton's remains one of the world's leading ski
schools.

The *Skihaserl*, or ski bunny, as the beginner is called, usually
joins a class on St. Anton's good "nursery" slopes, where he or
she will have plenty of often very distinguished company. Once
past the Skihaserl stage, skiers go higher in the Arlberg mountains to the superlative runs from the top of the Galzig and the
2,800-meter (9,100-ft) Valluga above it. Check with your hotel
or at ski-lift ticket offices about an **Arlberg-Skipass,** which is
good on cable cars and lifts in St. Anton and St. Christoph on
the Tirol side and on those in Zürs, Lech, Oberlech, and Stuben
in Vorarlberg—77 in all. You can find downhill skiing and, increasingly, cross-country throughout Tirol. Equipment is
available for rent, though the selection and quality will vary
from place to place.

Dining and Lodging

Dining   In many small towns you'll find country inns that have dining
rooms, but there are few if any separate restaurants. Prices for
meals include taxes and a service charge but not the customary
small additional tip.

Highly recommended restaurants are indicated by a star ★.

Category	Cost*
Very Expensive	over AS500
Expensive	AS300–AS500
Moderate	AS200–AS300
Inexpensive	under AS200

*per person for a typical 3-course meal, with a glass of house
wine*

Lodging   In the popular resort towns, many hotels operate on a half-
board basis (breakfast and one meal a day must be taken) during the ski season, and some take no credit cards. Summer
prices are often as much as 50% lower. It's a good idea to find
lodgings in small towns nearby, rather than in the resorts
themselves; local tourist offices may be able to help you, possibly even with accommodations in private homes if you book well
ahead. Prices include tax and service. Highly recommended
lodgings are indicated by a star ★ .

Category	Resorts*	Small Towns*
Very Expensive	over AS2,200	over AS1,000
Expensive	AS1,500–AS2,200	AS800–AS1,000
Moderate	AS900–AS1,500	AS500–AS800
Inexpensive	under AS900	under AS500

*per person for a standard double room with bath, including
breakfast except in Very Expensive hotels*

Achenkirch
Dining and Lodging

Posthotel. This comfortable alpine chalet is also a health center; you'll find every convenience for taking care of fitness, weight-loss and exercise programs; half or full board only. Rooms are in typical Tirolean country style. *A–6215, tel. 05246/6205. 123 rooms. Facilities: restaurant, indoor and outdoor pools, sauna, solarium, fitness room, tennis, riding, kindergarten. Closed mid-Nov.–mid-Dec. DC. Expensive.*

Alpbach
Dining and Lodging

Alpbacher Hof. The massive fireplace sets the keynote in the public rooms of this typical chalet hotel, and the welcoming feeling carries over to the bedrooms. *A–6236, tel. 05336/5237. 55 rooms. Facilities: restaurant, indoor pool. No credit cards. Closed Apr., Oct., Nov. Expensive.*

★ **Böglerhof.** Much of the original character has been preserved in this beautifully restored old double chalet, with its heavily beamed ceilings and stonework. The rooms are attractively decorated in Tirolean style. The excellent restaurant, with its small *Stuben* (side rooms), is known for such Austrian special-ties as cabbage soup or fillet points in light garlic sauce. The restaurant is a member of the Romantik Hotels group. *A–6236, tel. 05336/5227. 50 rooms. Facilities: restaurant (reservations advised, jacket and tie required), bar, indoor and outdoor pools, sauna, solarium, tennis, garage. Closed mid-Oct.–mid-Dec. MC, V. Expensive.*

Brixlegg
Dining and Lodging

Brixleggerhof. This house is small, but all the amenities are there. In the restaurant, the standard dishes—the roast pork and schnitzel—are the favorites. *A–6230, tel. 05337/2630. 10 rooms. Facilities: restaurant (closed Thurs., Fri. lunch), bar. No credit cards. Closed early June, Oct. Inexpensive.*

Ehrwald
Dining and Lodging

Alpenhof. The wood paneling and beamed ceilings of the house create an immediate friendly impression. Rooms are spacious and pleasantly furnished, and there's a children's playroom. *A–6632, tel. 05673/2345. 46 rooms. Facilities: restaurant, indoor and outdoor pools, sauna, solarium, garage, tennis. No credit cards. Closed late Apr., Nov. Expensive.*

Spielmann. This family-run house outside the center of town is attractively furnished in Tirolean style, with Oriental carpets as accents on the plain carpet. The restaurant, with four inti-mate, rustic rooms, is a special attraction: Christian Spielmann offers such dishes as his prized stuffed veal schnitzel with moz-zarella. *Wettersteinstr. 24, A–6632, tel. 05673/2225. 30 rooms. Facilities: restaurant (reservations advised, jacket advised). V. Closed mid-Apr.–May, Nov.–mid-Dec. Expensive.*

★ **Sonnenspitze.** This massive 19th-century house is loaded with gorgeous flower-filled balconies. The rooms are as inviting as the main lobby, with its stonework and warm colors. *Kirchplatz 14, A–6632, tel. 05673/2208. 26 rooms. Facilities: restaurant, garage. AE, MC, V. Closed mid-Apr.–mid-May, mid-Oct.–mid-Dec. Moderate.*

Ellmau
Dining and Lodging
★

Der Bär. Within walking distance of the village center, the Bear is known throughout Austria as one of the foremost coun-try inns. An elegant but friendly atmosphere pervades, with relaxed comfort in every respect, attractive bedrooms in Tiro-lean style included. The restaurant, a member of the Relais & Châteaux group, features local specialties; try roast lamb or game. *A–6352, tel. 05358/2395. 62 rooms. Facilities: restau-rant (reservations advised, jacket and tie advised), indoor and outdoor pools, sauna, solarium, fitness room. No credit cards. Closed May–early June, Nov.–mid-Dec. Very Expensive.*

Fulpmes
Dining and Lodging

Sporthotel Cristall. The alpine decor of wood and tiles emphasizes the friendly family atmosphere; there's a supervised playroom for children. The rooms have attractive wood paneling.
*A–6166, tel. 05225/3424. 30 rooms. Facilities: restaurant, bar,
playroom, indoor and outdoor pools, sauna, solarium, fitness
room, garage. No credit cards. Expensive.*
Alte Post. You'll be pleased at the value in this typical colorful
Tirolean hotel, with rooms that are modern and comfortably
furnished with overstuffed chairs. *A–6166, tel. 05225/2358. 40
rooms. Facilities: restaurant, bar, indoor pool, sauna, solarium, fitness room. AE, DC. Moderate.*

Gerlos
Dining and Lodging

Almhof. In typical Tirolean style, this alpine inn offers a friendly reception area and comfortable rooms. *A–6281, tel. 05284/
5323. 45 rooms. Facilities: restaurant, indoor pool, sauna, solarium, fitness room, tennis, garage. No credit cards. Closed
May–mid-June, mid-Oct.–mid-Dec. Expensive.*
Gaspingerhof. The three alpine chalets that make up this rustically furnished complex are connected by underground passages. Rooms are done in the bright local custom, with natural
woods and colorful fabrics. The nightlife is active. *A–6281, tel.
05284/5216. 65 rooms. Facilities: restaurant, indoor pool, sauna, solarium, tennis. No credit cards. Closed mid-Apr.–mid-
May, mid-Oct.–mid-Dec. Expensive.*

Going
Dining
★

Rautnerwirt. In its two small rooms with seven tables, this attractive restaurant in a country house offers imaginative local
cuisine; depending on the season, you might find roast young
goat or braised venison in a delicate mushroom sauce. *A–6353,
tel. 05358/2784. Reservations required. Jacket and tie advised.
AE, DC, MC, V. Closed Mon. and Tues. lunch; closed June–
early July. Expensive.*

Lodging

Stanglwirt. A 300-year-old coaching inn forms the core of this
health-and-fitness complex that's also a popular mealtime stop
for tour buses. Rooms in the new section are spacious; some are
studios with old-fashioned ceramic stoves, in keeping with the
Tirolean decor. Guests can ride, swim, or play tennis and
squash, indoor and out. *A–6353, tel. 05358/2000. 73 rooms. Facilities: restaurant, stables, tennis courts, indoor and outdoor
pools, sauna, solarium, fitness room, golf, hot-air ballooning.
AE, DC, MC, V. Expensive.*

Hintertux
Dining and Lodging

Rindererhof. This comfortable alpine lodge at the end of the
line is a good starting point for either climbing or skiing. *A–
6294, tel. 05287/501. 39 rooms. Facilities: restaurant, bar, sauna, solarium. No credit cards. Expensive.*

Imst
Dining and Lodging

Linserhof. This double-chalet hotel is outside town, set in a lush
alpine meadow at the base of a wooded hillside. The attractive
rooms are in rustic Tirolean decor, with much natural wood. *A–
6460 Imst/Teilwiesen, tel. 05412/2415. 40 rooms. Facilities: restaurant, indoor pool, sauna, fitness room, lake swimming,
tennis. AE, DC, MC, V. Closed Nov. Expensive.*
★ **Post.** A 15th-century former castle, complete with onion-dome
tower and set in a large park, is the heart of this member of the
Romantik Hotels group. The friendly interior is furnished with
antiques, the modern bedrooms are cheerful. *A–6460, tel.
05412/2554. 37 rooms. Facilities: restaurant, indoor pool, fitness room, garage. AE, DC, MC, V. Closed Nov.–mid-Dec.
Expensive.*
Stern. This rustic chalet is decorated with hunting trophies and

other oddities, which makes a pleasantly informal atmosphere.
The bedrooms continue this theme, in typical Tirolean style.
*A–6460, tel. 05412/3342. 25 rooms. Facilities: restaurant, sau-
na, fitness room, garage. AE, DC, MC, V. Closed Nov.–mid-
Dec. Expensive.*

Zum Hirschen. This comfortable *Gasthof-Pension*, attractively
renovated last year, pays particular attention to families with
children. *Th.-Walsch-Str. 3, A–6460, tel. 05412/2209. 41 rooms.
Facilities: restaurant, bar, sauna, solarium. AE, DC, MC, V.
Moderate.*

Ischgl
Dining and Lodging

Madlein. This modern chalet-style hotel is the place to stay for
sheer alpine elegance and to see the town's action. The rooms
are attractive, but you'll be tempted to spend your time in such
places as the beamed Wunderbar with its large dance floor and
friendly atmosphere. *A–6561, tel. 05444/5226. 65 rooms. Facilities: 2 restaurants, bar, nightclub, indoor pool, sauna, solarium, garage. No credit cards. Closed May–June, Oct.–Nov.
Expensive.*

Kitzbühel
Dining
★

Unterberger Stuben. In this former residence done up in typical
Tirolean fashion, with beige and red decor, you may have to reserve weeks ahead to get a table; the celebrities keep the place
booked solid. The international cuisine is among the best in
Tirol, offering such temptations as lobster risotto with water-
cress; lamb cutlets; and a number of fish specialties. *Wehrgasse
2, tel. 05356/2101. Reservations required; be punctual! Jacket
and tie advised. No credit cards. Closed mid-May–mid-June,
Nov. Expensive.*

★ **Praxmair.** Après-ski can't begin early enough for the crowds
who pile into this famous pastry shop-café, known also for its
florentines. *Vorderstadt, tel. 05356/2646. Reservations not required. Dress: casual chic. AE, DC, MC, V. Closed Apr., Nov.
Moderate.*

Lodging
★

Goldener Greif. The original building dates to 1271; renovations in the '50s gave the house a more contemporary but still
traditional Tirolean charm, emphasized by the magnificent
vaulted lobby with open fireplaces and antiques. The rooms,
too, are charming, some with four-posters, and a few apartments have fireplaces. The hotel is the locale of the Kitzbühel
casino. *A–6370, tel. 05356/4311. 55 rooms. Facilities: restaurant, casino, wine cellar, sauna, solarium. AE, DC, MC, V.
Closed Apr.–May, Oct.–Nov. Very Expensive.*

Schloss Lebenberg. A onetime 16th-century castle on a hilltop
outside town has been transformed into a wholly modern own-
er-managed family hotel, with few traces of its past. The bedrooms are in modern decor. You can literally start skiing at the
front door, and if the youngsters are too small to go along,
there's a kindergarten. The restaurant has a good reputation
for local specialties; try the sautéed breast of chicken in mushroom cream sauce. *A–6370, tel. 05356/4301. 109 rooms. Facilities: restaurant (reservations advised, jacket advised),
kindergarten, indoor pool, sauna, solarium, fitness room, tennis court, garage. AE, DC, MC, V. Closed Nov. Very Expensive.*

★ **Tennerhof.** Hidden away slightly out of the center, this
Romantik hotel is an elegant old mansion set in a huge garden
near the golf course. Emphasis here is on family; there's a special supervised children's room. The bedrooms are done in Tirolean country furnishings, all different, some with ceramic

stoves, some with hunting trophies. The restaurant enjoys a top reputation on its own; try any of the local specialties, such as the roast lamb with herbs from the garden outside the door. *A–6370, tel. 05356/3181. 44 rooms. Facilities: restaurant (reservations advised, jacket and tie advised), playroom, indoor and outdoor pools, sauna, solarium, garage. MC. Closed Apr.–May, mid-Oct.–mid-Dec. Very Expensive.*

Maria Theresia. Under the same management as the Goldener Greif, this fairly new six-floor chalet has elegant dark wood paneling and comfortable bedrooms. *A–6370, tel. 05356/4711. 108 rooms. Facilities: restaurant, sauna, solarium, fitness room, garage. AE, DC, MC, V. Closed Apr.–May, Oct.–Nov. Expensive (summer)–Very Expensive (winter).*

★ **Schloss Münichau.** Four km (2½ mi) outside town, just beyond the romantic Schwarzsee on the road to Reith, you'll find this quaint 15th-century hunting lodge from which you can still go hunting and fishing. The rooms are individual, with much Tirolean wood-carving in evidence. *A–6370 Reith bei Kitzbühel, tel. 05356/3248. 58 rooms. Facilities: restaurant. AE, DC, V. Closed Apr.–May, Oct.–Nov. Expensive.*

Weisses Rössl. This elegant but friendly hotel in the middle of town has open fireplaces ablaze in winter. The spacious rooms display much light pine and are particularly comfortable. *A–6370, tel. 05356/2541. 37 rooms. Facilities: restaurant, bars, disco, tennis, garage. AE, DC, MC, V. Closed mid-Oct.–early Dec. Expensive.*

Kufstein
Dining and Lodging
★
Alpenrose. This recently renovated house, on the edge of town in green surroundings, welcomes you immediately with its friendly lobby that seems to continue the outdoors; the feeling of relaxed comfort carries over into the attractive bedrooms as well. The restaurant is one of the best in the area; the *Tafelspitz* (boiled beef) and Wiener schnitzel are particularly recommended. *Weissachstr. 47, A–6330, tel. 05372/2122. 18 rooms. Facilities: restaurant (reservations advised, jacket advised), garage. MC. Expensive.*

Landeck
Dining and Lodging
Post-Tourotel. This attractive old house in the heart of town has been renovated from top to bottom and fortunately lost none of its charm in the process. The rooms now are functional-modern but comfortable, with clean lines and slick formica throughout. *Malser Str. 19, A–6500, tel. 05442/6911. 88 rooms. Facilities: restaurant, sauna, solarium, garage. AE, DC, MC, V. Expensive.*

Schrofenstein. Directly in the middle of town, this friendly older house still shows its original beamed ceilings and marble floors in the public areas. The rooms are comfortably modern. *Malser Str. 31, A–6500, tel. 05442/62395. 56 rooms. Facilities: restaurant, garage. AE, DC, V. Closed Nov.–mid-Dec. Moderate.*

Schwarzer Adler. Virtually in the shadow of the town castle, this traditional family-run hotel offers solid comfort in typical Tirolean style, with red checks and light wood. *Malser Str. 8, A–6500, tel. 05442/62316. 30 rooms. Facilities: restaurant. DC. Closed Nov.–mid-Dec. Moderate.*

Lanersbach
Dining and Lodging
Tuxerhof. The welcoming open fireplace in the lounge sets the relaxed style for this attractive alpine inn, and the rooms are comfortably appointed. *A–6293, tel. 05287/211. 50 rooms. Facilities: restaurant, bar, supervised children's room, sauna,*

solarium, garage. No credit cards. Closed June. Very Expensive.

Forelle. This friendly mountain inn offers comfortable rooms in typical alpine decor and a good restaurant specializing in trout. *A–6293, tel. 05287/214. 34 rooms. Facilities: restaurant, bar, indoor pool, sauna. No credit cards. Closed mid-Apr.–May, Nov.–mid-Dec. Moderate.*

Lermoos
Dining and Lodging

Post. The rather eclectic furnishings in the lobby set the style for this informal, relaxed hotel, but the rooms are complete and comfortable. *A–6631, tel. 05673/2281. 52 rooms. Facilities: restaurant, indoor pool, sauna, solarium, garage. MC, V. Closed Apr.–mid-May, mid-Oct.–mid-Dec. Expensive.*

Drei Mohren. This typical alpine house, with its white shuttered facade and overhanging eaves, is a great base for sports; the hotel offers fishing in the nearby river, and the lifts and cross-country ski trails begin at the back door. Rooms are comfortable in Tirolean style, and there's a kindergarten. The restaurant specializes in local fish. *A–6631, tel. 05673/2362. 50 rooms. Facilities: restaurant, kindergarten, solarium, fitness room, garage. AE, DC, MC, V. Closed Apr., mid-Nov.–mid-Dec. Moderate.*

Mayrhofen
Dining
★

Wirtshaus zum Griena. The restaurant tucked into this 400-year-old building is about 10 minutes' drive above Mayrhofen and the route is not simple, but everybody knows Griena's. Ask at your hotel for directions. Once you get there, you'll find yourself in rustic surroundings of natural wood paneling. Such local favorites as beer soup, pasta dishes, and schnitzel are tempting. The white wines come from Austria, the excellent reds from South Tirol. *Dorfhaus 768, tel. 05285/2778. Reservations recommended for dinner. Jacket advised. No credit cards. Closed June, Nov. Expensive.*

Lodging

Elisabeth. This newish house, in Tirolean style, radiates elegance without being too formal. The same is true of the well-decorated bedrooms, which have every amenity, including room safes. In addition to the main restaurant, also done in natural woods and reds, the house has an Italian restaurant that serves pizza and pasta. *Einfahrt Mitte 432, A–6290, tel. 05285/2929. 36 rooms. Facilities: 2 restaurants, bar, disco, indoor pool, sauna, solarium, fitness room, garage. No credit cards. Closed Nov. Expensive.*

★ **Kramerwirt.** Here's the center of the action in Mayrhofen, where the crowd gathers. The welcoming warmth of natural wood in the lobby and *Stuben* is accented by the Oriental carpets and occasional Tirolean antiques. You'll feel equally at home in the comfortable rooms. *Am Marienbrunnen 346, A–6290, tel. 05285/2615. 80 rooms. Facilities: restaurant (closed Nov.–Dec.), bar, sauna, solarium, fitness room, garage. No credit cards. Closed 2 weeks in Dec. Expensive.*

★ **Neue Post.** This typically Tirolean house, dating to 1626, has particularly comfortable, sunny bedrooms in its newer section. The bar draws a lively crowd in the evening. *Hauptstr., A–6290, tel. 05285/2131. 75 rooms. Facilities: restaurant, bar, garage. No credit cards. Closed Nov. Moderate.*

Nassereith
Lodging

Post. This newly renovated and expanded Tirolean house is a good base from which to explore the surrounding countryside. You'll also find ample evening entertainment in the hotel. *A–6465, tel. 05265/5202. 60 rooms. Facilities: restaurant, bar, sauna, solarium, outdoor pool. AE, MC, V. Moderate.*

Nauders
Dining and Lodging

Astoria. The bar of this alpine chalet in the center of town is the hub of après-ski and evening entertainment. The wood-paneled public rooms, in subdued colors, are cozy; the main dining room is somewhat formal, but there's an informal *Weinstube* as well. *A–6543, tel. 05473/310. 25 rooms. Facilities: 2 restaurants, bar, indoor pool, sauna, solarium, fitness room. No credit cards. Closed Apr., mid-Oct.–mid-Dec. Expensive.*

Neustift
Lodging

Alpenhof. In Neder Neustift, about 2 km (1 mi) before you reach Neustift proper, you'll find a pair of alpine chalets with ample wood-paneled public rooms and a particularly friendly staff. The rooms are furnished in a slick, contemporary version of Tirolean country style. *A–6167, tel. 05226/2711. 60 rooms. Facilities: restaurant (no credit cards), bar, indoor pool, sauna, solarium, fitness room. DC, MC, V. Closed early May, early Dec. Moderate.*

Obergurgl
Dining and Lodging
★

Bellevue. This friendly alpine chalet lives up to its name in every respect: Is there another Bellevue among the millions in the world with a vista to equal this one? You can ski right out the front door. Rooms are cozily comfortable, but you'll have to take half-board. *A–6456, tel. 05256/228. 26 rooms. Facilities: restaurant, indoor pool, sauna, solarium, fitness room. No credit cards. Closed May–June, Sept.–mid-Dec. Expensive.*

★

Edelweiss und Gurgl. Traditionally, this is *the* place to stay. Renovations have turned the massive house into an excellent family-run hotel with a comfortable, relaxed ambience. The cheery rooms have attractive natural-wood touches. *A–6456, tel. 05256/223. 105 rooms. Facilities: restaurant, bar, indoor pool, sauna, solarium, garage. AE, DC, MC. Closed Oct.–Nov. Expensive.*

Laurin. At the next level up toward Hochgurgl, you'll find this smaller house set cozily into the protective hillside. You'll have that same comfortable sheltered feeling inside. The rooms are attractive, in Tirolean decor. *A–6456 Obergurgl/Hochgurgl, tel. 05256/227. 32 rooms. Facilities: restaurant, bar, sauna, solarium, fitness room, garage. No credit cards. Closed May, Oct. Expensive.*

Ötz
Dining and Lodging

Alpenhotel. This solid house fits the center of town well; you'll find the traditional country warmth and friendliness and comfortable rooms as well. *Bielefeldstr. 4, A–6433, tel. 05252/6232. 45 rooms. Facilities: restaurant. No credit cards. Closed mid-Apr.–May, Oct.–mid-Dec. Moderate.*

Drei Mohren. You can't miss this collection of odd towers and onion domes. Fortunately, the interior is less exotic; the comfortable rooms are elegantly paneled, most have balconies, and you don't see the towers and domes. The paneled restaurant, offering standard local fare, is tastefully decorated with old etchings. *Hauptstr. 54, A–6433, tel. 05252/6301. 22 rooms. Facilities: restaurant, garage, tennis court. No credit cards. Closed Oct.–mid-Dec. Moderate.*

Pertisau
Dining and Lodging
★

Fürstenhaus. Duke Sigmund the Wealthy knew what he was doing when he built this massive house for himself in 1469; elegant it is, and directly on the lake; the hotel has its own boats. A later Sigmund, Freud, stayed here in 1900. The rooms are spacious and luxurious. *A–6213, tel. 05243/5442. 60 rooms. Facilities: restaurant, indoor pool, sauna, solarium, fitness room. AE, DC, MC, V. Closed Apr., Nov.–mid-Dec. Expensive.*

Kristall. This chalet lodge offers friendly comfort in ample, elegant public rooms and cheerfully decorated bedrooms. You can take half-board or not, and the restaurant is open to the public. *A–6213, tel. 05243/5490. 53 rooms. Facilities: restaurant (DC, MC, V), outdoor pool, sauna, solarium, fitness room. No credit cards. Closed Nov. Expensive.*

Rieser. As if the lake weren't enough, this large chalet has a swimming pool and bowling to keep you amused. The beamed-ceiling lobby and the extensive use of natural woods in the bedrooms create a warm atmosphere. The restaurant is well known for its steaks. *A–6213, tel. 05243/5251. 94 rooms. Facilities: restaurant, indoor pool, sauna, bowling alley, solarium, indoor and outdoor tennis, squash. No credit cards. Closed Nov.–early Dec. Expensive.*

Reutte/Plansee
Dining and Lodging

Ammerwald. This typical chalet-style house is located slightly out of the center of Reutte toward the Plansee. The interior color scheme is in browns and oranges, which are repeated in the comfortable, quiet rooms. A cross-country ski trail begins right at the door, and the restaurant has a growing reputation for its game. *Grenzstr., A–6600, tel. 05672/8131. 100 rooms. Facilities: restaurant (reservations advised, jacket advised), bar, indoor pool, sauna, solarium, bowling alley, garage. AE, DC, MC, V. Closed late Jan. Moderate.*

St. Anton
Dining
★

Brunnenhof. Set in the intimate homey atmosphere of an old farmhouse in nearby St. Jakob is one of the best restaurants in the area. From the excellent Tirolean and international menu you might choose a mushroom, garlic, or cheese soup and follow it with roast rack of lamb in an herb crust. The wine list is good. *St. Anton/St. Jakob, tel. 05446/2293. Reservations required. Jacket and tie advised. No credit cards. No lunch. Closed June–Nov. Expensive.*

Lodging
★

Arlberg Hospiz. This huge pink building re-creates much of the legendary ancient hospice that stood here until a tragic fire in the 1950s. Carved wood paneling and rich Oriental carpets abound. The rooms are luxurious in the extreme; service is attentive but not obtrusive. The restaurant has an elegant atmosphere and has earned a reputation for creative cooking: You might be offered cream of lobster or oyster soup, lamb or venison, or a variety of fish dishes. *A–6580 St. Anton/St. Christoph, tel. 05446/26110. 100 rooms. Facilities: restaurant (reservations advised; jacket and tie advised; AE, DC, MC, V in summer), indoor pool, sauna, solarium, garage. No credit cards. Closed May, Oct.–Nov. Very Expensive.*

★ **Schwarzer Adler.** The beautifully frescoed facade of this 420-year-old inn in the center of town creates the right setting for the open fireplaces, Tirolean antiques, and colorful Oriental carpets inside. Rooms are tastefully furnished in alpine style and fully equipped. An annex across the street has somewhat less elegant (and cheaper) rooms. The lively Disco Klause is in the basement of the main house. *A–6580, tel. 05446/2244. 50 rooms in main house, 13 in annex. Facilities: restaurant, café, sauna, solarium. No credit cards. Closed mid-Apr.–May, Oct.–Nov. Very Expensive.*

Sporthotel. The dark weathered wood and balconied front immediately identify the Sporthotel. Directly in the center, the modern house attracts the indoor as well as the outdoor crowd, so there's always activity. The rooms are decorated individually and range from cozy to elegant. The ski lifts are just two minutes away, so between the skiing, the indoor swimming pool (with waterfall), and two discos (Drop In is probably the hottest place in town), you won't be bored. *A–6580, tel. 05446/ 3111. 53 rooms. Facilities: 2 restaurants, 2 bars, 2 discos, indoor pool, sauna, solarium, garage. AE, DC, MC, V. Closed May, Oct.–Nov. Very Expensive.*

★ **Arlberg.** Built in 1970, this stylish, modern chalet, a bit out of the center, has now come of age. The wood-paneled lobby with its bar, the friendly staff, and the comfortable balconied rooms in Tirolean decor all contribute to a relaxed holiday atmosphere. The Zinnstube, open as a public restaurant, features Austrian standard fare of good quality. *A–6580, tel. 05446/ 2210. 75 rooms. Facilities: restaurant, bar, indoor pool, sauna, solarium, fitness room, tennis court. AE, MC, V. Closed mid-Apr.–May, Oct.–mid-Dec. Moderate (summer)–Very Expensive (winter).*

★ **Berghaus Maria.** This house in Oberndorf is away from the center of town, but a shuttle bus will take you back and forth. The welcoming fireplace and the friendly lobby bar set the ambience in the hotel. The smallish bedrooms are comfortable, with their rather run-of-the-mill furnishings, but the place is best known for its restaurant. The three Tirolean *Stuben*, with their ceramic tile stoves, the array of pewter, and the Oriental carpets, create an appealing setting for excellent food. Choose game, if it's available, or a specialty like the fillet of lamb with thyme sauce. *A–6580, tel. 05446/20050. 32 rooms. Facilities: restaurant (reservations advised, jacket and tie advised), indoor pool, sauna, solarium. AE, DC, MC, V. Closed May– Nov. Expensive.*

Karl Schranz. Your first impression of this new and spacious alpine lodge is the lobby, with its welcoming fireplace—a showcase for trophies won by the champion skier and owner-manager, Karl Schranz. A house bus will take you to and from the center of town. The rooms are large and modern, with elegant wood paneling. The Jägerstube restaurant features Austrian and Tirolean fare. *A–6580, tel. 05446/25550. 23 rooms. Facilities: restaurant, sauna, solarium, garage. No credit cards. Closed May–Nov. Moderate.*

St. Johann in Tirol
Lodging

Europa. This apartment hotel next to the recreation center (swimming, sauna, tennis) is attractively furnished in Baroque and local decor. Many rooms have a Tirolean four-poster and a furnished kitchenette. The great feature for exhausted skiers is that breakfast is served until 11 AM. *A–6380, tel. 05352/ 22850. 17 apartments. AE, DC. Closed mid-Apr.–mid-May, Oct.–mid-Dec. Expensive.*

Seefeld
Dining
★

Sir Richard. The view out over the restaurant garden and off toward the surrounding peaks is great, but the food here deserves the attention. Freshly baked bread is only one indication; try a game, lamb, or fish specialty to test the kitchen. Table settings are elegant, and the service and atmosphere are personal. *Tel. 05212/2093. Reservations advised. Jacket and tie suggested. AE, DC. Closed Mon., Tues. lunch; closed June. Expensive.*

Lodging
★

Klosterbräu. This quiet hotel in the pedestrian zone, built around a 16th-century cloister, is the town's premier inn. Its thick walls, vaulting, extensive stone, and wood paneling have been cleverly combined to provide a luxurious setting. The rooms are equally welcoming; most have balconies with flowers. The nightclub features dancing to live music with a revue, and the several restaurants are among the best in town. You can choose from the country-style Bräukeller, the rustic-elegant Tirolean room, and the more formal Ritter Oswald Stube. In the latter, you might select beef fillet in Café de Paris sauce or duck in orange sauce. *Klosterstr. 30, A–6100, tel. 05212/2621. 114 rooms. Facilities: 3 restaurants (reservations advised, jacket and tie advised), café, indoor and outdoor pools, sauna, solarium, fitness room, garage, tennis. AE, DC, MC, V. Closed Apr.–May, Oct.–mid-Dec. Very Expensive.*

★ **Tümmlerhof.** The atmosphere is friendly-casual, but every luxury is available at this charming chalet complex that meanders over the green hillside. The balconied rooms are individually furnished, with much warm wood. You can enjoy piano music in the bar at cocktail hour. The resaurant is rated one of the top dozen in Austria. *A–6100, tel. 05212/2571. 70 rooms. Facilities: restaurant (reservations advised, jacket advised), bar, indoor and outdoor pools, sauna, solarium, garage. No credit cards. Closed Apr.–May, Oct.–mid-Nov. Very Expensive.*

Astoria. This luxurious double chalet has views out over the Alps. The rooms are contemporary modern, with balconies, and are pleasant if somewhat conservative. The hotel restaurant is good without being extravagant; game, roast pork, and veal are featured. Golfers can use the nearby course. *A–6100, tel. 05212/2272. 60 rooms. Facilities: restaurant (jacket and tie advised), indoor pool, sauna, solarium, fitness room. No credit cards. Closed Apr.–May, Oct.–mid-Dec. Expensive.*

Dreitorspitz. You'll get a good view of the mountains from the balcony of your room in this family-run chalet-style house. It's done up in attractive light woods, with strong red accents, and is set in a large garden. *A–6100, tel. 05212/2951. 53 rooms. Facilities: restaurant, indoor pool, sauna, garage, putting green. AE, DC, MC, V. Closed Apr.–May, Sept.–Oct. Expensive.*

Karwendelhof. You'll find this large and elegant yet *gemütlich* chalet at the train station. The rooms are attractively furnished in modern Tirolean style, with much warm natural wood in evidence. The owner-managers are particularly friendly. Small children are looked after in a playroom. The hotel has its own 6-hole golf course and driving range and in winter a *Keller* nightclub and houses the town's casino. *A–6100, tel. 05212/2655. 43 rooms. Facilities: restaurant, nightclub, casino, sauna, solarium, golf course. AE, DC, MC, V. Closed Apr.–May, Oct.–mid-Dec. Expensive.*

Post. This tall, balconied chalet with a double roof is family managed. The modern bedrooms are comfortably furnished. There's an in-house disco for evening entertainment. *A–6100, tel. 05212/2201. 86 rooms. Facilities: café-bar, sauna, solarium, fitness room, garage. No credit cards. Expensive.*

Serfaus
Dining and Lodging

Cervosa. The center of action in Serfaus focuses on this typical double chalet close to the center of town. The family owners have preserved the hotel's informal ambience despite its rather elegant reconstruction. Rooms are welcoming and modern; there are apartments of various sizes as well. *A–6534, tel. 05476/6212. 70 rooms. Facilities: restaurant, indoor and outdoor pools, 2 saunas, solarium, fitness room, bowling, garage. DC, V. Closed mid-Apr.–May, mid-Oct.–mid-Dec. Expensive.*

Lowen. The attractive painted facade of this hotel in the heart of town conceals a virtually new building, yet it has not lost its typical Tirolean country charm. The rooms are cheerfully furnished and the management is unusually friendly and welcoming to families. The excellent restaurant is generally reserved for hotel guests alone, but if you phone ahead and are willing to take potluck, you might get a table. *A–6534, tel. 05476/6204. 53 rooms. Facilities: restaurant, indoor pool, sauna, solarium, fitness room, garage. No credit cards. Closed mid-Apr.–June, mid-Oct.–mid-Dec. Expensive.*

Maximilian. The transformation of a former Serfaus Gasthof into a modern hotel seems to have worked, successfully blending the old and the new. Rooms in the new section, some with open fireplaces, are more spacious, but all are comfortable, and there's a children's playroom. The excellent public restaurant, with a salad bar, is open evenings only. *A–6534, tel. 05476/6520. 36 rooms. Facilities: restaurant, indoor pool, sauna, solarium, fitness room, garage. No credit cards. Closed Oct.–mid-Dec., May. Expensive.*

Sölden
Dining and Lodging

Alpina. Tucked into a hillside, this typical alpine house offers a paneled interior and compact, comfortable rooms. *A–6450, tel. 05254/2559. 55 rooms. Facilities: restaurant, sauna, solarium. AE, DC. Expensive.*

Central. Huge arches and heavy wooden timbers accent the antique furniture and set the atmosphere in this massive riverside hotel where the prominent gather. The bedrooms are spacious and luxuriously furnished. *A–6450, tel. 05254/2260. 70 rooms. Facilities: restaurant, indoor pool, sauna, solarium, fitness room. No credit cards. Closed May–mid-July. Expensive.*

Sonne. You'll be right next to the chair lift to Hochsölden if you stay in this reconstructed half-timbered chalet. Its atmosphere is rustic, and the paneled rooms are cozy. *A–6450, tel. 05254/2203. 66 rooms. Facilities: restaurant, disco, sauna, solarium. No credit cards. Closed May. Moderate (summer)–Expensive (winter).*

Telfes
Lodging

Interalpen Tyrol. This new resort, outside town at 1,200 meters (3,900 ft), is simply huge, from the lobby with its vast expanse of carpet to the modern rooms. But the lobby's crackling fire is welcoming, and you'll find this a far quieter, more relaxing spot than you might guess from its original impression. *A–6410, tel. 05262/6060. 285 rooms. Facilities: restaurant, indoor pool, sauna, solarium, fitness room, spa, indoor and outdoor tennis, garage. AE, DC, MC, V. Closed Apr.–mid-May, Nov.–mid-Dec. Very Expensive.*

Zell am Ziller
Dining and Lodging

Zellerhof. This variation on the traditional alpine chalet has recently added a sauna and health club. It is tastefully decorated in the local style, with ample natural wood, and the Tirolean ambience carries over to the comfortable rooms. The hotel can arrange fishing. The intimate restaurant upstairs is excellent; ask for fish from the hotel's own ponds. *Bahnhofstr. 3, A–6280, tel. 05282/2612. 32 rooms. Facilities: restaurant, bar, nightclub, sauna, solarium, garage. No credit cards. Closed Nov. Expensive.*

★ **Bräu.** The heart of this thick-walled, five-story, frescoed building in the center of town dates to the 16th century; subsequent renovations have brought it quite up to date, with a new wing added in 1985. The rooms are decorated in warm alpine style, in beiges, greens, and brown. The hotel can arrange fishing trips. The three-room restaurant complex serves fine food, with emphasis on fish and game. Reserve for the *Bräustübl*, and enjoy the house beer; the house brewery is also the source of the *Gauderbier. A–6289, tel. 05282/2313. 36 rooms. Facilities: restaurant, sauna, solarium. No credit cards. Closed Apr., Nov.–mid-Dec. Moderate.*

Nightlife

Kitzbühel Much activity centers on the **casino** in the **Goldener Greif** hotel, where you'll find baccarat, blackjack, roulette, and one-armed bandits galore. There's a restaurant and a bar. *Tel. 05356/2300. Jacket and tie recommended. Open nightly Christmas–March, July–mid-Sept. Passport required.*

The **Tenne** has for generations been *the* evening spot in Kitz. It's partly because of the friendly atmosphere, the capacity, and the music (live), but most of all it's because you can meet people here. There's food, but emphasis is on drink and dance. *Hotel zur Tenne, A–6370, tel. 05356/4444. Dress: casual chic. AE, DC, MC, V. Open 9 PM–3 AM, closed May–July, Sept.–Dec. 25.*

Disco action currently centers on **Drop In,** in the **Weisses Rössl** hotel. You can drop in anytime up to closing at 5 AM and dance the rest of the night (morning) away in the mirrored surroundings. *Tel. 05356/2541. Dress: casual chic. AE, DC, MC, V. Open 10 PM–5 AM. Closed May–July, Sept.–Dec. 25.*

Seefeld The **casino** (tel. 05212/2340) in the gabled **Karwendelhof** by the railroad station is a center of evening activity, featuring American and French roulette, blackjack, baccarat, and slot machines. *Bring your passport. Jacket and tie advised. Closed Good Friday, Easter.*

You'll find the most sophisticated nightlife in the nightclub of the **Klosterbräu** hotel, where from 9 PM to 3 AM there's an international orchestra and floor show. In ski season, the club opens at 5 PM for tea dancing.

St. Anton For some visitors to St. Anton, the show, not the snow, is the thing. Nobody complains about lack of action! Check out the **Post Keller** (Hotel Post, tel. 05446/22130) for drinking, **Hotel Alte Post** (tel. 05446/58265) for disco, and **St. Anton Bar** (tel. 05446/3320) for dancing.

Vorarlberg

Vorarlberg has much in common with neighboring Switzerland. Not only are the dialects similar, but the landscape flows across the border with never a difference. Both peoples descended from the same ancient German Allemanic tribes that flourished in the 3rd century BC. Both have the same characteristics of thrift, hard work, and a deep-rooted instinct for democracy and independence. Travelers approaching from the Western Alps take the tunnel under the Arlberg mountain range into Vorarlberg.

Essential Information

Tourist Information Headquarters for information about Vorarlberg is at Römerstrasse 7, A–6901 Bregenz, tel. 05574/425250. Other tourist offices (*Verkehrsamt, Verkehrsverein,* or *Fremdenverkehrsamt*) are:

Bezau (Platz 39, A–6870, tel. 05514/2295 or 05514/3129)
Bludenz (Werdenberger Str. 42, A–6700, tel. 05552/62170)
Bregenz (Inselstr. 15, A–6900, tel. 05574/43391)
Feldkirch (Herrengasse 12, A–6800, tel. 05522/23467)
Lech (A–6764, tel. 05583/216112)
Montafon Valley (Silbertalerstr. 1, A–6780 Schruns, tel. 05556/2253)
Zürs (A–6763, tel. 05583/2245)

Arriving and Departing
By Plane The closest major airport is Zurich, 120 km (75 mi) away. Munich is 190 km (119 mi) away, and Innsbruck, 200 km (125 mi). Several trains a day serve Bregenz from the Zurich Kloten airport. In winter a bus leaves the airport at 12:30 PM on weekends for resorts in the Arlberg and Montafon regions. You can book through Swissair. On the Austrian side, call **Arlberg Express** (tel. 05582/226) for train information and bookings. The fare is AS400 one way, AS700 round-trip, Zurich–Zurs/Lech.

Rheintalflug flies twice daily each way between Vienna and Altenrhein on Lake Constance in Switzerland. A direct bus service takes passengers from the airport to Bregenz, Dornbirn, and Feldkirch at no charge. *Tel., in Vienna, 0222/513–9546, in Vorarlberg, 05576/3222, in Switzerland, 071/435120.*

By Car From Germany the autobahn (Route A–14/E–17) takes you into Bregenz; roads from Switzerland lead to Lustenau and Hohenems; from Liechtenstein, Route 16 (Route 191 in Austria) goes to Feldkirch; and routes A–12/E–60 from eastern Austria and 315 from Italy meet at Landeck and as Route 316/E–60 head westward through the Arlberg auto tunnel (toll AS150). Alternatively, your car (and you) can get to Vorarlberg on the car train that runs to Feldkirch from Vienna, Graz, or Villach.

By Train The main rail line connecting with Vienna and Innsbruck enters Vorarlberg at Langen after coming through the Arlberg tunnel. Both the *Arlberg* and *Orient Express* trains follow this route, which then swings through Bludenz to Feldkirch. There the line splits, with the Arlberg Express going south into Liechtenstein and Switzerland, the other branch through Dornbirn to Bregenz and on to Lindau in Germany.

By Ship From May to October, passenger ships of the Austrian railroad's Bodensee **White Fleet** (tel. 05574/42868) connect Bregenz with Lindau, Friedrichshafen, Meersburg, and Konstanz on the German side of the lake. The Eurailpass and Austrian railpasses are valid on these ships.

Getting Around
By Car A car is the most flexible way of getting about in Vorarlberg, but the roads are tricky to treacherous in winter. You are not allowed on some mountain roads in the Arlberg without chains, which you can rent from a number of service stations.

By Train The railroads connect the main centers of Vorarlberg remarkably well; besides the lines described above, the Montafoner electric (with occasional steam) rail line runs from Bludenz parallel to the highway southeast to Schruns.

By Bus Post office, railroad, and private bus services connect all the towns and villages not served by the railroad, using tracked vehicles when necessary in winter. Even so, some of the highest roads become impassable, and the only transportation is via helicopter or horse-drawn sleigh.

Exploring Vorarlberg

Our first itinerary takes us through Bregenz, at the eastern end of the Bodensee (Lake Constance), on a walking tour. On Tour 2 we wander the Bregenzerwald to Bludenz, follow the Inn valley to Feldkirch, and head north again to Bregenz. Tour 3 visits the Arlberg ski resorts.

Highlights Opera on the lake in **Bregenz** (Tour 1)
Medieval **Feldkirch** (Tour 2)
Skiing at **Oberlech** (Tour 3)

Numbers in the margin correspond with points of interest on the Vorarlberg map.

Tour 1: Bregenz **Bregenz** has been the capital of Vorarlberg since 1819 and seat
36 of the provincial government. The face of the town has changed dramatically in recent years, owing to much building in the lower or "new" section of the city. The rail yards were relocated outside town and the main highway and railroad were put into tunnels, thereby allowing the development of acres of lakeside land as a recreation area and connected the town to the waterfront.

Bregenz is pleasant at any time of year, but the best time to visit it is during the summer music festival (*see* The Arts and Nightlife, below). The festival's main feature is an opera, operetta, or musical comedy—this year, a repeat of the highly successful *Carmen* production of 1991—performed on a huge stage on the lake itself, an exciting spectacle.

Most of the important sights can be seen in the course of a walk of about 1½ hours. Start at the Tourist Information office and cross to the lake shore. To your right is the quay where the lake steamers dock. At its end stands the meteorological column, whose intriguing instruments measure the weather and lake water. Turn left up the promenade, and you'll come first to the horseshoe-shape **Music Pavilion,** where outdoor concerts are held in summer. Beyond the minigolf course on your right looms the massive Festival Hall and Congress Center, built in 1980 and designed so that in bad weather, at least half of those in the 4,200 seats outside can be accommodated in the hall. Turning back, stroll along the promenade once again, then turn left into the Seestrasse, where you'll see the turn-of-the-century main **Post Office** building at No. 5. Behind the post office on the Kaspar-Moosbrugger-Platz is the **Nepomukkapelle** of 1757, now used as the Hungarian church and open Saturday afternoons only. Turning right on the Kornmarktstrasse, you come to the **Gasthof Kornmesser,** a gorgeous example of a Baroque townhouse built in 1720 and renovated in 1960. Just after the alley simply marked "Theater," you'll reach the **Theater am Kornmarkt,** built in 1838 as a grain storehouse, when Bregenz was an important commercial port; in 1954 the granary was converted into a 700-seat theater. Next door is the **Landesmuseum** (provincial museum), another turn-of-the-century building, exhibiting, among other items, relics of Brigantium, the Roman administrative city that once stood where Bregenz is today. *Kornmarktplatz 1, tel. 05574/46050. Admission: AS15. Open Tues.–Sun. 9–noon and 2–5.*

Turning left into the Rathausstrasse, you'll find the **Rathaus,** also built (in 1685) as a grain warehouse. Given over to administration in 1720, the house got its ornate front and tower only in

Vorarlberg

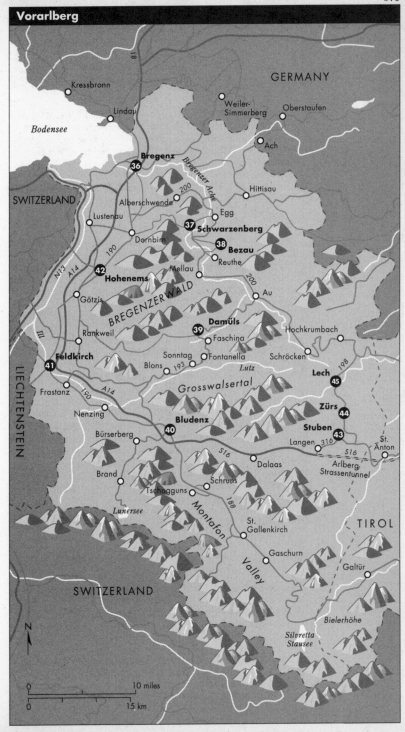

GERMANY

Kressbronn

Lindau

Bodensee

Weiler-
Simmerberg

Oberstaufen

Ach

Bregenz

36

Bregenzer Ache

Hittisau

SWITZERLAND

Alberschwende

200

Egg

Lustenau

Schwarzenberg

37

Dornbirn

38 **Bezau**

190

Reuthe

Mellau

42 **Hohenems**

200

Au

N13 A14

Götzis

BREGENZERWALD

Hochkrumbach

Rankweil

39 **Damüls**

Faschina

III

Sonntag

Schröcken

198

Feldkirch

Blons

193

Fontanella

Lutz

Lech

41

45

Frastanz

190

A14

Grosswalsertal

Zürs

Nenzing

44

Stuben

Bürserberg

40 **Bludenz**

43

Langen

316

St. Anton

LIECHTENSTEIN

Brand

Lunersee

Tschagguns

Schruns

S16

Dalaas

*Arlberg
Strassentunnel*

S16

188

St.
Gallenkirch

Montafon

TIROL

SWITZERLAND

Gaschurn

Galtür

Valley

Bielerhöhe

N

*Silvretta
Stausee*

0   10 miles

0   15 km

1898. The **Seekapelle** next door, with its onion dome, was put up over the graves of a defeated band of Swiss, who in 1408 attempted to incorporate Bregenz into Switzerland.

Time Out Behind the Seekapelle is the **Gösserbrau Restaurant** (Anton-Schneider-Gasse 1). This might be just the moment for a cool beer, a cup of coffee, or even something more substantial.

Take the pedestrian subway, and come up in the Maurachgasse. Turn left on the Belrupstrasse and walk to the base station of the **Pfänderbahn,** a cable car that takes you up to the 1,064-meter (3,460-ft) peak overlooking the city. You can see four countries from here, and the restaurant is open from June to mid-September. If you have time, you can take a 30-minute circular hike to a small outdoor zoo, with deer, alpine goats, moufflon, and wild boar. Entrance is free. *Pfänderbahn, tel. 05574/42160. Round-trip fare: AS94 adults, AS63 children. Open Oct.–Mar., daily 9–6, Apr.–Sept., daily 8:30–8 (some days in fine weather, till 10:30).*

Back on the Belrupstrasse, we come to the **Sacred Heart church,** built in 1908 in brick Gothic style with notable stained-glass windows. Walk back up the Maurachgasse, and you'll come to the **stone gate** to the upper (old) city, bearing the emblem of a Celtic-Roman equine goddess (the original is now in the Landesmuseum). Inside the gate are the coats of arms of the dukes of Bregenz and of the dukes of Montfort, the latter crest now the Vorarlberg provincial emblem. Turning left into Martinsplatz, you find the **Martinskirche,** a tiny chapel with 14th-century frescoes inside. To its right is a tower, the **Martinsturm** (1599–1602), the symbol of Bregenz and the first Baroque construction on Lake Constance, boasting the largest onion dome in central Europe. To the left of the Martinsgasse and Graf Wilhemstrasse is a piece of the old defense passageway and the city wall; on the first house on the right, notice the coats of arms of Bregenz families. Ahead on the right is the **Altes Rathaus** (1622), in ornate half-timbered construction and brightly shuttered. At the head of the Eponastrasse stands the former **Gesellenspital** (laborers' hospital); remnants of a fresco still visible on its wall depict Saint Christopher, Saint Peter, and a kneeling abbot. At the Ehre-Guta-Platz stands the **Montfortbrunnen,** a fountain to honor the minnesinger Hugo von Montfort, who was born in the old city in 1357. Every Ash Wednesday the fountain is the scene of a ritual washing of wallets and change purses, when the carnival jesters clean out their empty pockets and spin tales about the events of the previous year.

The three small parallel streets running uphill from Ehre-Guta-Platz roughly outline the boundaries of the town in the Middle Ages. Left of the fountain is the **Deuringschlösschen,** onetime residence of a noble family, now housing one of Austria's finest restaurants and a small, elegant hotel (*see* Dining and Lodging, below). Walk past the residence to the **Meissnerstiege** (Meissner steps), via the Thalbachgasse around to the 14th-century **parish church of Saint Gallus.** Note the high Baroque altar of red-brown marble. Walk over the stone bridge and left along the wall to the Kapuzinergasse, then turn left at the end to **Kunstlerhaus Thürn und Taxis,** an interesting building, now a modern gallery, set in the Thurn- und Taxispark.

Turn right on Wolfeggstrasse, continue down Kirchstrasse into Kaiserstrasse, and you're back in the new town again.

Tour 2: Through the Bregenzerwald to Bludenz and Feldkirch Bordering Bregenz on the south and southeast lies the **Bregenzerwald** (Bregenz Forest), a beautiful area of densely wooded highlands, sweeping valleys, and lush meadows radiant in summer with wildflowers, all set against a backdrop of mountains.

In the Bregenzerwald you see Vorarlberg women still wearing the handsome, stiffly starched folk dress of their ancestors. On festive occasions the girls wear a golden headdress shaped like a small crown, and the married women, a black or white pointed cap. Men's costume is worn by local band musicians (which seems to include nearly everyone), with the shape of the cap and the color of various parts of the clothing differing from town to town.

As you leave Bregenz headed south (Route 190), turn left sharply after crossing the river on a road marked to Wolfurt and Schwarzach. About 21 km (13 mi) farther, at Alberschwende, you will come to Route 200; follow the signs for **Egg,** where you should note the old country houses.

㊲ Head on from Egg to **Schwarzenberg,** one of the area's most colorful villages. The artist Angelika Kaufmann (1741–1807), who spent much of her time in England, considered this her home. Few people in Austria east of the Arlberg mountains knew of her until her picture appeared on a new issue of Austrian currency a few years ago. You can see several of her larger works in the Baroque village church, including an altar painting from about 1800. The Landesmuseum in Bregenz has her portrait of the Duke of Wellington. The town has a room dedicated to her. *Hof 765, tel. 05512/3166. Admission: AS25 adults, AS5 children. Open Tues., Thurs., weekends 2–4 or by appointment.*

Time Out The **Hirschen** (Hof 14), a Gasthof in a shuttered building in the center of town, is a fine place for a meal.

㊳ Shortly after leaving Schwarzenberg you'll come to a small road on your left, marked to **Bezau.** It's a particularly scenic stretch. Local history relates that the district hall here was built on tall columns and was accessible only by ladder; once the councillors were gathered inside, the ladder was removed until they came to a decision. The **Heimatmuseum,** slightly south of the center, contains more on the town's interesting past, including local folk costumes. *Ellenbogen 181, tel. 05514/2559 or 2295. Admission: AS15 adults, AS10 children. Open June–Sept., Tues., Thurs., Sat. 2–4, Wed. 10–noon.*

Bezau is also headquarters for the **Bregenzerwald Museumsbahn,** all that is left of the onetime narrow-gauge railroad that ran from Bregenz to Bezau and was abandoned in 1980. The museum has managed to preserve more than 6 km (almost 4 mi) of track to Bersbuch, beyond Schwarzenau, and runs diesel and steam excursions from mid-May to mid-October. *Bahnhof 147, tel. 05514/3174. Round-trip (steam) AS70 adults, AS30 children; (diesel) AS50 adults, AS20 children. Departures weekdays and holidays at 11, 2, 3:30; Thurs. (July–Aug.) at 11, 2.*

Reuthe, the next town just before you rejoin Route 200, has one of the area's oldest churches, with 15th-century frescoes inside. As you go along through the valley, you come across one town after another with *au* (meaning meadow) in its name: As the area developed, names were given to the meadows in which settlements were established.

39 At Au, turn right onto Route 193 and start upward toward **Damüls.** The road is narrow, with a 14-degree gradient at one point, but when you reach Damüls, you'll agree that the climb has been worth it; you're at 1,414 meters (4,640 ft), the top of the Bregenzerwald. This is great skiing country in winter. There are enough slopes and lifts, and the crowds are generally elsewhere. In summer the area is knee-deep in wildflowers, but don't pick them; it's against the law. Check the frescoes in the parish church, which date to 1490, just after the church was built, but were rediscovered under later plaster only about 40 years ago.

From Damüls, the way into the **Grosswalsertal** (Great Walliser valley) continues on Route 193, following signs to Faschina and over to Fontanella and Sonntag. The stretch down the valley from here is extremely scenic; as you start the descent, look across at the Saint Gerold monastery to your right, but after reaching Blons, look at the road: It's full of hairpin turns.

40 Route 193 brings you into **Bludenz,** which is full of architectural surprises: late 17th-century houses and relics of the ancient town defenses, arcaded shopping streets, and old buildings, all sheltered by mountains rising on the edge of the city. Bludenz sits at the heart of five valleys, all of which are well endowed with lifts, good slopes, and hiking trails. People here are pleased when you ask for a hot chocolate instead of coffee; Bludenz is a major chocolate-producing center, as you may detect if the wind is from the direction of the factories.

A detour on Route 188 southeast out of Bludenz—or on the Montafonerbahn electric rail line—will bring you to the Schruns-Tschagguns skiing area in the Montafon valley. Ernest Hemingway spent many winters here. Today neither of the towns is as fashionable as the resorts on the Arlberg, but the views over the Ferwall Alps to the east and the mighty Rätikon on the western side of the valley are unsurpassed anywhere in Austria. In winter the powdery snow provides wonderful skiing. In summer the heights are given over to climbers and hikers, the mountain streams to the trout fishermen, and the lowlands to the tennis players.

Time Out Hidden down a small street in Schruns, you'll find the **Café Feuerstein** at Dorfstrasse 4. It is furnished with antiques, particularly in the upstairs rooms, but the main attractions are its ice cream and pastries.

Heading northwest out of Bludenz toward Feldkirch, on Route 190 or on the train (both share the valley with the Ill river and the autobahn), the first village you'll come across is **Nenzing.** This is the jumping-off spot for the wildly romantic Gamperdonatal, the valley of the Meng river, which rises where the peaks are 2,000 meters (6,500 ft) or more. The valley is hikable, but it's barely passable for cars. The top is called *Nenzinger Himmel,* literally Nenzing Heaven.

Farther up the Ill valley at **Frastanz,** the relatively new but interesting neo-Gothic church (1888) was designed by Friedrich

Schmidt, the same architect responsible for the elegantly neo-Gothic city hall in Vienna.

41 **Feldkirch** is Vorarlberg's oldest town, with parts dating from the Middle Ages that contribute greatly to the town's romantic character. Picturesque arcades line the narrow main street. Marvelous towers and onion domes top some of the buildings, and the town is watched over by an assembly of imposing stone blockhouses which comprise the Schattenburg castle complex just above the town.

An easy walk around the center of Feldkirch will take you to most of the town's highlights. Start at the **St. Nicholas cathedral** on Domplatz. The mystical light in this church built in 1478 comes through the unusual glass windows. From the cathedral, walk toward the river past the district government offices (once a Jesuit monastery) and past the bishop's palace, a block back of the Herrengasse, to the **Katzenturm** (literally, "cat's tower," figuratively, "the clergy"), reconstructed by Emperor Maximilian I (1491–1507). This is the most prominent remnant of the town's fortifications and now holds the 7½-ton town bell. Down the Hirschgraben, you'll come to the Chur gate and beside it the **Frauenkirche** (women's church), dedicated to Saint Sebastian in 1473. Head down the Montfortgasse to where the **Wasserturm** (water tower) and the **Diebsturm** (thieves' tower) stand guard over the Schillerstrasse bridge. Wander down Vorstadt to the **Pulverturm** (powder tower) and across to the **Mühlenturm** (mill tower), whose contrast to the modern Leonhardsplatz is considerable. Turning left, you'll find the St. Johann Church (1218) and, behind it, the **market square** (market days Tuesday and Saturday), with its arcades, and at the far end, a five-story half-timbered house. The square is the site of the annual wine festival during the second week of July. Across the pedestrian zone you'll come to the Liechtenstein Palace, once the administrative center. On your right is the **Rathaus** of 1493 with its frescoes and paneled rooms. In the Neustadt, another series of opposing arcades forms a frame for the view up to the 12th-century **Schattenburg,** the massive castle that overlooks the town. *Burggasse 1, tel. 05522/21982 or 26689. Admission: AS20 adults, AS10 children. Open Tues.–Sun. 9–noon, 1–5. Closed Nov.*

42 Continuing on Route 190, you reach **Hohenems,** a small town now famous for the annual **Schubertiade** in the second half of June, considered one of the finest musical events in Europe. (Schubert had no connection with the town; the decision to emphasize his works was made arbitrarily.) In 1992 the festival takes place in Feldkirch; Schubertiade Hohenems (Schweizer Str. 1, A–6845 Hohenems, tel. 05576/2091) can furnish details.

Back on Route 190, the last stop on our way back to Bregenz is **Dornbirn,** the industrial center of Vorarlberg, specializing in textiles. The annual Dornbirn Fair in the first week of August shows a range of goods and technologies, but textiles are featured.

Tour 3: The Arlberg Resorts If you're traveling by train, **Langen** is the stop closest to the ski resorts; Route S–16/316 takes you by car from Bludenz to Langen and beyond to Route 198 heading north.

43 Before turning off Route 316 onto 198, you come to **Stuben,** the birthplace of Hannes Schneider, pioneer of alpine ski techniques. The magnificent skiing at 1,400 meters (4,600 ft) from

December to the end of April makes Stuben popular with the serious skiers who are willing to forgo the stylish resorts up the road.

Just past Stuben the Flexen road (Route 198) over the pass begins. For much of its length the road is protected from avalanches by concrete or timbered roofing. A triumph of engineering, it looks like a giant caterpillar crawling along the face of the cliffs. In summer the treeless slopes are covered with alpine flora.

㊹ For all its reputation as the chosen resort of royalty and show business on this side of the Arlberg, **Zürs** is little more than a collection of large hotels. It is strictly a winter-sports community; when the season is over, the hotels close. But Zürs is more exclusive than Lech and certainly more so than Gstaad or St. Moritz in Switzerland. In most hotels you'll be asked to take full board, so there are relatively few "public" restaurants in town and little chance to dine around. But the hotel dining rooms are elegant; in many, jacket and tie are de rigueur in the evening.

㊺ **Lech,** 5 km (3 mi) up the road from Zurs, is a full-fledged community; some argue that this detracts from its fashionableness. But there are more hotels in Lech, better tourist facilities, bigger ski schools, more shops, more nightlife, and prices nearly as high as those in Zürs. Zürs has the advantage of altitude, but Lech is a less artificial and very pretty alpine village. Be sure to check with the hotel of your choice about meal arrangements; as in Zürs, the hotels often require you to take full board.

What to See and Do with Children

Just outside Feldkirch (take the path and steps from the end of the Widnau/Fidelisstrasse intersection or drive south out the Churerstrasse and follow the signs that swing you around north) is the **Wildpark** (tel. 05522/24105), an expansive, natural setting with such local animals as deer, lynx, fox, wild boar, and a great variety of birds, even a snowy owl. A contribution is requested, and the park is open daily around the clock.

The **Bregenzerwaldbahn** (steam railway) (*see* Tour 2).

The **Hohentwiel,** a restored old-time paddle-wheel lake steamship, cruises Lake Constance out of Hard, southwest of Bregenz. Sailings are scheduled irregularly; for information call 05/071–413521.

Shopping

Vorarlberg's specialties are textiles, local costumes, and woven straw. If you've not yet bought your alpine hat, go to the Capo hat and cap works factory outlet in Egg (tel. 05512/23810; open weekdays 1–4:30 PM). It sells fashionable headgear as well as alpine styles.

Sports

Hiking and Climbing Tourist offices throughout Vorarlberg can direct you to a multitude of trails in varying degrees of difficulty.

Skiing In addition to the resorts in Tour 3, skiers head for the Pfander mountain, literally in the backyard of Bregenz, which has a cable tramway and two drag lifts.

Bezau has four regular trails for cross-country skiers and one lift that takes downhill skiers up to the 1,631-meter (5,300-ft) Baumgartenhohe.

Water Sports With the vast lake at the doorstep, Bregenz offers a variety of water sports. You can even learn to sail, although a minimum two weeks is required for a full course at Bodensee Segelschule Lochau. *Box 7, Alte Fahre, tel. 05574/252793.*

Dining and Lodging

Dining In small towns throughout the region, restaurants are often the dining rooms of country inns. The bill will include service and taxes, but it is customary to leave a small additional tip. Highly recommended restaurants are indicated by a star ★.

Category	Cost*
Very Expensive	over AS500
Expensive	AS300–AS500
Moderate	AS150–AS300
Inexpensive	under AS150

for a typical three-course meal with a glass of house wine, service, and tax, but excluding additional tip

Lodging In ski resorts in Vorarlberg, hotel rates in season are often well above the range of our chart. At most of those hotels, the price includes a mandatory two meals a day, and sometimes no credit cards are accepted. The tourist offices can usually help lead you to more moderate lodgings in private houses. In summer you can often find bargain rates at 50% of the winter tariff. In other towns, such as Bregenz, summer is the high season. Highly recommended lodgings are indicated by a star ★.

Category	Cost*
Very Expensive	over AS1,600
Expensive	AS1,000–AS1,600
Moderate	AS700–AS1,000
Inexpensive	under AS700

for a standard double room with bath in high season, including breakfast, service charge of 10%, and tax

Bezau **Engel.** Finding adventurous cooking in a small country inn is
Dining surprise enough, and this food arrives in country portions. Try
★ the excellent split-pea soup, the potato soup with sour cream, or the boiled beef with pan-fried potatoes. The wine list, too, is astonishing for the simple but pleasant surroundings. *Platz 29, tel. 05514/2203. Reservations advised. Jacket suggested. AE, MC, V. Closed Tues., Wed. lunch, and mid-Nov.–mid-Dec. Moderate.*

Lodging ★ **Gasthof Gams.** Dating to the 17th century, this friendly house in the center of town offers every comfort and is a great spot as a base. The rooms are in attractive beige and brown country-rustic decor, and the hotel welcomes families. *Platz 44, A–6870, tel. 05514/2220 or 05514/2421. 40 rooms. Facilities: restaurant, bar, outdoor pool, sauna, solarium, fitness room, tennis courts. No credit cards. Closed early Dec. Expensive.*

Bludenz
Lodging ★ **Schlosshotel.** Perched on a hill above the castle and overlooking the town, this modern hotel with balconies offers splendid views of the Rätikon mountain range to the south, on the Swiss border; ask for a room in the front above the café terrace. The pseudo rustic decor of the house (lots of plastic) continues into the guest rooms, whose clean lines and modern furnishings are, in fact, attractive. *A–6700, tel. 05552/63016. 42 rooms. Facilities: restaurant, café, bar, minigolf, garage. AE, DC, MC, V. Expensive.*

Bregenz
Dining ★ **Deuring-Schlössle.** The Huber family, responsible for what was once judged Austria's top restaurant, has moved it to new quarters in this historic old residence in the oldest part of Bregenz. Though some critics say the kitchen has suffered, it still ranks among Austria's six best. Everything is absolutely fresh and the cuisine is imaginative; Austrian "standards" become exquisite. The wine list is outstanding. *Ehre-Guta-Platz 4, tel. 05574/47800. Reservations advised. Jacket and tie advised. AE, DC, MC, V. Expensive.*

★ **Ilge-Weinstube.** This cozy, intimate *Keller* is old Bregenz at its best: rustic decor in the basement of a 300-year-old house close to the oldest section of town. The *Tafelspitz* (boiled beef) is particularly good, and the wine list excellent. *Maurachstr. 6, tel. 05574/43609. Reservations advised. Dress: casual chic. No credit cards. Closed Sun. dinner. Expensive.*

Neptune. The "in" crowd gathers here, looking only for a basic meal and a place to talk. But the food is good; try the melt-in-your-mouth schnitzel. *Deuringerstr. 3, tel. 05574/46325. Reservations advised. Dress: casual chic. V. Closed Sun. and Jan.–Feb. Moderate.*

Goldener Hirschen. Allegedly the oldest tavern in Bregenz and close to the oldest part of town, this restaurant offers good food and drink in a lively atmosphere. Try any of the roast meats. *Kirchstr. 8, tel. 05574/42815. Reservations not required. Dress: casual. No credit cards. Closed Tues. Inexpensive.*

Lodging ★ **Deuring-Schlössle.** As if running one of Austria's best restaurants weren't enough, the Huber family has now gone into the hotel business as well. The rooms in this more than 400-year-old castle set in a park are luxuriously furnished in rather formal antiques, which fit perfectly with the inlaid floors and the plaster ceiling ornamentation. And, of course, there's the restaurant. *Ehre-Guta-Platz 4, A–6900, tel. 05574/47800. 13 rooms. Facilities: restaurant, parking. AE, DC, MC, V. Very Expensive.*

Central. This modern, friendly hotel in the pedestrian zone is just steps away from the railroad station and in the middle of things. The room decor is contemporary; some rooms have balconies. *Kaiserstr. 26, A–6900, tel. 05574/42947. 41 rooms. Facilities: garage. AE, MC, V. Closed mid-Dec.–Feb. Expensive.*

Mercure. Adjacent to the festival hall and housing the casino, this is a good choice if you're in Bregenz mainly for the music or the money. The house is typical of the chain: functionally modern, all rooms with balconies. Rooms looking out over the lake are best. *Platz der Wiener Symphoniker, A–6900, tel. 05574/ 46100. 94 rooms. Facilities: 2 restaurants. AE, DC, MC, V. Expensive.*

★ **Schwärzler.** You'll need to drive from here to the center, but it's a quick trip. You'll be in a quiet location, adjacent to a park, in a traditional house often used by the festival stars. Rooms are comfortable, and some have a view of the mountains. *Landstr. 9, A–6900, tel. 05574/4990 or 05574/42422. 82 rooms. Facilities: restaurant, bar, indoor pool, sauna, solarium, garage. AE, DC, MC, V. Expensive.*

Weisses Kreuz. Here a traditional, family-run, turn-of-the-century house has been renovated with care and charm. The location is central, and the staff is particularly friendly. The rooms are comfortable and modern; those overlooking the private park out back are quieter. *Römerstr. 5, A–6900, tel. 05574/ 49880. 44 rooms. Facilities: restaurant, garage. AE, DC, MC, V. Expensive.*

Damüls
Lodging

Damülser-Hof. This group of chalets, spread over a meadow, forms an elegant but friendly hotel complex. It's warmly decorated and cozy, with brick, exposed wood, carpets, and open fireplaces. The rooms—also in country rustic decor—in the older section have been renovated, the ones in the new section are well designed and executed. *A–6884, tel. 05510/210. 37 rooms. Facilities: restaurant, café, bar, indoor pool, sauna, solarium, bowling, tennis court. DC. Closed 2 weeks early Nov. Expensive.*

Mittagspitze. Warm wood paneling sets the tone in this attractive chalet, which welcomes families. Many of the rooms have balconies; all are furnished in comfortable rustic style. *A–6884, tel. 05510/211. 26 rooms. Facilities: restaurant, bar, sauna, solarium, garage. AE, DC, MC, V. Closed Nov. Moderate.*

Dornbirn
Dining

Krone. The ambience is right for the excellent lamb, chicken, and other specialties of the house; everything is fresh from the market. You'll find attractive tables, friendly service, and a good wine card. *Hatlerstr. 2, tel. 05572/22720. Reservations advised. Jacket recommended. AE, DC, MC, V. Closed Sat. lunch, Sun. Moderate.*

★ **Rotes Haus.** The "red" in the name of this 1639 gabled wood house in the center of town refers to bull's blood, originally used as pigment for the facade, which is still basically red, with decorative panels. Traditional cuisine is served here, in a series of charming small rooms. You'll find lamb, game, and fish on the unusual menu. *Marktplatz 13, tel. 05572/31555. Reservations advised. Jacket and tie advised. AE, DC, MC, V. Closed Sun. Moderate.*

Feldkirch
Dining
★

Schäfle. Tucked away in the heart of the old town, this former Gasthaus has emerged as the best restaurant in town. The tables are elegantly set, and you can expect such regional fare as tongue, beef fillet, or perch from Lake Constance, all with delicate sauces and a fine touch. *Marktgasse 15, tel. 05522/22203. Reservations required. Jacket and tie advised. No credit cards. Closed Thurs., Fri. lunch, and mid-Dec.–mid-Jan. Expensive.*

Lodging

Illpark. The contrast between this contemporary hotel and the ancient square outside is startling, and you're in the center of town as well. *Leonhardsplatz 2, A–6800, tel. 05522/24600. 92* rooms. *Facilities: restaurant, bar, indoor pool, sauna, solarium, garage. AE, DC, MC, V. Expensive.*

★ **Alpenrose.** This charming old burgher house in the center of the old town has been renovated outside and in and offers unusually personal service. Rooms are tastefully done in period furnishings. *Rosengasse 6, A–6800, tel. 05522/221750. 24 rooms. AE, DC, MC, V. Moderate.*

Lech/Arlberg
Dining
★ **Brunnenhof.** This cozy restaurant in the hotel of the same name, slightly north of the center, has gotten increasingly better in recent years. The menu has offered such innovative dishes as beet soup with caviar and fish pieces, and roast lamb under a potato-zucchini crust. Be sure to reserve well in advance, for this is one of the two best restaurants in town, and it's regularly full. *Tel. 05583/2349. Reservations required. Jacket and tie advised. DC. Closed May–Dec. Very Expensive.*

Dining and Lodging **Arlberg.** This large rustic chalet manages the difficult balance between casualness and elegance: The public rooms are spacious and welcoming, the paneled guest rooms warm and comfortable. Many rooms have balconies, and you're right in the center of town. The restaurant is one of the best, offering game, lamb, and fish among other specialties. *A–6764, tel. 05583/2134. 55 rooms. Facilities: restaurant (reservations required, jacket and tie advised; AE, DC, MC). No credit cards in hotel. Closed Apr.–June, mid-Sept.–Nov. Very Expensive.*

★ **Gasthof Post.** A *gemütlich* atmosphere dominates in this green-shuttered chalet hotel, with murals and flower boxes, and a paneled wood interior. The kitchen is now in the hands of a capable Belgian who last served at the Palais Schwarzenberg in Vienna. *Tel. 05583/22060. 40 rooms. Facilities: restaurant (reservations required, jacket and tie advised), bar, indoor pool, solarium. AE, V. Closed mid-Apr.–mid-June, mid-Sept.–Nov. Very Expensive.*

Kristiania. About a five-minute walk from the center, this quiet hotel is perhaps better suited to the cross-country than the downhill skier; there are two cross-country trails nearby. Run by Othmar Schneider, the Olympic ski champion, the hotel is rustic-comfortable without ostentation. Two meals are included in the price. A separate restaurant caters to nonguests. *A–6764, tel. 05583/35000. 35 rooms. Facilities: 2 restaurants, sauna, solarium, fitness room, garage. AE, DC, MC, V. Closed May–Nov. Very Expensive.*

★ **Angela.** You're a bit above the town in this homey hotel, but you'll have to fight for a booking with the regulars who come back year after year. Half-board is mandatory in ski season. The rooms are tastefully decorated; the slopes are literally at the door. The hotel is a member of the Silencehotel group. *A–6764, tel. 05583/2407. 25 rooms. Facilities: restaurant, sauna, solarium, garage. No credit cards. Closed May–mid-July, mid-Sept.–Nov. Expensive (summer)–Very Expensive (winter).*

★ **Montana.** In Oberlech, just above the town, you'll find this easy-going hotel, run by an outgoing expatriate Alsatian. He has installed a *Vinothek*, or "wine library," where tastings are held and wine is sold by the glass or bottle. The bright interior colors contrast well with the weathered wood; the rooms are friendly and snug. The restaurant, Zur Kanne, is remarkable for its attention to detail, both in the kitchen and in the table settings. Ingredients are fresh daily, and dishes range from frog's legs to poached salmon and Black Angus steaks. *A–6764,* *tel. 05583/24600. 46 rooms. Facilities: restaurant (reservations required, jacket and tie advised), wine bar, indoor pool, sauna, solarium, fitness room, garage. No credit cards. Closed May– Nov. Expensive (restaurant)–Very Expensive (hotel, with breakfast and 1 meal).*

Solaria. This hillside chalet, fairly close to the center of town, is not far from the lower station of two of the lifts, one of which runs in summer as well. The hotel is family-run and friendly; the rooms are cheerful and cozy. Half-board is mandatory in winter. *A–6764, tel. 05583/2214. 22 rooms, not all with bath. Facilities: restaurant, fitness room. No credit cards. Closed May–Nov. Expensive–Very Expensive.*

Krone. Directly across the street from two of the main lifts, this family-managed hotel grew out of a 250-year-old house and now belongs to the Romantik-Hotel group. The adaptations and modernization have not affected the general ambience of comfort and well-being that's reflected in the beamed ceilings, tile stoves, and Oriental carpets. The rooms too have tile floors with Oriental rugs. The restaurant is noted for its game. And try the restaurant at noon, when prices are lower. *A–6764, tel. 05583/2551. 55 rooms. Facilities: restaurant (reservations advised, jacket advised), piano bar, sauna, solarium, fitness room, garage. No credit cards. Closed May–June, mid-Sept.– Nov. Moderate (summer)–Very Expensive (winter).*

Schruns-Tschagguns
Dining and Lodging

Löwen. The modified chalet design of this hotel in the center of town makes it look huge, but inside, the country style works well and the rustic dark-wood exterior is carried over elegantly into the modern balconied rooms. The hotel is set in the center of a grassy garden platform, which forms a green belt around the main building and serves as a roof for the ground-floor pool and restaurants. The fine French restaurant, with its graceful table settings (candlelit at night), also serves regional specialties, but with a flair. You might be offered grilled river trout or stuffed hare; the menu is created daily, depending on market availabilities. *Silverettastr. 8, A–6780, tel. 05556/3141. 85 rooms. Facilities: 2 restaurants (reservations advised, jacket and tie advised; no lunch), bar, disco, indoor pool, sauna, solarium, fitness room, garage. AE, DC, MC, V. Closed mid-Apr.–mid-May, Nov.–mid-Dec. Very Expensive.*

Alpenhof Messmer. Set on a lush green hillside slightly out of the center, this oversize double chalet welcomes you with fireplaces and comfortable rustic furnishings. Most of the imaginatively decorated rooms have balconies with a view over the town. It is a member of the Silencehotel group. *Grappaweg 6, A–6780, tel. 05556/2664. 35 rooms. Facilities: restaurant, indoor pool, sauna, solarium, fitness room, garage. No credit cards. Expensive.*

Montafoner Hof. The impression you get from the outside, of a large private house, carries over when you enter the welcoming lobby, with much light pine wood. The cheerful rooms have the same feeling of space and comfort. The restaurant is becoming known for its regional specialties, for example, rack of venison. The wine list is thorough, with emphasis on Austrian labels. *Dorf 282, A–6744 Tschagguns, tel. 05556/4400. 43 rooms. Facilities: restaurant (reservations advised, jacket and tie advised), bar, indoor and outdoor pools, sauna, solarium, fitness room. No credit cards. Closed Wed. and Easter–mid-May, mid-Nov.–mid-Dec. Expensive.*

Zürs
Dining and Lodging

Alpenhof. The timber-frame windows here open up a great panorama, but who has time to admire the scenery? If you're not on the slopes (the ski school is next door), the house offers dozens of other diversions. The Oriental carpets alone are worthy of a palace. The rooms are elegant yet comfortable. *A–6763, tel. 05583/2191. 41 rooms. Facilities: restaurant, piano bar, indoor pool, sauna, solarium, fitness room, movie theater, garage. No credit cards. Closed Easter–mid-Dec. Very Expensive (includes half-board).*

★ **Alpenrose-Post.** This sprawling chalet, with a facade of dark wood, draws a lot of celebrities, in part because of the friendly reception by the family management. The rooms vary from spacious to compact, from elegant (four-posters) to simple but comfortable; some have balconies. Ask for a room on the south side. *A–6763, tel. 05583/2271. 81 rooms. Facilities: restaurant, bar, indoor pool, sauna, solarium, garage. MC, V. Closed Easter–mid-Dec. Very Expensive (includes half-board).*

Central-Sporthotel Edelweiss. This 19th-century house has received an agreeable face-lift, giving it a colorful, contemporary interior, including the guest rooms. The restaurant (Chesa Verde) is the best in town, offering fresh fish, game, and regional standards. *A–6763, tel. 05583/26620. 77 rooms. Facilities: restaurant, sauna, solarium, fitness room, garage. No credit cards. Closed May–Nov. Very Expensive (includes half-board).*

Lorünser. The hospitable elegance of this hotel draws royalty and celebrities. In the reception area, carved ceiling beams, open fireplaces, and attractive accessories create a welcoming ambience. Rustic wood is used to good effect in the stylish guest rooms. The dining room is open to hotel guests only. *A–6763, tel. 05583/22540. 78 rooms. Facilities: restaurant, sauna, solarium, fitness room, garage. No credit cards. Closed May–Nov. Very Expensive (includes full board; half-board by arrangement).*

★ **Zürserhof.** Five chalets at the north end of town have been brought together into a luxurious complex. About a third of the accommodations are elegant, spacious apartments or suites; many have fireplaces, the newer ones have Roman baths. The family-run house has nevertheless managed to preserve the intimate atmosphere. *A–6763, tel. 05583/2513. 109 rooms, suites, or apartments. Facilities: restaurant, bar, disco, indoor pool, sauna, solarium, fitness room, bowling, indoor tennis, indoor driving range, hairdresser. No credit cards. Closed May–mid-Dec. Very Expensive (includes half-board).*

The Arts and Nightlife

The big cultural event in Bregenz is the **Bregenzer Festspiele,** held mid-July to mid-August. For information and tickets, contact the festival office (Box 311, A–6900, tel. 05574/492–0224). Tickets are also available at the Bregenz tourist office.

Much activity goes on in the **casino.** *Platz der Wiener Symphoniker, A–6900 Bregenz, tel. 05574/45127. Jacket and tie advised. The house opens at 3 PM. Bring your passport.*

For information and tickets for the **Schubertiade Hohenems,** contact the theater office (Box 100, Schweizer Str. 1, A–6845 Hohenems, tel. 05576/2091.)

Lech is known almost as much for après-ski and nightlife as for the snow and the slopes. You can join the crowd as early as 11 AM at the outdoor **Red Umbrella** snack and drinks bar at the Petersboden Sport Hotel at Oberlech (tel. 05583/3232). Activity continues at the late afternoon tea-dance at the **Tannbergerhof** (tel. 05583/2202). The popular place for a mid-evening drink (starting at 9:30) is the **Scotch Bar** in the basement of the Hotel Kristberg (tel. 05583/2488). The **Kronen Bar** in the Hotel Krone (tel. 05583/2551) is the only spot in town with live music, opening at 9 PM and going until 2 or 3 AM. Prices vary from place to place, but in general, you'll pay AS60–AS75 for a mixed drink such as gin and tonic.

German Vocabulary

To people who have studied only romance languages in school, the very sight of written German is terrifying—particularly when it's printed in that Gothic script that resembles old English lettering. Take heart, you are not alone. Mark Twain once wrote a funny piece called "The Horrible German Language," expounding on the German habit of tacking pieces of words together until the result fills an entire line. But never mind—you won't be required to speak it, and the section below will help.

Remember that the Austrians sometimes have just as much trouble speaking (and writing) English as you do with German. Witness the sign in a ski-resort hotel:

Not to perambulate the corridors
in the hours of repose
in the boots of ascension

An asterisk (*) denotes common usage in Austria.

Words and Phrases

	English	German	Pronunciation
Basics	Yes/no	Ja/nein	yah/nine
	Please	Bitte	**bit**-uh
	May I?	Darf ich?	darf ich?
	Thank you (very much)	Danke (vielen Dank)	**dahn**-kuh (**fee**-lun dahnk)
	You're welcome	Bitte, gern geschehen	**bit**-uh, gairn geshay-un
	Excuse me	Entschuldigen Sie	ent-**shool**-di-gen zee
	What? (What did you say?)	Wie, bitte?	vee, **bit**-uh?
	Can you tell me?	Können Sie mir sagen?	kunnen zee meer **sah**-gen?
	Do you know __?	Wissen Sie __?	**vee**-sen zee
	I'm sorry	Es tut mir leid.	es toot meer lite
	Good day	Guten Tag	**goo**-ten tahk
	Goodbye	Auf Wiedersehen	owf **vee**-der-zane
	Good morning	Guten Morgen	**goo**-ten **mor**-gen
	Good evening	Guten Abend	**goo**-ten **ah**-bend
	Good night	Gute Nacht	**goo**-tuh nahkt
	Mr./Mrs.	Herr/Frau	hair/frow
	Miss	Fräulein	**froy**-line
	Pleased to meet you	Sehr erfreut.	zair air-**froyt**
	How are you?	Wie geht es Ihnen?	vee **gate** es **ee**-nen?
	Very well, thanks.	Sehr gut, danke.	sair goot, **dahn**-kuh
	And you?	Und Ihnen?	oont **ee**-nen?
	Hi!	Servus!	**sair**-voos
	Hello! (on the telephone)	Hallo!	**hah**-lo
Numbers	1 eins	eints	6 sechs	zex
	2 zwei	tsvy	7 sieben	**zee**-bun

3 drei	dry			8 acht	ahkt
4 vier	fear			9 neun	noyn
5 fünf	foonf			10 zehn	tsane

11 elf	elf			16 sechszehn	**zex**-tsane
12 zwölf	tsvoolf			17 siebzehn	**zeeb**-tsane
13 dreizehn	**dry**-tsane			18 achtzehn	**ahkt**-tsane
14 vierzehn	**fear**-tsane			19 neunzehn	**noyn**-tsane
15 fünfzehn	**foonf**-sane			20 zwanzig	**tsvahn**-tsig

30 dreissig	**dry**-tsig			80 achtzig	**ahkt**-sig
40 vierzig	**fear**-tsig			90 neunzig	**noyn**-tsig
50 fünfzig	**foonf**-zig			100 hundert	**hoon**-dairt
60 sechszig	**zex**-sig			500 fünfhundert	foonf-**hoon**-dairt
70 siebzig	**zeeb**-sig				

Colors

black	schwarz	schvarts	pink	rosa	**row**-sa
blue	blau	blauw	purple	violett	vee-o-**let**
brown	braun	brown	red	rot	wrote
green	grün	groohn	white	weiss	vice
orange	orange	o-**rahn**-jun	yellow	gelb	gelb

Days of the Week

Sunday	Sonntag	**zohn**-tahk
Monday	Montag	**moan**-tahk
Tuesday	Dienstag	**deens**-tahk
Wednesday	Mittwoch	**mitt**-voak
Thursday	Donnerstag	**doe**-ners-tahk
Friday	Freitag	**fry**-tahk
Saturday	Samstag	**zahm**-stahk

Months

January	Januar	**yahn**-yu-ar
	*Jänner	**ye**-ner
February	Februar	**feb**-ru-ar
	*Feber	**fe**-ber
March	März	marts
April	April	ah-**pril**
May	Mai	**ma**-ee
June	Juni	**yoo**-nee
July	Juli	**yoo**-lee
August	August	ow-**goost**
September	September	sep-**tehm**-ber
October	Oktober	oc-**toe**-ber
November	November	no-**vehm**-ber
December	Dezember	day-**tsem**-ber

Useful Phrases

Do you speak English?	Sprechen Sie Englisch?	**shprek**-hun zee **eng**-glisch?
I don't speak German.	Ich spreche kein Deutsch.	ich **shprek**-uh kine doych
Please speak slowly.	Bitte sprechen Sie langsam.	**bit**-uh **shprek**-en zee **lahng**-zahm
I don't understand	Ich verstehe nicht	ich fair-**shtay**-uh nicht
I understand	Ich verstehe	ich fair-**shtay**-uh
I don't know	Ich weiss nicht	ich vice nicht
Excuse me/sorry	Entschuldigen Sie	ent-**shool**-di-gen zee

I am American/ British	Ich bin Amerikaner(in)/Engländer(in)	ich bin a-mer-i-**kahn**-er(in)/**eng**-glen-der(in)
What is your name?	Wie heissen Sie?	vee high-sen zee
My name is . . .	Ich heiße . . .	ich **high**-suh
What time is it?	Wieviel Uhr ist es? *Wie spät ist es? es?	**vee**-feel oor ist es **vee**shpate ist es
It is one, two, three . . . o'clock.	Es ist ein, zwei, drei . . . Uhr.	es ist ine, tsvy, dry . . . oor
Yes, please/ No, thank you	Ja, bitte/ Nein, danke	yah **bi**-tuh/ **nine** dahng-kuh
How?	Wie?	vee
When?	Wann? (as conjunction, als)	vahn (ahls)
This/next week	Diese/nächste Woche	**dee**-zuh/ **nehks**-tuh **vo**-kuh
This/next year	Dieses/nächstes Jahr	**dee**-zuz/ **nehks**-tuhs yahr
Yesterday/today/ tomorrow	Gestern/heute/ morgen	**ge-stairn/ hoy**-tuh/**mor**-gen
This morning/ afternoon	Heute morgen/ nachmittag	**hoy**-tuh **mor**-gen/ **nahk**-mit-tog
Tonight	Heute Nacht	**hoy**-tuh nahkt
What?	Wie?	vee
What is it?	Was ist es?	**vahss** ist es
Why?	Warum?	vah-**rum**
Who/whom?	Wer/wen?	vair/vane
I'd like to have . . . a room the key a newspaper a stamp a map a city map	Ich hätte gerne . . . ein Zimmer den Schlüssel eine Zeitung eine Briefmarke eine Karte ein Stadtplan	ich **het**-uh gairn ine **tsim**-er den **shluh**-sul i-nuh **tsy**-toong i-nuh **breef**-mark-uh i-nuh **cart**-uh ine **staad**-plahn
I'd like to buy . . . cigarettes matches a dictionary soap a toothbrush toothpaste a magazine paper	ich möchte . . . kaufen Zigaretten Streichholzer *Zünder ein Wörterbuch Seife eine Zahnbürste Zahnpaste eine Zeitschrift Papier	ich **merhk**-tuh **cow**-fen tzig-ah-**ret**-en **shtrike**-hult-suh **zoon**-der ine **vert**-tair-boo-k **sigh**-fuh i-nuh **tsahn**-burst-tuh **tsahn**-pasta i-nuh **tsite**-shrift pa-**peer**

an envelope	ein Briefumschlag	ine **breef**-um-schlahg
	*ein Kuvert	ine **koo**-vair
a postcard	eine Postkarte	I-nuh **post**-car-tuh

I'd like to exchange . . .	Ich möchte . . . wechseln	ich **merhk**-tuh . . . **vex**-eln/
dollars to schillings	Dollars in Schillinge	**dohl**-lars in **shil**-ling-uh
pounds to schillings	Pfünde in Schillinge	pfoonde in **shil**-ling-uh

| How much is it? | Wieviel kostet das? | vee-feel **cost**-et dahss? |

| It's expensive/cheap | Es ist teuer/billig | es ist **toy**-uh/**bill**-ig |

| A little/a lot | ein wenig/sehr | ine **ven**-ig/sair |

| More/less | mehr/weniger | mair/**vehn**-ig-er |

| Enough/too much/too little | genug/zuviel/zuwenig | geh-**noog**/tsoo-**feel**/tsoo-**vehn**-ig |

| Telegram | Telegramm | tel-uh-**gram** |

| I am ill/sick | Ich bin krank | ich bin krahnk |

I need . . .	Ich brauche . . .	ich **brow**-khuh
a doctor	einen Arzt	I-nen artst
the police	die Polizei	dee po-li-**tsai**
help	Hilfe	**hilf**-uh

| Stop! | Halt! | hahlt |

| Fire! | Feuer! | **foy**-er |

| Caution/Look out! | Achtung!/Vorsicht! | **ahk**-tung/**for**-zicht |

| Is this bus/train/subway going to . . . ? | Fährt dieser Bus/dieser Zug/diese U-Bahn nach . . . ? | fayrt **deezer** buhs/**deez**-er tsook/**deez**-uh **oo**-bahn nahk . . . |

Getting Around

Where is . . .	Wo ist . . .	**vo** ist
the train station?	der Bahnhof?	dare **bahn**-hof
the subway station?	die U-Bahn-Station?	dee oo-bahn-**staht**-sion
the bus stop?	die Bushaltestelle?	dee **booss**-hahlt-uh-**shtel**-uh
the airport?	der Flugplatz?	dare **floog**-plats
	*der Flughafen?	dare **floog**-hafen
the post office?	die Post?	dee **post**
the bank?	die Bank?	dee **banhk**
the American/British/Canadian consulate?	das Amerikanische/Britische/Kanadische Konsulat?	dahs a-mare-i-**kahn**-ish-uh/**brit**-ish-uh/kah-**nah**-dish-eh cone-tsoo-**laht**
the police station?	die Polizeistation?	dee po-lee-**tsai**-staht-**sion**
the . . . hotel?	das . . . Hotel?	dahs . . . ho-**tel**
the store?	das Geschäft?	dahs geh-**sheft**
the cashier?	die Kasse?	dee **kah**-suh

the . . . museum?	das . . . Museum	dahs moo-**zay**-um
the hospital?	das Krankenhaus?	dahs **krahnk**-en-house
the elevator?	der Aufzug?	dare owf-**tsoog**
the telephone?	das Telefon?	dahs te-le-**fone**
the rest room?	die Toilette?	dee twah-**let**-uh
a hairdresser/barber?	ein Friseur?	ine frih-**zerh**
a supermarket?	ein Supermarkt?	ine zoo-per-**mahrkt**/
	SB-Geschäft?	es-Bay geh-**sheft**
Here/there	hier/da	here/dah
Open/closed	offen/geschlossen	o-fen/geh-**shloss**-en
Left/right	links/rechts	links/rechts
Straight ahead	geradeaus	geh-**rah**-day-owss
Is it near/far?	Ist es in der Nähe/Ist es weit?	ist es in dare **nay**-uh/ist es vite
highway	Autobahn	**ow**-to-bahn
road, paved highway	Landstrasse, asphaltierte Landstrasse/Autobahn	**land**-strah-suh, asphalt-**tier**-tuh **land**-strah-suh
route	Strecke, Route	**strek**-kuh, **roo**-tuh
road	Strasse	**strah**-suh
street	Strasse, Gasse	**strah**-suh, **gah**-suh
tree-lined boulevard	Allee	ahl-lay
waterfront promenade	See-/Flusspromenade	**say**-/**floos**-pro-meh-**nah**-duh
wharf	Kai	kah-ee
square	Platz	plats
the zoo	Tiergarten	**teer**-gahr-ten
church	die Kirche	dee **keerkh**-uh
cathedral	der Dom	dare **dome**
neighborhood	Gegend, Umgebung	**geh**-gend, **oom**-geh-boong
foreign exchange shop	Geldwechsel *Change	**geld**-vek-sel chainj
city hall	Rathaus	**raht**-house
main square	Hauptplatz	**howpt**-plats
traffic circle	Kreisverkehr	**krice**-fehr-care
the marketplace	der Marktplatz	dare **markt**-plats
an inn	ein Gasthaus	ine **gast**-house
taxi	Taxi	**tahk**-see
a department store	ein Kaufhaus	ine **kauwf**-house

Dining Out

A bottle of . . .	eine Flasche . . .	I-nuh **flash**-uh
A cup of . . .	eine Tasse . . .	I-nuh **tahs**-uh
A glass of . . .	ein Glas . . .	ein glahss
Appetizers	Vorspeisen	for-**shpies**-un
Ashtray	der Aschenbecher	dare Ahsh-en-bekh-er
Bill/check	die Rechnung	dee **rekh**-nung
Breakfast	Frühstück	**fruh**-stuck
Cheers!	Prost! (for wine, zum Wohl!)	prost (tsoom **vole**)
Cocktail	Cocktail	**cock**-tail
Coffee shop	Kaffeehaus	**kah**-fay-house
Cold	kalt	kahlt
Depending on the season	je nach Saison	yay nahk sehy-**zone**
Desserts	Nachspeisen	**nakh**-shpie-zen
Dinner	Abendessen	**ah**-bund-**es**-en
Dish	Speise	**shpie**-zeh
Dish of the day	Tagesmenü	**tah**-guhs-meh-**nyuh**
Do you have . . . ?	Haben Sie . . . ?	**hah**-ben zee
Drink included	Getränke inbegriffen	geh-**trehn**-kuh in-buh-grif-un
Enjoy	Geniessen Sie	geh-**nee**-sen zee
Entrées	Hauptspeisen	howpt-**shpie**-zen
Extra charge	*Zuschlag	**zoo**-shlag
Fixed-price menu	Menü	meh-**nyuh**
Food	Essen	**es**-en
A fork	eine Gabel	i-nuh **gah**-bul
Homemade	Hausgemacht	**house**-geh-mahkt
Hot	heiß	hice
I am a diabetic.	Ich bin Diabetiker.	ich bin dee-ah-**bet**-ik-er
I am on a diet.	Ich halte Diät.	ich **hahl**-tuh dee-**et**
I am a vegetarian.	Ich bin Vegetarier.	ich bin ve-guh-**tah**-ree-er
I cannot eat . . .	Ich kann . . . nicht essen.	ich kan . . . nicht **es**-en
I'd like to order	Ich möchte bestellen . . .	ich **mohr**-shtuh buh-shtel-en
In season	in Saison	in sehy-**zone**

Is the service included?	Ist die Bedienung inbegriffen?	ist dee beh-**dee**-nung **in**-beh-grif-en
A knife	ein Messer	ine **mes**-er
Local specialties	Lokalspezialitäten	lo-**kahl**-**shpeh**-tsi-ahl-i-teyh-ten
Lunch	Lunch, Mittagessen	lunch, **mit**-tahg-es-en
Lunch menu	Mittagsmenü	**mit**-tahgs-meh-**nyuh**
Made to order	Auf Bestellung	owf beh-**shtel**-ung
Menu	die Speisekarte	dee **shpie**-zeh-**car**-tuh
Napkin	die Serviette	dee zair-vee-**eh**-tuh
. . . (not) included	. . . (nicht) inbegriffen	(nicht) **in**-beh-grif-en
Pepper	Pfeffer	**pfef**-er
Please give me	Bitte geben Sie mir	bit-uh **geh**-ben zee meer
Prices are . . .	Preise sind . . .	**prize**-uh sind
Salt	Salz	sahlts
Self-service restaurant	Selbstbedienungs-restaurant	selbst-be**dee**-nungs res-tauw-**rahnt**
Separate/ all together	Getrennt/ alles zusammen	ge-**trent**/ah-les tsu-**zah**-men
Service included	inklusive Bedienung	in-**kloo**-siv-uh beh-**dee**-nung
Set menu	Menü	men-**nyuh**
Side dishes	Beilagen	**bye**-lahg-en
Snack bar or stand	Imbisstube	**im**-biss-**shtoo**-buh
Soup of the day	Tagessuppe	**tahg**-es-**zuh**-puh
Special of the day	Spezialität des Tages	**shpeh**-tsi-ahl-i-**teyh**-ten des **tahg**-es
Specialty of the house	Spezialität des Hauses	**shpe**-tsi-ahl-i-**teyht** des **hous**-es
A spoon	ein Löffel	ine **luf**-el
Sugar	Zucker	**sook**-er
Value-added tax included	inklusive Mehrwertsteuer (Mwst.)	in-kloo-**seev**-uh **mair**-vairt-**stoy**-er
A waiter/waitress	Ein Kellner/ Eine Kellnerin	ine **kel**-ner/ i-nuh **kel**-ner-in
Waiter!/Waitress!	Herr Ober!/ Fräulein!	hair **o**-bair/ **froy**-line
When available	Falls verfügbar	fals fair-**foohg**-bar

Menu Guide

English	German

Breakfast

English	German
Toast	Toast
Bread	Brot
Roll(s)	Brötchen
Sweet rolls or bread	Plundergebäck
White bread	Weißbrot
Whole-wheat bread	Vollweizenbrot
Butter	Butter
Jam	Konfitüre
Honey/syrup	Honig/Sirup
Eggs	Eier
Boiled egg	Gekochtes Ei
Scrambled eggs	*Eierspeise
Bacon	Speck
Bacon and eggs	Speck und Ei
Ham and eggs	*Schinkeneierspeise
Fried eggs	Spiegelei
Orange juice	Orangensaft
Lemon	Zitrone
Sugar	Zucker

Snacks

English	German
German meatloaf in a roll	Leberkässemmerl
Cold cuts in a roll	Wurst Semmerl
Frankfurters	Würstel
Ham and cheese toast	Schinken-käse Toast, *Spezialtoast
Tarts, cakes	Torten, Kuchen
Cheese danish	*Topfengolatschen
Nut crescent	*Nusskipferl
Danish, cinnamon roll	Zimtschnecken

Soups

English	German
Stew	Eintopf
Semolina dumpling soup	Grießnockerlsuppe
Goulash soup	Gulaschsuppe
Chicken soup	Hühnersuppe
Potato soup	Kartoffelsuppe
Liver dumpling soup	Leberknödelsuppe
Oxtail soup	Ochsenschwanzsuppe
Tomato soup	Tomatensuppe
Onion soup	Zwiebelsuppe

Methods of Preparation

English	German
Blue (boiled in salt and vinegar)	Blau
Baked	Gebacken
Fried	Gebraten
Steamed	Gedämpft
Grilled (broiled)	Gegrillt
Boiled	Gekocht

Sautéed	In Butter geschwenkt
Breaded	Paniert
Raw	Roh

When ordering steak, the English words "rare, medium, (well) done" are used and understood in German. The German equivalents in Austria are: sehr Englisch (very rare), Englisch (rare), etwas durch (medium), durch (done), sehr durch (well done). When you want a steak rare or medium rare, you'll have to insist on it; the usual preparation is done to well done.

Vegetables

Eggplant	Aubergine
Red cabbage	Blaukraut
Cauliflower	*Karfiol, Blumenkohl
Beans	Bohnen
green	*grüne*
white	*weiße*
Button mushrooms	Champignons
Peas	Erbsen
Cucumber	Gurke
Cabbage	*Kraut, Kohl, Weisskohl
Lettuce	Kopfsalat
Leek	*Poree, Lauch
Peas and carrots	*Englisches Gemüse
Corn	Mais
Carrots	*Karotten
Peppers	Paprika
Chanterelle mushrooms	Pfifferlinge
Mushrooms	Champignons
Brussels sprouts	*Kohlsprossen
Red beets	*Rote Ruben
Red cabbage	Rotkohl(kraut)
Celery	Sellerie
Asparagus (tips)	Spargel(spitzen)
Tomatoes	Tomaten
Onions	Zwiebeln
Garlic	Knoblauch

Starches

Potato(es)	Kartoffel(n), Erdäpfel(n)
fried	*Brat . . .*
boiled in their jackets	*Pell . . .*
with parsley	*Petersilien . . .*
fried	*Röst . . .*
boiled in saltwater	*Salz . . .*
mashed	*. . . *puree*
dumplings	*. . . klöße (knödel)*
pancakes	*. . . puffer*
salad	*. . . salat*
Pasta	Nudeln
French fries	Pommes Frites
Rice	Reis
buttered	*Butter . . .*
steamed	*gedämpfter . . .*

Fish and Seafood

Eel	Aal
Oysters	Austern
Trout	Forelle
Flounder	Flunder
Prawns	Garnelen
Halibut	Heilbutt
Lobster	Hummer
Scallops	Jakobsmuscheln
Cod	Kabeljau
Crawfish	Krebs
Salmon	Lachs
Spiny lobster	Languste
Mackerel	Makerele
Herring	Matjes, Heringe
Mussels	Muscheln
Red sea bass	Rotbarsch
Sole	Seezunge
Squid	Tintenfisch
Tuna	Thunfisch

Meat

Mutton	Hammel
Veal	Kalb(s)
Lamb	Lamm
Beef	Rind(er)
Pork	Schwein(e)

Cuts of Meat

Example: For "Lammkeule" see "Lamm" (above) + ". . . keule" (below)

breast	. . . brust
scallopini	. . . geschnetzeltes
knuckle	. . . haxe
leg	. . . keule
liver	. . . leber
tenderloin	. . . lende
kidney	. . . niere
rib	. . . rippe
Meat patty	*Faschiertes Laibchen
Meat loaf	*Stefanibraten
Spare ribs	Schweinsrippchen
Liver meatloaf	Leberkäse
Ham	Schinken
Sausage and cold cut platter	Schlachtplatte
Sausage and hot meat platter	Bauernschmaus
Boiled beef with horseradish and cream sauce	Tafelspitz

Game and Poultry

Duck	Ente
Pheasant	Fasan
Goose	Gans
Chicken	*Hendl, Huhn
Hare	Hase
Deer	Hirsch
Rabbit	Kaninchen

Capon	Kapaun
Venison	Reh
Pigeon	Taube
Turkey	Truthahn
Quail	Wachtel

Condiments

Basil	Basilikum
Vinegar	Essig
Spice	Gewürz
Garlic	Knoblauch
Herbs	Kräuter
Caraway	Kümmel
Bay leaf	Lorbeer
Horseradish	*Kren, Meerettich
Nutmeg	Muskatnuß
Oil	Öl
Parsley	Petersilie
Saffron	Safran
Sage	Salbei
Chives	Schnittlauch
Mustard	Senf
Artificial sweetener	*Kandisin, Süßstoff
Cinnamon	Zimt
Sugar	Zucker

Cheese / Käse

Mild:	Appenzeller, Camembert, Emmentaler, Gervais (creamy), Gouda, Greyerzer, Hüttenkäse (cottage cheese), Kümmelkäse (with carraway seeds), Quark, Räucherkäse (smoked cheese), Tilsiter.
Sharp:	Bergkäse, Limburger.
curd	frisch
hard	hart
mild	mild
ripe	reif
sharp	scharf
soft	weich

Fruits

Apple	Apfel
Orange	*Orange(n)
Apricot	*Marillen, Aprikose
Blueberry	*Heidelbeere
Blackberry	Brombeere
Strawberry	Erdbeere
Raspberry	Himbeere
Cherry	Kirsche
Grapefruit	*Grapefruit, Pampelmuse
Cranberry	Preiselbeere
Raisin	Rosine
Grape	Trauben, Weintraube

Nuts

Peanuts	Erdnüsse
Hazelnuts	Haselnüsse
Coconut	Kokosnuß
Almonds	Mandeln
Chestnuts	Maronen
Walnuts	Walnüsse

Desserts

. . . soufflé	. . . auflauf
. . . ice cream	. . . eis
. . . cake	. . . kuchen
Honey-almond cake	Bienenstich
Fruit cocktail	Obstsalat
Whipped cream	*Schlagobers, Obers, (Schlag)sahne
Chocolate cake	Sacher Torte
with cream	*mit Schlagobers

Beverages

coffee	kaffee
decaffeinated	koffeinfrei
water	wasser
mineral water	Mineralwasser
soft drink	*Limonade, Soda
fruit juice	Fruchtsaft
milk	Milch
tea	Tee
beer	Bier
draft beer	vom Fass
a dark beer	Ein Dunkles
chilled	eiskalt
with/without ice	mit/ohne Eis
with/without water	mit/ohne Wasser
straight	pur
room temperature	Zimmertemperatur
. . . brandy	. . . geist
whiskey	Whisky (Scotch, Bourbon)
. . . liqueur	. . . likör
. . . schnapps	. . . schnapps
Scotch	Scotch
Egg liquor	Eierlikör
Mulled claret	Glühwein
Caraway flavored liquor	Kümmel
Fruit brandy	Obstler
Vermouth	Wermut
1/8 liter (usually wine)	Achterl
1/4 liter (usually wine)	Viertel
1/3 liter beer	*Seidl
1/2 liter beer	*Krügerl

When ordering a martini, you have to specify "gin (vodka) and vermouth"; otherwise you will be given a vermouth (Martini & Rossi).

Index

normal

Personal Itinerary

Departure *Date*

Time

Transportation

Arrival *Date*   *Time*

Departure *Date*   *Time*

Transportation

Accommodations

Arrival *Date*   *Time*

Departure *Date*   *Time*

Transportation

Accommodations

Arrival *Date*   *Time*

Departure *Date*   *Time*

Transportation

Accommodations

Addresses

Name	*Name*
Address	*Address*
Telephone	*Telephone*
Name	*Name*
Address	*Address*
Telephone	*Telephone*
Name	*Name*
Address	*Address*
Telephone	*Telephone*
Name	*Name*
Address	*Address*
Telephone	*Telephone*
Name	*Name*
Address	*Address*
Telephone	*Telephone*
Name	*Name*
Address	*Address*
Telephone	*Telephone*
Name	*Name*
Address	*Address*
Telephone	*Telephone*
Name	*Name*
Address	*Address*
Telephone	*Telephone*

Fodor's Travel Guides

U.S. Guides

Alaska
Arizona
Boston
California
Cape Cod, Martha's
  Vineyard, Nantucket
The Carolinas & the
  Georgia Coast
The Chesapeake
  Region
Chicago
Colorado
Disney World & the
  Orlando Area
Florida
Hawaii

Las Vegas, Reno,
  Tahoe
Los Angeles
Maine, Vermont,
  New Hampshire
Maui
Miami & the
  Keys
National Parks
  of the West
New England
New Mexico
New Orleans
New York City
New York City
  (Pocket Guide)

Pacific North Coast
Philadelphia & the
  Pennsylvania
  Dutch Country
Puerto Rico
  (Pocket Guide)
The Rockies
San Diego
San Francisco
San Francisco
  (Pocket Guide)
The South
Santa Fe, Taos,
  Albuquerque
Seattle &
  Vancouver

Texas
USA
The U. S. & British
  Virgin Islands
The Upper Great
  Lakes Region
Vacations in
  New York State
Vacations on the
  Jersey Shore
Virginia & Maryland
Waikiki
Washington, D.C.
Washington, D.C.
  (Pocket Guide)

Foreign Guides

Acapulco
Amsterdam
Australia
Austria
The Bahamas
The Bahamas
  (Pocket Guide)
Baja & Mexico's Pacific
  Coast Resorts
Barbados
Barcelona, Madrid,
  Seville
Belgium &
  Luxembourg
Berlin
Bermuda
Brazil
Budapest
Budget Europe
Canada
Canada's Atlantic
  Provinces

Cancun, Cozumel,
  Yucatan Peninsula
Caribbean
Central America
China
Czechoslovakia
Eastern Europe
Egypt
Europe
Europe's Great Cities
France
Germany
Great Britain
Greece
The Himalayan
  Countries
Holland
Hong Kong
India
Ireland
Israel
Italy

Italy 's Great Cities
Jamaica
Japan
Kenya, Tanzania,
  Seychelles
Korea
London
London
  (Pocket Guide)
London Companion
Mexico
Mexico City
Montreal &
  Quebec City
Morocco
New Zealand
Norway
Nova Scotia,
  New Brunswick,
  Prince Edward
  Island
Paris

Paris (Pocket Guide)
Portugal
Rome
Scandinavia
Scandinavian Cities
Scotland
Singapore
South America
South Pacific
Southeast Asia
Soviet Union
Spain
Sweden
Switzerland
Sydney
Thailand
Tokyo
Toronto
Turkey
Vienna & the Danube
  Valley
Yugoslavia

Wall Street Journal Guides to Business Travel

Europe

International Cities

Pacific Rim

USA & Canada

Special-Interest Guides

Bed & Breakfast and
Country Inn Guides:
Mid-Atlantic Region
New England
The South
The West

Cruises and Ports
  of Call
Healthy Escapes
Fodor's Flashmaps
  New York

Fodor's Flashmaps
  Washington, D.C.
Shopping in Europe
Skiing in the USA &
  Canada

Smart Shopper's
  Guide to London
Sunday in New York
Touring Europe
Touring USA